KNIVES
2010

Edited by
Joe Kertzman

©2009 Krause Publications, Inc., a subsidiary of F+W Media, Inc.

Published by

kp **krause publications**
A subsidiary of F+W Media, Inc.

700 East State Street • Iola, WI 54990-0001
715-445-2214 • 888-457-2873
www.krausebooks.com

Our toll-free number to place an order or obtain
a free catalog is (800) 258-0929.

ISSN 0277-0725

ISBN 13-digit: 978-0-89689-855-4
ISBN 10-digit: 0-89689-855-5

Designed by Kara Grundman
Edited by Corrina Peterson

Printed in the United States of America

Dedication and Acknowledgments

Our conversations go something like this. My office phone rings and, when I answer, a voice on the other end says, "Ken Warner here." I reply, "Well, hello, Ken. How are you?" He answers, and then inquires about *BLADE Magazine*, Editor Steve Shackleford, the horses that my wife and I keep, the *Knives* annual book, how things are at Krause Publications in Iola, Wis., and whether I'm keeping my chin up. Ken usually has a business reason for his phone calls, but not always. And he doesn't call often, maybe once every four-to-six months or so.

On more than one occasion, Mr. Warner said, to paraphrase, "I haven't had time to look over the entire book, but the *Knives* annual looks good, Joe. Let me say that if anyone ever gives you grief about the book, or compares your writing, knowledge or style to mine, it's really not fair, like comparing apples to oranges. You have your own way of tackling the subject matter, you're doing a fine job, and remember that it is an honor to edit and write the book. Keep up the good work."

Ken, of course, spent 20 years of his life gathering knife photos, writing and editing the *Knives* annual book, and is responsible for its inception, style, format and formula. He made the annual title what it is today, and he did as much for custom, handmade knives as anyone in the business. He is also a gentleman, scholar and true knife enthusiast. I dedicate this edition, *Knives 2010*, to Ken Warner. I thank him for his advice, friendship, constructive criticism and professionalism. And I acknowledge his writing

and editing abilities, knife knowledge and contributions to the world of knives.

I also want to dedicate this book to my parents, Jack and Cathy Kertzman, who, even though I was a scoundrel of a teenager and young adult, showed me unconditional love, understanding, support and encouragement. My father helped me land my first publishing job at Reiman Publications in Greendale, Wis., and has been there for me every day of my life. Thank you, Mom and Dad. I love you.

Knifemakers, you deserve special recognition. I have never met a harder working group of people, and those who are so dedicated to their craft. If the rest of the general populace were as driven and motivated about their passions as you are, the world would be a better, and safer, place to live.

Finally, to my wife and children who are far better people than I will ever be. When a father and husband strives to be more like his wife, son and daughter, that says a lot about the type of people they are. I'm so very proud and am not afraid to use you three, Tricia, Danny and Cora, as my writing, editing and publishing inspiration. I am one lucky *Knives* editor.

Joe Kertzman

On the Cover

If spectacular artistry and quality cutting tools are what you seek in a knife or collection, then the front cover of *Knives 2010* fulfills your fantasies, starting with the Steve Jernigan folder at top left. The way Steve cut, shaped and inlaid green sea snail in the Mike Norris damascus handle, and kept the theme going with the damascus blade, inlaying shell into the pivot pin head and back band, is an accomplishment of cut. Below it stands Owen Wood's "Empire State Building" art deco masterpiece engraved by Amayak Stepanyan. The knife is one in a series depicting the great art deco buildings of New York, and includes a composite-damascus blade, Damasteel bolsters and titanium liners. Mace Vitale set out to forge a damascus bowie, and did just that, outfitting his with a curly maple handle and tasteful silver-wire inlay, not to mention a copasetic copper guard. To the far right is something rarely seen in the knife world—a fixed-blade dagger from the hands of Stan Fujisaka that incorporates an imported snuff bottle, in this case with English setters in the heat of the hunt, as the handle. Mr. C.J. Cai lent his engraving skills to the six-inch dagger blade, guard and butt cap. Four fine knives make a good start to a breakout edition of the *Knives* annual book.

Contents

Introduction

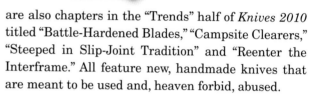

It is a blessing, not a dilemma. The situation is akin to being a guest at the cleanest house in the neighborhood. Ringing the bell and stepping into the foyer (not a mudroom, but a foyer), you notice the sparkling tiles, spotless paint and pristine, white carpet—the neat houses always have white carpet. It is so clean you're not only afraid to tread within, but also consider your shoes or boots unworthy of plodding through the entryway (an entryway, not a front door).

Then there's the businessman who couldn't hire the most qualified candidate because she was so stunningly beautiful, he knew if his wife ever laid eyes on her, he'd be in deep. Have you ever ducked out of a restaurant because it was too fancy? Or a dinner party because it was too stuffy?

In the knife industry, it's the handmade knives that get the comments. Part of casual conversation with knife enthusiasts often includes, "Most of my knives are in the $25-$75 range. I bought one for $150, and it's so nice I'm afraid to use it." Another example goes like this, "I bought the prettiest pearl-handle folder with action as smooth as silk. I show all my friends, but when it comes to working in the garage, I take out the pocketknife I bought at the hardware store."

One comment shared among knife magazine and book editors, one they've heard from readers in recent years, can best be paraphrased like this: "Something has happened to the knife magazines and books. All of the knives are high art pieces, and there aren't as many good, old-fashioned using pocketknives and straight blades as there used to be."

Why is that? Have low-paid, hard-working, poorly dressed editors with stains on their shirts gone sophisticated and highfalutin? Are they rubbing elbows with mayors, congressmen and high-society folks?

Or could it be, just maybe, that the knives, even the tactical, practical, chopping, lopping, camping, hunting, skinning, field dressing, whittling and pocket-bulging edged utility blades showcase finer fits and finishes? Do they parade modern materials, exotic handles and high-tech steel blades? Are the parts fashioned and painstakingly assembled on more technologically advanced machinery than ever before in the history of cut? Do the wood-handle hunters look like fine pieces of craftsmanship?

Flip the pages of this book to the chapter on "Fish & Game Wardens," and see for yourself. There are also chapters in the "Trends" half of *Knives 2010* titled "Battle-Hardened Blades," "Campsite Clearers," "Steeped in Slip-Joint Tradition" and "Reenter the Interframe." All feature new, handmade knives that are meant to be used and, heaven forbid, abused.

Sure, there are pearl-handled beauties shown in the "Edged Translucency" chapter, and other sections titled "21st Century Japan," "Studies in Stone" and "Quillion and Other Keen Daggers." In the "State Of The Art" half of the *Knives* book reside edged art knives beset with jewels and parading carving, etching, engraving, scrimshaw, mosaic-damascus blades, and gold and silver wire inlay.

Perhaps the debate is custom versus factory. While most knife magazines feature a fair share of handmade and factory pieces, the *Knives* annual concentrates almost entirely on custom knives, and has been successfully doing so for three decades.

Another part of the equation is how photos are chosen for the book. The methodology includes sending letters, faxes and emails to nearly 2,500 knifemakers around the world asking for photos of their best work. A representative sampling is then chosen of the best of the best, and not all pieces can be included. Some of those excluded are the most fancy of scrimshawed, jewel-inlaid, engraved and honed works of art, and others are straightforward yet clean, well-made, even gorgeous hunters, folders, camp knives and utility blades.

All, in this editor's opinion, are museum-quality masterpieces. And that's what makes the industry, the market, the craftsmanship and, yes, even the book, so alluring. The knives themselves are deeply moving and so very satisfying. Please enjoy yourselves as you delve into this, the newest edition of *Knives*. Be careful or you'll end up buying and using one of the fine, edged pieces.

STATE OF THE ART

FACTORY TRENDS

DIRECTORY

2010 WOODEN SWORD AWARD

Creative men escape to solitude, a place where they will be undisturbed to practice their craft, whether words on paper, paint on canvas, musical notes, woodwork or bladesmithing. Their vision is translated onto a medium others can understand, appreciate and enjoy. In some respects, they are interpreters between their own creative geniuses and the reactionary minds of art aficionados and laymen alike.

This is their undertaking. Some dare to go beyond a single objet d'art, breathing life into two, three or even four works, rousing the audience with a cacophony of creativity and having the audaciousness to fashion a handful of inspiring centerpieces. Few go for seven. That would be absurd. But that's just what our friend Richard Rogers set out to accomplish and succeeded with all the prowess of a master.

Sink your teeth into the Michael Price-style dagger with mother-of-pearl handle, domed pins, 14k-gold shield, and sterling silver handle wrap and

sheath engraved by Simon Lytton. Wrap your mind around the matching push dagger, the multi-blade folder and pocket watch. Open your senses to the match safe, watch fob and pocket-watch chain, and rest easy in the knowledge that Richard and Simon emerged from it all unscathed, and with nary a lasting aftereffect.

For their feat of daring and resulting embellished Gentleman's Set, the editor of *Knives* awards Richard Rogers and Simon Lytton the 2010 Wooden Sword Award. Congratulations on a job well executed.

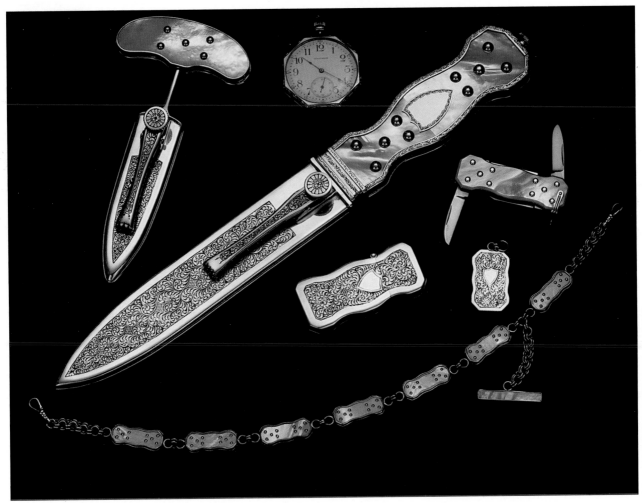

It's a Flip Fest

The fastest folders with the smoothest action become winners in the modern knife arena

By Michael Burch

No thumb stud, no thumb disc, just an extension of the blade tang protruding from between the handle slabs on the back of a closed folding knife. I went to push the steel tab, or extension, and nothing happened—uh oh.

There I was at the 2007 BLADE Show and I was handling my first real "flipper" folder, made by the young and talented Gerry McGinnis. Though I was trying to play it cool because I was at the big show, Gerry saw my discomfort and jokingly told me to "put some manpower behind it." I applied more pressure with my index finger, and I wondered if the beautiful blade was going to fly out of my hand in front of all the knife enthusiasts. Then my finger pressure finally overrode the detent pressure, and the small blade flew open with a loud "thwack." A huge grin crossed my face and I was officially hooked on flippers.

Before that moment, I had handled some folders, or folding knives, that needed a flick of the wrist to help propel the blades into the open position, and I presumed that's how a "flipper" operated. One of the big differences between a well-made flipper and a "wrist flipper" is having a strong detent.

In a frame-lock folder or a LinerLock®, as opposed to a flipper, a ball detent is nested into a small pocket when the blade is in the closed position, thus preventing the blade from accidental opening or engaging. For a flipper, a strong detent involves a ball that nests deeper into the pocket so that when pressure is placed on the flipper tab, pent-up pressure overrides the detent and releases a lot of energy over a small space. Couple this with the smooth action of a fine folder, and a blade flies open at automatic speed.

The detent is just one part of the flipper puzzle. There is a delicate balance between the right amount of lock-bar pressure and how the face of the lock is finished. Achieving that balance means the folder won't suffer from a "sticky" lock.

Gerry McGinnis's "Mini-Vicarious" features a 3-inch, hand-rubbed, Mike Norris stainless-damascus blade, and a Timascus and mother-of-pearl handle.

Designing a flipper can be problematic, and some makers have incorporated an "internal stop pin." A stop pin is exactly what its name implies—a pin that stops the blade when it is propelled into the fully open position. An internal stop pin juts through a semicircle cutout machined in the blade. With such a design, there isn't an exterior stop pin to hinder the blade tang extension—the flipper—from rotating unhindered. Some knifemakers, like Phil Boguszewski, fashion flippers with pins built into the

The Phil Boguszewski "Cobra" sports a 3 7/8-inch BG-42 blade, a "windowed" titanium frame, and stingray skin inlays. *(Martin Reingold photo)*

blades instead of the handles, and the cutouts in the handles. Either way works.

Flippers are often pricier than lock-back or locking-liner folders. There is a lot that goes into the design and manufacture of the knives, and a well-built flipper is worth the money.

The First Flippers

I researched the origins of the flipper and came up with more questions than answers. I would have had an easier time finding Sasquatch. In my search for the first flipper, I consulted knife purveyor Les Robertson, who attributed the idea of the flipper to early friction folders.

Robertson says the first flippers he came across were made by Mel Pardue in the late 1980s. From there, Pardue taught Randy Gilbreath the ins and outs of the design. Gilbreath fashioned the "Toggle Lock," and, in turn, gave permission to Kit Carson to incorporate the idea into his folders.

Other sources credit the late

Robert Hayes for making a Button Lock Flipper in the mid-1970s, but I couldn't locate a picture of said knife. However it came about, many people credit Carson for bringing the flipper into prominence. His M16 folder—the handmade version and the Columbia River Knife & Tool model—played a huge part in bringing flippers into the limelight, as did Ken Onion's SpeedSafe⊠ flipper folders, including those offered by Kershaw Knives.

There are plenty of knifemakers fashioning flippers, and the choices are abundant when shopping for one of the fun and functional blades. Though many of the makers aren't taking orders, or have large backlogs of orders, there are plenty of flippers to choose from on the aftermarket.

When someone posts a poll on an Internet forum (and there have been many) about the "smoothest flipper," there are a few names repeated over and over—and one of them is Boguszewski. A professional saxophonist in the 1980s, Phil became a full-time knifemaker in 1983. In the late '80s, Phil made a stiletto with double

guards integral to the blade.

The customer who bought the folding stiletto later told Phil that he was able to flip the blade open using the guard. Phil still enjoys fashioning stilettos, and in 2000 he became serious about making flippers. Since then, he's had a huge impact on the flipper world, with his blades highly sought after because of their uniqueness, fit and finish, and smooth operation. He credits precision parts and a lot of handwork for their smooth operation.

Though he builds many flippers, he makes more of the "Cobra" model than any other, and high demand makes obtaining one tough. He doesn't take orders, selling his blades at knife shows through a lottery system, with prices starting at $800 apiece.

Rotating Heli Blades ...

Another popular name in "smooth flipper" making is R.J. Martin, a knifemaker who's always been intrigued by metal and heat treatment. Martin pursued an engineering degree, and worked on helicopters for 17 years.

Eventually R.J. became

Matt Cuchiarra's "El Dorado" flipper employs a clip-point, bowie-style blade, 4 inches long and 5/32-inch thick, of Mike Norris stainless damascus, and a contoured-Timascus grip.

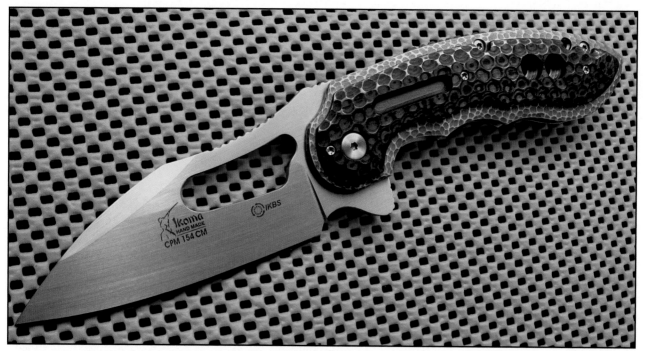

Among other amenities, the Flavio Ikoma "Harrier 425" showcases a 4 ¼-inch blade, a multi-position opening slot, and a carbon fiber and orange G-10 handle with coral texturing.

interested in knifemaking, attending his first big show in New York City in 1987, and becoming a full-time knifemaker in 2001. Now, as an eight-year veteran at building flippers, R.J. has it down pat. He relies on precision parts to make flippers fly, but also utilizes special thrust bearings around the pivot pin that greatly reduce friction yet still allow for tight-fitting folders.

R.J was prodded by Robertson to make a flipper, and that is how the Q-36 model came into being. His favorite materials are those used to design helicopter airframes—carbon fiber and titanium. As he said, "They are awesome materials in a knife, and special to me because they remind me of my 'previous life.'" R.J. utilizes the CPM blade steels and Devin Thomas damascus. His preferred natural handle materials include stag for its "character and feel," but also ancient ivory, ironwood and African blackwood.

In regards to the Q-36, he says, "I like the elegance and the simplicity." Obviously he's not alone with that line of thinking, as it garnered the "Best Tactical Folder" award at the 2007 BLADE Show.

R.J.'s flipper prices range from $375 to $1,200 apiece, with his mid-size knives running

The Lee Williams "Kickstop" flipper operates using a 4 ½-inch blade and a carved-titanium handle.

between $575 and $775.

Though fairly new to the knifemaking world, Tim Galyean made an impressive entrance with his great designs and beautiful blade grinds and machine work.

Tim started working as a machinist for Kershaw Knives in 2001, but after meeting Onion, his interest in custom knives peaked. In 2003, Tim visited Ken's shop in Hawaii and started getting serious about knifemaking. Two years later, he built a flipper.

Kershaw makes a production version of Galyean's "Junkyard Dawg" model, and Tim attributes the smoothness of his flippers to creating absolutely precision parts. He utilizes a variety of high-end stainless steels, as well as titanium, Micarta® and exotic handle materials. He does machining and handwork to create the unique textures and lines on his folders. A good example of his texturing creativity is the "Lahar" model that features titanium that has been jigged to look like bone.

J.L. "Lee" Williams already had a shop full of machinery and tools so, in November of 2001, he decided to make knives for friends and family for Christmas. His initial batch of Christmas fixed blades turned from 10 to 30. After that, Lee turned his machining

skills and extreme attention to detail into making folders. He gained much information from the Internet, got his hands on the quintessential Bob Terzuola book, "The Tactical Folding Knife," and made his first flipper—the "Rhino"—in 2002.

Being a fan of slim lines on a folder, Lee wanted to eliminate the "flipper tab" on his blades, so he created a "Kickstop" system that utilizes a floating stop pin. Some of his favorite materials include titanium, stainless damascus, meteorite and mother-of-pearl. Lee carves and files his blades to create unique finishes and textures.

Young Little Flipper

Definitely the youngest of the group, but far from the least talented, McGinnis began making knives in the fall of 2004, due to the desire for a better hunting knife. Like most knifemakers, he started with files and sandpaper, heat treating with a torch, and just making fixed blades. Eventually he acquired new tools, and worked with knifemaker Alan Folts to create his first LinerLock. He quickly took a liking to flippers and began to teach himself how to make them.

Then, in 2006, McGinnis met Williams and Matt Cucchiara, a

knifemaking duo who taught him how to build an internal stop pin and create the right detent for a flipper. Today, McGinnis prefers fashioning flippers over all other folders because of the "ease of opening, and functionality by pure design."

McGinnis utilizes unique blade shapes and has an ability to pack a lot of blade into his handles. His Mini-Vicarious model, for example, is only about 3 7/8 inches closed, but packs a big-knife punch.

His knives start at $450 each, but most of his carved flippers range for between $800 and $950 apiece.

Hailing from Brazil, Flavio Ikoma not only creates unique flippers, he also helped invent the I.K.B.S. (Ikoma-Korth Bearing System), which utilizes small ball bearings within a race around the pivot. The end result is smooth folder action, and many makers (myself included) now incorporate the I.K.B.S. design into their flippers, butterfly knives and regular folders for little-to-no resistance in blade opening.

Flavio has a unique style that combines clean lines with layers and texturing. He amazingly does it with a minimal amount of machinery.

Flavio started making knives

Illustrated is how the blade is milled out for an internal or "hidden" stop pin. The detent hole has been "feathered" on the backside so the detent ball falls into the hole without touching the back of the hole. According to Barry Davis, damascus folders were Schmidt's forte. Early on, Schmidt did not use a surface grinder but rather handfiled the blades to make them fit just so in the handles of his folders. The fact that he went to such trouble is a fete in itself. The fact that the folders were the epitome of the genre is testimony to his brilliance. This is Schmidt's "Touch of Midas." *(from the Pierluigi Peroni collection; Peroni photo)*

Harrier offers various opening options and various grips. The Harrier blade can be flicked open via the extended tang or tab, via a hole in the handle, or can be reversed in the hand by the "pivot."

The Flowing Flippers

Cuchiarra has a style all his own. His blades flow as if they were formed out of liquid metal. A mechanic for 18 years, Cuchiarra started making flippers only a month after he began building knives in 2003. He credits Jerry Hossom for getting him started and Tom Mayo for answering questions. He is "pretty much full-time" now and mainly works on flippers.

One feature that sets Cuchiarra's work apart from others is his unique carving, and he credits Onion's early work as a main influence. Matt likes working with CPM 154 and Mike Norris stainless damascus blade steels, as well as titanium, green/translucent G-10 and Timascus handles. Knife prices start at $400 apiece, but his carved knives carry price tags of $950 and up.

No, there are no thumb studs, discs, pegs or holes, just extensions of the blade tangs protruding from between the handle slabs and begging for someone to flip them, propelling blades into the open positions faster than jets leaving runways, or new flipper folders hitting a primed market.

Other Flipper Folder Makers*

Todd Begg

Peter Carey

Derek Fraley

Brian Tighe

Les Voorhies

Mikkel Willumsen

*There are many others.

for the Brazilian market in 1993, but didn't start selling into the U.S. market on a regular basis until 2003, after meeting Duane Dwyer of EDC Custom Knives. Flavio likes using high-tech, high-strength materials such as carbon fiber, G-10 and titanium, but will also work with wood and mother-of-pearl for his dressed-up blades.

Of all his models, Flavio's favorite is the Harrier 425, a unique take on flippers. The

Top Chefs Reveal Their Favorite Knives

From street-front cafes to five-star restaurants, gourmet cooks rely on the blades at hand

By Jordan Clary

A number of years ago I shared a household with an amateur chef. One warm autumn afternoon I made myself a BLT sandwich, set the knife on the counter to wash later and went out on the porch to enjoy lunch. A few minutes later, my normally even-tempered housemate came out visibly rattled, knife in hand.

In the short time it takes to fry some bacon and slap it on a piece of bread with lettuce, tomato and mayonnaise, I had made a number of grave errors, the worst of which was neglecting to wipe the blade down immediately, instead leaving it on the counter where acid from the tomato would wreak havoc on the high-carbon-steel blade.

I've never looked at kitchen knives the same way since.

Over the years I've met other chefs and observed them with their knives. I married a man who likes to cook. His cutlery collection is probably worth more than my car. Each chef has his or her own likes and dislikes, quirks as to a favorite knife to use in the kitchen. During this past year I decided to survey chefs about their cutlery, what they like, what

they don't. What are the trends in knives among chefs these days?

For a year I talked to chefs around the country, as well as on a trip to Taiwan. From small street-front cafes to five-star restaurants, the resident chefs all had something to say about their knives. And I did notice a definite trend. By and large, most chefs are moving away from German knives and leaning toward Japanese-style cutlery these days.

German-born Chef Hans Susser, who during his illustrious career has held positions as executive chef, sous chef, and chef de partie, among other titles, in countries around the world, says, "Japanese knife. German knife. It doesn't matter. A knife is only as good as its handler.

"I came in contact with Japanese knives 40 years ago and they are very good," Susser allows, "but I would not say that Japanese knives are better than any others. Some are easier to use than others, or more adapted to a certain cut. It has to do with the material, with the edge, whether a knife [edge] is one or two sided [has one or

two bevels]. Still you can take the best knife in the world, put it in the hands of an inexperienced chef and he'll destroy it in a matter of hours."

Susser, who has visited 129 countries and lived in several of them, delving into their culinary customs, is now teaching aspiring chefs at the Miami branch of the prestigious culinary institute Le Cordon Bleu. He says the knives the institute uses are American

Brian Malarkey, award-winning executive chef of San Diego's Oceanaire Restaurant, says many of the chefs in his kitchen use Kershaw Shuns because they "have real thin blades and come in a variety of shapes and sizes." *(Chantelle Marie Photography)*

made but forged in the German style. "A chef should use the knife that he or she is comfortable with. For a chef, your knife is an extension of the hand or arm," Susser notes.

The knife as an extension of self resonates with Hiroshi Shima, executive sushi chef at Sushi Roku/Katana in Los Angeles. Shima comes from Hokkaido, Japan's northernmost and least developed island. As well as fresh seafood, Hokkaido is famous for its Sapporo beer from the city of the same name. It was in Sapporo that Shima first began developing the art of sushi.

Spirit Blade

Through his translator, Vernon Cardenas, another accomplished chef who works with a fusion of Latino and Japanese food, Shima tells me, "Japanese chefs are taught that your knife and your cutting board are part of yourself. They're an extension of the spirit. They become close to your heart and you treat them like family."

Shima says this extends to Japanese knifemakers who bring that element of spirit to their craftsmanship. They bring other qualities to it as well, such as innovation. The driving force behind the Japanese knife trend is that they were able to produce a quality stainless steel knife that was superior to stain-resistant carbon blades, thus prompting a move of the entire chef's knife market toward Japanese design.

"Japanese knives often need more care," Shima says. "They should be oiled and sharpened regularly even though they hold their edge well. The metal needs special care. Japanese knives usually have wooden handles. They are more delicate." He says that, when choosing a knife, he considers length and balance, as well as finding a reputable company. He currently uses a long yanagi for fish and sushi, and a usuba, made by Suisin, for vegetables.

Junro Aoki, the son of the Aoki Knife Craft family, developed Suisin knives. He spent 20 years learning to craft knives that combined traditional qualities with modern designs. The Suisin Collection entered the market in 1990 and has garnered a reputation of quality among many chefs.

Praise for Japanese knives is heard in kitchens throughout the country. Fernando Desa, executive chef and product development manager for Goya Foods, Inc., the largest Hispanic-owned food

Between the appetizer and main course at Barclay Prime, a Philadelphia luxury boutique steakhouse, the servers approach their guests with a selection of steak knives to choose from: Henkel, Shun, Global, Wusthuf, Chroma or Furi.
(photos courtesy of Starr Restaurants)

Deborah Scott, executive chef of San Diego's Island Prime Restaurant, says that a lot of the younger prep chefs, especially those just out of school, use German-made Wusthof kitchen knives. *(photos courtesy of The Cohn Restaurant Group)*

distributer in the United States, says, "I still have my Bickies that I got in culinary school and use them at home, but I use Japanese knives professionally."

Desa says he began to notice the trend turn toward Japanese knives about 10 years ago. "There are a couple reasons. One, the Japanese knives are lighter, and two, they were able to capitalize on new developments of stainless steel as compared to carbon or low-quality stainless steel," he notes. "They hold their edge well."

Desa likes to use a Global santoku, which is shorter than most kitchen knives and easy to work with. Chef Susser also praises Global knives and says they are one of his favorites in the cutlery realm.

Global introduced its first knives designed by Komin Yamada in 1985. Since then,

Global knives have become popular with chefs for the reasons Desa already noted—they are light with razor-sharp blades, and Global offers a large selection including the santoku, which means "three virtues." This finely balanced knife comes with a hollow handle that the manufacturer fills with sand to achieve just the right balance.

Knife Finesse

Brian Malarkey, award-winning executive chef of San Diego's Oceanaire Restaurant, which has garnered numerous awards, concurs that Japanese knives "have finesse, balance, they're more versatile." He adds, "The metal is very responsive to a stone. German knives are like big, old workhorses."

Malarkey says many of the chefs in his kitchen use Kershaw

Shun knives because they "have real thin blades and come in a variety of shapes and sizes."

Shun knives are one of the fastest selling high-end cooking knives on the market. Kershaw manufactures a number of lines such as the Shun Elite, the Shun Classic and the Shun Pro, and a line developed by Ken Onion—the Shun Ken Onion. Onion's designs are distinguished by their curved handles and ripple design on the blades. All Shun knives incorporate high-carbon stainless steel blades and are known to hold their edges for an exceptionally long time.

While Chef Malarkey appreciates Japanese knives, he also says that one of the best things about being a celebrity chef is that he gets a lot of free knives. After he was one of the top finalists on the television show

"America's Top Chefs," he regularly gets sent samples, so he gets to "coast around trying different ones." He also gives away a lot of knives.

Chef Desa says, "Any knife can work as long as it's well-cared for. When you take care of a knife, keep the blade sharp and keep it clean, it works."

Practicality is a major component of favoritism and in many parts of the world the cleaver reigns. Developed in China, the basic cleaver is still the blade of choice throughout China and Taiwan from five-star restaurants to outdoor makeshift barbeques. It is also one of the most common knives in the world. This basic, all-round functional tool is the only knife used by many Chinese chefs. They chop vegetables with it, dice meat and carve duck.

Of the chefs I spoke to in Taiwan, all had nothing but praise for the cleaver. "I grew up watching my mother use it," one chef in a small roadside restaurant told me. "It's the perfect instrument and can be used for everything. I don't even remember not knowing how to use one."

The cleaver has its fans in the United States, as well. Chef Susser believes the cleaver is underappreciated here. He claims that, "The cleavers opened a whole new world of understanding for me," when he was first introduced to them in Hong Kong and Singapore in 1973. He mentions their versatility in all stages of food creation.

Another of San Diego's esteemed chefs, Deborah Scott, executive chef and partner in three San Diego distinctive Cohn Restaurant Group's restaurants— Kemo Sabe, Indigo Grill and Island Prime/C-level—also loves the cleaver as a basic all-round kitchen knife.

"Mine is not a name brand," she says. "In fact, we order a dozen at a time from the Asian market. It's great for prep; the weight, the size, the ease of handling and its span, all make it ideal. You don't have to push down as much; the weight of the blade does the work for you. They hold their sharpness fairly well."

Practical Is the Cleaver

Scott says that a lot of the younger prep chefs, especially those just out of school, are still using German-made Wusthof kitchen knives. She admits that Wusthofs are great knives, reasoning, "If you rode horses, a Wusthof would be an English saddle and a cleaver would be a Western saddle. The cleaver is more rustic, but also more practical."

One chef that any old knife won't work for is Daniel Kremin of Barclay Prime, a Philadelphia luxury boutique steakhouse. He has all of his primary knives custom made for the left hand. Currently he's using a Mishomoto. Kremin explains, "I used a Kershaw knife for a long time and found I was getting a blister. I did a lot of research as to which knife felt better." He said the Shuns were nice, but he finally decided on the Mishomoto because it "fit my hand better."

Barclay Prime is an example of a growing trend in steakhouses to take its cutlery seriously. Between the appetizer and main course, the servers approach their guests with a selection of steak knives to choose from: Henkel, Shun, Global, Wusthof, Chroma or Furi. They give a short presentation on the different knives, stating the advantages and disadvantages of each, and will often include a recommendation of their personal favorite.

Hiroshi Shima, executive sushi chef at Sushi Roku/Katana in Los Angeles, currently uses a long yanagi for fish and sushi, and a usuba, made by Suisin, for vegetables. (*photos by Nash Yoshimura and Hiroshi Shima*)

A sous chef at Silks House Restaurant in the Grand Fermosa Regency in Taipei, Taiwan, demonstrates one of many uses for professional cutlery.

German-born Chef Hans Susser, says, "Japanese knife. German knife. It doesn't matter. A knife is only as good as its handler." *(photo courtesy of Hans Susser)*

Salvatore Giuliano, executive chef at Temecula Creek Inn in southern California's premier wine region, has a fondness for pastries. He says, "I personally use knives with a larger clearance between the handle and the return. The reason for this is so my fingers don't hit the sheet of mini pastries as I cut down on them." He says that pastry chefs "also like using paring knives for doing detail cuts on fruit and berries for garnishes."

My husband likes to tell about the blade he bought at a yard sale in Los Angeles. It had no handle and the carbon blade had clearly been hand forged. The people he bought it from said it came from the kitchen of a European baron. He made a wooden handle for it and while it's a bit heavy for everyday use, he brings it out when he wants a knife with character.

Chef Shima says that at 16 years old, when he began apprenticing under his mentor, Mr. Asami, in Kyoto, Japan, he was not allowed near the cutting board or the knife. He washed dishes, cleaned vegetables and wiped counters. When Mr. Asami finally presented him with his first knife, it was a great honor, the equivalent of "getting an award or present." Shima still has the knife and considers it one of his most valued possessions.

The perfect kitchen knife probably doesn't exist, but the idea of the knife as an extension of the self in the culinary world seems universal. Chef Susser says, "Some people will tell you that you have to hold a knife a certain way for the best results. It's not true. You need to cut a piece of food. You have to be comfortable with the knife in your hand."

The servers go through an intensive orientation learning about the knives and food preparation. After they are hired, they have to spend a week in the kitchen following a chef around to get a feel for the process.

As for the customers, most of the guests are intrigued by the mini-lesson on cutlery, but sometimes they don't care. "Occasion-ally someone will say, 'just give me a knife and get it over with,'" laughs Kremin.

While versatility is a common trait that chefs look for, what makes a versatile knife varies. Chef Malarkey likes the finesse of a Japanese blade while chefs Scott and Susser enjoy the practicality of a cleaver. Different disciplines also require certain blades.

A Lifestyle, Not Just a Hobby

Knife aficionado Phil Lobred discusses the Buster Warenski King Tut dagger, Elvis, the Art Knife Invitational and more

By Steve Shackleford

When it comes to the modern handmade knife movement, few have had more impact than Phil Lobred. A devoted collector since the late 1960s, among other things he has designed and made knives, coordinated one of the world's most elite knife shows, the Art Knife Invitational, and commissioned perhaps the pre-eminent knife of the modern handmade era—Buster Warenski's King Tut Dagger.

Perhaps the most significant knife of the modern handmade era: the Buster Warenski King Tut Dagger. The granulation technique alone—the small beads on the handle—was something only a few goldsmiths living at the time could do. Phil Lobred and Warenski *(right)* stand by the Warenski Tut display at Solvang. *(knife photos by SharpByCoop.com; photo of Lobred and Warenski by Weyer International)*

The exhibitors and coordinator of the first Art Knife Invitational in 1983, front row, from left: *BLADE®* Magazine Cutlery Hall-Of-Famers© Ron Lake and Bill Moran; Henry Frank; Ted Dowell; Phil Lobred; Jim Schmidt; Royal Hanson and Billy Mace Imel. Back row, from left: Larry Hendricks; Ron Skaggs; Herman Schneider; Jim Hardenbrook; Marad Sayen; Lynton McKenzie; Fred Carter; Cutlery Hall-Of-Famer Buster Warenski; Dwight Towell and Bob Lum. *(photo courtesy of Phil Lobred)*

Two old friends: Phil Lobred *(left)* and Blade Magazine Cutlery Hall-Of-Famer© Gil Hibben. *(photo courtesy of Phil Lobred)*

Inside Lobred lies a passion for custom knives that has burned hot and bright for over four decades and shows no signs of abating.

He has collected knives since he was about 10 years old. In the 1950s, he would ride his bike to a local antique store and buy bayonets. At decade's end, his family moved to Anchorage, Alaska. "I amassed any knife that came my way and started buying factory-made knives in about 1964," he notes.

He first learned of handmade knives through gun magazines. Many stores in Anchorage had knives by Rudy Ruana, but it was in a downtown gun store where Lobred found hunters by Ralph Bone and G.W. Stone. "That's what really got me started," he recounts. After that, he located a Gil Hibben knife. "The next few years are a blur," Lobred indicates. "I ordered a knife from any maker I got an address on and the custom knives started rolling in. I stopped buying factory-made knives. Most of the handmades were in the $50 range at that time but a few were $100 or more. That was expensive!"

His initial handmade knife collection was essentially a one-from-each-maker compilation of hunters and skinners that eventually reached 200. Among them was a straight hunter by Bob Loveless that foreshadowed Lobred's belief that certain knives can be art.

A friend of Lobred's named Bill Thomas ordered the knife from Loveless for a friend going on a polar bear hunt. When Lobred saw the knife, he knew he had to have it. "I was overwhelmed," he recalls. "Whether he got a polar bear or not, I wanted to get my hands on that knife." As it turned out, the knife was too small for Thomas' friend's taste, so the friend returned it to Thomas. "I told Bill when that knife came back, I had to have it," Lobred says. "To me, it was art." He traded Thomas three knives—including a hunter by Bill Moran—and $125 for the Loveless. It was Lobred's first Loveless knife.

In 1971, Lobred learned of the Knifemakers' Guild and that its 1972 show would be in Kansas City. "I had to go," he recollects. "I had knives and/or orders with most all the makers and had spoken to most on the phone, but had never met any of them in person. I believe the forming of the Guild and the first few Guild shows were probably the most important factors in the beginning to establishing a collector market.

"Second to the formation of the Guild in early importance was the publishing of *The American Blade* magazine [today's *BLADE*®] in 1973. Wow, now we had a whole magazine devoted solely to knives. That added legitimacy to knife collecting."

Hibben in His Garage!

Lobred's life changed shortly after the 1972 Guild Show, where he had met Hibben. A few months later Hibben moved his family to Anchorage and, for the next few years, Lobred's two-car garage was the Hibben knife shop. It was there Lobred tried his hand at both designing and making knives.

"I had my own idea of what I liked in a knife," he reflects. "Gil and I worked close. I was always trying to push him into ideas I liked. I worked side by side with him for almost four years. I learned the business from the inside out. Not many get a chance to do something like that."

The experience also gave Lobred a keen perspective on the practice of paying a maker a deposit for a custom-ordered knife before it was made.

"If a maker accepts a deposit, he can't just put the money in the bank and sit on it," he opines.

Replete in mutton-chop sideburns, Lobred checks out a bowie by *Blade Magazine* Cutlery Hall-Of-Famer© Jimmy Lile under the watchful gaze of the maker at the 1972 Knifemakers' Guild Show in Kansas City. *(photo courtesy of Phil Lobred)*

According to Lobred, this 1850s Will & Finck San Francisco knife in his collection is "arguably the fanciest known." *(Point Seven photo)*

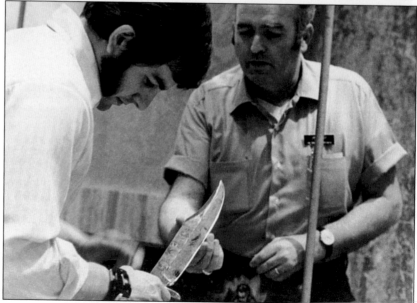

Kyle Ford, Lobred's 13-year-old grandson, hangs out with Blade Magazine Cutlery Hall-Of-Famer© Bob Loveless in the Loveless shop. "He has knives, he likes knives, hopefully he will grow up to be a knife collector," Lobred notes of Kyle. "After all, he obviously knows Bob Loveless!" *(photo courtesy of Phil Lobred)*

"I used to pay for knives up front thinking that would put pressure on the maker to get my knife done. All it really did was put him behind the eight ball. He's spent the [deposit] money and he doesn't have time to make the knife."

In '74, Lobred accompanied Hibben on a private audience with Presley. Hibben knew Ed Parker, the renowned Kenpo martial arts instructor who, in addition to being Presley's karate instructor, also had been one of the King's bodyguards. Hibben made a Kenpo knife in which Presley had expressed interest, so Parker arranged for Hibben to meet Presley and present one of the knives to him, and Lobred was invited along for the presentation. Lobred expected a quick handshake and that would be it, but he says Presley was a most gracious host. They all stayed up until 2 a.m. talking anything and everything, including knives.

By 1973, Lobred was collecting a style potpourri, from bowies to folders. About 1975, he switched to all full-tang knives, mostly drop-point hunters. "I began to slowly sell off the first collection to find room and money to continue to upgrade," he explains.

It was around then that he became interested in San Francisco knives—small dress bowies popularized by Michael Price, Will & Finck and others in the mid-19th century. "Within a short period of time I was collecting only San Francisco knives," he remembers.

Warenski's King Tut

The King Tut exhibit came to Los Angeles in 1982, and Lobred was interested in having a reproduction made of one of the two knives—the gold one—found on the Tut mummy. "As a sole authorship project, there was only one knifemaker at that time capable of pulling it off, and that was my friend, Buster Warenski," Lobred recalls.

Lobred remembers that, though Warenski was intrigued, at first he was not convinced he should take on such a massive undertaking. Meanwhile, Lobred would have to sell most of his collection of full-tang knives to pay for the project. He began to study books on Tut and was drawn deeper.

"It was all-consuming for a couple of years. It drained me," Lobred explains. "It took every spare nickel I could get my hands on. I had to liquidate my prized collection to do it."

Lobred spoke with Warenski several times and Warenski started to get excited about making the knife. "It required goldsmithing skills he did not have then, and some of these skills were almost lost over time," Lobred states. "Only a few living goldsmiths were known to still do granulation work, for instance."

Lobred gave 10 or 12 one-ounce Canadian gold maple leaf coins to Buster to melt down to start the blade. In the end it took 33 ounces of gold to complete. For over a year, they studied pictures of the knife and talked endlessly and studied everything Tut-related they could find. It was difficult to find published pictures of every part of the knife and, as far as the Egyptians were concerned, it was strictly forbidden to photograph the knife.

After a five-year ordeal, Warenski finished the repro and it was exhibited at the 1987 Guild Show. It was a sensation, making the cover of *BLADE* and otherwise taking the handmade world by storm.

During the early 1980s it became increasingly apparent to Lobred that a niche for art knives was unfilled. Makers knew they could make several hunting knives and sell them easily at the Guild Show but, if they took art knives to the show, they might come home with the same knives unsold. As a result, Lobred broached the idea of the Art Knife Invitational.

With support and help from Ted and Betty Dowell, he put on the first Art Knife Invitational in 1983 at the MGM Grand in Reno, Nev., and again in 1984. The 1983 show consisted of 16 of the world's top makers, each of whom brought the best art knives they could make for sale to a small but discerning group of collectors. The collectors could submit one bid per knife. Though only a smattering of collectors attended, sales were great. The 1984 show was also a sales success. Nonetheless, Lobred experienced trouble getting the commitment he needed from some of the participating makers, so he put the AKI "into mothballs" for a time.

By the early 1990s, sentiment began to grow to resurrect the show, only instead of an annual event it would be held every other year. In 1993 the AKI reappeared, this time at the Marriott and Marina in San Diego, Calif. Once again, sales were excellent and the event has been held every other year since.

Tips from The Top

Lobred has watched the handmade knife movement evolve over the years and, as he notes, while some things have transformed, others have not.

"I don't think collecting has changed much from the early days. Prices have," he observes. "Knives have certainly evolved from those early days. Certainly knife steels have changed over the last 40 years, but handle materi-

Amidst some of his handmades sometime in the early 1970s, Lobred puts pen to paper. *(Sid Latham photo)*

als have not. About everything known to man has been used or tried as a knife handle right from the start."

His collecting rule No. 1: Buy what you like. "Go to shows and look at knives. Read everything you can and learn something about the item you want to collect," he points out.

He says purveyors are extremely important in the handmade knife world. "There have always been only a handful of stores that carry handmade knives. The purveyors are the galleries, so to speak, for the knifemaker," he observes. "The only difference I see in the knife collector of today and the collector of the '70s is that with the wealth of information in the mainstream now, most new collectors are better prepared, better informed," he assesses.

At the forefront of the modern

communication phenomenon is the internet. "It is the information highway," he opines. "The internet sells knives for makers, collectors and purveyors alike. The internet shows off collections worldwide. The forums make it possible for people all over the world to sit and chat like they were in the same room, to share ideas and ask questions, to learn."

Still, he offers one caveat to the Worldwide Web.

"The internet is a shopping aid compared to a knife show, which is a hands-on experience that cannot be beat," he emphasizes.

Whatever the form of communication, as long as collectors are communicating, knife collecting will continue to flourish.

"This networking and camaraderie keeps knife people collecting years longer than they might otherwise. It becomes a lifestyle," he concludes, "not just a hobby."

Goo-Goo-Eyed for Gemstone Knives

Precious stone inlays enliven knives, build character and enhance the pieces

By Mike Haskew

They dazzle and delight. They glitter and gleam. Gemstones captivate the knifemaker and the knife enthusiast alike. Those who create cutlery that incorporates precious and semiprecious stones are something of a breed apart, an uncommon clan within the greater family.

The combination of stone and steel is timeless, as evidenced in the Legacy Series by the late master Buster Warenski. The knives, including the King Tut Dagger and the Gem of the Orient, not only conveyed history but made history as well.

Why gemstones? The question is simple in the asking, yet the answers are as varied as the stones themselves. For Texan Bill Keller, the response is quick and decisive.

"Flash!" he responded. "You've gotta have some glitz in there every once in a while, right? I like red, so I use a lot of rubies, and I am working with agates and jaspers now."

Kellers utilizes preset stones from Signity, and works with precision drill equipment to prepare the seats, securing the settings, stones and bezels to the pieces. His tour de force is a pearl-handle, double-action automatic knife with topaz, ruby and blue sapphire accents.

"That was the first one I did, and I was just proud as punch over it," he remembered.

For more than 30 years, Jot Singh Khalsa has conveyed an artistic, moral and religious message in his work with knives and gemstones. Like numerous other knifemakers, he began his artistic career as a jewelry maker.

"I started making knives in 1979," Khalsa recalled. "I was in college studying jewelry making at the state university in New Paltz, New York. Also, I was becoming involved in yoga and meditation, and because my teacher was a Sikh, I learned that among them there is a long tradition of living as protectors of the weak and the innocent. One of the symbols of the Sikh religion is the kirpan, a knife that serves as a reminder to protect the innocent."

The Jeweled Sword

Khalsa believes his real gifts have always been related to artistic capabilities. His jeweled sword—in 24-karat gold zirconium with lapis, sterling silver, and patches of diamonds and garnets set throughout the handle—won best of show in Chicago last year and revealed his artistic prowess. The overall length of the sword is 42 inches, and the blade is

Jot Singh Khalsa's "The Clown" button-lock folding knife sports a nickel-damascus blade, jasper handle with black-pearl accents, engraving and gold inlay by Rick Eaton, and a carved spine inlaid with black-lip mother-of-pearl. *(SharpByCoop.com photo)*

exquisite Devin Thomas twist-pattern damascus.

"Every piece of stone is rather unique," commented Jot. "If you hunt out exciting minerals, they can lend a whole new excitement to a piece with the possibilities of patterns and colors you can get. There are many possibilities in finding the one with the right temperament, not too brittle or soft.

"Jaspers are probably the most suitable stones for handles," Jot added, "and they are related to agate. Agates are very hard, and the jaspers are hard as well, but they are also very tough and resilient."

Cutting and polishing the handle materials himself, Jot purchases cut diamonds, rubies, garnets and emeralds. Taking great care, he guards against any costly misstep.

"I think unexpected breakage is the biggest challenge in working with gemstones," he commented, "because you can be working with a $1,000 piece of mineral and if it breaks in some fashion you must find new."

The Rhode Island School of Design gave John Lewis Jensen the basis of his knifemaking genesis, and knifemaker George Dailey, a fellow graduate of the school, added fuel to the fire. With a degree in fine arts in jewelry making and metalsmithing, Jensen was nevertheless unsure about the path his career would take.

"At the time I was really interested in the process and techniques of making jewelry but knew I didn't necessarily want to make wearable pieces," he said. "During that time, I met George at an alumni association event and discovered that he was

Dellana developed knifemaking skill while leveraging a background in high-end jewelry making. She credits her mentor Jim Schmidt for heightening her skills and sharing techniques. (PointSeven photo)

a part-time knifemaker. I connected with him, and he showed me the ropes."

From learning the knifemaking ropes, Jensen has progressed rapidly in little more than a decade. Today, he employs gemstones on just about every knife.

Using a variety of gemstones, with sapphires, garnets, and peridot as favorites, Jensen allows the stones to complement

Black-lip pearl handle scales and Turkish Twist-pattern damascus blade steel are accented by iolite stones and garnets set in 18-karat gold on Nuibiru, a creation by John Lewis Jensen. The bolsters are etched and hot-blued composite Gibeon meteorite with citrine, peridot, and garnet insets. Abalone inlays and iolite complement the titanium tang wrap.

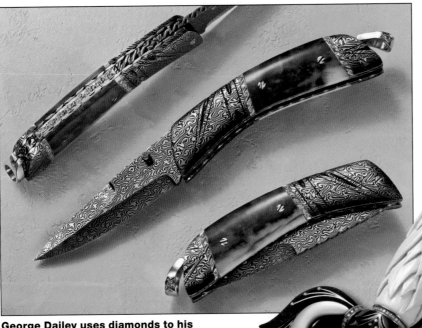

Van Barnett's "Garden of Eden" boasts 124 diamonds totally 3.4 carats set in 14k gold, a carved-ivory handle, carved and hot-blued steel guard and pommel and a ladder-pattern damascus blade. *(PointSeven photo)*

George Dailey uses diamonds to his advantage by inlaying them in gold at the ends of the handle slabs, along the fileworked back spacer and liners, in the thumb stud and on the gold dangler of the damascus locking-liner folder. *(SharpByCoop.com photo)*

the overall knife through form, function and aesthetics. For John, the actual selection of stones comes late in the knifemaking process. First, he draws the knife on paper, placing the gems conceptually. Then, the piece is constructed.

Informed by the Knife

"Not until the titanium is anodized, the mother of pearl polished and the damascus etched does the knife inform me as to the stones that I will use," he said. "The gems are the cherry on top. I use them in every single piece I make. They are a huge part of the overall aesthetic. Another dimension is the style of construction that I use. I build all my knives as sort of a layered

sandwich, so everything is put together with screws that are never seen. I can use the stones to cover the screws."

Although the ruby is red, the garnet, he says, is a deeper hue and therefore a favorite. The green of the emerald is a bit garish, but the tourmaline and peridot suit his tastes nicely.

"I am a painter, as well, and have been all my life," said John. "I definitely approach knives very much from a painting perspective. If you look at my work in comparison to a lot of knifemakers, it is pretty colorful. It is more important to use the stone that works with the piece than to use the stone for the sake of the stone."

One of Jensen's most recent

works may in fact become his most memorable. The dagger includes a blade of Daryl Meier Turkish Twist damascus, deeply etched and blackened through a process similar to bluing, which results in hints of purple and bronze. The tang wrap is a slab of titanium, and the liners are titanium as well. The handle and bolsters are hot-blued meteorite and composite black-lip pearl. The base has nearly 40 stones in it, including garnet, citrine, iolite, peridot, blue topaz and amethyst.

When the plywood mill he worked in closed its doors 18 years ago, Rainy Vallotton accepted an invitation from his father, Butch, to learn knifemaking. Working with stones is a fairly recent development, but has begun to fit nicely with Rainy's style.

"It's only been about two-and-a-half years," he commented. "A customer had some stones and asked me to give it a shot. I used many from him, cut stones to cabochons, rubies to black opals. Stones are very fragile and can be temperamental. I broke a few trying to learn and found that I had a lot more to learn about how and what to do and use in my settings."

Rainy credits a young man named Torston Bull with helping him learn more about working with gemstones. Polished with a flat side, cabochons are his favorite, as opposed to cut stones. The glisten and sparkle of rubies and sapphires are high on his list.

"I like to use stones in bolsters, buttons and back springs," remarked Rainy. "They are the parts that show off best to me. Darrel Ralph pushed me into doing file work, and I soon found that it accented the stones like a wedding ring, adding sparkle and glitz to something that made my knives even more stylish."

A Single Sapphire

Some time ago, Rainy was one of several knifemakers who participated in a tribute to Jerry Rados and his fine Turkish damascus. Rainy contributed the setting of a single sapphire in the front bolster to accent the damascus.

When Van Barnett married his wife, Dellana, in 1999, the two knifemakers quickly discovered that their collaborations, and their own distinctive styles could coexist and even reach new levels of expression. Van is a veteran knifemaker, primarily self-taught in rural West Virginia. Dellana developed knifemaking skill while leveraging a background in high-end jewelry making.

"I had started out early doing art knives and did some elaborate ones," remembered Van, "but I never incorporated gemstones until I met Dellana in 1997. Personally, I believe gemstones tend to give more depth, three dimensionality, and life to a piece. Actually, I like to use diamonds, sapphires and rubies, and I also cut opals."

Among other amenities, Curt Erickson's dagger features a fluted-ancient-ivory handle, engraving by Julie Warenski-Erickson, and garnets inlaid in gold on the guard and engraved sheath. (SharpByCoop.com photo)

A two-time winner of the W.W. Cronk Award from The Knifemakers' Guild, Van cites the Garden Of Eden dagger as one of his most memorable works. The 19-inch knife includes a ladder-pattern damascus blade, 24-karat gold inlay, carved ivory, blued steel fittings and 124 diamonds.

Not only does Dellana accent her knives with gemstones, she also maintains an extensive personal collection. "I have always just loved gemstones in jewelry for the color they can bring into a metal piece. I don't use stones just to blob them on so I can charge extra," she related. "The whole design has to flow. Gemstones are magic. They are beautiful, and my whole design concept revolves around beauty."

A lover of diamonds, rubies, sapphires and emeralds, Dellana is also partial to black opals, cutting and polishing her own stones.

One of her most memorable pieces is the Golden Heart sword, a collaborative effort with Van. A *Knives 2009* Wooden Sword Award winner, the Golden Heart was a four-year project incorporating more than four pounds of 14-karat gold, 30 karats of diamonds, and a bevy of rubies.

"With my folders, I think the 'gold-melted' ones are special," she commented, "and I always add gemstones to those. These folders really flow organically and literally look like the gold melted down onto something. I want to do a knife that has a handle that is like puddles of gorgeous black opal showing through melted gold."

The attraction of the gemstone is stronger than a magnet, inexorably pulling the knifemaker and the knife purchaser closer. Whatever its color, cut or clarity, a gemstone augments a piece with sparkle and personality plus.

Discovered! The Fine Art of Guilloché

The author demonstrates an art form that seems to attract a discerning clientele of knife collectors

By Allen Elishewitz

Some historians believe that guilloché is derived from ornamental turning of medieval times. Ornamental turners were, and are, craftsmen who turn wood, ivory and some soft metals using a special type of lathe. The lathe rotates on a floating drum and employs rosettes that manipulate the drum in specific patterns. Separate from the spindle, a rotary cutter shapes the material as the lathe is spinning. Such lathes work in a similar manner to today's CNC (Computer Numerically Controlled) lathes with live tooling.

In medieval times, ornamental turners shaped material into complex and elaborate designs that were used in everyday items like bedposts, pillars, vases and plates.

Guilloché differs from ornamental turning because it is accomplished using a fixed cutter. The cutter has a very specific shape, and the degree of sharpness is essential to the quality of the cut. Guilloché is a combination of engraving and pantograph designs. The engraving results from the cutter and how it removes material. The pantograph function allows the design of the patterns (rosettes) to be duplicated or manipulated to give a slightly different appearance. These images can be simple or complex, and even three-dimensional. Guilloché is traditionally used on soft materials, such as brass, silver and gold,

The author's fancy "E-Lock Pirate" folding knife showcases fine spiral-wave-pattern guilloché.

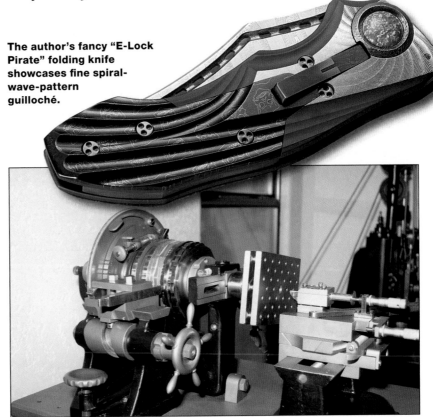

The rose engine is an American-made Charles Field machine from Providence, RI.

The Lienhard straight line is a rare Swiss-made machine.

The author uses a Glendo Accu-Finish diamond grinder to sharpen the guilloché cutters.

After achieving the proper angles and polishing, the author sets the machine at 90 degrees (a flat surface on the cutting edge) to produce a tool that will cut and burnish the material at the same time.

Knifemaker Allen Elishewitz inspects the cutter for proper finish, shape and cutting angles.

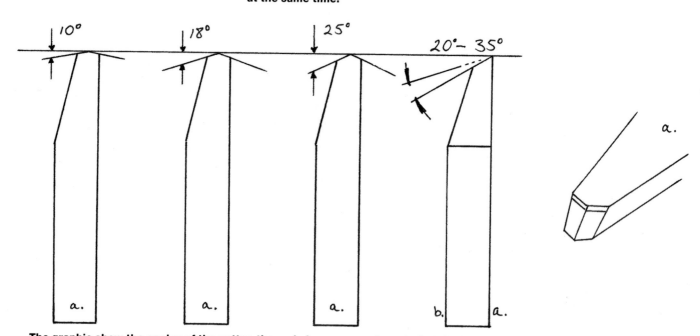

The graphic show the angles of the cutter, the end clearance angle and what the front of the cutter should look like.

but the author has been known to work with titanium, which is a hard medium.

There are two styles of guilloché machines: One is a rose engine, and the other is called a "straight line." Both machines operate in a similar fashion for basic functions. The main difference between the two is that the rose engine works like a lathe with the material rotating on it; while the straight-line machine acts as a shaper with the material moving up and down in a straight line. Illustrated are some examples of rose engine and straight-line machines made in the early 1900s.

The sharpness of the cutter plays an important role in the final appearance of the design on the piece, just as the finish on the cutter dictates the finish of the engraving on the material. For example, if the cutter is rough, the finish on the material will be rough. This is why "guillochéurs"

A rose engine features coarse and fine cam adjustments, and the photo shows a coarse adjustment used for making zigzag-pattern guilloché.

This is the fine worm gear adjustment typically used to create moiré patterns (wavelike patterns). The knob is usually notched to give the guillochéur a reference as to how much the pattern has been shifted.

Here is a close-up of a rubber making contact with a rosette. As the spindle rotates, the pattern of the rosette is transferred to the material.

can range from 20 to 35 degrees. The steepness of the angle is due to the fact that the spindle not only turns in a circular motion, but also moves in a linear direction. One of the most important but rarely mentioned techniques in tool sharpening is putting a 90-degree flat surface on the cutting edge. Contrary to what one might think, the slight dulling of the cutter actually produces a tool that will cut and burnish the material at the same time.

Guilloché machines are basically hand-powered miniature lathes. Each one integrates some kind of hand- or foot-powered lever connected to a flywheel. The flywheel powers the drum through the use of leather belts, and the drum is what holds the rosettes and the cam mechanism on the spindle. The drum and rosettes are on moving carriages that tilt left to right, movement that allows the rosettes and spindle to rotate freely.

The rosettes have different patterns or designs that the guillochéur attempts to duplicate. A rubber—a piece of steel that rubs against the rosettes to transfer the pattern to the rotating spindle—remains in contact with the rosettes, basically acting as a giant "Spirograph." There are usually two sets of cams incorporated into the operation of the drum/spindle. One cam is a worm gear for fine adjustments and offsets, and the other a coarser offset, which is usually faster and easier to use than the worm gear.

The cams can manipulate the patterns and create 3-D or even more complex designs. As the worm gear or coarse notches are used, the rosettes are shifted out of their phase: In other words, the patterns can be moved side to side.

spend a lot of time sharpening and polishing their cutters.

The angles of the cutting surface of the cutter can range from 130 to 160 degrees. That leaves only a 10-to-25-degree variance from side to side. The 130-to-160-degree angle is wide enough to allow light to reflect

out of each cut. If the cutter left a sharper angle, the reflection of the design would be dull.

An end clearance angle is the angle in front of the cutter where the material is cleared while cutting. The end clearance angle is usually very steep, more so than on a typical lathe tool, and

The cross-slide is a completely separate unit from the lathe/guilloché machine. The main purpose of the cross-slide is to hold the engraving tool or cutter, to control its depth of cut and its side-to-side movement. The cutter is held firmly in place next to the guide, and the purpose of the guide is to control the depth that the engraving tool cuts.

The art knife starts of with a straight guilloché pattern and turns into a moiré.

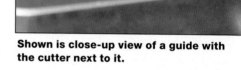

Shown is close-up view of a guide with the cutter next to it.

The author modified his machine with a micrometer head to precisely control the movement of the guide. The radius worm gear that's visible allows the machine operator to change the angle of the cutter so he or she can apply guilloché to curved surfaces.

On a Charles Field cross-slide, the knob to move the carriage has a ratchet attached to it. By moving the two screws and bolts located on the frame, one can control the amount of movement of the cross-slide. There are different versions of cross-slides, but they all achieve the same purpose.

With the guide in front of the cutter, the engraving tool cannot cut the material. The guide is usually located about .002-inch behind the cutter, and once the guide makes contact with the material, the cutter stops cutting. A radius adjustment worm gear on the cross-slide allows the guilochéur to control the cutter while guilloché is applied on a curved surface.

The cutter, guide and worm gear are mounted on top of a cross-slide in the X-axis (left to right). The cross-slide can be set up on a ratcheting system to allow the guillochéur to move it in one direction only. Not only can it travel in one particular direction, but the amount of travel can also be controlled. For example, if a knifemaker or machinist wanted each of the engraved cuts to be .015-inch side by side, he or she would set up the ratchet so it only allowed to the operator to move the carriage .015-inch at a time.

Guilloché is applied. In the background to the right in the photo, the rubber makes contact with the pattern bar, while in front, the cutter removes a nice piece of material. The guide controlling the depth of cut resides next to the cutter. The pattern begins to develop as each cut is completed and the cross-slide is moved.

Guilloché on the dial of the sterling silver watch is in a spiral basket-weave pattern.

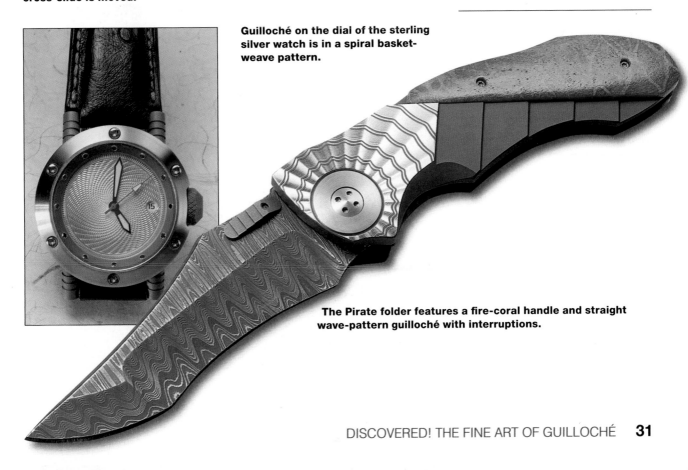

The Pirate folder features a fire-coral handle and straight wave-pattern guilloché with interruptions.

Fine Knives from the Far North

Strømeng blades exude and embody the tradition of Norwegian knifemaking

By Roderick T. Halvorsen

Nearly 200 years ago, some of my ancestors left the crags and fjords of Norway and commenced wandering to other lands. Despite the distance and time, many cultural aspects of the Old Country grab my attention, and the unique and ancient craft of Norwegian knifemaking is surely one of them.

Many traditional knives of Fenno-Scandinavia possess similar traits. Stick tangs, carved birch handles, pocket sheaths and slim, trim, utilitarian blades round out the common features. Many Americans are unfamiliar with such knives and the advantages each one offers.

And few, no doubt, have even heard of Strømeng knives.

Located far north above the Arctic Circle in the Land of the Midnight Sun, and nestled in the town of Karasjok, Norway, "Knivsmed Strømeng" has been building blades for the Sami (indigenous people of northern Sweden, Norway, Finland and the Kola Peninsula) since the 1700s.

The hardy Sami (pronounced Sah-meh), more commonly known to Americans as the Lapps, have relied on Strømeng knives for performing the myriad tasks required in their age-old work herding reindeer, and due to where they live, merely surviving in the Arctic.

In today's world, few people practice millennia-old traditions like the Sami do, and fewer still family-owned businesses can boast continuous services to one group of people for hundreds of years

The author developed a real fondness for the Strømeng KS7, which he describes as a splitting wedge, a machete and a 3-inch fillet knife all wrapped into one.

The "Krumkniv," or "arched knife," is the reindeer-hunting knife of the Sami.

The "Krumkniv," or "arched knife," is the reindeer-hunting knife of the Sami.

brass ferrules at the hilts, the latter for strength and to prevent the wood from splitting at high stress points. Unlike many common Scandinavian knives, the special Strømeng Lapp knives boast tangs that extend the full lengths of the grips, with the ends peened to brass butt plates in an effort to prevent chipping or cracking of the handles if dropped.

Hunting Season & Home on the Ranch

I had the privilege of examining and putting to work several Strømeng knives in the field during hunting season and at home on the ranch.

I greatly enjoyed the features that earned Strømeng such a high level of respect among the company's main customers—the Sami herders.

Specifically, I obtained a model KS7 with a 7 1/8-inch blade; a KS8F sporting an 8 1/8-inch blade; and the highly specialized K1 featuring a 5 3/8-inch blade.

First-time handlers of traditional Nordic knives frequently comment on how light they feel, and may even be deceived into believing them delicate. Indeed, none of the Strømeng knives I tested fall into the common, blocky, "sharpened pry-bar" genre of some American survival knives. The long KS8F tipped the postal scale at only 10 ounces, with the KS7 going 7.5 ounces, and the KS1 a full three ounces lighter yet. For contrast, a U.S.

From skinning and gutting to butchering, the KS8F did it all on this bear.

as can the Strømeng family! For much of that time, located in a small forging shop, the Strømeng family also made other tools and even steel runners for sledges, but today the business remains focused on knives.

Strømeng knives are stamped from 74NiCr2 steel. Commonly considered saw steel, with a .70 percent carbon content, my experience with it indicates similar working qualities to 1080 blade steel. It will rust but is easily sharpened at a Rockwell hardness of 58RC, exhibiting excellent edge-holding characteristics.

A new file will bite the edge, and similar to simple carbon steels like 1060 and 1095, stone-work is a breeze. The knives feature arctic birch handles and

Featured from left to right are three Strømeng models, the K1 Krumkniv, the KS7 and the KS8F.

Navy MK2, with a similar blade length to the KS7, is three ounces heavier.

Used in their traditional locales under the most rigorous and taxing circumstances, Strømeng's products represent true, working survival knives. Setting them apart from other Nordic types, the knives have longer blades, and they handle similar to light machetes. For common hunting and camping tasks, the blades I tested blend the chopping efficiency of machetes with the handling of kitchen, skinning and boning knives.

As is common with many traditional Nordic edged tools, the Strømeng models do not possess finger guards or cross guards of any type. This feature frequently concerns first-time users who are accustomed to knives with finger guards, and who may choke up on the handles until their index fingers rest against the guards.

With traditional Nordic knives, users must keep their fingers away from the edges! I myself have employed such knives for many years and have never cut myself due to my hand creeping up on the edge, but certainly it could happen with less care.

For those who simply cannot get comfortable with a guard-less knife, Strømeng makes a series of models with brass cross guards. Yet knives without guards are the most traditional of Norse tools. I suspect that those who reject such tradition must deny the pleasures of eating lutefisk too!

The narrow, stick tang common to Nordic knives allows the wooden handles to be carved and shaped into highly ergonomic grips. In my opinion, full-tang knives rarely compare in comfort to the traditional Scandinavian type for long hours of use.

Stickiness of Birch Grips

I found Strømeng knives to exhibit the best in hand purchase under a wide variety of conditions. Even when I was working with cold, wet, bloody and greasy hands, the Strømeng knives remained steady. Like other forms of wood handles, the birch grips possess a certain stickiness under all conditions in which I have used them.

Scabbard designs of the Strømeng knives reflect centuries of Norwegian dedication to the pocket sheath. Leather sheaths are made with a seam running up the back of the scabbard that lies against the flat of the blade. Such a design allows the blade edge to lie against one layer of leather, which can unfortunately result in penetration of the scabbard by the blade if care is not taken in withdrawing and sheathing the edge.

The proper technique for inserting or withdrawing a blade from such a sheath is to use two hands, one to pull the knife out and the

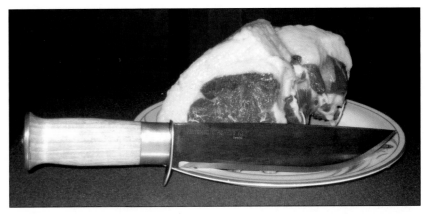

Whether designed with black bear in mind or not, the KS8F easily made fine steaks, chops and roasts.

Pinching the scabbard prevents cutting it when withdrawing or inserting the knife.

other to pinch the opening of the scabbard, thereby preventing the blade edge from contacting the mouth of the scabbard and cutting it. In practice, once sheathed, the upper part of the sheath grips the spine of the blade and prevents the steel edge from lying against the scabbard, and if a bit of care is given, a well-made pocket sheath can last a long time.

On my daily hikes, while hunting and butchering over the course of a month, I spent quite a bit of time using all three of the models I obtained. The KS8F boasts a long, axe-ground blade that is .112 inches thick with a matte-black blade finish resulting from a nickel penetrate. This finish prevents rust and seems to hold up quite well. No doubt this feature was required when the knife became standard issue for the Norwegian military as a survival tool.

As a military knife, it possesses features somewhat uncommon to many other Strømeng knives. For example, it is fitted with a brass finger guard. The guard, of course, precludes the use of a full pocket sheath, but the makers have provided an ingenious design with a flap that not only retains the knife, but also holds it snugly in the sheath. The closure is Velcro, and while certainly not in keeping with materials of ancient tradition, works well indeed!

I carried the knife extensively and built a number of blinds, cleared shooting lanes around them and then used the knife for gutting, skinning and butchering a black bear I had shot. I did not sharpen the edge except for occasionally drawing it against a steel, and at the end of the day I could still pop hairs off the back of my hand anywhere on the edge.

For a knife with a steeply ground edge with which the makers encourage opening soup cans, I found this most impressive! I should add that all three of my kids have owned KS8F knives since receiving them as Christmas gifts from a Norwegian friend a year ago. The knife trio has been used for butchering and trail-clearing tasks while hunting, skiing and hiking for the better part of a year

now, and all are holding up well.

One salient feature that allows the KS8F to be used as such an effective chopping tool is the design of the handle butt. A wide swell at the end of the handle is designed to, and does, act as a secondary grip, allowing the user to slide his hand down and grasp it with the last two or three fingers, thereby gaining full length and leverage of the blade and a part of the grip itself. Using a whipping motion, the 8-inch blade, in essence, acts as an 11 ¼-inch blade and gains all the added cutting force of a machete.

Loyal to Sami Tradition

Unlike the military KS8F, the KS7 knife remains completely loyal to Sami tradition. It represents the quintessential "samekniv" and is even used as a gift in a Lutheran church confirmation rite among the Sami people. The KS7 serves as a common model for an all-around camp, hunting and "field kitchen" knife. The blade thickness is .110 inches and features a unique edge grind that blends characteristics of a flat and cannel grind.

The edge has three separate levels of sharpness. Nearest the grip it is more or less dull. The grind extends for about two inches whereupon the edge transitioned into a sharper grind that would not pop hair. Finally, the last three or so inches to the tip were given an absolute razor fine sharpness.

This then is the secret of the samekniv! In effect, the knife is a splitting wedge, a machete and a 3-inch fillet knife all wrapped into one!

Mentioned in the company's literature, the edge closest to the grip is used for such tasks as splitting kindling. The middle section is designed for chopping chores like clearing heavy brush or small trees, or splitting the pelvis of a reindeer. Again, protection of the blade is the purpose of the semi-sharp midsection.

The rest of the blade to the tip is kept for superfine work like cleaning fish, filleting, cutting meat, skinning, and other jobs where a very fine, sharp edge is required. Certainly unique, the design of the samekniv blade speaks to hundreds of years of actual field use and the resultant preferences developed by the Sami themselves.

These are not knives designed by computer graphics in a marketing department and sold as new advances, but rather are made according to the demands placed before the company by the users.

Reverse "Madison Avenue" to be sure! I myself found the "triple-edge" to accomplish everything for which it is it is advertised, but ultimately, after much wood cutting and blind making with the knife, for personal preference reasons largely involving my common use of the knife for cutting rope and twine up close to the grip, I found it easier to merely sharpen the entire edge.

Even though the resulting edge was thinner, very sharp and theoretically, at least, "weaker," I found I could split a butcher sheep's pelvis and deer chest, and also chop through deer neck vertebrae without dulling the blade. For chopping chores involving tough materials like serviceberry, mountain maple and animal bone, the KS7 was the definition of efficiency, particularly so because it, too, possesses a flared butt end. Using the low grip on the handle swell near the butt, the 7-inch blade gains over three inches. I have developed a real fondness for the KS7 knife.

Object Lesson in Tool Design

The KS1 is an object lesson in specialty tool design. Known in Norwegian as "krumkniv," or "arched knife," it is the reindeer-

hunting knife of the Sami. Reindeer are, and have been for millennia, the main source of life-sustaining protein, furs and leather for the Sami people, and the tradition of reindeer herding is still very much alive. It speaks to the high moral standards of a people that they'd think out a knife design that would most quickly and humanely dispatch stock in the remoteness of their high Arctic environs.

The heavy, .309-inch-thick, hook-shaped, almost triangular blade sports an edge on the inner curve of the concave blade, and it is wielded point down. Gripped with the thumb in the finger choil, this knife is used for butchering reindeer behind the head where the blade's point can easily enter and penetrate. During butchering here on the ranch, I found that it works well.

Holding a Strømeng knife in one's hand is holding hundreds of years of tradition and the refinement of practical design. We in America frequently find ourselves looking for new ideas and improvements to our gear, so it is refreshing to find knives that are the end result of hundreds of years of hard use, those that represent designs the users themselves see no need to improve. Indeed, after using Strømeng knives, it is difficult for me to see where they could be improved upon, even if tradition was thrown to the wind.

Strømeng knives can be ordered through Ragweed Forge, P.O. Box 326 Sanborn, NY 14132, www.ragweedforge.com/Stro-mengCatalog.html, ragnar@ragweedforge.com.

Gripping the swell at the handle butt on the KS7 knife and slightly bending the branches while cutting made for easy clearing of tough brush.

Road Trips Gave Birth to the Souvenir Knife

Experience the grandeur of the country through the novelty of tourist blades

By Richard D. White

Travel and tourism have changed dramatically over the years, and yet, in some ways, stayed relatively the same. The leisurely automobile road trip has often been replaced by a jet blast to a distant location and back, all within the same weekend. Presently, the cost of gasoline and general lack of family time have put additional dampers on vacationers who still wish to view the grandeur of this United States from road level.

For those who have experienced at least one "road trip," it is hard to forget the details of the adventure, not the least of which are the landmarks that continue to dot the landscape from the Great Smoky Mountains to Yosemite National Monument. It seems that everywhere travelers gather, a plethora of tourist traps and souvenir shops are there to greet them. From the Lake of the Ozarks to Estes Park, souvenir shops are sure to provide travelers with everything from ice water to Native American drums, and from polished agates to butterscotch fudge.

It is in these places that the souvenir or tourist knife was born.

My own memories of family road trips include the inevitable souvenir shops, loaded with a plethora of fringed-leather buckskin jackets, paperweights, rubber spears, and cactus jelly; and the predictable bins full of rubber

Western Cutlery offered goldstone-celluloid handles on souvenir knives such as these featuring famous tourist attractions in the greater Colorado Springs, Colo., area.

The outstanding Daniel Peres souvenir knives showcase not only famous Washington, D.C., landmarks, but also fine craftsmanship. The embossed handles depict Mount Vernon—the home of George Washington—and the Washington Monument.

spiders and snakes, turquoise bracelets, gags of all sorts, postcards and shot glasses.

Most of the gift stores also carried displays of pocketknives or small decorated sheath knives, embossed with the names of the nearest national parks or geographical monoliths. The knives were generally of poor quality, some made in the United States, but many from foreign countries, even during the 1950s and '60s. Of course knives and boys are a natural combination, and lucky was the father who escaped the shops without having to purchase at least one knife from the proprietor.

Souvenir knives were not always cheaply made. There was a time when tourist knives were finely crafted, using tempered steel, embossing, and with quality sheaths or pouches, and such early edged objects are the true focus of serious collectors.

One of the earliest tourist destinations was our nation's capital, Washington, D.C., a popular place to travel even before the advent of automobiles and interstates. Architecture viewed at the 1891 Columbian Exposition became a driving force behind the beautification of Washington, D.C., and the modeling of the capital after great European cities, which established D.C. as a focus of civic and national pride.

Plans included the impressive public mall, anchored at one end by the Washington Monument and at the other by the White House and Capitol Building; a major bridge leading to Arlington Cemetery; the Jefferson Monument to honor our founding fathers; the Lincoln Memorial; and fountains, statues and tree-lined boulevards.

Our nation's capitol is the subject of these two Daniel Peres watch fob knives that show intricate detail that mirrors the architectural design of the building.

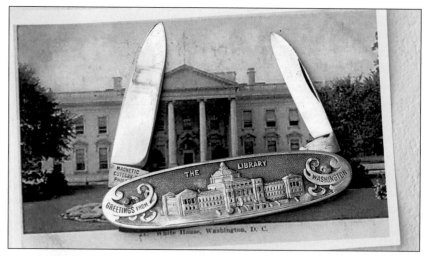

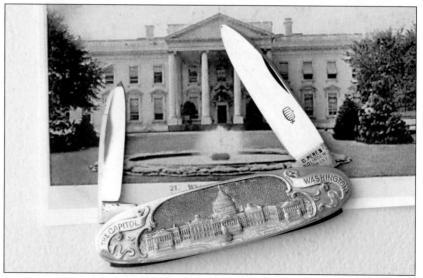

An outstanding Daniel Peres swell-center penknife features yet another view of our nation's capitol in Washington, D.C., with the reverse showing the National Library, all surrounded by a fleur-de-leis pattern.

In the 1930s, Camillus Cutlery offered souvenir knives touting cities throughout the United States, but largely in the eastern half of the country.

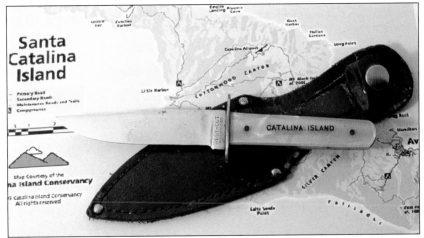

Offered as a souvenir on Catalina Island, just off of California's West Coast, the rare Western Cutlery boys' knife is true in every aspect to its full-size counterpart. Dark lettering pops off the yellow "cracked-ice"-celluloid handle.

Points of Interest in Washington, D.C.

This great American dreamscape also led to the first serious souvenir knives manufactured by Daniel Peres & Co., of Solingen, Germany. Identified by its famous "ale barrel" logo, the company offered intricately stamped knives depicting capital landmarks in a way theretofore unseen. Daniel Peres knives remain sought after for their embellished renderings of the buildings in our nation's capital.

As early as 1805, the company established itself as a manufacturer of fine penknives, and was elected into the Cutler's Guild along with other German blade makers. Since that time, the name Daniel Peres has been associated not only with exquisite penknives, but also with multi-blade folders and bartender's knives, many sporting genuine pearl handles. Daniel Peres is also widely known, however, for making small souvenir knives showcasing stamped or embossed aluminum scales. As

a lightweight, malleable metal that resists corrosion, aluminum proved to be the perfect medium for intricate etchings and embossing.

The knives sold in and around the capital city were of the finest ever produced by Daniel Peres. Made small to fit into vest pockets or attached to watch fob chains, they depict famous Washington, D.C., landmarks from the turn of the century.

The smallest of the watch fob knives are engraved on one side: "Greetings from Washington," with raised, ornate scroll and a floral pattern over a pebbled background. On the reverse side is an accurate rendering of the nation's capitol within a fleur-de-leis outline.

Slightly larger examples of Peres knives depict not only the White House and nation's capitol, but also the Mount Vernon Mansion and Washington Monument. The handle stampings are accurate renderings of the buildings themselves.

In an era of limited photographic capabilities, the knives provided visitors to Washington, D.C., finely crafted examples of the ornate architecture they'd find throughout the unique urban setting. And tourists soon discovered the usefulness of the knives, many of which featured multiple Solingen steel blades and fingernail files. Today, knife and advertising collectors seek out the knives, and the once overlooked blades have moved to the top of many wish lists.

Even though other cities in the United States boast fewer attractions than Washington, D.C., many were also immortalized in handle etchings of pocketknives and small sheath knives. Travelers to almost every major city in the country can find collectible souvenir knives that generally feature celluloid handles of various colors and patterns. Light-mottled-yellow "cracked ice" celluloid was a perennial favorite of tourist knife manufacturers because it provided a light palette for dark lettering.

In all probability, companies like Kutmaster, Imperial, Colonial, Western Cutlery and others made millions of souvenir knives in the 19th century and up through the 1950s. Although we generally think of tourist knives as touting an attraction, like Pikes Peak or the Grand Canyon, many are embossed with only the name of a city.

Tourist Knives in Droves

Utica Cutlery, doing business under its Kutmaster tang stamp, capitalized on local pride by manufacturing thousands of knives embossed with the names of cities all across the United States, but primarily in the East. Among examples are souvenir knives touting Baltimore, Louisville and Rochester.

The Western Cutlery Co., originally located in Boulder, Colo., known also as Western States Cutlery and Manufacturing Co., was a significant manufacturer of souvenir knives. Because of its proximity to the Rocky Mountains, collectors find Western Cutlery knives featuring Pikes Peak, Seven Falls, Grand Lake and Colorado Springs. Although most knife companies offered souvenir knives with neutral white or yellow handles so that dark lettering was easy to read, Western opted for "goldstone" celluloid handles, char-

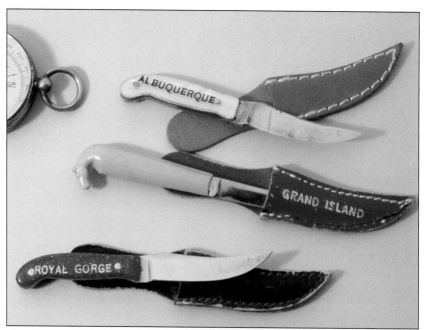

The Western Cutlery miniatures were generally not stamped with the Western logo, making them a true find for serious collectors.

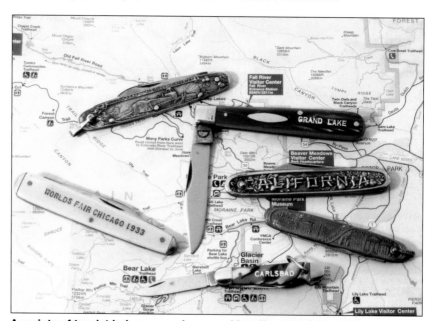

A variety of tourist knives came in several handle materials and sizes, including a brass-handle folder touting Pikes Peak, a Western States celluloid-handle model from Grand Lake, Colo., and a small, mottled-green knife depicting Carlsbad Caverns.

acterized by an orange color with flecks of gold glitter embedded into the material. In order to make the names of cities and attractions stand out clearly, Western chose white paint for the lettering.

Goldstone celluloid, when polished, is a flashy material, and just the thing to attract the eyes of visitors to the Colorado Rocky Mountains. The choice of goldstone may also have been a nod to the many goldmines dotting the Colorado landscape.

Most of Western's goldstone-handle tourist knives are traditional senator penknives, rather small, and featuring two blades. Each with single back springs operating two offsetting blades, the knives were ideal for mass production. Western, however, manufactured another strikingly handsome souvenir knife that is almost impossible to find, and eagerly sought after by Western collectors. Known as the Model 51, it is a small fixed blade or sheath knife, generally not marked with the "Western States Cutlery" tang stamp. It was a Western knife, nonetheless, as early catalogs attest.

The Model 51, with its radical upswept blade, is a miniature of another Western full-sized, production sheath knife, the Model 39, manufactured in the tens of thousands for use by hunters and sportsmen.

The rare, mini versions of the Western sheath knives are only about two inches in length, yet come with sewn-leather sheaths. Made from the same steel as the full-sized models, even more rare are the versions with etched handles showcasing tourist attractions.

The fact that the knives were unmarked gives collectors familiar with early Western States knives a distinct advantage. Those without Western tang stamps often turn up in batches of letter openers or old knife lots. In the past few months, I have seen at least two of the rare knives appear on eBay auctions in lots of "miniature knives." A serious collector of Western knives purchased both eBay pieces because he had a sharp eye, and watched the lots for just such knives. He also had deep pockets, and could afford to put in top bids at the last minute.

Sharp Souvenirs for the Boys

Two unusual Western Cutlery souvenir knives have become real showstoppers. Significantly larger than miniatures, but noticeably smaller than full-size sheath knives, they can only be described as "boys' knives." In our current culture of knife legislation and countrywide fear of children carrying knives, it's refreshing to remember that boys' knives were once made for utilitarian use by adolescents and teens. In addition to Western, KA-BAR was also known for is production of small sheath knives for boys.

The Western Cutlery examples feature cracked-ice-celluloid (so named because of the inclusions that run through the material) handles, one with yellow cracked ice, and the other with lighter, almost white celluloid. Each sheath knife is stamped with a tourist destination on the side of the handle, and outfitted with a nickel silver guard and the same blade steel as full-size models.

The first example, etched "Catalina Island," carries a "WEST-CUT" tang stamp, one that Western Cutlery employed for less expensive knives in the 1930s. Catalina Island is located 22 miles from the California coast, and was a major tourist attraction in the 1920s. In 1929, the gorgeous Casino dancehall was built, largely through donations from chewing gum magnate William Wrigley Jr., to promote tourism. Presently, it is the site of California's first permanent desalination plant.

The second sheath knife, stamped "DEER RIDGE," is made with Western's characteristic upswept blade, and black and red spacers. An exceptional example of Western's quality knife production,

the tang stamp reads "Western, Boulder, Colorado," with a patent number that dates it to the 1930s. The leather sheath, also stamped "WESTERN," has the original price penciled on the back as $1.35. In today's market, it would likely bring upwards of $100.

The location of "DEER RIDGE" is itself somewhat of a mystery. Although there is a Deer Ridge Mountain Resort in Gatlinburg, Tenn., Western Cutlery rarely did business east of the Mississippi River. Other attractions named Deere Ridge include golf courses, vineyards, subdivisions, fishing camps, towns, communities, a campground, and even a correctional institution.

It would take some effort to see which of these locations was established as early as the 1930s, and which went to the trouble of commissioning an advertising knife.

Whether as keepsakes for vacationers traveling throughout the country, or for souvenir knife collectors, the edged mementos provide a glimpse into destinations commemorated in etchings, stampings and embossing. Many souvenir knives were made with the same care as their full-size counterparts.

Somewhat like advertising knives, another subcategory of cutlery collecting, souvenir knives can still be found in mint or near mint condition. Collectors frequently overlook souvenir knives, yet because of the wide scope of the edged keepsakes, a collector could specialize in knives made by a specific cutlery company, or collect only knives commemorating National Parks, monuments or major cities. Souvenir knives open yet another avenue into cutlery collecting that has, until now, been underappreciated.

Walkabout In Werewolf Country

Regardless of whether werewolves are myth or legend, the story and knives are true

By James Morgan Ayres

Have you ever wished for a magical blade to protect you from werewolves and other creatures of legend? I did once, while being menaced by a creature from a nightmare during a moonstruck night while traveling in remote Italian mountains.

The Le Marche region runs along Italy's east coast. The Adriatic's turquoise waters wash its golden beaches. The Romans who flee here to escape the hoards of tourists that overrun their city each summer call the area "Tuscany without the tourists." But the Romans don't venture more than a mile from the beaches. The mountains of the interior have little in common with tamed and manicured Tuscany.

The Sibylline Mountains, part of the Apennine Range, straddle Le Marche. These remote hills and hidden valleys are wrapped in myth and legend. Over the centuries the area became home to healers and herbalists, sorcerers who could call up storms, and legend had it, werewolves.

Today Le Marche is still rumored to be home to wild magic. When I mentioned to one of my friends in Italy, an anthropologist, that we planned to do some foraging for wild edible plants during our walkabout in the Sibylline, she warned us to never dig up a mandrake root for fear of causing a

Mist rises from the werewolf's valley—the valley of Monteleone, Le Marche, Italy. The remote hills and valleys of the Sibylline Mountains are wrapped in myth and legend.

storm that could wash away roads, flood valleys and send boulders tumbling down mountainsides.

Before leaving, I had read up on the area's fauna and learned that the Sibylline mountains were in fact home to one of Europe largest population of wild wolves, with packs running free and taking down deer, sheep and sometimes cows. There had been no mention

of werewolves in the biology text.

I was in the company of MaryLou, who goes by M.L., lovely wife and faithful companion of a hundred adventures, stalwart in emergencies and tolerant of my tendency to get us into situations. We intended to wander through the hills, mostly on foot and unencumbered by reservations.

We were equipped for our

From top are the knives the author's wife, MaryLou, took on a long hike into the valley of Monteleone: a Wayne Goddard "Little Bitty Knife," a Spyderco Fred Perrin Street Beat and a Spyderco Cricket.

While traveling in the remote Italian Mountains, the author opted to carry, from top, a Chris Reeve Sebenza, a Fallkniven F1 and a Victorinox Swiss Army Knife.

journey with small rucksacks, a change of clothing for each of us, and some simple camping gear. And of course, knives. Lots of knives. Our first line of defense against evil sorcerers and ravening predators was M.L.'s Spyderco Cricket. Even a werewolf wouldn't mess with M.L. when she's got her Cricket in hand and her dander up. In real life M.L. uses the tiny folder for everything from slicing bread to peeling potatoes.

Fixed Blade Advocate

Anyone who's been reading my scribble in *BLADE Magazine*® knows that I advocate for a strong, handy sized, fixed-blade survival knife. For this trip I chose an old Fallkniven F1. The sturdy little knife is well used. But I keep a good edge on it, and I know it has a reserve of strength if needed.

To avoid my nagging about having a fixed blade, M.L. travels with either a Spyderco Fred Perrin Street Beat, a terrific little knife for daily use, or a Wayne Goddard "Little Bitty Knife," a marvelous pocket-sized fixed blade.

I did not think we would really run into any bad tempered wild animals, shape changers or sorcerers, but I was pretty sure we would encounter more than one bottle of local wine. Against that eventuality I tucked away a Victornox Rucksack, with the all-important corkscrew, in my rucksack.

As an all-purpose folder I brought one of Chris Reeve's Sebenzas, the standard size, classic model. There's something about a Sebenza, tough tool, modern minimal design. I used the Sebenza hard for weeks and never had to touch the edge to a stone.

Like many others I prefer using a folder around town; people accept a folder as an ordinary daily tool, whereas any fixed blade will often stimulate unwelcome comments. When my fixed blade was stashed in my bag I used the Sebenza for almost everything.

Suitably outfitted for our adventure and setting aside our friend's warnings, we hit the road, planning to camp out most nights and stay in an inexpensive country inn every few days. Things didn't turn out quite that way.

Our routine was to rise early and intrepidly trek through the hills each day for at least an hour, sometimes two. One day, overcome by the beauty of the hills with their covering of umber wheat, olive trees with leaves fluttering in mountain winds, and the smell of wine-sweet grapes growing in rows next to the road, we forgot ourselves and pressed on hour after hour.

Howling, Slavering Dogs

In early evening, after dawdling along a country road picking fruit and flowers, we would usually approach a farmhouse to ask if we could camp at the edge of their field. This is a perfectly normal request and acceptable in every European country. Sometimes it was difficult to approach the farmhouses because they were often guarded by howling, slavering dogs, mongrels of uncertain ancestry and fierce disposition straining at their chains and displaying a heartfelt desire to tear us limb from limb.

Until M.L. smiled at them, and told them what good dogs they were, and what a good job they were doing guarding the homestead, and asked them if they would they like her to pet them. They invariably did, rolling over in helpless adoration to have their bellies rubbed, or nuzzling her knee to have their ears scratched. This happens the world over.

M.L. has some kind of dog magic; it works on cats and horses too. You see my strategy now. It was M.L. and her critter magic, not so much her Cricket that was our first line of defense against fierce creatures. I wasn't sure the same magic would work with werewolves but I was willing to give it a try.

No one wanted us camp to in their fields. Everyone insisted that we stay in their homes and take dinner with them and sample the local wine and get to know the whole family. Le Marche is home to a scattering of expatriate Brits, all of who were hospitable and good for great conversation and much fun. We usually helped with preparing dinner, and because people always

have dull kitchen knives, we used our own, and loaned them to our hosts, which sometimes occasioned comment regarding sharpness and design. "What kind of knife is that?" And, "Ouch! Bloody thing is like a razor!" And so on.

When we wearied of our arduous pace we hopped on a local bus, or simply raised a hand for a ride when a vehicle passed by, wandering from stone village to tumbledown Roman ruins, to medieval palaces and windswept mountaintops.

We foraged fresh greens and herbs for salads, all growing wild on the margins of cultivated

The author foraged chicory using a Fallkniven F1 knife.

MaryLou used a Spyderco Cricket to gather figs.

In the shadows of Mount Sibylline, the butcher and his wife, Mario and Estella, plied their trade in the traditional way, working with razor-sharp knives and seasoning pork with wild herbs grown on the hill behind their shop.

fields. Uncultivated fig and plum trees flourished. One evening we stopped in the overgrown yard of an abandoned farm to watch the setting sun set the sky aflame and decided to stay there for the night. We wanted to be alone, and out of doors, and to watch the moon rise and the stars blink on.

As the color faded from the sky, M.L. sliced bread with her tiny Cricket by cutting in a circle around the loaf. We had prosciutto, and tomatos plucked from a roadside garden and sliced with my Fallkniven. M.L. dressed our salad of foraged greens with olive oil and balsamic. The figs went with the last of the Sangovese from the bottle in my pack.

A Flash of Fangs

I awakened during the night to the sound of rustling in the bushes at the edge of the clearing around the house. The noise from the brush grew louder. I was a little foggy from the Sangovese. Anyway, I was pretty sure I saw a flash of fangs in the moonlight. Could this be the creature of legend and nightmares?

A low growling came from the bushes. M.L. woke and asked, "What's that noise?"

"Probably a werewolf."

"Right," she said, turning over to go back to sleep.

Then I saw it: a dark shape, fangs definitely flashing in the moonlight. The creature threw back its head and howled, a long, wavering wail, sending chills up my back. A werewolf for sure. I reached for my Sebenza with my left hand, the Fallkniven clenched in my right.

M.L., hearing the blood-curdling cry, sat up quickly and peered at the bushes, "Here puppy," she said. A whine came from the bushes. "Oh come on over here."

A monster the size of a Fiat 500 slinked out of the shadows. Revealed in moonlight, it looked like a cross between a timber wolf and a Tasmanian devil. Hair bristled on its back. Its tongue hung from a fanged muzzle. The beast stalked slowly towards us. It could have pounced any second.

"There's a nice doggie," M.L. said. "Are you hungry? Want some water?"

The brute licked her hand and, of course, rolled over on its back for a belly rub. M.L. got up and poured water into our single pot, which the animal lapped up while gazing worshipfully at her. She dug out our salami, and prosciutto, and bread, all of which the creature gobbled up with those fangs, and all the while M.L. kept up a patter, "Poor puppy, so hungry, you're such a good dog, and so handsome, are you lost, have some more prosciutto, do you like salami?"

Me? I'm holding onto the knives. Finally the love fest was over and M.L. got back in our sleeping bag. The "poor puppy" snuffled around for a while then lied down at our feet and went to sleep. I dozed off to the sound of its snoring, aware that it could turn savage and go for our throats in the night.

Into the Night

We awakened with sunlight on our faces. Our nighttime visitor had disappeared. Probably hiding from the sun, as werewolves do. We packed up our gear and strolled to a hilltop village in search of coffee. On the way to the café we stopped in a butcher shop for more salami. The butcher plied his trade in the traditional way, working with razor-sharp knives and seasoning his pork with wild herbs he grew on the hill behind his shop. His knives reminded me that we were supposed to do a story on Maniago, the town where knives are made in Italy.

I broke the news to M.L. as

MaryLou cut a walking stick with the Wayne Goddard "Little Bitty Knife."

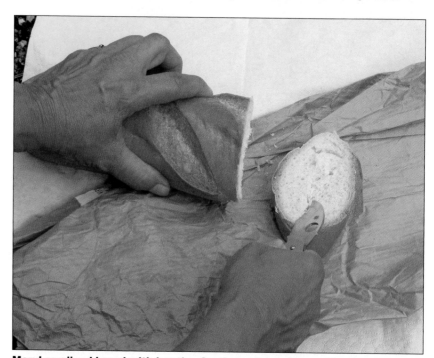

MaryLou sliced bread with her tiny Spyderco Cricket by cutting in a circle around the loaf.

we had coffee on a café terrace overlooking Mount Sibylline. Duty called. We should leave the hills and catch a train; find a hotel in Maniago; call on the Chamber of Commerce; set up interviews and factory tours; make notes and take photos; do things; work.

On the other hand, "There might be a sorcerer who can call up storms in the next valley," I said. "The one over that mountain," pointing to snow-capped Sibylline.

M.L. looked at the beckoning mountain and set down her tiny espresso cup.

"Let's go," she said.

Chips off the Old Rock

Making blades the ancient way revives the native stone smith experience

By William Hovey Smith

The first cutting tools, what early man wrapped his strong, dirty fingers around and used to cut, were formed from stone, wood, shell, bone and obsidian.

Modern "flint knappers," those who chip or knap edges from obsidian, flint, novaculite and other hard, brittle rocks, give insight into the ancient techniques of making blades. The resulting edged implements were once widely used in all cultures, as attested by billions of flint fragments, projectile points and blades found all over the world.

"The Stone Age" was aptly named but somewhat oversimplified, because early man graduated to using metals such as copper (found in its native state) and iron (from meteorites), each of which proved useful, to say nothing of hardwoods, shell and bone.

Favored game observation sites are often littered with tiny

Knifemaker Ken Austin flint knapped the obsidian knife that is shown here on buffalo hide.

flint fragments where hundreds, or thousands, of years ago our stone-using predecessors passed the time by making a few points while scanning the horizon for game. Although commonly known as arrowheads, only the smallest of these points were used on arrows.

As most modern archers can attest, lightweight points fly better, have longer range and are more accurate than ponderous stone heads. In the ancient Southeast, even the hard, sharp scales from the alligator gar made excellent arrow points in ancient times.

Larger points were affixed to short wooden handles as knives, on longer shafts as atlatl (a device made of wood with a handgrip and a hook opposite the grip used to propel a spear) points and on heavier poles as spears and lances. Smaller "micro-blades" were also imbedded into wood to form slashing and cutting implements.

From the point of view of efficiently killing game, the larger the cutting surface and the deeper it could be thrust into an animal, the more effective the result. Lances and spears killed faster than arrows because of their larger points and better penetration.

Although there was trading for favored materials, most native cultures depended on local rock sources to make cutting tools. Many of these were made from minerals of the quartz family, including flint, jasper, chert, vein quartz and occasionally even rock crystal.

Careful workmen in the western United States employed obsidian, a natural volcanic glass, to produce wide, thin and long blades, but these were so brittle as to be considered "art pieces." Even slight sideways blows could break the attractive blades.

The practical useful length limit of a stone blade is about six inches, unless it is made undesirably thick to resist breakage. Modern flint knappers heat treat the primitive-style blades to make the stone easier to work and give

a waxy finish to the surface, but the downside is that the finished product is more likely to break.

Necked and Smooth Points

Much can be told by feeling traditional flint-knapped knives. If the points are necked and feel smooth, they were likely lashed onto shafts with the sides dulled to keep from cutting the lashing sinew. Carrying pointed, stone arrows in quivers also blunted them, making it mandatory to periodically refresh the points. Some stone edges lasted longer than others. Granular materials like quartzite dulled more rapidly, although these tools could be sharp when freshly worked.

Ken Austin of Raleigh, Miss., has been making stone points and blades for more than nine years, and has discovered quite a bit about the practicalities of fashioning and using stone blades.

"I can show you that the Indians heat treated their rocks just

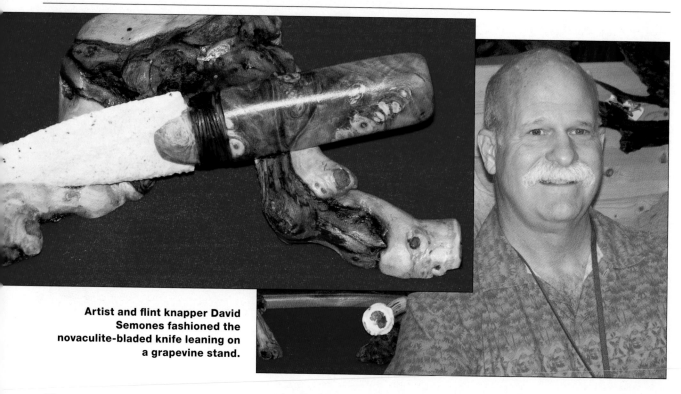

Artist and flint knapper David Semones fashioned the novaculite-bladed knife leaning on a grapevine stand.

From left to right, top, are a jasper arrowhead, a spearhead drill, a knife and a second arrowhead. A mace (war club) is shown at bottom.

as I do to achieve material that was easier to flake with the tip of a deer antler. The local chert, for example, is yellow. Yet, the worked points that I find are red, indicating that they have been exposed to fire," Austin allows.

"These stone-tipped arrows and spears were strictly short-range propositions when used for hunting," he adds. "It was impossible to make the points [of equal weights so that they would] fly [in similar patterns to each other], even when shot from the same bow. If an archer who shoots stone arrows can group them within a pie-plate diameter from 20 yards, he is doing well.

"I am also convinced that spears, except for atlatl points, were jabbed into animals like buffalo at close range, rather than thrown," Austin notes, "because a thrown spear has much less penetration than one powered into an animal with the weight of a man behind it."

Austin said that in the southern states, spear shafts were sometimes fashioned from cane, with the points being attached to short, detachable shafts that slid into the hollow cane segments. Once a thrust was made into a heavy animal, the short shaft and point remained in the animal. The longer part of the spear could be retained, another detachable point inserted and subsequent points pushed into the animal's vitals until it succumbed. Thus a hunter needed to be encumbered with only one spear shaft that could be used with several points.

Try as he might, Austin said that he has yet to produce micro flaking on blade edges without using metal tools. "Deer antler is too soft. I strongly suspect that the fine edges found on ancient blades were made using native copper tools," he notes. "We find copper in North American Indian burials, and I cannot do this sort of work using traditional hammer stones and antler points. I believe that they found and used native copper as a flaking tool, although professional archeologists disagree with me."

Hog Wild in San Saba

Wanting to see how effective stone blades are, I asked Austin to make me a stone-bladed knife to use on game. The first opportunity came on a Texas hog, which I took with a flintlock smoothbore muzzleloader near San Saba. Although I skinned the animal with a steel knife, I used a deer-antler-knapped blade of Knife River flint from North Dakota to cut the meat. Fellow writer Sharon Estes Henson and I were impressed with the efficiency with which the blade butchered the small hog. The cuts were sharp and straight, with the principal difference being that it took a bit more energy for the thicker stone blade to make deep cuts.

I carried the blade in a nylon sheath on my belt, but unfortunately the knife blade broke just forward of the sinew lashings on the handle when it pressed against the steering wheel of my truck as I got in. Any Indian would have reworked this point and fastened it to another handle but, lacking these skills, I discontinued use of the knife except to make the initial cuts against the sternum of a Georgia deer.

The deer was a 90-pound doe taken with another muzzleloader. Fortunately the kill was made early in the day allowing ample time to skin and cut it up using an obsidian-bladed knife provided by Austin. The knife had a 4½-inch, flint-knapped blade attached by sinew and glue to a deer antler handle. Care was taken that the stone blade was used to make only straight jabs and cuts through the hide and muscle tissue. I employed a steel knife to work around the joints, and a saw to cut through the pelvis, sternum and backbone.

Although I did take more time and care than I would have with a steel-bladed knife, the obsidian blade effectively cut the hide once an initial opening had been made. I had no problem with making the slicing cuts necessary when severing the connective tissue between the hide and carcass, and the obsidian blade performed well in separating the meat from the bone.

This process took a bit longer with the stone than with a steel blade. Periodically I had to clean the blade of hair and fat that stuck to the many irregularities of the obsidian blade, but this was a minor inconvenience. The tiny micro-serrations on the blade aided cutting.

Buffalo Skinner

A mature American buffalo is an intimidating animal. Even when dead and lying on its side, the carcass is over three feet high at the hump and over six feet long. This is not an animal that one man can drag anywhere. Small wonder that the Indians sometimes moved camp to the buffalo rather than the other way around. Depending on the time of year, a buffalo's typical coat of twisted brown hair could be over two inches thick and the hide four inches thick at the shoulders.

I shot my buffalo with a smooth-bore .75-caliber ball fired from a flintlock fowler using an English flint at a range of about 40 yards. Now that the buffalo was dead, I wanted to see if Austin's stone knives could assist in processing it. I quickly discovered that there was no hope of pushing the stone blade

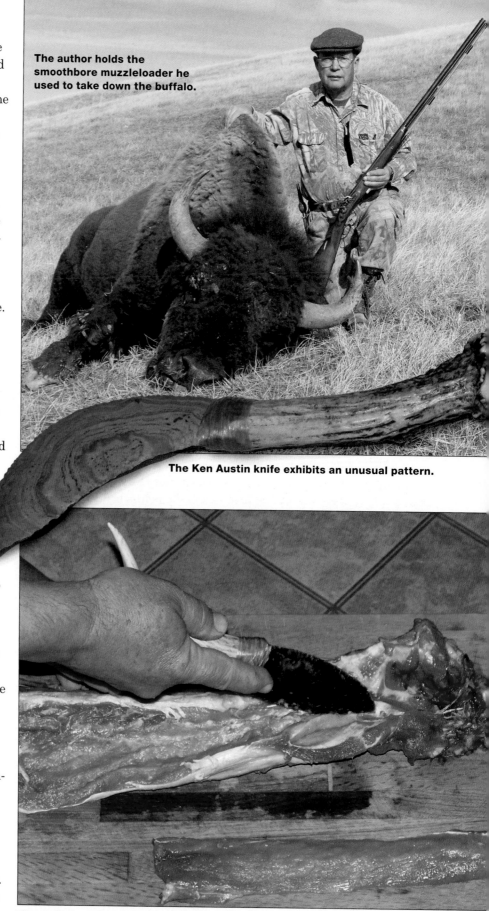

The author holds the smoothbore muzzleloader he used to take down the buffalo.

The Ken Austin knife exhibits an unusual pattern.

The author employs a stone knife to cut back straps from a Texas hog.

The stone points show varying degrees of tempering, with the reddest of the bunch (bottom) having been exposed longest to the fire.

through the thick hide. I could only puncture the thin hide of the underbelly to start the skinning process. And only by laboriously parting the hair and slicing the hide could the thicker portions be cut.

If fat and hair matting on the stone blade had been something of a problem with the smaller deer and hogs, it was an even greater problem working up buffalo meat. To keep the meat clean and the stone edges cutting, the blades had to be constantly wiped.

Heavy stone maces made of tough rocks like andesite or diabase were traditionally used to chop through the ribs and break the heavy bones to extract the marrow, while the more delicate stone knife blades were employed to slice the meat for drying or cooking. The rich, fatty smell of buffalo would have permeated everyone and nearly everything during the butchering process. This was not a bad smell, but difficult to be rid of in a culture that did not have modern soaps. Although some meat was dried and smoked, the usual procedure was that buffalo was eaten until it was gone.

Among the better cuts is buf-falo tongue, which I skinned with the stone knives and smoked. This proved to make an excellent base for a rich soup, to which I added onions and rice. Buffalo Bill was correct when he claimed that this was the best part of the buffalo, and he often reserved the tongue for himself.

Stone Tool Déjavu

People who like knives often experience an eerie feeling of prior existence when sizing up a stone blade. Although they have not touched the object, they feel as if they know the cool feel of the conchoidally fractured stone and the micro-serrations of the edge.

The old stone has cultural appeal and many knappers today make blades from obsidian, flint and other natural materials using the ancient techniques of spalling and pressure flaking. Their chief concession to modernity is that they work from blanks sawn with diamond-impregnated wheels to help reduce wastage. Not only do these stone-bladed knives partly replicate past techniques and represent works of art, many are also useful tools for those interested in the past.

Modern flint knappers use many of the same techniques as primitive cultures to produce objects, mostly knives, seen in trade shows. They make arrow points, spear points and art objects. Many are quite accomplished, and the best work equals that of the Aztecs who used flint to knap elaborate profiles of their nobility wearing feather headdresses.

David Semones, of Deland, Fla., is not only adept at flint knapping, but he also carves bone, creates cypress sculptures of native wildlife, and paints and scrimshaws. This formidable skill set enables him to make knife blades of materials as diverse as native chert, several colors of obsidian, Arkansas novaculite and flints from all over the world. He credits lace mahogany obsidian as his best-selling blade material, and he often outfits the blades with bone, horn, mastodon- or elephant-ivory handles, frequently scrimshawing animals on the handles for a unique touch.

Always seeking to stretch his artistic vision, Semones carves knife handles into three-dimensional wildlife shapes, producing one-of-a-kind knives with fish-, duck- or alligator-shaped grips.

Plain knives of readily available materials and even those with exotic handles and from costly materials, perhaps carved or scrimshawed, carry price ranges between $150-$400. Considering the historic, artistic and functional appeal of stone-bladed knives, it should come as no surprise that Semones, Austin and other knappers have slowly built up demand for the edged, utilitarian tools. It's a harkening back to a craft as relative today as it was thousands of years ago.

William Hovey Smith is a retired geologist who has worked all over North America and frequently hunts with primitive tools. His most recent books are Crossbow Hunting (Stackpole, 2006) and Practical Bowfishing (Stoeger, 2004).

Ken Austin
591 Highway 481
Releigh, MS 30159
(601) 536-3579

David Semones
295 Deerfoot Road
Deland, FL 32720
dave@dswildart.com
(386) 736-5733

Plug Bayonets— Last-Ditch Weapons

Out of powder but not fight, they rammed hunting knives into muskets to continue battle

By Greg Bean

Fix bayonets! Charge! From out of a dense hail of randomly fired musket balls and an even denser cloud of black-powder smoke, a disciplined line of red-coated troops materialize with their Brown Bess's transformed into pikes, charge through the ranks of some heathen rabble until their line breaks and scatters, giving up their position to the charging British. In the 18th century this worked for the English and the French who developed a successful, offensive tactic from what started and ultimately ended as a defensive and last-ditch weapon. Last ditch, when talking about bayonet usage, was often more than a metaphor.

The term bayonet is attributed to the French town of Bayonne where Basque peasants, out of powder but not the will to fight, rammed hunting knives into their muskets to continue the battle. The plug bayonet was born from this conflict and noticed by the French military. Soon after, the bayonet was added to the French arsenal.

The first bayonets were simple daggers with tapered, round grips that plugged into the musket barrels like corks in bottles. When close combat was imminent and there was not time to reload, the soldiers rammed the plug bayonets into position after the muskets were fired. The tapered grips allowed the bayonets to fit into

Some things never change. The hammer and tongs are exactly as they would have looked and been used in the 17th century. The steel would have come in much cruder bar stock, but the wood for the handles would have been from a sawed block. Coal is coal even if it's just a backdrop.

many sizes of barrels, usually with a maximum size of .75 caliber.

The handles were typically wood, with the tangs going through the grips and fixed with end caps.

Each bayonet incorporated a guard, usually of brass, allowing it to be used as a tactical weapon and preventing the user's hand from sliding onto the blade. The steel blade stretched about a foot long. With a 5-foot musket, the weapon was about the length of an infantry spear and long enough to deal with charging horses or taking cavalry soldiers off their mounts.

The first firearms were single-shot, slow to reload and vulnerable during the reload. They had to be protected from cavalry and charging foot soldiers by pike men. The development of the bayonet-enhanced musket freed up the pike men to be issued muskets, effectively doubling the firepower of the infantry. Transforming an empy musket back into an effective weapon was too good to be passed up, even for militaries that were slow to embrace innovation.

The plug bayonet had its problems, though. It was slow to place when in a melee, leaving a window of opportunity for the opposing

Halfway there, the blade still needs to be ground and sharpened, the grip turned, the guard shaped and welded, and the pieces put together.

Stock removal provides uniformity to the blade, taking out those unsightly hammer dings.

forces to catch the defenders with their weapons off-line. Ramming it in too securely ensured the musket couldn't quickly be returned to fire duty. If it wasn't secure, it could be left in the body of a skewered enemy or dislodged in battle.

Like all other armies to use the plug bayonet, the French found its flaws through losses, catastrophes and near-catastrophes. The French evolved to using an offset, fixed bayonet in place of the plug. The rest of Europe, not wanting to be left out, adopted the socket bayonet and its techniques as standard practice.

Fixing Blade to Weapon

The next 300 years saw incremental changes that included multiple ways of fixing the blade to the weapon. The first changes included different forms of attachments to mount the bayonet to the firearm, but still allowing it to be removed. Another permutation was to permanently attach the bayonet with a hinge mechanism to swing the blade under the barrel and out of the way when firing. The bayonet progressed from a knife blade or spear point into a short sword, then a piercing weapon, a "triangular" needle blade and back again to a hafted blade.

"Fix bayonets" were the last words heard by many British soldiers at Killiecrankie, in 1689, in a battle against a Scottish uprising that also wedded the Scots to their chaotic Highland charge. The battle may have been the first use of the bayonet by the British. The disciplined methods of the British, with the soldiers working in formation and following commands to "fire," "reload," "fix bayonets" and the like, worked against them in the battle with Scottish forces loyal to William the Orange, as it gave the opportunistic Highlanders an opening to charge as the British forces were placing their plug bayonets.

The defeat drove the bayonet's development into an offensive weapon that served the British well and became a standard part of their tactics for the next 200 years.

The commander of the British forces, Gen. Hugh Mackay, used the edged tool to his advantage, and developed a bayonet with a ring or sleeve to suspend it below the barrel of the musket. It didn't interfere with the firing of the musket, and with the bayonet secured, the transform to a pike was instant. Reloading with the bayonet in place provided its own issues, and there were sure to have been some hand injuries, but this became a matter of technique and an aspect of training.

The first uses of the bayonet were defensive. With infantry massed several layers deep and arrayed in a square formation, they could defend their position while allowing each line the chance to reload while covered by the other lines of soldiers. As long as one line of soldiers maintained itself ready to use their muskets as pikes, there was a defense against cavalry and being overrun by other infantry. This wasn't the most glorious use of the bayonet, however, and not the right way to expand an empire.

Pounding at the anvil is the great common to all blacksmithing and is the first step in getting the blade into shape.

Water is essential to the process if you want a blade that won't bend under duress.

Fix Bayonets! It is an easy job in training, although slightly more anxious when you're being overrun.

Illustrated is the 1717 French military musket, cartridge case and bayonet.

The bayonet eventually became part of a system that created an advantage out of one of weaknesses of period firearms. The single-shot, black powder weapons blew a lot of smoke, and standing in the acrid clouds of even one volley was an eye-stinging, cough-inducing event. Numerous volleys made the situation worse.

British tactics called for a rapid advance to get into an optimum musket range and discharging their firearms, taking out as many as possible and creating a dense, opaque smoke screen. The infantry then charged out of this with their bayonet-loaded muskets. When it worked right, the effect devastated the enemy's moral and defensive line, causing enough chaos that they couldn't muster an organized retreat.

Paul Smith, military historian and former U.S. Marine, says, "Until modern warfare, more people have been killed in retreat than in standing combat. When you run, you can't shoot. If you want to run faster you start dropping things. Like your rifle."

Limited Bayonet Usage

European warfare followed this pattern into the 19th century, when rifled barrels and repeating firearms kept most combat activity beyond a hand-weapon's distance, unless something was going terribly wrong. Running out of ammunition and being run over by the enemy were the two circumstances calling for bayonet usage.

At the battle of the Somme in World War I, the 18th-century tactics of a close-order advance with fixed bayonets was an optimistic but losing proposition against hardened concrete bunkers and the German MG08. It was also one of the last uses of the bayonet as an offensive weapon. Machine guns and concertina wire made obsolete the bayonet charge and returned the bayonet to a defensive weapon. Over-the-top trench warfare became back-against-the-wall desperation, and tanks became the infantry's new best friend.

The modern military has little need for the bayonet, as combat is being conducted from greater and greater distances, although. There are occasional tales of bayonet usage, in the Falkland Island fighting the British are said to have resorted to a few bayonet charges. There are a couple of instances in both Iraq wars in which the Sutherland and Argyll Highlanders from the British Army took part in fighting that included bayonets.

Paul Smith, who joined the Marines in 1981 and was in the first Gulf war, used a mounted bayonet only once while in Iraq. "I was walking across our position when I saw a snake," Smith begins. "I pulled out my bayonet and attached it to my M-16 and stuck it through the snake. About 20 or 30 yards away was an officer we called Buck, who was digging a foxhole. He was well into this task with his back to me.

"I decided I was going to show him my snake, held out my rifle with the snake wiggling around on the end and said, 'Captain Rogers, I've brought your dinner,'" Smith continues. "He turned around and with his face about a foot from that wiggling snake, he cursed, jumped backwards and grabbed for his pistol. He said I was lucky he didn't shoot me."

Mike McCrae, a knifemaker who forged a plug bayonet, is a former Marine who went through boot camp at Parris Island in 1967 and served in Vietnam. McCrae

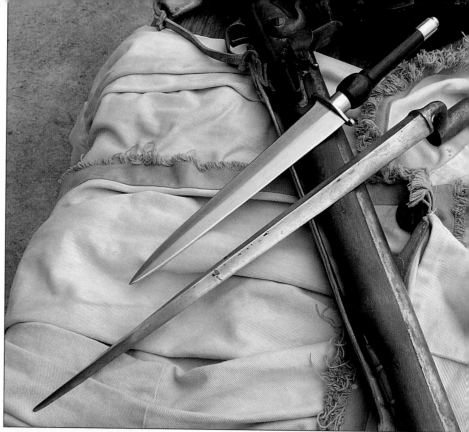

Later technology did away with the plug's shortcomings, but didn't look nearly as good.

was trained for bayonet using practice dummies and pugil sticks, knowing there was a real possibility he may need the training. The pugil stick, a padded stick with one end representing the bayonet and the other end serving as the gun butt, is a safe alternative to actual gunstocks and sharp blades while building the skills and endurance needed for this physically demanding form of sparring.

Pugil Stick Training

"Pugil stick training," says McCrae, "is the only way you're going to get physical bayonet training with a live target. If you're going to train with a live opponent they're not going to let you go up against someone with an M-14 and a bayonet. Boot camp was hard enough as it was."

An authority on edged weapons, McCrae says, "You'd have a lot fewer wars if it had to be done at bayonet distance. Once out of

boot camp, the only time I ever heard 'Fix bayonets' was in parade formations."

For that, he could have simply used a plug bayonet.

About the knifemaker:

Michael McRae, from Mint Hill, N.C., is a knifemaker and jeweler specializing in Scottish weaponry. More can be learned about Mike and his knives at www.scotia-works.com.

About the "soldier" modeling bayonet usage in the accompanying photographs:

David Ford, from Great Falls, S.C., is a soldier of the New Acquisition Militia, a group of living historians named for an actual militia from the time of the American Revolution and active in the South Carolina and North Carolina area. More information is available at www.newacquisition-militia.com.

TRENDS

Did you see what that hussy hunting knife is wearing? Well, practically nothing, but she's flaunting her turquoise handle and stainless steel butt as if she was a common dime store switchblade. I've heard pearl is all the rage and that any folder worth its weight is wearing it. Yeah, and fashions don't change, they just come back. I can't believe I saw an Interframe the other day, and some edgy dude pimping camping attire that was so last year.

You get the point, or direction, in which this is going. Knife fashion is much like human fashion. Trends are set, changed, borrowed, rehashed, redone from the ground up, torn down and rebuilt all over again. Once in awhile a new trend emerges, something that's never been seen before, and that makes edged art all the more worthy of full participation.

It is astounding, really, the creative people who have devoted themselves to knife handcraft. It's no stretch to say that some of today's custom cutlers fashion museum-quality pieces. It is the care, time and dedication put into each knife, along with "sweat equity," that allows the industry to stretch its steel tips, to grow, thrive and expand into new areas. And the trends keep coming.

This year, blades built in the style of Bob Loveless are plentiful. Quillion daggers have come back into the fray, "Battle-Hardened Blades" see new light, "Bowie Hybrids" are thriving and slip joints have proven themselves steadfast and true. Knifemakers aren't just using parts they find in their backyards, but incorporating the most exotic materials, state-of-the-art steels and daring designs their minds can imagine.

Trends are what keep a traditional industry like the knife business exciting and fun. Besides, take a good look at that floozy down the street parading a nut-brown birch grip that wouldn't cover a miniature blade's bolster, much less an entire tang. What the new knives won't wear these days!

Ancient Ivory & Mammoth Molars

Recognizing beauty, whether stopping to enjoy a breathtaking view of a dewy, lush, green valley in the morning, or incurably intrigued, excited by the rare beauty of a lovely lady, everyone is attracted to comeliness.

So does that make it an open invitation to stop and stare? In some cases, yes, and in others the act will only land you in trouble. Yet recognizing elegance, grace and symmetry, whatever it may be, is akin to hope or aspiration. It gives us something for which to live and strive.

In trees we find outer beauty in the way light reflects off the leaves, how moisture clings to branches, and internally, how grain, rings and color swirl within the wood itself. That is similar to the prettiness of ancient ivory and mammoth molars. It's in the disintegration that the real splendor surfaces. Thousands of years of outside elements have morphed ancient ivory into cracked, disfigured,

colored and even stained slabs of richness and texture.

Be they green, blue, beige, orange, yellow or black, Grandma's teeth never looked this good. These are hubba-hubba hunks of tusks and teeth.

Give knifemakers credit. It is the recognition of beauty, whether understanding the allure of translucent pearl or the godliness of inlaid gold that should be credited for bringing handcraftsmanship into the realm of artistry. Only those who see it for

what it is, who allow themselves to be swept away by rare beauty can also bring it before an appreciate audience and pronounce it good. They are the diehard romantics of blade building, and we all know how hard it is to talk sense into smitten softies.

▶ **STEVE CULVER:** As good as the master smith is, he couldn't paint a picture as pretty as the mammoth ivory that grips the damascus folding dagger. *(Ward photo)*

▶ **TERRY VANDEVENTER:** Unlike ice taken from the freezer and warmed, the crackled mammoth ivory won't break under pressure, but adds strength and depth to the small mosaic damascus hunter. *(SharpByCoop.com photo)*

▶ **THOMAS HASLINGER:** Only sculpted 10k-gold pins sufficed for the mammoth-ivory handle of the solid hunting knife. It features a Mike Norris damascus blade and Gerome Weinand "horses and horseshoes" damascus bolsters.

► **MIKE MILLER:** The mammoth-ivory gent's knife is nice and tight. *(Ward photo)*

▲ **DON HETHCOAT:** Inclusions in the mammoth ivory resemble barbed wire wrapping itself around a damascus locking-liner folder. *(PointSeven photo)*

▲ **PETER MARTIN:** Bark mammoth ivory and twist mosaic damascus are the yin and the yang of the slip-joint folder. *(Cory Martin Imaging)*

▲ **ANDRE THORBURN:** The character of the fossil mammoth ivory complements the Heimskringla pattern of the stainless damascus bolsters and even the unblemished 12C27 blade. *(BladeGallery. com photo)*

◄ **CHRIS GIARDIA:** Where the Devin Thomas raindrop-pattern damascus stops and the mammoth molar begins remains relatively insignificant. *(BladeGallery.com photo)*

▶ **JIM KRAUSE:** Few knifemakers have combined mammoth tooth with wood, in this case ebony, and fewer still carried on with a Damasteel blade, damascus bolsters, a carved back strap and fileworked liners. *(PointSeven photo)*

▶ **JOSH SMITH:** It takes a pretty piece of fossil ivory to compete with the "tiger-stripe" damascus and the sapphire in the thumb stud. *(PointSeven photo)*

◀ **RON HEMBROOK:** The personal protection knife is done up in Doug Ponzio mosaic damascus and a handle of mammoth tooth. The knife comes with a J. Kelley leather sheath.

▶ **TOMMY GANN:** Mammoth ivory handle scales proved a solid choice for the hand-forged damascus gent's bowie/hunter. *(BladeGallery.com photo)*

CLIFF POLK: After scaring up some colorful mammoth ivory, Cliff forged a "spider-and-web" damascus blade and bolsters for the folder. *(Ward photo)*

PETE TRUNCALE: The mammoth tooth put dents in the bolsters of the ATS-34 folder. *(PointSeven photo)*

STEVE DUNN: Steve's been around long enough to select the right mammoth ivory. He inlaid gold, engraved steel and forged a fun "Halloween" damascus blade. *(PointSeven photo)*

CURT ERICKSON: Julie Warenski engraving and mosaic pins highlight the 440C fighter with the orange-tinted mammoth-ivory handle. *(Ward photo)*

▶ **RICK DUNKERLEY:** Rick "blued out all the stops" for this mosaic masterpiece, engraving the back bar, fileworking the liners and inlaying the thumb stud with a diamond. *(PointSeven photo)*

▲ **R.W. WILSON:** Damascus, mokumé and ancient ivory are the core, heart and soul of an upswept hunter and skinner. *(Cory Martin Imaging)*

◀ **STEVE JOHNSON and FRANCESCO PACHI:** The blue mammoth ivory pretties up the only S.R. Johnson and Francesco Pachi knife known to exist.

▶ **DAVE KELLY:** Recognizing the colors and inherent beauty of the mammoth ivory, Dave outfitted the knife with a complementary bronze frame, copper fittings and a clay-hardened 1095 blade.

▲ **KYLE ROYER:** The pretty, patterned, fileworked fighter in 1084-15N20-and-German-silver damascus was an ideal candidate for a mammoth-ivory grip. *(SharpByCoop.com photo)*

▲ **ROBERT DODD:** The "Black Mammoth" folder isn't nearly as intimidating as its name suggests.

◄▼ TIM BRITTON: The teardrop jackknife showcases a BG-42 blade, a long nail nick and a spectacular mammoth-ivory handle. *(Ward photo)*

▲ GARY MULKEY: The chocolate mastodon-bark ivory is the sticky sweetness of the clip-point hunter. *(Ward photo)*

◄ BRUCE D. BUMP: While the "Wild Fire" damascus spreads across the blade, blue mammoth ivory enlivens the handle. *(PointSeven photo)*

► MARK NEVLING: The grizzly on the mosaic-damascus bolster emerges from a landscape of green and gold. *(Ward photo)*

► DON HANSON III: Within the framework of a large auto dagger are a mosaic-damascus blade, solid 18k-gold screws, a titanium frame and North Sea mammoth ivory handle scales. *(SharpByCoop.com photo)*

Grab-Worthy Guards

▼**GRAZYNA SHAW COLLECTION:** A sextet of Elmer Keith-style knives includes highly guarded pieces by Buster Warenski, Gil Hibben, D.E. Friedly and Harvey Draper. *(Ward photo)*

▲**RICHARD S. WRIGHT:** The Greystoke bowie is beset with mammoth ivory, sterling silver, and a Jerry Rados Turkish-twist-damascus blade and cross-guard.

▼**LLOYD HALE:** To go along with the silver chains inset into the fluted ebony handle is a carved and sculpted 440C guard, a crown-like pommel and a 9-inch dagger blade. *(SharpByCoop.com photo)*

▶**PAUL JARVIS:** Three carved silver and bronze crowns cap each end of the guard and pommel, each inset with garnets and complemented by a sea-cow-bone hilt and a 16-inch damascus blade.

► **MIKE RUTH:** The light reflecting off the stainless steel clamshell guard will halt the troops long enough to appreciate the damascus blade and ivory handle before resuming the charge. *(Ward photo)*

◄ **MICHAEL RADER:** It is hard to imagine what would feel better, the curly-maple, Peruvian-walnut and brown-mesquite handle, or the curlicue guard of the damascus hand-and-a-half sword. *(BladeGallery.com photo)*

► **DAN GRAVES:** Dan forged a 16 ½-inch damascus blade and D-guard for the African-blackwood-hilted piece. *(SharpByCoop.com photo)*

► **BILL BURKE:** An all-damascus and mammoth-ivory mini sword has a mighty fine guard at that. *(BladeGallery.com photo)*

► **KENT HICKS:** The blued-steel guard of the ebony-handle fighter would deflect sword blades, knives and all enemy edges. Sherry Lott fashioned a leather sheath for the piece. *(Ward photo)*

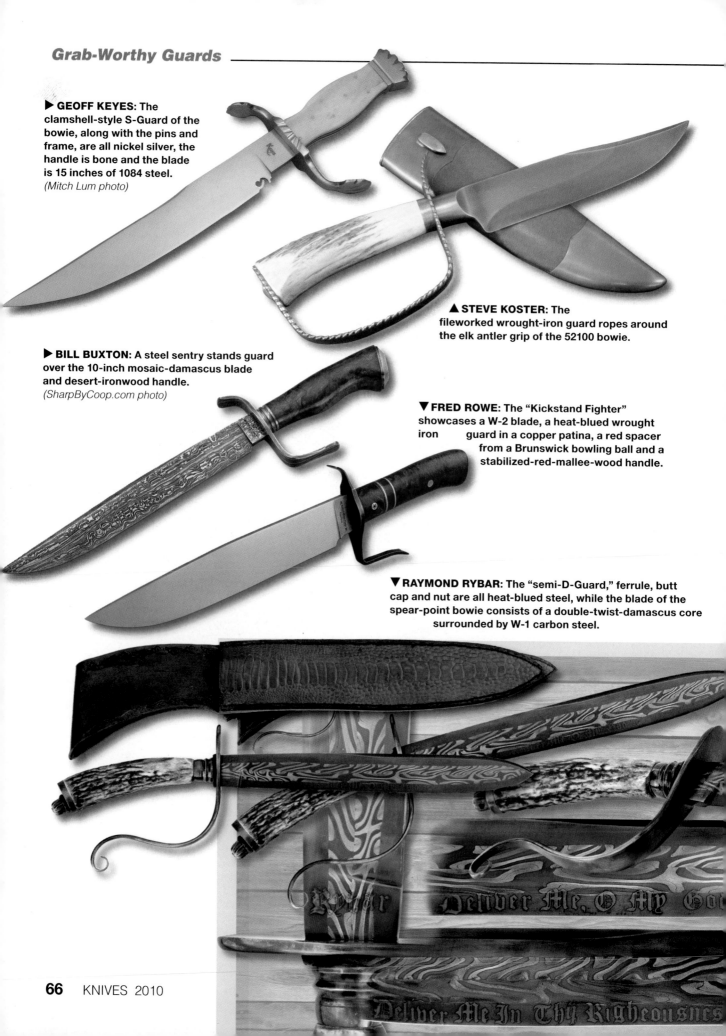

► **GEOFF KEYES:** The clamshell-style S-Guard of the bowie, along with the pins and frame, are all nickel silver, the handle is bone and the blade is 15 inches of 1084 steel. *(Mitch Lum photo)*

▲ **STEVE KOSTER:** The fileworked wrought-iron guard ropes around the elk antler grip of the 52100 bowie.

► **BILL BUXTON:** A steel sentry stands guard over the 10-inch mosaic-damascus blade and desert-ironwood handle. *(SharpByCoop.com photo)*

▼ **FRED ROWE:** The "Kickstand Fighter" showcases a W-2 blade, a heat-blued wrought iron guard in a copper patina, a red spacer from a Brunswick bowling ball and a stabilized-red-mallee-wood handle.

▼ **RAYMOND RYBAR:** The "semi-D-Guard," ferrule, butt cap and nut are all heat-blued steel, while the blade of the spear-point bowie consists of a double-twist-damascus core surrounded by W-1 carbon steel.

Steeped In Slip-Joint Tradition

In just about every industry, when a young generation of workers comes into the fray, it results in new ways of doing things, fresh products, innovative approaches and technology. The knife arena is no different in that respect, but with one major exception—tradition.

Makers of traditional pocketknife patterns use time-honored techniques, materials and in some cases antiquated tools. Everything from coat-sleeve jackknives to whittlers, elephant toenails, slimline trappers and doctor's knives are being studied, fashioned by hand and perfected.

The folders don't clip to blue jeans because there are no pocket clips. They don't open with one hand because it takes a fingernail to pull the blade or blades open via the "nail nicks." Traditional slip-joint pocketknives do not fly open with the tug of a disc, the handles do not swing or pivot, they are rarely made with modern, bullet-proof materials, no blade coatings, pictures forged into the steel or futuristic blade grinds, grooved grips or modified-tanto tips.

Such knives are old fashioned, fashioned slowly and seemingly unfashionable. Or are they?

Collectors, even young, modern, trendy, aware and advanced knife collectors, are buying up the old-school edges, and for good reason. To build a traditional pocketknife takes handwork, patience, precision, perfect fit and finish and an artist's eye. They are quality pieces that will last a lifetime. They remain true to form, reminiscent of a bygone era and handcrafted in fine fashion. They are steeped in slip-joint tradition, and not even a water-jet, computer-numerically controlled, laser-enhanced supercomputer can accomplish that feat.

▶ **MIKE ZSCHERNY:** The stag- and Remington-bone-handle folders sport CPM 154 blades and stainless frames, bolsters and handle shields. (SharpByCoop.com photo)

◀ **BARRY GALLAGER:** The exquisite coat-sleeve jackknife is done up in brown jigged bone.

▲ **MATSUSAKI TAKESHI:** Among the many steel implements are a saw, scissors, band saw, hook, tweezers, two blades, a file, corkscrew, drill and compass. And the pearl handle isn't bad, either.

◀ **BILL RUPLE:** One whittler, one canoe and a lot of love. Even the liners are filed, and the bolsters grooved. *(SharpByCoop. com photo)*

◀ **SHANE SLOAN:** Here's a sheep-horn-handle, slip-joint folder that will sheer anything. *(Todd Brewer photo)*

▶ **JERALD NICKELS:** Rare is the saddle-horn trapper with a damascus blade, and rarer still the engraved-bolster breed. Brad Vice is credited for forging the damascus. *(Ward photo)*

◀▼ **JEFF CLAIBORNE:** The 52100 blades of the swell-center toenail are forged to shape, given eyelash nail nicks and treated to India stag handle slabs. *(Hoffman photo)*

▲ **JOHNNY STOUT:** The clip and spay blades of the slip-joint trapper are CPM 154 steel, satin finished, of course, and butted up against stainless bolsters and a red-jigged-bone grip.

▶ **DAN BURKE:** Dan planted petals of pearl and three blades grew. *(PointSeven photo)*

▲ **ANDREW MCLURKIN:** Mammoth ivory and 154CM blade steel are just what the doctor ordered.

▼ **TONY and REESE BOSE:** One knife professional said that the biggest compliment he could pay Tony's son Reese is that most collectors wouldn't be able to tell the difference between their knives if the tang stamps were absent from the blades. So, which is whose? *(Ward photo)*

▲ **DON MORROW:** Filework and dyed stag highlight the double-blade trapper, and the hand-rubbed finish and Kathy Morrow engraved shield are equally fine touches. *(Johnny Stout photo)*

◀ **RON NEWTON:** The barrel knife is loaded with ATS-34 steel and white ivory. *(Ward photo)*

▼ **BEN MIDGLEY:** The liquidity of abalone gives the saddle-horn trapper even more movement than is inherent in the flowing pattern. *(Ward photo)*

◄ **C. GRAY TAYLOR:** There's artwork—carved and checkered black-lip pearl—on the artwork—a pair of three-blade orange blossom folders, one large and one small. *(Mitch Lum photo)*

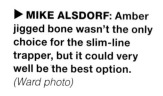

► **MIKE ALSDORF:** Amber jigged bone wasn't the only choice for the slim-line trapper, but it could very well be the best option. *(Ward photo)*

▲ **JOEL CHAMBLIN:** Whether the checkered pearl, piqué work, 14k-gold pins or mammoth ivory is most appealing, the CPM 154 blades remain sharpest of the lot. *(PointSeven photo)*

◄ **RAYMOND SMITH:** Touches like filework, an extended, rattail pommel that's reminiscent of decorative wrought iron, and a stabilized-maple-burl handle rubbed until it reflects light raise the bar on slip joints. *(SharpByCoop.com photo)*

▲ RICHARD ROGERS: The swell-center congress in ATS-34, black-lip pearl and gold is more swell than Congress. *(Mitch Lum photo)*

▶ BILL BURKE: Mammoth ivory makes a bid for most valuable player on a 52100 slip-joint folder. *(PointSeven photo)*

▶ STEVE DUNN: Traditional, enlightened engraving, proven stag, slip-joint patterns and skill beyond the ordinary result in three fine folders. *(PointSeven photo)*

◀ BRET DOWELL: The pattern of the ATS-34 slip joint and the way the ancient ivory is shaped give the jack a sway back. *(Chuck Ward photo)*

◀ TIM BRITTON: It flows from the round end to the pointy one. *(SharpByCoop. com photo)*

Futuristic Folders

Oh there's a future. And it's not as bleak as the picture painted by modern doomsday portrayers, financial analysts and broken Wall Street brokers. I'm reminded of a friend who referred to his lady boss as "an optimist because and her husband had three kids." He insinuated that, because she had children, it went to reason that she had faith in the future and a better world than we live in today. Something tells me a good number of custom knifemakers agree with the lady boss.

If pessimism prevailed, then designs of handmade knives would remain stagnant. There would be no innovation, forward thinking or healthy competition to exceed expectations. No one would create, invent or advance. The methods of knifemaking would not improve, and make no mistake about it, they are constantly improving.

Folders are easier to open, faster, sharper, and stay sharper, than ever before. The materials last longer, the designs are the definition of "21st century," and knife junkies are given more gadgets to play with than they can possibly grasp. Springs and bushings share space with locks, buttons, switches, pivots and pins. Smooth is the name of the game, and friction is forgotten like yesterdays boxy tactical folders.

Yes, there's a future. And it's not as ugly as some slow-to-change factory bosses might tell you, nor as dull, difficult to navigate or hard to handle. The futuristic folders of the new millennium are positioned to take an industry by storm. Hang onto your collective hats. It's going to be as tumultuous as high-carbon steel in a brand-new blade tumbler.

▶ **PAT and WES CRAWFORD:** The Crawfords went with a "Wild One" done up in Mike Norris damascus, titanium and wooly-mammoth ivory, complete with jewels in the bolsters and filework along the spine, spacers, clip and liners.
(SharpByCoop.com photo)

◀ **ERIC ELSON:** Yah mon, the "Dreadlock Lite" earns respect via a ladder-pattern Damasteel blade and a carbon fiber handle with the personality of a Rastafarian.
(SharpByCoop.com photo)

◀ **KIT CARSON:** The one-blade folder with the anodized-titanium bolsters and Micarta® grip switches and locks, while the pearl-handle, two-blade damascus folder swings and rocks.
(SharpByCoop.com photo)

▶ **JOHN KUBASEK:** The "Creditor II" exudes optimism with its chisel-ground 440C-and-carbon-fiber laminated blade, and titanium handle with carbon-fiber "tip protector" overlays. *(SharpByCoop.com photo)*

▶ **JEREMY KRAMMES:** The CPM 154 blade, titanium bolsters and carbon-fiber and silver-G-10 handle of the "Cricket" chirp a cool, catchy tune. *(SharpByCoop.com photo)*

▲ **WALLY HAYES:** The double-hollow-ground art folder showcases damascus, titanium, ebony and black-lip pearl. *(SharpByCoop. com photo)*

◀ **PETER CAREY:** Carbon fiber and twist damascus grab the spotlight and shine it toward the sharpened CPM 154 steel.

◀ **MICHAEL WALKER:** An early folding knife innovator, Michael stays ahead of the pack with his newest titanium-frame Damasteel folder, including inlays of 22k gold, and silver-Shakado mokumé. *(SharpByCoop.com photo)*

▶ **SCOT MATSUOKA:** Gripping and cutting is the titanium and steel flipper folder. *(PointSeven photo)*

▶ **R.J. MARTIN:** The Rampage II won the "Best Tactical Knife" award at the 2008 BLADE Show. *(SharpByCoop.com photo)*

▶ **JIM HAMMOND:** The locking-liner folder with anodized-titanium frame and overlays comes with a choice of fossil-walrus ivory, sheep horn, mammoth-ivory or stag *(shown)* handle slabs. *(Balance Digital photo)*

▶ **LOURENS PRINSLOO:** The damascus crocodile would cut through the water with nary a ripple. *(SharpByCoop. com photo)*

▶ **TOM WATSON:** Even Tom thinks it's scary, calling it "Spook," and a ghostly one at that, wearing a white- and blue-G-10 handle and bolsters, and a D2 blade.

▼ **ALLEN ELISHEWITZ:** The fire coral is reminiscent of where the Chad Nichols damascus was forged. The E-Lock sports a bi-metal rocker.

▼ **LYLE BRUNCKHORST:** It's only a CPM 154 "Side Kick" with a titanium frame, carbon fiber handle, finger flipper and Xross-Bar Lock designed by Dan Perreault. No big deal.
(SharpByCoop.com photo)

▲ **DARREL RALPH:** If the San Mai blade with a VG-10 core doesn't slay ya, then the fluted damascus grip probably won't float your boat, either.
(SharpByCoop.com photo)

▲ **STAN WILSON:** Desert ironwood blends beautifully into the blued 1095 bolsters and CPM S90V blade of the dual-action, semi-auto folder. What a looker!
(SharpByCoop.com photo)

Futuristic Folders

▲ TODD BEGG: The "Ring Dagger" is a Liong Mah design, and built properly with a CPM S30V blade, and a G-10 handle with Koa-wood overlays. *(Mitch Lum photo)*

▼ LYLE BRUNCKHORST: The red-and-black G-10 handle of the Star Fighter is a fiery treat, the "flipper" mechanism doubles as a finger guard, and the lock works like a LinerLock® but is not dependant on lockup with the radius of the tang. *(SharpByCoop.com photo)*

▲ RICK HANEY: The S30V and black-G-10 "Kraken" butterfly knife has an upswept blade, down-sloped grip and a well-rounded look and feel. *(PointSeven photo)*

▶ GREG LIGHTFOOT: He calls the damascus folders "Extreme Jewelry," and they wear ironwood, mammoth ivory and carbon fiber with pride. *(Mitch Lum photo)*

▶ **ANDRE VAN HEERDEN:** White G-10 is dovetailed to the black carbon fiber bolsters, finished to perfection, and coupled with a satin-finished 12C27 stainless steel blade. *(BladeGallery.com photo)*

▶ **KIRK REXROAT:** Damascus and G-10 make for a deadly combination. *(PointSeven photo)*

▶ **BRIAN TIGHE:** Brian says the "Tighe One On" is on top, and the "Twist Tighe" on the bottom, both with carbon-fiber handles and fluted G-10 inlays. *(Mitch Lum photo)*

▶ **MIKE FRANKLIN:** It pierces, cuts, hurts and harbors bad feelings, but the tactical folder, or "El Diablo," has a stylish blued-titanium blade overlay and handle frame, and a shapely synthetic grip.

▲ **TIM GALYEAN:** "Mega Moab" dons a gun-grade, black DLC coat and a business-like demeanor. *(Mitch Lum photo)*

21st-Century Japan

▲ **DAVID GOLDBERG:** A wispy temper line dances along the edge of the Japanese-style fighting knife, or "Kuma Killer" (bear killer), with the upper half of the 1095 blade hammer finished. *(PointSeven photo)*

▲ **SCOTT SLOBODIAN:** The name "Whirlpool" likely refers to the 15-inch carbon steel blade with wavy temper line, complemented by copper fittings and a leather-wrapped stingray skin handle. The engraving is from the hand of Barbara Slobodian.

◄ **MIKE MOONEY:** The Japanese-style "Personal Chef" knife employs a Devin Thomas quilted-damascus blade for chopping duties, and an octagonal stabilized-amboyna-burl handle to, well, stabilize things.

◄ **DAVID GOLDBERG:** The sterling silver fittings of "The Red Dragon" accentuate the high-carbon-steel blade of the unapologetically imperial wakizashi.
(PointSeven photo)

▶ **BILL BURKE:** The crimson silk wrap of the musk-ox grip brings out the golden hues of the mokumé gane habaki (blade collar), and contrasts with the blade and cloudy temper line. *(PointSeven photo)*

▼ **TOM FERRY:** The "Koi Tanto" tempts the senses using its exciting damascus blade, carved wooly-mammoth-ivory grip and engraved, golden koi fish. *(Ward photo)*

◀ **JAN DOX:** The triple-hardened steel is forged from an old diamond saw blade, and blends into a black over-blue, stingray-skin handle.

◀ **DON POLZIEN:** Enemy dispatching is accomplished through 2,000 layers of damascus, a red-cinnabar-lacquered grip and sterling silver fittings, the latter to keep up appearances, of course.

▼ **GREG LIGHTFOOT:** The "21st Century San Mai" parades a carbon-fiber and damascus, laminated blade butted up against a cord-wrapped, python-skin handle and shark tooth handle charm. *(Mitch Lum photo)*

◀ **MICHAEL RADER:** The katana sports more than 27 inches of "Marquenched" damascus forged from 15N20 and 8660 carbon steels, and is anchored by a Peruvian walnut handle with brown mesquite accents. *(BladeGallery.com photo)*

WALLY HAYES: The long, 15-inch tanto features a forged blade and silver-and-wrought-iron guard, as well as a silk-wrapped stingray skin grip. *(SharpByCoop.com photo)*

▲ **STEVE SCHWARZER:** The gold-plated habaki *(blade collar)* is treated to a 13-inch 1086 blade with distinct temper line on one side, and a leather-wrapped stingray-skin handle with gold menuki (handle charm) on the other. *(PointSeven photo)*

◄ **COLLABORATIVE EFFORT:** The Peter Martin damascus blade was forged to shape by Jerry Rados, ground by Michael Kanter, fileworked by Ron Rosenbaugh, heat treated and tempered by Bob Rossdeutscher, and hand finished, etched and sharpened by Karl Andersen. Tim Horan did the handle wrap, Affeelean Nevling fashioned the glass bead dangler, Mary Rose scrimshawed the sheath decoration, and Spen Stelzer made the sheath. *(Cory Martin Imaging)*

▲ **BAILEY BRADSHAW:** The forged W-1 blade of the katana is married to a mild-steel tsuba (guard) and silk-wrapped wood handle. Antique menuki (handle decoration) furthers a fisherman theme. *(SharpByCoop.com photo)*

Fish & Game Wardens

The pride is there. It's in the hands of the hunter who not only wants to bag a trophy buck but rely on his own ingenuity and wits in the woods, field dressing the downed animal, quartering it, removing it from the wilderness to be processed. Pride is in the hands of the knifemaker who builds his tools to succeed, accomplish their job and excel.

Dignified are those who weigh the animal, measure it and tag it. Respectful are the photographer and newspaper reporter who show pictures of the big 10-pointer in the local press and write photo captions identifying the skilled hunter who dragged it out of the woods. Pride is in the readers who recognize the fellow and feel comfortable living in a community that celebrates its own.

They are all fish and game wardens: the hunter, the knife, knifemaker, processors, press, readers, neighbors and friends. The smart, conscientious and dignified ones self-regulate themselves. They don't trespass on other peoples' property, take more than they can eat, share or donate, kill for thrill or bring the game in too small or out of season.

In the center of it all is the knife, one of only a few tools used in the timeless ritual. Sure, hunters are as susceptible to marketers as anyone else, buying Humvees, four-wheelers, scents, netting, GPS units, locators, face paint, tree stands and hand warmers. Some are necessary, but not all. Yet the gun, knife, ammo, natural instincts, experience and knowledge are the only tools he or she needs. And nothing but quality tools will do, like the edged fish and game wardens that made their way onto these pages … quietly, without leaving a scent, a trail or a trace.

▼ **JERRY MOEN:** The exquisite demeanor of the CPM154 hunter comes from the Kevin Elkins engraving, orange/brown ironwood, leather lanyard and matching wood bead with red spacers. *(Ward photo)*

◄ **R.L. WELLING:** Ron works in the style of William Scagel, grinding a clean blade with a slender false edge, and stacking leather, brass and axis-deer-antler for the handle. *(Ward photo)*

◄ **MIKE RUTH:** It's a straightforward hunter, orchestrated in stag and damascus, with clean lines and nice fit and finish. *(Ward photo)*

▶ **DAN FARR:** It is a brown-on-brown, steel package of stag, walnut, nickel silver, and the maker's own forging and engraving. *(SharpByCoop.com photo)*

▶ **JOHN BARTLOW:** Like the fossil walrus ivory grip it wears, the ATS-34 hunter is full of character, including Jere Davidson engraving on the stainless steel guard. *(SharpByCoop.com photo)*

▶ **ROB BROWN:** The curvature of the ATS-34 blade and desert ironwood handle gives this one the right look, and the tapered tang achieves the correct weight, balance and feel. *(Kam Singh photo)*

◀ **DAVID SYLVESTER:** The transition from the W-2 blade to the integral bolster and ironwood handle is seamless, smooth and fine. *(SharpByCoop.com photo)*

▲ **JASON KNIGHT:** Texturing and shaping the blackwood grip, complete with a nice handle swell, goes a long way in furthering the craftsmanship of the piece. *(SharpByCoop.com photo)*

▲ **CHARLIE and HARRY MATHEWS:** A proven pattern, the Michael Price-style skinner features a 5-inch CPM S30V blade, an ivory handle and a leather sheath. *(SharpByCoop.com photo)*

▶ **JACK JONES:** A pair of hollow-ground, drop-point hunters showcase 3 ¾-inch ATS-34 blades, and desert-ironwood and green-canvas-Micarta® handles. *(SharpByCoop.com photo)*

▶ **HARVEY DEAN:** The engraved sheep-horn-handle hunter sports a 4 ½-inch 1084 blade and a hot look. *(Ward photo)*

▼ **JERRY MCCLURE:** The bronze-colored mosaic-damascus bolsters bring out similar hues in the giraffe-bone handle of the 7 7/8-inch damascus skinner. Take a tug on the horsehair lanyard. *(Ward photo)*

◀ **JIM FERGUSON:** The thumb print knives hold an appeal all their own, and when married with the right slab of amboyna burl and a nicely finished ATS-34 blade, they can be downright pretty to look at. *(Johnny Stout image)*

▲ **DAVE KELLY:** Measuring up to the stag grip and clay-tempered, polished 1084 blade is a bronze guard and file-worked ferrule.

▶ **E. JAY HENDRICKSON:** Calling it a "high-clip Nanook Hunter," because of the high-clip-point blade, Jay beset the piece with an ivory handle and vine file work from his own hand. *(SharpByCoop.com photo)*

◀ **JERRY RALPH RICHARDS:** It's not just ironwood and damascus but the presentation that earns accolades. *(Ward photo)*

▲ **CHARLIE WEISS:** From left to right are a bird-and-trout knife, skinner and small hunter, all with full, extended tangs, ivory handles and stainless steel bolsters or finger guards. *(Buddy Thomason photo)*

▲ **LIN RHEA:** The sun lit up the ironwood like a Christmas tree and Santa left a hot little hunter. *(Ward photo)*

▲ **KENT CARTER:** The bone is carved to resemble stag, the blade mirror polished, and the hunting knife finely fit and finished. *(Johnny Stout photo)*

► **MIKE MOSSINGTON:** The Canadian knifemaker left a maple leaf in the center of the mosaic-damascus, and dovetailed bolsters that fit snugly against the wood grip and steel blade. *(PointSeven photo)*

Mossington *Canada*

◄ **BILL KENNEDY JR.:** My friends would be so busy ogling the fillet knife with the buckeye-burl grip that I'd catch all the fish. *(Ward photo)*

► **TONY DAUGHERTY:** The palpable blackwood grip is secured to the full tang of the ATS-34 blade with mosaic pins, and to the hand with leather lanyard. *(PointSeven photo)*

a

F STALCUP GALLUP, N.M.

◄ **EDDIE STALCUP:** It wasn't enough that the maker ingeniously mated a stag grip with cape-buffalo-horn bolsters that are jigged to resemble the stag, attached with mosaic pins, but then he fashioned the tang of the bird-and-trout knife into a wing and leg notch, and the choil into a backbone scraper. *(Hoffman photo)*

▲ **RICK DUNKERLEY:** Just when you thought the wheel couldn't be reinvented, Rick comes along with a damascus hunter with an amber-stag handle and engraved guard that's unlike anything we've ever seen. *(PointSeven photo)*

▶ **BILL AMOUREUX:** Combining L-6 and nickel wire for the bolsters results in a soothing look and perfect respite between jigged bone and stainless steel. *(BladeGallery. com photo)*

▲ **JAMES CROWELL:** The stag-handle hunter with a drop-point 1084 blade was not complete until Steve Dunn engraved the guard and butt cap. *(Ward photo)*

▼ **MICHAEL RADER:** The curly maple handle with koa-wood accents meanders endearingly while the 52100 carbon steel blade remains straight and true. *(BladeGallery.com photo)*

▲ **RON RICHERSON:** The wide leaf-shape, spear-point damascus blade and curvaceous rosewood handle are so shapely, it took a Sherry Lott leather sheath with alligator inlay to contain the piece. *(Hoffman photo)*

◀ **DICK FAUST:** Stag is a sly choice for a stainless bird-and-trout knife.

▶ **JAMES SPONAUGLE:** The "Turkey Skinner" comes with all the trimmings—giraffe-bone and two kinds of stainless steel. (Ward photo)

▼ **DANIEL WINKLER:** Copper highlights are forged into the damascus blade of Daniel's "Morning Star Hunter," a frontier-style knife with a mammoth-ivory grip and a rawhide-wrapped guard. The sheath is by Karen Shook. (Hiro Seto photo)

▲ **EDMUND DAVIDSON:** The BG-42 and ironwood semi-skinner is as soft as a doe's ear. (PointSeven photo)

Quillion & Keen Daggers

► **KEVIN CASHEN:** Kingwood was a fine choice for a damascus dagger with a guard reminiscent of a knight's sword. *(SharpByCoop.com photo)*

◄ **HERMAN SCHNEIDER:** It is classy and royal, damascus and engraved, ivory and fluted, keen and clean. *(Hiro Soga photo)*

► **SHAWN MCINTYRE:** From the patterned damascus to the straight, as opposed to spiral, fluting of the wood, blued fittings and shapely guard and pommel, this one is truly a keen dagger. *(SharpByCoop.com photo)*

◄ **RUSS ANDREWS:** The ladder-pattern-damascus dagger is dashing in a quillion-style damascus guard, fluted-mammoth-ivory handle and 14k-gold wire inlay. *(SharpByCoop.com photo)*

► **WOLFGANG LOERCHNER:** Master artist Martin Butler added gold inlay and engraving to the dynamic dagger that also sports a fluted-mammoth-ivory handle and a sculpted guard and pommel. *(SharpByCoop.com photo)*

► **HENRY TORRES:** From pointy pommel to damascus tip, the quillion dagger honors its ancestry. *(PointSeven photo)*

◄ **MIKE O'BRIEN:** Natural forms, including a leaf-shaped blade, define the 440C and ebony dagger. *(SharpByCoop.com photo)*

▼ **JOHN HORRIGAN:** Taken in a literal sense, "quillion" means "guarded" or parts of a cross guard, and this damascus and fluted-ironwood dagger features the blued-steel variety of armament. *(BladeGallery.com photo)*

► **KEVIN HARVEY:** If it hadn't been carefully placed between 24k-gold-inlaid, gun-blued-damascus bolsters, the stabilized box elder wood handle would have stolen the show from the "explosion"-pattern-damascus dagger. *(BladeGallery.com photo)*

► **VAN ZYL and DE WET:** The European-style quillion dagger blends brass fittings with a fluted red-ebony handle and twisted-brass-wire inlay. It's classically designed and given an antiqued finish. *(BladeGallery.com photo)*

▶ **LEE FERGUSON:** The engraved and gold-inlaid blued-steel guard is the centerpiece that brings a leaf-shaped blade together with a wire-inlaid, fluted-walrus-ivory grip. *(Ward photo)*

◀ **GERT VAN DEN ELSEN:** The Viking/Saxon dagger with an Achim Wirtz damascus blade is trimmed in silver pins, an amber pommel bead and a sea-cow-bone handle.

▼ **DAN GRAVES:** The quillions and "skull crusher pommel" are changeable, but the damascus blade and pre-ban-elephant-ivory handle are permanent fixtures. *(SharpByCoop.com photo)*

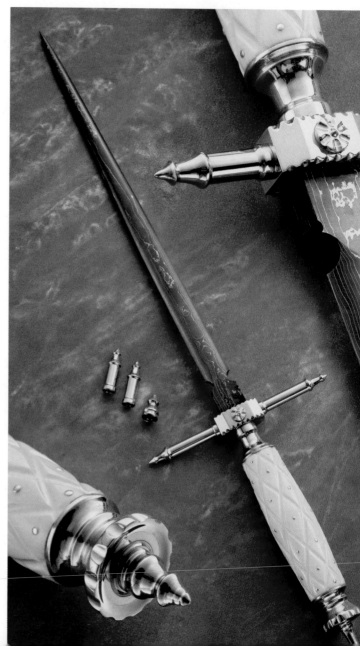

▲ **RAYMOND RYBAR:** Thirteen inches of the 18-inch "Forester's Dagger" are devoted to a "French Truffles"-pattern mosaic-damascus blade, and complemented by a forged guard with acorn tips, a popcorn-stag handle, and a lost-wax-cast silver bronze pommel showing acorns and oak leaves.

THOMAS HASLINGER: A narwhal tusk graces the handle of the large dagger, also outfitted with a Mike Norris stainless-damascus blade, sculpted 14k-gold spacer rings, and ammonites inset into the guard and pommel. The dagger can be fully disassembled by removing the pommel.

RUSTY POLK: Equal billing goes to the damascus blade and the fluted-mammoth-ivory handle, the latter with twisted-wire inlay and copper accents. *(Ward photo)*

J. NEILSON: Damascus, handle fluting and wood are common modern quillion dagger ingredients. *(Ward photo)*

GEORGE HERRON: Two Herron daggers with natural handles are clean and true. *(Cory Martin Imaging)*

Reenter the Interframe

Like so many great inventions, innovations and technological advances, it seems so simple now, but was revolutionary in its time. What is so difficult about creating a folding knife with a frame that completely surrounds and secures handle inlays? What was so revolutionary about making a glass bulb with a thin filament in it that, when hit with electricity, lit up?

There is more to the interframe than the handle inlays and surrounding knife frame. There's also a "lockback" mechanism integral to the originals that Ron Lake built. Ron fashioned his folders with lock bars that held the folding blades securely in the "open" position.

The lock was disengaged by pushing down on the spring, accessible via a cutout on the back of the handle, or spine, of the knife, enabling the user to close the blade. And that, my friends, is the interframe, lockback folding knife, well, not quite ... did I mention the impeccable fit and finish, incredible artistry, smooth lines and seamless operation of Ron Lake's lockback folders?

Knifemakers across the board continue to build interframe folders in the likeness of those Ron Lake first fashioned decades ago, including Lake himself, and that alone is testament to a knife well designed, a useful tool, a perfect pallet for artistic renderings and quality craftsmanship. Reenter the interframe and celebrate the ingenuity of the knife industry.

▶ **RON LAKE: Here's a smooth steel interframe with a stag grip and a look that took an industry by storm.** *(Francesco Pachi photo)*

▶ **GAYLE BRADLEY: The black-lip pearl transitions beautifully into the stainless steel handle of the CPM 154 folder.** *(Ward photo)*

▶ **RON LAKE: Ron's set of "Sierra" interframe folders boast semi-boot-style blades that are each marked #1, and perfectly matched big-horn-sheep inlays.** *(Francesco Pachi photo)*

◄ RUSS SUTTON: Engraving, gold inlay and black-lip pearl seem to be a theme in modern interframe folders, and none are fashioned finer than this piece. *(PointSeven photo)*

▼ FRITS SCHNEIDER: Rarely does black-lip pearl emit such brown hues, and seldom is a damascus interframe folder done up so handsomely in a titanium frame.

▼ ANDRE THORBURN: The ironwood interframe folder features a locking liner rather than a lockback mechanism, and a hand-rubbed, satin-finished, folding-dagger-style 12C27 stainless steel blade. *(BladeGallery.com photo)*

► HOWARD HITCHMOUGH: Not a traditional interframe, but rather a locking-liner folder, the look furthers the Ron Lake tradition, this one in Damasteel, black-lip pearl, and Tim George's gold inlay and engraving. *(PointSeven photo)*

▲ DWIGHT TOWELL: A seraphinite stone surrounded by engraving and 24k-gold inlay highlights the interframe folder.

The Loveless Legacy

Do painters copy Rembrandt? I suppose they do. I know singers and music groups borrow songs, lyrics and melodies from each other. Conductors, I'm sure, share notes. As a writer and editor, I can tell you that, even though I insist my style is my own, it's undoubtedly influenced by what I've read by others. And you know fashion designers disguise themselves with fake mustaches and overcoats to catch glimpses at the competitors' newest runway styles.

So why not knifemakers?

It is the ultimate compliment, after all, to pay homage to another knifemaker by emulating his or her patterns, lines and designs. Credit should be given when credit is due, and most conscientious blade builders oblige by naming their influences, collaborators, mentors and heroes.

Bob Loveless is one of the most copied of all. He's the master, the one who popularized the drop-point hunter, brought ATS-34 to the United States, is practically a rock star in Japanese knife circles, furthered the popularity of the sub-hilt fighter and created the chute knife as it is known today. Articles and books have been written by and about Bob, and if you care to go up to www.wikipedia.com, the largest Internet encyclopedia, you can read all about Robert Waldorf (R.W.) Loveless.

As far as accomplishments and legacies go, perhaps the largest would be for a knife collector to look at a knife and know who built it before seeing the name on the tang of the blade. The same would go for songs by musicians, orchestral pieces by conductors, feature articles by writers ... and Rembrandt paintings. It is certainly true in regards to the knives and style of Bob Loveless, and thus is the Loveless legacy.

▲ RON NEWTON: The sentry stand guard, in this case two Loveless-style fighters and a hunter, bladed in CPM 154 steel and handled in ringed gidgee wood, and black and green Micarta®. *(Ward photo)*

◄ STEVE GATLIN: The "New York Special" is delivered in green canvas Micarta® and an ATS-34 blade, ala the way Loveless does it. *(PointSeven photo)*

◄ C.L. WEISS: The original chute knife was built by Bob Loveless for a Spec Ops parachute jumper as a way to cut himself out of the cord, or down from a tree, if necessary. The C.L. Weiss version employs a checkered French walnut handle, engraved 416 stainless steel guard and 440C blade. *(Thomason photo)*

► **JOHN YOUNG:** The beautiful tapered-tang fighter with ancient-ivory handle is made by John Young but has Bob Loveless written all over it. *(SharpByCoop.com photo)*

► **EDMUND DAVIDSON:** Edmund loved the Loveless design so much he hand rubbed the blade and outfitted it in stag. *(PointSeven photo)*

▲ **CHARLES VESTAL:** The "Loveless Style Hideout" sports an ironwood grip and a CPM 154CM blade. *(SharpByCoop.com photo)*

▲ **STEVE JOHNSON:** The quintessential Bob Loveless-style boot knife substitutes a musk-ox-horn grip for the Micarta® Loveless uses, but remains true with an ATS-34 blade. *(PointSeven photo)*

▲ **DAVID LANG:** Here's a chute knife in desert ironwood and a Thomas Brothers damascus blade. *(Balance Digital photo)*

◀ **R.W. LOVELESS:** The nude semi-skinner was invited to a stag party. *(Francesco Pachi photo)*

◀ **RON NEWTON:** The drop-point hunter (thank you, Bob) is striking in amber, dyed Sambar stag and a CPM T440V blade. *(Ward photo)*

▲ **MICHAEL LOVETT:** Bob's Mini Semi-Skinner model is fashioned in ancient ivory and a 154CM blade with Bob's double-nude logo.

◀ **R.W. LOVELESS:** His style is all his own, and this prototype skinner, made in 1970, sports a walnut handle and an open thong slot. *(Francesco Pachi photo)*

▲ **MICHAEL LOVETT:** The "Big Bear," possibly one of Bob Loveless's most recognizable models, has a 154CM blade and a standard green-Micarta® grip.

Battle-Hardened Blades

▶ **MIKKEL WILLUMSEN:** The "Wolverine" features a wicked rock-tumble-finished RWL-34 stainless steel blade, a contoured-G-10 handle and a grooved finger-hole pommel. *(BladeGallery.com photo)*

▲**TOM WATSON:** With its damascus stinger at the ready, the "Wasp I" has a honey of a G-10 handle. Mike Norris is credited for the damascus.

▲ **RANDY DOUCETTE:** The three battle-hardened soldiers are steel, G-10 and carbon fiber.

▲ **MAGNUS AXELSON:** Underneath the open-spine, wet-molded leather sheath, the radical full-integral tactical is Damasteel from point to pointed pommel and sports a leather-wrapped grip. *(PointSeven photo)*

Bowie Hybrids

How dare you refer to my exact replica of a Daniel Searles bowie a "hybrid?" Have you no appreciation for art, craftsmanship, tradition or culture? How can a historically accurate piece be a hybrid, as if comparing it to some half-gas/half-electric, lightweight, no-power, no-speed modern incarnation of an automobile from a factory that closed two days after it came off the assembly line?

Well, they are all hybrids, renditions, if you think about it. There are theories—some of them researched and documented—of what the original knife Col. James Bowie carried looked like, how it appeared and handled. Knifemakers investigate the materials that went into it, how it was shaped and ground, its length, the heft and feel. There are at least two gentlemen and a museum claiming the original bowie knife. But no one really knows, now, do they?

And some of the modern incarnations of bowies are downright gorgeous pieces, improved upon, really, and all pay homage to the original knife or knives that reportedly came out of James Black's shop. In fact, I'd wager a guess that some of the examples that follow are technically advanced, fine-tuned, better-balanced, more user friendly, further-adorned fixed blades than the James Bowie blade.

What remains important is that the bowie knife is an American icon, an edged tool born from necessity, and that it survives today because the style or pattern motivated people, made a lasting impression upon them and intrigued them. If today's bowie hybrids are not perfected patterns, they are about as close you can come to the Sandbar Bowie without actually drinking water from the river.

◀ **HENRY TORRES:** The coffin-shaped ironwood handle gives way to a stainless steel guard and swooping, clip-point 52100 blade. *(SharpByCoop.com photo)*

▶ **MATT DISKIN:** One bowie variation comes in the Mississippi dog-bone style with a walrus-tusk handle, sterling silver pins, and a mokumé throat, ferrule, guard and escutcheon plates. *(PointSeven photo)*

◀ **TERRY VENDEVENTER:** A notched false edge, file work along the tang, an oval guard and escutcheon plates, and shapely African blackwood handle are just a few amenities. *(SharpByCoop.com photo)*

▶ **JOHN PERRY:** A sizeable 1056 blade, S-shaped guard, white mother-of-pearl handle, rectangular escutcheon plate and embellished coffin pommel parade before admiring eyes. *(Ward photo)*

▶ **HERMAN SCHNEIDER:** When you have an ATS-34 blade that reaches for the stars like this convex-ground beauty, it takes a hefty guard and African blackwood handle to anchor the piece. *(Hiro Soga photo)*

◀ **ERIK FRITZ:** In the coffin-handle style comes a cocobolo and 5160 bowie including simple but elegant domed pins, an octagonal ferrule and oval guard. *(PointSeven photo)*

▶ **WALTER BREND:** They wore 'em big in the west, and this Devin Thomas damascus bladed bowie with a stag grip would have measured up nicely. Floyd Byrd fashioned a sheath for the piece. *(SharpByCoop.com photo)*

▶ **GARY MULKEY:** The milky white, fossil-walrus-ivory handle and plain steel blade make for a clean presentation. *(Ward photo)*

◀ **CHARLIE and HARRY MATHEWS:** In the old days, they forged 5160 steel, fashioned wrought-iron guards and employed stag for handles, similar to how they do it today. *(SharpByCoop.com photo)*

▶ **JERRY FISK:** Bowies are supposed to be made with clipped-point blades, false edges, oval guards and ivory handles, much like the "Bandolero" in damascus and niter-blued fittings. *(Ward photo)*

▶ **GORDON GRAHAM:** Fifteen inches of stag and damascus are done up bowie style. *(Ward photo)*

◀ **KYLE ROYER:** The D-guard bowie sports the most colorful ironwood handle this side of the hornbeam forest, and a damascus blade of which Col. James himself would have been proud. *(Ward photo)*

▶ **JOSH SMITH:** The Searles Bowie features a three-bar, composite-damascus blade in twist and snowflake patterns, a matching damascus guard and an African blackwood handle. Steve Dunn engraved the bowie and Paul Long fashioned a sheath for the piece. *(SharpByCoop.com photo)*

◀ **BUSTER WARENSKI:** Buster busted out a fancy English bowie showcasing a 440C blade, engraved nickel-silver guard and fittings, an ebony handle with engraved, oval escutcheon plate, and an engraved nickel silver throat-and-tip sheath. *(SharpByCoop.com)*

LARRY FUEGEN: Say howdy to the "Buckaroo Bowie" in fossil-walrus ivory, a carved and antiqued guard, engraved sterling silver ferrule and 5160 blade. It comes with a leather and engraved-sterling-silver throat and tip sheath. *(PointSeven photo)*

RUSTY POLK: The natural bend of the stag grip was perfectly suited to the clip-point 5160 bowie blade. *(Ward photo)*

RICHARD EPTING: Stag, damascus fittings and a blued-steel spacer color up the traditional cut. *(Ward photo)*

TIM HANCOCK: A damascus dog-bone bowie doesn't sound all that special, until one sees it done right, complete with domed pins, bowtie guard, file-worked liners and rectangle escutcheon plates. *(SharpByCoop.com photo)*

▼**ED BRANDSEY:** The red dots show you where the file work is, and transition your eye from the curvaceous 440C blade to the S-guard, and stag and ironwood handle. The buckskin sheath features an arrowhead carved from buffalo horn, and a buffalo-head nickel on the strap. *(Ward photo)*

◄**JAMES BATSON:** The silver is German, the stag of the Sambar variety, the knife itself in the Woodhead style and the bowie as American as apple pie. *(Ward photo)*

►**STEPHAN FOWLER:** The wrought iron guard brings out the color of the Sambar stag grip and enhances the ripple effect of the wavy temper line. *(SharpByCoop. com photo)*

▼**MICHAEL MCCLURE:** The Woodhead-style bowie dons a forged O-1 blade, mammoth-ivory handle and nickel-silver hardware. *(BladeGallery.com photo)*

►**GAETAN BEAUCHAMP:** Brass adds class to the ATS-34 and ironwood bowie, not that it needed much attention.

▶ **RALPH RICHARDS:** The little touches—a file-worked guard, blade spine and butt plate—benefit the stag bowie. *(Ward photo)*

▶ **LIN RHEA:** The Musso-style bowie boasts a foot of 5160 steel, a large S-guard and a handful of walnut. *(Ward photo)*

◀ **TIM TABOR:** If the giraffe bone doesn't blow you away, the damascus blade is sure to knock your socks off. *(PointSeven photo)*

▶ **DON HANSON III:** The temper line rolls along the W-2 blade like high tide on the mammoth-ivory coast. *(SharpByCoop. com photo)*

▶ **JOE MANDT:** What's better than a stag and W-2 bowie? Two stag and W-2 bowies, of course. *(SharpByCoop.com photo)*

▶ **FRANS VAN ELDIK:** Engraved silver fittings and a plain ATS-34 blade are nice counterparts on a full-tang, stag-handle bowie. The incredible engraved throat-and-tip sheath is the bowie de gras.

▲ **CHARLES STOUT:** A little anodized titanium goes a long way in embellishing a damascus and mammoth-ivory bowie. *(Ward photo)*

▼ **E. JAY HENDRICKSON:** A silver dogwood flower sprouts from the curly maple handle of the damascus bowie. *(SharpByCoop.com photo)*

▶ **W.E. ANKROM:** Gil Rudolph engraved and gold inlaid the "Urban Bowie," a nice, damascus, stag-handle hybrid of the American bowie knife. *(Hiro Soga photo)*

JERRY VAN EIZENGA: Kings, queens and Cherokee Chiefs alike would gravitate toward the Tah-Chee bowie with coffin-shaped blackwood handle and 5160 blade. *(PointSeven photo)*

BILL BURKE: It's blued and brown and bowie all over. *(SharpByCoop.com photo)*

STEVEN RAPP: Could this be bowie Rappsody? It is if you love mother-of-pearl, steel, New Orleans bowie knives and Steven Rapp, and who doesn't? *(PointSeven photo)*

HENRY TORRES: Neither the 52100 blade nor the black-ebony handle ever stop bending. *(PointSeven photo)*

Studies In Stone

▶ **MEL NISHIUCHI:** Petrified coral qualifies as stone in this case, knock-dead-gorgeous stone, and from Indonesia at that, then married to a Devin Thomas damascus blade and bolsters, and titanium liners. *(Mitch Lum photo)*

▼ **SCOTT SAWBY:** Marian Sawby endeavored to engrave orchid leaves around the jade handle of the button-lock folder, a worthwhile endeavor at that.

▶ **AL CRENSHAW:** The saddleback trapper features turquoise handle inlays, arrowhead and acorn handle shields, file-worked blade spines and spacers, and carved 416 stainless steel bolsters. *(Ward photo)*

◀ **MICHAEL MILLER:** Malachite recon stone is the green that groups the African blackwood grip and the scenic ladder-pattern-damascus blade, the latter featuring mosaic floral patterns that have been inlayed and forge-welded in place prior to forging.

◀ **RUSTY PRESTON:** Red coral, the stone-hard kind, is the rust that the file-worked back spacers and hand-rubbed, satin-finished blades of the folding trapper do not have. The file work is of the Roman knot variety. *(Johnny Stout photo)*

◀ **MIKE FRANKLIN:** It would be a pleasure to grab hold of the push dagger by its composite turquoise handle, and wrap fingers around the neck of the double-hollow-ground ATS-34 blade.

▶ **NORMAN BARDSLEY:** Check out the Navajo village in raised, three-dimensional jasper, mastodon ivory, mother-of-pearl and camel bone, all with a Nevada turquoise sky and abalone sun. One almost ignores the Nick Smolen damascus blade and Richard Marks damascus bolsters … almost.

▶ **STEVE JERNIGAN:** The British Columbia jade is sea green and gorgeous, especially when mated skillfully with the chocolaty mokumé bolsters and grooved 12C27 blade. *(Ward photo)*

◀ **T.C. ROBERTS:** The ocean jasper is aptly named, divided by pearl, and surrounded by steel. *(Ward photo)*

◀ **MARK KNAPP:** The chainsaw-damascus blade is patterned similarly to the blue-sheep-horn handle with amber (fossil resin turned semi-stone) spacers. Brass adds more class. *(BladeGallery.com photo)*

Edged Translucency

I t's the cocktail dress of knives, the Porsche of custom cutlery, the Frank Lloyd Wright of handmade blades. Pearl is a surefire way to class up a knife. It bespeaks quality, style and grace, and can be as mesmerizing as a classical play with a perfect score, top-notch actors and a fascinating storyline.

You can get lost in pearl. It reflects the ocean, pounding sands and the mollusks that once made it home. It has captured the colors of the sea and brought them to light in its nacreous luster. Few cameras have frozen the ocean in time as well as pearl. It is a perfect reflection and as natural as a sea snake slithering along a coral reef.

Pearl is hard, durable and easily worked. It is cool to the touch, smooth, palpable and pleasant. The colors are not startling or gaudy, but rather rich, vibrant and easy on the eyes. No synthetic, manmade material can compete with pearl, just as a Hollywood movie set has nothing over the great, Western Plains. There is nothing like the mother of all materials, nature's best, the translucent, illustrious and nacreous pearl. You go, girl!

▶ **CHARLES WEISS:** Gold-lined engraving and translucent pearl enhance a well-executed gent's knife. *(Buddy Thomason photo)*

◀ **BUTCH BALL:** Black-lip pearl, gold-lip pearl and abalone invite you into the realm of damascus folding knives, with Chad Nichols and Larry Donnelly doing the damascus honors. *(SharpByCoop.com photo)*

▲ **JERRY MCCLURE:** "Mercedes" was a pretty black-lip-pearl girl in Damasteel bolsters, a twist-Damasteel blade and gold buttons.

▶ **DAN CHINNOCK:** For their good looks, the "Fishtail" models rely on mother-of-pearl handles, Larry Donnelly damascus blades and gold screws. *(Ward photo)*

▶ **LEE FERGUSON:** The white, bronze, blue, black and gray color scheme sends the locking-liner folder to market in style. Devin Thomas forged a little damascus for the occasion. *(Ward photo)*

▶ **WARREN OSBORNE:** A match-up between black-lip pearl and Mike Norris damascus resulted in a winsome folding dagger. *(SharpByCoop.com photo)*

▲ **TIM BRITTON:** A colorful bit of nacre beckoned for gold-inlaid and engraved bolsters like only Jim Small could accomplish. *(SharpByCoop.com photo)*

◀ **STEVEN RAPP:** Cutting, fitting and matching mother-of-pearl, abalone and black-lip pearl for hours is how one achieves such a perfect set of California-style CPM154 fixed blades. *(BladeGallery.com photo)*

JERRY FISK: People dream about owning a pearl-handle fixed blade, and the damascus piece with engraved bolsters is what dreams are made of. *(Ward photo)*

JEFF CLAIBORNE: Take a long pull on the blades, grab hold of the pearl and crush a few pills with the butt of the 52100 doctor's knife. *(Hoffman photo)*

DON HETHCOAT: The colorful pearl concerto includes performances by pattern-welded-steel bolsters and blade, and an engraved back spacer. *(PointSeven photo)*

KEN ONION: Not only was pearl planted in the gold-anodized-titanium handle frame, but along the spacer where it shared the limelight with little ball bearings. The flipper blade of the "Packrat" is CPM154 steel. *(Mitch Lum photo)*

JIM and JOYCE MINNICK: File work, gold inlay, and gold buttons and pins highlight the stunning folding daggers in two flavors of mother-of-pearl. *(PointSeven photo)*

MICK PENFOLD: The job of protecting the pearl was giving to a file-worked and grooved nickel silver guard and his Grosserosen Damasteel blade. This is the kind of stuff found in fairytales and castles.

RODGER ECHOLS: To forge the damascus, checker the pearl, file-work the liners and flute the gold pins, for this is our mission, and this we shall achieve. *(Ward photo)*

STEVE JOHNSON: Steve gave pearl a whirl for the asymmetrical dirk with satisfactory results. *(Francesco Pachi photo)*

REINHARD TSCHAGER: Bedecked in ruby, sapphire, gold and mother-of-pearl is the bedazzling semi-integral knife.

GRACE HORNE: She has so much going for her—a laminated-steel blade with veins of pure silver, wrought iron bolsters and a black-lip mother-of-pearl handle. What a looker! *(PointSeven photo)*

Fixin' for a Fight

The question invariably arises, "Well who really fights with knives anymore?" And the answer is, "That's not the point." It's rare for people to arm themselves with baskethilt swords, cutlasses, maces, sabers or Roman gladii, but the exotic blades are reproduced, meticulously copied and improved upon to retain their tradition and flavor. Not many people kill rabbits with slingshots, but we give the rubber-banded Y-sticks to our children as toys, and teach them proper use and care.

Few folks heat their houses with wood-burning fireplaces, yet the mesmerizing flames radiate another kind of warmth, a nostalgic glow, a longing for a simpler time and a feeling of comfort in the home. There would be no dire consequences if black-powder rifles ceased to exist, but don't tell outdoorsmen that. Thousands of hunters carry them annually and get a charge out of the hobby. Try to stop a fox hunt in the English countryside and you're likely to end up an unwilling participant in the Queen's Army.

There's another reason to hand-fashion fighters. Their lines are as mesmerizing as those dancing flames in the fireplace. Straight-back little soldiers, theirs is a piercing way of combat, including hand guards, long slender blades and slim, slashing builds.

Another aspect of the allure is in crafting fighters because we can. The mountain is there, so we climb it. And the allure of fighters includes a bit of rebellious attitude. Knifemakers are an indignantly optimistic bunch, a bit set in their ways, like English fox hunters. Only the knifemakers have the tools, and they know how to use them.

▶ **RICARDO VELARDE:** Fully integral is the sub-hilt fighter and wholly beautiful. *(PointSeven photo)*

▶ **JOHN WHITE:** John was serious about making a fighter, handpicking mammoth-ivory slabs, shaping an oval damascus guard, and forging, clay tempering and hand rubbing an 11-inch W-2 blade. *(Ward photo)*

▲ **DAN GRAVES:** Smart parts make up the fighter, like a rounded damascus guard, ferrule and end cap, elongated, tapered blade, and smooth, pre-ban elephant ivory handle. *(SharpByCoop.com photo)*

▶ **TOM FERRY:** Random-pattern damascus and the maker's own engraving make a sub-hilt fighter fashionable. *(Mitch Lum photo)*

▲ **THAD BUCHANAN:** Curly koa wood doesn't attempt to tame the CPM 154 fighter. *(Mitch Lum photo)*

▲ **JASON KNIGHT:** Good Knight! A fighter in sanded, buffed, shaped and polished ironwood sports a sharp blade with a radical false edge. *(SharpByCoop.com photo)*

▲ **WALTER BREND:** Well the fighting knife master just made his mark again, this time in mammoth tooth, a CPM 154 blade and an impeccable pattern. Floyd Byrd fashioned a sheath for the piece. *(Ward photo)*

▲ **CHARLES VESTAL:** Follow the grinds of the Bob Loveless-style fighter and chute knives straight to the tips and back to the green-canvas-Micarata® grips. *(SharpByCoop.com photo)*

▶ **FRANK GAMBLE:** Frank's thumbprint is on more than just the bolsters of the stag-and-stainless steel fighter. *(BladeGallery.com photo)*

◀ **MICHAEL MCCLURE:** The knifemaker proved up to the task of competing with the bark mammoth ivory by properly pinning it, and then forging a flawless high-carbon-steel blade. *(BladeGallery.com photo)*

▶ **STEPHAN A. FOWLER:** The slim fighter with wispy temper line is treated to a California buckeye burl handle with some swirling dervishes of its own. *(SharpByCoop.com photo)*

◀ **MARK NEVLING:** Damascus, oosic and mokumé. Need we say more?

▶ **KIRK REXROAT:** Kirk combined an oosic handle with 10 inches of damascus, and blue-anodized, fileworked fittings. *(PointSeven photo)*

◀ **ANDERS HOGSTROM:** Anders antiqued and textured the sterling silver furniture of the "Invalidator Bowie" and then forged and clay tempered a bad-ass blade. The fossil-walrus grip has attitude, too. *(SharpByCoop.com photo)*

◀ **JOE MANDT:** The convex-ground W-2 blade rises to the occasion, as does the curly maple grip of the fighter. *(SharpByCoop.com photo)*

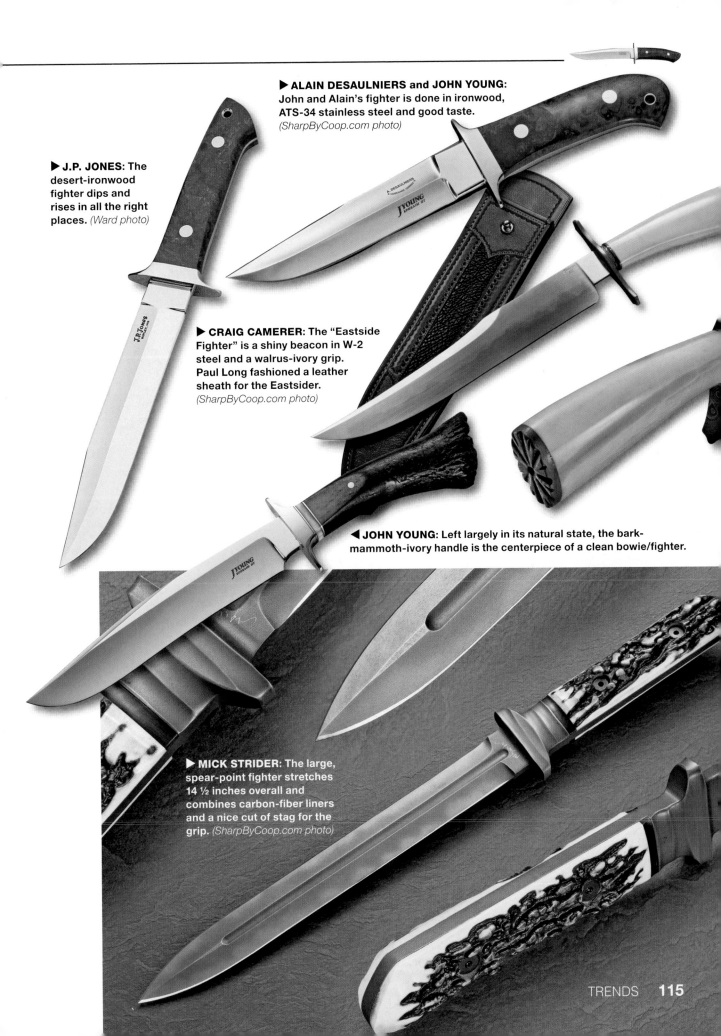

▶ **ALAIN DESAULNIERS and JOHN YOUNG:** John and Alain's fighter is done in ironwood, ATS-34 stainless steel and good taste. *(SharpByCoop.com photo)*

▶ **J.P. JONES:** The desert-ironwood fighter dips and rises in all the right places. *(Ward photo)*

▶ **CRAIG CAMERER:** The "Eastside Fighter" is a shiny beacon in W-2 steel and a walrus-ivory grip. Paul Long fashioned a leather sheath for the Eastsider. *(SharpByCoop.com photo)*

◀ **JOHN YOUNG:** Left largely in its natural state, the bark-mammoth-ivory handle is the centerpiece of a clean bowie/fighter.

▶ **MICK STRIDER:** The large, spear-point fighter stretches 14 ½ inches overall and combines carbon-fiber liners and a nice cut of stag for the grip. *(SharpByCoop.com photo)*

◀ CURT ERICKSON: Golden engraving by Julie Warenski-Erickson highlights the guard, pinheads and sheath of the stag and stainless fighter. *(Ward photo)*

▶ J.R. COOK: Amber stag and the knifemaker's winning attitude elevate the 5160 fighter to new heights. *(Ward photo)*

◀ DON HANSON III: If Don really forged the temper line into that 1086M blade, and he did, then he's the reigning champion of fighting knives, stag handled or not. Don Long created a sheath (not shown) for the piece. *(SharpByCoop.com photo)*

◀ MAGNUS AXELSON: There's a whole lot of fight left in the D-2 and Damasteel fixed blade with a silver-vine handle. An open-spine leather sheath completes the package. *(PointSeven photo)*

▶ **J.R. REEVES:** Strategic filework, a tactile design and fine craftsmanship. That's all a 1084 fighter could ask for, and maybe some curly maple for good measure. *(Ward photo)*

▲ **DAVID BROADWELL:** The lines of the fighting knives, carved grips and shaped guards, along with the highly patterned wood, create a complete package. *(SharpByCoop.com photo)*

▶ **OLEKSANDER BOGDANOVICH:** More than geometric shapes, the mokumé handles and damascus guards of the fighters have futuristic yet utilitarian forms. *(SharpByCoop.com photo)*

Nut-Brown Knives

How does that saying go? Even a blind squirrel finds a nut once in a while? Well, that has nothing to do with the talented knifemakers fashioning gorgeous wood-handle cutlery, except that they recognize fine nut-brown grains when they see them. And such are the beginnings of woodworkers toiling with sandpaper, buffing compounds, stains, varnishes, saws and drills … and all other vises, glues, pins and spacers.

These are the guys with cluttered workbenches, but good lighting, screws and other hardware separated by sizes and diameters, a clamp for every occasion and various sizes of wood blocks ready and waiting to be wrapped with fine-grit buffing paper and lathered with elbow grease.

If you close your eyes, you can smell the sawdust, feel the friction of sandpaper on pulp, hear the grits bite down and see the light filter through air born wood particles. It is a scene right out of Dad's workshop, a Sunday Mr. Fixit show or a high school woodshop class. Whatever the case may be, nostalgia reigns supreme and the scene is set for traditional toiling and lots of oiling.

Then there are the finished products. They make the work worthwhile, and if the craftsman knows his wood lathe from a band saw, the results could be anywhere from spectacular to breathtaking, and likely too good for any old career in cabinetry or flooring.

The nut-brown knives are akin to handcrafted wood furniture, wardrobes, armoires and china cabinets. Their sheer beauty is smooth to the touch, elegant to the eye and stately in its being. These are the wood-grain finishers of the knife industry and not any old cuts or slabs will do for such highly-figured finery.

◄ **DICK FAUST:** Spalted maple does its best calico cat impression on a 154CM hunter that stretches 9 inches overall.

► **GEORGE COUSINO:** He laid some wood upon the blade and walked away contented. That would be Afzalia lay wood and 440C steel for those of you paying attention. (PointSeven photo)

► **BRIAN THIE:** Stained wood of the 15-inch, 5160 bowie emits orange and red hues that complement the light-brown basket-weave sheath. The maker's own engraving tops off the pretty package. (Ward photo)

▶ **KEVIN CASEY:** Some like how the hamon (temper line) ebbs and flows, while others dig the waves awash within the eucalyptus grip. *(PointSeven photo)*

▼ **CHRISTOPHER MEYER:** The full-tang, O-1 "Mimosa" kitchen/utility knife is handled in stabilized mimosa wood, and with care.

▶ **BRION TOMBERLIN:** The "Black Rapids Recurve," in an ironwood handle and a stately 9260 H steel blade with etched hamon (temper line), won the 2008 Best Fighter Award at the Oklahoma Custom Knife Show. *(Ward photo)*

◀ **DON HANSON III and RUSS ANDREWS:** Missouri black walnut makes its debut on a W-2 fighter with a damascus hand guard. *(SharpByCoop.com photo)*

◀ **MICHAEL RADER:** Stabilized maple burl and curly maple are fitted together with walnut accents to create the grip of the integral, 52100 Santoku kitchen knife. *(BladeGallery.com photo)*

▶ **PERCY RICHARDSON:** Maple-burl handle scales sandwich the full-tang skinner. *(Johnny Stout photo)*

▲ **GARTH HINDMARCH:** It's OK to palm the palm wood.

▲ **DAN FARR and GREG NEELY:** Two masters team on a carved walnut hunter with oak leaf engravings. *(PointSeven photo)*

◀ **EDMUND DAVIDSON:** An all-integral 440C fighter is treated to a stabilized California buckeye burl handle and Edmund's many grits and sizes of sandpaper, files and buffers. *(PointSeven photo)*

▶ **THOMAS HASLINGER:** Haslinger the former hash slinger *(really)* debuts the "New Generation Chef's Knife" sporting a CPM 154CM blade and a smokin' spalted-curly-maple grip.

◄ GERT VAN DEN ELSEN: The Puukko is done up in CPM 420 steel and exhibition-grade Massur birch with spacers of reindeer horn and blued mild steel.

► FRANCESCO PACHI: Snakewood shows its skin, while the knifemaker shows his prowess.

▲ MIKE WILLIAMS: The talented Mike Williams builds an Ouachita Hunter in maple burl and 1084 blade steel. *(Ward photo)*

► ALBERT TRUJILLO: ATS-34 hunters are outfitted in maple- and amboyna-burl handles. The filework is a finishing touch. *(PointSeven photo)*

▲ RON REEVES: The "Yukon Skinner," in a fileworked 5160 blade and mosaic pins, dons a dyed box elder handle that's to die for. *(Ward photo)*

▼**DANIEL ERICKSON:** The beautiful form of the "Phalanx" is accentuated by the spalted-maple and Afzalia-wood handle, the stretching, reaching, hand-forged damascus blade and copasetic copper pins. *(BladeGallery.com photo)*

◀**MIKE MOONEY:** The trailing-point skinning knife parades a black-ash and African-blackwood grip that won't stop.

◀**STEVEN KOSTER:** The kingwood handle is fit and finished for a king.

▲ **ANDRE VAN HEERDEN:** Exhibition-grade desert ironwood is like the cork in a pricey Damasteel wine bottle. *(BladeGallery.com photo)*

▶ **ERIK FRITZ:** Eucalyptus burl was the outstanding wood of choice for a random-pattern-damascus fixed blade. *(PointSeven photo)*

◀ **JOHN PARKS:** The classic knife pattern is usurped only by the Thuya burl patterning. *(PointSeven photo)*

◀ **CRAIG CAMERER:** A lot of W-2 fighter and a long temper line deserve an equitable length of desert ironwood. *(Ward photo)*

◀ **LIN RHEA:** Ironwood swirls around the oval guard and tastefully engraved ferrule of the 5160 bowie. *(Ward photo)*

▼ **J.R. COOK:** Grab hold of the grainy walnut dagger and do some damage. The sheath is a beauty and the engraving is done in good taste. *(Ward photo)*

The Color Of Cut

Color for the sake of color is counterproductive. It's why people still make black-and-white movies, take black-and-white photos and draw in pencil. The effect one wishes to achieve dictates the medium used. Artists understand that, and the knifemakers who built the brilliant edges that follow are true artists in every sense of the word.

Theirs was not a fashioning of gaudy showpieces that would attract customers who are unconcerned with how the knives perform. Just the opposite, the artisans whose examples are paraded here before the eyes of *Knives 2010* readers first aspired to utility and performance, peak performance, and to aesthetic beauty as a secondary benefit of their skill sets. Each of the pieces is fit and finished with precision, yet embellished with a full array of colors to the delight of knife collectors across the board.

Titanium has not only allowed knifemakers to forge, grind and buff their work, but also to paint it. Modern heat-coloration methods undertaken by the world's finest blade smiths add color to the steel, and particularly mosaic damascus, but to single-alloy steels, as well. Add in a little mammoth tooth, giraffe bone, pearl and a few gemstones, and voila, craftsmen achieve the ultimate color of cut. What an industry!

▼**SCOT MATSUOKA:** This little wrath of grape comes in the form of a dyed box-elder-burl grip trying to secure a wicked Devin Thomas damascus blade and bolsters. *(BladeGallery.com photo)*

◄**TIM GALYEAN:** The "Digital" folders features an anodized-titanium grip in an Art-Deco-style geometric pattern that complements the angular CPM 154 blade. *(SharpByCoop.com photo)*

◄**KEN ONION:** Meandering coral-reef-like textured and anodized titanium handles breathe life into the "Dragster" folders. *(Mitch Lum photo)*

▶ **PHIL ERNEST:** The colorful cast of cutlery characters includes a green mammoth tooth handle, purple blade and blue bolsters. *(PointSeven photo)*

◀ **JOSH SMITH:** Blued mosaic damascus electrifies the blade, handle and even the file-worked back spacer of the locking-liner folder. *(PointSeven photo)*

◀ **RICK DUNKERLEY:** The blue, white and purple mosaic damascus frames in the gold-lip mother-of-pearl in a colorful cut of craftsmanship. *(PointSeven photo)*

▶ **PETE CAREY:** A green-anodized-titanium frame radiates through the translucent G-10 handle scales of the "Executive" locking-liner folder.

◀ **STAN WILSON:** A kaleidoscope of colors splash across the "dragon-skin"-pattern damascus blade of the dual-action auto, mimicking a land where dragons tread and fire lights up the landscape. Gold-lip pearl is the calming force. *(SharpByCoop.com photo)*

◀ **GARY HOUSE:** Heat-blued "dancing zebra"-pattern damascus emboldens the miniature, 4 ¼-inch sword with a gold "radials"-pattern damascus guard and mammoth-ivory handle. *(BaldeGallery.com photo)*

▶ **ED CAFFREY:** Floral engraving on anodized and textured titanium, along with gold-plated screws and a back spacer inset with rubies, add more than a touch of colorful class to a damascus folder.

▼ **DAVE AMMONS:** The dyed-maple handle of the damascus hunter will blend in perfectly with its wooded surroundings. *(Balance Digital photo)*

◀ **STAN FUJISAKA:** What so proudly we hailed by the titanium's last gleaming. The engraving is by **Bruce Shaw.** *(Mitch Lum photo)*

◀ **BRIAN TIGHE:** Blue and purple bats flitter across the handle of a damascus folder with double, integral guard. If you'd like, Brian can supply a matching belt buckle with the knife. *(PointSeven photo)*

◀ **RICK HANEY:** Orange G-10 is the backbone of the "Vertebrae" folding knife with a 3.65-inch S30V blade. *(PointSeven photo)*

◀ **SAL MANARO:** Mokumé and fossil ivory make their milky way across the handle and bolsters of a locking-liner folder. Phillip Jones forged the mokumé, and David Abramson fashioned a leather pouch. *(SharpByCoop.com photo)*

▶ **WALLY HAYES:** A dragon graces the red-hot handle and breathes down the neck of a damascus blade. *(PointSeven photo)*

◀ **MICHAEL WALKER:** Pink and pearl go together like the "zipped" blade steels of the folder. *(PointSeven photo)*

▼ **ERIC ELSON:** Wearing blaze orange is always a good idea during hunting season, and this stone-washed CPM 154 "Dread Lock Light" folder would be a handy companion. *(SharpByCoop.com photo)*

◀ **GARY ROOT:** Red, white and blue were fitting color choices for a patriotic spear-point fixed blade. *(SharpByCoop.com photo)*

Hafted 'Hawks & Hatchets

There can be innovation in knives, but a tomahawk is a tomahawk, and an axe is an axe. Who ever heard of a talking 'hawk, a walking hatchet, an art axe or a high-tech wood splitter? Lest you forget, we're talking knifemakers here, and when it comes to the blade builders, there is no scrimping, dogging it or taking the easy way out.

Nope, knifemakers overbuild everything they make. They're a lot like Tim "The Tool Man" Taylor in that way. Tim always used the highest-powered equipment, the most tricked-out, built-up, bored-out, custom power tools he could get his testosterone-fueled hands on, and knifemakers are kin to the Tool Man.

They use a tool, aren't completely satisfied with the way it performs, conjure up ways to make it better, and the next thing you know, all activities are postponed for the day while they're in the shop grinding, sanding, drilling, honing and buffing. The drawing board has more erase marks on it than the government's budget proposal, and the band saw just got a new blade.

The tomahawks and hatchets look good, too, while they're chopping, splitting, shaving kindling or whistling

through the air at some hand-crafted target. Their hafts are strong, well refined and taken to a high sheen. The heads are driven on with power hammers, honed to hair-splitting sharpness, and the decorations are enough to make a war general's toes curl. These are the hafted 'hawks and axes of the knife industry, not some Boy Scout hatchets with fake-leather snap sheaths.

▼ LIN RHEA: The belt axe benefits from a 5160 head and a bronze bolster and cap, the latter hand carved to simulate the grooves of the stag grip. *(Ward photo)*

► TERRY RODGERS: The knifemaker's heart went into, and pierced through, the 5160 head of the William Scagel-style tomahawk that is anchored by a crown-stag and bois-de-arc haft. *(Ward photo)*

◄ ALAN TIENSVOLD: Topped with an engraved bronze cap, this 'hawk is a beauty from its curly-maple haft to its 5160 head. *(PointSeven photo)*

▲ ED CAFFREY: This twist-pattern-damascus tomahawk wears beaver fur, brain-tanned deer hide, 1800s trade beads, ivory and a turkey feather.

▲ DANIEL WINKLER: The spike 'hawk/war 'hawk can be made with a rubber-coated handle for use in wet environs, or a carved wooden haft, each with Kydex® sheaths, Tek-Lok™ clips and built-in, knotted bungee cords to further secure the sheaths to the heads. *(SharpByCoop.com photo)*

▲ GREG LIGHTFOOT: Not satisfied with the double-bit axe head? Switch it out for the spike-hawk head using the Torx™ wrench and screws provided, oiling the threads with "Lightfoot Lube." Then hold onto that leather-wrapped handle and let 'er rip.

◀ J. NEILSON: Measuring nearly 9 inches from spike to cutting edge, the head of the "Shorty Tomahawk" is forged from 200 layers of twist-pattern damascus and driven onto a curly maple haft. Decorations include Turk's-head knots, buffalo horn caps, black spacers and nickel silver tacks.

▶ JACK FULLER: The pipe tomahawk takes smoking to new levels, considering its forged head with tool-steel bit, buffalo horn mouthpiece and cleanout plug, and copper-wire-wrapped curly maple haft.

Foreign Flavor

▲ **ALBERTO SYMONDS:** The Mattias Styrefors and Jonny Walker Nilsson, heat-colored, mosaic-damascus blade rests easily against a carved sterling silver guard, black palm spacers and an axis-stag and Thuya-burl handle.

◀ **SCOTT SLOBODIAN:** The Chinese gold fittings are carved by Barbara Slobodian, and the forged 1050 carbon steel blade and boxwood handle fashioned by Scott himself.

▲ **PAUL COOPER:** The Persian struts its curvaceous stuff in damascus and wildwood. *(PointSeven photo)*

▲ **MAIHKEL EKLUND:** The gun-blued, gold-inlaid carbon steel blade is straight and true, as the stabilized-birch handle is solid and palpable.

▶ **MICHAEL RADER:** The Dha draws its influence from Eastern style, complete with a dramatic, 28 ½-inch damascus blade, a Peruvian walnut and curly maple handle, and African blackwood accents. *(BladeGallery.com photo)*

▶ **PEKKA TUOMINEN:** The puukko parades a forged blade, birch-bark handle and brass bolsters.

▶ **ANDERS HOGSTROM:** In traditional Japanese style, the 1050 fixed blade with the liquid-like temper line comes apart by removing a peg in the ebony handle. A birch sheath with silk tassels silences the piece. *(PointSeven photo)*

▲ **VINCE EVANS:** Via a 32-inch, 1,024-layer-damascus blade, bronze habaki (blade collar), carved tsuba (guard) and a leather cord-wrapped handle, the Chinese "Willow Leaf Saber" makes the air sing around it. *(PointSeven photo)*

◀ **MEL NISHIUCHI:** One pretty Persian folder, she showcases an ATS-34 blade, Devin Thomas "Spirograph"-damascus bolsters and an Afghanistan lapis handle.

▼ **RICHARD VAN DIJK:** The dirk and sgian dubh are large and small, respectively, but take on similar forms, and materials that include file-worked damascus, carved ebony and sterling silver.

Campsite Clearers

▶ **GEOFF KEYES:** The crown stag literally wears a brass crown and beautifies a 1084 "Mountain Man Camp Knife" that reaches a full 13 inches overall. *(Mitch Lum photo)*

▲ **DANIEL WINKLER:** Daniel built the camp knife to be used in cutting competition, outfitting it with a curly-maple handle, full, tapered tang and braided leather lanyard. *(SharpByCoop.com photo)*

◀ **GARY RODEWALD:** The above-standard camp supplies include a stabilized-masur-birch handle, hand-forged, satin-finished O-1 blade, distal-tapered tang, stainless steel rivets and a lanyard hole. *(BladeGallery.com photo)*

▶ **DR. JIM LUCIE:** The William Scagel-style camp knife sports a hand-forged 1084 blade and a stacked-leather handle with a crown-stag butt. Engraved on the end of the crown stag is "To Buddy Thomason In Friendship From The Maker Oct. 2006." *(Thomason photo)*

▲ **JODY MULLER:** The mammoth-ivory camp knife showcases a handsome, clay-tempered damascus blade and engraved stainless steel guard. *(BladeGallery.com photo)*

STATE OF THE ART

The long-running television program "60 Minutes" recently ran a segment on Wilmington, Ohio, where a DHL plant closed, leaving thousands of townspeople out of work. One of the unfortunate ex-employees was then part-time knifemaker Michael O'Machearley.

When CBS and "60 Minutes" interviewed O'Machearley and asked what he planned to do now that he was unemployed, he said that he'd be forced to make his part-time knifemaking hobby a full-time career. CBS was intrigued. Add to that the fact that O'Machearley had suffered a horrendous loss years earlier when his son was killed in action in Iraq, and CBS had a story. The broadcasting corporation sent reporters to O'Machearley's house and knifemaking shop, filmed him at the grinder, and talked to his wife and former coworkers.

Shortly after the segment aired, O'Machearley experienced an outpouring of generosity from the American viewing public, who ordered more than 200 knives from Michael within 24 hours of the show. Emails flooded in, and one in particular made an impression on O'Machearley. It was from a gentleman who ordered a $500 knife from Michael and then proceeded to tell him that he had never even heard of custom knives before the broadcast. Imagine that. He was unfamiliar with handmade knives.

What an eye-opener it must be for the uninitiated to see a program like "60 Minutes," open a book like *Knives 2010*, visit a museum displaying handmade knives and swords, or attend the BLADE Show or Knifemakers' Guild Show with a friend and be awakened to the incredible artistry, craftsmanship and technical beauty of knives, embellished or not.

Further that by looking at some of the engraved, scrimshawed, sculpted, jeweled or pattern-welded pieces that modern knifemakers are so adept at fashioning, and the tongue must hang so low it touches the earth. Admittedly, there is some satisfaction in being part of something few know about, a trade that brings joy, furthers art, promotes American ingenuity and hard work, and helps society. It's the "State Of The Art" in knives, and it's a euphoric state of a nirvana-like magnitude.

Sheath Beauty

◄ KENNY ROWE: The matching leather belt and sheath feature engraved buckles, Conchos, loops and straps. *(Ward photo)*

▼ ANDREA PULISOVA: She looked at boxwood and saw bears, thus the reason why knifemaker Vladimir Pulis chose Andrea to carve the handle and sheath of his damascus hunter.

◄ KENNY ROWE: The carved steer head, engraved Concho and stitched leather sheath are ready for the California-buckeye-burl-handled "Southwest Utility" knife by John Holley. *(Ward photo)*

▼ KAREN SHOOK: The tasseled, fringed-leather sheath is a perfect match for the leather-wrapped stag handle of Daniel Winkler's hunter. *(Ward photo)*

▼SHERRY LOTT: Ostrich leather inlay and decorative stitching were the embellishments of choice for the leather sheath, and scrimshaw for the ivory-handle bowie by R.W. Wilson. *(Hoffman photo)*

▲R. CAPECE: Only a ruby would suffice to embellish the R. Capece-engraved silver throat and tip of the black-leather sheath. The stag-handle bowie is the work of Frans Van Eldik.

▶LARRY PARSONS: To complement a Jerry McClure damascus knife, only a leather sheath with a bronze Concho, and stingray- and alligator-skin inlays would suffice. *(Ward photo)*

▲RONALD WELLING: The damascus hunter with a mammoth ivory grip slides easily into its carved, stitched and stamped leather belt sheath, complete with abalone arrowhead and engraved silver inlays. *(Ward photo)*

▶JOANN KELLEY: Two-tone, stippled leather is adorned with an engraved sterling silver "blossom" Concho.

Groove Masters

▶ **PETER MARTIN:** The bog oak handles have more grooves than a jive album, and are matched up against damascus bolsters and ladder-pattern-damascus blades. *(Cory Martin Imaging)*

▼ **ALLEN ELISHEWITZ:** The titanium and Doug Ponzio "skulls"-pattern-damascus handle is given the groove treatment to compete with the high, multi grinds of the Chad Nichols damascus blade.

▶ **LEON TREIBER:** With not only the mother-of-pearl grooved, but also the bolsters, and the back spacer and spine file worked, it gives the impression of movement and translucency. *(Ward photo)*

◀ **BRIAN TIGHE:** Brian did his groovin' in purple, like Jimi Hendrix, and his grippin' and grindin' in damascus, like a steel smith. *(PointSeven photo)*

◀ **TODD BEGG:** The grooved "Glimpse" folder features a Gerome Weinand damascus blade and a Damasteel handle frame. *(Mitch Lum Photography)*

◀ **DAN DUGDALE:** The hard-anodized-aluminum handle is machined and grooved for grip, and it's a good thing—to open the knife, the user holds the outside of the pivot and rotates the handle away from the blade. *(SharpByCoop.com photo)*

Scrimmed & Proper

A canvas and paint would be nice, or a potter's wheel, some clay and a kiln. But what am I supposed to do with these needles, inkpot and ink? And where's the paper? Who took the easel? I thought this was supposed to be an art studio. You're giving me nothing to work with here.

That would be the way most artists would feel about the tools scrimshanders—those who practice scrimshaw—work with to create pictures. Similar to watercolors that soak into paper, scrimshaw becomes part of ivory, bone, stag or ivory Micarta®, embedded beneath the surface in the pores of the medium. A scrimshaw artist uses needles to paint pictures, with each needle prick leaving a tiny dot of ink within the pores of, in this case, a knife handle. The scenes, wildlife, people, places and events are immortalized one needle prick at a time.

That's what makes scrimshaw so awe inspiring, particularly when animals, human faces and fantastic figures have character or evoke emotion. It's one thing to use a pencil, paintbrush or chisel to express oneself, but ink and needles, now that's a challenge. Yet there are talented scrimshanders whose art captures the essence and meaning of life, shares experiences, is full of feeling and moves people to laughter, tears, elation or surprise. It is yet another method of expression, one that was born on ship by sailors looking to pass time at sea.

Early scrimshaw artists buried ink beneath the surface of whale teeth. The salty open air became their art studio, and they used materials found aboard sailing vessels. Artists cannot be stopped from expressing themselves, and that is as beautiful as a scrimshawed scene of a buck following a curious doe into a misty meadow.

▶ **NKOSI JUBANE:** Color scrimshaw on the elephant-ivory handle of A.R. Mahomedy's hunter reveals a strelitzia reginae—the national flower of the South African province of Natal. The knife also features Elke Henley bolster engraving and gold inlay.

▼ **LINDA KARST STONE:** The bull elk sounds a warning on the mammoth-ivory grip of a Jerry Moen hunter in CPM 154 steel and engraving by Kevin Elkins.
(Ward photo)

▶ **LINDA KARST STONE:** Among the color scrimshaw of an African landscape and wildlife, and the Jere Davidson engraving is a slick Edmund Davidson re-curved sub-hilt fighter.
(PointSeven photo)

Scrimmed & Proper

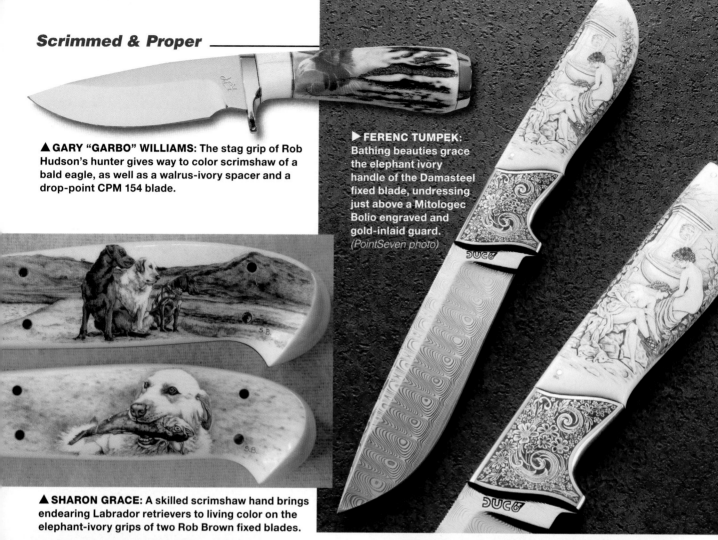

▲ **GARY "GARBO" WILLIAMS:** The stag grip of Rob Hudson's hunter gives way to color scrimshaw of a bald eagle, as well as a walrus-ivory spacer and a drop-point CPM 154 blade.

▶ **FERENC TUMPEK:** Bathing beauties grace the elephant ivory handle of the Damasteel fixed blade, undressing just above a Mitologec Bolio engraved and gold-inlaid guard. *(PointSeven photo)*

▲ **SHARON GRACE:** A skilled scrimshaw hand brings endearing Labrador retrievers to living color on the elephant-ivory grips of two Rob Brown fixed blades.

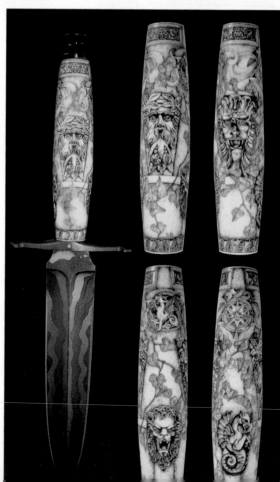

◀ **DARREL MORRIS:** Black and white scrimshaw of two lovely ladies enlivens the ivory handles of a Herman Schneider knife, fork and spoon set, all accompanied by Fritz Schneider damascus and Julie Warenski-Erickson gold inlay. *(Hiro Soga photo)*

▶ **SHARON GRACE:** Gracing the Theuns Prinsloo dagger and its multiple handle incarnations is color and black-and-white gargoyle scrimshaw on elephant ivory.

▲ **GAETAN BEAUCHAMP:** Take me to your model, done up in full, living, breathing color on the mammoth ivory handle, and accompanied by a Devin Thomas stainless damascus blade. *(Alain Miville-Deschenes photo)*

◄ **FAUSTINA MEAD:** The stoic Native American stares out from the elephant-ivory handle of a Don Lozier hunter engraved by Julie Warenski-Erickson. *(Weyer photo)*

► **RONI DIETRICH:** The hairstyle, dress and fashionable lady are captured on the ancient-ivory handle of a blued-damascus folder.

► **FAUSTINA MEAD:** The colorful court jester does his jig upon the elephant-ivory grip of a Don Lozier art dagger that also showcases a Jerry Rados Turkish-damascus blade, ruby inlays, and a nickel-silver guard and butt cap engraved by Julie Warenski-Erickson. *(PointSeven photo)*

▲ **GAETAN BEAUCHAMP:** To illustrate Albert Einstein, it took two knives, each with Mike Norris stainless damascus blades and mammoth-ivory and buffalo-horn handles.

Wispy Wire Inlay

It is wispy but controlled. Those who are connoisseurs of wire inlay look for smooth, even, non-jerky lines and curves. They admire flow and fluidity. The scroll must be symmetrical yet alive and rolling, like waves, clouds, billowing blankets and blowing sands. It is an art from, not a utilitarian enhancement, an embellishment and statement, not a precise, measured technology. And wire inlay is aesthetically superior.

Add silver wire to ironwood, and one highlights the grain and structure. Inlay gold within maple burl, and the pulp is paraded before kings and queens. The shine of metal meets the character of highly figured hardwood and results in gorgeous, gleaming grains, embellished and beautified burls. The look suits knives,

and complements the steely blades like no other enhancement.

Some knifemakers excel and specialize in wispy wire inlay, choosing to adorn most wood-handle blades with gold or silver. Others pick and choose the knives that will be enhanced in such a matter. The wood often speaks to them, and the spirit moves them. This is the way of the creative mind, the genius of the species, and wispy wire inlay answers the call, enhances knives and makes blades into beautiful beings. What a wild and wispy world in which we live.

◄ **JERRY LAIRSON:** The curvature of the wire inlay of the maple handle is repeated through etching of the damascus bowie blade. *(Ward photo)*

▶ **JAY HENDRICKSON:** One of those mentioned above who specialize in wire inlay, Jay's knives are recognized as his own by knife collectors long before looking at the tang stamps on the blades, and that's a complement to any knifemaker. *(PointSeven photo)*

▲ **WES WHIPPLE:** There is more wire in the tiger maple handle than on most spools, yet inlaid in a most spectacular fashion, reminding one of Mother Nature's perfection. *(PointSeven photo)*

▲ JEFFREY DRISCOLL: Mattias Styrefors forged the multi-bar, mosaic-damascus blade, and the knifemaker complemented his work with a sculpted-African-blackwood handle, and fine silver and copper inlay, creating the tail of a dragon whose head becomes a sheath for the steely creature. *(BladeGallery.com photo)*

◀ JEFFREY HARKINS: Gold wire is the spark that fires the automatic damascus dagger blade. *(SharpByCoop.com photo)*

▲ JOE KEESLAR: Where the flower is planted, vines grow and enliven the wood they wrap themselves around. The vine file work on the blade spine and tang furthers the theme. *(PointSeven photo)*

▶ CHRIS OWEN: The carved curly maple features fine silver inlay that, when coupled with the multi-bar, composite-damascus blade, becomes a handsome hunter in all respects. *(BladeGallery.com photo)*

▶ JACK FULLER: The way the rust-brown-finished guard bends is no accident considering the wispy wire inlay of the maple handle, and the file work along the spine of the 5160 blade.

Art Nouveau & Art Deco

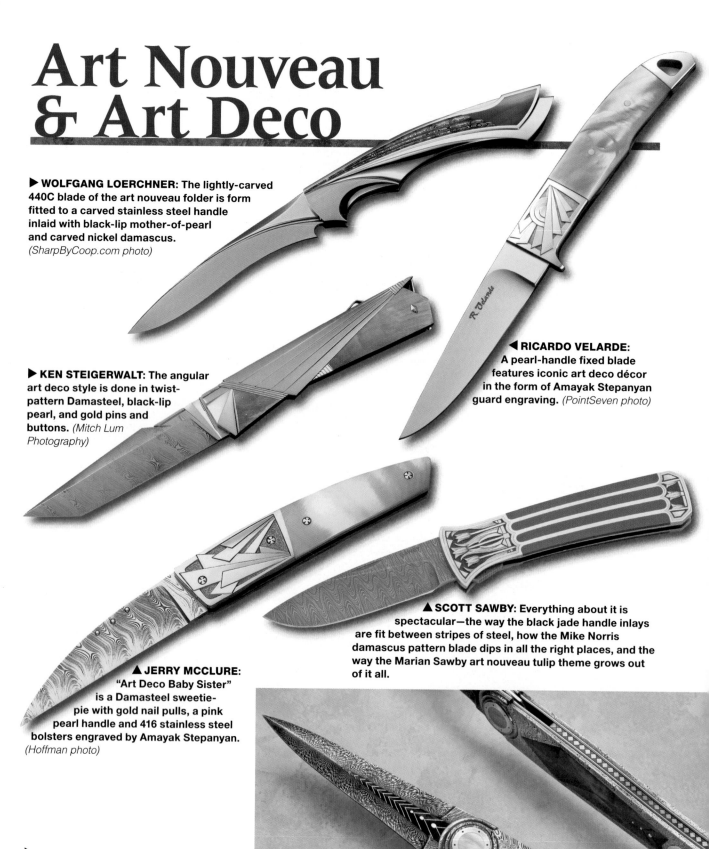

▶ **WOLFGANG LOERCHNER:** The lightly-carved 440C blade of the art nouveau folder is form fitted to a carved stainless steel handle inlaid with black-lip mother-of-pearl and carved nickel damascus. *(SharpByCoop.com photo)*

▶ **KEN STEIGERWALT:** The angular art deco style is done in twist-pattern Damasteel, black-lip pearl, and gold pins and buttons. *(Mitch Lum Photography)*

◀ **RICARDO VELARDE:** A pearl-handle fixed blade features iconic art deco décor in the form of Amayak Stepanyan guard engraving. *(PointSeven photo)*

▲ **JERRY MCCLURE:** "Art Deco Baby Sister" is a Damasteel sweetie-pie with gold nail pulls, a pink pearl handle and 416 stainless steel bolsters engraved by Amayak Stepanyan. *(Hoffman photo)*

▲ **SCOTT SAWBY:** Everything about it is spectacular—the way the black jade handle inlays are fit between stripes of steel, how the Mike Norris damascus pattern blade dips in all the right places, and the way the Marian Sawby art nouveau tulip theme grows out of it all.

▶ **OWEN WOOD:** The art deco handle was achieved by cutting and fitting black-lip pearl, Damasteel, 18k gold and stainless steel over a titanium frame, and the blade is composed of "herringbone"- and "explosion"-pattern damascus. *(SharpByCoop.com photo)*

A Metallic Mosaic

There are classes on carving. Colleges offer engraving courses, and if you're interested, you can attend a GRS Engraving workshop at the GRS Training Center. Nearly every accredited university that offers Bachelors Of Art degrees has painting, sculpting, pottery making and abstract art electives. Yet, there aren't too many formal classes or schools set up to teach mosaic-damascus forging.

In recent years, there have been seminars, hammer-ins and American Bladesmith Society classes on forging mosaic damascus, all taught by veteran blade smiths to budding blade smiths. That doesn't mean that mosaic damascus making has become part of mainstream culture, and in fact, it's just the opposite. The forging art isn't universally taught, known or easy to learn. Mosaic-damascus making is one of the best-kept secrets in the knife industry.

It makes you feel good, doesn't it? Being exposed to the incredible art of blade steel forged to resemble masterful mosaic tiles and tapestries of the world is akin to seeing the inside of King Tut's Tomb. Not many people experience it, know about it or can relate to the experience. It's an exclusive club of people who are familiar with mosaic damascus.

Welcome, and please, feel free to enjoy the visual experience known as mosaic damascus, a metallic mosaic that revels Arabian tapestries and the marble mosaics of Italian mosques.

◄ JEREMY MARSH: The "Fancy Fatty" model is all about patterns—the Robert Eggerling mosaic damascus that resembles tiles of an alfresco courtyard, and the mammoth-tooth-ivory grip. *(SharpByCoop.com photo)*

► J.W. RANDALL: The "Fox Hunter" shows a horseman on the bolsters, equine imagery forged into the blade, and a pearl of a grip. *(Tammy Randall photo)*

► J. NEILSON: The knifemaker fit the entire state of Texas, and a few stars, in the confines of a 10 ½-inch bowie blade, complemented by a desert-ironwood handle and mokumé fittings. *(Ward photo)*

► TOM FERRY: Whether sparklers, stars, angelic forms, plants or animal life, the damascus blade definitely adds character to the ivory-handle fighter featuring engraved and case-hardened furniture. *(PointSeven photo)*

◀ **CLIFF PARKER:** "Walrus-mosaic-damascus" bolsters hint as to where the ivory handle originated. *(PointSeven photo)*

▲ **DENNIS FRIEDLY:** A controlled forging frenzy resulted in the disciplined *but* frenetic multi-bar, composite-damascus blade, protected by a carved *(see the faces looking down toward the blade)*, engraved and gold-inlaid guard, an ancient-ivory grip, and a gemstone and more engraving on the handle butt. *(PointSeven photo)*

▶ **DAVID LISCH:** They call it a pattern-welded blade, but it's more like a power point presentation, complete with ironwood platform. *(BladeGallery.com photo)*

◀ **GAYLE BRADLEY:** Purple and blue pool together in the Chris Marks mosaic-damascus bolsters of the locking-liner folder that sports a gray-blue mammoth ivory handle and a "TNT-pattern" Damasteel blade. *(Custom Knife Gallery of Colorado photo)*

▶ **KEVIN HARVEY:** For his rendition of a Searles/Fowler-style bowie, the knifemaker forged a "4th Of July pattern," multi-bar, mosaic-damascus blade, celebrating the occasion with an exhibition-grade, fossil-walrus-ivory handle pinned to a nickel silver frame. *(BaldeGallery.com photo)*

◄▼ JON CHRISTENSEN: The "leaf-mosaic-damascus" push dagger blade, "surge-damascus" handle, quilted-maple (one side of the handle) and fossil-ivory (other side) inlays and textured nickel-silver spacers are why museums are built in the first place. *(SharpByCoop.com)*

▲ RICK DUNKERLEY: The gold inlay ties the colors of the black-lip pearl and the patterns of the mosaic-damascus blade together in one artistic achievement. *(PointSeven photo)*

◄ PHIL ERNEST: To paint it would be difficult enough, but to forge weld it this way, heat color it, shape it, forge it and file work it, that's edgy art 21st-century style. Pearl contrasts nicely. *(PointSeven photo)*

◄ JOHN DAVIS: There's something about the tight, repeating mosaic-damascus patterning that bespeaks quality, as do dovetailed bolsters, fileworked liners and mammoth-ivory grips. *(SharpByCoop.com photo)*

▶ **PETER MARTIN:** Forging the "spider web" mosaic damascus was only the first step. Splitting the blade down the middle was a stroke of genius, and the buffalo-horn upper body, red acrylic inlay, walrus ivory lower, damascus head, 14k-gold settings, black diamond eyes, gold fangs and mokumé rocker bar release were added revelations. *(Cory Martin Imaging)*

▶ **RAY RYBAR:** Along the edges of the blade are "In The Beginning God Created The Heaven And The Earth Genesis 1:1," and then Ray shows us what those places look like in the blade steel. *(PointSeven photo)*

▶ **DON MAXWELL:** The heat-colored Chris Marks mosaic damascus make's one smile upon the fossil-wooly-mammoth ivory handle, citrine thumb stud, knife and life in general.

▶ **RICHARD EPTING:** It's amazing what you can do with mother-of-pearl, damascus and mosaic damascus, not to mention some file work, hand rubbing and a little elbow grease. *(Ward photo)*

◀ **RON HEMBROOK:** A real giant of a bowie, the Doug Ponzio mosaic-damascus blade deserved a heat-blued guard and a mammoth-bark-ivory handle.

◀ CHRIS OWEN: "Radial-pattern" damascus, on bolsters and blade, gives exhibition-grade mother-of-pearl a run for its money. Even the thumb stud and pivot pinhead are mosaic masterpieces. *(BaldeGallery.com photo)*

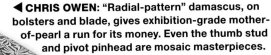

▶ FRANCESCO PACHI: Pink pearl was positively the proper handle choice to accompany the purple, blue and red mosaic-damascus blade and bolsters of the locking-liner folder.

◀ MIKE FELLOWS: The "Baroness" struts her mosaic-damascus, elephant ivory and textured-nickel-silver stuff.

▶ ANDRE VAN HEERDEN: Ettoré Gianferarri forged a mosaic-damascus blade pattern that is exotic and exciting, the perfect match for the pearl-inlaid locking-liner folder with more damascus grip inlays. *(BladeGallery.com photo)*

◀ JOE OLSON: The hand-forged "guitar-pattern" damascus is made even more relevant by inlaid handle elements that represent the favorite musical memories of the collector who bought the knife. *(BladeGallery.com photo)*

A Metallic Mosaic

▶ **SHANE TAYLOR:** We told Shane not to go batty, but he couldn't help forging the night creatures into the blade and bolsters, and carving winged grips. *(PointSeven photo)*

◀ **RON NEWTON:** Fire opal inlays add color to the prettily patterned, "turkeys and leaves" mosaic-damascus folder. *(Ward photo)*

▶ **HANK KNICKMEYER:** Of San Mai construction, the "running deer pattern" mosaic-damascus blade is reminiscent of cave paintings, and thus it follows that the fossil-walrus-ivory grip was a logical choice. *(PointSeven photo)*

◀ **MIKE MOSSINGTON:** Maple leaves are appropriate attire for the forged fixed blade of a knifemaker who grew up in Northern Ontario. Stag isn't a bad choice, either. *(PointSeven photo)*

▲ **BILL COFFEY:** The "flag steel" shows all the right colors. *(PointSeven photo)*

KELLY CARLSON: The Robert Eggerling mosaic-damascus blade and double bolsters combine with the buffalo horn handle scales to put the "black" in the "Black Barracuda" folder.

LOURENS PRINSLOO: He said he was going to add a warthog-tusk (one side of the handle) and mammoth-ivory (other side) grip to the mosaic damascus folder, but no one could have foreseen the beautiful form it would take. *(SharpByCoop.com photo)*

ANDERS HEDLUND: Mattias Styrefors and Jonny Walker Nilsson forged the "reindeer and polar bear" mosaic-damascus bolsters, with Jonny also engraving the reindeer-horn handle, and Conny Persson creating the mosaic-damascus blade.

Damascus Digs

▶ **TINUS KLAASE:** An electrifying random-pattern-damascus blade highlights a replica of the Puma "White Hunter," complemented by engraved brass bolsters and a buffalo horn handle.

◀ **JOHN PERRY:** Damascus rushes over the blade and bolsters of the pearl-handle mid-lock folder. *(PointSeven photo)*

▶ **MICHAEL VAGNINO:** Damascus feathers out from the blade's center grind line and from the pins of the bolsters, while a mammoth-ivory handle inlay anchors the piece. *(Ward photo)*

▶ **TOM WATSON:** Lines of the Mike Norris damascus lead straight to the tip, and back to the G-10 handle scales.

▲ **BRIAN TIGHE:** Expectations are such that damascus patterning, in this case Damasteel, is no longer good enough, but that it also must match the pattern of the knife and of the handle material, here a fluted tortoise shell. *(Mitch Lum photo)*

◀ **JERRY FISK:** The fixed blade features damascus patterning from spine to edge, integral bolsters, a stag handle and engraved butt cap. *(SharpByCoop. com photo)*

▶ **JODY MULLER:** The lines of a topographical map were never so interesting as those on the toothy blade of "The Executioner," complete with a dimpled mammoth-ivory handle and file-worked titanium back spacer. *(SharpByCoop.com photo)*

▶ **RUSS ANDREWS:** The San Mai damascus of the sub-hilt fighter washes along the blade edge in a carefree manner until it reaches the damascus guard and walrus-tusk handle. *(SharpByCoop. com photo)*

▲ **KEVIN CASEY:** The nice, tight, feather-like pattern of the damascus blade and bolsters are a perfect match for the grains of the eucalyptus-fiddle-burl grip. *(SharpByCoop.com photo)*

▶ **JERRY MCCLURE:** Sometimes it takes two to tango—"Durango twist" and "cracked ice" damascus patterns, separated by a center line. The handle is Sambar stag with carved mammoth-ivory spacers.

▶ **GARY ROOT:** Forging steels together until molten lava flows, hardening them, grinding, etching, polishing, sharpening and capping them off with crown-stag butts. This is the way of the blade smith. *(SharpByCoop.com photo)*

▶ **MIKE RUTH:** Splayed out from center of the blade spine, the damascus pattern reaches every inch of edge. *(Ward photo)*

▶ **KYLE ROYER:** The damascus pattern is so stunning, one almost forgets to appreciate the re-curve of the clip-point blade, the smoothness of the ironwood grip and the rounded guard and butt cap. *(SharpByCoop. com photo)*

▲ **STEVE CULVER:** Shocking, just shocking! *(Ward photo)*

▶ **JERRY LAIRSON:** I believe that etching the "shark's tooth"-damascus blade so it matches the silver wire inlay of the curly maple grip qualifies as cheating, and thus any awards must be returned. *(Ward photo)*

◀ **SHAWN ELLIS:** The hot-blued damascus skin of the steel serpent is slithering sharp, guarded by fangs and harnessed by a leather sheath, inlaid with snakeskin, of course. *(Ward photo)*

▶ **SCOTT SLOBODIAN:** The shape of the "Mogul Dagger" called for an equally swooping Jim Ferguson damascus pattern, and a silver-and-steel handle and sheath that can only be described as "sheik." Barbara Slobodian engraved the Mandela on the knife box.

◀ **DAVID LISCH:** Blackwood and wrought iron make an admirable attempt at wrapping themselves around an 11 3/4-inch 15N20-and1080-damascus blade. *(BladeGallery.com photo)*

Damascus Digs

▶ **HENRY TORRES:** The big damascus blade called for a stag grip and a damascus butt cap filed to follow the grooves of the deer antler. *(PointSeven photo)*

▼ **J.W. RANDALL:** The composite-damascus blade features a feather-damascus core and is grouped with a clamshell guard and a premium blue-mammoth-ivory grip. *(Hoffman photo)*

▶ **WESLEY DAVIS:** Feather-pattern damascus and mammoth ivory are a lively pair that couldn't be pinned down with anything other than 18k-gold tacks. *(Ward photo)*

▼ **RON NEWTON:** Only brown-lip-pearl and 24k-gold inlays could compete with the chevron-pattern damascus blade of the auto dagger. *(Ward photo)*

▲ **HARVEY DEAN:** Don't be fooled by the feather-pattern damascus—it doesn't tickle—but the stag grip feels good and the engraving is amazing. *(SharpByCoop.com photo)*

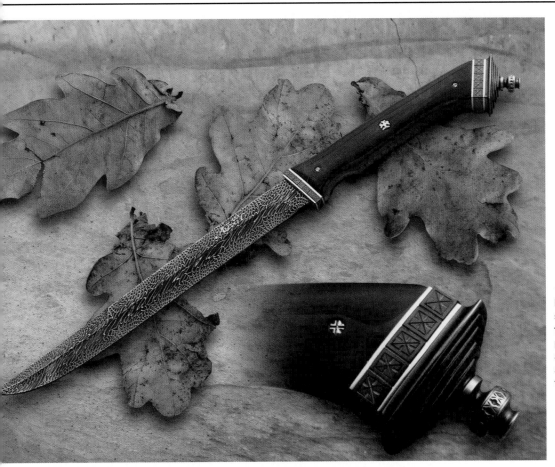

◄ MIKE FELLOWS: The Persian fighter has a slight Oriental flavor and features a "ripple-twist"-pattern damascus blade, a buffalo-horn handle and heat-blued and fileworked bolsters.

► KELLY CARLSON: The "Barracuda" cuts through the water with a pointy chevron-pattern damascus blade, one sapphire eye on its prey, and a body the color of the sea.

▲ BERTIE RIETVELD: The chatoyant five-bar Turkish-twist blade averts the eyes only momentarily away from the 24k-gold lotus flower on the heat-colored steel handle. A stanhope lens can be viewed by unscrewing the anodized-titanium pommel. *(Francesco Pachi photo)*

Damascus Digs

▶ **DES HORN:** All the Damasteel was hardened, and then sub-zero quenched in liquid nitrogen and double-tempered for maximum strength and edge holding.

▶ **MIKE MOONEY:** When you start with a 10-inch Devin Thomas "shark's-tooth"-damascus blade, there's danger of an overbite unless you reign it in with an ironwood handle and fileworked nickel-silver guard. *(Balance Digital photo)*

▶ **TIM HANCOCK:** Which is shapelier, the 11 7/8-inch composite-damascus blade or the ironwood handle? *(PointSeven photo)*

◀ **TOMMY LEE:** The etched damascus pattern follows the lines of the blade, creating its own wavy movement along the way. The engraved bolster and clean handle are finishing touches. *(PointSeven photo)*

A Certain Class Of Carved

It's a dangerous business. Every time you pick up a carving tool and remove material from any medium, you expose yourself to critique and criticism. The only way to avoid it would be to squirrel away whatever you've carved for eternity, never showing it to anyone, anywhere, any time. To avoid scrutiny, all carvings would be stowed away like castaways on seaward schooners.

Of course, that rarely happens. The artwork is shared. People view it. Some observers have skills of their own, and others are not creative types, or if they are, they do not carve. There you stand, naked as a jaybird, all your parts exposed. It's that kind of feeling. You've allowed yourself to create, an outpouring of expression, a piece of you in every carving. You've shaped something

with tools and your own hands, and now the world watches, scrutinizing what you made, and maybe even commenting on it.

It's not much different from being the person who says they're never dating again because they've been burned too many times. That constant fire licking at them strikes fear in their heart.

Maybe it isn't so bad if what you carve is truly good, if you are not ashamed of it, but proud, if you want to show people, and possibly sell it to an appreciative collector. If it has a knife blade attached, and if you know how to grind, forge, shape, buff and hone, then that's a bonus. This is what skilled craftsmen do, yet few can carve. Fewer still engrave, and scrimshaw is reserved for the fortunate few.

None of the carvers and knifemakers whose creations grace this and the following pages are ashamed. They shouldn't be anyway. Theirs is a certain class of carved born

from creative genius and practiced at length. Allow the carvings to sweep you away like a ship at sea, bobbing up and down, sternward and aft, and always forward, lilting toward the horizon, the sun, the stars and sparkling moon.

◄ SHANE TAYLOR: The lizard-looking grip of the blued-damascus fixed blade is carved ivory of the highest order, a certain class of carved, if you will, and complemented by gold-wire inlay. *(PointSeven photo)*

► HARRY LEO SMITH: Totem poles have nothing over the ceremonial dagger in Native motif, carved from walrus ivory, black walnut and rosewood, and adorned with carved copper spacers. *(PointSeven photo)*

◄ WILLIAM LLOYD: The "Green Man Folder" has malachite eyes, a bearded face carved from deer antler, and a forged damascus blade. *(PointSeven photo)*

A Certain Class Of Carved

▼**JOSEPH CARR:** The carved-stag eagle head of the handmade hunter looks one way, and the Doug Ponzio damascus blade points another direction. *(Cory Martin Imaging)*

▲**R.W. WILSON:** A talented artist by the name of Normal J. Caeser carved the desert ironwood elephant head of the 4-inch drop-point hunter. *(Cory Martin Imaging)*

◄**VLADIMIR BURKOVSKI:** In true war club fashion, the carved bone handle with red-coral and diamond inlays makes ready a damascus dagger sporting a guard of silver and white gold. *(PointSeven photo)*

▲**J.R. COOK:** The damascus bowie broke out in elephantiasis, but it's a blessing, not a disease, and the etching of the pachyderm on the blade ain't bad, either. *(Ward photo)*

◄**PAUL COOPER:** The carved-wood grip is reminiscent of Celtic knot work, and the carved blade with blue patina similar to a bamboo leaf. *(PointSeven photo)*

JULIUS MOJZIS: The bear carved into and pierced through the fixed blade follows its nose toward an edged fantasy world of plants, butterflies and good things to eat.

CLIFF PARKER: An angel wing of pearl dips naturally into a damascus blade and bolsters. *(SharpByCoop.com photo)*

AL DIPPOLD: Minimalist art doesn't diminish its effectiveness, and such is the case with the carved ebony grip and lightly file-worked, clip-point blade. *(PointSeven photo)*

JOSEF RUSNAK: The art deco-inspired lady in mammoth tusk and 18k gold seduces a folding knife with silver bolsters and an RWL-34 blade. *(SharpByCoop.com photo)*

VLADIMIR PULIS: A hunting party took up residence within the deer bone and silver handle of the mosaic-damascus knife. The snakewood sheath shows more of their activity and features fox teeth as danglers.

◀ **LARRY FUEGEN:** The carved, ladder-pattern-damascus blade is the twisted tail that leads to a carved North American deer-antler handle turned fire-breathing dragon, a fantastic dragon with fossil-walrus-ivory fangs and a 14k-gold split tongue. (SharpByCoop.com photo)

◀ **RICK DUNKERLEY:** The textured and carved black lip pearl is colorful enough to compete with the blue, brown and white damascus blade. (PointSeven photo)

▶ **JAMES RODEBAUGH:** The "Brothel Dagger" sports a fluted-ivory grip as smooth as silk sheets. (PointSeven photo)

▶ **HARUMI HIRAYAMA:** A pair of "Moth Knives" is metamorphosed from stag, silver and 440C stainless steel. One moth shows the undersides of its wings as an alerting signal.

▲ **STEPHEN OLSZEWSKI:** She's shy and secretive, subtle and lovely, carved from mammoth ivory in Art Deco fashion, and born from a Lalique perfume bottle of the 1920s. Such a sensuous art dagger she has become. (PointSeven photo)

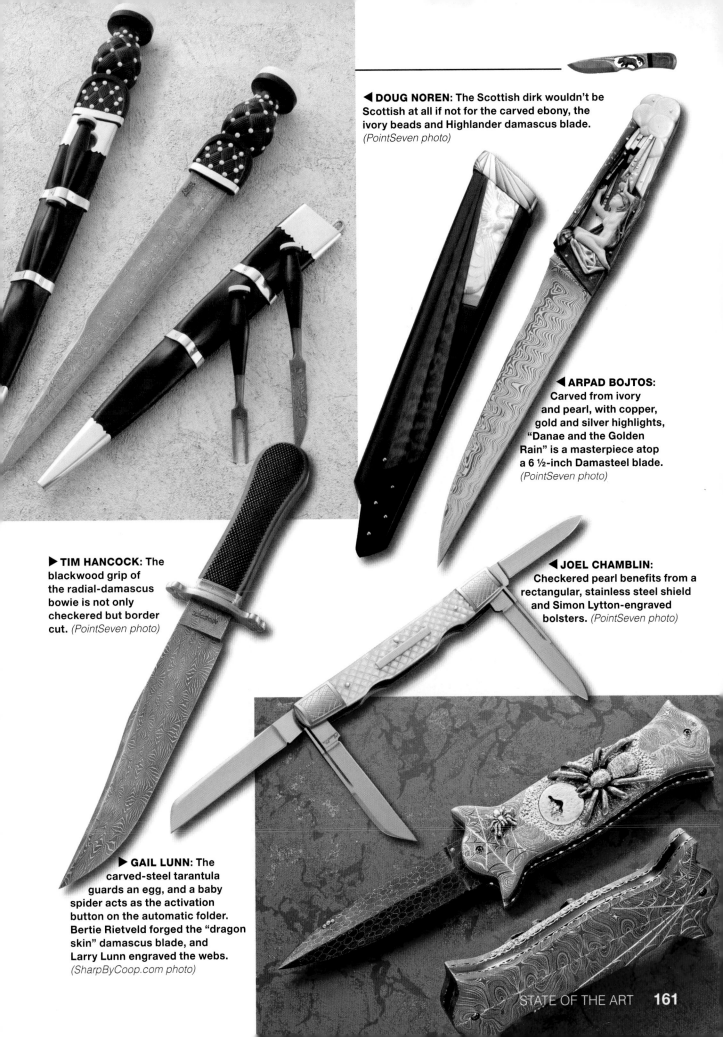

◄ **DOUG NOREN:** The Scottish dirk wouldn't be Scottish at all if not for the carved ebony, the ivory beads and Highlander damascus blade. (PointSeven photo)

◄ **ARPAD BOJTOS:** Carved from ivory and pearl, with copper, gold and silver highlights, "Danae and the Golden Rain" is a masterpiece atop a 6 ½-inch Damasteel blade. (PointSeven photo)

► **TIM HANCOCK:** The blackwood grip of the radial-damascus bowie is not only checkered but border cut. (PointSeven photo)

◄ **JOEL CHAMBLIN:** Checkered pearl benefits from a rectangular, stainless steel shield and Simon Lytton-engraved bolsters. (PointSeven photo)

► **GAIL LUNN:** The carved-steel tarantula guards an egg, and a baby spider acts as the activation button on the automatic folder. Bertie Rietveld forged the "dragon skin" damascus blade, and Larry Lunn engraved the webs. (SharpByCoop.com photo)

Sculpted Steel

▶ **KEN STEIGERWALT:** When you have black-lip mother-of-pearl of this magnitude, you sculpt a steel frame for it, add carved damascus, inlay it with gold and give it a dagger blade. *(SharpByCoop.com photo)*

◀ **BILL TUCH:** The all-stainless "Pelican" folder is such a pretty bird it won the "Best Handle Design" award at the 2008 BLADE Show. *(SharpByCoop.com photo)*

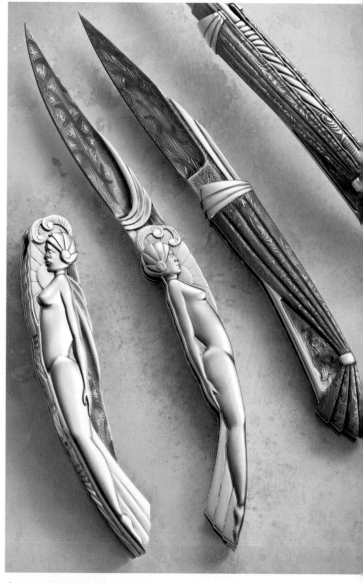

▲ **JULIUS MOJZIS:** A girl contemplates the goings on below her—the dragon, knight, damascus dagger, and castle-like surroundings.

▲ **STEPHEN OLSZEWSKI:** A pair of folders, each with Robert Eggerling damascus blades, features deep relief carving of an art deco woman on one knife, and a pearl-inlaid "window" partially concealed by "drapes" on the second knife. *(SharpByCoop.com photo)*

▼**MARK LARAMIE:** The "Chameleon" figural automatic showcases a tongue-like Devin Thomas "basket-weave"-pattern damascus blade, and a reptilian handle with green-ripple mosaic abalone inlays. *(SharpByCoop.com photo)*

▲**WOLFGANG LOERCHNER:** The "Armadillo" integral dagger is hand carved from a solid piece of 440C steel and parades extensive engraving and gold inlay by master engraver Martin Butler. *(SharpByCoop.com photo)*

▶**DONALD BELL:** Scrolled to perfection, the pierced Devin Thomas damascus handle and blade are highlighted by abalone inlays, a gold bail and a diamond-inlaid gold thumb stud. *(SharpByCoop.com photo)*

▶**ARPAD BOJTOS:** "Leda" lies on her stomach, the swan astride her, soaring into a point of no return, and followed only by the gold and mammoth ivory they carry. *(PointSeven photo)*

▶**GARRI DADYAN:** Hand-chasing with small chisels, and working in solid sterling silver, the filigree work is complemented by peridot and ruby inlays, a carved serpent's head and a Hank Knickmeyer mosaic-damascus blade. *(BladeGallery.com photo)*

Sculpted Steel

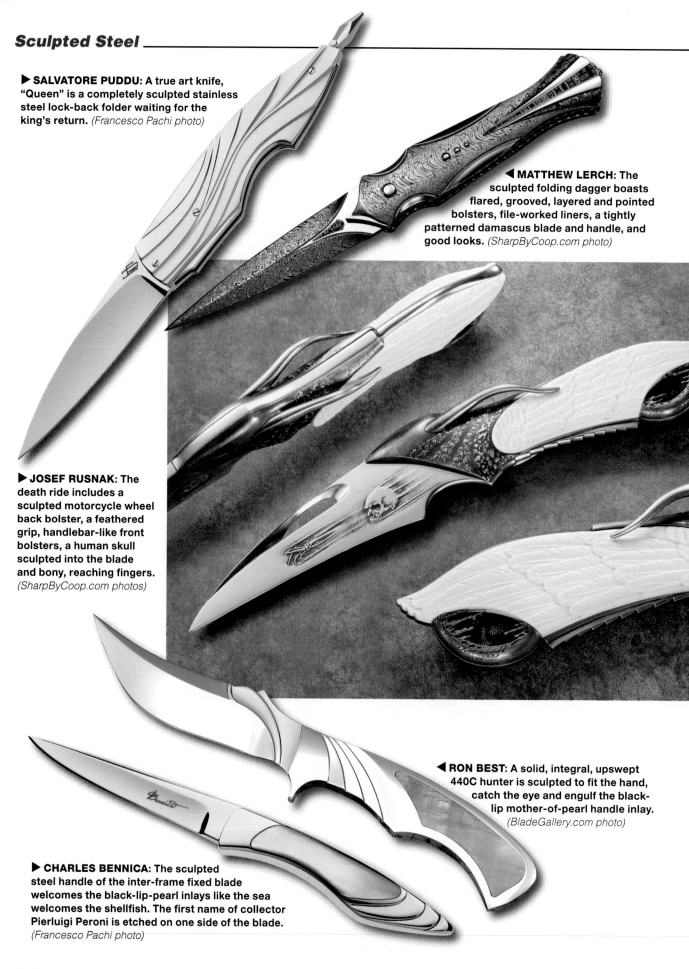

▶ **SALVATORE PUDDU:** A true art knife, "Queen" is a completely sculpted stainless steel lock-back folder waiting for the king's return. *(Francesco Pachi photo)*

◀ **MATTHEW LERCH:** The sculpted folding dagger boasts flared, grooved, layered and pointed bolsters, file-worked liners, a tightly patterned damascus blade and handle, and good looks. *(SharpByCoop.com photo)*

▶ **JOSEF RUSNAK:** The death ride includes a sculpted motorcycle wheel back bolster, a feathered grip, handlebar-like front bolsters, a human skull sculpted into the blade and bony, reaching fingers. *(SharpByCoop.com photos)*

◀ **RON BEST:** A solid, integral, upswept 440C hunter is sculpted to fit the hand, catch the eye and engulf the black-lip mother-of-pearl handle inlay. *(BladeGallery.com photo)*

▶ **CHARLES BENNICA:** The sculpted steel handle of the inter-frame fixed blade welcomes the black-lip-pearl inlays like the sea welcomes the shellfish. The first name of collector Pierluigi Peroni is etched on one side of the blade. *(Francesco Pachi photo)*

World-Class Engraving

▶ **JERE DAVIDSON:** Wherever he could find room on the upswept Ronald Best integral fixed blade, Jere left his magnificent marks, like all around the **Madrone-burl grip.** *(SharpByCoop. com photo)*

▶ **C.J. CAI:** Knifemaker Koji Hara's signature bamboo-style handle, this time in black-lip pearl, called for golden Japanese engraving on the bolsters. *(SharpByCoop.com photo)*

▼ **SHAUN and SHARLA HANSEN:** Gold inlay and engraving not only portray the goldilocks girl on the auto button, and a sea of scroll below her, but also help to group the moss agate inlay with the Turkish damascus blade. *(PointSeven photo)*

▲ **JIM SMALL:** The Don Cowles pearl-handle fixed blade is the lucky recipient of Jim's Celtic engraving and Don Ponzio's damascus. *(SharpByCoop. com photo)*

◀ **TIM HERMAN:** The color engraving and gorgeous subject matter sexy up Billy Mace Imel's pearl-handle folder. *(SharpByCoop.com photo)*

▼**DAVID PERDUE:** The Jot Singh Khalsa "Kirpan" *(ceremonial knife)* is a study in black and white engraving, damascus and mother-of-pearl. *(SharpByCoop.com photo)*

▶**JOE MASON:** It takes a lot of engraving and gold inlay to compete with the "chevron" and "explosion" blade patterning of the T.R. Overeynder folding dagger, let alone the Russian Charoite handle. *(SharpByCoop.com photo)*

▼**JOE MASON:** The collaborative effort between knifemakers Steve Johnson and Michael J. Smith called for special bolster engraving and gold inlay. *(SharpByCoop.com photo)*

▲**TIM HERMAN:** One bug is a lady and the other an arachnid on the ATS-34 "Sliver Stinger." *(PointSeven photo)*

▶ **JIM SMALL:** If goldenrods grew in the sea, they'd resemble the engraved Robert Eggerling damascus handle of Johnny Stout's double-action auto folder, which also parades a Chad Nichols snakeskin-damascus blade. *(SharpByCoop.com photo)*

▶ **BRUCE SHAW:** A triceratops, unicorn and griffin are the three engraved gifts given to a trio of Keith Ouye locking-liner folders. *(SharpByCoop.com photo)*

▶ **JODY MULLER:** The warriors in headdress and on horseback reign over an ivory and mosaic landscape. *(SharpByCoop.com photo)*

▲ **STEVE DUNN:** The damascus and mammoth-ivory bowie is garnished with gold inlay and engraving in an exquisite floral pattern. *(PointSeven photo)*

▶ **C.J. CAI:** A dragon lit the titanium handle of a Scot Matsuoka Flipper folder on fire. Devin Thomas did the damascus damage. *(SharpByCoop.com photo)*

▶ **DWAYNE DUSHANE:** The distinct damascus pattern gives way to bolster engraving and a West Texas mesquite-burl grip. *(SharpByCoop.com photo)*

◀ **TOM FERRY:** Practicing sole authorship means the knifemaker forged the mosaic-damascus blade, inlaid the pearl and engraved the koi-fish scene. *(Mitch Lum photo)*

◀ **GIL RUDOLPH:** Gold engraving and diamond insets embellish W.E. Ankrom's full-size takedown fighter with auxiliary chute-knife blade, and the accompanying, matching folder. Nathan Rudolph built a box for the occasion, and Paul Long performed sheath work. *(Hiro Soga photo)*

▶ **DENNIS FRIEDLY:** Engraving, gold inlay, gold-wire wrap and a fluted-ivory handle grace the dagger. *(PointSeven photo)*

◄ **JERRY CORBIT:** The colors of the coral reef come alive in the gold inlay and engraving, the abalone inlay and the mosaic-damascus blade. *(PointSeven photo)*

► **RON NEWTON:** The bolster engraving grew into a golden guard that protects the fingers from the damascus blade and keeps the hand on the ironwood grip. *(Ward photo)*

▲ **NORIMI:** After getting by the jungle monster on the titanium handle of the Stan Fujisaka damascus folder, one nearly misses the half-sphere Marcite stone inlay. *(Mitch Lum photo)*

► **TIM GEORGE:** Luck be a lady tonight! Warren Osborne's damascus lockback is stone-cold sexy. *(SharpByCoop.com photo)*

BRUCE CHRISTENSEN: The David Lang push dagger is presented with a 440C blade, inviting carved-ivory grip, and engraved stainless steel torso and sheath. *(Balance Digital photo)*

JULIE WARENSKI-ERICKSON: The carved mother-of-pearl handle inlay of Curt Erickson's 440C dagger is highlighted by gold inlay and engraving. *(PointSeven photo)*

TIM GEORGE: Knifemaker Joe Kious created the Persian pattern, complete with blue-mammoth-ivory handle inlay and upswept, carved damascus blade, on which Tim worked his engraving and gold inlay magic. *(PointSeven photo)*

STEVE DUNN: The ivory-handle, damascus lockback folder by Jim Crowell deserved some gold inlay and scroll engraving by the master Dunn himself. *(Ward photo)*

STEVEN RAPP: A gangster captures the engraved girl within the confines of the gold- and copper-inlaid California-style CPM 154 dagger. *(BladeGallery.com photo)*

▶ **JIM** and **JOYCE MINNICK:** Pegasus, a helmed bird and other fantastic creatures are engraved and gold inlaid around the stone handle insert of a damascus folding art dagger. *(PointSeven photo)*

▲ **DAVID GIULIETTI:** Only a concubine among flowering trees would suffice for a Dan Burk three-blade pocketknife. *(PointSeven photo)*

◀ **ARMIN WINKLER:** The gold-inlaid and engraved guard is the flower garden of A.R. Mahomedy's fighter/chute knife, the handle being the ironwood grove, and the blade the steely horizon.

▲ **MARIAN SAWBY:** The engraved scarlet swallowtail butterfly lit upon a lemon tree, finding the perfect home just above the Royal Sahara jasper handle inlay of Scott Sawby's folding dagger.

▶ **C.J. CAI:** "Deadsexy" is more morbid than sensuous, yet knifemaker Ken Onion can make any of his damascus Flipper folders sexy, and there's no arguing with success. *(Mitch Lum photo)*

FACTORY TRENDS

You hear it all the time. The car industry is tripping over itself trying to sell off the gas-guzzling SUVs and build more fuel-efficient, lightweight hybrid cars to meet whatever demand might come about when the economy finally rebounds. Research and development is higher on the priority list than saving the jobs of factory workers who have been employed by the big automakers for decades. Layoffs abound as the scurry for technologically advanced cars reigns.

Power companies mail letters to customers encouraging them to shore up drafty windows and doors, insulate, take advantage of wind and solar energy and become more efficient. You hear about "carbon footprints" and "living green."

The knife industry also innovates, yet it does it in a much different manner. High-tech blade steels, folding knife locks, assisted-opening devices, durable handle materials, fresh designs, modern blade shapes, technologically advanced coatings and more ergonomically friendly knife handles are the order of the day. Like the automakers and energy companies, the knife industry also has research and development teams. Perhaps the biggest difference isn't in how advanced or modern the end product is, but instead the fact that in the auto and energy industries, new developments equate to environmentally friendly designs and methods. Whereas, in the blade realm, the new knives are just a whole lot of fun to show to friends, employ, cut with and generally use. They are state-of-the-art, fine knives that make people smile. That's nice.

Knives of the Great American Gun Makers

Guns and knives from the same manufacturers—it doesn't get any better than that

By Evan F. Nappen, Esq.

When folks ask me what guns or knives I like to collect, I tell them, "I have to strictly limit myself—it's got to cut or shoot for me to like it." Some of my favorite knives are those made by gun manufacturers. Gun company knives provide a great way to collect Colts, Smith & Wessons, Remingtons, Winchesters, Rugers, Ithacas and Brownings without any paperwork required.

Such knives carry the reputation of the gun manufacturers with every blade. Knives usually cost less than firearms, so it's not as hard on the wallet to build a nice collection. Certain blades have novel features, such as the Colt Barry Wood Folder that opens in an unusual way.

A number of knives are commemoratives, honoring people, events or anything else worth memorializing. Others showcase unique functions that relate back to the guns themselves. For example, the Remington Waterfowler pocketknife, in addition to a blade, features a choke-tube wrench and a pin punch to take down Remington shotguns.

Knives are sometimes used to promote gun sales. With its "Size Matters" promotion, Smith & Wesson offered a free bowie knife to each of those who purchased Smith & Wesson .500 Magnum revolvers. Other times, knives have been sold together with guns as sets. Colt offered a .357 magnum revolver, a Colt folding knife and a Colt belt buckle as a cased set.

It is a fun exercise to study the various knives offered by top American gun makers.

The Browning name has been synonymous with guns since John Browning revolutionized the firearms industry through many innovations.

In 1978, Browning manufactured the Browning USA Centennial 1878-1978 set of three pocketknives, including canoe, stockman and lockback patterns. All showcase stag handles, single etched blades and locking walnut display cases. Throughout the years, Browning has offered

The first-production-run Ruger "All Weather" automatic knife would be a nice addition to a collection of blades offered by famous American gun companies.

Gun companies have been known to offer commemorative blades, such as Marlin's 125th anniversary knife.

various sporting knives under its brand, from folders to fixed blades.

One of my favorites is the "Living History" set of knives. The fixed blades honor famous people or places, incorporating handles of wood cut from trees in historically significant locales. The handles add significant flavor to each Living History knife.

The first in the series is the "Liberty Tree" knife with a handle fashioned from one of the last remaining liberty trees of the American Revolution era. Browning also offered a Bowie knife with a grip of wood taken from the Alamo, and a D-guard Bowie honoring Robert E. Lee and featuring wood from his home in Arlington, Va.

Ingenious Colt Folder

The Colt brand has stood the test of time thanks in large part to the genius of Samuel Colt, who excelled at promoting fine firearms. Colt did not enter the knife business until 1971, at which time the company began offering one of the most unique folding knives of the day.

Designed by Barry Wood, Colt distributed approximately 15,000 folders, each featuring a handle that opened and rotated 360 degrees, locking in place and exposing the blade.

Colt also introduced a line of fixed blades made in Sheffield, England, and a Sportsman's line of fixed-blade knives made by Olson.

Buck also offered other Colt knives, such as the etched and serial numbered Model 125 Frontiersman, which is quite rare and worth approximately $2,000 today.

Schrade made a number of

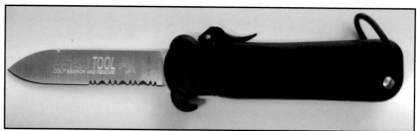
The German-made gravity knife is a Colt Search and Rescue tool.

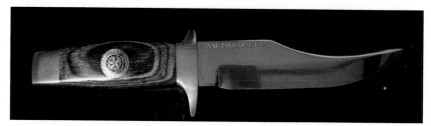
Twenty thousand Texas Ranger Bowies were produced and marketed by Smith & Wesson.

knives for Colt, including the LB7 folding knife and a few nylon-handle folders. Schrade also manufactured DE555 multi-blades with the Colt logo. Colonial Knife Co. produced a multi-blade utility knife for Colt showcasing a "Colt The Legend Lives" handle etching.

In 1993, United Cutlery was licensed to produce a large line of Colt knives, both fixed blades and folders. One of the more unique offerings is the CT2, a hand axe with a fixed blade housed in its handle. United also offered the CT8 Liberty Dagger, a double-edge blade with certain boot knife qualities about it. The wide variety of edges from famous American companies makes collecting Colt knives a fun challenge.

Ithaca Gun Co. was founded in 1883 when William Henry Baker and his partners began offering side-by-side shotguns. The most famous Ithaca gun remains the Model 37 pump shotgun, designed by John Browning. Though Ithaca has been bought and sold a number of times, in the early 1970s the company, under its "Ithacagun" brand, produced a nice series of

fixed blades called "Track Knives."

The custom-quality knives feature wood and laminate handles in incredible modern styling. Although only produced for a few years, they are desirable collectors' items. One of the most striking designs is the "Two Medicine" with a sweeping blade and finger-grooved handle. Each Track Knife sports a paw print trademark on the blade.

Marlin Firearms Co. opened for business in 1870, offering lever-action rifles that retain their popularity today. Marlin sold a few knives as well. One of the most desirable was offered in 1984 when Marlin and the First National Bank of Powell, Wyo., collaborated on a commemorative rifle and knife set to celebrate the bank's 75th anniversary. The commemorative edge is a Gerber Hunting Knife featuring an etched and serial numbered blade. Although the knives are marked "1 of 500," "2 of 500," and so on, only 350 were produced.

An Eliphalet in the Room

Eliphalet Remington founded Remington Arms in 1816, with the company growing to become one of the largest gun manufacturers in the United States. The year 1920 ushered in the first Remington knife, model R-103, and by 1931 Remington Cutlery had progressed to offering nearly three million knives a year.

In 1940, Remington sold off its cutlery division to Pal Blade Co. and went back to strictly making guns. It would take an entire book to list all of the Remington knives offered throughout the years. The company came out with every conceivable pattern of folding knife and fixed blade, yet Remington's most famous and collectible knives are known simply as "bullet knives," featuring handle shields in the shapes of firearms cartridges.

Remington debuted the original bullet knives in 1922, keeping them in the company catalog until the cutlery division was sold.

In 1982, Remington contracted with Camillus to produce "Year Knives" modeled after old Remington patterns.

In 1949, William B. Ruger founded Sturm, Ruger and Co. in partnership with Alexander Sturm (the son-in-law of Alice Roosevelt Longworth).

Many Ruger knives are rare. At one point, Zippo offered a small Ruger folding knife. And a 1960s hunting knife program proved short-lived, though interesting in its own right. Using castings from the Pine Tree division of Ruger, the 1960s blades were combinations of chromium/molybdenum 4140 and beryllium/copper alloy steels. Although prototypes were made, no complete knives were ever produced. Most fascinating was the discovery that beryllium blades were almost impossible to break. Yet, the project was terminated when Ruger discovered that a poisonous gas was released in the blade polishing process.

Somehow an automatic knife with a black nylon handle made its way into the marketplace, complete with the famous Ruger eagle logo and an etched blade touting "Ruger All-Weather," but

it remains unconfirmed whether Ruger ever authorized the knife. In 2004, the company did license Case Cutlery Co. to produce a line of Ruger Knives.

Smith & Wesson opened operations in 1852. In 1972 Smith & Wesson teamed up with Blackie Collins. That same year, the Texas Ranger Commission approached Smith & Wesson to build a commemorative revolver honoring the commission's 150th anniversary.

Texas Ranger Bowie

The Texas Ranger Commission also chose to have Smith & Wesson produce a Bowie knife, eventually becoming known as the Texas Ranger Bowie. Twenty thousand Texas Ranger Bowies were produced and marketed by Smith & Wesson, each serial-numbered near the top of the blade from "TR1" to "TR20,000." Eight thousand of the 20,000 Texas Ranger Bowies were sold with commemorative Model 19 .357 revolvers.

Smith & Wesson expanded the Blackie Collins line of knives to include a non-Texas-Ranger Bowie, in all offering 15,000 pieces worldwide. Other knives in the Blackie Collins line include a special Missouri Highway Patrol Bowie; the Outdoorsman, the Survival, of which 17,500 were created; the Collector Series, a four-knife set engraved with eagles, deer, bear and rams, of which 800 sets were produced; the Skinner, of which 15,500 were made; the Filet, of which 4,500 were made; the Fisherman, of which 4,500 were made; and the folding Hunter, of which 35,000 were made, including a special Police Marksman Assoc. commemorative version.

In 1980 Smith & Wesson manufactured a mid-range line of knives starting with the Maverick,

The Remington Waterfowler pocketknife features a choke-tube wrench and a pin punch to take down Remington shotguns.

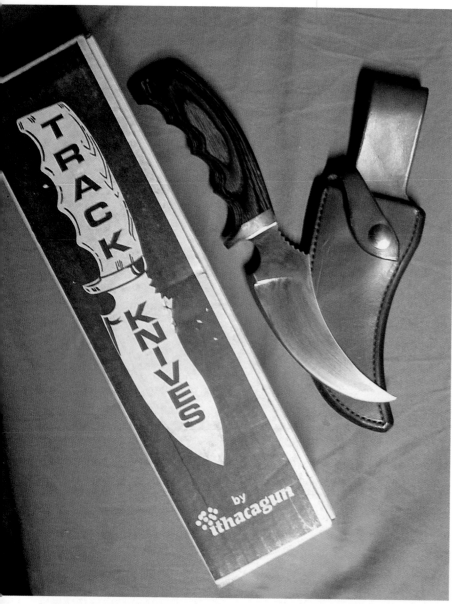

In the early 1970s Ithaca produced a nice series of fixed blades called "Track Knives."

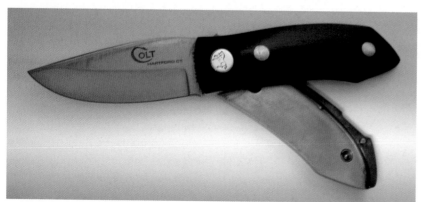

Designed by Barry Wood, Colt distributed approximately 15,000 folders, each featuring a handle that opened and rotated 360 degrees, locking in place and exposing the blade.

a general-purpose folding knife, and later the Ultra-Thin, which was a small, stainless steel lock-back pocketknife. Smith & Wesson later expanded its knife designs to a style called the Swing-blade. Swing-blades exploded in popularity, and the company focused its production solely on the new series of popular-priced knives.

Today Smith & Wesson has teamed up with Taylor Cutlery to produce hundreds of knife models and styles. Many sport innovative features, and most of the knives are imported and competitively priced.

Founded in 1866, the Winchester Repeating Arms Co. eventually merged, in 1922, with the Simmons Hardware Co. In 1919, Winchester acquired the Eagle Pocketknife and Napanoch Knife companies. With these acquisitions, the Winchester brand suddenly appeared on hundreds of knives.

Winchester stopped producing its own knives in the 1940s. In the late 1980s, Blue Grass Cutlery was licensed to make Winchester knives. Winchester knives can be found in every conceivable pattern, utilizing amazing variations of handle materials and blade shapes.

There are many, highly collectible Winchester knife accessories, including knife boxes, display cases and even pocketknife purses that protected pocketknives.

The history and variety of gun manufacturers' knives makes for a fascinating collecting segment of the combined industries. The gun maker brands always assure value, and a nice representative collection can be assembled at reasonable cost. Collecting the knives ensures that you'll always have something from your favorite gun maker in your pocket.

Factory Autos

▼ The Spyderco "C121 Embassy" comes with a back-up safety switch situated next to the push button on the aluminum handle frame, just above the G-10 inlay.

▲ One of the latest autos from Pro-Tech is the "Runt J4" featuring a Robert Eggerling mosaic-damascus blade, and abalone handle inserts to match an abalone-inlaid push button.

▶ The Al Mar "Auto SERE" sports a 3 ½-inch CPM S30V blade in a black finish, and an aircraft-aluminum handle.

▼ A slim, snappy folder, the "SOG-TAC" from SOG Specialty Knives includes a 3 ½-inch AUS-8 stainless steel blade and is also available in a smaller version with a 3-inch blade.

▶ To open the blade of the Meyerco "X-Ray 18," one slides the push button forward in the slot, at which point the button is ready to be pressed. This way, the opening, closing and "safe" position all require only one motion.

Black Tactical Fixed Blades

▶ A.G. Russell's "Shopmade Chute Knife" is a sweet design with a "swedge"-ground 154CM stainless steel blade, a double finger guard and an Ebony Rucarta™ handle.

◀ Benchmade's "CSKII" combat/survival knife features a palpable, black Santoprene™ rubber handle, and a 6-inch, black 1095 high-carbon-steel blade.

▶ Also in the black realm is the Blackhawk Blades "Razorback-Trocar," an AUS-8A stainless fixed-blade tanto with a fiberglass-reinforced, injection-molded nylon handle.

▶ Gerber says the serrations on the black, 420HC dagger blade of the "Mark II" are easily honed in the field using a standard, flat sharpener.

▶ Chris Reeve Knives makes the "Green Beret Knife" available in a partially serrated CPM S30V blade with a black KG Gun-kote coating, and a sandblasted black-canvas-Micarta® handle.

◀ Check out the textured tire-rubber handle of the Mantis "TA-2 Seymore" tactical/skinning knife.

▼ SOG Specialty Knives offers the "SERE Operator" saw-back fixed blade in CPM S30V steel, a Prylon™ handle and a synthetic sheath with secondary rubber retainer.

▲ The Waffentechnik "KM2K" model sports a partially serrated, black, tanto blade, an oval handle with sectioned grip and an integral guard featuring finger notches for added purchase.

▲ Notches machined into the full, extended tang of Boker's "Armed Forces Tactical Tanto Fixed Blade" completely surround the G-10 handle.

▲ Black-and-gray camouflage defines the 440A stainless steel blade of the UZI/Hallmark "Ops Commander Tactical Fixed Blade-Camo," which also dons a contoured G-10 handle and extended, exposed tang.

Happy Huntin' Knives

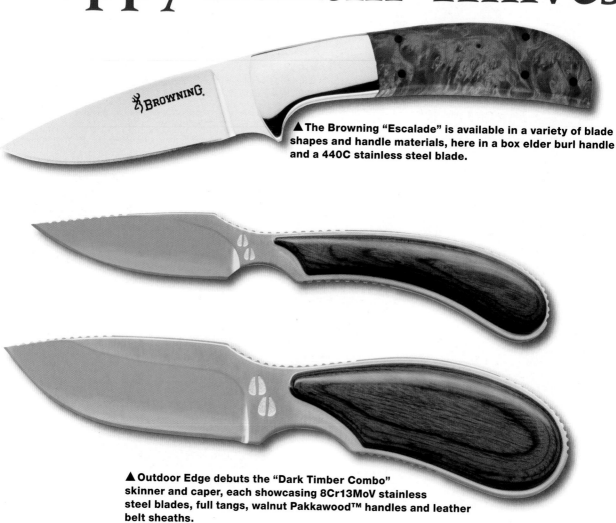

▲ The Browning "Escalade" is available in a variety of blade shapes and handle materials, here in a box elder burl handle and a 440C stainless steel blade.

▲ Outdoor Edge debuts the "Dark Timber Combo" skinner and caper, each showcasing 8Cr13MoV stainless steel blades, full tangs, walnut Pakkawood™ handles and leather belt sheaths.

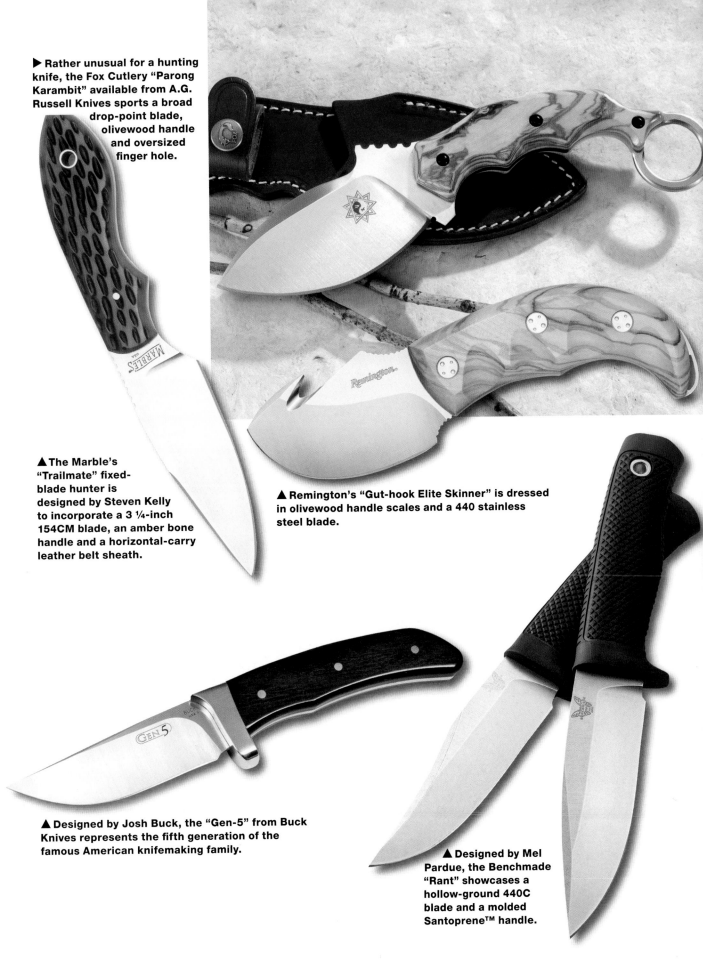

▶ Rather unusual for a hunting knife, the Fox Cutlery "Parong Karambit" available from A.G. Russell Knives sports a broad drop-point blade, olivewood handle and oversized finger hole.

▲ The Marble's "Trailmate" fixed-blade hunter is designed by Steven Kelly to incorporate a 3 ¼-inch 154CM blade, an amber bone handle and a horizontal-carry leather belt sheath.

▲ Remington's "Gut-hook Elite Skinner" is dressed in olivewood handle scales and a 440 stainless steel blade.

▲ Designed by Josh Buck, the "Gen-5" from Buck Knives represents the fifth generation of the famous American knifemaking family.

▲ Designed by Mel Pardue, the Benchmade "Rant" showcases a hollow-ground 440C blade and a molded Santoprene™ handle.

Soldiers' Steel

▶ In Ontario Knife Co.'s Ranger Series is the "Afghan," a Justin Gingrich design in a texture-powder-coated 5160 blade and a tan-Micarta® handle.

▲ The Benchmade "Mini-Griptilian Tanto" boasts a 2.91-inch blade of 154CM stainless steel in a black coating, a black Valox™ handle and an Axis™ lock.

◀ The revised Spyderco "Endura" folder features the Ernest Emerson "Wave" pocket-opening/blade-spine feature for ease of opening the blade while simultaneously pulling the knife from a pocket.

◀ Columbia River Knife & Tool's Kit Carson-designed "M-16 Desert Dog" gives GIs the option of a sand-colored camouflage handle and blade, and the design is improved with a secondary lock—the Lake And Walker Knife Safety (LAWKS).

▶ The military-only black oxide "Surge" from Leatherman Tool Group, top left, satisfies soldiers' multi-tool needs, while the full-size, partially serrated Ka-Bar USMC fighting/utility knife (middle) and new SOG Specialty Knives "Aegis" with a blackened blade and "Digi-Cam" camouflage handle provide fixed-blade and folder options.

▲ Jim Wehrs of Lone Wolf Knives said a number of U.S. servicemen in Afghanistan indicate they like the Lone Wolf/Bill Harsey D2 double-action auto for its large size and double-action feature.

▲ The Cold Steel "SRK" (top) and "Recon Tanto" models, in all black, are popular with active military members.

Hair-Poppin' Pinkies

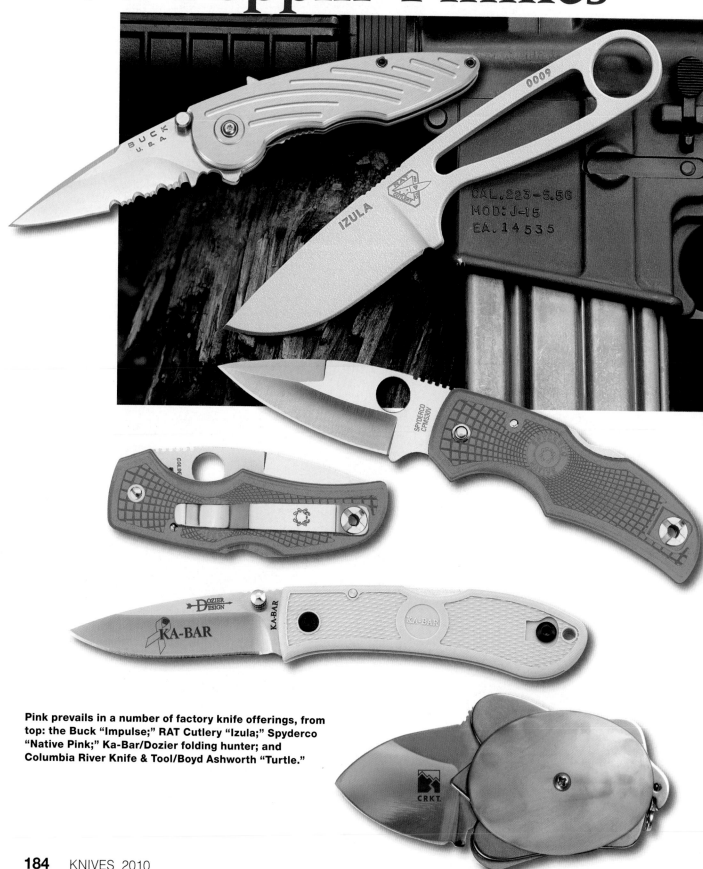

Pink prevails in a number of factory knife offerings, from top: the Buck "Impulse;" RAT Cutlery "Izula;" Spyderco "Native Pink;" Ka-Bar/Dozier folding hunter; and Columbia River Knife & Tool/Boyd Ashworth "Turtle."

KNIVES MARKETPLACE

INTERESTING PRODUCT NEWS FOR BOTH THE CUTLER AND THE KNIFE ENTHUSIAST

The companies and individuals represented on the following pages will be happy to provide additional information — feel free to contact them.

WARTHOG SHARPENERS - USA

Featuring the **Warthog V-Sharp**, a user friendly, empowering tool which allows a person to sharpen their straight edge knife blades to factory sharp condition with no special skill required. Ideal for hunting, fishing, kitchen, or working blades. Diamond rods, adjustable angles, and spring tension, all work together to put the perfect edge on each side of the blade simultaneously.

Warthog Multi-Sharpener Systems, are designed to sharpen scissors, chisels, planer blades, serrated edges, as well as fine collectible and working knives.

Dealer Inquiries Invited: Retailers, Gun & Knife Show Dealers, Outdoor Show Exhibitors & Dealers.

Call John Ring @ 954-275-6872
or visit our web site at **http://www.warthogsharp.com**
for more information or to locate the dealer nearest you.

KNIVES MARKETPLACE

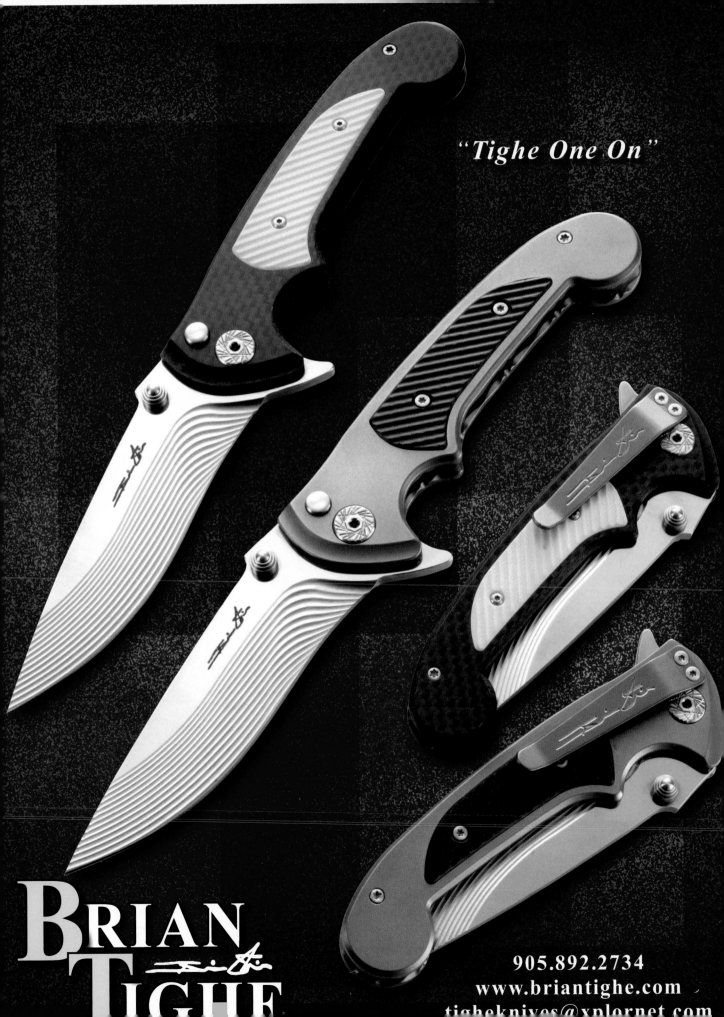

More Titles Worth Wielding!

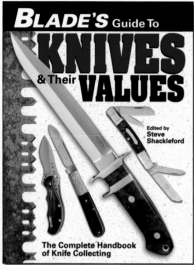
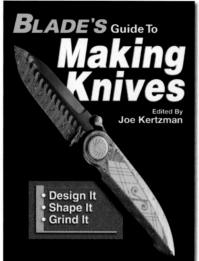
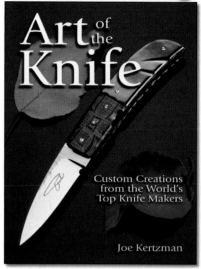

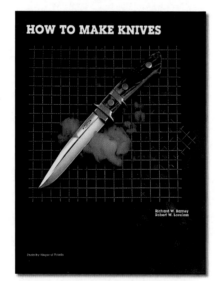

DIRECTORY

A

ABEGG, ARNIE,
5992 Kenwick Cr, Huntington Beach, CA 92648, Phone: 714-848-5697

ABERNATHY, PAUL J,
3033 Park St., Eureka, CA 95501, Phone: 707- 442-3593
Specialties: Period pieces and traditional straight knives of his design and in standard patterns. **Patterns:** Miniature daggers, fighters and swords. **Technical:** Forges and files SS, brass and sterling silver. **Prices:** $100 to $250; some to $500. **Remarks:** Part-time maker. Doing business as Abernathy's Miniatures. **Mark:** Stylized initials.

ACCAWI, FUAD,
131 Bethel Rd, Clinton, TN 37716, Phone: 865-414- 4836, gaccawi@comcast. net; Web: www.acremetalworks.com
Specialties: I create one of a kind pieces from small working knives to performance blades and swords. **Patterns:** Styles include, and not limited to hunters, Bowies, daggers, swords, folders and camp knives. **Technical:** I forge primarily 5160, produces own Damascus and does own heat treating. **Prices:** $150 to $3000. **Remarks:** I am a full-time bladesmith. I enjoy producing Persian and historically influenced work. **Mark:** My mark is an eight sided Middle Eastern star with initials in the center.

ACKERSON, ROBIN E,
119 W Smith St, Buchanan, MI 49107, Phone: 616-695-2911

ADAMS, JIM,
322 Parkway Dr., Scottsville, KY 42164, Phone: 270-622- 8776, jim@blacktoeknives.com
Specialties: Fixed blades in classic design. **Patterns:** Hunters, fighters, and Bowies. **Technical:** Grinds Damascus, O1, others as requested. **Prices:** Starting at $150. **Remarks:** Full-time maker. **Mark:** J. Adams, Scottsville, KY.

ADAMS, LES,
6413 NW 200 St, Hialeah, FL 33015, Phone: 305-625- 1699
Specialties: Working straight knives of his design. **Patterns:** Fighters, tactical folders, law enforcing autos. **Technical:** Grinds ATS-34, 440C and D2. **Prices:** $100 to $500. **Remarks:** Part-time maker; first knife sold in 1989. **Mark:** First initial, last name, Custom Knives.

ADAMS, WILLIAM D,
PO Box 439, Burton, TX 77835, Phone: 713-855- 5643, Fax: 713-855-5638
Specialties: Hunter scalpels and utility knives of his design. **Patterns:** Hunters and utility/camp knives. **Technical:** Grinds 1095, 440C and 440V. Uses stabilized wood and other stabilized materials. **Prices:** $100 to $200. **Remarks:** Part-time maker; first knife sold in 1994. **Mark:** Last name in script.

ADDISON, KYLE A,
588 Atkins Trail, Hazel, KY 42049-8629, Phone: 270-492-8120, kylest2@yahoo.com
Specialties: Hand forged blades including Bowies, fighters and hunters. **Patterns:** Custom leather sheaths. **Technical:** Forges 5160, 1084, and his own Damascus. **Prices:** $175 to $1500. **Remarks:** Part-time maker, first knife sold in 1996. ABS member. **Mark:** First and middle initial, last name under "Trident" with knife and hammer.

ADKINS, LARRY,
10714 East County Rd. 100S, Indianapolis, IN 46231, Phone: 317-838-7292
Specialties: Single blade slip joint folders. Bear Jaw Damascus hunters, Bowies, and fighters. Handles from stag, ossic, pearl, bone, mastodon-mammoth elephant. **Technical:** Forges own Damascus and all high carbon steels. Grinds 5160, 52100, 1095, O1 and L6. **Prices:** $150 and up. **Remarks:** Part-time maker, first knife sold in 2001. **Mark:** L. Adkins.

ADKINS, RICHARD L,
138 California Ct, Mission Viejo, CA 92692-4079

AIDA, YOSHIHITO,
26-7 Narimasu 2-chome, Itabashi-ku, Tokyo 175- 0094, JAPAN, Phone: 81-3-3939-0052, Fax: 81-3-3939-0058
Specialties: High-tech working straight knives and folders of his design. **Patterns:** Bowies, lockbacks, hunters, fighters, fishing knives, boots. **Technical:** Grinds CV-134, ATS-34; buys Damascus; works in traditional Japanese fashion for some handles and sheaths. **Prices:** $700 to $1200; some higher. **Remarks:** Full-time maker; first knife sold in 1978. **Mark:** Initial logo and Riverside West.

ALBERICCI, EMILIO,
19 Via Masone, 24100, Bergamo, ITALY, Phone: 01139-35-215120
Specialties: Folders and Bowies. **Patterns:** Collector knives. **Technical:** Uses stock removal with extreme accuracy; offers exotic and high-tech materials. **Prices:** Not currently selling. **Remarks:** Part-time maker. **Mark:** None.

ALBERT, STEFAN,
U Lucenecka 434/4, Filakovo 98604, SLOVAK REPUBLIC, stefan.albert@post.sk; Web: www.albertknives.com
Specialties: Art Knives, miniatures, Scrimshaw. **Prices:** From USD $300 to USD $2000. **Mark:** A.

ALDERMAN, ROBERT,
2655 Jewel Lake Rd., Sagle, ID 83860, Phone: 208-263-5996
Specialties: Classic and traditional working straight knives in standard patterns or to customer specs and his design; period pieces. **Patterns:** Bowies, fighters, hunters and utility/camp knives. **Technical:** Casts, forges and grinds 1084; forges and grinds L6 and O1. Prefers an old appearance. **Prices:** $100 to $350; some to $700. **Remarks:** Full-time maker; first knife sold in 1975. Doing business as Trackers Forge. Knife- making school. Two-week course for beginners; covers forging, stock removal, hardening, tempering, case making. All materials supplied; $1250. **Mark:** Deer track.

ALDRETE, BOB,
PO Box 1471, Lomita, CA 90717, Phone: 310-326- 3041

ALEXANDER, DARREL,
Box 381, Ten Sleep, WY 82442, Phone: 307- 366-2699, dalexwyo@tctwest. net
Specialties: Traditional working straight knives. **Patterns:** Hunters, boots and fishing knives. **Technical:** Grinds D2, 440C, ATS-34 and 154CM. **Prices:** $75 to $120; some to $250. **Remarks:** Full-time maker; first knife sold in 1983. **Mark:** Name, city, state.

ALEXANDER, EUGENE,
Box 540, Ganado, TX 77962-0540, Phone: 512-771-3727

ALEXANDER, OLEG, Cossack Blades,
15460 Stapleton Way, Wellington, FL 33414, Phone: 443-676-6111, Web: www.cossackblades.com
Technical: All knives are made from hand-forged Damascus (3-4 types of steel are used to create the Damascus) and have a HRC of 60-62. Handle materials are all natural, including various types of wood, horn, bone and leather. Embellishments include the use of precious metals and stones, including gold, silver, diamonds, rubies, sapphires and other unique materials. All knives include hand-made leather sheaths, and some models include wooden presentation boxes and display stands. **Prices:** $395 to over $10,000, depending on design and materials used. **Remarks:** Full-time maker, first knife sold in 1993. **Mark:** Rectangle enclosing a stylized Cyrillic letter "O" overlapping a stylized Cyrillic "K."

ALLEN, MIKE "WHISKERS",
12745 Fontenot Acres Rd, Malakoff, TX 75148, Phone: 903-489-1026, whiskersknives@aol.com; Web: www.whiskersknives.com
Specialties: Working and collector-quality lockbacks, liner locks and automatic folders to customer specs. **Patterns:** Folders, hunters, tantos, bowies and miniatures. **Technical:** Grinds Damascus, 440C and ATS- 34, engraves. **Prices:** $200 and up. **Remarks:** Full-time maker; first knife sold in 1984. **Mark:** Whiskers and date.

ALLRED, BRUCE F,
1764 N. Alder, Layton, UT 84041, Phone: 801-825- 4612, allredbf@msn.com
Specialties: Custom hunting and utility knives. **Patterns:** Custom designs that include a unique grind line, thumb and mosaic pins. **Technical:** ATS-34, 154CM and 440C. **Remarks:** The handle material includes but not limited to Micarta (in various colors), natural woods and reconstituted stone.

ALLRED, ELVAN,
31 Spring Terrace Court, St. Charles, MO 63303, Phone: 636-936-8871, allredknives@yahoo.com; Web: www.allredcustomknives.com
Specialties: Innovative sculpted folding knives designed by Elvan's son Scott that are mostly one of a kind. **Patterns:** Mostly folders but some high-end straight knives. **Technical:** ATS-34 SS, 440C SS, stainless Damascus, S30V, 154cm; inlays are mostly natural materials such as pearl, coral, ivory, jade, lapis, and other precious stone. **Prices:** $500 to $4000, some higher. **Remarks:** Started making knives in the shop of Dr. Fred Carter in the early 1990s. Full-time maker since 2006, first knife sold in 1993. Take some orders but work mainly on one-of-a-kind art knives. **Mark:** Small oval with signature Eallred in the center and handmade above.

ALVERSON, TIM (R.V.),
622 Homestead St., Moscow, ID 83843, Phone: 208-874-2277, alvie35@yahoo.com
Specialties: Fancy working knives to customer specs; other types on request. **Patterns:** Bowies, daggers, folders and miniatures. **Technical:** Grinds 440C, ATS-34; buys some Damascus. **Prices:** Start at $100. **Remarks:** Full-time maker; first knife sold in 1981. **Mark:** R.V.A. around rosebud.

AMERI, MAURO,
Via Riaello No. 20, Trensasco St Olcese, 16010 Genova, ITALY, Phone: 010-8357077
Specialties: Working and using knives of his design. Patterns: Hunters, Bowies and utility/camp knives. Technical: Grinds 440C, ATS-34 and 154CM. Handles in wood or Micarta; offers sheaths. Prices: $200 to $1200. Remarks: Spare-time maker; first knife sold in 1982. Mark: Last name, city.

AMMONS, DAVID C,
6225 N. Tucson Mtn. Dr, Tucson, AZ 85743, Phone: 520-307-3585
Specialties: Will build to suit. **Patterns:** Yours or his. **Prices:** $250 to $2000. **Mark:** AMMONS.

AMOUREUX, A W,
PO Box 776, Northport, WA 99157, Phone: 509-732- 6292
Specialties: Heavy-duty working straight knives. Patterns: Bowies, fighters, camp knives and hunters for world-wide use. Technical: Grinds 440C, ATS-34 and 154CM. Prices: $80 to $2000. Remarks: Full-time maker; first knife sold in 1974. Mark: ALSTAR.

ANDERS, DAVID,
157 Barnes Dr, Center Ridge, AR 72027, Phone: 501- 893-2294
Specialties: Working straight knives of his design. **Patterns:** Bowies, fighters and hunters. **Technical:** Forges 5160, 1080 and Damascus. **Prices:** $225 to $3200. **Remarks:** Part-time maker; first knife sold in 1988. Doing business as Anders Knives. **Mark:** Last name/MS.

ANDERS, JEROME,
14560 SW 37th St, Miramar, FL 33027, Phone: 305-613-2990, web:www. andersknives.com
Specialties: Case handles and pin work. **Patterns:** Layered and mosiac steel. **Prices:** $275 and up. **Remarks:** All his knives are truly one-of-a- kind. **Mark:** J. Anders in half moon.

ANDERSEN, HENRIK LEFOLII,
Jagtvej 8, Groenholt, 3480, Fredensborg, DENMARK, Phone: 0011-45-48483026
Specialties: Hunters and matched pairs for the serious hunter. **Technical:** Grinds A2; uses materials native to Scandinavia. **Prices:** Start at $250. **Remarks:** Part-time maker; first knife sold in 1985. **Mark:** Initials with arrow.

ANDERSON, GARY D,
2816 Reservoir Rd, Spring Grove, PA 17362- 9802, Phone: 717-229-2665
Specialties: From working knives to collectors quality blades, some folders. **Patterns:** Traditional and classic designs; customer patterns welcome. **Technical:** Forges Damascus carbon and stainless steels. Offers silver inlay, mokume, filework, checkering. **Prices:** $250 and up. **Remarks:** Part-time maker; first knife sold in 1985. Some engraving, scrimshaw and stone work. **Mark:** GAND, MS.

ANDERSON, MARK ALAN,
1176 Poplar St, Denver, CO 80220, mcantdrive95@comcast.net; Web: www. malancustomknives.com
Specialties: Stilettos. Automatics of several varieties and release mechanisms. **Patterns:** Drop point hunters, sub hilt fighters & drop point camp knives. **Technical:** Almost all my blades are hollow ground. **Prices:** $200 to $1800. **Remarks:** Focusing on fixed blade hunting, skinning & fighting knives now. **Mark:** Dragon head.

ANDERSON, MEL,
29505 P 50 Rd, Hotchkiss, CO 81419-8203, Phone: 970-872-4882, Fax: 970-872-4882, artnedge1@wmconnect.com
Specialties: Full-size, miniature and one-of-a-kind straight knives and folders of his design. **Patterns:** Tantos, Bowies, daggers, fighters, hunters and pressure folders. **Technical:** Grinds 440C, 5160, D2, 1095. **Prices:** Start at $145. **Remarks:** Knifemaker and sculptor, full-time maker; first knife sold in 1987. **Mark:** Scratchy Hand.

ANDREWS, ERIC,
132 Halbert Street, Grand Ledge, MI 48837, Phone: 517-627-7304
Specialties: Traditional working and using straight knives of his design. **Patterns:** Full-tang hunters, skinners and utility knives. **Technical:** Forges carbon steel; heat-treats. All knives come with sheath; most handles are of wood. **Prices:** $80 to $160. **Remarks:** Part-time maker; first knife sold in 1990. Doing business as The Tinkers Bench.

ANDREWS, RUSS,
PO Box 7732, Sugar Creek, MO 64054, Phone: 816- 252-3344, russandrews@ sbcglobal.net; Web:wwwrussandrewsknives.com
Specialties: Hand forged bowies & hunters. **Mark:** E. R. Andrews II. ERAII.

ANGELL, JON,
22516 East C R1474, Hawthorne, FL 32640, Phone: 352-475-5380, syrjon@ aol.com

ANKROM, W.E.,
14 Marquette Dr, Cody, WY 82414, Phone: 307-587- 3017, Fax: 307-587-3017, weankrom@hotmail.com
Specialties: Best quality folding knives of his design. Bowies, fighters, chute knives, boots and hunters. **Patterns:** Lock backs, liner locks, single high art. **Technical:** ATS-34 commercial Damascus, CPM 154 steel. **Prices:** $500 and up. **Remarks:** Full-time maker; first knife sold in 1975. **Mark:** Name or name, city, state.

ANSO, JENS,
GL. Skanderborgvej, 116, 8472 Sporup, DENMARK, Phone: 45 86968826, info@ansoknives.com; Web: www.ansoknives.com
Specialties: Working knives of his own design. **Patterns:** Balisongs, swords, folders, drop-points, sheepsfoots, hawkbill, tanto, recurve. **Technical:** Grinds RWL-34 Damasteel S30V, CPM 154CM. Handrubbed or beadblasted finish. **Price:** $400 to $1200, some up to $3500. **Remarks:** Full-time maker since January 2002. First knife sold 1997. Doing business as ANSOKNIVES. **Mark:** ANSO and/or ANSO with logo.

ANTONIO JR., WILLIAM J,
6 Michigan State Dr, Newark, DE 19713- 1161, Phone: 302-368-8211, antonioknives@aol.com
Specialties: Fancy working straight knives of his design. **Patterns:** Hunting, survival and fishing knives. **Technical:** Grinds D2, 440C and 154CM; offers stainless Damascus. **Prices:** $125 to $395; some to $900. **Remarks:** Part-time maker; first knife sold in 1978. **Mark:** Last name.

APELT, STACY E,
8076 Moose Ave, Norfolk, VA 23518, Phone: 757- 583-5872, sapelt@cox.net
Specialties: Exotic wood and burls, ivories, Bowies, custom made knives to order. **Patterns:** Bowies, hunters, fillet, professional cutlery and Japanese style blades and swords. **Technical:** Hand forging, stock removal, scrimshaw, carbon, stainless and Damascus steels. **Prices:** $65 to $5000. **Remarks:** Professional Goldsmith. **Mark:** Stacy E. Apelt - Norfolk VA.

APPLEBY, ROBERT,
746 Municipal Rd, Shickshinny, PA 18655, Phone: 570-864-0879, applebyknives@yahoo.com; Web: www.applebyknives.com
Specialties: Working using straight knives and folders of his own and popular and historical designs. **Patterns:** Variety of straight knives and folders. **Technical:** Hand forged or grinds O1, 1084, 5160, 440C, ATS-34, commercial Damascus, makes own sheaths. **Prices:** Starting at $75. **Remarks:** Part-time maker, first knife sold in 1995. **Mark:** APPLEBY over SHICKSHINNY, PA.

APPLETON, RON,
315 Glenn St, Bluff Dale, TX 76433, Phone: 254-728- 3039, ron@helovesher.com; Web: http://community.webshots.com/user/ angelic574
Specialties: One-of-a-kind folding knives. **Patterns:** Unique folding multi-locks and high-tech patterns. **Technical:** All parts machined, D2, S7, 416, 440C, 6A14V et.al. **Prices:** Start at $9500. **Remarks:** Spare- time maker; first knife sold in 1996. **Mark:** Initials with anvil or initials within arrowhead, signed and dated.

ARBUCKLE, JAMES M,
114 Jonathan Jct, Yorktown, VA 23693, Phone: 757-867-9578, a_r_bukckle@ hotmail.com
Specialties: One-of-a-kind of his design; working knives. **Patterns:** Mostly chef's knives and hunters. **Technical:** Forged and stock removal blades using exotic hardwoods, natural materials, Micarta and stabilized woods. Forge 5160, 1084 and O1; stock remove D2, ATS-34, 440C. Makes own pattern welded steel. **Prices:** $175 to $900. **Remarks:** Forge, grind, heat-treat, finish and embellish all knives himself. Does own leatherwork. Part-time maker. ABS Journeyman smith 2007; ASM member. **Mark:** J. Arbuckle or Arbuckle with maker below it.

ARCHER, RAY AND TERRI,
4207 South 28 St., Omaha, NE 68107, Phone: 402-505-3084, archerrt@cox.net
Specialties: Back to basics high finish working knives and upscale. **Patterns:** Hunters/skinners, camping. **Technical:** Flat grinds ATS-34, 440C, S30V. Buys Damascus. **Price:** $100 to $500, some higher. **Remarks:** Full time makers. Make own sheaths; first knife sold 1994. Member of PKA & OK CA (Oregon Knife Collector Assoc.). **Mark:** Last name over city and state.

ARDWIN, COREY,
4700 North Cedar, North Little Rock, AR 72116, Phone: 501-791-0301, Fax: 501-791-2974, Boog@hotmail.com

ARM-KO KNIVES,
PO Box 76280, Marble Ray 4035 KZN, SOUTH AFRICA, Phone: 27 31 5771451, arm-koknives.co.za; Web: www.arm- koknives.co.za
Specialties: They will make what your fastidious taste desires. Be it cool collector or tenacious tactical with handles of mother-of-pearl, fossil & local ivories. Exotic dye/stabilized burls, giraffe bone, horns, carbon fiber, g10, and titanium etc. **Technical:** Via stock removal, grinding Damasteel, carbon & mosaic. Damascus, ATS-34, N690, 440A, 440B, 12C27, RWL34 and high carbon EN 8, 5160 all heat treated in house. **Prices:** From $200 and up. **Remarks:** Father a part-time maker for well over 10 years and member of Knifemakers Guild in SA. Son full-time maker over 3 years. **Mark:** Logo of initials A R M and H A R M "Edged Tools."

ARMS, ERIC,
11153 7 Mile Road, Tustin, MI 49688, Phone: 231-829- 3726, ericarms@ netonecom.net
Specialties: Working hunters, high performance straight knives. **Patterns:** Variety of hunters, scagel style, Ed Fowler design and drop point. **Technical:** Forge 52100, 5160, 1084 hand grind, heat treat, natural handle, stag horn, elk, big horn, flat grind, convex, all leather sheath work. **Prices:** Starting at $150 **Remarks:** Part-time maker **Mark:** Eric Arms

ARNOLD, JOE,
47 Patience Cres, London, Ont., CANADA N6E 2K7, Phone: 519-686-2623
Specialties: Traditional working and using straight knives of his design and to customer specs. **Patterns:** Fighters, hunters and Bowies. **Technical:** Grinds 440C, ATS-34 and 5160. **Prices:** $75 to $500; some to $2500. **Remarks:** Part-time maker; first knife sold in 1988. **Mark:** Last name, country.

ARROWOOD, DALE,
556 Lassetter Rd, Sharpsburg, GA 30277, Phone: 404-253-9672
Specialties: Fancy and traditional straight knives of his design and to customer specs. Patterns: Bowies, fighters and hunters. Technical: Grinds ATS-34 and 440C; forges high-carbon steel. Engraves and scrimshaws. Prices: $125 to $200; some to $245. Remarks: Part-time maker; first knife sold in 1989. Mark: Anvil with an arrow through it; Old English "Arrowood Knives."

ASHBY, DOUGLAS,
10123 Deermont, Dallas, TX 75243, Phone: 972- 238-7531
Specialties: Traditional and fancy straight knives of his design or to customer specs. Patterns: Hunters, fighters and utility/camp knives. Technical: Grinds ATS-34 and commercial Damascus. Prices: $75 to $200; some to $500. Remarks: Part-time maker; first knife sold in 1990. Mark: Name, city.

ASHWORTH, BOYD,
1510 Bullard Place, Powder Springs, GA 30127, Phone: 770-422-9826, boydashworth@comcast.net; Web: www.boydashworthknives.com
Specialties: Turtle folders. Fancy Damascus locking folders. Patterns: Fighters, hunters and gents. Technical: Forges own Damascus; offers filework; uses exotic handle materials. Prices: $500 to $2500. Remarks: Part-time maker; first knife sold in 1993. Mark: Last name.

ATHEY, STEVE,
3153 Danube Way, Riverside, CA 92503, Phone: 951- 850-8612, stevelonnie@yahoo.com
Specialties: Stock removal. Patterns: Hunters & Bowies. Prices: $100 to $500. Remarks: Part-time maker. Mark: Last name with number on blade.

ATKINSON, DICK,
General Delivery, Wausau, FL 32463, Phone: 850- 638-8524
Specialties: Working straight knives and folders of his design; some fancy. Patterns: Hunters, fighters, boots; locking folders in interframes. Technical: Grinds A2, 440C and 154CM. Likes filework. Prices: $85 to $300; some exceptional knives. Remarks: Full-time maker; first knife sold in 1977. Mark: Name, city, state.

AYARRAGARAY, CRISTIAN L.,
Buenos Aires 250, (3100) Parana- Entre Rios, ARGENTINA, Phone: 043-231753
Specialties: Traditional working straight knives of his design. Patterns: Fishing and hunting knives. Technical: Grinds and forges carbon steel. Uses native Argentine woods and deer antler. Prices: $150 to $250; some to $400. Remarks: Full-time maker; first knife sold in 1980. Mark: Last name, signature.

B

BAARTMAN, GEORGE,
PO Box 1116, Bela-Bela 0480, Limpopo, SOUTH AFRICA, Phone: 27 14 736 4036, Fax: 086 636 3408, thabathipa@gmail.com
Specialties: Fancy and working LinerLock® folders of own design and to customers specs. Specialize in pattern filework on liners. Patterns: LinerLock® folders. Technical: Grinds 12C27, ATS-34, and Damascus, prefer working with stainless damasteel. Hollow grinds to hand-rubbed and polished satin finish. Enjoys working with mammoth, warthog tusk and pearls. Prices: Folders from $380 to $1000. Remarks: Part-time maker. Member of the Knifemakers Guild of South Africa since 1993. Mark: BAARTMAN.

BACHE-WIIG, TOM,
N-5966, Eivindvik, NORWAY, Phone: 475-778- 4290, Fax: 475-778-1099, tom.bache-wiig@enivest.net; Web: tombaschewiig.com
Specialties: High-art and working knives of his design. Patterns: Hunters, utility knives, hatchets, axes and art knives. Technical: Grinds Uddeholm Elmax, powder metallurgy tool stainless steel. Handles made of rear burls of Nordic woods stabilized with vacuum/high-pressure technique. Prices: $430 to $900; some to $2300. Remarks: Part-time maker; first knife sold 1988. Mark: Etched name and eagle head.

BACON, DAVID R.,
906 136th St E, Bradenton, FL 34202-9694, Phone: 813-996-4289

BAGLEY, R. KEITH,
OLD PINE FORGE, 4415 Hope Acres Dr, White Plains, MD 20695, Phone: 301-932-0990, oldpineforge@hotmail.com
Specialties: Hand-made Damascus hunters, skinners, Bowies. Technical: Use ATS-34, 5160, O1, 1085, 1095. Patterns: Ladder-wave lightning bolt. Price: $275 to 750. Remarks: Farrier for 25 years, blacksmith for 25 years, knifemaker for 10 years. Mark: KB inside horseshoe and anvil.

BAILEY, I.R.,
Lamorna Cottage, Common End, Norfolk, ENGLAND NR21&JD, Phone: 01-328-856-183, irbailey1975@tiscali.co.uk
Specialties: Hunters, utilities, Bowies, camp knives, fighters. Mainly influenced by Moran, Loveless and Lile. Technical: Primarily grinds cisrcular saw blades. All flat ground with convex edge. Occasionally forges, including own Damascus. Uses exotic and native hardwoods, stag, leather, micarta, and other synthetic handle materials, with brass fittings. Does some fileword and leather tooling. Does own heat treating. Remarks: Part-time maker since 2005. All knives and sheaths are sole authorship. Mark: Last name stamped.

BAILEY, JOSEPH D.,
3213 Jonesboro Dr, Nashville, TN 37214, Phone: 615-889-3172, jbknfemkr@aol.com
Specialties: Working and using straight knives; collector pieces. Patterns: Bowies, hunters, tactical, folders. Technical: 440C, ATS-34, Damascus and wire Damascus. Offers scrimshaw. Prices: $85 to $1200. Remarks: Part-time maker; first knife sold in 1988. Mark: Joseph D Bailey Nashville Tennessee.

BAILEY, RYAN,
4185 S. St. Rt. 605, Galena, OH 43021, Phone: 740- 965-9970, dr@darrelralph.com; Web: www.darrelralph.com
Specialties: Fancy, high-art, high-tech, collectible straight knives and folders of his design and to customer specs; unique mechanisms, some disassemble. Patterns: Daggers, fighters and swords. Technical: Does own Damascus and forging from high-carbon. Embellishes with file work and gold work. Prices: $200 to $2500. Remarks: Full-time maker; first knife sold in 1999. Doing business as Briar Knives. Mark: RLB.

BAKER, HERB,
14104 NC 87 N, Eden, NC 27288, Phone: 336-627- 0338

BAKER, RAY,
PO Box 303, Sapulpa, OK 74067, Phone: 918-224-8013
Specialties: High-tech working straight knives. Patterns: Hunters, fighters, Bowies, skinners and boots of his design and to customer specs. Technical: Grinds 440C, 1095 spring steel or customer request; heat-treats. Custom-made scabbards for any knife. Prices: $125 to $500; some to $1000. Remarks: Full-time maker; first knife sold in 1981. Mark: First initial, last name.

BAKER, VANCE,
574 Co. Rd 675, Riceville, TN 37370, Phone: 423-745- 9157
Specialties: Traditional working straight knives of his design and to customer specs. Prefers drop-point hunters and small Bowies. Patterns: Hunters, utility and kitchen knives. Technical: Forges Damascus, cable, L6 and 5160. Prices: $100 to $250; some to $500. Remarks: Part-time maker; first knife sold in 1985. Mark: Initials connected.

BAKER, WILD BILL,
Box 361, Boiceville, NY 12412, Phone: 914-657- 8646
Specialties: Primitive knives, buckskinners. Patterns: Skinners, camp knives and Bowies. Technical: Works with L6, files and rasps. Prices: $100 to $350. Remarks: Part-time maker; first knife sold in 1989. Mark: Wild Bill Baker, Oak Leaf Forge, or both.

BALBACH, MARKUS,
Heinrich - Worner - Str 3, 35789 Weilmunster- Laubuseschbach/Ts., GERMANY 06475-8911, Fax: 912986, Web: www.schmiede-balbach.de
Specialties: High-art knives and working/using straight knives and folders of his design and to customer specs. Patterns: Hunters and daggers. Technical: Stainless steel, one of Germany's greatest Smithies. Supplier for the forges of Solingen. Remarks: Full-time maker; first knife sold in 1984. Doing business as Schmiedewerkstatte M. Balbach. Mark: Initials stamped inside the handle.

BALL, KEN,
127 Sundown Manor, Mooresville, IN 46158, Phone: 317- 834-4803
Specialties: Classic working/using straight knives of his design and to customer specs. Patterns: Hunters and utility/camp knives. Technical: Flat-grinds ATS-34. Offers filework. Prices: $150 to $400. Remarks: Part-time maker; first knife sold in 1994. Doing business as Ball Custom Knives. Mark: Last name.

BALLESTRA, SANTINO,
via D. Tempesta 11/17, 18039 Ventimiglia (IM), ITALY 0184-215228, ladasin@libero.it
Specialties: Using and collecting straight knives. Patterns: Hunting, fighting, skinners, Bowies, medieval daggers and knives. Technical: Forges ATS-34, D2, O2, 1060 and his own Damascus. Uses ivory and silver. Prices: $500 to $2000; some higher. Remarks: Full-time maker; first knife sold in 1979. Mark: First initial, last name.

BALLEW, DALE,
PO Box 1277, Bowling Green, VA 22427, Phone: 804- 633-5701
Specialties: Miniatures only to customer specs. Patterns: Bowies, daggers and fighters. Technical: Files 440C stainless; uses ivory, abalone, exotic woods and some precious stones. Prices: $100 to $800. Remarks: Part-time maker; first knife sold in 1988. Mark: Initials and last name.

BANKS, DAVID L.,
99 Blackfoot Ave, Riverton, WY 82501, Phone: 307- 856-3154/Cell: 307-851-5599
Specialties: Heavy-duty working straight knives. Patterns: Hunters, Bowies and camp knives. Technical: Forges Damascus 1084-15N20, L6-W1 pure nickel, 5160, 52100 and his own Damascus; differential heat treat and tempers. Handles made of horn, antlers and exotic wood. Hand- stitched harness leather sheaths. Prices: $300 to $2000. Remarks: Part- time maker. Mark: Banks Blackfoot forged Dave Banks and initials connected.

BARBARA BASKETT CUSTOM KNIVES,
427 Sutzer Ck Rd, Eastview, KY 42732, Phone: 270-862-5019, baskettknives@windstream; Web: www.geocities.com/baskettknives
Specialties: Fancy working knives and fantasy pieces, often set up in desk stands. Patterns: Fighters, Bowies and survival knives; locking folders and traditional styles. Technical: Liner locks. Cutting competition knives. Grinds O1, 440C, S30V, power CPM 154, CPM 4 buys Damascus. Filework provided on most knives. Prices: Start at $250 and up. Remarks: Part-time maker; first knife sold in 1980. Mark: B. Baskett.

BARDSLEY, NORMAN P.,
197 Cottage St, Pawtucket, RI 02860, Phone: 401-725-9132, norman.bardsley@verizon.net
 Specialties: Working and fantasy knives. **Patterns:** Fighters, boots, fantasy, renaissance and native American in upscale and presentation fashion. **Technical:** Grinds all steels and Damascus. Uses exotic hides for sheaths. **Prices:** $100 to $15,000. **Remarks:** Full-time maker. **Mark:** Last name in script with logo.

BAREFOOT, JOE W.,
1654 Honey Hill, Wilmington, NC 28442, Phone: 910-641-1143
 Specialties: Working straight knives of his design. **Patterns:** Hunters, fighters and boots; tantos and survival knives. **Technical:** Grinds D2, 440C and ATS-34. Mirror finishes. Uses ivory and stag on customer request only. **Prices:** $50 to $160; some to $500. **Remarks:** Part-time maker; first knife sold in 1980. **Mark:** Bare footprint.

BARKER, REGGIE,
603 S Park Dr, Springhill, LA 71075, Phone: 318- 539-2958, wrbarker@cmaaccess.com; Web: www.reggiebarkerknives.com
 Specialties: Camp knives and hatchets. **Patterns:** Bowie, skinning, hunting, camping, fighters, kitchen or customer design. **Technical:** Forges carbon steel and own pattern welded steels. **Prices:** $225 to $2000. **Remarks:** Full-time maker. Winner of 1999 and 2000 Spring Hammering Cutting contest. Winner of Best Value of Show 2001; Arkansas Knife Show and Journeyman Smith. Border Guard Forge. **Mark:** Barker JS.

BARKER, ROBERT G.,
2311 Branch Rd, Bishop, GA 30621, Phone: 706-769-7827
 Specialties: Traditional working/using straight knives of his design. **Patterns:** Bowies, hunters and utility knives, ABS Journeyman Smith. **Technical:** Hand forged carbon and Damascus. Forges to shape high-carbon 5160, cable and chain. Differentially heat-treats. **Prices:** $200 to $500; some to $1000. **Remarks:** Spare-time maker; first knife sold in 1987. **Mark:** BARKER/J.S.

BARKES, TERRY,
14844 N. Bluff Rd., Edinburgh, IN 46124, Phone: 812-526-6390, knifenpocket@sbcglobal.net; Web:http:// my.hsonline.net/ wizard/TerryBarkesKnives.htm
 Specialties: Traditional working straight knives of his designs. **Patterns:** Drop point hunters, boot knives, skinning, fighter, utility, all purpose, camp, and grill knives. **Technical:** Grinds 1095 - 1084 - 52100 - 01, Hollow grinds and flat grinds. Hand rubbed finish from 400 to 2000 grit or High polish buff. Hard edge and soft back, heat treat by maker. Likes File work, natural handle material, bone, stag, water buffalo horn, wildbeast bone, ironwood. **Prices:** $200 and up **Remarks:** Full-time maker, first knifge sold in 2005. Doing business as Barkes Knife Shop. **Marks:** Barkes - USA, Barkes Double Arrow - USA

BARLOW, JANA POIRIER,
3820 Borland Cir, Anchorage, AK 99517, Phone: 907-243-4581

BARNES, AUBREY G.,
11341 Rock Hill Rd, Hagerstown, MD 21740, Phone: 301-223-4587, a.barnes@myactv.net
 Specialties: Classic Moran style reproductions and using knives of his own design. **Patterns:** Bowies, hunters, fighters, daggers and utility/ camping knives. **Technical:** Forges 5160, 1085, L6 and Damascus, Silver wire inlays. **Prices:** $500 to $5000. **Remarks:** Full-time maker; first knife sold in 1992. Doing business as Falling Waters Forge. **Mark:** First and middle initials, last name, M.S.

BARNES, GARY L.,
Box 138, New Windsor, MD 21776-0138, Phone: 410-635-6243, Fax: 410-635-6243, mail@glbarnes.com; Web: www.glbarnes.com or www.barnespneumatic.com
 Specialties: Ornate button lock Damascus folders. **Patterns:** Barnes original. **Technical:** Forges own Damascus. **Prices:** Average $2500. **Remarks:** ABS Master Smith since 1983. **Mark:** Hand engraved logo of letter B pierced by dagger.

BARNES, GREGORY,
266 W Calaveras St, Altadena, CA 91001, Phone: 626-398-0053, snake@annex.com

BARNES, JACK,
PO Box 1315, Whitefish, MT 59937-1315, Phone: 406- 862-6078

BARNES, MARLEN R.,
904 Crestview Dr S, Atlanta, TX 75551-1854, Phone: 903-796-3668, MRBlives@worldnet.att.net
 Specialties: Hammer forges random and mosaic Damascus. **Patterns:** Hatchets, straight and folding knives. **Technical:** Hammer forges carbon steel using 5160, 1084 and 52100 with 15N20 and 203E nickel. **Prices:** $150 and up. **Remarks:** Part-time maker; first knife sold 1999. **Mark:** Script M.R.B., other side J.S.

BARNES, WENDELL,
PO Box 272, Clinton, MT 59825, Phone: 406-825- 0908
 Specialties: Working straight knives. Patterns: Hunters, folders, neck knives. Technical: Grinds 440C, ATS-34, D2 and Damascus. Prices: Start at $75. Remarks: Spare-time maker; first knife sold in 1996. Mark: First initial and last name around broken heart.

BARNES, WILLIAM,
591 Barnes Rd, Wallingford, CT 06492-1805, Phone: 860-349-0443

BARNES JR., CECIL C.,
141 Barnes Dr, Center Ridge, AR 72027, Phone: 501-893-2267

BARNETT, VAN,
BARNETT INT'L INC, 1135 Terminal Way Ste #209, Reno, NV 89502, Phone: 304-727-5512, artknife@suddenlink.net; Web: www.VanBarnett.com
 Specialties: Collector grade one-of-a-kind / embellished high art daggers and art folders. **Patterns:** Art daggers and folders. **Technical:** Forges and grinds own Damascus. **Prices:** Upscale. **Remarks:** Designs and makes one-of-a-kind highly embellished art knives using high karat gold, diamonds and other gemstones, pearls, stone and fossil ivories, carved steel guards and blades, all knives are carved and or engraved, does own engraving, carving and other embellishments, sole authorship; full- time maker since 1981. Does one high art collaboration a year with Dellana. Member of ABS. Member Art Knife Invitational Group (AKI) **Mark:** V. H. Barnett or Van Barnett in script.

BARR, A.T.,
153 Madonna Dr, Nicholasville, KY 40356, Phone: 859-887- 5400, Web: www.customknives.com
 Specialties: Fine gent's user and collector grade LinerLock® folders and sheath knives. **Patterns:** LinerLock® folders and sheath knives. **Technical:** Flat grinds S30V, ATS-34, D2 commercial Damascus; all knives have a hand rubbed satin finish. Does all leather work. **Prices:** Start at $250 for folders and $200 for sheath knives. **Remarks:** Full-time maker, first knife sold in 1979. Knifemakers' Guild voting member. "Don't you buy no ugly knife." **Mark:** Full name.

BARR, JUDSON C.,
1905 Pickwick Circle, Irving, TX 75060, Phone: 972-790-7195, judsonbarrknives@yahoo.com
 Specialties: Bowies. **Patterns:** Sheffield and Early American. **Technical:** Forged carbon steel and Damascus. Also stock removal. **Remarks:** Journeyman member of ABS. **Mark:** Barr.

BARRETT, CECIL TERRY,
2514 Linda Lane, Colorado Springs, CO 80909, Phone: 719-473-8325
 Specialties: Working and using straight knives and folders of his design, to customer specs and in standard patterns. **Patterns:** Bowies, hunters, kitchen knives, locking folders and slip-joint folders. **Technical:** Grinds 440C, D2 and ATS-34. Wood and leather sheaths. **Prices:** $65 to $500; some to $750. **Remarks:** Full-time maker. **Mark:** Stamped middle name.

BARRETT, RICK L. (TOSHI HISA),
18943 CR 18, Goshen, IN 46528, Phone: 574-533-4297, barrettrick@hotmail.com
 Specialties: Japanese-style blades from sushi knives to katana and fantasy pieces. **Patterns:** Swords, axes, spears/lances, hunter and utility knives. **Technical:** Forges and grinds Damascus and carbon steels, occasionally uses stainless. **Prices:** $250 to $4000+. **Remarks:** Full-time bladesmith, jeweler. **Mark:** Japanese mei on Japanese pieces and stylized initials.

BARRON, BRIAN,
123 12th Ave, San Mateo, CA 94402, Phone: 650- 341-2683
 Specialties: Traditional straight knives. **Patterns:** Daggers, hunters and swords. **Technical:** Grinds 440C, ATS-34 and 1095. Sculpts bolsters using an S-curve. **Prices:** $130 to $270; some to $1500. **Remarks:** Part- time maker; first knife sold in 1993. **Mark:** Diamond Drag "Barron."

BARRY, SCOTT,
Box 354, Laramie, WY 82073, Phone: 307-721-8038, scottyb@uwyo.edu
 Specialties: Currently producing mostly folders, also make fixed blade hunters & fillet knives. **Technical:** Steels used are 440/C, ATS/34, 154/ CM, S30V, Damasteel & Mike Norris stainless Damascus. **Prices:** Range from $300 $1000. **Remarks:** Part-time maker. First knife sold in 1972. **Mark:** DSBarry, etched on blade.

BARRY III, JAMES J.,
115 Flagler Promenade No., West Palm Beach, FL 33405, Phone: 561-832-4197
 Specialties: High-art working straight knives of his design also high art tomahawks. **Patterns:** Hunters, daggers and fishing knives. **Technical:** Grinds 440C only. Prefers exotic materials for handles. Most knives embellished with filework, carving and scrimshaw. Many pieces designed to stand unassisted. **Prices:** $500 to $10,000. **Remarks:** Part-time maker; first knife sold in 1975. Guild member (Knifemakers) since 1991. **Mark:** Branded initials as a J and B together.

BARTH, J.D.,
101 4th St, PO Box 186, Alberton, MT 59820, Phone: 406- 722-4557, mtdeerhunter@blackfoot.net; Web: www.jdbarthcustomknives.com
 Specialties: Working and fancy straight knives of his design. LinerLock® folders, stainless and Damascus, fully file worked, nitre bluing. Technical: Grinds ATS-34, 440-C, stainless and carbon Damascus. Uses variety of natural handle materials and Micarta. Likes dovetailed bolsters. Filework on most knives, full and tapered tangs. Makes custom fit sheaths for each knife. Mark: Name over maker, city and state.

custom knifemakers

BARTLOW, JOHN,
5078 Coffeen Ave, Sheridan, WY 82801, Phone: 307 673-4941, bartlow@bresnan.net
Specialties: Working hunters, greenriver skinners, classic capers and bird & trouts. **Technical:** ATS-34, CPM154, Damascus available on all linerlocks. **Prices:** Full-time maker, guild member from 1988. **Mark:** Bartlow, Sheridan WYO.

BARTRUG, HUGH E.,
2701 34th St N #142, St. Petersburg, FL 33713, Phone: 813-323-1136
Specialties: Inlaid straight knives and exotic folders; high-art knives and period pieces. **Patterns:** Hunters, Bowies and daggers; traditional patterns. **Technical:** Diffuses mokume. Forges 100 percent nickel, wrought iron, mosaic Damascus, shokeedo and O1 tool steel; grinds. **Prices:** $210 to $2500; some to $5000. **Remarks:** Retired maker; first knife sold in 1980. **Mark:** Ashley Forge or name.

BASKETT, BARBARA,
Custom Knives, 427 Sutzer Ck Rd, Eastview, KY 42732, Phone: 270-862-5019, baskettknives@windstream.net
Specialties: Hunters and LinerLocks. **Technical:** 440-C, CPM 154, S30V. **Prices:** $250 and up. **Mark:** B. Baskett.

BASSETT, DAVID J.,
P.O. Box 69-102, Glendene, Auckland 0645, NEW ZEALAND, Phone: 64 9 818 9083, Fax: 64 9 818 9013, david@customknifemaking.co.nz; Web:www.customknifemaking.co.nz
Specialties: Working/using knives. **Patterns:** Hunters, fighters, boot, skinners, tanto. **Technical:** Grinds 440C, 12C27, D2 and some Damascus via stock removal method. **Prices:** $150 to $500. **Remarks:** Part- time maker, first knife sold in 2006. Also carries range of natural and synthetic handle material, pin stock etc. for sale. **Mark:** Name over country in semi-circular design.

BATLEY, MARK S.,
PO Box 217, Wake, VA 23176, Phone: 804 776- 7794

BATSON, JAMES,
176 Brentwood Lane, Madison, AL 35758
Specialties: Forged Damascus blades and fittings in collectible period pieces. **Patterns:** Integral art knives, Bowies, folders, American-styled blades and miniatures. **Technical:** Forges carbon steel and his Damascus. **Prices:** $150 to $1800; some to $4500. **Remarks:** Semi retired full-time maker; first knife sold in 1978. **Mark:** Name, bladesmith with horse's head.

BATSON, RICHARD G.,
6591 Waterford Rd, Rixeyville, VA 22737, Phone: 540-937-2318
Specialties: Military, utility and fighting knives in working and presentation grade. **Patterns:** Daggers, combat and utility knives. **Technical:** Grinds O1, 1095 and 440C. Etches and scrimshaws; offers polished, Parkerized finishes. **Prices:** $350 to $1500. **Remarks:** Semi-retired, limit production. First knife sold in 1958. **Mark:** Bat in circle, hand-signed and serial numbered.

BATTS, KEITH,
450 Manning Rd, Hooks, TX 75561, Phone: 903-277- 8466, kbatts@valornet.com
Specialties: Working straight knives of his design or to customer specs. **Patterns:** Bowies, hunters, skinners, camp knives and others. **Technical:** Forges 5160 and his Damascus; offers filework. **Prices:** $245 to $895. **Remarks:** Part-time maker; first knife sold in 1988. **Mark:** Last name.

BAUCHOP, ROBERT,
PO Box 330, Munster, Kwazulu-Natal 4278, SOUTH AFRICA, Phone: +27 39 3192449
Specialties: Fantasy knives; working and using knives of his design and to customer specs. **Patterns:** Hunters, swords, utility/camp knives, diver's knives and large swords. **Technical:** Grinds Sandvick 12C27, D2, 440C. Uses South African hardwoods red ivory, wild olive, African blackwood, etc. on handles. **Prices:** $200 to $800; some to $2000. **Remarks:** Full-time maker; first knife sold in 1986. Doing business as Bauchop Custom Knives and Swords. **Mark:** Viking helmet with Bauchop (bow and chopper) crest.

BAUMGARDNER, ED,
PO Box 81, Glendale, KY 42740, Phone: 502- 435-2675
Specialties: Working fixed blades, some folders. **Patterns:** Drop point and clip point hunters, fighters, small Bowies, traditional slip joint folders, lockbacks, Liner locks and art folders with gold & gemstone inlays. **Technical:** Grinds O1, 154CM, ATS-34, and Damascus likes using natural handle materials. **Prices:** $100 to $2000. **Remarks:** Part-time maker, first knife sold in 2001. **Mark:** Last name.

BAXTER, DALE,
291 County Rd 547, Trinity, AL 35673, Phone: 256- 355-3626, dale@baxterknives.com
Specialties: Bowies, fighters, and hunters. **Patterns:** No patterns: all unique true customs. **Technical:** Hand forge and hand finish. Steels: 1095 and L6 for carbon blades, 1095/L6 for Damascus. **Remarks:** Full- time bladesmith and sold first knife in 1998. **Mark:** Dale Baxter (script) and J.S. on reverse.

BEAM, JOHN R.,
1310 Foothills Rd, Kalispell, MT 59901, Phone: 406- 755-2593
Specialties: Classic, high-art and working straight knives of his design. **Patterns:** Bowies and hunters. **Technical:** Grinds 440C, Damascus and scrap. **Prices:** $175 to $600; some to $3000. **Remarks:** Part-time maker; first knife sold in 1950. Doing business as Beam's Knives. **Mark:** Beam's Knives.

BEASLEY, GENEO,
PO Box 339, Wadsworth, NV 89442, Phone: 775- 575-2584

BEATTY, GORDON H.,
121 Petty Rd, Seneca, SC 29672, Phone: 864- 882-6278
Specialties: Working straight knives, some fancy. **Patterns:** Traditional patterns, mini-skinners and letter openers. **Technical:** Grinds 440C, D2 and ATS-34; makes knives one-at-a-time. **Prices:** $75 to $450. **Remarks:** Part-time maker; first knife sold in 1982. **Mark:** Name.

BEATY, ROBERT B.,
CUTLER, 1995 Big Flat Rd, Missoula, MT 59804, Phone: 406-549-1818
Specialties: Plain and fancy working knives and collector pieces; will accept custom orders. **Patterns:** Hunters, Bowies, utility, kitchen and camp knives; locking folders. **Technical:** Grinds D-2, ATS-34, Dendritie D-2, makes all tool steel Damascus, forges 1095, 5160, 52100. **Prices:** $150 to $600, some to $1100. **Remarks:** Full-time maker; first knife sold 1995. **Mark:** Stainless: First name, middle initial, last name, city and state. Carbon: Last name stamped on Ricasso.

BEAUCHAMP, GAETAN,
125 de la Rivire, Stoneham, PQ, CANADA G3C 0P6, Phone: 418-848-1914, Fax: 418-848-6859, knives@gbeauchamp.ca; Web: www.gbeauchamp.ca
Specialties: Working knives and folders of his design and to customer specs. **Patterns:** Hunters, fighters, fantasy knives. **Technical:** Grinds ATS-34, 440C, Damascus. Scrimshaws on ivory; specializes in buffalo horn and black backgrounds. Offers a variety of handle materials. **Prices:** Start at $250. **Remarks:** Full-time maker; first knife sold in 1992. **Mark:** Signature etched on blade.

BECKER, FRANZ,
AM Kreuzberg 2, 84533, Marktl/Inn, GERMANY 08678-8020
Specialties: Stainless steel knives in working sizes. **Patterns:** Semi- and full-integral knives; interframe folders. **Technical:** Grinds stainless steels; likes natural handle materials. **Prices:** $200 to $2000. **Mark:** Name, country.

BEERS, RAY,
2501 Lakefront Dr, Lake Wales, FL 33898, Phone: Winter 863-696-3036, rbknives@copper.net

BEERS, RAY,
8 Manorbrook Rd, Monkton, MD 21111, Phone: Summer 410-472-2229

BEETS, MARTY,
390 N 5th Ave, Williams Lake, BC, CANADA V2G 2G4, Phone: 250-392-7199
Specialties: Working and collectable straight knives of his own design. **Patterns:** Hunter, skinners, Bowies and utility knives. **Technical:** Grinds 440C-does all his own work including heat treating. Uses a variety of handle material specializing in exotic hardwoods, antler and horn. **Price:** $125 to $400. **Remarks:** Wife, Sandy does handmade/hand stitched sheaths. First knife sold in 1988. Business name Beets Handmade Knives.

BEGG, TODD M.,
420 169 St S, Spanaway, WA 98387, Phone: 253- 531-2113, web:www.beggknives.com
Specialties: Hand rubbed satin finished 440c stainless steel. Mirror polished 426 stainless steel. Stabilized mardrone wood.

BEHNKE, WILLIAM,
8478 Dell Rd, Kingsley, MI 49649, Phone: 231-263-7447, wbehnke@michweb.net
Specialties: Hunters, belt knives, folders, hatchets and tomahawks. **Patterns:** Traditional styling in moderate-sized straight and folding knives. **Technical:** Forges his own Damascus, W-2 and 1095; likes natural material. **Prices:** $150 to $2000. **Remarks:** Part-time maker. **Mark:** Bill Behnke Knives.

BELL, DON,
Box 98, Lincoln, MT 59639, Phone: 406-362-3208, dlb@linctel.net
Patterns: Folders, hunters and custom orders. **Technical:** Carbon steel 52100, 5160, 1095, 1084. Making own Damascus. Flat grinds. Natural handle material including fossil. ivory, pearl, & ironwork. **Remarks:** Full-time maker. First knife sold in 1999. **Mark:** Last name.

BELL, DONALD,
2 Division St, Bedford, Nova Scotia, CANADA B4A 1Y8, Phone: 902-835-2623, donbell@accesswave.ca; Web: www.bellknives.com
Specialties: Fancy knives: carved and pierced folders of his own design. **Patterns:** Locking folders, pendant knives, jewelry knives. **Technical:** Grinds Damascus, pierces and carves blades. **Prices:** $500 to $2000, some to $3000. **Remarks:** Spare-time maker; first knife sold in 1993. **Mark:** Bell symbol with first initial inside.

BELL, MICHAEL,
88321 N Bank Lane, Coquille, OR 97423, Phone: 541- 396-3605, michael@dragonflyforge.com; Web: www. Dragonflyforge.com
Specialties: Full line of combat quality Japanese swords. Patterns: Traditional tanto to katana. Technical: Handmade steel and welded cable. Prices: Swords from bare blades to complete high art $4500 to $28,000. Remarks: Studied with Japanese master Nakajima Muneyoshi. Instruction in sword crafts. Mark: Dragonfly in shield or tombo kunimitsu.

BELL, TONY,
PO Box 24, Woodland, AL 36280, Phone: 256-449-2655, tbell905@aol.com
Specialties: Hand forged period knives and tomahawks. Art knives and knives made for everyday use. Technical: Makes own Damascus. Forges 1095, 5160,1080,L6 steels. Does own heat treating. Prices: $75-$1200. Remarks: Full time maker. Mark: Bell symbol with initial T in the middle.

BENDIK, JOHN,
7076 Fitch Rd, Olmsted Falls, OH 44138

BENJAMIN JR., GEORGE,
3001 Foxy Ln, Kissimmee, FL 34746, Phone: 407-846-7259
Specialties: Fighters in various styles to include Persian, Moro and military. Patterns: Daggers, skinners and one-of-a-kind grinds. Technical: Forges O1, D2, A2, 5160 and Damascus. Favors Pakkawood, Micarta, and mirror or Parkerized finishes. Makes unique para-military leather sheaths. Prices: $150 to $600; some to $1200. Remarks: Doing business as The Leather Box. Mark: Southern Pride Knives.

BENNETT, BRETT C,
4717 Sullivan St, Cheyenne, WY 82009, Phone: 307-220-3919, brett@bennettknives.com; Web: www.bennettknives.com
Specialties: Hand-rubbed finish on all blades. Patterns: Most fixed blade patterns. Technical: ATS-34, D-2, 1084/15N20 Damascus, 1084 forged. Prices: $100 and up. Mark: "B.C. Bennett" in script or "Bennett" stamped in script.

BENNETT, GLEN C,
5821 S Stewart Blvd, Tucson, AZ 85706

BENNETT, PETER,
PO Box 143, Engadine N.S.W. 2233, AUSTRALIA, Phone: 02-520-4975 (home), Fax: 02-528-8219 (work)
Specialties: Fancy and embellished working and using straight knives to customer specs and in standard patterns. Patterns: Fighters, hunters, bird/trout and fillet knives. Technical: Grinds 440C, ATS-34 and Damascus. Uses rare Australian desert timbers for handles. Prices: $90 to $500; some to $1500. Remarks: Full-time maker; first knife sold in 1985. Mark: First and middle initials, last name; country.

BENNICA, CHARLES,
11 Chemin du Salet, 34190 Moules et Baucels, FRANCE, Phone: +33 4 67 73 42 40, cbennica@bennica-knives.com; Web: www.bennica-knives.com
Specialties: Fixed blades and folding knives; the latter with slick closing mechanisms with push buttons to unlock blades. Unique handle shapes, signature to the maker. Technical: 416 stainless steel frames for folders and ATS-34 blades. Also specializes in Damascus.

BENSON, DON,
2505 Jackson St #112, Escalon, CA 95320, Phone: 209-838-7921
Specialties: Working straight knives of his design. Patterns: Axes, Bowies, tantos and hunters. Technical: Grinds 440C. Prices: $100 to $150; some to $400. Remarks: Spare-time maker; first knife sold in 1980. Mark: Name.

BENTLEY, C L,
2405 Hilltop Dr, Albany, GA 31707, Phone: 912-432- 6656

BENTZEN, LEIF,
15 Apdalsvej, Aarhus N, DENMARK 8200
Technical: Blades are ground from Thyradur 2842 steel. Remarks: Part-time knifemaker and mostly makes hunter or collectors knives. Prices: $250 to $1600.

BER, DAVE,
656 Miller Rd, San Juan Island, WA 98250, Phone: 206- 378-7230
Specialties: Working straight and folding knives for the sportsman; welcomes customer designs. Patterns: Hunters, skinners, Bowies, kitchen and fishing knives. Technical: Forges and grinds saw blade steel, wire Damascus, O1, L6, 5160 and 440C. Prices: $100 to $300; some to $500. Remarks: Full-time maker; first knife sold in 1985. Mark: Last name.

BERG, LOTHAR,
37 Hillcrest Ln, Kitchener ON, CANADA NZK 1S9, Phone: 519-745-3260; 519-745-3260

BERGER, MAX A.,
5716 John Richard Ct, Carmichael, CA 95608, Phone: 916-972-9229, bergerknives@aol.com
Specialties: Fantasy and working/using straight knives of his design. Patterns: Fighters, hunters and utility/camp knives. Technical: Grinds ATS-34 and 440C. Offers fileworks and combinations of mirror polish and satin finish blades. Prices: $200 to $600; some to $2500. Remarks: Part-time maker; first knife sold in 1992. Mark: Last name.

BERGH, ROGER,
Dalkarlsa 291, 91598 Bygdea, SWEDEN, Phone: 469-343-0061, knivroger@hotmail.com; Web: www.rogerbergh.com
Specialties: Collectible all-purpose straight-blade knives. Damascus steel blades, carving and artistic design knives are heavily influenced by nature and have an organic hand crafted feel.

BERGLIN, BRUCE D,
17441 Lake Terrace Place, Mount Vernon, WA 98274, Phone: 360-422-8603, bruce@berglins.com
Specialties: Working and using fixed blades and folders of his own design. Patterns: Hunters, boots, bowies, utility, liner locks and slip joints some with vintage finish. Technical: Forges carbon steel, grinds carbon steel. Prefers natural handle material and Micarta. Prices: Start at $300. Remarks: Part-time maker since 1998. Mark: First initial, middle initial and last name, sometimes surrounded with an oval.

BERTOLAMI, JUAN CARLOS,
Av San Juan 575, Neuquen, ARGENTINA 8300, fliabertolami@infovia.com.ar
Specialties: Hunting and country labor knives. All of them unique high quality pieces and supplies collectors too. Technical: Austrian stainless steel and elephant, hippopotamus and orca ivory, as well as ebony and other fine woods for the handles.

BERTUZZI, ETTORE,
Via Partigiani 3, 24068 Seriate (Bergamo), ITALY, Phone: 035-294262, Fax: 035-294262
Specialties: Classic straight knives and folders of his design, to customer specs and in standard patterns. Patterns: Bowies, hunters and locking folders. Technical: Grinds ATS-34, D3, D2 and various Damascus. Prices: $300 to $500. Remarks: Part-time maker; first knife sold in 1993. Mark: Name etched on ricasso.

BESEDICK, FRANK E,
195 Stillwagon Rd, Ruffsdale, PA 15679, Phone: 724-696-3312, bxtr.bez3@verizon.net
Specialties: Traditional working and using straight knives of his design. Patterns: Hunters, utility/camp knives and miniatures; buckskinner blades and tomahawks. Technical: Forges and grinds 5160, O1 and Damascus. Offers filework and scrimshaw. Prices: $75 to $300; some to $750. Remarks: Part-time maker; first knife sold in 1990. Mark: Name or initials.

BESHARA, BRENT (BESH),
207 Cedar St, PO Box 1046, Stayner, Ont., CANADA L0M 1S0, Phone: 705-428-3152, beshknives@sympatico.ca; Web: www.beshknives.com
Specialties: Tactical fighting fixed knives. Patterns: Tantos, fighters, neck and custom designs. Technical: Grinds 0-1, L6 and stainless upon request. Offers Kydex sheaths, does own Paragon heat treating. Prices: Start at $150. Remarks: Inventor of Besh wedge™. Part-time maker. Active serving military bomb disposal driver. Mark: "BESH" stamped.

BEST, RON,
1489 Adams Lane, Stokes, NC 27884, Phone: 252-714- 1264, ronbestknives@msn.com; Web: www.ronbestknives.com
Specialties: All integral fixed blades, interframe. Patterns: Bowies, hunters, fighters, fantasy, daggers & swords. Technical: Grinds 440C, D-2 and ATS-34. Prices: $600 to $8000.

BETANCOURT, ANTONIO L.,
5718 Beefwood Ct., St. Louis, MO 63129, Phone: 314-306-1869, bet2001@charter.net
Specialties: One-of-a-kind fixed blades and art knives. Patterns: Hunters and Bowies with embellished handles. Technical: Uses cast sterling silver and lapidary with fine gemstones, fossil ivory, and scrimshaw. Grinds Damascus and 440C. Prices: $100 to $800. Remarks: Part-time maker, first knife sold in 1974. Mark: Initials in cursive.

BETHKE, LORA SUE,
13420 Lincoln St, Grand Haven, MI 49417, Phone: 616-842-8268
Specialties: Scagel style knives. Patterns: Hunters and miniatures Technical: Forges 1084 and Damascus. Prices: Start at $400. Remarks: Part-time maker; first knife sold in 1997. Journeyman Bladesmith, American Bladesmith Society. Mark: Full name - JS on reverse side.

BEUKES, TINUS,
83 Henry St, Risiville, Vereeniging 1939, SOUTH AFRICA, Phone: 27 16 423 2053
Specialties: Working straight knives. Patterns: Hunters, skinners and kitchen knives. Technical: Grinds D2, 440C and chain, cable and stainless Damascus. Prices: $80 to $180. Remarks: Part-time maker; first knife sold in 1993. Mark: Full name, city, logo.

BEVERLY II, LARRY H,
PO Box 741, Spotsylvania, VA 22553, Phone: 540-898-3951
Specialties: Working straight knives, slip-joints and liner locks. Welcomes customer designs. Patterns: Bowies, hunters, guard less fighters and miniatures. Technical: Grinds 440C, A2 and O1. Prices: $125 to $1000. Remarks: Part-time maker; first knife sold in 1986. Mark: Initials or last name in script.

BEZUIDENHOUT, BUZZ,
30 Surlingham Ave, Malvern, Queensburgh, Natal 4093, SOUTH AFRICA, Phone: 031-4632827, Fax: 031-3631259
Specialties: Traditional working and using straight knives of his design and to customer specs. **Patterns:** Boots, hunters, kitchen knives and utility/camp knives. **Technical:** Grinds 12C27, 440C and ATS-34. Uses local hardwoods, horn: kudu, impala, buffalo, giraffe bone and ivory for handles. **Prices:** $150 to $200; some to $1500. **Remarks:** Spare-time maker; first knife sold in 1988. **Mark:** First name with a bee emblem.

BIGGERS, GARY,
VENTURA KNIVES, 1278 Colina Vista, Ventura, CA 93003, Phone: 805-658-6610, Fax: 805-658-6610
Specialties: Fixed blade knives of his design. **Patterns:** Hunters, boots/fighters, Bowies and utility knives. **Technical:** Grinds ATS-34, O1 and commercial Damascus. **Prices:** $150 to $550. **Remarks:** Part-time maker: first knife sold in 1996. Doing business as Ventura Knives. **Mark:** First and last name, city and state.

BILLGREN, PER,
Stallgatan 9, S815 76 Soderfors, SWEDEN, Phone: +46 293 30600, Fax: +46 293 30124, mail@damasteel.se Web:www.damasteel.se
Specialties: Damasteel, stainless Damascus steels. **Patterns:** Bluetongue, Heimskringla, Muhammad's ladder, Rose, Twist, Odin's eye, Vinland, Hakkapelliitta. **Technical:** Modern Damascus steel made by patented powder metallurgy method. **Prices:** $80 to $180. **Remarks:** Damasteel is available through distributors around the globe.

BIRDWELL, IRA LEE,
PO Box 1448, Congress, AZ 85332, Phone: 928- 925-3258, heli.ira@gmail.com
Specialties: Special orders. **Mark:** Engraved signature.

BIRNBAUM, EDWIN,
9715 Hamocks Blvd I 206, Miami, FL 33196

BISH, HAL,
9347 Sweetbriar Trace, Jonesboro, GA 30236, Phone: 770- 477-2422, halbish@hp.com

BIZZELL, ROBERT,
145 Missoula Ave, Butte, MT 59701, Phone: 406- 782-4403, patternweld@yahoo.com
Specialties: Damascus Bowies. **Patterns:** Composite, mosaic and traditional. **Technical:** Fixed blades & LinerLock® folders. **Prices:** Fixed blades start at $275. Folders start at $500. **Remarks:** Currently not taking orders. **Mark:** Hand signed.

BLACK, EARL,
3466 South, 700 East, Salt Lake City, UT 84106, Phone: 801-466-8395
Specialties: High-art straight knives and folders; period pieces. **Patterns:** Boots, Bowies and daggers; lockers and gents. **Technical:** Grinds 440C and 154CM. Buys some Damascus. Scrimshaws and engraves. **Prices:** $200 to $1800; some to $2500 and higher. **Remarks:** Full-time maker; first knife sold in 1980. **Mark:** Name, city, state.

BLACK, SCOTT,
570 Malcom Rd, Covington, GA 30209
Specialties: Working/using folders of his design. **Patterns:** Daggers, hunters, utility/camp knives and friction folders. **Technical:** Forges pattern welded, cable, 1095, O1 and 5160. **Prices:** $100 to $500. **Remarks:** Part-time maker; first knife sold in 1992. Doing business as Copperhead Forge. **Mark:** Hot mark on blade, copperhead snake.

BLACK, SCOTT,
27100 Leetown Rd, Picayune, MS 39466, Phone: 601- 799-5939, copperheadforge@telepak.net
Specialties: Friction folders; fighters. **Patterns:** Bowies, fighters, hunters, smoke hawks, friction folders, daggers. **Technical:** All forged, all work done by him, own hand-stitched leather work; own heat-treating. **Prices:** $100 to $2200. **Remarks:** ABS Journeyman Smith. Cabel / Damascus/ High Carbone. **Mark:** Hot Mark - Copperhead Snake.

BLACK, TOM,
921 Grecian NW, Albuquerque, NM 87107, Phone: 505- 344-2549, tblackknives@aol.com
Specialties: Working knives to fancy straight knives of his design. **Patterns:** Drop-point skinners, folders, using knives, Bowies and daggers. **Technical:** Grinds 440C, 154CM, ATS-34, A2, D2 and Damascus. Offers engraving and scrimshaw. **Prices:** $250 and up; some over $8500. **Remarks:** Full-time maker; first knife sold in 1970. **Mark:** Name, city.

BLACKWOOD, NEIL,
7032 Willow Run, Lakeland, FL 33813, Phone: 863-701-0126, neil@blackwoodknives.com; Web: www.blackwoodknives.com
Specialties: Fixed blades and folders. **Technical:** Blade steels D2 Talonite, Stellite, CPM S30V and RWL 34. Handle materials: G-10 carbon fiber and Micarta in the synthetics: giraffe bone and exotic woods on the natural side. **Remarks:** Makes everything from the frames to the stop pins, pivot pins: everything but the stainless screws; one factory/custom collaboration (the Hybrid Hunter) with Outdoor Edge is in place and negotiations are under way for one with Benchmade.

BLANCHARD, G R (GARY),
PO Box 709, Pigeon Forge, TN 37868, Phone: 865-908-7466, Fax: 865-908-7466, blanchardscutlery@yahoo.com; Web: www.blanchardscutlery.com
Specialties: Fancy folders with patented button blade release and high- art straight knives of his design. **Patterns:** Boots, daggers and locking folders. **Technical:** Grinds 440C and ATS-34 and Damascus. Engraves his knives. **Prices:** $1500 to $18,000 or more. **Remarks:** Full-time maker; first knife sold in 1989. **Mark:** First and middle initials, last name or last name only.

BLASINGAME, ROBERT,
281 Swanson, Kilgore, TX 75662, Phone: 903-984-8144, rbblademastger@cablelynx.com Web:www.blasingameknives.com
Specialties: Classic working and using straight knives and folders of his design and to customer specs. **Patterns:** Bowies, daggers, fighters and hunters; one-of-a-kind historic reproductions. **Technical:** Hand-forges P.W. Damascus, cable Damascus and chain Damascus. **Prices:** $150 to $1000; some to $2000. **Remarks:** Full-time maker; first knife sold in 1968. **Mark:** 'B' inside anvil.

BLAUM, ROY,
319 N Columbia St, Covington, LA 70433, Phone: 985- 893-1060
Specialties: Working straight knives and folders of his design; lightweight easy-open knives. **Patterns:** Hunters, boots, fishing and woodcarving/whittling knives. **Technical:** Grinds A2, D2, O1, 154CM and ATS- 34. Offers leatherwork. **Prices:** $40 to $800; some higher. **Remarks:** Full-time maker; first knife sold in 1976. **Mark:** Engraved signature or etched logo.

BLOOMER, ALAN T,
PO Box 154, 116 E 6th St, Maquon, IL 61458, Phone: 309-875-3583, alant.bloomer@winco.net
Specialties: Folders & straight knives & custom pen maker. **Patterns:** All kinds. **Technical:** Does own heat treating. **Prices:** $400 to $1000. **Remarks:** Part-time maker. No orders. **Mark:** Stamp Bloomer.

BLUM, CHUCK,
743 S Brea Blvd #10, Brea, CA 92621, Phone: 714-529- 0484
Specialties: Art and investment daggers and Bowies. **Technical:** Flat-grinds; hollow-grinds 440C, ATS-34 on working knives. **Prices:** $125 to $8500. **Remarks:** Part-time maker; first knife sold in 1985. **Mark:** First and middle initials and last name with sailboat logo.

BLUM, KENNETH,
1729 Burleson, Brenham, TX 77833, Phone: 979- 836-9577
Specialties: Traditional working straight knives of his design. **Patterns:** Camp knives, hunters and Bowies. **Technical:** Forges 5160; grinds 440C and D2. Uses exotic woods and Micarta for handles. **Prices:** $150 to $300. **Remarks:** Part-time maker; first knife sold in 1978. **Mark:** Last name on ricasso.

BOARDMAN, GUY,
39 Mountain Ridge R, New Germany 3619, SOUTH AFRICA, Phone: 031-726-921
Specialties: American and South African-styles. **Patterns:** Bowies, American and South African hunters, plus more. **Technical:** Grinds Bohler steels, some ATS-34. **Prices:** $100 to $600. **Remarks:** Part-time maker; first knife sold in 1986. **Mark:** Name, city, country.

BOCHMAN, BRUCE,
183 Howard Place, Grants Pass, OR 97526, Phone: 541-471-1985
Specialties: Working straight knives in standard patterns. **Patterns:** Bowies, hunters, fishing and bird knives. **Technical:** ATS34, 154CM, 5160, mirror or satin finish. **Prices:** $200 to $350; some to $750. **Remarks:** Part-time maker; first knife sold in 1977. **Mark:** Custom blades by B. Bochman.

BODEN, HARRY,
Via Gellia Mill, Bonsall Matlock, Derbyshire DE4 2AJ, ENGLAND, Phone: 0629-825176
Specialties: Traditional working straight knives and folders of his design. **Patterns:** Hunters, locking folders and utility/camp knives. **Technical:** Grinds Sandvik 12C27, D2 and O1. **Prices:** £70 to £150; some to £300. **Remarks:** Full-time maker; first knife sold in 1986. **Mark:** Full name.

BODNER, GERALD "JERRY",
4102 Spyglass Ct, Louisville, KY 40229, Phone: 502-968-5946
Specialties: Fantasy straight knives in standard patterns. **Patterns:** Bowies, fighters, hunters and micro-miniature knives. **Technical:** Grinds Damascus, 440C and D2. Offers filework. **Prices:** $35 to $180. **Remarks:** Part-time maker; first knife sold in 1993. **Mark:** Last name in script and JAB in oval above knives.

BODOLAY, ANTAL,
Rua Wilson Soares Fernandes #31, Planalto, Belo Horizonte MG-31730-700, BRAZIL, Phone: 031-494-1885
Specialties: Working folders and fixed blades of his design or to customer specs; some art daggers and period pieces. **Patterns:** Daggers, hunters, locking folders, utility knives and Khukris. **Technical:** Grinds D6, high-carbon steels and 420 stainless. Forges files on request. **Prices:** $30 to $350. **Remarks:** Full-time maker; first knife sold in 1965. **Mark:** Last name in script.

BOEHLKE, GUENTER,
Parkstrasse 2, 56412 Grossholbach, GERMANY 2602-5440, Boehlke-Messer@t-online.de; Web: www.boehlke- messer.de
   Specialties: Classic working/using straight knives of his design. **Patterns:** Hunters, utility/camp knives and ancient remakes. **Technical:** Grinds Damascus, CPM-T-440V and 440C. Inlays gemstones and ivory. **Prices:** $220 to $700; some to $2000. **Remarks:** Spare-time maker; first knife sold in 1985. **Mark:** Name, address and bow and arrow.

BOGUSZEWSKI, PHIL,
PO Box 99329, Lakewood, WA 98499, Phone: 253-581-7096, knives01@aol.com
   Specialties: Working folders—some fancy—mostly of his design. **Patterns:** Folders, slip-joints and lockers; also makes anodized titanium frame folders. **Technical:** Grinds BG42 and Damascus; offers filework. **Prices:** $550 to $3000. **Remarks:** Full-time maker; first knife sold in 1979. **Mark:** Name, city and state.

BOJTOS, ARPAD,
Dobsinskeho 10, 98403 Lucenec, SLOVAKIA, Phone: 00421-47 4333512, botjos@stonline.sk; Web: www.arpadbojtos.sk
   Specialties: Art knives. **Patterns:** Daggers, fighters and hunters. **Technical:** Grinds ATS-34. Carves on steel, handle materials and sheaths. **Prices:** $5000 to $10,000; some over. **Remarks:** Full-time maker; first knife sold in 1990. **Mark:** AB.

BOLEWARE, DAVID,
PO Box 96, Carson, MS 39427, Phone: 601-943- 5372
   Specialties: Traditional and working/using straight knives of his design, to customer specs and in standard patterns. **Patterns:** Bowies, hunters and utility/camp knives. **Technical:** Grinds ATS-34, 440C and Damascus. **Prices:** $85 to $350; some to $600. **Remarks:** Part-time maker; first knife sold in 1989. **Mark:** First and last name, city, state.

BOLEY, JAMIE,
PO Box 477, Parker, SD 57053, Phone: 605-297-0014, jamie@polarbearforge.com
   Specialties: Working knives and historical influenced reproductions. **Patterns:** Hunters, skinners, scramasaxes, and others.**Technical:** Forges 5160, O1, L6, 52100, W1, W2 makes own Damascus. **Prices:** Starts at $125. **Remarks:** Part-time maker. **Mark:** Polar bear paw print with name on the left side and Polar Bear Forge on the right.

BONASSI, FRANCO,
Via Nicoletta 4, Pordenone 33170, ITALY, Phone: 0434-550821; f.bonassi@faridindustrie.it
   Specialties: Fancy and working one-of-a-kind folder knives of his design. **Patterns:** Folders, linerlocks and back locks. **Technical:** Grinds CPM, ATS-34, 154CM and commercial Damascus. Uses only titanium foreguards and pommels. **Prices:** Start at $350. **Remarks:** Spare-time maker; first knife sold in 1988. Has made cutlery for several celebrities; Gen. Schwarzkopf, Fuzzy Zoeller, etc. **Mark:** FRANK.

BOOCO, GORDON,
175 Ash St, PO Box 174, Hayden, CO 81639, Phone: 970-276-3195
   Specialties: Fancy working straight knives of his design and to customer specs. **Patterns:** Hunters and Bowies. **Technical:** Grinds 440C, D2 and A2. Heat-treats. **Prices:** $150 to $350; some $600 and higher. **Remarks:** Part-time maker; first knife sold in 1984. **Mark:** Last name with push dagger artwork.

BOOS, RALPH,
6018-37A Avenue NW, Edmonton, Alberta, CANADA T6L 1H4, Phone: 780-463-7094
   Specialties: Classic, fancy and fantasy miniature knives and swords of his design or to customer specs. **Patterns:** Bowies, daggers and swords. **Technical:** Hand files O1, stainless and Damascus. Engraves and carves. Does heat bluing and acid etching. **Prices:** $125 to $350; some to $1000. **Remarks:** Part-time maker; first knife sold in 1982. **Mark:** First initials back to back.

BOOTH, PHILIP W,
301 S Jeffery Ave, Ithaca, MI 48847, Phone: 989- 875-2844, Web: wwwphilipbooth.com
   Specialties: Automatics and lock back. Folding knives of his design, some liner locks. **Patterns:** Auto lock backs, liner locks, classic pattern multi-blades. **Technical:** Grinds ATS-34, 440C, 1095 and commercial Damascus. Prefers natural materials, offers file work and scrimshaw. **Prices:** $200 and up. **Remarks:** Part-time maker, first knife sold in 1991. **Mark:** Last name or name with city and map logo.

BORGER, WOLF,
Benzstrasse 8, 76676 Graben-Neudorf, GERMANY, Phone: 07255-72303, Fax: 07255-72304, wolf@messerschmied.de; Web: www.messerschmied.de
   Specialties: High-tech working and using straight knives and folders, many with corkscrews or other tools, of his design. **Patterns:** Hunters, Bowies and folders with various locking systems. **Technical:** Grinds 440C, ATS-34 and CPM. Uses stainless Damascus. **Prices:** $250 to $900; some to $1500. **Remarks:** Full-time maker; first knife sold in 1975. **Mark:** Howling wolf and name; first name on Damascus blades.

BOSE, REESE,
PO Box 61, Shelburn, IN 47879, Phone: 812-397-5114
   Specialties: Traditional working and using knives in standard patterns and multi-blade folders. **Patterns:** Multi-blade slip-joints. **Technical:** ATS-34, D2 and CPM 440V. **Prices:** $275 to $1500. **Remarks:** Full-time maker; first knife sold in 1992. Photos by Jack Busfield. **Mark:** R. Bose.

BOSE, TONY,
7252 N. County Rd, 300 E., Shelburn, IN 47879-9778, Phone: 812-397-5114
   Specialties: Traditional working and using knives in standard patterns; multi-blade folders. **Patterns:** Multi-blade slip-joints. **Technical:** Grinds commercial Damascus, ATS-34 and D2. **Prices:** $400 to $1200. **Remarks:** Full-time maker; first knife sold in 1972. **Mark:** First initial, last name, city, state.

BOSSAERTS, CARL,
Rua Albert Einstein 906, 14051-110, Ribeirao Preto, S.P., BRAZIL, Phone: 016 633 7063
   Specialties: Working and using straight knives of his design, to customer specs and in standard patterns. **Patterns:** Hunters, fighters and utility/camp knives. **Technical:** Grinds ATS-34, 440V and 440C; does filework. **Prices:** 60 to $400. **Remarks:** Part-time maker; first knife sold in 1992. **Mark:** Initials joined together.

BOST, ROGER E,
30511 Cartier Dr, Palos Verdes, CA 90275-5629, Phone: 310- 541-6833, rogerbost@cox.net
   Specialties: Hunters, fighters, boot, utility. **Patterns:** Loveless-style. **Technical:** ATS-34, 60-61RC, stock removal and forge. **Prices:** $300 and up. **Remarks:** First knife sold in 1990. Cal. Knifemakers Assn., ABS. **Mark:** Diamond with initials inside and Palos Verdes California around outside.

BOSWORTH, DEAN,
329 Mahogany Dr, Key Largo, FL 33037, Phone: 305-451-1564
   Specialties: Free hand hollow ground working knives with hand rubbed satin finish, filework and inlays. **Patterns:** Bird and Trout, hunters, skinners, fillet, Bowies, miniatures. **Technical:** Using 440C, ATS-34, D2, Meier Damascus, custom wet formed sheaths. **Prices:** $250 and up. **Remarks:** Part-time maker; first knife made in 1985. Member Florida Knifemakers Assoc. **Mark:** BOZ stamped in block letters.

BOURBEAU, JEAN YVES,
15 Rue Remillard, Notre Dame, Ile Perrot, Quebec, CANADA J7V 8M9, Phone: 514-453-1069
   Specialties: Fancy/embellished and fantasy folders of his design. **Patterns:** Bowies, fighters and locking folders. **Technical:** Grinds 440C, ATS-34 and Damascus. Carves precious wood for handles. **Prices:** $150 to $1000. **Remarks:** Part-time maker; first knife sold in 1994. **Mark:** Interlaced initials.

BOUSE, D. MICHAEL,
1010 Victoria Pl, Waldorf, MD 20602, Phone: 301-843-0449
   Specialties: Traditional and working/using straight knives of his design. **Patterns:** Daggers, fighters and hunters. **Technical:** Forges 5160 and Damascus; grinds D2; differential hardened blades; decorative handle pins. **Prices:** $125 to $350. **Remarks:** Spare-time maker; first knife sold in 1992. Doing business as Michael's Handmade Knives. **Mark:** Etched last name.

BOWEN, TILTON,
189 Mt Olive Rd, Baker, WV 26801, Phone: 304-897- 6159
   Specialties: Straight, stout working knives. **Patterns:** Hunters, fighters and boots; also offers buckskinner and throwing knives. All his D2-blades since 1st of year, 1997 are Deep Cryogenic processed. **Technical:** Grinds D2 and 4140. **Prices:** $70 to $295. **Remarks:** Full-time maker; first knife sold in 1982-1983. Sells wholesale to dealers. **Mark:** Initials and BOWEN BLADES, WV.

BOWLES, CHRIS,
PO Box 985, Reform, AL 35481, Phone: 205-375- 6162
   Specialties: Working/using straight knives, and period pieces. **Patterns:** Utility, tactical, hunting, neck knives, machetes, and swords. **Grinds:** 0-1, 154 cm, BG-42, 440V. **Prices:** $50 to $400 some higher. **Remarks:** Full-time maker. **Mark:** Bowles stamped or Bowles etched in script.

BOXER, BO,
LEGEND FORGE, 6477 Hwy 93 S #134, Whitefish, MT 59937, Phone: 505-799-0173, legendforge@aol.com; Web: www.legendforgesknives.com
   Specialties: Handmade hunting knives, Damascus hunters. Most are antler handled. Also, hand forged Damascus steel. **Patterns:** Hunters and Bowies. **Prices:** $125 to $2500 on some very exceptional Damascus knives. **Remarks:** Makes his own custom leather sheath stamped with maker stamp. His knives are used by the outdoorsman of the Smoky Mountains, North Carolina, and the Rockies of Montana and New Mexico. Spends one-half of the year in Montana and the other part of the year in Taos, New Mexico. **Mark:** The name "Legend Forge" hand engraved on every blade.

BOYD, FRANCIS,
1811 Prince St, Berkeley, CA 94703, Phone: 510-841- 7210
   Specialties: Folders and kitchen knives, Japanese swords. **Patterns:** Push-button sturdy locking folders; San Francisco-style chef's knives. **Technical:** Forges and grinds; mostly uses high-carbon steels. **Prices:** Moderate to heavy. **Remarks:** Designer. **Mark:** Name.

BOYE—BROADWELL

BOYE, DAVID,
PO Box 1238, Dolan Springs, AZ 86441, Phone: 800- 853-1617, Fax: 928-767-4273, boye@cltlink.net; Web: www.boyeknives.com
Specialties: Folders and Boye Basics. Forerunner in the use of dendritic steel and dendritic cobalt for blades. **Patterns:** Lockback folders and fixed blade sheath knives in cobalt. **Technical:** Casts blades in cobalt. **Prices:** From $129 to $360. **Remarks:** Part-time maker; author of *Step- by-Step Knifemaking*. **Mark:** Name.

BOYER, MARK,
10515 Woodinville Dr #17, Bothell, WA 98011, Phone: 206-487-9370, boyerbl@mail.eskimo.com
Specialties: High-tech and working/using straight knives of his design. **Patterns:** Fighters and utility/camp knives. **Technical:** Grinds 1095 and D2. Offers Kydex sheaths; heat-treats. **Prices:** $45 to $120. **Remarks:** Part-time maker; first knife sold in 1994. Doing business as Boyer Blades. **Mark:** Eagle holding two swords with name.

BOYES, TOM,
731 Jean Ct, Addison, WI 53002, Phone: 262-391-2172
Specialties: Hunters, working knives. **Technical:** Grinds ATS-34, 440C, O1 tool steel and Damascus. **Prices:** $60 to $1000. **Remarks:** First knife sold in 1998. Doing business as R. Boyes Knives.

BOYSEN, RAYMOND A,
125 E St Patrick, Rapid Ciy, SD 57701, Phone: 605-341-7752
Specialties: Hunters and Bowies. **Technical:** High performance blades forged from 52100 and 5160. **Prices:** $200 and up. **Remarks:** American Bladesmith Society Journeyman Smith. Part-time bladesmith. **Mark:** BOYSEN.

BRACK, DOUGLAS D,
1591 Los Angeles Ave #8, Ventura, CA 93004, Phone: 805-659-1505
Specialties: Fighters, daggers, boots, Bowies. **Patterns:** One of a kind. **Technical:** Grinds 440-ATS, own Damascus. **Prices:** $300 to $3000. **Remarks:** Full-time maker; first knife sold in 1984. **Mark:** tat.

BRADBURN, GARY,
BRADBURN CUSTOM CUTLERY, 1714 Park Place, Wichita, KS 67203, Phone: 316-640-5684, gary@bradburnknives.com; Web:www.bradburnknives.com
Specialties: Specialize in clay-tempered Japanese-style knives and swords. **Patterns:** Also Bowies and fighters. **Technical:** Forge and/or grind carbon steel only. **Prices:** $150 to $1200. **Mark:** Initials GB stylized to look like Japanese character.

BRADFORD, GARRICK,
582 Guelph St, Kitchener ON, CANADA N2H- 5Y4, Phone: 519-576-9863

BRADLEY, DENNIS,
2410 Bradley Acres Rd, Blairsville, GA 30512, Phone: 706-745-4364
Specialties: Working straight knives and folders, some high-art. **Patterns:** Hunters, boots and daggers; slip-joints and two-blades. **Technical:** Grinds ATS-34, D2, 440C and commercial Damascus. **Prices:** $100 to $500; some to $2000. **Remarks:** Part-time maker; first knife sold in 1973. **Mark:** BRADLEY KNIVES in double heart logo.

BRADLEY, JOHN,
PO Box 33, Pomona Park, FL 32181, Phone: 904- 649-4739, yeldarbj@bellsouth.net
Specialties: Fixed-blade using knives. **Patterns:** Skinners, Bowies, camp knives and primitive knives. **Technical:** Hand forged from 52100, 1095 and own Damascus. **Prices:** $150 to $1000; some higher. **Remarks:** Part-time maker; first knife sold in 1988. **Mark:** Last name.

BRADSHAW, BAILEY,
PO Box 564, Diana, TX 75640, Phone: 903-968-2029, bailey@bradshawcutlery.com
Specialties: Traditional folders and contemporary front lock folders. **Patterns:** Single or multi-blade folders, Bowies. **Technical:** Grind CPM 3V, CPM 440V, CPM 420V, Forge Damascus, 52100. **Prices:** $250 to $3000. **Remarks:** Engraves, carves and does sterling silver sheaths. **Mark:** Tori arch over initials back to back.

BRANDON, MATTHEW,
4435 Meade St, Denver, CO 80211, Phone: 303-458-0786, mtbrandon@hotmail.com
Specialties: Hunters, skinners, full-tang Bowies. **Prices:** $150 to $1000. **Remarks:** Satisfaction or full refund. **Mark:** MTB.

BRANDSEY, EDWARD P,
4441 Hawkridge Ct, Janesville, WI 53546, Phone: 608-868-9010, ebrandsey@centurytel.com
Patterns: Large bowies, hunters, neck knives and buckskinner-styles. Native American influence on some. An occasional tanto, art piece. Does own scrimshaw. See Egnath's second book. Now making locking liner folders. **Technical:** ATS-34, S530V, 440-C, 0-1, and some Damascus. Paul Bos treating past 20 years. **Prices:** $250 to $600; some to $3000. **Remarks:** Full-time maker. First knife sold in 1973. **Mark:** Initials connected - registered Wisc. Trademark since March 1983.

BRANDT, MARTIN W,
833 Kelly Blvd, Springfield, OR 97477, Phone: 541-747-5422, oubob747@aol.com

BRANTON, ROBERT,
4976 Seewee Rd, Awendaw, SC 29429, Phone: 843-928-3624
Specialties: Working straight knives of his design or to customer specs; throwing knives. **Patterns:** Hunters, fighters and some miniatures. **Technical:** Grinds ATS-34, A2 and 1050; forges 5160, O1. Offers hollow- or convex-grinds. **Prices:** $25 to $400. **Remarks:** Part-time maker; first knife sold in 1985. Doing business as Pro-Flyte, Inc. **Mark:** Last name; or first and last name, city, state.

BRASCHLER, CRAIG W.,
HC4 Box 667, Doniphan, MO 63935, Phone: 593-996-5058
Specialties: Art knives, Bowies, utility hunters, slip joints, miniatures, engraving. **Technical:** Flat grinds. Does own selective heat treating. Does own engraving. **Prices:** Starting at $200. **Remarks:** Full-time maker since 2003. **Mark:** Braschler over Martin Oval stamped.

BRATCHER, BRETT,
11816 County Rd 302, Plantersville, TX 77363, Phone: 936-894-3788, Fax: (936) 894-3790, brett_bratcher@msn.com
Specialties: Hunting and skinning knives. **Patterns:** Clip and drop point. Hand forged. **Technical:** Material 5160, D2, 1095 and Damascus. **Price:** $200 to $500. **Mark:** Bratcher.

BRAY JR., W LOWELL,
6931 Manor Beach Rd, New Port Richey, FL 34652, Phone: 727-846-0830, brayknives@aol.com
Specialties: Traditional working and using straight knives and folders of his design. **Patterns:** Hunters, fighters and utility knives. **Technical:** Grinds 440C and ATS-34; forges 52100 and Damascus. **Prices:** $125 to $800. **Remarks:** Spare-time maker; first knife sold in 1992. **Mark:** Lowell Bray Knives in shield or Bray Primitive in shield.

BREED, KIM,
733 Jace Dr, Clarksville, TN 37040, Phone: 931-645-9171, sfbreed@yahoo.com
Specialties: High end through working folders and straight knives. **Patterns:** Hunters, fighters, daggers, Bowies. His design or customers. Likes one-of-a-kind designs. **Technical:** Makes own Mosiac and regular Damascus, but will use stainless steels. Offers filework and sculpted material. **Prices:** $150 to $2000. **Remarks:** Full-time maker. First knife sold in 1990. **Mark:** Last name.

BREND, WALTER,
353 Co Rd 1373, Vinemont, AL 35179, Phone: 256- 739-1987, walterbrend@hotmail.com
Specialties: Tactical-style knives, fighters, automatics. **Technical:** Grinds D-Z and 440C blade steels, 154CM steel. **Prices:** Micarta handles, titanium handles.

BRENNAN, JUDSON,
PO Box 1165, Delta Junction, AK 99737, Phone: 907-895-5153, Fax: 907-895-5404
Specialties: Period pieces. **Patterns:** All kinds of Bowies, rifle knives, daggers. **Technical:** Forges miscellaneous steels. **Prices:** Upscale, good value. **Remarks:** Muzzle-loading gunsmith; first knife sold in 1978. **Mark:** Name.

BRESHEARS, CLINT,
1261 Keats, Manhattan Beach, CA 90266, Phone: 310-372-0739, Fax: 310-372-0739, breshears1@verizon.net; Web: www.clintknives.com
Specialties: Working straight knives and folders. **Patterns:** Hunters, Bowies and survival knives. Folders are mostly hunters. **Technical:** Grinds 440C, 154CM and ATS-34; prefers mirror finishes. **Prices:** $125 to $750; some to $1800. **Remarks:** Part-time maker; first knife sold in 1978. **Mark:** First name.

BREUER, LONNIE,
PO Box 877384, Wasilla, AK 99687-7384
Specialties: Fancy working straight knives. **Patterns:** Hunters, camp knives and axes, folders and Bowies. **Technical:** Grinds 440C, AEB-L and D2; likes wire inlay, scrimshaw, decorative filing. **Prices:** $60 to $150; some to $300. **Remarks:** Part-time maker; first knife sold in 1977. **Mark:** Signature.

BRITTON, TIM,
PO Box 71, Bethania, NC 27010, Phone: 366-923-2062; 336-922-9582, timbritton@yahoo.com; Web: www.timbritton.com
Specialties: Small and simple working knives, sgian dubhs, slip joint folders and special tactical designs. **Technical:** Forges and grinds stainless steel. **Prices:** $165 to ???. **Remarks:** Veteran knifemaker. **Mark:** Etched signature.

BROADWELL, DAVID,
PO Box 4314, Wichita Falls, TX 76308, Phone: 940-692-1727, Fax: 940-692-4003, david@broadwell.com; Web: www.david.broadwell.com
Specialties: Sculpted high-art straight and folding knives. **Patterns:** Daggers, sub-hilted fighters, folders, sculpted art knives and some Bowies. **Technical:** Grinds mostly Damascus; carves; prefers natural handle materials, including stone. Some embellishment. **Prices:** $350 to $3000; some

higher. **Remarks:** Full-time maker; first knife sold in 1982. **Mark:** Stylized emblem bisecting "B"/with last name below.

BROCK, KENNETH L,
PO Box 375, 207 N Skinner Rd, Allenspark, CO 80510, Phone: 303-747-2547, brockknives@nedernet.net
Specialties: Custom designs, full-tang working knives and button lock folders of his design. **Patterns:** Hunters, miniatures and minis. **Technical:** Flat-grinds D2 and 440C; makes own sheaths; heat-treats. **Prices:** $75 to $800. **Remarks:** Full-time maker; first knife sold in 1978. **Mark:** Last name, city, state and serial number.

BRODZIAK, DAVID,
27 Stewart St, Albany, Western Australia, AUSTRALIA 6330, Phone: 61 8 9841 3314, Fax: 61898115065, brodziakomninet.net.au; Web: www.brodziakcustomknives.com

BROMLEY, PETER,
BROMLEY KNIVES, 1408 S Bettman, Spokane, WA 99212, Phone: 509-534-4235, Fax: 509-536-2666
Specialties: Period Bowies, folder, hunting knives; all sizes and shapes. **Patterns:** Bowies, boot knives, hunters, utility, folder, working knives. **Technical:** High-carbon steel (1084, 1095 and 5160). Stock removal and forge. **Prices:** $85 to $750. **Remarks:** Almost full-time, first knife sold in 1987. A.B.S. Journeyman Smith. **Mark:** Bromley, Spokane, WA.

BROOKER, DENNIS,
Rt 1, Box 12A, Derby, IA 50068, Phone: 515-533- 2103
Specialties: Fancy straight knives and folders of his design. **Patterns:** Hunters, folders and boots. **Technical:** Forges and grinds. Full-time engraver and designer; instruction available. **Prices:** Moderate to upscale. **Remarks:** Part-time maker. Takes no orders; sells only completed work. **Mark:** Name.

BROOKS, BUZZ,
2345 Yosemite Dr, Los Angles, CA 90041, Phone: 323-256-2892

BROOKS, MICHAEL,
2811 64th St, Lubbock, TX 79413, Phone: 806- 799-3088, chiang@nts-online.net
Specialties: Working straight knives of his design or to customer specs. **Patterns:** Martial art, Bowies, hunters, and fighters. **Technical:** Grinds 440C, D2 and ATS-34; offers wide variety of handle materials. **Prices:** $75 & up. **Remarks:** Part-time maker; first knife sold in 1985. **Mark:** Initials.

BROOKS, STEVE R,
1610 Dunn Ave, Walkerville, MT 59701, Phone: 406-782-5114, Fax: 406-782-5114, steve@brooksmoulds.com; Web: brooksmoulds.com
Specialties: Working straight knives and folders; period pieces. **Patterns:** Hunters, Bowies and camp knives; folding lockers; axes, tomahawks and buckskinner knives; swords and stilettos. **Technical:** Damascus and mosaic Damascus. Some knives come embellished. **Prices:** $400 to $2000. **Remarks:** Full-time maker; first knife sold in 1982. **Mark:** Lazy initials.

BROOME, THOMAS A,
1212 E. Aliak Ave, Kenai, AK 99611-8205, Phone: 907-283-9128, tomlei@ptialaska.ent; Web: www.alaskanknives.com
Specialties: Working hunters and folders **Patterns:** Traditional and custom orders. **Technical:** Grinds ATS-34, BG-42, CPM-S30V. **Prices:** $175 to $350. **Remarks:** Full-time maker; first knife sold in 1979. Doing business as Thom's Custom Knives, Alaskan Man O; Steel Knives. **Mark:** Full name, city, state.

BROTHERS, ROBERT L,
989 Philpott Rd, Colville, WA 99114, Phone: 509-684-8922
Specialties: Traditional working and using straight knives and folders of his design and to customer specs. **Patterns:** Bowies, fighters and hunters. **Technical:** Grinds D2; forges Damascus. Makes own Damascus from saw steel wire rope and chain; part-time goldsmith and stone-setter. **Prices:** $100 to $400; some higher. **Remarks:** Part-time maker; first knife sold in 1986. **Mark:** Initials and year made.

BROWER, MAX,
2016 Story St, Boone, IA 50036, Phone: 515-432-2938, mbrower@mchsi.com
Specialties: Working/using straight knives. **Patterns:** Bowies, hunters and boots. **Technical:** Grinds 440C and ATS-34. **Prices:** Start at $150. **Remarks:** Spare-time maker; first knife sold in 1981. **Mark:** Last name.

BROWN, DENNIS G,
1633 N 197th Pl, Shoreline, WA 98133, Phone: 206-542-3997, denjilbro@msn.com

BROWN, HAROLD E,
3654 NW Hwy 72, Arcadia, FL 34266, Phone: 863-494-7514, brknives@strato.net
Specialties: Fancy and exotic working knives. **Patterns:** Folders, slip-lock, locking several kinds. **Technical:** Grinds D2 and ATS-34. Embellishment available. **Prices:** $175 to $1000. **Remarks:** Part-time maker; first knife sold in 1976. **Mark:** Name and city with logo.

BROWN, JIM,
1097 Fernleigh Cove, Little Rock, AR 72210

BROWN, ROB E,
PO Box 15107, Emerald Hill 6011, Port Elizabeth, SOUTH AFRICA, Phone: 27-41-3661086, Fax: 27-41-4511731, rbknives@global.co.za
Specialties: Contemporary-designed straight knives and period pieces. **Patterns:** Utility knives, hunters, boots, fighters and daggers. **Technical:** Grinds 440C, D2, ATS-34 and commercial Damascus. Knives mostly mirror finished; African handle materials. **Prices:** $100 to $1500. **Remarks:** Full-time maker; first knife sold in 1985. **Mark:** Name and country.

BROWNE, RICK,
980 West 13th St, Upland, CA 91786, Phone: 909- 985-1728
Specialties: Sheffield pattern pocket knives. **Patterns:** Hunters, fighters and daggers. No heavy-duty knives. **Technical:** Grinds ATS-34. **Prices:** Start at $450. **Remarks:** Part-time maker; first knife sold in 1975. **Mark:** R.E. Browne, Upland, CA.

BROWNING, STEVEN W,
3400 Harrison Rd, Benton, AR 72015, Phone: 501-316-2450

BRUNCKHORST, LYLE,
COUNTRY VILLAGE, 23706 7th Ave SE Ste B, Bothell, WA 98021, Phone: 425-402-3484, bronks@bronksknifeworks.com; Web: www.bronksknifeworks.com
Specialties: Forges own Damascus with 1084 and 15N20, forges 5160, 52100. Grinds CPM 154 CM, ATS-34, S30V. Hosts Biannual Northwest School of Knifemaking and Northwest Hammer In. Offers online and in-house sharpening services and knife sharpeners. Maker of the Double L Hoofknife. Traditional working and using knives, the new patent pending Xross-Bar Lock folders, tomahawks and irridescent RR spike knives. **Patterns:** Damascus Bowies, hunters, locking folders and featuring the ultra strong locking tactical folding knnives. **Prices:** $185 to $1500; some to $3750. **Remarks:** Full-time maker; first knife made in 1976. **Mark:** Bucking horse or bronk.

BRUNER JR., FRED BRUNER BLADES,
E10910W Hilldale Dr, Fall Creek, WI 54742, Phone: 715-877-2496, brunerblades@msn.com
Specialties: Pipe tomahawks, swords, makes his own. **Patterns:** Drop point hunters. **Prices:** $65 to $1500. **Remarks:** Voting member of the Knifemakers Guild. **Mark:** Fred Bruner.

BRUNETTA, DAVID,
PO Box 4972, Laguna Beach, CA 92652, Phone: 714-497-9611
Specialties: Straights, folders and art knives. **Patterns:** Bowies, camp/hunting, folders, fighters. **Technical:** Grinds ATS-34, D2, BG42. forges O1, 52100, 5160, 1095, makes own Damascus. **Prices:** $300 to $9000. **Mark:** Circle DB logo with last name straight or curved.

BRYAN, TOM,
14822 S Gilbert Rd, Gilbert, AZ 85296, Phone: 480-812- 8529
Specialties: Straight and folding knives. **Patterns:** Drop-point hunter fighters. **Technical:** ATS-34, 154CM, 440C and A2. **Prices:** $150 to $800. **Remarks:** Part-time maker; sold first knife in 1994. DBA as T. Bryan Knives. **Mark:** T. Bryan.

BUCHANAN, THAD,
THAD BUCHANAN CUSTOM KNIVES, 915 NW Perennial Way, Prineville, OR 97754, Phone: 541-416-2556, knives@crestviewcable.com; Web: www.buchananblades.com
Specialties: Fixed blades. **Patterns:** Various hunters, trout, bird, utility, boots & fighters. **Technical:** Stock removal, high polish, variety handle materials. **Prices:** $450 to $1100. **Remarks:** 2005 and 2008 Blade in magazine handmade award for hunter/utility. 2006 Blade West best fixed blade award; 2008 Blade West best hunter/utility. **Mark:** Thad Buchanan Oregon USA.

BUCHMAN, BILL,
63312 South Rd, Bend, OR 97701-9027, Phone: 541- 382-8851
Specialties: Leather cutting knives for saddle makers and leather crafters. **Patterns:** Many. **Technical:** Sandkik-Swedish carbon steel. **Prices:** Varies: $35 to $130. **Remarks:** Full-time maker; first knife sold in 1982. **Mark:** BB & # of knife on large knives - no mark on small knives.

BUCHNER, BILL,
PO Box 73, Idleyld Park, OR 97447, Phone: 541-498- 2247, blazinhammer@earthlink.net; Web: www.home.earthlin.net/~blazinghammer
Specialties: Working straight knives, kitchen knives and high-art knives of his design. **Technical:** Uses W1, L6 and his own Damascus. Invented "spectrum metal" for letter openers, folder handles and jewelry. Likes sculpturing and carving in Damascus. **Prices:** $40 to $3000; some higher. **Remarks:** Full-time maker; first knife sold in 1978. **Mark:** Signature.

BUCHOLZ, MARK A,
PO Box 82, Holualoa, HI 96725, Phone: 808-322- 4045
Specialties: LinerLock® folders. **Patterns:** Hunters and fighters. **Technical:** Grinds ATS-34. **Prices:** Upscale. **Remarks:** Full-time maker; first knife sold in 1976. **Mark:** Name, city and state in buffalo skull logo or signature.

BUCKBEE, DONALD M,
243 South Jackson Trail, Grayling, MI 49738, Phone: 517-348-1386
Specialties: Working straight knives, some fancy, in standard patterns; concentrating on kitchen knives. **Patterns:** Kitchen knives, hunters, Bowies. **Technical:** Grinds D2, 440C, ATS-34. Makes ultra-lights in hunter patterns. **Prices:** $100 to $250; some to $350. **Remarks:** Part-time maker; first knife sold in 1984. **Mark:** Antlered bee—a buck bee.

BUCKNER, JIMMIE H,
PO Box 162, Putney, GA 31782, Phone: 229- 436-4182
Specialties: Camp knives, Bowies (one-of-a-kind), liner-lock folders, tomahawks, camp axes, neck knives for law enforcement and hide-out knives for body guards and professional people. **Patterns:** Hunters, camp knives, Bowies. **Technical:** Forges 1084, 5160 and Damascus (own), own heat treats. **Prices:** $195 to $795 and up. **Remarks:** Full-time maker; first knife sold in 1980, ABS Master Smith. **Mark:** Name over spade.

BUEBENDORF, ROBERT E,
108 Lazybrooke Rd, Monroe, CT 06468, Phone: 203-452-1769
Specialties: Traditional and fancy straight knives of his design. **Patterns:** Hand-makes and embellishes belt buckle knives. **Technical:** Forges and grinds 440C, O1, W2, 1095, his own Damascus and 154CM. **Prices:** $200 to $500. **Remarks:** Full-time maker; first knife sold in 1978. **Mark:** First and middle initials, last name and MAKER.

BULLARD, BILL,
Rt 5, Box 35, Andalusia, AL 36420, Phone: 334-222- 9003
Specialties: Traditional working and using straight knives and folders of his design. **Patterns:** Hunters, slip-joint folders and utility/camp knives and folders to customer specs. **Technical:** Forges Damascus, cable. Offers filework. **Prices:** $100 to $500; some to $1500. **Remarks:** Part- time maker; first knife sold in 1974. Doing business as Five Runs Forge. **Mark:** Last name stamped on ricasso.

BULLARD, RANDALL,
7 Mesa Dr., Canyon, TX 79015, Phone: 806- 655-0590
Specialties: Working/using straight knives and folders of his design or to customer specs. **Patterns:** Hunters, locking folders and slip-joint folders. **Technical:** Grinds O1, ATS-34 and 440C. Does file work. **Prices:** $125 to $300; some to $500. **Remarks:** Part-time maker; first knife sold in 1993. Doing business as Bullard Custom Knives. **Mark:** First and middle initials, last name, maker, city and state.

BULLARD, TOM,
117 MC 8068, Flippin, AR 72634, Phone: 870-453-3421, tbullard@southshore.com; Web: www.southshore.com/~tombullard
Specialties: Traditional folders and hunters. **Patterns:** Bowies, hunters, single and 2-blade trappers, lockback folders. **Technical:** Grinds 440-C, ATS-34, 0-1, commercial Damascus. **Prices:** $150 and up. **Remarks:** Offers filework and engraving by Norvell Foster and Terry Thies. Does not make screw-together knives. **Mark:** T Bullard.

BUMP, BRUCE D.,
1103 Rex Ln, Walla Walla, WA 99362, Phone: 509 522-2219, bruceandkaye@charter.net; Web: www.brucebumpknives.com
Specialties: Complete range of knives from field grade to "one-of-a-kind" cut and shoots. **Patterns:** Black Powder pistol/folders, "Brutus" axe/gun, shooting swords. **Technical:** Dual threat weapons of his own design inspired from early centuries. **Prices:** $250 to $20,000. **Remarks:** Full- time maker ABS mastersmith 2003. **Mark:** Bruce D. Bump, Bruce D Bump Custom Walla Walla WA.

BURDEN, JAMES,
405 Kelly St, Burkburnett, TX 76354

BURGER, FRED,
Box 436, Munster 4278, Kwa-Zulu Natal, SOUTH AFRICA, Phone: 27 39 3192316, info@swordcane.com; Web: www.swordcane.com
Specialties: Sword canes, folders, and fixed blades. **Patterns:** 440C and carbon steel blades. **Technical:** Double hollow ground and Poniard-style blades. **Prices:** $300 to $3000. **Remarks:** Full-time maker with son, Barry, since 1987. Member South African Guild. **Mark:** Last name in oval pierced by a dagger.

BURGER, PON,
12 Glenwood Ave, Woodlands, Bulawayo, ZIMBABWE 75514
Specialties: Collector's items. **Patterns:** Fighters, locking folders of traditional styles, buckles. **Technical:** Scrimshaws 440C blade. Uses polished buffalo horn with brass fittings. Cased in buffalo hide book. **Prices:** $450 to $1100. **Remarks:** Full-time maker; first knife sold in 1973. Doing business as Burger Products. **Mark:** Spirit of Africa.

BURKE, BILL,
12 Chapman In, Boise, ID 83716, Phone: 208-756-3797, burke531@salmoninternet.com
Specialties: Hand-forged working knives. **Patterns:** Fowler pronghorn, clip point and drop point hunters. **Technical:** Forges 52100 and 5160. Makes own Damascus from 15N20 and 1084. **Prices:** $450 and up. **Remarks:** Dedicated to fixed-blade high-performance knives. ABS Journeyman. Also makes "Ed Fowler" miniatures. **Mark:** Initials connected.

BURKE, DAN,
22001 Ole Barn Rd, Edmond, OK 73003, Phone: 405- 341-3406, Fax: 405-340-3333, burkeknives@aol.com
Specialties: Slip joint folders. **Patterns:** Traditional folders. **Technical:** Grinds D2 and BG-42. Prefers natural handle materials; heat-treats. **Prices:** $440 to $1900. **Remarks:** Full-time maker; first knife sold in 1976. **Mark:** First initial and last name.

BURRIS, PATRICK R,
11078 Crystal Lynn Ct, Jacksonville, FL 32226, Phone: 904-757-3938, keenedge@comcast.net
Specialties: Traditional straight knives. **Patterns:** Hunters, Bowies, locking liner folders. **Technical:** Flat grinds CPM stainless and Damascus. **Remarks:** Offers filework, embellishment, exotic materials and Damascus **Mark:** Last name in script.

BURROWS, CHUCK,
WILD ROSE TRADING CO, 289 La Posta Canyon Rd, Durango, CO 81303, Phone: 970-259-8396, chuck@wrtcleather.com; Web: www.wrtcleather.com
Specialties: Presentation knives, hawks, and sheaths based on the styles of the American frontier incorporating carving, beadwork, rawhide, braintan, and other period correct materials. Also makes other period style knives such as Scottish Dirks and Moorish jambiyahs. **Patterns:** Bowies, Dags, tomahawks, war clubs, and all other 18th and 19th century frontier style edged weapons and tools. **Technical:** Carbon steel only: 5160, 1080/1084, 1095, O1, Damascus-Our Frontier Shear Steel, plus other styles available on request. Forged knives, hawks, etc. are made in collaborations with bladesmiths. Gib Guignard (under the name of Cactus Rose) and Mark Williams (under the name UB Forged). Blades are usually forge finished and all items are given an aged period look. **Prices:** $500 plus. **Remarks:** Full-time maker, first knife sold in 1973. 40+ years experience working leather. **Mark:** A lazy eight or lazy eight with a capital T at the center. On leather either the lazy eight with T or a WRTC makers stamp.

BURROWS, STEPHEN R,
1020 Osage St, Humboldt, KS 66748, Phone: 816-921-1573
Specialties: Fantasy straight knives of his design, to customer specs and in standard patterns; period pieces. **Patterns:** Fantasy, bird and trout knives, daggers, fighters and hunters. **Technical:** Forges 5160 and 1095 high-carbon steel, O1 and his Damascus. Offers lost wax casting in bronze or silver of cross guards and pommels. **Prices:** $65 to $600; some to $2000. **Remarks:** Full-time maker; first knife sold in 1983. Doing business as Gypsy Silk. **Mark:** Etched name.

BUSCH, STEVE,
1989 Old Town Loop, Oakland, OR 97462, Phone: 541-459-2833, steve@buschcustomknives.com; Web: wwwbuschcustomknives.blademakers.com
Specialties: D/A automatic right and left handed, folders, fixed blade working mainly in Damascus file work, functional art knives, nitrate bluing, heat bluing most all scale materials. **Prices:** $150 to $2000. **Remarks:** Trained under Vallotton family 3 1/2 years on own since 2002. **Mark:** Signature and date of completion on all knives.

BUSFIELD, JOHN,
153 Devonshire Circle, Roanoke Rapids, NC 27870, Phone: 252-537-3949, Fax: 252-537-8704, busfield@charter.net; Web: www.busfieldknives.com
Specialties: Investor-grade folders; high-grade working straight knives. **Patterns:** Original price-style and trailing-point interframe and sculpted-frame folders, drop-point hunters and semi-skinners. **Technical:** Grinds 154CM and ATS-34. Offers interframes, gold frames and inlays; uses jade, agate and lapis. **Prices:** $275 to $2000. **Remarks:** Full-time maker; first knife sold in 1979. **Mark:** Last name and address.

BUSSE, JERRY,
11651 Co Rd 12, Wauseon, OH 43567, Phone: 419- 923-6471
Specialties: Working straight knives. **Patterns:** Heavy combat knives and camp knives. **Technical:** Grinds D2, A2, INFI. **Prices:** $1100 to $3500. **Remarks:** Full-time maker; first knife sold in 1983. **Mark:** Last name in logo.

BUTLER, BART,
822 Seventh St, Ramona, CA 92065, Phone: 760-789- 6431

BUTLER, JOHN,
777 Tyre Rd, Havana, FL 32333, Phone: 850-539-5742
Specialties: Hunters, Bowies, period. **Technical:** Damascus, 52100, 5160, L6 steels. **Prices:** $80 and up. **Remarks:** Making knives since 1986. Journeyman (ABS). **Mark:** JB.

BUTLER, JOHN R,
20162 6th Ave N E, Shoreline, WA 98155, Phone: 206-362-3847, rjjjrb@sprynet.com

BUXTON, BILL,
155 Oak Bend Rd, Kaiser, MO 65047, Phone: 573-348- 3577, camper@yhti.net; Web: www.geocities.com/buxtonknives
Specialties: Forged fancy and working straight knives and folders. Mostly one-of-a-kind pieces. **Patterns:** Fighters, daggers, Bowies, hunters, liner-lock folders, axes and tomahawks. **Technical:** Forges 52100, 0- 1, 1080. Makes own Damascus (mosaic and random patterns) from 1080, 1095, 15n20, and powdered metals 1084 and 4800a. Offers sterling silver inlay, n/s pin patterning and pewter pouring on axe and hawk handles. **Prices:** $300 to $1500. **Remarks:** Full-time maker, sold first knife in 1998. **Mark:** First and last name.

BYBEE, BARRY J,
795 Lock Rd. E, Cadiz, KY 42211-8615
Specialties: Working straight knives of his design. **Patterns:** Hunters, fighters, boot knives, tantos and Bowies. **Technical:** Grinds ATS-34, 440C. Likes stag and Micarta for handle materials. **Prices:** $125 to $200; some

to $1000. **Remarks:** Part-time maker; first knife sold in 1968. **Mark:** Arrowhead logo with name, city and state.

BYRD, WESLEY L,
189 Countryside Dr, Evensville, TN 37332, Phone: 423-775-3826, w.l.byrd@worldnet.att.net
    Specialties: Hunters, fighters, Bowies, dirks, sgian dubh, utility, and camp knives. **Patterns:** Wire rope, random patterns. Twists, W's, Ladder, Kite Tail. **Technical:** Uses 52100, 1084, 5160, L6, and 15n20. **Prices:** Starting at $180. **Remarks:** Prefer to work with customer for their design preferences. ABS Journeyman Smith. **Mark:** BYRD, WB <X.

C

CABE, JERRY (BUDDY),
62 McClaren Ln, Hattieville, AR 72063, Phone: 501-354-3581

CABRERA, SERGIO B,
24500 Broad Ave, Wilmington, CA 90744

CAFFREY, EDWARD J,
2608 Central Ave West, Great Falls, MT 59404, Phone: 406-727-9102, caffreyknives@gmail.com; Web: www.caffreyknives.net
    Specialties: One-of-a-kind using and collector quality pieces. Will accept some customer designs. **Patterns:** Bowies, folders, hunters, fighters, camp/utility, tomahawks and hatchets. **Technical:** Forges all types of Damascus, specializing in Mosaic Damascus, 52100, 5160, 1080/1084 and most other commonly forged steels. **Prices:** Starting at $185; typical hunters start at $400; collector pieces can range into the thousands. **Remarks:** Offers one-on-one basic and advanced bladesmithing classes. ABS Mastersmith. Full-time maker. **Mark:** Stamped last name and MS on straight knives. Etched last name with MS on folders.

CALDWELL, BILL,
255 Rebecca, West Monroe, LA 71292, Phone: 318-323-3025
    Specialties: Straight knives and folders with machined bolsters and liners. **Patterns:** Fighters, Bowies, survival knives, tomahawks, razors and push knives. **Technical:** Owns and operates a very large, well-equipped blacksmith and bladesmith shop with six large forges and eight power hammers. **Prices:** $400 to $3500; some to $10,000. **Remarks:** Full-time maker and self-styled blacksmith; first knife sold in 1962. **Mark:** Wild Bill and Sons.

CALLAHAN, F TERRY,
PO Box 880, Boerne, TX 78006, Phone: 830-981-8274, Fax: 830-981-8279, ftclaw@gvtc.com
    Specialties: Custom hand-forged edged knives, collectible and functional. **Patterns:** Bowies, folders, daggers, hunters & camp knives . **Technical:** Forges 5160, 1095 and his own Damascus. Offers filework and handmade sheaths. **Prices:** $125 to $2000. **Remarks:** First knife sold in 1990. ABS/Journeyman Bladesmith. **Mark:** Initials inside a keystone symbol.

CALVERT JR., ROBERT W (BOB),
911 Julia, PO Box 858, Rayville, LA 71269, Phone: 318-728-4113, Fax: (318) 728-0000, rcalvert@fredmorganins.com
    Specialties: Using and hunting knives; your design or his. Since 1990. **Patterns:** Forges own Damascus; all patterns. **Technical:** 5160, D2, 52100, 1084. Prefers natural handle material. **Prices:** $250 and up. **Remarks:** TOMB Member ABS, Journeyman Smith. Board of directors- ABS. **Mark:** Calvert (Block) J S.

CAMERER, CRAIG,
3766 Rockbridge Rd, Chesterfield, IL 62630, Phone: 618-753-2147, craig@camererknives.com; Web: www.camererknives.com
    Specialties: Everyday carry knives, hunters and Bowies. **Patterns:** D-guard, historical recreations and fighters. **Technical:** Most of his knives are forged to shape. **Prices:** $100 and up. **Remarks:** Member of the ABS and PKA. Journeymen Smith ABS.

CAMERON, RON G,
PO Box 183, Logandale, NV 89021, Phone: 702-398-3356, rntcameron@mvdsl.com
    Specialties: Fancy and embellished working/using straight knives and folders of his design. **Patterns:** Bowies, hunters and utility/camp knives. **Technical:** Grinds ATS-34, AEB-L and Devin Thomas Damascus or own Damascus from 1084 and 15N20. Does filework, fancy pins, mokume fittings. Uses exotic hardwoods, stag and Micarta for handles. Pearl & mammoth ivory. **Prices:** $175 to $850 some to $1000. **Remarks:** Part-time maker; first knife sold in 1994. Doing business as Cameron Handmade Knives. **Mark:** Last name, town, state or last name.

CAMERON HOUSE,
2001 Delaney Rd Se, Salem, OR 97306, Phone: 503-585-3286
    Specialties: Working straight knives. **Patterns:** Hunters, Bowies, fighters. **Technical:** Grinds ATS-34, 530V, 154CM. **Remarks:** Part-time maker, first knife sold in 1993. **Prices:** $150 and up. **Mark:** HOUSE.

CAMPBELL, COURTNAY M,
PO Box 23009, Columbia, SC 29224, Phone: 803-787-0151

CAMPBELL, DICK,
196 Graham Rd, Colville, WA 99114, Phone: 509-684-6080, dicksknives@aol.com
    Specialties: Working straight knives, folders & period pieces. **Patterns:**

Hunters, fighters, boots: 19th century Bowies, Japanese swords and daggers. **Technical:** Grinds 440C, 154CM. **Prices:** $200 to $2500. **Remarks:** Full-time maker. First knife sold in 1975. **Mark:** Name.

CAMPOS, IVAN,
R.XI de Agosto 107, Tatui, SP, BRAZIL 18270-000, Phone: 00-55-15-2518092, Fax: 00-55-15-2594368, ivan@ivancampos.com; Web: www.ivancompos.com
    Specialties: Brazilian handmade and antique knives.

CANDRELLA, JOE,
1219 Barness Dr, Warminster, PA 18974, Phone: 215-675-0143
    Specialties: Working straight knives, some fancy. **Patterns:** Daggers, boots, Bowies. **Technical:** Grinds 440C and 154CM. **Prices:** $100 to $200; some to $1000. **Remarks:** Part-time maker; first knife sold in 1985. Does business as Franjo. **Mark:** FRANJO with knife as J.

CANNADY, DANIEL L,
Box 301, 358 Parkwood Terrace, Allendale, SC 29810, Phone: 803-584-2813, Fax: 803-584-2813
    Specialties: Working straight knives and folders in standard patterns. **Patterns:** Drop-point hunters, Bowies, skinners, fishing knives with concave grind, steak knives and kitchen cutlery. **Technical:** Grinds D2, 440C and ATS-34. **Prices:** $65 to $325; some to $1000. **Remarks:** Full-time maker; first knife sold in 1980. **Mark:** Last name above Allendale, S.C.

CANNON, RAYMOND W,
PO Box 1412, Homer, AK 99603, Phone: 907-235-7779, Web: www.cannon@xyz.net
    Specialties: Fancy working knives, folders and swords of his design or to customer specs; many one-of-a-kind pieces. **Patterns:** Bowies, daggers and skinners. **Technical:** Forges & grinds O1, A6, 52100, 5160, 1050, 1084 and his own combinations for Damascus. **Remarks:** First knife sold in 1984. **Mark:** Cannon Alaska or "Hand forged by Wes Cannon."

CANOY, ANDREW B,
3420 Fruchey Ranch Rd, Hubbard Lake, MI 49747, Phone: 810-266-6039, canoy1@shianet.org

CANTER, RONALD E,
96 Bon Air Circle, Jackson, TN 38305, Phone: 731-668-1780, canterr@charter.net
    Specialties: Traditional working knives to customer specs. **Patterns:** Beavertail skinners, Bowies, hand axes and folding lockers. **Technical:** Grinds 440C, Micarta & deer antler. **Prices:** $75 and up. **Remarks:** Spare-time maker; first knife sold in 1973. **Mark:** Three last initials intertwined.

CANTRELL, KITTY D,
19720 Hwy 78, Ramona, CA 92076, Phone: 760-788-8304

CAPDEPON, RANDY,
553 Joli Rd, Carencro, LA 70520, Phone: 318-896-4113, Fax: 318-896-8753
    Specialties: Straight knives and folders of his design. **Patterns:** Hunters and locking folders. **Technical:** Grinds ATS-34, 440C and D2. **Prices:** $200 to $600. **Remarks:** Part-time maker; first knife made in 1992. Doing business as Capdepon Knives. **Mark:** Last name.

CAPDEPON, ROBERT,
829 Vatican Rd, Carencro, LA 70520, Phone: 337-896-8753, Fax: 318-896-8753
    Specialties: Traditional straight knives and folders of his design. **Patterns:** Boots, hunters and locking folders. **Technical:** Grinds ATS-34, 440C and D2. Hand-rubbed finish on blades. Likes natural horn materials for handles, including ivory. Offers engraving. **Prices:** $250 to $750. **Remarks:** Full-time maker; first knife made in 1992. **Mark:** Last name.

CAREY, PETER,
P.O. Box 4712, Lago Vista, TX 78645, Phone: 512-358-4839, Web: www.careyblade.com
    Specialties: Tactical folders, Every Day Carry to presentation grade. Working straight knives, hunters, and tactical. **Patterns:** High-tech patterns of his own design, Linerlocks, Framelocks, Flippers. **Technical:** Hollow grings CPM154, S30V, 154cm, stainless Damascus, Talonite, Stellite. Uses titanium, carbon fiber, G10, and select natural handle materials. **Prices:** Starting at $400. **Remarks:** Full-time maker, first knife sold in 2002. **Mark:** Last name in diamond.

CARLISLE, JEFF,
PO Box 282 12753 Hwy 200, Simms, MT 59477, Phone: 406-264-5693

CARLSON, KELLY,
54 S Holt Hill, Antrim, NH 03440, Phone: 603-588-2765, kellycarlson@tds.net; Web: www.carlsonknives.com
    Specialties: Unique folders of maker's own design. **Patterns:** One-of-a-kind, artistic folders, mostly of liner-lock design, along with interpretations of traditional designs. **Technical:** Grinds and heat treats S30V, D2, ATS-34, stainless and carbon Damascus steels. Prefers hand sanded finishes and natural ivories and pearls, in conjunction with decorative accents obtained from mosaic Damascus, Damascus and various exotic materials. **Prices:** $400 to $4000. **Remarks:** Full-time maker as of 2002, first knife sold in 1975. New mechanism designs include assisted openers, top locks, and galvanic slipjoints powered by neodymium magnets, patent pending. **Mark:** "Carlson," usually inside backspacer.

CAROLINA CUSTOM KNIVES, SEE TOMMY MCNABB,

CARPENTER, RONALD W,
Rt. 4 Box 323, Jasper, TX 75951, Phone: 409-384-4087

CARR, JOSEPH E.,
W183 N8974 Maryhill Drive, Menomonee Falls, WI 53051, Phone: 920-625-3607, carsmith1@SBCGlobal.net; Web: Hembrook3607@charter.net
Specialties: JC knives. **Patterns:** Hunters, Bowies, fighting knives, every day carries. **Technical:** Grinds ATS-34 and Damascus. **Prices:** $200 to $750. **Remarks:** Full-time maker for 2 years, being taught by Ron Hembrook.

CARR, TIM,
3660 Pillon Rd, Muskegon, MI 49445, Phone: 231-766-3582
Specialties: Hunters, camp knives. **Patterns:** His or yours. **Technical:** Hand forges 5160, 52100 and Damascus. **Prices:** $125 to $700. **Remarks:** Part-time maker. **Mark:** The letter combined from maker's initials TRC.

CARRILLO, DWAINE,
C/O AIRKAT KNIVES, 1021 SW 15th St, Moore, OK 73160, Phone: 405-503-5879, Web: www.airkatknives.com

CARROLL, CHAD,
12182 McClelland, Grant, MI 49327, Phone: 231-834-9183, CHAD724@msn.com
Specialties: Hunters, Bowies, folders, swords, tomahawks. **Patterns:** Fixed blades, folders. **Prices:** $100 to $2000. **Remarks:** ABS Journeyman May 2002. **Mark:** A backwards C next to a forward C, maker's initials.

CARSON, HAROLD J "KIT",
1076 Brizendine Lane, Vine Grove, KY 40175, Phone: 270 877-6300, Fax: 270 877 6338, KCKnives@bbtel.com; Web: www.kitcarsonknives.com/album
Specialties: Military fixed blades and folders; art pieces. **Patterns:** Fighters, D handles, daggers, combat folders and Crosslock-styles, tactical folders, tactical fixed blades. **Technical:** Grinds Stellite 6K, Talonite, CPM steels, Damascus. **Prices:** $400 to $750; some to $5000. **Remarks:** Full-time maker; first knife sold in 1973. **Mark:** Name stamped or engraved.

CARTER, FRED,
5219 Deer Creek Rd, Wichita Falls, TX 76302, Phone: 904-723-4020
Specialties: High-art investor-class straight knives; some working hunters and fighters. **Patterns:** Classic daggers, Bowies; interframe, stainless and blued steel folders with gold inlay. **Technical:** Grinds a variety of steels. Uses no glue or solder. Engraves and inlays. **Prices:** Generally upscale. **Remarks:** Full-time maker. **Mark:** Signature in oval logo.

CARTER, MURRAY M,
PO Box 307, Vernonia, OR 97064, Phone: 503-429-0447, murray@cartercutlery.com; Web:www.cartercutlery.com
Specialties: Traditional Japanese cutlery, utilizing San soh ko (three layer) or Kata-ha (two layer) blade construction. Laminated neck knives, traditional Japanese etc. **Patterns:** Works from over 200 standard Japanese and North American designs. **Technical:** Hot forges and cold forges Hitachi white steel #1, Hitachi blue super steel exclusively. **Prices:** $800 to $10,000. **Remarks:** Owns and operates North America's most exclusive traditional Japanese bladesmithing school; web site available at which viewers can subscribe to 10 free knife sharpening and maintenance reports. **Mark:** Name in cursive, often appearing with Japanese characters. **Other:** Very interestng and informative monthly newsletter.

CASEY, KEVIN,
10583 N. 42nd St., Hickory Corners, MI 49060, Phone: 269-719-7412, kevincasey@tds.net; Web: www.kevincaseycustomknives.com
Specialties: Fixed blades and folders. **Patterns:** Liner lock folders and feather Damascus pattern, mammoth ivory. **Technical:** Forges Damascus and carbon steels. **Prices:** Starting at $700. **Remarks:** Member ABS, Knifemakers Guild, Custom Knifemakers Collectors Association.

CASHEN, KEVIN R,
5615 Tyler St, Hubbardston, MI 48845, Phone: 989-981-6780, kevin@cashenblades.com; Web: www.cashenblades.com
Specialties: Working straight knives, high art pattern welded swords, traditional renaissance and ethnic pieces. **Patterns:** Hunters, Bowies, utility knives, swords, daggers. **Technical:** Forges 1095, 1084 and his own O1/ L6 Damascus. **Prices:** $100 to $4000+. **Remarks:** Full-time maker; first knife sold in 1985. Doing business as Matherton Forge. **Mark:** Black letter Old English initials and Master Smith stamp.

CASTEEL, DIANNA,
PO Box 63, Monteagle, TN 37356, Phone: 931-212-4341, ddcasteel@charter.net; Web: www.casteelcustomknives.com
Specialties: Small, delicate daggers and miniatures; most knives one-of-a-kind. **Patterns:** Daggers, boot knives, fighters and miniatures. **Technical:** Grinds 440C. Offers stainless Damascus. **Prices:** Start at $350; miniatures start at $250. **Remarks:** Full-time maker. **Mark:** Di in script.

CASTEEL, DOUGLAS,
PO Box 63, Monteagle, TN 37356, Phone: 931-212-4341, Fax: 931-723-1856, ddcasteel@charter.net; Web: www.casteelcustomknives.com
Specialties: One-of-a-kind collector-class period pieces. **Patterns:** Daggers, Bowies, swords and folders. **Technical:** Grinds 440C. Offers gold and silver castings.Offers stainless Damascus **Prices:** Upscale. **Remarks:** Full-time maker; first knife sold in 1982. **Mark:** Last name.

CASTELLUCIO, RICH,
220 Stairs Rd, Amsterdam, NY 12010, Phone: 518-843-5540, rcastellucio@nycap.rr.com
Patterns: Bowies, push daggers, and fantasy knives. **Technical:** Uses ATS-34, 440C, 154CM. I use stabilized wood, bone for the handles. Guards are made of copper, brass, stainless, nickle, and mokume.

CASTON, DARRIEL,
3725 Duran Circle, Sacramento, CA 95821, Phone: 916-359-0613, dcaston@surewest.net
Specialties: Investment grade jade handle folders of his design and gentleman folders. **Patterns:** Folders: slipjoints and lockback. Will be making linerlocks in the near future. **Technical:** Small gentleman folders for office and desk warriors. Grinds ATS-34, 154CM, S30V and Damascus. **Prices:** $250 to $900. **Remarks:** Part-time maker; won best new maker at first show in Sept 2004. **Mark:** Etched rocket ship with "Darriel Caston" or just "Caston" on inside spring on Damascus and engraved knives.

CASWELL, JOE,
173 S Ventu Park Rd, Newbury, CA 91320, Phone: 805-499-0707, Web:www.caswellknives.com
Specialties: Historic pattern welded knives and swords, hand forged. Also high precision folding and fixed blade "gentleman" and "tactical" knives of his design, period firearms. Inventor of the "In-Line" retractable pocket clip for folding knives. **Patterns:** Hunters, tactical/utility, fighters, bowies, daggers, pattern welded medieval swords, precision folders. **Technical:** Forges own Damascus especially historic forms. Sometimes uses modern stainless steels and Damascus of other makers. Makes some pieces entirely by hand, others using the latest CNC techniques and by hand. Makes sheaths too.**Prices:**$100-$5,500. **Remarks:**Full time makers since 1995. Making mostly historic recreations for exclusive clientele. Recently moving into folding knives and 'modern' designs. **Mark:**CASWELL or CASWELL USA Accompanied by a mounted knight logo.

CATOE, DAVID R,
4024 Heutte Dr, Norfolk, VA 23518, Phone: 757-480-3191
Technical: Does own forging, Damascus and heat treatments. **Price:** $200 to $500; some higher. **Remarks:** Part-time maker; trained by Dan Maragni 1985-1988; first knife sold 1989. **Mark:** Leaf of a camellia.

CAWTHORNE, CHRISTOPHER A,
PO Box 604, Wrangell, AK 99929, Phone: 661-902-3724, chriscawthorne@hotmail.com
Specialties: High-carbon steel, cable wire rope, silver wire inlay. **Patterns:** Forge welded Damascus and wire rope, random pattern. **Technical:** Hand forged, 50 lb. little giant power hammer, W-2, 0-1, L6, 1095. **Prices:** $650 to $2500. **Remarks:** School ABS 1985 w/Bill Moran, hand forged, heat treat. **Mark:** Cawthorne, forged in stamp.

CENTOFANTE, FRANK,
PO Box 928, Madisonville, TN 37354-0928, Phone: 423-442-5767, Fax: 423-420-0871, frankcentofante@bellsouth.net
Specialties: Fancy working folders. **Patterns:** Lockers and liner locks. **Technical:** Grinds ATS-34 and CPM154; hand-rubbed satin finish on blades. **Prices:** $600 to $1200. **Remarks:** Full-time maker; first knife sold in 1968. **Mark:** Name, city, state.

CEPRANO, PETER J.,
213 Townsend Brooke Rd., Auburn, ME 04210, Phone: 207-786-5322, bpknives@gmail.com
Specialties: Traditional working/using straight knives; tactical/defense straight knives. Own designs or to a customer's specs. **Patterns:** Hunters, skinners, utility, Bowies, fighters, camp and survival, neck knives. **Technical:** Forges 1095, 5160, W2, 52100 and old files; grinds CPM154cm, ATS-34, 440C, D2, CPMs30v, Damascus from other makes and other tool steels. Hand-sewn and tooled leather and Kydex sheaths. **Prices:** Starting at $125. **Remarks:** Full-time maker, first knife sold in 2001. Doing business as Big Pete Knives. **Mark:** Bold BPK over small BigPeteKnivesUSA.

CHAFFEE, JEFF L,
14314 N. Washington St, PO Box 1, Morris, IN 47033, Phone: 812-934-6350
Specialties: Fancy working and utility folders and straight knives. **Patterns:** Fighters, dagger, hunter and locking folders. **Technical:** Grinds commercial Damascus, 440C, ATS-34, D2 and O1. Prefers natural handle materials. **Prices:** $350 to $2000. **Remarks:** Part-time maker; first knife sold in 1988. **Mark:** Last name.

CHAMBERLAIN, CHARLES R,
PO Box 156, Barren Springs, VA 24313-0156, Phone: 703-381-5137

CHAMBERLAIN, JON A,
15 S. Lombard, E. Wenatchee, WA 98802, Phone: 509-884-6591
Specialties: Working and kitchen knives to customer specs; exotics on special order. **Patterns:** Over 100 patterns in stock. **Technical:** Prefers ATS-34, D2, L6 and Damascus. **Prices:** Start at $50. **Remarks:** First knife sold in 1986. Doing business as Johnny Custom Knifemakers. **Mark:** Name in oval with city and state enclosing.

CHAMBERLIN, JOHN A,
11535 Our Rd., Anchorage, AK 99516, Phone: 907-346-1524, Fax: 907-562-4583
Specialties: Art and working knives. **Patterns:** Daggers and hunters; some folders. **Technical:** Grinds ATS-34, 440C, A2, D2 and Damascus. Uses

Alaskan handle materials such as oosic, jade, whale jawbone, fossil ivory. **Prices:** Start at $150. **Remarks:** Does own heat treating and cryogenic deep freeze. Full-time maker; first knife sold in 1984. **Mark:** Name over English shield and dagger.

CHAMBLIN, JOEL,
960 New Hebron Church Rd, Concord, GA 30206, Phone: 770-884-9055, Web: chamblinknives.com
   Specialties: Fancy and working folders. **Patterns:** Fancy locking folders, traditional, multi-blades and utility. **Technical:** Grinds ATS-34, 440V, BG- 42 and commercial Damascus. Offers filework. **Prices:** Start at $300. **Remarks:** Full-time maker; first knife sold in 1989. **Mark:** Last name.

CHAMPION, ROBERT,
7001 Red Rock Rd., Amarillo, TX 79118, Phone: 806-622-3970
   Specialties: Traditional working straight knives. **Patterns:** Hunters, skinners, camp knives, Bowies, daggers. **Technical:** Grinds 440C and D2. **Prices:** $100 to $600. **Remarks:** Part-time maker; first knife sold in 1979. Stream-line hunters. **Mark:** Last name with dagger logo, city and state.

CHAPO, WILLIAM G,
45 Wildridge Rd, Wilton, CT 06897, Phone: 203- 544-9424
   Specialties: Classic straight knives and folders of his design and to customer specs; period pieces. **Patterns:** Boots, Bowies and locking folders. **Technical:** Forges stainless Damascus. Offers filework. **Prices:** $750 and up. **Remarks:** Full-time maker; first knife sold in 1989. **Mark:** First and middle initials, last name, city, state.

CHARD, GORDON R,
104 S. Holiday Lane, Iola, KS 66749, Phone: 620- 365-2311, Fax: 620-365-2311, gchard@cox.net
   Specialties: High tech folding knives in one-of-a-kind styles. **Patterns:** Liner locking folders of own design. Also fixed blade Art Knives. **Technical:** Clean work with attention to fit and finish. Blade steel mostly ATS-34 and 154CM, some CPM440V Vaso Wear and Damascus. **Prices:** $150 to $2500. **Remarks:** First knife sold in 1983. **Mark:** Name, city and state surrounded by wheat on each side.

CHASE, ALEX,
208 E. Pennsylvania Ave., DeLand, FL 32724, Phone: 386-734-9918, chase8578@bellsouth.net
   Specialties: Historical steels, classic and traditional straight knives of his design and to customer specs. **Patterns:** Art, fighters, hunters and Japanese style. **Technical:** Forges O1-L6 Damascus, meteoric Damascus, 52100, 5160; uses fossil walrus and mastodon ivory etc. **Prices:** $150 to $1000; some to $3500. **Remarks:** Full-time maker; Guild member since 1996. Doing business as Confederate Forge. **Mark:** Stylized initials-A.C.

CHASE, JOHN E,
217 Walnut, Aledo, TX 76008, Phone: 817-441-8331, jchaseknives@sbcglobal.net
   Specialties: Straight high-tech working knives in standard patterns or to customer specs. **Patterns:** Hunters, fighters, daggers and Bowies. **Technical:** Grinds D2, O1, 440C; offers mostly satin finishes. **Prices:** Start at $265. **Remarks:** Part-time maker; first knife sold in 1974. **Mark:** Last name in logo.

CHAUVIN, JOHN,
200 Anna St, Scott, LA 70583, Phone: 337-237-6138, Fax: 337-230-7980
   Specialties: Traditional working and using straight knives of his design, to customer specs and in standard patterns. **Patterns:** Bowies, fighters, and hunters. **Technical:** Grinds ATS-34, 440C and O1 high-carbon. Paul Bos heat treating. Uses ivory, stag, and stabilized Louisiana swamp maple for handle materials. Makes sheaths using alligator and ostrich. **Prices:** $200 and up. Bowies start at $500. **Remarks:** Part-time maker; first knife sold in 1995. **Mark:** Full name, city, state.

CHAUZY, ALAIN,
1 Rue de Paris, 21140 Seur-en-Auxios, FRANCE, Phone: 03-80-97-03-30, Fax: 03-80-97-34-14
   Specialties: Fixed blades, folders, hunters, Bowies-scagel-style. **Technical:** Forged blades only. Steels used XC65, 07C, and own Damascus. **Prices:** Contact maker for quote. **Remarks:** Part-time maker. **Mark:** Number 2 crossed by an arrow and name.

CHEATHAM, BILL,
PO Box 636, Laveen, AZ 85339, Phone: 602-237- 2786, blademan76@aol.com
   Specialties: Working straight knives and folders. **Patterns:** Hunters, fighters, boots and axes; locking folders. **Technical:** Grinds 440C. **Prices:** $150 to $350; exceptional knives to $600. **Remarks:** Full-time maker; first knife sold in 1976. **Mark:** Name, city, state.

CHERRY, FRANK J,
3412 Tiley N.E., Albuquerque, NM 87110, Phone: 505-883-8643

CHEW, LARRY,
515 Cleveland Rd Unit A-9, Granbury, TX 76049, Phone: 817-573-8035, chewman@swbell.net; Web: www.voodooinside.com
   Specialties: High-tech folding knives. **Patterns:** Double action automatic and manual folding patterns of his design. **Technical:** CAD designed folders utilizing roller bearing pivot design known as "VooDoo." Double action automatic folders with a variety of obvious and disguised release mechanisms, some with lock-outs. **Prices:** Manual folders start at $475, double action autos start at $750. **Remarks:** Made and sold first knife in 1988, first folder in 1989. Full-time maker since 1997. **Mark:** Name and location etched in blade, Damascus autos marked on spring inside frame. Earliest knives stamped LC.

CHOATE, MILTON,
1665 W. County 17-1/2, Somerton, AZ 85350, Phone: 928-627-7251, mccustom@juno.com
   Specialties: Classic working and using straight knives of his design, to customer specs and in standard patterns. **Patterns:** Bowies, hunters and utility/camp knives. **Technical:** Grinds 440C; grinds and forges 1095 and 5160. Does filework on top and guards on request. **Prices:** $200 to $800. **Remarks:** Full-time maker, first knife made in 1990. All knives come with handmade sheaths by Judy Choate. **Mark:** Knives marked "Choate."

CHRISTENSEN, JON P,
7814 Spear Dr, Shepherd, MT 59079, Phone: 406-373-0253, jpcknives@gmail.com; Web: www.jonchristensenknives.com
   Specialties: Patch knives, hunter/utility knives, Bowies, tomahawks. **Technical:** All blades forged, does all own work including sheaths. Forges O1, 1084, 52100, 5160. Damascus from 1084/15N20. **Prices:** $220 and up. **Remarks:** ABS Mastersmith, first knife sold in 1999. **Mark:** First and middle initial surrounded by last initial.

CHURCHMAN, T W (TIM),
475 Saddle Horn Drive, Bandera, TX 78003, Phone: 830-796-8350
   Specialties: Fancy and traditional straight knives and single blade liner locking folders. Bird/trout knives of his design and to customer specs. **Patterns:** Bird/trout knives, Bowies, daggers, fighters, boot knives, some miniatures. **Technical:** Grinds 440C, D2 and 154CM. Offers stainless fittings, fancy filework, exotic and stabilized woods and hand sewed lined sheaths. Also flower pins as a style. **Prices:** $80 to $650; some to $1500. **Remarks:** Part-time maker; first knife made in 1981 after reading "*KNIVES '81.*" Doing business as "Custom Knives Churchman Made." **Mark:** Last name, dagger.

CLAIBORNE, JEFF,
1470 Roberts Rd, Franklin, IN 46131, Phone: 317- 736-7443, jeff@claiborneknives.com; Web: www.claiborneknives.com
   Specialties: Multi blade slip joint folders. All one-of-a-kind by hand, no jigs or fixtures, swords, straight knives, period pieces, camp knives, hunters, fighters, ethnic swords all periods. Handle: uses stag, pearl, oosic, bone ivory, mastadon-mammoth, elephant or exotic woods. **Technical:** Forges high-carbon steel, makes Damascus, forges cable grinds, O1, 1095, 5160, 52100, L6. **Prices:** $250 and up. **Remarks:** Part-time maker; first knife sold in 1989. **Mark:** Stylized initials in an oval.

CLAIBORNE, RON,
2918 Ellistown Rd, Knox, TN 37924, Phone: 615- 524-2054, Bowie@icy.net
   Specialties: Multi-blade slip joints, swords, straight knives. **Patterns:** Hunters, daggers, folders. **Technical:** Forges Damascus: mosaic, powder mosaic. Prefers bone and natural handle materials; some exotic woods. **Prices:** $125 to $2500. **Remarks:** Part-time maker; first knife sold in 1979. Doing business as Thunder Mountain Forge Claiborne Knives. **Mark:** Claiborne.

CLARK, D E (LUCKY),
413 Lyman Lane, Johnstown, PA 15909-1409
   Specialties: Working straight knives and folders to customer specs. **Patterns:** Customer designs. **Technical:** Grinds D2, 440C, 154CM. **Prices:** $100 to $200; some higher. **Remarks:** Part-time maker; first knife sold in 1975. **Mark:** Name on one side; "Lucky" on other.

CLARK, HOWARD F,
115 35th Pl, Runnells, IA 50237, Phone: 515-966- 2126, howard@mvforge.com; Web: mvforge.com
   Specialties: Currently Japanese-style swords. **Patterns:** Katana. **Technical:** Forges L6 and 1086. **Prices:** $1200 to 5000. **Remarks:** Full-time maker; first knife sold in 1979. Doing business as Morgan Valley Forge. **Prior Mark:** Block letters and serial number on folders; anvil/initials logo on straight knives. **Current Mark:** Two character kanji "Big Ear."

CLARK, NATE,
604 Baird Dr, Yoncalla, OR 97499, nateclarkknives@hotmail.com; Web: www.nateclarkknives.com
   Specialties: Automatics (push button and hidden release) ATS-34 mirror polish or satin finish, Damascus, pearl, ivory, abalone, woods, bone, Micarta, G-10, filework and carving and sheath knives. **Prices:** $100 to $2500. **Remarks:** Full-time knifemaker since 1996. **Mark:** Nate Clark on spring, spacer or blade.

CLARK, R W,
R.W. CLARK CUSTOM KNIVES, 17602 W. Eugene Terrace, Surprise, AZ 85388-5047, Phone: 909-279-3494, info@rwclarkknives.com
   Specialties: Military field knives and Asian hybrids. Hand carved leather sheaths. **Patterns:** Fixed blade hunters, field utility and military. Also presentation and collector grade knives. **Technical:** First maker to use liquid metals LM1 material in knives. Other materials include S30V, O1, stainless and carbon Damascus. **Prices:** $75 to $2000. Average price $300. **Remarks:** Started knifemaking in 1990, full-time in 2000. **Mark:** R.W. Clark, Custom, Corona, CA in standard football shape. Also uses three Japanese characters, spelling Clark, on Asian Hybrids.

CLAY, WAYNE,
Box 125B, Pelham, TN 37366, Phone: 931-467-3472, Fax: 931-467-3076
Specialties: Working straight knives and folders in standard patterns. **Patterns:** Hunters and kitchen knives; gents and hunter patterns. **Technical:** Grinds ATS-34. **Prices:** $125 to $500; some to $1000. **Remarks:** Full-time maker; first knife sold in 1978. **Mark:** Name.

COATS, KEN,
317 5th Ave, Stevens Point, WI 54481, Phone: 715-544- 0115, kandk_c@ charter.net
Technical: Grinds ATS-34, 440C. Stainless blades and backsprings. Does all own heat treating and freeze cycle. Blades are drawn to 60RC. Nickel silver or brass bolsters on folders are soldered, neutralized and pinned. Handles are jigged bone, hardwoods antler, and Micarta. Cuts and jigs own bone, usually shades of brown or green.

COCKERHAM, LLOYD,
1717 Carolyn Ave, Denham Springs, IA 70726, Phone: 225-665-1565

COFFEY, BILL,
68 Joshua Ave, Clovis, CA 93611, Phone: 559-299- 4259
Specialties: Working and fancy straight knives and folders of his design. **Patterns:** Hunters, fighters, utility, LinerLock® folders and fantasy knives. **Technical:** Grinds 440C, ATS-34, A-Z and commercial Damascus. **Prices:** $250 to $1000; some to $2500. **Remarks:** Full-time maker. First knife sold in 1993. **Mark:** First and last name, city, state.

COFFMAN, DANNY,
541 Angel Dr S, Jacksonville, AL 36265-5787, Phone: 256-435-1619
Specialties: Straight knives and folders of his design. Now making liner locks for $650 to $1200 with natural handles and contrasting Damascus blades and bolsters. **Patterns:** Hunters, locking and slip-joint folders. **Technical:** Grinds Damascus, 440C and D2. Offers filework and engraving. **Prices:** $100 to $400; some to $800. **Remarks:** Spare-time maker; first knife sold in 1992. Doing business as Customs by Coffman. **Mark:** Last name stamped or engraved.

COHEN, N J (NORM),
2408 Sugarcone Rd, Baltimore, MD 21209, Phone: 410-484-3841, njcohen@ verizon.net; Web:www.njcknives.com
Specialties: Working class knives. **Patterns:** Hunters, skinners, bird knives, push daggers, boots, kitchen and practical customer designs. **Technical:** Stock removal 440C, ATS-34. Uses Micarta, Corian. Some woods in handles. **Prices:** $50 to $250. **Remarks:** Part-time maker; first knife sold in 1982. **Mark:** NJC engraved.

COHEN, TERRY A,
PO Box 406, Laytonville, CA 95454
Specialties: Working straight knives and folders. **Patterns:** Bowies to boot knives and locking folders; mini-boot knives. **Technical:** Grinds stainless; hand rubs; tries for good balance. **Prices:** $85 to $150; some to $325. **Remarks:** Part-time maker; first knife sold in 1983. **Mark:** TERRY KNIVES, city and state.

COIL, JIMMIE J,
2936 Asbury Pl, Owensboro, KY 42303, Phone: 270- 684-7827
Specialties: Traditional working and straight knives of his design. **Patterns:** Hunters, Bowies and fighters. **Technical:** Grinds 440C, ATS-34 and D2. Blades are flat-ground with brush finish; most have tapered tang. Offers filework. **Prices:** $65 to $250; some to $750. **Remarks:** Spare- time maker; first knife sold in 1974. **Mark:** Name.

COLE, DAVE,
620 Poinsetta Dr, Satellite Beach, FL 32937, Phone: 321- 773-1687, Web: www.dcknivesandleather.blademakers.com
Specialties: Fixed blades and friction folders of his design or customers. **Patterns:** Utility, hunters, and Bowies. **Technical:** Grinds O1, 1095. 440C stainless Damascus; prefers natural handle materials, handmade sheaths. **Prices:** $100 and up. **Remarks:** Part-time maker, custom sheath services for others; first knife sold in 1991. **Mark:** D Cole.

COLE, JAMES M,
505 Stonewood Blvd, Bartonville, TX 76226, Phone: 817-430-0302, dogcole@ swbell.net

COLE, WELBORN I,
365 Crystal Ct, Athens, GA 30606, Phone: 404- 261-3977
Specialties: Traditional straight knives of his design. **Patterns:** Hunters. **Technical:** Grinds 440C, ATS-34 and D2. Good wood scales. **Prices:** NA. **Remarks:** Full-time maker; first knife sold in 1983. **Mark:** Script initials.

COLEMAN, JOHN A,
7233 Camel Rock Way, Citrus Heightss, CA 95610, Phone: 916-335-1568
Specialties: Traditional working straight knives of his design or yours. **Patterns:** Plain to fancy file back working knives hunters, bird, trout, camp knives, skinners. Trout knives miniatures of Bowies and cappers. **Technical:** Grinds 440C, ATS-34, 145CM and D2. Exotic woods bone, antler and some ivory. **Prices:** $80 to $200, some to $450. **Remarks:** Part-time maker. First knife sold in 1989. Doing business as Slim's Custom Knives. Enjoys making knives to your specs; all knives come with handmade sheath by Slim's Leather. **Mark:** Cowboy setting on log whittling Slim's Custom Knives above cowboy and name and state under cowboy.

COLLINS, LYNN M,
138 Berkley Dr, Elyria, OH 44035, Phone: 440-366- 7101
Specialties: Working straight knives. **Patterns:** Field knives, boots and fighters. **Technical:** Grinds D2, 154CM and 440C. **Prices:** Start at $150. **Remarks:** Spare-time maker; first knife sold in 1980. **Mark:** Initials, asterisks.

COLTER, WADE,
PO Box 2340, Colstrip, MT 59323, Phone: 406-748- 4573
Specialties: Fancy and embellished straight knives, folders and swords of his design; historical and period pieces. **Patterns:** Bowies, swords and folders. **Technical:** Hand forges 52100 ball bearing steel and L6, 1090, cable and chain Damascus from 5N20 and 1084. Carves and makes sheaths. **Prices:** $250 to $3500. **Remarks:** Part-time maker; first knife sold in 1990. Doing business as "Colter's Hell" Forge. **Mark:** Initials on left side ricasso.

COLTRAIN, LARRY D,
PO Box 1331, Buxton, NC 27920

CONKLIN, GEORGE L,
Box 902, Ft. Benton, MT 59442, Phone: 406- 622-3268, Fax: 406-622-3410, 7bbgrus@3rivers.net
Specialties: Designer and manufacturer of the "Brisket Breaker." **Patterns:** Hunters, utility/camp knives and hatchets. **Technical:** Grinds 440C, ATS-34, D2, 1095, 154CM and 5160. Offers some forging and heat-treats for others. Offers some jewelling. **Prices:** $65 to $200; some to $1000. **Remarks:** Full-time maker. Doing business as Rocky Mountain Knives. **Mark:** Last name in script.

CONLEY, BOB,
1013 Creasy Rd, Jonesboro, TN 37659, Phone: 423- 753-3302
Specialties: Working straight knives and folders. **Patterns:** Lockers, two-blades, gents, hunters, traditional-styles, straight hunters. **Technical:** Grinds 440C, 154CM and ATS-34. Engraves. **Prices:** $250 to $450; some to $600. **Remarks:** Full-time maker; first knife sold in 1979. **Mark:** Full name, city, state.

CONN JR., C T,
206 Highland Ave, Attalla, AL 35954, Phone: 205-538- 7688
Specialties: Working folders, some fancy. **Patterns:** Full range of folding knives. **Technical:** Grinds O2, 440C and 154CM. **Prices:** $125 to $300; some to $600. **Remarks:** Part-time maker; first knife sold in 1982. **Mark:** Name.

CONNOLLY, JAMES,
2486 Oro-Quincy Hwy, Oroville, CA 95966, Phone: 530-534-5363, rjconnolly@ sbcglobal.net
Specialties: Classic working and using knives of his design. **Patterns:** Boots, Bowies, daggers and swords. **Technical:** Grinds ATS-34, BG42, A2, O1. **Prices:** $100 to $500; some to $1500. **Remarks:** Part-time maker; first knife sold in 1980. Doing business as Gold Rush Designs. **Mark:** First initial, last name, Handmade.

CONNOR, JOHN W,
PO Box 12981, Odessa, TX 79768-2981, Phone: 915-362-6901

CONNOR, MICHAEL,
Box 502, Winters, TX 79567, Phone: 915-754- 5602
Specialties: Straight knives, period pieces, some folders. **Patterns:** Hunters to camp knives to traditional locking folders to Bowies. **Technical:** Forges 5160, O1, 1084 steels and his own Damascus. **Prices:** Moderate to upscale. **Remarks:** Spare-time maker; first knife sold in 1974. ABS Master Smith 1983. **Mark:** Last name, M.S.

CONTI, JEFFREY D,
21104 75th St E, Bonney Lake, WA 98390, Phone: 253-447-4660, Fax: 253- 512-8629
Specialties: Working straight knives. **Patterns:** Fighters and survival knives; hunters, camp knives and fishing knives. **Technical:** Grinds D2, 154CM and O1. Engraves. **Prices:** Start at $80. **Remarks:** Part-time maker; first knife sold in 1980. Does own heat treating. **Mark:** Initials, year, steel type, name and number of knife.

CONWAY, JOHN,
13301 100th Place NE, Kirkland, WA 98034, Phone: 425-823-2821, jcknives@ verizon.net
Specialties: Folders; working and Damascus. Straight knives, camp, utility and fighting knives. **Patterns:** LinerLock® folders of own design. Hidden tang straight knives of own design. **Technical:** Flat grinds forged carbon steels and own Damascus steel, including mosaic. **Prices:** $300 to $850. **Remarks:** Part-time maker since 1999. **Mark:** Oval with stylized initials J C inset.

COOGAN, ROBERT,
1560 Craft Center Dr, Smithville, TN 37166, Phone: 615-597-6801, http://iweb. tntech.edu/rcoogan/
Specialties: One-of-a-kind knives. **Patterns:** Unique items like ulu-style Appalachian herb knives. **Technical:** Forges; his Damascus is made from nickel steel and W1. **Prices:** Start at $100. **Remarks:** Part-time maker; first knife sold in 1979. **Mark:** Initials or last name in script.

COOK, JAMES R,
455 Anderson Rd, Nashville, AR 71852, Phone: 870 845 5173, jr@jrcookknives. com; Web: www.jrcookknives.com
Specialties: Working straight knives and folders of his design or to cus-

tomer specs. **Patterns:** Bowies, hunters and camp knives. **Technical:** Forges 1084 and high-carbon Damascus. **Prices:** $195 to $5500. **Remarks:** Full-time maker; first knife sold in 1986. **Mark:** First and middle initials, last name.

COOK, LOUISE,
475 Robinson Ln, Ozark, IL 62972, Phone: 618-777-2932
    Specialties: Working and using straight knives of her design and to customer specs; period pieces. **Patterns:** Bowies, hunters and utility/camp knives. **Technical:** Forges 5160. Filework; pin work; silver wire inlay. **Prices:** Start at $50/inch. **Remarks:** Part-time maker; first knife sold in 1990. Doing business as Panther Creek Forge. **Mark:** First name and Journeyman stamp on one side; panther head on the other.

COOK, MIKE,
475 Robinson Ln, Ozark, IL 62972, Phone: 618-777-2932
    Specialties: Traditional working and using straight knives of his design and to customer specs. **Patterns:** Bowies, hunters and utility/camp knives. **Technical:** Forges 5160. Filework; pin work. **Prices:** Start at $50/ inch. **Remarks:** Spare-time maker; first knife sold in 1991. **Mark:** First initial, last name and Journeyman stamp on one side; panther head on the other.

COOK, MIKE A,
10927 Shilton Rd, Portland, MI 48875, Phone: 517-647- 2518
    Specialties: Fancy/embellished and period pieces of his design. **Patterns:** Daggers, fighters and hunters. **Technical:** Stone bladed knives in agate, obsidian and jasper. Scrimshaws; opal inlays. **Prices:** $60 to $300; some to $800. **Remarks:** Part-time maker; first knife sold in 1988. Doing business as Art of Ishi. **Mark:** Initials and year.

COOMBS JR., LAMONT,
546 State Rt 46, Bucksport, ME 04416, Phone: 207-469-3057, Fax: 207-469-3057, theknifemaker@hotmail.com; Web: www.knivesby.com/coomb-knives.html
    Specialties: Classic fancy and embellished straight knives; traditional working and using straight knives. Knives of his design and to customer specs. **Patterns:** Hunters, folders and utility/camp knives. **Technical:** Hollow- and flat-grinds ATS-34, 440C, A2, D2 and O1; grinds Damascus from other makers. **Prices:** $100 to $500; some to $3500. **Remarks:** Full-time maker; first knife sold in 1988. **Mark:** Last name on banner, handmade underneath.

COON, RAYMOND C,
21135 S.E. Tillstrom Rd, Gresham, OR 97080, Phone: 503-658-2252, Raymond@damascusknife.com; Web: Damascusknife.com
    Specialties: Working straight knives in standard patterns. **Patterns:** Hunters, Bowies, daggers, boots and axes. **Technical:** Forges high-carbon steel and Damascus or 97089. **Prices:** Start at $235. **Remarks:** Full- time maker; does own leatherwork, makes own Damascus, daggers; first knife sold in 1995. **Mark:** First initial, last name.

COPELAND, THOM,
171 Country Line Rd S, Nashville, AR 71852, tcope@cswnet.com
    Specialties: Hand forged fixed blades; hunters, Bowies and camp knives. **Remarks:** Member of ABS and AKA (Arkansas Knifemakers Association). **Mark:** Copeland.

COPPINS, DANIEL,
7303 Sherrard Rd, Cambridge, OH 43725, Phone: 740-439-4199
    Specialties: Grinds 440 C, D-2. Antler handles. **Patterns:** Drop point hunters, fighters, Bowies, bird and trout daggers. **Prices:** $40 to $800. **Remarks:** Sold first knife in 2002. **Mark:** DC.

CORBY, HAROLD,
218 Brandonwood Dr, Johnson City, TN 37604, Phone: 423-926-9781
    Specialties: Large fighters and Bowies; self-protection knives; art knives. Along with art knives and combat knives, Corby now has a all new automatic MO.PB1, also side lock MO LL-1 with titanium liners G-10 handles. **Patterns:** Sub-hilt fighters and hunters. **Technical:** Grinds 154CM, ATS- 34 and 440C. **Prices:** $200 to $6000. **Remarks:** Full-time maker; first knife sold in 1969. Doing business as Knives by Corby. **Mark:** Last name.

CORDOVA, JOSEPH G,
PO Box 977, Peralta, NM 87042, Phone: 505- 869-3912, kcordova@rt66.com
    Specialties: One-of-a-kind designs, some to customer specs. **Patterns:** Fighter called the 'Gladiator', hunters, boots and cutlery. **Technical:** Forges 1095, 5160; grinds ATS-34, 440C and 154CM. **Prices:** Moderate to upscale. **Remarks:** Full-time maker; first knife sold in 1953. Past chairman of American Bladesmith Society. **Mark:** Cordova made.

CORKUM, STEVE,
34 Basehoar School Rd, Littlestown, PA 17340, Phone: 717-359-9563, sco7129849@aol.com; Web: www.hawknives.com

COSGROVE, CHARLES G,
7606 Willow Oak Ln, Arlington, TX 76001, Phone: 817-472-6505, charles.barchar@gmail.com
    Specialties: Traditional fixed or locking blade working knives. **Patterns:** Hunters, Bowies and locking folders. **Technical:** Stock removal using 440C, ATS-34 and D2. Makes heavy, hand-stitched sheaths. **Prices:** $250 to $2500. **Remarks:** Full-time maker; first knife sold in 1968. No longer accepting customer designs. **Mark:** C. Cosgrove.

COSTA, SCOTT,
409 Coventry Rd, Spicewood, TX 78669, Phone: 830- 693-3431
    Specialties: Working straight knives. **Patterns:** Hunters, skinners, axes, trophy sets, custom boxed steak sets, carving sets and bar sets. **Technical:** Grinds D2, ATS-34, 440 and Damascus. Heat-treats. **Prices:** $225 to $2000. **Remarks:** Full-time maker; first knife sold in 1985. **Mark:** Initials connected.

COTTRILL, JAMES I,
1776 Ransburg Ave, Columbus, OH 43223, Phone: 614-274-0020
    Specialties: Working straight knives of his design. **Patterns:** Caters to the boating and hunting crowd; cutlery. **Technical:** Grinds O1, D2 and 440C. Likes filework. **Prices:** $95 to $250; some to $500. **Remarks:** Full- time maker; first knife sold in 1977. **Mark:** Name, city, state, in oval logo.

COURTNEY, ELDON,
2718 Bullinger, Wichita, KS 67204, Phone: 316- 838-4053
    Specialties: Working straight knives of his design. **Patterns:** Hunters, fighters and one-of-a-kinds. **Technical:** Grinds and tempers L6, 440C and spring steel. **Prices:** $100 to $500; some to $1500. **Remarks:** Full- time maker; first knife sold in 1977. **Mark:** Full name, city and state.

COURTOIS, BRYAN,
3 Lawn Ave, Saco, ME 04072, Phone: 207-282- 3977, bryancourtois@verizon.net; Web: http://mysite.verizon.net/ vzeui2z01
    Specialties: Working straight knives; prefers customer designs, no standard patterns. **Patterns:** Functional hunters; everyday knives. **Technical:** Grinds 440C or customer request. Hollow-grinds with a variety of finishes. Specializes in granite handles and custom skeleton knives. **Prices:** Start at $75. **Remarks:** Part-time maker; first knife sold in 1988. Doing business as Castle Knives. **Mark:** A rook chess piece machined into blade using electrical discharge process.

COUSINO, GEORGE,
7818 Norfolk, Onsted, MI 49265, Phone: 517-467- 4911, gcousino@frontiernet.net; Web: www.cousinoknives.com
    Specialties: Hunters, Bowies using knives. **Patterns:** Hunters, Bowies, buckskinners, folders and daggers. **Technical:** Grinds 440C. **Prices:** $95 to $300. **Remarks:** Part-time maker; first knife sold in 1981. **Mark:** Last name.

COVER, RAYMOND A,
1206 N Third St, Festus, MO 63028-1628, Phone: 636-937-5955
    Specialties: High-tech working straight knives and folders in standard patterns. **Patterns:** Slip joint folders, two-bladed folders. **Technical:** Grinds D2, and ATS-34. **Prices:** $165 to $250; some to $400. **Remarks:** Part-time maker; first knife sold in 1974. **Mark:** Name.

COWLES, DON,
1026 Lawndale Dr, Royal Oak, MI 48067, Phone: 248- 541-4619, don@cowlesknives.com; Web: www.cowlesknives.com
    Specialties: Straight, non-folding pocket knives of his design. **Patterns:** Gentlemen's pocket knives. **Technical:** Grinds CPM154, S30V, Damascus, Talonite. Engraves; pearl inlays in some handles. **Prices:** Start at $300. **Remarks:** Full-time maker; first knife sold in 1994. **Mark:** Full name with oak leaf.

COX, COLIN J,
107 N. Oxford Dr, Raymore, MO 64083, Phone: 816- 322-1977, colin4knives@aol.com; Web: www.colincoxknives.com
    Specialties: Working straight knives and folders of his design; period pieces. **Patterns:** Hunters, fighters and survival knives. Folders, two-blades, gents and hunters. **Technical:** Grinds D2, 440C, 154CM and ATS-34. **Prices:** $125 to $750; some to $4000. **Remarks:** Full-time maker; first knife sold in 1981. **Mark:** Full name, city and state.

COX, SAM,
1756 Love Springs Rd, Gaffney, SC 29341, Phone: 864-489- 1892, Fax: 864-489-0403, artcutlery@yahoo.com; Web: www.samcox.us
    Specialties: Classic high-art working straight knives of his design. Duck knives copyrighted. **Patterns:** Diverse. **Technical:** Grinds 154CM and S30V. **Prices:** $300 to $1400. **Remarks:** Full-time maker; first knife sold in 1983. **Mark:** Cox Call, Sam, Sam Cox, unique 2000 logo, artistic cutlery logo (beginning 2007).

CRAIG, ROGER L,
2617 SW Seabrook Ave, Topeka, KS 66614, Phone: 785-249-4109
    Specialties: Working and camp knives, some fantasy; all his design. **Patterns:** Fighters, hunter. **Technical:** Grinds 1095 and 5160. Most knives have file work. **Prices:** $50 to $250. **Remarks:** Part-time maker; first knife sold in 1991. Doing business as Craig Knives. **Mark:** Last name-Craig.

CRAIN, JACK W,
PO Box 212, Granbury, TX 76048, Phone: 817-599- 6414, Web: www.crainknives.com - Site 9291 jackwcrain@crainknives.com
    Specialties: Fantasy and period knives; combat and survival knives. **Patterns:** One-of-a-kind art or fantasy daggers, swords and Bowies; survival knives. **Technical:** Forges Damascus; grinds stainless steel. Carves. **Prices:** $350 to $2500; some to $20,000. **Remarks:** Full-time maker; first knife sold in 1969. Designer and maker of the knives seen in the films *Dracula 2000*, *Executive Decision*, *Demolition Man*, *Predator I* and *II*, *Commando*, *Die Hard I* and *II*, *Road House*, *Ford Fairlane* and *Action Jackson*, and television shows *War of the Worlds*, *Air Wolf*, *Kung Fu: The Legend Cont.* and *Tales of the Crypt*. **Mark:** Stylized crane.

CRAWFORD, PAT AND WES,
205N. Center, WestMemphis, AR72301, Phone:870-732-2452, patcrawford1@earthlink.com; Web: www.crawfordknives.com
Specialties: Stainless steel Damascus. High-tech working self-defense and combat types and folders. **Patterns:** Tactical-more fancy knives now. **Technical:** Grinds S30V. **Prices:** $400 to $2000. **Remarks:** Full-time maker; first knife sold in 1973. **Mark:** Last name.

CRAWLEY, BRUCE R,
16 Binbrook Dr, Croydon 3136 Victoria, AUSTRALIA
Specialties: Folders. **Patterns:** Hunters, lockback folders and Bowies. **Technical:** Grinds 440C, ATS-34 and commercial Damascus. Offers file-work and mirror polish. **Prices:** $160 to $3500. **Remarks:** Part-time maker; first knife sold in 1990. **Mark:** Initials.

CRENSHAW, AL,
Rt 1 Box 717, Eufaula, OK 74432, Phone: 918-452- 2128
Specialties: Folders of his design and in standard patterns. **Patterns:** Hunters, locking folders, slip-joint folders, multi blade folders. **Technical:** Grinds 440C, D2 and ATS-34. Does filework on back springs and blades; offers scrimshaw on some handles. **Prices:** $150 to $300; some higher. **Remarks:** Full-time maker; first knife sold in 1981. Doing business as A. Crenshaw Knives. **Mark:** First initial, last name, Lake Eufaula, state stamped; first initial last name in rainbow; Lake Eufaula across bottom with Okla. in middle.

CROCKFORD, JACK,
1859 Harts Mill Rd, Chamblee, GA 30341, Phone: 770-457-4680
Specialties: Lockback folders. **Patterns:** Hunters, fishing and camp knives, traditional folders. **Technical:** Grinds A2, D2, ATS-34 and 440C. Engraves and scrimshaws. **Prices:** Start at $175. **Remarks:** Part-time maker; first knife sold in 1975. **Mark:** Name.

CROSS, ROBERT,
RMB 200B, Manilla Rd, Tamworth 2340, NSW, AUSTRALIA, Phone: 067-618385

CROWDER, ROBERT,
Box 1374, Thompson Falls, MT 59873, Phone: 406-827-4754
Specialties: Traditional working knives to customer specs. **Patterns:** Hunters, Bowies, fighters and fillets. **Technical:** Grinds ATS-34, 154CM, 440C, Vascowear and commercial Damascus. **Prices:** $225 to $500; some to $2500. **Remarks:** Full-time maker; first knife sold in 1985. **Mark:** R Crowder signature & Montana.

CROWELL, JAMES L,
PO Box 822, 676 Newnata Cutoff, Mtn. View, AR 72560, Phone: 870-746-4215, crowellknives@yahoo.com
Specialties: Bowie knives; fighters and working knives. **Patterns:** Hunters, fighters, Bowies, daggers and folders. Period pieces: War hammers, Japanese and European. **Technical:** Forges 10 series carbon steels as well as O1, L6 and his own Damascus. **Prices:** $425 to $4500; some to $7500. **Remarks:** Full-time maker; first knife sold in 1980. Earned ABS Master Bladesmith in 1986. **Mark:** A shooting star.

CROWL, PETER,
5786 County Road 10, Waterloo, IN 46793, Phone: 260-488-2532, Email: pete@petecrowlknives.com; Web: www.petecrowlknives.com

CROWTHERS, MARK F,
PO Box 4641, Rolling Bay, WA 98061-0641, Phone: 206-842-7501

CULPEPPER, JOHN,
2102 Spencer Ave, Monroe, LA 71201, Phone: 318-323-3636
Specialties: Working straight knives. **Patterns:** Hunters, Bowies and camp knives in heavy-duty patterns. **Technical:** Grinds O1, D2 and 440C; hollow-grinds. **Prices:** $75 to $200; some to $300. **Remarks:** Part- time maker; first knife sold in 1970. Doing business as Pepper Knives. **Mark:** Pepper.

CULVER, STEVE,
5682 94th St, Meriden, KS 66512, Phone: 866-505- 0146, Web: www.culverart.com
Specialties: Edged tools and weapons, collectible and functional. **Patterns:** Bowies, daggers, swords, hunters, folders and edged tools. **Technical:** Forges carbon steels and his own pattern welded steels. **Prices:** $200 to $1500; some to $4000. **Remarks:** Full-time maker; first knife sold in 1989. **Mark:** Last name, M. S.

CUMMING, BOB,
CUMMING KNIVES, 35 Manana Dr, Cedar Crest, NM 87008, Phone: 505-286-0509, cumming@comcast.net; Web: www.cummingknives.com
Specialties: One-of-a-kind exhibition grade custom Bowie knives, exhibition grade and working hunters, bird & trout knives, salt and fresh water fillet knives. Low country oyster knives, custom tanto's plains Indian style sheaths & custom leather, all types of exotic handle materials, scrimshaw and engraving. Added folders in 2006. **Prices:** $90 to $2500 and up. **Remarks:** Mentored by the late Jim Nolen, sold first knife in 1978 in Denmark. Retired U.S. Foreign Service Officer. Member NCCKG. **Mark:** Stylized CUMMING.

CURTISS, STEVE L,
PO Box 448, Eureka, MT 59914, Phone: 406-889- 5510, Fax: 406-889-5510, slc@bladerigger.com; Web: http://www.bladerigger.com
Specialties: True custom and semi-custom production (SCP), specialized concealment blades; advanced sheaths and tailored body harnessing systems. **Patterns:** Tactical/personal defense fighters, swords, utility and custom patterns. **Technical:** Grinds A2 and Talonite®; heat-treats. Sheaths: Kydex or Kydex-lined leather laminated or Kydex-lined with Rigger Coat™. Exotic materials available. **Prices:** $50 to $10,000. **Remarks:** Full-time maker. Doing business as Blade Rigger L.L.C. Martial artist and unique defense industry tools and equipment. **Mark:** For true custom: Initials and for SCP: Blade Rigger.

CUTE, THOMAS,
State Rt 90-7071, Cortland, NY 13045, Phone: 607- 749-4055
Specialties: Working straight knives. **Patterns:** Hunters, Bowies and fighters. **Technical:** Grinds O1, 440C and ATS-34. **Prices:** $100 to $1000. **Remarks:** Full-time maker; first knife sold in 1974. **Mark:** Full name.

CUTTING EDGE, THE, Mark,
1971 Fox Ave, Fairbanks, AK 99701, Phone: 907-452-7477, cuttingedge@gcil. net www.markknappcustomeknives.com
Specialties: Mosaic handles of exotic natural materials from Alaska and around the world. Folders, fixed blades, full and hidden tangs. **Patterns:** Folders, hunters, skinners and camp knives. **Technical:** Forges own Damascus, uses both forging and stock removal with ATS-34, 154CM, stainless Damascus, carbon steel and carbon Damascus. **Prices:** $800-$2000. **Remarks:** Full time maker, sold first knife in 2000. **Mark:** Mark Knapp Custom Knives Fairbanks AK.

D

DAILEY, G E,
577 Lincoln St, Seekonk, MA 02771, Phone: 508-336- 5088, gedailey@msn. com; Web: www.gedailey.com
Specialties: One-of-a-kind exotic designed edged weapons. **Patterns:** Folders, daggers and swords. **Technical:** Reforges and grinds Damascus; prefers hollow-grinding. Engraves, carves, offers filework and sets stones and uses exotic gems and gold. **Prices:** Start at $1100. **Remarks:** Full-time maker. First knife sold in 1982. **Mark:** Last name or stylized initialed logo.

DAKE, C M,
19759 Chef Menteur Hwy, New Orleans, LA 70129-9602, Phone: 504-254-0357, Fax: 504-254-9501
Specialties: Fancy working folders. **Patterns:** Front-lock lockbacks, button-lock folders. **Technical:** Grinds ATS-34 and Damascus. **Prices:** $500 to $2500; some higher. **Remarks:** Full-time maker; first knife sold in 1988. Doing business as Bayou Custom Cutlery. **Mark:** Last name.

DAKE, MARY H,
Rt 5 Box 287A, New Orleans, LA 70129, Phone: 504- 254-0357

DALLYN, KELLY,
14695 Deerridge Dr SE, Calgary, AB, CANADA T2J 6A8, Phone: 403-278-3056

DAMASTEEL STAINLESS DAMASCUS,
3052 Isim Rd., Norman, OK 73026, Phone: 888-804-0683; 405-321-3614, damascus@newmex.com; Web: www.ssdamacus.com
Patterns: Rose, Odin's eye, 5, 20, 30 twists Hakkapelitta, TNT, and infinity

DAMLOVAC, SAVA,
10292 Bradbury Dr, Indianapolis, IN 46231, Phone: 317-839-4952
Specialties: Period pieces, fantasy, Viking, Moran type all Damascus daggers. **Patterns:** Bowies, fighters, daggers, Persian-style knives. **Technical:** Uses own Damascus, some stainless, mostly hand forges. **Prices:** $150 to $2500; some higher. **Remarks:** Full-time maker; first knife sold in 1993. Specialty, Bill Moran all Damascus dagger sets, in Moran-style wood case. **Mark:** "Sava" stamped in Damascus or etched in stainless.

D'ANDREA, JOHN,
8517 N Linwood Loop, Citrus Springs, FL 34433- 5045, Phone: 352-489-2803, jpda@optonline.net
Specialties: Fancy working straight knives and folders with filework and distinctive leatherwork. **Patterns:** Hunters, fighters, daggers, folders and an occasional sword. **Technical:** Grinds ATS-34, 154CM, 440C and D2. **Prices:** $180 to $600; some to $1000. **Remarks:** Part-time maker; first knife sold in 1986. **Mark:** First name, last initial imposed on samurai sword.

D'ANGELO, LAURENCE,
14703 NE 17th Ave, Vancouver, WA 98686, Phone: 360-573-0546
Specialties: Straight knives of his design. **Patterns:** Bowies, hunters and locking folders. **Technical:** Grinds D2, ATS-34 and 440C. Hand makes all sheaths. **Prices:** $100 to $200. **Remarks:** Full-time maker; first knife sold in 1987. **Mark:** Football logo—first and middle initials, last name, city, state, Maker.

DANIEL, TRAVIS E,
1655 Carrow Rd, Chocowinity, NC 27817, Phone: 252-940-0807, tedsknives@mail.com
Specialties: Traditional working straight knives of his design or to customer specs. **Patterns:** Hunters, fighters and utility/camp knives. **Technical:** Grinds ATS-34, 440-C, 154CM, forges his own Damascus. Stock removal. **Prices:** $90 to $1200. **Remarks:** Full-time maker; first knife sold in 1976. **Mark:** TED.

DANIELS, ALEX,
1416 County Rd 415, Town Creek, AL 35672, Phone: 256-685-0943, akdknives@aol.com
Specialties: Working and using straight knives and folders; period pieces, reproduction Bowies. **Patterns:** Mostly reproduction Bowies but offers full line of knives. **Technical:** Now also using BG-42 along with 440C and ATS-34. **Prices:** $200 to $2500. **Remarks:** Full-time maker; first knife sold in 1963. **Mark:** First and middle initials, last name, city and state.

DANNEMANN, RANDY,
RIM RANCH, 27752 P25 Rd, Hotchkiss, CO 81419
Specialties: Classic pattern working hunters, skinners, bird, trout, kitchen & utility knives. **Technical:** Grinds 440C, 154CM, & D2 steel, in house heat treating and cryogenic enhancement. Most are full tapered tang with finger guard and working satin finish. Custom fitted leather sheath for every hunting style knife, both serialized. Uses imported hardwoods, stag, or Micarta for handles. **Price:** $140 to $240 some higher. **Remarks:** First knife sold 1974. **Mark:** R. Dannemann Colorado or stamped Dannemann.

DARBY, DAVID T,
30652 S 533 Rd, Cookson, OK 74427, Phone: 918- 457-4868, knfmkr@fullnet.net
Specialties: Forged blades only, all styles. **Prices:** $350 and up. **Remarks:** ABS Journeyman Smith. **Mark:** Stylized quillion dagger incorporates last name (Darby).

DARBY, JED,
7878 E Co Rd 50 N, Greensburg, IN 47240, Phone: 812- 663-2696
Specialties: Traditional working/using straight knives of his design and to customer specs. **Patterns:** Bowies, hunters and utility/camp knives. **Technical:** Grinds 440C, ATS-34 and Damascus. **Prices:** $70 to $550; some to $1000. **Remarks:** Full-time maker; first knife sold in 1992. Doing business as Darby Knives. **Mark:** Last name and year.

DARBY, RICK,
71 Nestingrock Ln, Levittown, PA 19054
Specialties: Working straight knives. **Patterns:** Boots, fighters and hunters with mirror finish. **Technical:** Grinds 440C and CPM440V. **Prices:** $125 to $300. **Remarks:** Part-time maker; first knife sold in 1974. **Mark:** First and middle initials, last name.

DARCEY, CHESTER L,
1608 Dominik Dr, College Station, TX 77840, Phone: 979-696-1656, DarceyKnives@yahoo.com
Specialties: Lockback, LinerLock® and scale release folders. **Patterns:** Bowies, hunters and utilities. **Technical:** Stock removal on carbon and stainless steels, forge own Damascus. **Prices:** $200 to $1000. **Remarks:** Part-time maker, first knife sold in 1999. **Mark:** Last name in script.

DARK, ROBERT,
2218 Huntington Court, Oxford, AL 36203, Phone: 256-831-4645, dark@darkknives.com; Web: www.darknives.com
Specialties: Fixed blade working knives of maker's designs. Works with customer designed specifications. **Patterns:** Hunters, Bowies, camp knives, kitchen/utility, bird and trout. Standard patterns and customer designed. **Technical:** Forged and stock removal. Works with high carbon, stainless and Damascus steels. Hollow and flat grinds. **Prices:** $175 to $750. **Remarks:** Sole authorship knives and custom leather sheaths. Full-time maker. **Mark:** "R Dark" on left side of blade.

DARPINIAN, DAVE,
12484 S Greenwood St, Olathe, KS 66062, Phone: 913-244-7114, darpo1956@yahoo.com
Specialties: Working knives and fancy pieces to customer specs. **Patterns:** Full range of straight knives including art daggers and short swords. **Technical:** Art grinds ATS-34, 440C, 154 CM, 5160, 1095. **Prices:** $300 to $1000. **Remarks:** First knife sold in 1986, part-time maker. **Mark:** Last name.

DAVEY, KEVIN,
105 Joey Dr, Boerne, TX 78006, kevin_n_davey@yahoo.com; Web: www.coutelforge.com
Specialties: Bowies, camp, drop point hunters, forged integrals, daggers, mostly one-of-a-kind designs by maker, sole authorship. **Technical:** Bladesmith, forges mostly 52100 with flat or convex grinds but can also grind hollow, makes own pattern welded steel and own heat treatment. **Prices:** Between $200 to $800. **Remarks:** Part-time maker, current American Bladesmith Society Apprentice working towards journeyman status. See samples of work at www.coutelcutlery.com. **Mark:** Kevin Davey stamped in circle with 5 point star in center.

DAVIDSON, EDMUND,
3345 Virginia Ave, Goshen, VA 24439, Phone: 540-997-5651, Web: www.edmunddavidson.com
Specialties: Working straight knives; many integral patterns and upgraded models. **Patterns:** Heavy-duty skinners and camp knives. **Technical:** Grinds A2, ATS-34, BG-42, S7, 440C. **Prices:** $100 to infinity. **Remarks:** Full-time maker; first knife sold in 1986. **Mark:** Name in deer head or custom logos.

DAVIDSON, JEFF,
PO Box 14708, Haltom City, TX 76117, Phone: 8175282416, davidsonknives@sbcglobal.net; Web: davidsoncustomknives.net
Specialties: High-performance working fixed blades. **Patterns:** Hunters, camp knives and Bowies. **Technical:** Low temperature forged 5160 and 52100 blades. Multiple quench heat treating, handle materials hardwoods, deer, elk and other types of horn. Makes heavy duty hand stitched waxed harness leather pouch type sheaths. **Prices:** Start at $300. **Remarks:** Full-time maker dedicated to the high performance using knife. **Mark:** First and last name.

DAVIDSON, LARRY,
921 Bennett St, Cedar Hill, TX 75104, Phone: 972- 291-3904, dson@swbell.net; Web: www.davidsonknives.com

DAVIS, BARRY L,
4262 US 20, Castleton, NY 12033, Phone: 518-477-5036, daviscustomknives@yahoo.com
Specialties: Collector grade Damascus folders. Traditional designs with focus on turn-of-the-century techniques employed. Sole authorship. Forges own Damascus, does all carving, filework, gold work and piquet. Uses only natural handle material. Enjoys doing multi-blade as well as single blade folders and daggers. **Prices:** Prices range from $2000 to $7000. **Remarks:** First knife sold in 1980.

DAVIS, CHARLIE,
ANZA KNIVES, PO Box 710806, Santee, CA 92072, Phone: 619-561-9445, Fax: 619-390-6283, sales@anzaknives.com; Web: www.anzaknives.com
Specialties: Fancy and embellished working straight knives of his design. **Patterns:** Hunters, camp and utility knives. **Technical:** Grinds high-carbon files. **Prices:** $20 to $185, custom depends. **Remarks:** Full- time maker; first knife sold in 1980. Now offers custom. **Mark:** ANZA U.S.A.

DAVIS, DON,
8415 Coyote Run, Loveland, CO 80537-9665, Phone: 970- 669-9016, Fax: 970-669-8072
Specialties: Working straight knives in standard patterns or to customer specs. **Patterns:** Hunters, utility knives, skinners and survival knives. **Technical:** Grinds 440C, ATS-34. **Prices:** $75 to $250. **Remarks:** Full- time maker; first knife sold in 1985. **Mark:** Signature, city and state.

DAVIS, JESSE W,
7398A Hwy 3, Sarah, MS 38665, Phone: 662-382- 7332, jandddvais1@earthlink.net
Specialties: Working straight knives and boots in standard patterns and to customer specs. **Patterns:** Boot knives, daggers, fighters, subhilts & Bowies. **Technical:** Grinds A2, D2, 440C and commercial Damascus. **Prices:** $125 to $1000. **Remarks:** Full-time maker; first knife sold in 1977. Former member Knifemakers Guild (in good standing). **Mark:** Name or initials.

DAVIS, JOEL,
74538 165th, Albert Lea, MN 56007, Phone: 507-377- 0808, joelknives@yahoo.com
Specialties: Complete sole authorship presentation grade highly complex pattern-welded mosaic Damascus blade and bolster stock. **Patterns:** To date Joel has executed over 900 different mosaic Damascus patterns in the past four years. Anything conceived by maker's imagination. **Technical:** Uses various heat colorable "high vibrancy" steels, nickel 200 and some powdered metal for bolster stock only. Uses 1095, 1075 and 15N20. High carbon steels for cutting edge blade stock only. **Prices:** 15 to $50 per square inch and up depending on complexity of pattern. **Remarks:** Full-time mosaic Damascus metal smith focusing strictly on never-before-seen mosaic patterns. Most of maker's work is used for art knives ranging between $1500 to $4500.

DAVIS, JOHN,
235 Lampe Rd, Selah, WA 98942, Phone: 509-697-3845, 509-945-4570
Specialties: Damascus and mosaic Damascus, working knives, working folders, art knives and art folders. **Technical:** Some ATS-34 and stainless Damascus. Embellishes with fancy stabilized wood, mammoth and walrus ivory. **Prices:** Start at $150. **Remarks:** Part-time maker; first knife sold in 1996. **Mark:** Name city and state on Damascus stamp initials; name inside back RFR.

DAVIS, STEVE,
3370 Chatsworth Way, Powder Springs, GA 30127, Phone: 770-427-5740
Specialties: Traditional gents and ladies folders of his design and to customer specs. **Patterns:** Slip-joint folders, locking-liner folders, lock back folders. **Technical:** Grinds ATS-34, 440C and Damascus. Offers filework; prefers hand-rubbed finishes and natural handle materials. Uses pearl, ivory, stag and exotic woods. **Prices:** $250 to $600; some to $1500. **Remarks:** Part-time maker; first knife sold in 1988. Doing business as Custom Knives by Steve Davis. **Mark:** Name engraved on blade.

DAVIS, TERRY,
Box 111, Sumpter, OR 97877, Phone: 541-894-2307
Specialties: Traditional and contemporary folders. **Patterns:** Multi-blade folders, whittlers and interframe multiblades; sunfish patterns. **Technical:** Flat-grinds ATS-34. **Prices:** $400 to $1000; some higher. **Remarks:** Full-time maker; first knife sold in 1985. **Mark:** Name in logo.

DAVIS, VERNON M,
2020 Behrens Circle, Waco, TX 76705, Phone: 254-799-7671
Specialties: Presentation-grade straight knives. Patterns: Bowies, daggers, boots, fighters, hunters and utility knives. Technical: Hollow-grinds 440C, ATS-34 and D2. Grinds an aesthetic grind line near choil. Prices: $125 to $550; some to $5000. Remarks: Part-time maker; first knife sold in 1980. Mark: Last name and city inside outline of state.

DAVIS, W C,
1955 S 1251 Rd, El Dorado Springs, MO 64744, Phone: 417-876-1259
Specialties: Fancy working straight knives and folders. Patterns: Folding lockers and slip-joints; straight hunters, fighters and Bowies. Technical: Grinds A2, ATS-34, 154, CPM T490V and CPM 530V. Prices: $100 to $300; some to $1000. Remarks: Full-time maker; first knife sold in 1972. Mark: Name.

DAVIS JR., JIM,
5129 Ridge St, Zephyrhills, FL 33541, Phone: 813-779- 9213 813-469-4241 Cell, jimdavisknives@aol.com
Specialties: Presentation-grade fixed blade knives w/composite hidden tang handles. Employs a variety of ancient and contemporary ivories. Patterns: One-of-a-kind gents, personal, and executive knives and hunters w/unique cam-lock pouch sheaths and display stands. Technical: Flat grinds ATS-34 and stainless Damascus w/most work by hand w/ assorted files. Prices: $300 and up. Remarks: Full-time maker, first knives sold in 2000. Mark: Signature w/printed name over "HANDCRAFTED."

DAVISON, TODD A.,
415 So. Reed, Lyons, KS 67554, Phone: 620-894- 0402, crazyknifeblade@yahoo.com; Web: www.tadscustomknives.com
Specialties: Making working/using and collector folders of his design. All knives are truly made one of a kind. Each knife has a serial number inside the liner. Patterns: Single and double blade traditional slip-joint pocket knives. Technical: Free hand hollow ground blades, hand finished. Using only the very best materials possible. Holding the highest standards to fit & finish and detail. Does his own heat treating. ATS34 and D2 steel. Prices: $450 to $900, some higher. Remarks: Full time maker, first knife sold in 1981. Mark: T.A. DAVISON stamped.

DAWKINS, DUDLEY L,
221 NW Broadmoor Ave., Topeka, KS 66606- 1254, Phone: 785-235-0468, Fax: 785-235-3871, dawkind@sbcglobal.net
Specialties: Stylized old or "Dawkins Forged" with anvil in center. New tang stamps. Patterns: Straight knives. Technical: Mostly carbon steel; some Damascus-all knives forged. Prices: $175 and up. Remarks: All knives supplied with wood-lined sheaths. Also make custom wood-lined sheaths $55 and up. ABS Member, sole authorship. Mark: Stylized "DLD or Dawkins Forged with anvil in center.

DAWSON, BARRY,
10A Town Plaza Suite 303, Durango, CO 81301, lindad@northlink.com; Web: www.knives.com
Specialties: Samurai swords, combat knives, collector daggers, tactical, folding and hunting knives. Patterns: Offers over 60 different models. Technical: Grinds 440C, ATS-34, own heat-treatment. Prices: $75 to $1500; some to $5000. Remarks: Full-time maker; first knife sold in 1975. Mark: Last name, USA in print or last name in script.

DAWSON, LYNN,
7760 E Hwy 69 #C-5 157, Prescott Valley, AZ 86314, Phone: 928-713-7548/928/713/8493, Fax: 928-772-1729, lynnknives@commspeed.net; Web: www.lynnknives.com
Specialties: Swords, hunters, utility, and art pieces. Patterns: Over 25 patterns to choose from. Technical: Grinds 440C, ATS-34, own heat treating. Prices: $80 to $1000. Remarks: Custom work and her own designs. Mark: The name "Lynn" in print or script.

DE MARIA JR., ANGELO,
12 Boronda Rd, Carmel Valley, CA 93924, Phone: 831-659-3381, Fax: 831-659-1315, angelodemaria1@mac.com
Specialties: Damascus, fixed and folders, sheaths. Patterns: Mosiac and random. Technical: Forging 5160, 1084 and 15N20. Prices: $200+. Remarks: Part-time maker. Mark: Angelo de Maria Carmel Valley, CA etch or AdM stamp.

DEAN, HARVEY J,
3266 CR 232, Rockdale, TX 76567, Phone: 512-446-3111, Fax: 512-446-5060, dean@tex1.net; Web: www.harveydean.com
Specialties: Collectible, functional knives. Patterns: Bowies, hunters, folders, daggers, swords, battle axes, camp and combat knives. Technical: Forges 1095, O1 and his Damascus. Prices: $350 to $10,000. Remarks: Full-time maker; first knife sold in 1981. Mark: Last name and MS.

DEBRAGA, JOSE C,
229, de la Martiniere, Aux Lievres, Quebec, CANADA G1L 4G7, Phone: 418-948-0105, Fax: 418-948-0105, josecdebragaglovetrotter.net; Web: www.geocities.com/josedebraga
Specialties: Art knives, fantasy pieces and working knives of his design or to customer specs. Patterns: Knives with sculptured or carved handles, from miniatures to full-size working knives. Technical: Grinds and hand-files 440C and ATS-34. A variety of steels and handle materials available. Offers lost wax casting. Prices: Start at $300. Remarks: Full- time maker;

wax modeler, sculptor and knifemaker; first knife sold in 1984. Mark: Initials in stylized script and serial number.

DEBRAGA, JOVAN,
141 Notre Dame des Victoir, Quebec, CANADA G2G 1J3, Phone: 418-997-0819/418-877-1915, jovancdebraga@msn.com
Specialties: Art knives, fantasy pieces and working knives of his design or to customer specs. Patterns: Knives with sculptured or carved handles, from miniatures to full-sized working knives. Technical: Grinds and hand-files 440C, and ATS-34. A variety of steels and handle materials available. Prices: Start at $300. Remarks: Full time maker. Sculptor and knifemaker. First knife sold in 2003. Mark: Initials in stylized script and serial number.

DEL RASO, PETER,
28 Mayfield Dr, Mt. Waverly, Victoria, 3149, AUSTRALIA, Phone: 61398060644, delrasofamily@optusnet.com.au
Specialties: Fixed blades, some folders, art knives. Patterns: Daggers, Bowies, tactical, boot, personal and working knives. Technical: Grinds ATS-34, commercial Damascus and any other type of steel on request. Prices: $100 to $1500. Remarks: Part-time maker, first show in 1993. Mark: Maker's surname stamped.

DELAROSA, JIM,
2116 N Pontiac Dr, Janesville, WI 53545, Phone: 608- 754-1719, d-knife@hotmail.com
Specialties: Working straight knives and folders of his design or customer specs. Patterns: Hunters, skinners, fillets, utility and locking folders. Technical: Grinds ATS-34, 440-C, D2, O1 and commercial Damascus. Prices: $75 to $450; some higher. Remarks: Part-time maker. Mark: First and last name.

DELL, WOLFGANG,
Am Alten Berg 9, D-73277 Owen-Teck, GERMANY, Phone: 49-7021-81802, wolfgang@dell-knives.de; Web: www.dell-knives.de
Specialties: Fancy high-art straight of his design and to customer specs. Patterns: Fighters, hunters, Bowies and utility/camp knives. Technical: Grinds ATS-34, RWL-34, Elmax, Damascus (Fritz Schneider). Offers high gloss finish and engraving. Prices: $500 to $1000; some to $1600. Remarks: Full-time maker; first knife sold in 1992. Mark: Hopi hand of peace.

DELLANA,
STARLANI INT'L INC, 1135 Terminal Way Ste #209, Reno, NV 89502, Phone: 304-727-5512, dellana@dellana.cc; Web: www.dellana.cc
Specialties: Collector grade fancy/embellished high art folders and art daggers. Patterns: Locking folders and art daggers. Technical: Forges her own Damascus and W-2. Engraves, does stone setting, filework, carving and gold/platinum fabrication. Prefers exotic, high karat gold, platinum, silver, gemstone and mother-of-pearl handle materials. Price: Upscale. Remarks: Sole authorship, full-time maker, first knife sold in 1994. Also does one high art collaboration a year with Van Barnett. Member: Art Knife Invitational and ABS. Mark: First name.

DELONG, DICK,
17561 E. Ohio Circle, Aurora, CO 80017, Phone: 303- 745-2652
Specialties: Fancy working knives and fantasy pieces. Patterns: Hunters and small skinners. Technical: Grinds and files O1, D2, 440C and Damascus. Offers cocobolo and Osage orange for handles. Prices: Start at $50. Remarks: Part-time maker. Member of Art Knife Invitational. Voting member of Knifemakers Guild. Member of ABS. Mark: Last name; some unmarked.

DEMENT, LARRY,
PO Box 1807, Prince Fredrick, MD 20678, Phone: 410-586-9011
Specialties: Fixed blades. Technical: Forged and stock removal. Prices: $75 to $200. Remarks: Affordable, good feelin', quality knives. Part-time maker.

DEMPSEY, DAVID,
1644 Bass Rd, Apt 2202, Macon, GA 31210, Phone: 229-244-9101, dempsey@dempseyknives.com; Web: www.dempseyknives.com
Specialties: Tactical, utility, working, classic straight knives. Patterns: Fighters, tantos, hunters, neck, utility or customer design. Technical: Grinds carbon steel and stainless including S30V (differential heat treatment), stainless steel. Prices: Start at $150 for neck knives. Remarks: Full-time maker. First knife sold 1998. Mark: First and last name over knives.

DEMPSEY, GORDON S,
PO Box 7497, N. Kenai, AK 99635, Phone: 907-776-8425
Specialties: Working straight knives. Patterns: Pattern welded Damascus and carbon steel blades. Technical: Pattern welded Damascus and carbon steel. Prices: $80 to $250. Remarks: Part-time maker; first knife sold in 1974. Mark: Name.

DENNEHY, DAN,
PO Box 470, Del Norte, CO 81132, Phone: 719-657- 2545
Specialties: Working knives, fighting and military knives, throwing knives. Patterns: Full range of straight knives, tomahawks, buckle knives. Technical: Forges and grinds A2, 01 and D2. Prices: $200 to $500. Remarks: Full-time maker; first knife sold in 1942. Latest inductee into cutlery hall of fame, #44 Mark: First name and last initial, city, state and shamrock.

DENNEHY, JOHN D,
8463 Woodlands Way, Wellington, CO 80549, Phone: 970-568-3697, jd@ thewildirishrose.com
Specialties: Working straight knives, throwers, and leatherworker's knives. **Technical:** 440C, & O1, heat treats own blades, part-time maker, first knife sold in 1989. **Patterns:** Small hunting to presentation Bowies, leatherworks round and head knives. **Prices:** $200 and up. **Remarks:** Custom sheath maker, sheath making seminars at the Blade Show.

DENNING, GENO,
CAVEMAN ENGINEERING, 135 Allenvalley Rd, Gaston, SC 29053, Phone: 803-794-6067, cden101656@aol.com; Web: www.cavemanengineering. com
Specialties: Mirror finish. **Patterns:** Hunters, fighters, folders. **Technical:** ATS-34, 440V, S-30-V D2. **Prices:** $100 and up. **Remarks:** Full-time maker since 1996. Sole income since 1999. Instructor at Montgomery Community College (Grinding Blades). A director of SCAK: South Carolina Association of Knifemakers. **Mark:** Troy NC.

DERINGER, CHRISTOPH,
625 Chemin Lower, Cookshire, Quebec, CANADA J0B 1M0, Phone: 819-345-4260, cdsab@sympatico.ca
Specialties: Traditional working/using straight knives and folders of his design and to customer specs. **Patterns:** Boots, hunters, folders, art knives, kitchen knives and utility/camp knives. **Technical:** Forges 5160, O1 and Damascus. Offers a variety of filework. **Prices:** Start at $250. **Remarks:** Full-time maker; first knife sold in 1989. **Mark:** Last name stamped/engraved.

DERR, HERBERT,
413 Woodland Dr, St. Albans, WV 25177, Phone: 304-727-3866
Specialties: Damascus one-of-a-kind knives, carbon steels also. **Patterns:** Birdseye, ladder back, mosaics. **Technical:** All styles functional as well as artistically pleasing. **Prices:** $90 to $175 carbon, Damascus $250 to $800. **Remarks:** All Damascus made by maker. **Mark:** H.K. Derr.

DETMER, PHILLIP,
14140 Bluff Rd, Breese, IL 62230, Phone: 618-526- 4834, jpdetmer@att.net
Specialties: Working knives. **Patterns:** Bowies, daggers and hunters. **Technical:** Grinds ATS-34 and D2. **Prices:** $60 to $400. **Remarks:** Part-time maker; first knife sold in 1977. **Mark:** Last name with dagger.

DEUBEL, CHESTER J.,
6211 N. Van Ark Rd., Tucson, AZ 85743, Phone: 520-444-5246, clvcdeubel@ aol.com; Web: www.cjdeubel.com
Specialties: Fancy working straight knives and folders of his or customer design, with intricate filework. **Patterns:** Fighters, Bowies, daggers, hunters, camp knives, and cowboy. **Technical:** Flat guard, hollow grind, antiqued; all types Damascus, 154cpm Stainsteel, high carbon steel, 440c Stainsteel. **Prices:** From $250 to $3500. **Remarks:** Started making part-time in 1980; went to full-time in 2000. **Mark:** C.J. Deubel.

DI MARZO, RICHARD,
1417 10th St S, Birmingham, AL 35205, Phone: 205-252-3331
Specialties: Handle artist. Scrimshaw carvings.

DICK, DAN,
P.O. Box 2303, Hutchinson, KS 67504-2303, Phone: 620- 669-6805, Dan@ DanDickKnives.com; Web: www.dandickknives.com
Specialties: Working/using fixed bladed knives of maker's design. **Patterns:** Hunters, Skinners, Utility, Kitchen, Tactical, Bowies. **Technical:** Stock removal maker using D2, forges his own Damascus and is dabbling in forging knives. Prefers natural handle materials such as: exotic and fancy burl woods and some horn. Makes his own leather sheaths, many with tooling, also makes sheaths from Kydex for his tacticals. **Prices:** $80 and up. **Remarks:** Part-time maker since 2006. **Marks:** Dan Dick using one big D for beginning of first and last name, with first name over last name in rectangle.

DICKERSON, GAVIN,
PO Box 7672, Petit 1512, SOUTH AFRICA, Phone: +27 011-965-0988, Fax: +27 011-965-0988
Specialties: Straight knives of his design or to customer specs. **Patterns:** Hunters, skinners, fighters and Bowies. **Technical:** Hollow-grinds D2, 440C, ATS-34, 12C27 and Damascus upon request. Prefers natural handle materials; offers synthetic handle materials. **Prices:** $190 to $2500. **Remarks:** Part-time maker; first knife sold in 1982. **Mark:** Name in full.

DICKERSON, GORDON S,
47 S Maple St, New Augusta, MS 38462, Phone: 931-796-1187
Specialties: Traditional working straight knives; Civil War era period pieces. **Patterns:** Bowies, hunters, tactical, camp/utility knives; some folders. **Technical:** Forges carbon steel; pattern welded and cable Damascus. **Prices:** $150 to $500; some to $3000. ABS member. **Mark:** Last name.

DICKISON, SCOTT S,
179 Taylor Rd, Fisher Circle, Portsmouth, RI 02871, Phone: 401-847-7398, squared22@cox .net; Web: http://members.cox.net/squared22
Specialties: Working and using straight knives and locking folders of his design and automatics. **Patterns:** Trout knives, fishing and hunting knives. **Technical:** Forges and grinds commercial Damascus and D2, O1. Uses natural handle materials. **Prices:** $400 to $750; some higher. **Remarks:** Part-time maker; first knife sold in 1989. **Mark:** Stylized initials.

DICRISTOFANO, ANTHONY P,
PO Box 2369, Northlake, IL 60164, Phone: 847-845-9598, sukemitsu@ sbcglobal.net Web: www.namahagesword.com
Specialties: Japanese-style swords. **Patterns:** Katana, Wakizashi, Otanto, Kozuka. **Technical:** Tradition and some modern steels. All clay tempered and traditionally hand polished using Japanese wet stones. **Remarks:** Part-time maker. **Prices:** Varied, available on request. **Mark:** Blade tang signed in "SUKEMITSU."

DIETZ, HOWARD,
421 Range Rd, New Braunfels, TX 78132, Phone: 830-885-4662
Specialties: Lock-back folders, working straight knives. **Patterns:** Folding hunters, high-grade pocket knives. ATS-34, 440C, CPM 440V, D2 and stainless Damascus. **Prices:** $300 to $1000. **Remarks:** Full-time gun and knifemaker; first knife sold in 1995. **Mark:** Name, city, and state.

DIETZEL, BILL,
PO Box 1613, Middleburg, FL 32068, Phone: 904-282- 1091
Specialties: Forged straight knives and folders. **Patterns:** His interpretations. **Technical:** Forges his Damascus and other steels. **Prices:** Middle ranges. **Remarks:** Likes natural materials; uses titanium in folder liners. Master Smith (1997). **Mark:** Name.

DIGANGI, JOSEPH M,
Box 950, Santa Cruz, NM 87567, Phone: 505- 753-6414, Fax: 505-753-8144, Web: www.digangidesigns.com
Specialties: Kitchen and table cutlery. **Patterns:** French chef's knives, carving sets, steak knife sets, some camp knives and hunters. Holds patents and trademarks for "System II" kitchen cutlery set. **Technical:** Grinds ATS-34. **Prices:** $150 to $595; some to $1200. **Remarks:** Full- time maker; first knife sold in 1983. **Mark:** DiGangi Designs.

DILL, DAVE,
7404 NW 30th St, Bethany, OK 73008, Phone: 405-789- 0750
Specialties: Folders of his design. **Patterns:** Various patterns. **Technical:** Hand-grinds 440C, ATS-34. Offers engraving and filework on all folders. **Prices:** Starting at $450. **Remarks:** Full-time maker; first knife sold in 1987. **Mark:** First initial, last name.

DILL, ROBERT,
1812 Van Buren, Loveland, CO 80538, Phone: 970- 667-5144, Fax: 970-667-5144, dillcustomknives@msn.com
Specialties: Fancy and working knives of his design. **Patterns:** Hunters, Bowies and fighters. **Technical:** Grinds 440C and D2. **Prices:** $100 to $800. **Remarks:** Full-time maker; first knife sold in 1984. **Mark:** Logo stamped into blade.

DILLUVIO, FRANK J,
13611 Murthum, Warren, MI 48088, Phone: 586- 294-5280, frankscustomknives@hotmail.com; Web: www.fdilluviocustomknives.com
Specialties: Traditional working straight knives, some high-tech. **Patterns:** Hunters, Bowies, fishing knives, sub-hilts, LinerLock® folders and miniatures. **Technical:** Grinds D2, 440C, CPM; works for precision fits— no solder. **Prices:** $95 to $450; some to $800. **Remarks:** Full-time maker; first knife sold in 1984. **Mark:** Name and state.

DION, GREG,
3032 S Jackson St, Oxnard, CA 93033, Phone: 805-483- 1781
Specialties: Working straight knives, some fancy. Welcomes special orders. **Patterns:** Hunters, fighters, camp knives, Bowies and tantos. **Technical:** Grinds ATS-34, 154CM and 440C. **Prices:** $85 to $300; some to $600. **Remarks:** Part-time maker; first knife sold in 1985. **Mark:** Name.

DIOTTE, JEFF,
DIOTTE KNIVES, 159 Laurier Dr, LaSalle Ontario, CANADA N9J 1L4, Phone: 519-978-2764

DIPPOLD, AL,
90 Damascus Ln, Perryville, MO 63775, Phone: 573-547- 1119, adippold@ midwest.net
Specialties: Fancy one-of-a-kind locking folders. **Patterns:** Locking folders. **Technical:** Forges and grinds mosaic and pattern welded Damascus. Offers filework on all folders. **Prices:** $500 to $3500; some higher. **Remarks:** Full-time maker; first knife sold in 1980. **Mark:** Last name in logo inside of liner.

DISKIN, MATT,
PO Box 653, Freeland, WA 98249, Phone: 360-730- 0451
Specialties: Damascus autos. **Patterns:** Dirks and daggers. **Technical:** Forges mosaic Damascus using 15N20, 1084, 02, 06, L6; pure nickel. **Prices:** Start at $500. Remarks: Full-time maker. **Mark:** Last name.

DIXON JR., IRA E,
PO Box 2581, Ventura, CA 93002-2581, irasknives@yahoo.com
Specialties: Utilitarian straight knives of his design. **Patterns:** Camp, hunters, fighters, utility knives and art knives. **Technical:** Grinds CPM, S30V, 1095, Damascus and D2. **Prices:** $200 to $1500. **Remarks:** Part- time maker; first knife sold in 1993. **Mark:** First name, Handmade.

DODD, ROBERT F,
4340 E Canyon Dr, Camp Verde, AZ 86322, Phone: 928-567-3333, rfdknives@ commspeed.net; Web: www.rfdoddknives.com
Specialties: Folders, fixed blade hunter/skinners, Bowies, daggers. **Patterns:** Drop point. **Technical:** ATS-34 and Damascus. **Prices:** $250 and up. **Remarks:** Hand tooled leather sheaths. **Mark:** R. F. Dodd, Camp Verde AZ.

custom knifemakers

DOGGETT, BOB,
1310 Vinetree Rd, Brandon, FL 33510, Phone: 813- 786-9057, dogman@tampabay.rr.com; Web: www.doggettcustomknives.com
Specialties: Clean, functional working knives. **Patterns:** Classic-styled hunter, fighter and utility fixed blades; liner locking folders. **Technical:** Uses stainless steel and commercial Damascus, 416 stainless for bolsters and hardware, hand-rubbed satin finish, top quality handle materials and titanium liners on folders. **Prices:** Start at $175. **Remarks:** Part-time maker. **Mark:** Last name.

DOIRON, DONALD,
6 Chemin Petit Lac des Ced, Messines, PQ, CANADA J0X-2J0, Phone: 819-465-2489

DOLAN, ROBERT L.,
220—B Naalae Rd, Kula, HI 96790, Phone: 808- 878-6406
Specialties: Working straight knives in standard patterns, his designs or to customer specs. **Patterns:** Fixed blades and potter's tools, ceramic saws. **Technical:** Grinds O1, D2, 440C and ATS-34. Heat-treats and engraves. **Prices:** Start at $75. **Remarks:** Full-time tool and knifemaker; first knife sold in 1985. **Mark:** Last name, USA.

DOLE, ROGER,
DOLE CUSTOM KNIFE WORKS, PO Box 323, Buckley, WA 98321, Phone: 253-862-6770
Specialties: Folding knives. They include slip joint, lock back and locking liner type knives. Most have integral bolster and liners. The locking liner knives have a removable titanium side lock that is machined into the integral liner, they are also available with a split liner lock. **Technical:** Makes ATS-34, 440-C and BG-42 stainless steel. Has in stock or available all types of natural and synthetic handle materials. Uses 416, 303, and 304 stainless steel, 7075-T6 aluminum and titanium for the guards on the fixed blade knives and integral liners on the folding knives. The locking LinerLock® mechanisms are made from 6AL4V titanium. Uses the stock removal method to fabricate all of the blades produced. The blades are ground on a 2 X 72 inch belt grinder. Not a bladesmith. **Patterns:** 51 working designs for fixed blade knives. They include small bird and trout knives to skinning axes. Most are working designs. All come with hand crafted leather sheath Kydex sheaths; can be special ordered. **Remarks:** First knife sold in 1975.

DOMINY, CHUCK,
PO Box 593, Colleyville, TX 76034, Phone: 817-498- 4527
Specialties: Titanium LinerLock® folders. **Patterns:** Hunters, utility/camp knives and LinerLock® folders. **Technical:** Grinds 440C and ATS- 34. **Prices:** $250 to $3000. **Remarks:** Full-time maker; first knife sold in 1976. **Mark:** Last name.

DOOLITTLE, MIKE,
13 Denise Ct, Novato, CA 94947, Phone: 415-897- 3246
Specialties: Working straight knives in standard patterns. **Patterns:** Hunters and fishing knives. **Technical:** Grinds 440C, 154CM and ATS- 34. **Prices:** $125 to $200; some to $750. **Remarks:** Part-time maker; first knife sold in 1981. **Mark:** Name, city and state.

DORNELES, LUCIANO OLIVERIRA,
Rua 15 De Novembro 2222, Nova Petropolis, RS, BRAZIL 95150-000, Phone: 011-55-54-303-303-90, tchebufalo@hotmail.com
Specialties: Traditional "true" Brazilian-style working knives and to customer specs. **Patterns:** Brazilian hunters, utility and camp knives, Bowies, Dirk. A master at the making of the true "Faca Campeira Gaucha," the true camp knife of the famous Brazilian Gauchos. A Dorneles knife is 100 percent hand-forged with sledge hammers only. Can make spectacular Damascus hunters/daggers. **Technical:** Forges only 52100 and his own Damascus, can put silver wire inlay on customer design handles on special orders; uses only natural handle materials. **Prices:** $250 to $1000. **Mark:** Symbol with L. Dorneles.

DOTSON, TRACY,
1280 Hwy C-4A, Baker, FL 32531, Phone: 850-537- 2407
Specialties: Folding fighters and small folders. **Patterns:** LinerLock® and lockback folders. **Technical:** Hollow-grinds ATS-34 and commercial Damascus. **Prices:** Start at $250. **Remarks:** Part-time maker; first knife sold in 1995. **Mark:** Last name.

DOUCETTE, R,
CUSTOM KNIVES, 112 Memorial Dr, Brantford, Ont., CANADA N3R 5S3, Phone: 519-756-9040, randy@randydoucetteknives.com; Web: www.randydoucetteknives.com
Specialties: Filework, tactical designs, multiple grinds. **Patterns:** Tactical folders, fancy folders, daggers, tantos, karambits. **Technical:** All knives are handmade. The only outsourcing is heat treatment. **Prices:** $500 to $2,500. **Remarks:** Full-time knifemaker; 2-year waiting list. **Mark:** R. Doucette

DOUGLAS, JOHN J,
506 Powell Rd, Lynch Station, VA 24571, Phone: 804-369-7196
Specialties: Fancy and traditional straight knives and folders of his design and to customer specs. **Patterns:** Locking folders, swords and sgian dubhs. **Technical:** Grinds 440C stainless, ATS-34 stainless and customer's choice. Offers newly designed non-pivot uni-lock folders. Prefers highly polished finish. **Prices:** $160 to $1400. **Remarks:** Full-time maker; first knife sold in 1975. Doing business as Douglas Keltic. **Mark:** Stylized initial. Folders are numbered; customs are dated.

DOURSIN, GERARD,
Chemin des Croutoules, F 84210, Pernes les Fontaines, FRANCE
Specialties: Period pieces. **Patterns:** Liner locks and daggers. **Technical:** Forges mosaic Damascus. **Prices:** $600 to $4000. **Remarks:** First knife sold in 1983. **Mark:** First initial, last name and I stop the lion.

DOUSSOT, LAURENT,
1008 Montarville, St. Bruno, Quebec, CANADA J3V 3T1, Phone: 450-441-3298, doussot@skalja.com; Web: www.skalja.com, www.doussot-knives.com
Specialties: Fancy and embellished folders and fantasy knives. **Patterns:** Fighters and locking folders. **Technical:** Grinds ATS-34 and commercial Damascus. Scale carvings on all knives; most bolsters are carved titanium. **Prices:** $350 to $3000. **Remarks:** Part-time maker; first knife was sold in 1992. **Mark:** Stylized initials inside circle.

DOWELL, T M,
139 NW St Helen's Pl, Bend, OR 97701, Phone: 541- 382-8924, Fax: 541-382-8924, tmdknives@webtv.net
Specialties: Integral construction in hunting knives. **Patterns:** Limited to featherweights, lightweights, integral hilt and caps. **Technical:** Grinds D-2, BG-42 and Vasco wear. **Prices:** $275 and up. **Remarks:** Full-time maker; first knife sold in 1967. **Mark:** Initials logo.

DOWNIE, JAMES T,
10076 Estate Dr, Port Franks, Ont., CANADA N0M 2L0, Phone: 519-243-1488, Web: www.ckg.org (click on members page)
Specialties: Serviceable straight knives and folders; period pieces. **Patterns:** Hunters, Bowies, camp knives, fillet and miniatures. **Technical:** Grinds D2, 440C and ATS-34, Damasteel, stainless steel Damascus. **Prices:** $100 to $500; some higher. **Remarks:** Full-time maker, first knife sold in 1978. **Mark:** Signature of first and middle initials, last name.

DOWNING, LARRY,
12268 Hwy 181N, Bremen, KY 42325, Phone: 270- 525-3523, larrydowning@bellsouth.net; Web: www.downingcustomknives.com
Specialties: Working straight knives and folders. **Patterns:** From mini-knives to daggers, folding lockers to interframes. **Technical:** Forges and grinds 154CM, ATS-34 and his own Damascus. **Prices:** $195 to $950; some higher. **Remarks:** Part-time maker; first knife sold in 1979. **Mark:** Name in arrowhead.

DOWNING, TOM,
2675 12th St, Cuyahoga Falls, OH 44223, Phone: 330-923-7464
Specialties: Working straight knives; period pieces. **Patterns:** Hunters, fighters and tantos. **Technical:** Grinds 440C, ATs-34 and CPM-T-440V. Prefers natural handle materials. **Prices:** $150 to $900, some to $1500. **Remarks:** Part-time maker; first knife sold in 1979. **Mark:** First and middle initials, last name.

DOWNS, JAMES F,
2247 Summit View Rd, Powell, OH 43065, Phone: 614-766-5350, jfdowns1@yahoo.com
Specialties: Working straight knives of his design or to customer specs. **Patterns:** Folders, Bowies, boot, hunters, utility. **Technical:** Grinds 440C and other steels. Prefers mastodon ivory, all pearls, stabilized wood and elephant ivory. **Prices:** $75 to $1200. **Remarks:** Full-time maker; first knife sold in 1980. **Mark:** Last name.

DOX, JAN,
Zwanebloemlaan 27, B 2900 Schoten, BELGIUM, Phone: 32 3 658 77 43, jan.dox@scarlet.be
Specialties: Working/using knives, from kitchen to battlefield. **Patterns:** Own designs, some based on traditional ethnic patterns (Scots, Celtic, Scandinavian and Japanese) or to customer specs. **Technical:** Grinds D2/A2 and stainless, forges carbon steels, convex edges. Handles: Wrapped in modern or traditional patterns, resin impregnated if desired. Natural or synthetic materials, some carved. **Prices:** $50 and up. **Remarks:** Spare-time maker, first knife sold 2001. **Mark:** Name or stylized initials.

DOZIER, BOB,
PO Box 1941, Springdale, AR 72765, Phone: 888-823- 0023/479-756-0023, Fax: 479-756-9139, info@dozierknives.com; Web www.dozierknives.com
Specialties: Using knives (fixed blades and folders). **Patterns:** Using fine collector-grade knives. **Technical:** Uses D2. Prefers Micarta handle material. **Prices:** Using knives: $195 to $700. **Remarks:** Full-time maker; first knife sold in 1965. No longer doing semi-handmade line. **Mark:** State, made, last name in a circle (for fixed blades); Last name with arrow through 'D' and year over name (for folders).

DRAPER, AUDRA,
#10 Creek Dr, Riverton, WY 82501, Phone: 307-856- 6807 or 307-851-0426 cell, adraper@wyoming.com; Web: www.draperknives.com
Specialties: One-of-a-kind straight and folding knives. Also pendants, earring and bracelets of Damascus. **Patterns:** Design custom knives, using, Bowies, and minis. **Technical:** Forge Damascus; heat-treats all knives. **Prices:** Vary depending on item. **Remarks:** Full-time maker; master bladesmith in the ABS. Member of the PKA; first knife sold in 1995. **Mark:** Audra.

DRAPER, MIKE,
#10 Creek Dr, Riverton, WY 82501, Phone: 307-856-6807, adraper@wyoming.com
Specialties: Mainly folding knives in tactical fashion, occasonal fixed blade. **Patterns:** Hunters, Bowies and camp knives, tactical survival. **Technical:** Grinds S30V stainless steel. **Prices:** Starting at $250+. **Remarks:** Full-time maker; first knife sold in 1996. **Mark:** Initials M.J.D. or name, city and state.

DREW, GERALD,
213 Hawk Ridge Dr, Mill Spring, NC 28756, Phone: 828-713-4762
Specialties: Blade ATS-34 blades. Straight knives. **Patterns:** Hunters, camp knives, some Bowies and tactical. **Technical:** ATS-34 preferred. **Price:** $65 to $400. **Mark:** GL DREW.

DRISCOLL, MARK,
4115 Avoyer Pl, La Mesa, CA 91941, Phone: 619-670-0695
Specialties: High-art, period pieces and working/using knives of his design or to customer specs; some fancy. **Patterns:** Swords, Bowies, fighters, daggers, hunters and primitive (mountain man-styles). **Technical:** Forges 52100, 5160, O1, L6, 1095, and maker his own Damascus and mokume; also does multiple quench heat treating. Uses exotic hardwoods, ivory and horn, offers fancy file work, carving, scrimshaws. **Prices:** $150 to $550; some to $1500. **Remarks:** Part-time maker; first knife sold in 1986. Doing business as Mountain Man Knives. **Mark:** Double "M."

DROST, JASON D,
Rt 2 Box 49, French Creek, WV 26218, Phone: 304-472-7901
Specialties: Working/using straight knives of his design. **Patterns:** Hunters and utility/camp knives. **Technical:** Grinds 154CM and D2. **Prices:** $125 to $5000. **Remarks:** Spare-time maker; first knife sold in 1995. **Mark:** First and middle initials, last name, maker, city and state.

DROST, MICHAEL B,
Rt 2 Box 49, French Creek, WV 26218, Phone: 304-472-7901
Specialties: Working/using straight knives and folders of all designs. **Patterns:** Hunters, locking folders and utility/camp knives. **Technical:** Grinds ATS-34, D2 and CPM-T-440V. Offers dove-tailed bolsters and spacers, filework and scrimshaw. **Prices:** $125 to $400; some to $740. **Remarks:** Full-time maker; first knife sold in 1990. Doing business as Drost Custom Knives. **Mark:** Name, city and state.

DRUMM, ARMIN,
Lichtensteinstrasse 33, D-89160 Dornstadt, GERMANY, Phone: 49-163-632-2842, armin@drumm-knives.de; Web: www.drumm-knives.de
Specialties: One-of-a-kind forged and Damascus fixed blade knives and folders. **Patterns:** Classic Bowie knives, daggers, fighters, hunters, folders, swords. **Technical:** Forges own Damascus and carbon steels, filework, carved handles. **Prices:** $250 to $800, some higher. **Remarks:** First knife sold in 2001, member of the German Knifemakers Guild. **Mark:** First initial, last name.

DUBLIN, DENNIS,
728 Stanley St, Box 986, Enderby, B.C., CANADA V0E 1V0, Phone: 604-838-6753
Specialties: Working straight knives and folders, plain or fancy. **Patterns:** Hunters and Bowies, locking hunters, combination knives/axes. **Technical:** Forges and grinds high-carbon steels. **Prices:** $100 to $400; some higher. **Remarks:** Full-time maker; first knife sold in 1970. **Mark:** Name.

DUFF, BILL,
2801 Ash St, Poteau, OK 74953, Phone: 918-647-4458
Specialties: Straight knives and folders, some fancy. **Patterns:** Hunters, folders and miniatures. **Technical:** Grinds 440-C and commercial Damascus. **Prices:** $200 to $1000 some higher. **Remarks:** First knife some in 1976. **Mark:** Bill Duff.

DUFOUR, ARTHUR J,
8120 De Armoun Rd, Anchorage, AK 99516, Phone: 907-345-1701
Specialties: Working straight knives from standard patterns. **Patterns:** Hunters, Bowies, camp and fishing knives—grinded thin and pointed. **Technical:** Grinds 440C, ATS-34, AEB-L. Tempers 57-58R; hollow- grinds. **Prices:** $135; some to $250. **Remarks:** Part-time maker; first knife sold in 1970. **Mark:** Prospector logo.

DUGDALE, DANIEL J,
11 Eleanor Road, Walpole, MA 02081, Phone: 508-668-3528, dlpdugdale@comcast.net
Specialties: Button-lock and straight knives of his design. **Patterns:** Utilities, hunters, skinners, and tactical. **Technical:** Falt grinds D-2 and 440C, aluminum handles with anodized finishes. **Prices:** $150 to $500. **Remarks:** Part-time maker since 1977. **Mark:** Deer track with last name, town and state.

DUGGER, DAVE,
2504 West 51, Westwood, KS 66205, Phone: 913-831-2382
Specialties: Working straight knives; fantasy pieces. **Patterns:** Hunters, boots and daggers in one-of-a-kind styles. **Technical:** Grinds D2, 440C and 154CM. **Prices:** $75 to $350; some to $1200. **Remarks:** Part-time maker; first knife sold in 1979. Not currently accepting orders. Doing business as Dog Knives. **Mark:** DOG.

DUNKERLEY, RICK,
PO Box 582, Seeley Lake, MT 59868, Phone: 406- 677-5496, rick@dunkerleyhandmadeknives.com
Specialties: Mosaic Damascus folders and carbon steel utility knives. **Patterns:** One-of-a-kind folders, standard hunters and utility designs. **Technical:** Forges 52100, Damascus and mosaic Damascus. Prefers natural handle materials. **Prices:** $200 and up. **Remarks:** Full-time maker; first knife sold in 1984, ABS Master Smith. Doing business as Dunkerley Custom Knives. Dunkerley handmade knives, sole authorship. **Mark:** Dunkerley, MS.

DUNN, CHARLES K,
17740 GA Hwy 116, Shiloh, GA 31826, Phone: 706-846-2666
Specialties: Fancy and working straight knives and folders of his design and to customer specs. **Patterns:** Bowies, hunters and locking folders. **Technical:** Grinds 440C and ATS-34. Engraves; filework offered. **Prices:** $75 to $300. **Remarks:** Part-time maker; first knife sold in 1988. **Mark:** First initial, last name, city, state.

DUNN, STEVE,
376 Biggerstaff Rd, Smiths Grove, KY 42171, Phone: 270-563-9830, dunndeal@verizon.net; Web: www.stevedunnknives.com
Specialties: Working and using straight knives of his design; period pieces. Also offer engraving & gold inlays. **Patterns:** Hunters, skinners, Bowies, fighters, camp knives, folders, swords and battle axes. **Technical:** Forges own Damascus, 1075, 15N20, 52100, 1084, L6. **Prices:** Moderate to upscale. **Remarks:** Full-time maker; first knife sold in 1990. **Mark:** Last name and MS.

DURAN, JERRY T,
PO Box 80692, Albuquerque, NM 87198-0692, Phone: 505-873-4676, jtdknives@hotmail.com; Web: www.kmg.org/jtdknives
Specialties: Tactical folders, Bowies, fighters, liner locks, autopsy and hunters. **Patterns:** Folders, Bowies, hunters and tactical knives. **Technical:** Forges own Damascus and forges carbon steel. **Prices:** Moderate to upscale. **Remarks:** Full-time maker; first knife sold in 1978. **Mark:** Initials in elk rack logo.

DURHAM, KENNETH,
BUZZARD ROOST FORGE, 10495 White Pike, Cherokee, AL 35616, Phone: 256-359-4287, www.home.hiwaay.net/ ~jamesd/
Specialties: Bowies, dirks, hunters. **Patterns:** Traditional patterns. **Technical:** Forges 1095, 5160, 52100 and makes own Damascus. **Prices:** $85 to $1600. **Remarks:** Began making knives about 1995. Received Journeyman stamp 1999. Got Master Smith stamp in 2004. **Mark:** Bull's head with Ken Durham above and Cherokee AL below.

DURIO, FRED,
144 Gulino St, Opelousas, LA 70570, Phone: 337-948- 4831/cell 337-351-2652, fdurio@yahoo.com
Specialties: Folders. **Patterns:** Liner locks; plain and fancy. **Technical:** Makes own Damascus. **Prices:** Moderate to upscale. **Remarks:** Full- time maker. **Mark:** Last name-Durio.

DUVALL, FRED,
10715 Hwy 190, Benton, AR 72015, Phone: 501-778- 9360
Specialties: Working straight knives and folders. **Patterns:** Locking folders, slip joints, hunters, fighters and Bowies. **Technical:** Grinds D2 and CPM440V; forges 5160. **Prices:** $100 to $400; some to $800. **Remarks:** Part-time maker; first knife sold in 1973. **Mark:** Last name.

DYER, DAVID,
4531 Hunters Glen, Granbury, TX 76048, Phone: 817- 573-1198
Specialties: Working skinners and early period knives. **Patterns:** Customer designs, his own patterns. **Technical:** Coal forged blades; 5160 and 52100 steels. Grinds D2, 1095, L6. **Prices:** $150 for neck knives and small (3" to 3-1/2"). To $600 for large blades and specialty blades. **Mark:** Last name DYER electro etched.

DYESS, EDDIE,
1005 Hamilton, Roswell, NM 88201, Phone: 505-623- 5599, eddyess@msn.com
Specialties: Working and using straight knives in standard patterns. **Patterns:** Hunters and fighters. **Technical:** Grinds 440C, 154CM and D2 on request. **Prices:** $150 to $300, some higher. **Remarks:** Spare-time maker; first knife sold in 1980. **Mark:** Last name.

DYRNOE, PER,
Sydskraenten 10, Tulstrup, DK 3400 Hilleroed, DENMARK, Phone: +45 42287041
Specialties: Hand-crafted knives with zirconia ceramic blades. **Patterns:** Hunters, skinners, Norwegian-style tolle knives, most in animal-like ergonomic shapes. **Technical:** Handles of exotic hardwood, horn, fossil ivory, etc. Norwegian-style sheaths. **Prices:** Start at $500. **Remarks:** Part-time maker in cooperation with Hans J. Henriksen; first knife sold in 1993. **Mark:** Initial logo.

E

EAKER, ALLEN L,
416 Clinton Ave Dept KI, Paris, IL 61944, Phone: 217-466-5160
Specialties: Traditional straight knives and folders of his design. **Patterns:** Hunters, locking folders and slip-joint folders. **Technical:** Grinds 440C;

inlays. **Prices:** $125 to $325; some to $500. **Remarks:** Spare-time maker; first knife sold in 1994. **Mark:** Initials in tankard logo stamped on tang, serial number on back side.

EALY, DELBERT,
PO Box 121, Indian River, MI 49749, Phone: 231- 238-4705

EATON, FRANK L JR,
41 Vista Woods Rd, Stafford, VA 22556, Phone: 540-657-6160, FEton2@aol.com
Specialties: Full tang/hidden tang fixed working and art knives of his own design. **Patterns:** Hunters, skinners, fighters, Bowies, tacticals and daggers. **Technical:** Stock removal maker, prefer using natural materials. **Prices:** $175 to $400. **Remarks:** Part-time maker - Active Duty Airborn Ranger-Making 4 years. **Mark:** Name over 75th Ranger Regimental Crest.

EATON, RICK,
313 Dailey Rd, Broadview, MT 59015, Phone: 406-667- 2405, rick@eatonknives.com; Web: www.eatonknives.com
Specialties: Interframe folders and one-hand-opening side locks. **Patterns:** Bowies, daggers, fighters and folders. **Technical:** Grinds 154CM, ATS-34, 440C and other maker's Damascus. Offers high-quality hand engraving, Bulino and gold inlay. **Prices:** Upscale. **Remarks:** Full-time maker; first knife sold in 1982. **Mark:** Full name or full name and address.

EBISU, HIDESAKU,
3-39-7 Koi Osako Nishi Ku, Hiroshima City, JAPAN 733 0816

ECHOLS, ROGER,
46 Channing Rd, Nashville, AR 71852-8588, Phone: 870-451-9089, blademanechols@aol.com
Specialties: Liner locks, auto-scale release, lock backs. **Patterns:** His or yours. **Technical:** Autos. **Prices:** $500 to $1700. **Remarks:** Likes to use pearl, ivory and Damascus the most. Made first knife in 1984. Part-time maker; tool and die maker by trade. **Mark:** Name.

EDDY, HUGH E,
211 E Oak St, Caldwell, ID 83605, Phone: 208-459- 0536

EDEN, THOMAS,
PO Box 57, Cranbury, NJ 08512, Phone: 609-371- 0774, njirrigation@msn.com
Specialties: Chef's knives. **Patterns:** Fixed blade, working patterns, hand forged. **Technical:** Damascus. **Remarks:** ABS Smith. **Mark:** Eden (script).

EDGE, TOMMY,
1244 County Road 157, Cash, AR 72421, Phone: 501- 477-5210, tedge@tex.net
Specialties: Fancy/embellished working knives of his design. **Patterns:** Bowies, hunters and utility/camping knives. **Technical:** Grinds 440C, ATS-34 and D2. Makes own cable Damascus; offers filework. **Prices:** $70 to $250; some to $1500. **Remarks:** Part-time maker; first knife sold in 1973. **Mark:** Stamped first initial, last name and stenciled name, city and state in oval shape.

EDWARDS, FAIN E,
PO Box 280, Topton, NC 28781, Phone: 828-321- 3127

EDWARDS, MITCH,
303 New Salem Rd, Glasgow, KY 42141, Phone: 270-404-0758 / 270-404-0758, medwards@glasgow-ky.com; Web: www.traditionalknives.com
Specialties: Period pieces. **Patterns:** Neck knives, camp, rifleman and Bowie knives. **Technical:** All hand forged, forges own Damascus O1, 1084, 1095, L6, 15N20. **Prices:** $200 to $1000. **Remarks:** Journeyman Smith. **Mark:** Broken heart.

EHRENBERGER, DANIEL ROBERT,
1213 S Washington St, Mexico, MO 65265, Phone: 573-633-2010
Specialties: Affordable working/using straight knives of his design and to custom specs. **Patterns:** 10" western Bowie, fighters, hunting and skinning knives. **Technical:** Forges 1085, 1095, his own Damascus and cable Damascus. **Prices:** $80 to $500. **Remarks:** Full-time maker, first knife sold 1994. **Mark:** Ehrenberger JS.

EKLUND, MAIHKEL,
Fone Stam V9, S-820 41 Farila, SWEDEN, info@art-knives.com; Web: www.art-knives.com
Specialties: Collector-grade working straight knives. **Patterns:** Hunters, Bowies and fighters. **Technical:** Grinds ATS-34, Uddeholm and Dama steel. Engraves and scrimshaws. **Prices:** $200 to $2000. **Remarks:** Full-time maker; first knife sold in 1983. **Mark:** Initials or name.

ELDER JR., PERRY B,
1321 Garrettsburg Rd, Clarksville, TN 37042- 2516, Phone: 931-647-9416, pbebje@bellsouth.net
Specialties: Hunters, combat Bowies bird and trout. **Technical:** High- carbon steel and Damascus blades. **Prices:** $350 and up depending on blade desired. **Mark:** ELDER.

ELDRIDGE, ALLAN,
7731 Four Winds Dr, Ft. Worth, TX 76133, Phone: 817-370-7778
Specialties: Fancy classic straight knives in standard patterns. **Patterns:** Hunters, Bowies, fighters, folders and miniatures. **Technical:** Grinds O1 and Damascus. Engraves silver-wire inlays, pearl inlays, scrimshaws and offers filework. **Prices:** $50 to $500; some to $1200. **Remarks:** Spare-time maker; first knife sold in 1965. **Mark:** Initials.

ELISHEWITZ, ALLEN,
3960 Lariat Ridge, New Braunfels, TX 78132, Phone: 830-899-5356, allen@elishewitzknives.com; Web: elishewitzknives.com
Specialties: Collectible high-tech working straight knives and folders of his design. **Patterns:** Working, utility and tactical knives. **Technical:** Designs and uses innovative locking mechanisms. All designs drafted and field-tested. **Prices:** $600 to $1000. **Remarks:** Full-time maker; first knife sold in 1989. **Mark:** Gold medallion inlaid in blade.

ELKINS, VAN,
3596 New Monroe Rd., Bastrop, LA 71220, Phone: 318- 614-0543/318-283-2374
Specialties: Folders, from liner-locks to one-of-a-kind damascus button-locks. **Patterns:** Bowies and folders. **Technical:** Forges own damascus in several patterns. Uses high-tech stainless in tactical designs. **Prices:** $595 to $5800. **Remarks:** Believes in sole authorship. First knife sold in 1984. **Mark:** Elkins.

ELLEFSON, JOEL,
PO Box 1016, 310 S 1st St, Manhattan, MT 59741, Phone: 406-284-3111
Specialties: Working straight knives, fancy daggers and one-of-a-kinds. **Patterns:** Hunters, daggers and some folders. **Technical:** Grinds A2, 440C and ATS-34. Makes own mokume in bronze, brass, silver and shibuishi; makes brass/steel blades. **Prices:** $100 to $500; some to $2000. **Remarks:** Part-time maker; first knife sold in 1978. **Mark:** Stylized last initial.

ELLERBE, W B,
3871 Osceola Rd, Geneva, FL 32732, Phone: 407-349- 5818
Specialties: Period and primitive knives and sheaths. **Patterns:** Bowies to patch knives, some tomahawks. **Technical:** Grinds Sheffield O1 and files. **Prices:** Start at $35. **Remarks:** Full-time maker; first knife sold in 1971. Doing business as Cypress Bend Custom Knives. **Mark:** Last name or initials.

ELLIOTT, JERRY,
4507 Kanawha Ave, Charleston, WV 25304, Phone: 304-925-5045, elliottknives@verizon.net
Specialties: Classic and traditional straight knives and folders of his design and to customer specs. **Patterns:** Hunters, locking folders and Bowies. **Technical:** Grinds ATS-34, 154CM, O1, D2 and T-440-V. All guards silver-soldered; bolsters are pinned on straight knives, spot- welded on folders. **Prices:** $80 to $265; some to $1000. **Remarks:** Full- time maker; first knife sold in 1972. **Mark:** First and middle initials, last name, knife maker, city, state.

ELLIS, DAVE/ABS MASTERSMITH,
380 South Melrose Dr #407, Vista, CA 92083, Phone: 760-643-4032 Eves: 760-945-7177, www.exquisiteknives.com
Specialties: Bowies, utility and combat knives. **Patterns:** Using knives to art quality pieces. **Technical:** Forges 5160, L6, 52100, cable and his own Damascus steels. **Prices:** $300 to $4000. **Remarks:** Part-time maker. California's first ABS Master Smith. **Mark:** Dagger-Rose with name and M.S. mark.

ELLIS, WILLIAM DEAN,
2767 Edgar Ave, Sanger, CA 93657, Phone: 559-314-4459, urleebird@comcast.net; Web: www.billysblades.com
Specialties: Classic and fancy knives of his design. **Patterns:** Boots, fighters and utility knives. **Technical:** Grinds ATS-34, D2 and Damascus. Offers tapered tangs and six patterns of filework; tooled multi-colored sheaths. **Prices:** $250 to $500; some to $1500. **Remarks:** Part-time maker; first knife sold in 1991. Doing business as Billy's Blades. **Mark:** "B" in a five-point star next to "Billy," city and state within a rounded-corner rectangle.

ELLIS, WILLY B,
4941 Cardinal Trail, Palm Harbor, FL 34683, Phone: 727-942-6420, Web: www.willyb.com
Specialties: One-of-a-kind high art and fantasy knives of his design. Occasional customs full size and miniatures. **Patterns:** Bowies, fighters, hunters and others. **Technical:** Grinds 440C, ATS-34, 1095, carbon Damascus, ivory bone, stone and metal carving. **Prices:** $175 to $15,000. **Remarks:** Full-time maker, first knife made in 1973. Member Knifemakers Guild. Jewel setting inlays. **Mark:** Willy B. or WB'S C etched or carved.

ELROD, ROGER R,
58 Dale Ave, Enterprise, AL 36330, Phone: 334- 347-1863

EMBRETSEN, KAJ,
FALUVAGEN 67, S-82830 Edsbyn, SWEDEN, Phone: 46-271-21057, Fax: 46-271-22961, kay.embretsen@telia.com Web:www.embretsenknives.com
Specialties: Damascus folding knives. **Patterns:** Uses mammoth ivory and some pearl. **Technical:** Uses own Damascus steel. **Remarks:** Full time since 1983. **Prices:** $2500 to $8000. **Mark:** Name inside the folder.

EMERSON, ERNEST R,
PO Box 4180, Torrance, CA 90510-4180, Phone: 310-212-7455, info@emersonknives.com; Web: www.emersonknives.com
Specialties: High-tech folders and combat fighters. **Patterns:** Fighters, LinerLock® combat folders and SPECWAR combat knives. **Technical:** Grinds 154CM and Damascus. Makes folders with titanium fittings, liners and locks. Chisel grind specialist. **Prices:** $550 to $850; some to $10,000. **Remarks:** Full-time maker; first knife sold in 1983. **Mark:** Last name and Specwar knives.

ENCE, JIM,
145 S 200 East, Richfield, UT 84701, Phone: 435-896-6206
Specialties: High-art period pieces (spec in California knives) art knives. **Patterns:** Art, boot knives, fighters, Bowies and occasional folders. **Technical:** Grinds 440C for polish and beauty boys; makes own Damascus. **Prices:** Upscale. **Remarks:** Full-time maker; first knife sold in 1977. Does own engraving, gold work and stone work. Guild member since 1977. Founding member of the AKI. **Mark:** Ence, usually engraved.

ENGLAND, VIRGIL,
1340 Birchwood St, Anchorage, AK 99508, Phone: 907-274-9494, WEB:www.virgilengland.com
Specialties: Edged weapons and equipage, one-of-a-kind only. **Patterns:** Axes, swords, lances and body armor. **Technical:** Forges and grinds as pieces dictate. Offers stainless and Damascus. **Prices:** Upscale. **Remarks:** A veteran knifemaker. No commissions. **Mark:** Stylized initials.

ENGLE, WILLIAM,
16608 Oak Ridge Rd, Boonville, MO 65233, Phone: 816-882-6277
Specialties: Traditional working and using straight knives of his design. **Patterns:** Hunters, Bowies and fighters. **Technical:** Grinds 440C, ATS-34 and 154CM. **Prices:** $250 to $500; some higher. **Remarks:** Part-time maker; first knife sold in 1982. All knives come with certificate of authenticity. **Mark:** Last name in block lettering.

ENGLEBRETSON, GEORGE,
1209 NW 49th St, Oklahoma City, OK 73118, Phone: 405-840-4784
Specialties: Working straight knives. **Patterns:** Hunters and Bowies. **Technical:** Grinds A2, D2, 440C and ATS-34. **Prices:** Start at $150. **Remarks:** Full-time maker; first knife sold in 1967. **Mark:** "By George," name and city.

ENGLISH, JIM,
14586 Olive Vista Dr., Jamul, CA 91935, Phone: 619-669-0833
Specialties: High-quality working straight knives. **Patterns:** Hunters, fighters, skinners, tantos, utility and fillet knives, Bowies and *san-mai* Damascus Bowies. **Technical:** Hollow-grind 440C by hand. Feature linen Micarta handles, nickel-silver handle bolts and handmade sheaths. **Prices:** $65 to $270. **Remarks:** Company name is Mountain Home Knives. **Mark:** Mountain Home Knives.

ENGLISH, JIM,
14586 Olive Vista Dr, Jamul, CA 91935, Phone: 619-669-0833
Specialties: Traditional working straight knives to customer specs. **Patterns:** Hunters, Bowies, fighters, tantos, daggers, boot and utility/camp knives. **Technical:** Grinds 440C, ATS-34, commercial Damascus and customer choice. **Prices:** $130 to $350. **Remarks:** Part-time maker; first knife sold in 1985. In addition to custom line, also does business as Mountain Home Knives. **Mark:** Double "A," Double "J" logo.

ENNIS, RAY,
1220S 775E, Ogden, UT 84404, Phone: 800-410-7603, Fax: 501-621-2683, nifmakr@hotmail.com; Web:www.ennis-entrekusa.com

ENOS III, THOMAS M,
12302 State Rd 535, Orlando, FL 32836, Phone: 407-239-6205, tmenos3@att.net
Specialties: Heavy-duty working straight knives; unusual designs. **Patterns:** Swords, machetes, daggers, skinners, filleting, period pieces. **Technical:** Grinds 440C, D2, 154CM. **Prices:** $75 to $1500. **Remarks:** Full-time maker; first knife sold in 1972. No longer accepting custom requests. Will be making his own designs. Send SASE for listing of items for sale. **Mark:** Name in knife logo and year, type of steel and serial number.

ENTIN, ROBERT,
127 Pembroke St 1, Boston, MA 02118

EPTING, RICHARD,
4021 Cody Dr, College Station, TX 77845, Phone: 979-690-6496, rgeknives@hotmail.com; Web: www.eptingknives.com
Specialties: Folders and working straight knives. **Patterns:** Hunters, Bowies, and locking folders. **Technical:** Forges high-carbon steel and his own Damascus. **Prices:** $200 to $800; some to $1800. **Remarks:** Part-time maker, first knife sold 1996. **Mark:** Name in arch logo.

ERICKSON, L.M.,
1379 Black Mountain Cir, Ogden, UT 84404, Phone: 801-737-1930
Specialties: Straight knives; period pieces. **Patterns:** Bowies, fighters, boots and hunters. **Technical:** Grinds 440C, 154CM and commercial Damascus. **Prices:** $200 to $900; some to $5000. **Remarks:** Part-time maker; first knife sold in 1981. **Mark:** Name, city, state.

ERICKSON, WALTER E.,
22280 Shelton Tr, Atlanta, MI 49709, Phone: 989-785-5262, wberic@racc2000.com
Specialties: Unusual survival knives and high-tech working knives. **Patterns:** Butterflies, hunters, tantos. **Technical:** Grinds ATS-34 or customer choice. **Prices:** $150 to $500; some to $1500. **Remarks:** Full-time maker; first knife sold in 1981. **Mark:** Using pantograph with assorted fonts (no longer stamping).

ERIKSEN, JAMES THORLIEF,
dba VIKING KNIVES, 3830 Dividend Dr, Garland, TX 75042, Phone: 972-494-3667, Fax: 972-235-4932, VikingKnives@aol.com
Specialties: Heavy-duty working and using straight knives and folders utilizing traditional, Viking original and customer specification patterns. Some high-tech and fancy/embellished knives available. **Patterns:** Bowies, hunters, skinners, boot and belt knives, utility/camp knives, fighters, daggers, locking folders, slip-joint folders and kitchen knives. **Technical:** Hollow-grinds 440C, D2, ASP-23, ATS-34, 154CM, Vascowear. **Prices:** $150 to $600. **Remarks:** Full-time maker; first knife sold in 1985. Doing business as Viking Knives. For a color catalog showing 50 different models, mail $5 to above address. **Mark:** VIKING or VIKING USA for export.

ERNEST, PHIL (PJ),
PO Box 5240, Whittier, CA 90607-5240, Phone: 562-556-2324, hugger883562@yahoo.com; Web:www.ernestcustomknives.com
Specialties: Fixed blades. **Patterns:** Wide range. Many original as well as hunters, camp, fighters, daggers, bowies and tactical. Specialzin in Wharncliff's of all sizes. **Technical:** Grinds commercial Damascus, Mosaic Damascus. ATS-34, and 440C. Full Tangs with bolsters. Handle material includes all types of exotic hardwood, abalone, peal mammoth tooth, mammoth ivory, Damascus steel and Mosaic Damascus. **Remarks:** Full time maker. First knife sold in 1999. **Prices:** $200 to $1800. Some to $2500. **Mark:** Owl logo with PJ Ernest Whittier CA or PJ Ernest.

ESSEGIAN, RICHARD,
7387 E Tulare St, Fresno, CA 93727, Phone: 309-255-5950
Specialties: Fancy working knives of his design; art knives. **Patterns:** Bowies and some small hunters. **Technical:** Grinds A2, D2, 440C and 154CM. Engraves and inlays. **Prices:** Start at $600. **Remarks:** Part-time maker; first knife sold in 1986. **Mark:** Last name, city and state.

ETZLER, JOHN,
11200 N Island, Grafton, OH 44044, Phone: 440-748-2460, jetzler@bright.net; Web: members.tripod.com/~etzlerknives/
Specialties: High-art and fantasy straight knives and folders of his design and to customer specs. **Patterns:** Folders, daggers, fighters, utility knives. **Technical:** Forges and grinds nickel Damascus and tool steel; grinds stainless steels. Prefers exotic, natural materials. **Prices:** $250 to $1200; some to $6500. **Remarks:** Full-time maker; first knife sold in 1992. **Mark:** Name or initials.

EVANS, BRUCE A,
409 CR 1371, Booneville, MS 38829, Phone: 662-720-0193, beknives@avsia.com; Web: www.bruceevans.homestead.com/open.html
Specialties: Forges blades. **Patterns:** Hunters, Bowies, or will work with customer. **Technical:** 5160, cable Damascus, pattern welded Damascus. **Prices:** $200 and up. **Mark:** Bruce A. Evans Same with JS on reverse of blade.

EVANS, CARLTON,
PO Box 72, Fort Davis, TX 79734, Phone: 817-886-9231, carlton@carltonevans.com; Web: www.evanshandmakeknives.com
Specialties: High end folders and fixed blades. **Technical:** Uses the stock removal methods. The materials used are of the highest quality. **Remarks:** Full-time knifemaker, voting member of Knifemakers Guild, member of the Texas Knifemakers and Collectors Association.

EVANS, RONALD B,
209 Hoffer St, Middleton, PA 17057-2723, Phone: 717-944-5464

EVANS, VINCENT K AND GRACE,
35 Beaver Creek Rd, Cathlamet, WA 98612, Phone: 360-795-0096, evansvk@gmail.com
Specialties: Period pieces; swords. **Patterns:** Scottish, Viking, central Asian. **Technical:** Forges 5160 and his own Damascus. **Prices:** $700 to $4000; some to $8000. **Remarks:** Full-time maker; first knife sold in 1983. **Mark:** Last initial with fish logo.

EWING, JOHN H,
3276 Dutch Valley Rd, Clinton, TN 37716, Phone: 865-457-5757, johnja@comcast.net
Specialties: Working straight knives, hunters, camp knives. **Patterns:** Hunters. **Technical:** Grinds 440-D2. Forges 5160, 1095 prefers forging. **Prices:** $150 to $2000. **Remarks:** Part-time maker; first knife sold in 1985. **Mark:** First initial, last name, some embellishing done on knives.

F

FANT JR., GEORGE,
1983 CR 3214, Atlanta, TX 75551-6515, Phone: (903) 846-2938

FARID R, MEHR,
8 Sidney Close, Tunbridge Wells, Kent, ENGLAND TN2 5QQ, Phone: 011-44-1892 520345, farid@faridknives.com; Web: www.faridknives.com
Specialties: Hollow handle survival knives. High tech folders. **Patterns:** Flat grind blades & chisel ground LinerLock® folders. **Technical:** Grinds 440C, CPMT-440V, CPM-420V, CPM-15V, CPM5125V, and T-1 high speed steel. **Prices:** $550 to $5000. **Remarks:** Full-time maker; first knife sold in 1991. **Mark:** First name stamped.

FARR, DAN,
285 Glen Ellyn Way, Rochester, NY 14618, Phone: 585- 721-1388
 Specialties: Hunting, camping, fighting and utility. **Patterns:** Fixed blades. **Technical:** Forged or stock removal. **Prices:** $150 to $750.

FASSIO, MELVIN G,
420 Tyler Way, Lolo, MT 59847, Phone: 406-273- 9143
 Specialties: Working folders to customer specs. **Patterns:** Locking folders, hunters and traditional-style knives. **Technical:** Grinds 440C. **Prices:** $125 to $350. **Remarks:** Part-time maker; first knife sold in 1975. **Mark:** Name and city, dove logo.

FAUCHEAUX, HOWARD J,
PO Box 206, Loreauville, LA 70552, Phone: 318-229-6467
 Specialties: Working straight knives and folders; period pieces. Also a hatchet with capping knife in the handle. **Patterns:** Traditional locking folders, hunters, fighters and Bowies. **Technical:** Forges W2, 1095 and his own Damascus; stock removal D2. **Prices:** Start at $200. **Remarks:** Full-time maker; first knife sold in 1969. **Mark:** Last name.

FAUST, DICK,
624 Kings Hwy N, Rochester, NY, 14617, Phone: 585- 544-1948, dickfaustknives@mac.com
 Specialties: High-performance working straight knives. **Patterns:** Hunters and utility/camp knives. **Technical:** Hollow grinds 154CM full tang. Exotic woods, stag and Micarta handles. Provides a custom leather sheath with each knife. **Prices:** From $200 to $600, some higher. **Remarks:** Full-time maker. **Mark:** Signature.

FAUST, JOACHIM,
Kirchgasse 10, 95497 Goldkronach, GERMANY

FECAS, STEPHEN J,
1312 Shadow Lane, Anderson, SC 29625, Phone: 864-287-4834, Fax: 864-287-4834
 Specialties: Front release lock backs, liner locks. Folders only. **Patterns:** Gents folders. **Technical:** Grinds ATS-34, Damascus-Ivories and pearl handles. **Prices:** $650 to $1200. **Remarks:** Full-time maker since 1980. First knife sold in 1977. All knives hand finished to 1500 grit. **Mark:** Last name signature.

FELIX, ALEXANDER,
PO Box 4036, Torrance, CA 90510, Phone: 310- 320-1836, sgiandubh@dslextreme.com
 Specialties: Straight working knives, fancy ethnic designs. **Patterns:** Hunters, Bowies, daggers, period pieces. **Technical:** Forges carbon steel and Damascus; forged stainless and titanium jewelry, gold and silver casting. **Prices:** $110 and up. **Remarks:** Jeweler, ABS Journeyman Smith. **Mark:** Last name.

FELLOWS, MIKE,
PO Box 162, Mosselbay 6500, SOUTH AFRICA, Phone: 27 82 960 3868, karatshin@gmail.com
 Specialties: Miniatures, art knives and folders with occasionally hunters and skinners. **Patterns:** Own designs. **Technical:** Uses own Damascus. **Prices:** R2,000 and up. **Remarks:** Use only indigenous materials. Exotic hard woods, horn & ivory. Does all own embellishments. **Mark:** "SHIN" letter from Hebrew alphabet over Hebrew word "Karat." **Other:** Member of knifemakers guild of Southern Africa.

FERGUSON, JIM,
PO Box 301, San Angelo, TX 76902, Phone: 915-651- 6656
 Specialties: Straight working knives and folders. **Patterns:** Working belt knives, hunters, Bowies and some folders. **Technical:** Grinds ATS-34, D2 and Vascowear. Flat-grinds hunting knives. **Prices:** $200 to $600; some to $1000. **Remarks:** Full-time maker; first knife sold in 1987. **Mark:** First and middle initials, last name.

FERGUSON, JIM,
32131 Via Bande, Temecula, CA 92592, Phone: 325- 245-7106, Web: www.jimfergusonknives.com
 Specialties: Nickel Damascus, Bowies, daggers, push blades. **Patterns:** All styles. **Technical:** Forges Damascus and sells in U.S. and Canada. **Prices:** $350 to $600, some to $1000. **Remarks:** 1200 sq. ft. commercial shop, 75 ton press. Has made over 11,000 lbs of Damascus. **Mark:** Jim Ferguson over push blade. Also make swords, battle axes and utilities.

FERGUSON, LEE,
1993 Madison 7580, Hindsville, AR 72738, Phone: 479-443-0084, info@fergusonknives.com; Web: www.fergusonknives.com
 Specialties: Straight working knives and folders, some fancy. **Patterns:** Hunters, daggers, swords, locking folders and slip-joints. **Technical:** Grinds D2, 440C and ATS-34; heat-treats. **Prices:** $50 to $600; some to $4000. **Remarks:** Full-time maker; first knife sold in 1977. **Mark:** Full name.

FERGUSON, LINDA,
1993 Madison 7580, Hindsville, AR 72738, Phone: 479-443-0084, info@fergusonknives.com; Web: www.fergusonknives.com
 Specialties: Mini knives. **Patterns:** Daggers & hunters. **Technical:** Hollow ground, stainless steel or Damascus. **Prices:** $65 to $250. **Remarks:** 2004 member Knifemakers Guild, Miniature Knifemakers Society. **Mark:** LF inside a Roman numeral 2.

FERRARA, THOMAS,
122 Madison Dr, Naples, FL 33942, Phone: 813- 597-3363, Fax: 813-597-3363
 Specialties: High-art, traditional and working straight knives and folders of all designs. **Patterns:** Boots, Bowies, daggers, fighters and hunters. **Technical:** Grinds 440C, D2 and ATS-34; heat-treats. **Prices:** $100 to $700; some to $1300. **Remarks:** Part-time maker; first knife sold in 1983. **Mark:** Last name.

FERRIER, GREGORY K,
3119 Simpson Dr, Rapid City, SD 57702, Phone: 605-342-9280

FERRIS, BILL,
186 Thornton Dr, Palm Beach Garden, FL 33418

FERRY, TOM,
16005 SE 322nd St, Auburn, WA 98092, Phone: 253-217-2569, tomferryknives@Q.com; Web: www.tferryknives.com
 Specialties: Presentation grade knives. **Patterns:** Folders and fixed blades. **Technical:** Specialize in Damascus and engraving. **Prices:** $500 and up. **Remarks:** DBA: Soos Creek Ironworks. ABS Master Smith. **Mark:** Combined T and F in a circle and/or last name.

FIKES, JIMMY L,
PO Box 3457, Jasper, AL 35502, Phone: 205-387- 9302, Fax: 205-221-1980, oleyfermo@aol.com
 Specialties: High-art working knives; artifact knives; using knives with cord-wrapped handles; swords and combat weapons. **Patterns:** Axes to buckskinners, camp knives to miniatures, tantos to tomahawks; springless folders. **Technical:** Forges W2, O1 and his own Damascus. **Prices:** $135 to $3000; exceptional knives to $7000. **Remarks:** Full-time maker. **Mark:** Stylized initials.

FILIPPOU, IOANNIS-MINAS,
7 Krinis Str Nea Smyrni, Athens 17122, GREECE, Phone: (1) 935-2093

FINCH, RICKY D,
2446 Hwy. 191, West Liberty, KY 41472, Phone: 606- 743-7151, finchknives@mrtc.com; Web: www.finchknives.com
 Specialties: Traditional working/using straight knives of his design or to customer spec. **Patterns:** Hunters, skinners and utility/camp knives. LinerLock® of his design. **Technical:** Grinds 440C, ATS-34 and CPM154, hand rubbed stain finish, use Micarta, stabilized wood, natural and exotic. **Prices:** $85 to $225. **Remarks:** Part-time maker, first knife made 1994. Doing business as Finch Knives. **Mark:** Last name inside outline of state of Kentucky.

FIORINI, BILL,
E2173 Axlen Rd., DeSoto, WI 54624, Phone: 608-780- 5898, fiorini.will@uwlax.edu; Web: www.billfiorini.com
 Specialties: Fancy working knives. **Patterns:** Hunters, boots, Japanese-style knives and kitchen/utility knives and folders. **Technical:** Forges own Damascus, mosaic and mokune-gane. **Prices:** Full range. **Remarks:** Full-time metal smith researching pattern materials. **Mark:** Orchid crest with name KOKA in Japanese.

FISHER, JAY,
1405 Edwards, Clovis, NM 88101, Phone: 575-763-2268, jayfisher@jayfisher.com Web: www.JayFisher.com
 Specialties: High-art, working and collector's knives of his design and client's designs. Military working and commemoratives. **Patterns:** Hunters, daggers, folding knives, museum pieces and high-art sculptures. **Technical:** Grinds 440C, ATS-34, O1and D2. Prolific maker of stone-handled knives and swords. **Prices:** $400 to $50,000; some higher. **Remarks:** Full-time maker; first knife sold in 1980. High resolution etching, computer and manual engraving. **Mark:** Signature "JaFisher"

FISHER, THEO (TED),
8115 Modoc Lane, Montague, CA 96064, Phone: 916-459-3804
 Specialties: Moderately priced working knives in carbon steel. **Patterns:** Hunters, fighters, kitchen and buckskinner knives, Damascus miniatures. **Technical:** Grinds ATS-34, L6 and 440C. **Prices:** $65 to $165; exceptional knives to $300. **Remarks:** First knife sold in 1981. **Mark:** Name in banner logo.

FISK, JERRY,
10095 Hwy 278 W, Nashville, AR 71852, Phone: 870- 845-4456, jerry@fisk-knives.com; Web: wwwfisk-knives.com
 Specialties: Edged weapons, collectible and functional. **Patterns:** Bowies, daggers, swords, hunters, camp knives and others. **Technical:** Forges carbon steels and his own pattern welded steels. **Prices:** $250 to $15,000. **Remarks:** National living treasure. **Mark:** Name, MS.

FISTER, JIM,
PO Box 307, Simpsonville, KY 40067
 Specialties: One-of-a-kind collectibles and period pieces. **Patterns:** Bowies, camp knives, hunters, buckskinners, and daggers. **Technical:** Forges, 1085, 5160, 52100, his own Damascus, pattern and turkish. **Prices:** $150 to $2500. **Remarks:** Part-time maker; first knife sold in 1982. **Mark:** Name and MS.

FITCH, JOHN S,
45 Halbrook Rd, Clinton, AR 72031-8910, Phone: 501- 893-2020

FITZGERALD, DENNIS M,
4219 Alverado Dr, Fort Wayne, IN 46816- 2847, Phone: 219-447-1081
Specialties: One-of-a-kind collectibles and period pieces. **Patterns:** Skinners, fighters, camp and utility knives; period pieces. **Technical:** Forges 1085, 1095, L6, 5160, 52100, his own pattern and Turkish Damascus. **Prices:** $100 to $500. **Remarks:** Part-time maker; first knife sold in 1985. Doing business as The Ringing Circle. **Mark:** Name and circle logo.

FLINT, ROBERT,
2902 Aspen, Anchorage, AK 99517, Phone: 907-243- 6706
Specialties: Working straight knives and folders. **Patterns:** Utility, hunters, fighters and gents. **Technical:** Grinds ATS-34, BG-42, D2 and Damascus. **Prices:** $150 and up. **Remarks:** Part-time maker, first knife sold in 1998. **Mark:** Last name; stylized initials.

FLOURNOY, JOE,
5750 Lisbon Rd, El Dorado, AR 71730, Phone: 870- 863-7208, flournoy@ipa.net
Specialties: Working straight knives and folders. **Patterns:** Hunters, Bowies, camp knives, folders and daggers. **Technical:** Forges only high- carbon steel, steel cable and his own Damascus. **Prices:** $350 Plus. **Remarks:** First knife sold in 1977. **Mark:** Last name and MS in script.

FLYNT, ROBERT G,
15173 Christy Lane, Gulfport, MS 39503, flyntstoneknives@bellsouth.net
Web: www.flyntstoneknifeworks.com
Specialties:
All types of fixed blades: Drop point, clip point, trailing point, bull nose hunters, tactical, fighters and Bowies. Folders I've made include liner lock, slip joint and lock back styles.
Technical: Using 154 cm, cpm154, ats34, 440c, cpm3v and 52100 steel, most of my blades are made by stock removal, hollow and flat grind methods. I do forge some cable Damascus and use numerous types of Damascus that is purchased in billets from various makers. All file work and bluing is done by me.
I have made handles from a variety of wood, bone and horn materials, including some with wire inlay and other embellishments.
Most knives are sold with custom fit leather sheaves most include exotic skin inlay when appropriate.
Prices: $150 and up depending on embellishments on blade and sheath.
Remarks: Full time maker. First knife made in 1966.
Mark: Last name in cursive letters or a knife striking a flint stone.

FOGARIZZU, BOITEDDU,
via Crispi 6, 07016 Pattada, ITALY
Specialties: Traditional Italian straight knives and folders. **Patterns:** Collectible folders. **Technical:** forges and grinds 12C27, ATS-34 and his Damascus. **Prices:** $200 to $3000. **Remarks:** Full-time maker; first knife sold in 1958. **Mark:** Full name and registered logo.

FOGG, DON,
40 Alma Rd, Jasper, AL 35501-8813, Phone: 205-483- 0822, dfogg@dfoggknives.com; Web: www.dfoggknives.com
Specialties: Swords, daggers, Bowies and hunting knives. **Patterns:** Collectible folders. **Technical:** Hand-forged high-carbon and Damascus steel. **Prices:** $200 to $5000. **Remarks:** Full-time maker; first knife sold in 1976. **Mark:** 24K gold cherry blossom.

FONTENOT, GERALD J,
901 Maple Ave, Mamou, LA 70554, Phone: 318-468-3180

FORREST, BRIAN,
FORREST KNIVES, PO Box 203, Descanso, CA 91916, Phone: 619-445-6343, forrestknives@hotmail.com; Web: www.forrestknives.com
Specialties: Forged tomahawks, working knives, big Bowies. **Patterns:** Traditional and extra large Bowies. **Technical:** Hollow grinds: 440C, 1095, S160 Damascus. **Prices**"$125 and up. **Remarks:** Member of California Knifemakers Association. Full-time maker. First knife sold in 1971. **Mark:** Forrest USA/Tomahawks marked FF (Forrest Forge).

FORTHOFER, PETE,
5535 Hwy 93S, Whitefish, MT 59937, Phone: 406- 862-2674
Specialties: Interframes with checkered wood inlays; working straight knives. **Patterns:** Interframe folders and traditional-style knives; hunters, fighters and Bowies. **Technical:** Grinds D2, 440C, 154CM and ATS-34. **Prices:** $350 to $2500; some to $1500. **Remarks:** Part-time maker; full-time gunsmith. First knife sold in 1979. **Mark:** Name and logo.

FORTUNE PRODUCTS, INC.,
205 Hickory Creek Rd, Marble Falls, TX 78654, Phone: 830-693-6111, Fax: 830-693-6394, Web: www.accusharp.com
Specialties: Knife sharpeners.

FOSTER, AL,
118 Woodway Dr, Magnolia, TX 77355, Phone: 936-372- 9297
Specialties: Straight knives and folders. **Patterns:** Hunting, fishing, folders and Bowies. **Technical:** Grinds 440-C, ATS-34 and D2. **Prices:** $100 to $1000. **Remarks:** Full-time maker; first knife sold in 1981. **Mark:** Scorpion logo and name.

FOSTER, BURT,
23697 Archery Range Rd, Bristol, VA 24202, Phone: 276-669-0121, burtfoster@bvunet.net; Web: www.burt@burtfoster.com
Specialties: Working straight knives, laminated blades, and some art knives of his design. **Patterns:** Bowies, hunters, daggers. **Technical:** Forges 52100, W-2 and makes own Damascus. Does own heat treating. **Remarks:** ABS MasterSmith. Full-time maker, believes in sole authorship. **Mark:** Signed "BF" initials.

FOSTER, NORVELL C,
7945 Youngsford Rd, Marion, TX 78124-1713, Phone: 830-914-2078
Specialties: Engraving; ivory handle carving. **Patterns:** American-large and small scroll-oak leaf and acorns. **Prices:** $25 to $400. **Remarks:** Have been engraving since 1957. **Mark:** N.C. Foster - Marion - Tex and current year.

FOSTER, R L (BOB),
745 Glendale Blvd, Mansfield, OH 44907, Phone: 419-756-6294

FOSTER, RONNIE E,
95 Riverview Rd., Morrilton, AR 72110, Phone: 501-354-5389
Specialties: Working, using knives, some period pieces, work with customer specs. **Patterns:** Hunters, fighters, Bowies, liner-lock folders, camp knives. **Technical:** Forge-5160, 1084, O1, 15N20-makes own Damascus. **Prices:** $200 (start). **Remarks:** Part-time maker. First knife sold 1994. **Mark:** Ronnie Foster MS.

FOSTER, TIMOTHY L,
723 Sweet Gum Acres Rd, El Dorado, AR 71730, Phone: 870-863-6188

FOWLER, CHARLES R,
226 National Forest Rd 48, Ft McCoy, FL 32134-9624, Phone: 904-467-3215

FOWLER, ED A.,
Willow Bow Ranch, PO Box 1519, Riverton, WY 82501, Phone: 307-856-9815
Specialties: High-performance working and using straight knives. **Patterns:** Hunter, camp, bird, and trout knives and Bowies. New model, the gentleman's Pronghorn. **Technical:** Low temperature forged 52100 from virgin 5-1/2 round bars, multiple quench heat treating, engraves all knives, all handles domestic sheep horn processed and aged at least 5 years. Makes heavy duty hand-stitched waxed harness leather pouch type sheathes. **Prices:** $800 to $7000. **Remarks:** Full-time maker. First knife sold in 1962. **Mark:** Initials connected.

FOWLER, JERRY,
610 FM 1660 N, Hutto, TX 78634, Phone: 512-846- 2860, fowler@inetport.com
Specialties: Using straight knives of his design. **Patterns:** A variety of hunting and camp knives, combat knives. Custom designs considered. **Technical:** Forges 5160, his own Damascus and cable Damascus. Makes sheaths. Prefers natural handle materials. **Prices:** Start at $150. **Remarks:** Part-time maker; first knife sold in 1986. Doing business as Fowler Forge Knife Works. **Mark:** First initial, last name, date and J.S.

FOWLER, RICKY AND SUSAN,
FOWLER CUSTOM KNIVES, 18535-B Co. Rd. 48, Robertsdale, AL 36567, Phone: 251-947-5648, theknifeshop@gulftel.com; Web: www.fowlerknives.net
Specialties: Traditional working/using straight knives of his design or to customer specifications. **Patterns:** Skinners, fighters, tantos, Bowies and utility/camp knives. **Technical:** Grinds O1, exclusively. **Prices:** Start at $150. **Remarks:** Full-time maker; first knife sold in 1994. Doing business as Fowler Custom Knives. **Mark:** Last name tang stamped.

FOX, PAUL,
4721 Rock Barn Rd, Claremont, NC 28610, Phone: 828- 459-2000, pfox@charter.net
Specialties: Unique locking mechanisms. **Patterns:** Pen knives, one-of-a-kind tactical knives. **Technical:** All locking mechanisms are his. **Prices:** $350 and up. **Remarks:** First knife sold in 1976. Guild member since 1977. **Mark:** Fox, P Fox, Paul Fox. Cuts out all parts of knives in shop.

FRALEY, D B,
1355 Fairbanks Ct, Dixon, CA 95620, Phone: 707-678- 0393, dbtfnives@sbcglobal.net; Web:www.dbfraleyknives.com
Specialties Usable gentleman's fixed blades and folders. **Patterns:** Foure folders in four different sizes in liner lock and frame lock. **Technical:** Grinds CPMS30V, 154, 6K stellite. **Prices:** $250 and up. **Remarks:** Part time maker. First knife sold in 1990. **Mark:** First and middle initials, last name over a buffalo.

FRAMSKI, WALTER P,
24 Rek Ln, Prospect, CT 06712, Phone: 203- 758-5634

FRANCE, DAN,
Box 218, Cawood, KY 40815, Phone: 606-573-6104
Specialties: Traditional working and using straight knives of his design. **Patterns:** Hunters, Bowies and utility/camp knives. **Technical:** Forges and grinds O1, 5160 and L6. **Prices:** $35 to $125; some to $350. **Remarks:** Spare-time maker; first knife sold in 1985. **Mark:** First name.

FRANCIS, JOHN D,
FRANCIS KNIVES, 18 Miami St., Ft. Loramie, OH 45845, Phone: 937-295-3941, jdfrancis@roadrunner.com
Specialties: Utility and hunting-style fixed bladed knives of 440 C and ATS-34 steel; Micarta, exotic woods, and other types of handle materials. **Prices:** $90 to $150 range. **Remarks:** Exceptional quality and value at factory prices. **Mark:** Francis-Ft. Loramie, OH stamped on tang.

FRANK, HEINRICH H,
1147 SW Bryson St, Dallas, OR 97338, Phone: 503-831-1489, Fax: 503-831-1489
Specialties: High-art investor-class folders, handmade and engraved. **Patterns:** Folding daggers, hunter-size folders and gents. **Technical:** Grinds 07 and O1. **Prices:** $4800 to $16,000. **Remarks:** Full-time maker; first knife sold in 1965. Doing business as H.H. Frank Knives. **Mark:** Name, address and date.

FRANKLIN, MIKE,
9878 Big Run Rd, Aberdeen, OH 45101, Phone: 937- 549-2598, Web: www.mikefranklinknives.com, hawgcustomknives.com
Specialties: High-tech tactical folders. **Patterns:** Tactical folders. **Technical:** Grinds CPM-T-440V, 440-C, ATS-34; titanium liners and bolsters; carbon fiber scales. Uses radical grinds and severe serrations. **Prices:** $100 to $1000. **Remarks:** Full-time maker; first knife sold in 1969. All knives made one at a time, 100% by the maker. **Mark:** Stylized boar with HAWG.

FRAPS, JOHN R,
3810 Wyandotte Tr, Indianpolis, IN 46240-3422, Phone: 317-849-9419, Fax: 317-842-2224, jfraps@att.net; Web: www.frapsknives.com
Specialties: Working and collector grade LinerLock® and slip joint folders. **Patterns:** One-of-a kind linerlocks and traditional slip joints. **Technical:** Flat and hollow grinds ATS-34, Damascus, Talonite, CPM S30V, 154CM, Stellite 6K; hand rubbed or mirror finish. **Prices:** $200 to $1500, some higher. **Remarks:** Voting member of the Knifemaker's Guild; Full- time maker; first knife sold in 1997. **Mark:** Cougar Creek Knives and/or name.

FRAZIER, RON,
2107 Urbine Rd, Powhatan, VA 23139, Phone: 804- 794-8561
Specialties: Classy working knives of his design; some high-art straight knives. **Patterns:** Wide assortment of straight knives, including miniatures and push knives. **Technical:** Grinds 440C; offers satin, mirror or sand finishes. **Prices:** $85 to $700; some to $3000. **Remarks:** Full-time maker; first knife sold in 1976. **Mark:** Name in arch logo.

FRED, REED WYLE,
3149 X S, Sacramento, CA 95817, Phone: 916- 739-0237
Specialties: Working using straight knives of his design. **Patterns:** Hunting and camp knives. **Technical:** Forges any 10 series, old files and carbon steels. Offers initialing upon request; prefers natural handle materials. **Prices:** $30 to $300. **Remarks:** Part-time maker; first knife sold in 1994. Doing business as R.W. Fred Knifemaker. **Mark:** Engraved first and last initials.

FREDERICK, AARON,
459 Brooks Ln, West Liberty, KY 41472-8961, Phone: 606-7432015, aaronf@mrtc.com; Web: www.frederickknives.com
Specialties: Makes most types of knives, but as for now specializes in the Damascus folder. Does all own Damascus and forging of the steel. Also prefers natural handle material such as ivory and pearl. Prefers 14k gold screws in most of the knives he do. Also offer several types of file work on blades, spacers, and liners. Has just recently started doing carving and can do a limited amount of engraving.

FREER, RALPH,
114 12th St, Seal Beach, CA 90740, Phone: 562-493- 4925, Fax: same, ralphfreer@adelphia.net
Specialties: Exotic folders, liner locks, folding daggers, fixed blades. **Patters:** All original. **Technical:** Lots of Damascus, ivory, pearl, jeweled, thumb studs, carving ATS-34, 420V, 530V. **Prices:** $400 to $2500 and up. **Mark:** Freer in German-style text, also Freer shield.

FREILING, ALBERT J,
3700 Niner Rd, Finksburg, MD 21048, Phone: 301-795-2880
Specialties: Working straight knives and folders; some period pieces. **Patterns:** Boots, Bowies, survival knives and tomahawks in 4130 and 440C; some locking folders and interframes; ball-bearing folders. **Technical:** Grinds O1, 440C and 154CM. **Prices:** $100 to $300; some to $500. **Remarks:** Part-time maker; first knife sold in 1966. **Mark:** Initials connected.

FREY, STEVE,
19103 131st Drive SE, Snohomish, WA 98296, Phone: 360-668-7351, sfrey2@aol.com
Remarks: Custom crafted knives-all styles.

FREY JR., W FREDERICK,
305 Walnut St, Milton, PA 17847, Phone: 570-742-9576, wffrey@ptd.net
Specialties: Working straight knives and folders, some fancy. **Patterns:** Wide range miniatures, boot knives and lock back folders. **Technical:** Grinds A2, O1 and D2; vaseo wear, cru-wear and CPM S60V and CPM S90V. **Prices:** $100 to $250; some to $1200. **Remarks:** Spare-time maker; first knife sold in 1983. All knives include quality hand stitched sheaths. **Mark:** Last name in script.

FRIEDLY, DENNIS E,
12 Cottontail Ln E, Cody, WY 82414, Phone: 307- 527-6811, friedly_knives@hotmail.com
Specialties: Fancy working straight knives and daggers, lock back folders and liner locks. Also embellished bowies. **Patterns:** Hunters, fighters, short swords, minis and miniatures; new line of full-tang hunters/boots. **Technical:** Grinds 440C, commercial Damascus, mosaic Damascus and ATS-34 blades; prefers hidden tangs and full tangs. Both flat and hollow grinds. **Prices:** $350 to $2500. Some to $10,000. **Remarks:** Full-time maker; first knife sold in 1972. **Mark:** D.E. Friedly-Cody, WY. Friedly Knives

FRIGAULT, RICK,
3584 Rapidsview Dr, Niagara Falls, Ont., CANADA L2G 6C4, Phone: 905-295-6695, rfrigualt@cogeco.ca; Web: www.rfrigaultknives.com
Specialties: Fixed blades. **Patterns:** Hunting, tactical and large Bowies. **Technical:** Grinds ATS-34, 440-C, D-2, CPMS30V, CPMS60V, CPMS90V, BG42 and Damascus. Use G-10, Micarta, ivory, antler, ironwood and other stabilized woods for carbon fiber handle material. Makes leather sheaths by hand. Tactical blades include a Concealex sheath made by "On Scene Tactical." **Remarks:** Sold first knife in 1997. Member of Canadian Knifemakers Guild. **Mark:** RFRIGAULT.

FRITZ, ERIK L,
837 River St Box 1203, Forsyth, MT 59327, Phone: 406-351-1101, tacmedic45@yahoo.com
Specialties: Forges carbon steel 1084, 5160, 52100 and Damascus. **Patterns:** Hunters, camp knives, bowies and folders as well as forged tactical. **Technical:** Forges own Mosaic and pattern welded Damascus as well as doing own heat treat. **Prices:** A$200 and up. **Remarks:** Sole authorship knives and sheaths. Part time maker first knife sold in 2004. ABS member. **Mark:** E. Fritz in arc on left side ricasso.

FRITZ, JESSE,
900 S. 13th St, Slaton, TX 79364, Phone: 806-828-5083
Specialties: Working and using straight knives in standard patterns. **Patterns:** Hunters, utility/camp knives and skinners with gut hook, Bowie knives, kitchen carving sets by request. **Technical:** Grinds 440C, O1 and 1095. Uses 1095 steel. Fline-napped steel design, blued blades, filework and machine jewelling. Inlays handles with turquoise, coral and mother-of-pearl. Makes sheaths. **Prices:** $85 to $275; some to $500. **Mark:** Last name only (FRITZ).

FRIZZELL, TED,
14056 Low Gap Rd, West Fork, AR 72774, Phone: 501-839-2516
Specialties: Swords, axes and self-defense weapons. **Patterns:** Small skeleton knives to large swords. **Technical:** Grinds 5160 almost exclusively—1/4" to 1/2"— bars some O1 and A2 on request. All knives come with Kydex sheaths. **Prices:** $45 to $1200. **Remarks:** Full-time maker; first knife sold in 1984. Doing business as Mineral Mountain Hatchet Works. Wholesale orders welcome. **Mark:** A circle with line in the middle; MM and HW within the circle.

FRONEFIELD, DANIEL,
20270 Warriors Path, Peyton, CO 80831, Phone: 719-749-0226, dfronfld@hiwaay.com
Specialties: Fixed and folding knives featuring meteorites and other exotic materials. **Patterns:** San-mai Damascus, custom Damascus. **Prices:** $500 to $3000.

FROST, DEWAYNE,
1016 Van Buren Rd, Barnesville, GA 30204, Phone: 770-358-1426, lbrtyhill@aol.com
Specialties: Working straight knives and period knives. **Patterns:** Hunters, Bowies and utility knives. **Technical:** Forges own Damascus, cable, etc. as well as stock removal. **Prices:** $150 to $500. **Remarks:** Part-time maker ABS Journeyman Smith. **Mark:** Liberty Hill Forge Dewayne Frost w/liberty bell.

FRUHMANN, LUDWIG,
Stegerwaldstr 8, 84489 Burghausen, GERMANY
Specialties: High-tech and working straight knives of his design. **Patterns:** Hunters, fighters and boots. **Technical:** Grinds ATS-34, CPM-T- 440V and Schneider Damascus. Prefers natural handle materials. **Prices:** $200 to $1500. **Remarks:** Spare-time maker; first knife sold in 1990. **Mark:** First initial and last name.

FUEGEN, LARRY,
617 N Coulter Circle, Prescott, AZ 86303, Phone: 928-776-8777, fuegen@cableone.net; Web: www.larryfuegen.com
Specialties: High-art folders and classic and working straight knives. **Patterns:** Forged scroll folders, lockback folders and classic straight knives. **Technical:** Forges 5160, 1095 and his own Damascus. Works in exotic leather; offers elaborate filework and carving; likes natural handle materials, now offers own engraving. **Prices:** $575 to $9000. **Remarks:** Full-time maker; first knife sold in 1975. Sole authorship on all knives. ABS Mastersmith. **Mark:** Initials connected.

FUJIKAWA, SHUN,
Sawa 1157 Kaizuka, Osaka 597 0062, JAPAN, Phone: 81-724-23-4032, Fax: 81-726-23-9229
Specialties: Folders of his design and to customer specs. **Patterns:** Locking folders. **Technical:** Grinds his own steel. **Prices:** $450 to $2500; some to $3000. **Remarks:** Part-time maker.

FUJISAKA, STANLEY,
45-004 Holowai St, Kaneohe, HI 96744, Phone: 808-247-0017, s.fuj@earthlink.net
>**Specialties:** Fancy working straight knives and folders. **Patterns:** Hunters, boots, personal knives, daggers, collectible art knives. **Technical:** Grinds 440C, 154CM and ATS-34; clean lines, inlays. **Prices:** $400 to $2000; some to $6000. **Remarks:** Full-time maker; first knife sold in 1984. **Mark:** Name, city, state.

FUKUTA, TAK,
38-Umeagae-cho, Seki-City, Gifu-Pref, JAPAN, Phone: 0575-22-0264
>**Specialties:** Bench-made fancy straight knives and folders. **Patterns:** Sheffield-type folders, Bowies and fighters. **Technical:** Grinds commercial Damascus. **Prices:** Start at $300. **Remarks:** Full-time maker. **Mark:** Name in knife logo.

FULLER, BRUCE A,
1305 Airhart Dr, Baytown, TX 77520, Phone: 281- 427-1848, fullcoforg@aol.com
>**Specialties:** One-of-a-kind working/using straight knives and folders of his designs. **Patterns:** Bowies, hunters, folders, and utility/camp knives. **Technical:** Forges high-carbon steel and his own Damascus. Prefers El Solo Mesquite and natural materials. Offers filework. **Prices:** $200 to $500; some to $1800. **Remarks:** Spare-time maker; first knife sold in 1991. Doing business as Fullco Forge. **Mark:** Fullco, M.S.

FULLER, JACK A,
7103 Stretch Ct, New Market, MD 21774, Phone: 301-798-0119
>**Specialties:** Straight working knives of his design and to customer specs. **Patterns:** Fighters, camp knives, hunters, tomahawks and art knives. **Technical:** Forges 5160, O1, W2 and his own Damascus. Does silver wire inlay and own leather work, wood lined sheaths for big camp knives. **Prices:** $300 to $850. **Remarks:** Part-time maker. Master Smith in ABS; first knife sold in 1979. **Mark:** Fuller's Forge, MS.

FULTON, MICKEY,
406 S Shasta St, Willows, CA 95988, Phone: 530- 934-5780
>**Specialties:** Working straight knives and folders of his design. **Patterns:** Hunters, Bowies, lockback folders and steak knife sets. **Technical:** Hand-filed, sanded, buffed ATS-34, 440C and A2. **Prices:** $65 to $600; some to $1200. **Remarks:** Full-time maker; first knife sold in 1979. **Mark:** Signature.

G

GADBERRY, EMMET,
82 Purple Plum Dr, Hattieville, AR 72063, Phone: 501-354-4842

GADDY, GARY LEE,
205 Ridgewood Lane, Washington, NC 27889, Phone: 252-946-4359
>**Specialties:** Working/using straight knives of his design; period pieces. **Patterns:** Bowies, hunters, utility/camp knives. **Technical:** Grinds ATS- 34, O1; forges 1095. **Prices:** $100 to $225; some to $400. **Remarks:** Spare-time maker; first knife sold in 1991. **Mark:** Quarter moon logo.

GAETA, ANGELO,
R. Saldanha Marinho, 1295 Centro Jau, SP-17201- 310, BRAZIL, Phone: 0146-224543, Fax: 0146-224543
>**Specialties:** Straight using knives to customer specs. **Patterns:** Hunters, fighting, daggers, belt push dagger. **Technical:** Grinds D6, ATS-34 and 440C stainless. Titanium nitride golden finish upon request. **Prices:** $60 to $300. **Remarks:** Full-time maker; first knife sold in 1992. **Mark:** First initial, last name.

GAETA, ROBERTO,
Rua Mandissununga 41, Sao Paulo, BRAZIL 05619-010, Phone: 11-37684626, karlaseno@uol.com.br
>**Specialties:** Wide range of using knives. **Patterns:** Brazilian and North American hunting and fighting knives. **Technical:** Grinds stainless steel; likes natural handle materials. **Prices:** $500 to $800. **Remarks:** Full-time maker; first knife sold in 1979. **Mark:** BOB'G.

GAINES, BUDDY,
GAINES KNIVES, 155 Red Hill Rd., Commerce, GA 30530, Web: www.gainesknives.com
>**Specialties:** Collectible and working folders and straight knives. **Patterns:** Folders, hunters, Bowies, tactical knives. **Technical:** Forges own Damascus, grinds ATS-34, D2, commercial Damascus. Prefers mother- of-pearl and stag. **Prices:** Start at $200. **Remarks:** Part-time maker, sold first knife in 1985. **Mark:** Last name.

GAINEY, HAL,
904 Bucklevel Rd, Greenwood, SC 29649, Phone: 864- 223-0225, Web: www.scak.org
>**Specialties:** Traditional working and using straight knives and folders. **Patterns:** Hunters, slip-joint folders and utility/camp knives. **Technical:** Hollow-grinds ATS-34 and D2; makes sheaths. **Prices:** $95 to $145; some to $500. **Remarks:** Full-time maker; first knife sold in 1975. **Mark:** Eagle head and last name.

GALLAGHER, BARRY,
135 Park St, Lewistown, MT 59457, Phone: 406-538-7056, Web: www.gallagherknives.com
>**Specialties:** One-of-a-kind Damascus folders. **Patterns:** Folders, utility to high art, some straight knives, hunter, Bowies, and art pieces. **Technical:** Forges own mosaic Damascus and carbon steel, some stainless. **Prices:** $400 to $5000+. **Remarks:** Full-time maker; first knife sold in 1993. Doing business as Gallagher Custom Knives. **Mark:** Last name.

GAMBLE, FRANK,
4676 Commercial St SE #26, Salem, OR 97302, Phone: 503-581-7993, gamble6831@comcast.net
>**Specialties:** Fantasy and high-art straight knives and folders of his design. **Patterns:** Daggers, fighters, hunters and special locking folders. **Technical:** Grinds 440C and ATS-34; forges Damascus. Inlays; offers jewelling. Prices $150 to $10,000. **Remarks:** Full-time maker; first knife sold in 1976. **Mark:** First initial, last name.

GAMBLE, ROGER,
2801 65 Way N, St. Petersburg, FL 33710, Phone: 727-384-1470, rlgamble2@netzero.net
>**Specialties:** Traditional working/using straight knives and folders of his design. **Patterns:** Liner locks and hunters. **Technical:** Grinds ATS-34 and Damascus. **Prices:** $150 to $2000. **Remarks:** Part-time maker; first knife sold in 1982. Doing business as Gamble Knives. **Mark:** First name in a fan of cards over last name.

GANN, TOMMY,
2876 State Hwy. 198, Canton, TX 75103, Phone: 903- 848-9375
>**Specialties:** Art and working straight knives of my design or customer preferences/design. **Patterns:** Bowie, fighters, hunters, daggers. **Technical:** Forges Damascus 52100 and grinds ATS-34 and D2. **Prices:** $200 to $2500. **Remarks:** Full-time knifemaker, first knife sold in 2002. ABS journey bladesmith. **Mark:** TGANN.

GANSHORN, CAL,
123 Rogers Rd., Regina, Saskatchewan, CANADA S4S 6T7, Phone: 306-584-0524
>**Specialties:** Working and fancy fixed blade knives. **Patterns:** Bowies, hunters, daggers, and filleting. **Technical:** Makes own forged Damascus billets, ATS, salt heat treating, and custom forges and burners. **Prices:** $250 to $1500. **Remarks:** Part-time maker. **Mark:** Last name etched in ricasso area.

GANSTER, JEAN-PIERRE,
18, Rue du Vieil Hopital, F-67000 Strasbourg, FRANCE, Phone: (0033) 388 32 65 61, Fax: (0033) 388 32 52 79
>**Specialties:** Fancy and high-art miniatures of his design and to customer specs. **Patterns:** Bowies, daggers, fighters, hunters, locking folders and miniatures. **Technical:** Forges and grinds stainless Damascus, ATS-34, gold and silver. **Prices:** $100 to $380; some to $2500. **Remarks:** Part- time maker; first knife sold in 1972. **Mark:** Stylized first initials.

GARCIA, MARIO EIRAS,
R. Edmundo Scanapieco, 300 Caxingui, Sao Paulo SP-05516-070, BRAZIL, Fax: 011-37214528
>**Specialties:** Fantasy knives of his design; one-of-a-kind only. **Patterns:** Fighters, daggers, boots and two-bladed knives. **Technical:** Forges car leaf springs. Uses only natural handle material. **Prices:** $100 to $200. **Remarks:** Part-time maker; first knife sold in 1976. **Mark:** Two "B"s, one opposite the other.

GARNER, LARRY W,
13069 FM 14, Tyler, TX 75706, Phone: 903-597- 6045, lwgarner@classicnet.net
>**Specialties:** Fixed blade hunters and Bowies. **Patterns:** His designs or yours. **Technical:** Hand forges 5160. **Prices:** $200 to $500. **Remarks:** Apprentice bladesmith. **Mark:** Last name.

GARNER JR., WILLIAM O,
2803 East DeSoto St, Pensacola, FL 32503, Phone: 850-438-2009
>**Specialties:** Working straight and art knives. **Patterns:** Hunters and folders. **Technical:** Grinds 440C and ATS-34 steels. **Prices:** $235 to $600. **Remarks:** Full-time maker; first knife sold in 1985. **Mark:** First and last name in oval logo or last name.

GARVOCK, MARK W,
RR 1, Balderson, Ont., CANADA K1G 1A0, Phone: 613-833-2545, Fax: 613-833-2208, garvock@travel-net.com
>**Specialties:** Hunters, Bowies, Japanese, daggers and swords. **Patterns:** Cable Damascus, random pattern welded or to suit. **Technical:** Forged blades; hi-carbon. **Prices:** $250 to $900. **Remarks:** CKG member and ABS member. Shipping and taxes extra. **Mark:** Big G with M in middle.

GAUDETTE, LINDEN L,
5 Hitchcock Rd, Wilbraham, MA 01095, Phone: 413-596-4896
>**Specialties:** Traditional working knives in standard patterns. **Patterns:** Broad-bladed hunters, Bowies and camp knives; wood carver knives; locking folders. **Technical:** Grinds ATS-34, 440C and 154CM. **Prices:** $150 to $400; some higher. **Remarks:** Full-time maker; first knife sold in 1975. **Mark:** Last name in Gothic logo; used to be initials in circle.

GAULT, CLAY,
#1225 PR 7022, Lexington, TX 78947, Phone: 979-773- 3305
>**Specialties:** Classic straight and folding hunting knives and multi-blade folders of his design. **Patterns:** Folders and hunting knives. **Technical:** Grinds BX-NSM 174 steel, custom rolled from billets to his specifications. Uses exotic leathers for sheaths, and fine natural materials for all knives. **Prices:** $325 to $600; some higher. **Remarks:** Full-time maker; first knife sold in 1970. **Mark:** Name or name with cattle brand.

GEDRAITIS, CHARLES J,
GEDRAITIS HAND CRAFTED KNIVES, 444 Shrewsbury St, Holden, MA 01520, Phone: 508-963-1861, knifemaker_1999@yahoo.com; Web: www.gedraitisknives.com
Specialties: One-of-a-kind folders & automatics of his own design. **Patterns:** One-of-a-kind. **Technical:** Forges to shape mostly stock removal. **Prices:** $300 to $2500. **Remarks:** Full-time maker. **Mark:** 3 scallop shells with an initial inside each one: CJG.

GEISLER, GARY R,
PO Box 294, Clarksville, OH 45113, Phone: 937- 383-4055, ggeisler@in-touch.net
Specialties: Period Bowies and such; flat ground. **Patterns:** Working knives usually modeled close after an existing antique. **Technical:** Flat grinds 440C, A2 and ATS-34. **Prices:** $300 and up. **Remarks:** Part-time maker; first knife sold in 1982. **Mark:** G.R. Geisler Maker; usually in script on reverse side because maker is left-handed.

GENSKE, JAY,
283 Doty St, Fond du Lac, WI 54935, Phone: 920-921- 8019/Cell Phone 920-579-0144, jaygenske@hotmail.com
Specialties: Working/using knives and period pieces of his design and to customer specs. Patterns: Bowies, fighters, hunters. Technical: Grinds ATS-34 and 440C, O1 and 1095 forges and grinds Damascus and 1095. Offers custom-tooled sheaths, scabbards and hand carved handles. Prices: $95 to $500; some to $1000. Remarks: Full-time maker; first knife sold in 1985. Doing business as Genske Knives. Mark: Stamped or engraved last name.

GEORGE, HARRY,
3137 Old Camp Long Rd, Aiken, SC 29805, Phone: 803-649-1963, hdkkgeorge@scescape.net
Specialties: Working straight knives of his design or to customer specs. **Patterns:** Hunters, skinners and utility knives. **Technical:** Grinds ATS- 34. Prefers natural handle materials, hollow-grinds and mirror finishes. **Prices:** Start at $70. **Remarks:** Part-time maker; first knife sold in 1985. Trained under George Herron. Member SCAK. Member Knifemakers Guild. **Mark:** Name, city, state.

GEORGE, LES,
6521 Fenwick Dr., Corpus Christi, TX 78414, Phone: 361-288-9777, les@georgeknives.com; Web: www.georgeknives.com
Specialties: Tactical folders, balisongs, and fixed blades. **Patterns:** Folders, balisongs, and fixed blades. **Technical:** Grinds S30V, D2, A2, 3V, CPM154. **Prices:** $200 to $700. **Remarks:** Full-time maker, first knife sold in 1992. Doing business as www.georgeknives.com. **Mark:** Last name over logo.

GEORGE, TOM,
550 Aldbury Dr, Henderson, NV 89014, tagmaker@aol.com
Specialties: Working straight knives, display knives, custom meat cleavers, and folders of his design. **Patterns:** Hunters, Bowies, daggers, buck-skinners, swords and folders. **Technical:** Uses D2, 440C, ATS-34 and 154CM. **Prices:** $500 to $13,500. **Remarks:** Custom orders not accepted "at this time". Full-time maker. First knife1982; first 350 knives were numbered; after that no numbers. Almost all his knives today are Bowies and swords. **Mark:** Tom George maker.

GEPNER, DON,
2615 E Tecumseh, Norman, OK 73071, Phone: 405- 364-2750
Specialties: Traditional working and using straight knives of his design. **Patterns:** Bowies and daggers. **Technical:** Forges his Damascus, 1095 and 5160. **Prices:** $100 to $400; some to $1000. **Remarks:** Spare-time maker; first knife sold in 1991. Has been forging since 1954; first edged weapon made at 9 years old. **Mark:** Last initial.

GERNER, THOMAS,
PO Box 301 Walpole, Western Australia, AUSTRALIA 6398, gerner@bordernet.com.au; Web: www.deepriverforge.com
Specialties: Forged working knives; plain steel and pattern welded. **Patterns:** Tries most patterns heard or read about. **Technical:** 5160, L6, O1, 52100 steels; Australian hardwood handles. **Prices:** $220 and up. **Remarks:** Achieved ABS Master Smith rating in 2001. **Mark:** Like a standing arrow and a leaning cross, T.G. in the Runic (Viking) alphabet.

GEVEDON, HANNERS (HANK),
1410 John Cash Rd, Crab Orchard, KY 40419-9770
Specialties: Traditional working and using straight knives. **Patterns:** Hunters, swords, utility and camp knives. **Technical:** Forges and grinds his own Damascus, 5160 and L6. Cast aluminum handles. **Prices:** $50 to $250; some to $400. **Remarks:** Part-time maker; first knife sold in 1983. **Mark:** Initials and LBF tang stamp.

GIAGU, SALVATORE AND DEROMA MARIA ROSARIA,
Via V Emanuele 64, 07016 Pattada (SS), ITALY, Phone: 079-755918, Fax: 079-755918, coltelligiagu@jumpy.it
Specialties: Using and collecting traditional and new folders from Sardegna. **Patterns:** Folding, hunting, utility, skinners and kitchen knives. **Technical:** Forges ATS-34, 440, D2 and Damascus. **Prices:** $200 to $2000; some higher. **Mark:** First initial, last name and name of town and muflon's head.

GIBERT, PEDRO,
Gutierrez 5189, 5603 Rama Caida, San Rafael Mendoza, ARGENTINA, Phone: 054-2627-441138, rosademayo@infovia.com.ar
Specialties: Hand forges: Stock removal and integral. High quality artistic knives of his design and to customer specifications. **Patterns:** Country (Argentine gaucho-style), knives, folders, Bowies, daggers, hunters. Others upon request. **Technical:** Blade: Bohler k110 Austrian steel (high resistance to waste). Handles: (Natural materials) ivory elephant, killer whale, hippo, walrus tooth, deer antler, goat, ram, buffalo horn, bone, rhea, goat, sheep, cow, exotic woods (South America native woods) hand carved and engraved guards and blades. Stainless steel guards, finely polished: semi-matte or shiny finish. Sheaths: Raw or tanned leather, hand-stitched; rawhide or cotton yarn embroidered. Box: One wood piece, hand carved. Wooden hinges and locks. **Prices:** $400 and up. **Remarks:** Full-time maker. Supply contractors. **Mark:** Only a rose logo. Buyers initials upon request.

GIBO, GEORGE,
PO Box 4304, Hilo, HI 96720, Phone: 808-987-7002, geogibo@interpac.net
Specialties: Straight knives and folders. **Patterns:** Hunters, bird and trout, utility, gentlemen and tactical folders. **Technical:** Grinds ATS-34, BG-42, Talonite, Stainless Steel Damascus. **Prices:** $250 to $1000. **Remarks:** Spare-time maker; first knife sold in 1995. **Mark:** Name, city and state around Hawaiian "Shaka" sign.

GIBSON SR., JAMES HOOT,
90 Park Place Ave., Bunnell, FL 32110, Phone: 386-437-4383, hootsknives. aol.com
Specialties: Bowies, folders, daggers, and hunters. **Patterns:** Most all. **Technical:** ATS-440C hand cut and grind. Also traditional old fashioned folders. **Prices:** $250 to $3000. **Remarks:** 100 percent handmade. **Mark:** Hoot.

GILBERT, CHANTAL,
291 Rue Christophe-Colomb est #105, Quebec City Quebec, CANADA G1K 3T1, Phone: 418-525-6961, Fax: 418-525- 4666, gilbertc@medion.qc.ca; Web:www.chantalgilbert.com
Specialties: Straight art knives that may resemble creatures, often with wings, shells and antennae, always with a beak of some sort, fixed blades in a feminine style. **Technical:** ATS-34 and Damascus. Handle materials usually silver that she forms to shape via special molds and a press; ebony and fossil ivory. **Prices:** Range from $500 to $4000. **Remarks:** Often embellishes her art knives with rubies, meteorite, 18k gold and similar elements.

GILBREATH, RANDALL,
55 Crauswell Rd, Dora, AL 35062, Phone: 205-648-3902
Specialties: Damascus folders and fighters. **Patterns:** Folders and fixed blades. **Technical:** Forges Damascus and high-carbon; stock removal stainless steel. **Prices:** $300 to $1500. **Remarks:** Full-time maker; first knife sold in 1979. **Mark:** Name in ribbon.

GILJEVIC, BRANKO,
35 Hayley Crescent, Queanbeyan 2620, N.S.W., AUSTRALIA 0262977613
Specialties: Classic working straight knives and folders of his design. **Patterns:** Hunters, Bowies, skinners and locking folders. **Technical:** Grinds 440C. Offers acid etching, scrimshaw and leather carving. **Prices:** $150 to $1500. **Remarks:** Part-time maker; first knife sold in 1987. Doing business as Sambar Custom Knives. **Mark:** Company name in logo.

GIRAFFEBONE INC.,
3052 Isim Road, Norman, OK 73026, Phone: 888- 804-0683; 405-321-3614, sandy@giraffebone.com; Web: www.giraffebone.com
Specialties: Giraffebone, horns, African hardwoods, and mosaic Damascus

GIRTNER, JOE,
409 Catalpa Ave, Brea, CA 92821, Phone: 714-529- 2388, conceptsinknives@aol.com
Specialties: Art knives and miniatures. **Patterns:** Mainly Damascus (some carved). **Technical:** Many techniques and materials combines. **Prices:** $55 to $3000. **Mark:** Name.

GITTINGER, RAYMOND,
6940 S Rt 100, Tiffin, OH 44883, Phone: 419- 397-2517

GLOVER, RON,
7702 Misty Springs Ct, Mason, OH 45040, Phone: 513- 398-7857
Specialties: High-tech working straight knives and folders. **Patterns:** Hunters to Bowies; some interchangeable blade models; unique locking mechanisms. **Technical:** Grinds 440C, 154CM; buys Damascus. **Prices:** $70 to $500; some to $800. **Remarks:** Part-time maker; first knife sold in 1981. **Mark:** Name in script.

GLOVER, WARREN D,
dba BUBBA KNIVES, PO Box 475, Cleveland, GA 30528, Phone: 706-865-3998, Fax: 706-348-7176, warren@bubbaknives.net; Web: www.bubbaknives.net
Specialties: Traditional and custom working and using straight knives of his design and to customer request. **Patterns:** Hunters, skinners and bird and fish, utility and kitchen knives. **Technical:** Grinds 440, ATS-34 and stainless steel Damascus. **Prices:** $75 to $400 and up. **Remarks:** Full- time maker; sold first knife in 1995. **Mark:** Bubba, year, name, state.

GODDARD, WAYNE,
473 Durham Ave, Eugene, OR 97404, Phone: 541-689-8098, wgoddard44@comcast.net
Specialties: Working/using straight knives and folders. **Patterns:** Hunters and folders. **Technical:** Works exclusively with wire Damascus and his own-pattern welded material. **Prices:** $250 to $4000. **Remarks:** Full- time maker; first knife sold in 1963. **Mark:** Blocked initials on forged blades; regular capital initials on stock removal.

GODLESKY, BRUCE F.,
1002 School Rd., Apollo, PA 15613, Phone: 724-840-5786, brucegodlesky@yahoo.com; Web: www.birdforge.com
Specialties: Working/using straight knives and tomahawks, mostly forged. **Patterns:** Hunters, birds and trout, fighters and tomahawks. **Technical:** Most forged, some stock removal. Carbon steel only. 5160, O-1, W2, 10xx series. Makes own Damascus and welded cable. **Prices:** Starting at $75. **Mark:** BIRDOG FORGE.

GOERS, BRUCE,
3423 Royal Ct S, Lakeland, FL 33813, Phone: 941- 646-0984
Specialties: Fancy working and using straight knives of his design and to customer specs. **Patterns:** Hunters, fighters, Bowies and fantasy knives. **Technical:** Grinds ATS-34, some Damascus. **Prices:** $195 to $600; some to $1300. **Remarks:** Part-time maker; first knife sold in 1990. Doing business as Vulture Cutlery. **Mark:** Buzzard with initials.

GOFOURTH, JIM,
3776 Aliso Cyn Rd, Santa Paula, CA 93060, Phone: 805-659-3814
Specialties: Period pieces and working knives. **Patterns:** Bowies, locking folders, patent lockers and others. **Technical:** Grinds A2 and 154CM. **Prices:** Moderate. **Remarks:** Spare-time maker. **Mark:** Initials interconnected.

GOGUEN, SCOTT,
166 Goguen Rd, Newport, NC 28570, Phone: 252- 393-6013, goguenknives.com
Specialties: Classic and traditional working knives. **Patterns:** Kitchen, camp, hunters, Bowies. **Technical:** Forges high-carbon steel and own Damascus. Offers clay tempering and cord wrapped handles. **Prices:** $85 to $1500. **Remarks:** Spare-time maker; first knife sold in1988. **Mark:** Last name or name in Japanese characters.

GOLDBERG, DAVID,
321 Morris Rd, Ft Washington, PA 19034, Phone: 215-654-7117, david@goldmountainforge.com; Web: www.goldmountainforge.com
Specialties: Japanese-style designs, will work with special themes in Japanese genre. **Patterns:** Kozuka, Tanto, Wakazashi, Katana, Tachi, Sword canes, Yari and Naginata. **Technical:** Forges his own Damascus and makes his own handmade tamehagane steel from straw ash, iron, carbon and clay. Uses traditional materials, carves fittings handles and cases. Hardens all blades in traditional Japanese clay differential technique. **Remarks:** Full-time maker; first knife sold in 1987. Japanese swordsmanship teacher (jaido) and Japanese self-defense teach (aikido). **Mark:** Name (kinzan) in Japanese Kanji on Tang under handle.

GOLDEN, RANDY,
6492 Eastwood Glen Dr, Montgomery, AL 36117, Phone: 334-271-6429, rgolden1@mindspring.com
Specialties: Collectable quality hand rubbed finish, hunter, camp, Bowie straight knives, custom leather sheaths with exotic skin inlays and tooling. **Technical:** Stock removal ATS-34, CPM154, S30V and BG-42. Natural handle materials primarily stag and ivory. **Prices:** $250 to $1500. **Remarks:** Full-time maker, member Knifemakers Guild, first knife sold in 2000. **Mark:** R. R. Golden Montgomery, AL.

GOLTZ, WARREN L,
802 4th Ave E, Ada, MN 56510, Phone: 218-784- 7721, sspexp@loretel.net
Specialties: Fancy working knives in standard patterns. **Patterns:** Hunters, Bowies and camp knives. **Technical:** Grinds 440C and ATS-34. **Prices:** $120 to $595; some to $950. **Remarks:** Part-time maker; first knife sold in 1984. **Mark:** Last name.

GONZALEZ, LEONARDO WILLIAMS,
Ituzaingo 473, Maldonado, CP 20000, URUGUAY, Phone: 598 4222 1617, Fax: 598 4222 1617, willyknives@hotmail.com
Specialties: Classic high-art and fantasy straight knives; traditional working and using knives of his design, in standard patterns or to customer specs. **Patterns:** Hunters, Bowies, daggers, fighters, boots, swords and utility/camp knives. **Technical:** Forges and grinds high-carbon and stainless Bohler steels. **Prices:** $100 to $2500. **Remarks:** Full-time maker; first knife sold in 1985. **Mark:** Willy, whale, R.O.U.

GOO, TAI,
5920 W Windy Lou Ln, Tucson, AZ 85742, Phone: 520-744- 9777, taigoo@msn.com; Web: www.taigoo.com
Specialties: High art, neo-tribal, bush and fantasy. **Technical:** Hand forges, does own heat treating, makes own Damascus. **Prices:** $150 to $500 some to $10,000. **Remarks:** Full-time maker; first knife sold in 1978. **Mark:** Chiseled signature.

GOODE, BEAR,
PO Box 6474, Navajo Dam, NM 87419, Phone: 505- 632-8184
Specialties: Working/using straight knives of his design and in standard patterns. **Patterns:** Bowies, hunters and utility/camp knives. **Technical:** Grinds 440C, ATS-34, 154-CM; forges and grinds 1095, 5160 and other steels on request; uses Damascus. **Prices:** $60 to $225; some to $500 and up. **Remarks:** Part-time maker; first knife sold in 1993. Doing business as Bear Knives. **Mark:** First and last name with a three-toed paw print.

GOODE, BRIAN,
203 Gordon Ave, Shelby, NC 28152, Phone: 704-434- 6496, web:www.bgoodeknives.com
Specialties: Flat ground working knives with etched/antique or brushed finish. **Patterns:** Field, camp, hunters, skinners, survival, kitchen, maker's design or yours. Currently full tang only with supplied leather sheath. **Technical:** 0-1, D2 and other ground flat stock. Stock removal and differential heat treat preferred. Etched antique/etched satin working finish preferred. Micarta and hardwoods for strength. **Prices:** $150 to $700. **Remarks:** Part-time maker and full-time knife lover. First knife sold in 2004. **Mark:** B. Goode with NC separated by a feather.

GORDON, LARRY B,
23555 Newell Cir W, Farmington Hills, MI 48336, Phone: 248-477-5483, lbgordon1@aol.com
Specialties: Folders, small fixed blades. New design rotating scale release automatic. **Patterns:** Rotating handle locker. Ambidextrous fire (R&L) **Prices:** $450 minimum. **Remarks:** High line materials preferred. **Mark:** Gordon.

GORENFLO, GABE,
9145 Sullivan Rd, Baton Rouge, LA 70818, Phone: 504-261-5868

GORENFLO, JAMES T (JT),
9145 Sullivan Rd, Baton Rouge, LA 70818, Phone: 225-261-5868
Specialties: Traditional working and using straight knives of his design. **Patterns:** Bowies, hunters and utility/camp knives. **Technical:** Forges 5160, 1095, 52100 and his own Damascus. **Prices:** Start at $200. **Remarks:** Part-time maker; first knife sold in 1992. **Mark:** Last name or initials, J.S. on reverse.

GOSSMAN, SCOTT,
, PO Box 815, Forest Hill, MD 21050, Phone: 410- 452-8456, scott@gossmanknives.com Web:www.gossmanknives.com
Specialties: Heavy duty knives for big game hunting and survival. **Patterns:** Drop point spear point hunters. Large camp/survival knives. **Technical:** Grinds D-2, A2, O1 and 57 convex grinds and edges. **Price:** $100 to $350 some higher. **Remarks:** Full time maker does business as Gossman Knives. **Mark:** Gossman and steel type.

GOTTAGE, DANTE,
43227 Brooks Dr, Clinton Twp., MI 48038-5323, Phone: 810-286-7275
Specialties: Working knives of his design or to customer specs. **Patterns:** Large and small skinners, fighters, Bowies and fillet knives. **Technical:** Grinds O1, 440C and 154CM and ATS-34. **Prices:** $150 to $600. **Remarks:** Part-time maker; first knife sold in 1975. **Mark:** Full name in script letters.

GOTTAGE, JUDY,
43227 Brooks Dr, Clinton Twp., MI 48038-5323, Phone: 586-286-7275, jgottage@remaxmetropolitan.com
Specialties: Custom folders of her design or to customer specs. **Patterns:** Interframes or integral. **Technical:** Stock removal. **Prices:** $300 to $3000. **Remarks:** Full-time maker; first knife sold in 1980. **Mark:** Full name, maker in script.

GOTTSCHALK, GREGORY J,
12 First St. (Ft. Pitt), Carnegie, PA 15106, Phone: 412-279-6692
Specialties: Fancy working straight knives and folders to customer specs. **Patterns:** Hunters to tantos, locking folders to minis. **Technical:** Grinds 440C, 154CM, ATS-34. Now making own Damascus. Most knives have mirror finishes. **Prices:** Start at $150. **Remarks:** Part-time maker; first knife sold in 1977. **Mark:** Full name in crescent.

GOUKER, GARY B,
PO Box 955, Sitka, AK 99835, Phone: 907-747- 3476
Specialties: Hunting knives for hard use. **Patterns:** Skinners, semi-skinners, and such. **Technical:** Likes natural materials, inlays, stainless steel. **Prices:** Moderate. **Remarks:** New Alaskan maker. **Mark:** Name.

GRAHAM, GORDON,
3145 CR 4008, New Boston, TX 75570, Phone: 903-293-2610, Web: www.grahamknives.com
Prices: $325 to $850. **Mark:** Graham.

GRANGER, PAUL J,
704 13th Ct. SW, Largo, FL 33770-4471, grangerknives@hotmail.com
Specialties: Working straight knives of his own design and a few folders. **Patterns:** 2.75" to 4" work knives, skinners, tactical knives and Bowies from 5"-9." **Technical:** Forges 52100 and 5160 and his own carbon steel Damascus. Offers filework. **Prices:** $95 to $400. **Remarks:** Part-time maker since 1997. Sold first knife in 1997. Doing business as Granger Knives and Pale Horse Fighters. Member of ABS and OBG. **Mark:** "Granger" or "Palehorse Fighters."

GRAVELINE, PASCAL AND ISABELLE,
38, Rue de Kerbrezillic, 29350 Moelan-sur-Mer, FRANCE, Phone: 33 2 98 39 73 33, Fax: 33 2 98 39 73 33, atelier.graveline@wanadoo.fr; Web: www.graveline-couteliers.com
Specialties: French replicas from the 17th, 18th and 19th centuries. **Patterns:** Traditional folders and multi-blade pocket knives; traveling knives, fruit knives and fork sets; puzzle knives and friend's knives; rivet less knives. **Technical:** Grind 12C27, ATS-34, Damascus and carbon steel. **Prices:** $500 to $5000. **Remarks:** Full-time makers; first knife sold in 1992. **Mark:** Last name over head of ram.

GRAVES, DAN,
4887 Dixie Garden Loop, Shreveport, LA 71105, Phone: 318-865-8166, Web: wwwtheknifemaker.com
Specialties: Traditional forged blades and Damascus. **Patterns:** Bowies (D guard also), fighters, hunters, large and small daggers. **Remarks:** Full-time maker. **Mark:** Initials with circle around them.

GRAY, BOB,
8206 N Lucia Court, Spokane, WA 99208, Phone: 509- 468-3924
Specialties: Straight working knives of his own design or to customer specs. **Patterns:** Hunter, fillet and carving knives. **Technical:** Forges 5160, L6 and some 52100; grinds 440C. **Prices:** $100 to $600. **Remarks:** Part-time knifemaker; first knife sold in 1991. Doing business as Hi-Land Knives. **Mark:** HI-L.

GRAY, DANIEL,
GRAY KNIVES, 686 Main Rd., Brownville, ME 04414, Phone: 207-965-2191, mail@grayknives.com; Web: www.grayknives.com
Specialties: Straight knives, fantasy, folders, automatics and traditional of his own design. **Patterns:** Automatics, fighters, hunters. **Technical:** Grinds O1, 154CM and D2. **Prices:** From $155 to $750. **Remarks:** Full- time maker; first knife sold in 1974. **Mark:** Gray Knives.

GREBE, GORDON S,
PO Box 296, Anchor Point, AK 99556-0296, Phone: 907-235-8242
Specialties: Working straight knives and folders, some fancy. **Patterns:** Tantos, Bowies, boot fighter sets, locking folders. **Technical:** Grinds stainless steels; likes 1/4" inch stock and glass-bead finishes. **Prices:** $75 to $250; some to $2000. **Remarks:** Full-time maker; first knife sold in 1968. **Mark:** Initials in lightning logo.

GRECO, JOHN,
100 Mattie Jones Rd, Greensburg, KY 42743, Phone: 270-932-3335, Fax: 270-932-2225, johngreco@grecoknives.com; Web: www.grecoknives.com
Specialties: Limited edition knives and swords. **Patterns:** Tactical, fighters, camp knives, short swords. **Technical:** Stock removal carbon steel. **Prices:** Affordable. **Remarks:** Full-time maker since 1986. First knife sold in 1979. **Mark:** Greco and w/mo mark.

GREEN, BILL,
6621 Eastview Dr, Sachse, TX 75048, Phone: 972-463- 3147
Specialties: High-art and working straight knives and folders of his design and to customer specs. **Patterns:** Bowies, hunters, kitchen knives and locking folders. **Technical:** Grinds ATS-34, D2 and 440V. Hand- tooled custom sheaths. **Prices:** $70 to $350; some to $750. **Remarks:** Part-time maker; first knife sold in 1990. **Mark:** Last name.

GREEN, WILLIAM (BILL),
46 Warren Rd, View Bank Vic., AUSTRALIA 3084, Fax: 03-9459-1529
Specialties: Traditional high-tech straight knives and folders. **Patterns:** Japanese-influenced designs, hunters, Bowies, folders and miniatures. **Technical:** Forges O1, D2 and his own Damascus. Offers lost wax castings for bolsters and pommels. Likes natural handle materials, gems, silver and gold. **Prices:** $400 to $750; some to $1200. **Remarks:** Full-time maker. **Mark:** Initials.

GREENAWAY, DON,
3325 Dinsmore Tr, Fayetteville, AR 72704, Phone: 501-521-0323

GREENE, CHRIS,
707 Cherry Lane, Shelby, NC 28150, Phone: 704- 434-5620

GREENE, DAVID,
570 Malcom Rd, Covington, GA 30209, Phone: 770- 784-0657
Specialties: Straight working using knives. **Patterns:** Hunters. **Technical:** Forges mosaic and twist Damascus. Prefers stag and desert ironwood for handle material.

GREENE, STEVE,
DUNN KNIVES INC, PO Box 204, Rossville, KS 66533, Phone: 785-584-6856, Fax: 785-584-6020, s.greene@earthlink.net; Web: www.dunnknives.com
Specialties: Skinning & fillet knives. **Patterns:** Skinners, drop points, clip points and fillets. **Technical:** S60V, S90V and 20 CV powdered metal steel. **Prices:** $90 to $250. **Mark:** Dunn by Greene and year. **Remarks:** Full-time knifemaker. First knife sold in 1972.

GREENFIELD, G O,
2605 15th St #310, Everett, WA 98201, garyg1946@yahoo.com
Specialties: High-tech and working straight knives and folders of his design. **Patterns:** Boots, daggers, hunters and one-of-a-kinds. **Technical:** Grinds ATS-34, D2, 440C and T-440V. Makes sheaths for each knife. **Prices:** $100 to $800; some to $10,000. **Remarks:** Part-time maker; first knife sold in 1978. **Mark:** Springfield®, serial number.

GREGORY, MICHAEL,
211 Calhoun Rd, Belton, SC 29627, Phone: 864- 338-8898
Specialties: Working straight knives and folders. **Patterns:** Hunters, tantos, locking folders and slip-joints, boots and fighters. **Technical:** Grinds 440C, 154CM and ATS-34; mirror finishes. **Prices:** $95 to $200; some to $1000. **Remarks:** Part-time maker; first knife sold in 1980. **Mark:** Name, city in logo.

GREINER, RICHARD,
1073 E County Rd 32, Green Springs, OH 44836

GREISS, JOCKL,
Herrenwald 15, D 77773 Schenkenzell, GERMANY, Phone: +49 7836 95 71 69 or +49 7836 95 55 76, www.jocklgreiss@yahoo.com
Specialties: Classic and working using straight knives of his design. **Patterns:** Bowies, daggers and hunters. **Technical:** Uses only Jerry Rados Damascus. All knives are one-of-a-kind made by hand; no machines are used. **Prices:** $700 to $2000; some to $3000. **Remarks:** Full-time maker; first knife sold in 1984. **Mark:** An "X" with a long vertical line through it.

GREY, PIET,
PO Box 363, Naboomspruit 0560, SOUTH AFRICA, Phone: 014-743-3613
Specialties: Fancy working and using straight knives of his design. **Patterns:** Fighters, hunters and utility/camp knives. **Technical:** Grinds ATS-34 and AEB-L; forges and grinds Damascus. Solder less fitting of guards. Engraves and scrimshaws. **Prices:** $125 to $750; some to $1500. **Remarks:** Part-time maker; first knife sold in 1970. **Mark:** Last name.

GRIFFIN, RENDON AND MARK,
9706 Cedardale, Houston, TX 77055, Phone: 713-468-0436
Specialties: Working folders and automatics of their designs. **Patterns:** Standard lockers and slip-joints. **Technical:** Most blade steels; stock removal. **Prices:** Start at $350. **Remarks:** Rendon's first knife sold in 1966; Mark's in 1974. **Mark:** Last name logo.

GRIFFIN, THOMAS J,
591 Quevli Ave., Windom, MN 56101, Phone: 507-831-1089
Specialties: Period pieces and fantasy straight knives of his design. **Patterns:** Daggers and swords. **Technical:** Forges 1095, 52100 and L6. Most blades are his own Damascus; turned fittings and wire-wrapped grips. **Prices:** $250 to $800; some to $2000. **Remarks:** Full-time maker; first knife sold in 1991. Doing business as Griffin Knives. **Mark:** Last name etched.

GRIFFIN JR., HOWARD A,
14299 SW 31st Ct, Davie, FL 33330, Phone: 954-474-5406, mgriffin18@aol.com
Specialties: Working straight knives and folders. **Patterns:** Hunters, Bowies, locking folders with his own push-button lock design. **Technical:** Grinds 440C. **Prices:** $100 to $200; some to $500. **Remarks:** Part-time maker; first knife sold in 1983. **Mark:** Initials.

GROSPITCH, ERNIE,
18440 Amityville Dr, Orlando, FL 32820, Phone: 407-568-5438, shrpknife@aol.com; Web: www.erniesknives.com
Specialties: Bowies, hunting, fishing, kitchen, lockback folders, leather craft. **Patterns:** His design or customer. **Technical:** Stock removal using most available steels. **Prices:** $140 and up. **Remarks:** Full-time maker, sold first knife in 1990. Mark: Etched name/maker city and state.

GROSS, W W,
109 Dylan Scott Dr, Archdale, NC 27263-3858
Specialties: Working knives. **Patterns:** Hunters, boots, fighters. **Technical:** Grinds. **Prices:** Moderate. **Remarks:** Full-time maker. **Mark:** Name.

GROSSMAN, STEWART,
24 Water St #419, Clinton, MA 01510, Phone: 508-365-2291; 800-mysword
Specialties: Miniatures and full-size knives and swords. **Patterns:** One- of-a-kind miniatures—jewelry, replicas—and wire-wrapped figures. Full- size art, fantasy and combat knives, daggers and modular systems. **Technical:** Forges and grinds most metals and Damascus. Uses gems, crystals, electronics and motorized mechanisms. **Prices:** $20 to $300; some to $4500 and higher. **Remarks:** Full-time maker; first knife sold in 1985. **Mark:** G1.

GRUSSENMEYER, PAUL G,
310 Kresson Rd, Cherry Hill, NJ 08034, Phone: 856-428-1088, pgrussentne@comcast.net; Web: www.pgcarvings.com
Specialties: Assembling fancy and fantasy straight knives with his own carved handles. **Patterns:** Bowies, daggers, folders, swords, hunters and miniatures. **Technical:** Uses forged steel and Damascus, stock removal and knapped obsidian blades. **Prices:** $250 to $4000. **Remarks:** Spare- time maker; first knife sold in 1991. **Mark:** First and last initial hooked together on handle.

GUARNERA, ANTHONY R,
42034 Quail Creek Dr, Quartzhill, CA 93536, Phone: 661-722-4032
Patterns: Hunters, camp, Bowies, kitchen, fighter knives. **Technical:** Forged and stock removal. **Prices:** $100 and up.

GUIDRY, BRUCE,
24550 Adams Ave, Murrieta, CA 92562, Phone: 909- 677-2384

GUINN, TERRY,
958 US Hwy 82 W, Seymour, TX 76380, Phone: 940- 889-2437, Web: www.terryguinn.com
Specialties: Working fixed blades and balisongs. **Patterns:** Almost all types

of folding and fixed blades, from patterns and "one of a kind". **Technical:** Stock removal all types of blade steel with preference for air hardening steel. Does own heat treating, all knives Rockwell tested in shop. **Prices:** $200 to $2,000. **Remarks:** Part time maker since 1982, sold first knife 1990. **Mark:** Full name with cross in the middle.

GUNTER, BRAD,
13 Imnaha Rd., Tijeras, NM 87059, Phone: 505-281- 8080

GUNTHER, EDDIE,
11 Nedlands Pl Burswood, 2013 Auckland, NEW ZEALAND, Phone: 006492722373, eddit.gunther49@gmail.com
Specialties: Drop point hunters, boot, Bowies. All mirror finished. **Technical:** Grinds D2, 440C, 12c27. **Prices:** $250 to $800. **Remarks:** Part- time maker, first knife in 1986. **Mark:** Name, city, country.

GURGANUS, CAROL,
2553 NC 45 South, Colerain, NC 27924, Phone: 252-356-4831, Fax: 252-356-4650
Specialties: Working and using straight knives. **Patterns:** Fighters, hunters and kitchen knives. **Technical:** Grinds D2, ATS-34 and Damascus steel. Uses stag, and exotic wood handles. **Prices:** $100 to $300. **Remarks:** Part-time maker; first knife sold in 1992. **Mark:** Female symbol, last name, city, state.

GURGANUS, MELVIN H,
2553 NC 45 South, Colerain, NC 27924, Phone: 252-356-4831, Fax: 252-356-4650
Specialties: High-tech working folders. **Patterns:** Leaf-lock and back- lock designs, bolstered and interframe. **Technical:** D2 and 440C; Heat- treats, carves and offers lost wax casting. **Prices:** $300 to $3000. **Remarks:** Part-time maker; first knife sold in 1983. **Mark:** First initial, last name and maker.

GUTHRIE, GEORGE B,
1912 Puett Chapel Rd, Bassemer City, NC 28016, Phone: 704-629-3031
Specialties: Working knives of his design or to customer specs. **Patterns:** Hunters, boots, fighters, locking folders and slip-joints in traditional styles. **Technical:** Grinds D2, 440C and 154CM. **Prices:** $105 to $300; some to $450. **Remarks:** Part-time maker; first knife sold in 1978. **Mark:** Name in state.

H

HAGEN, DOC,
PO Box 58, 41780 Kansas Point Ln, Pelican Rapids, MN 56572, Phone: 218-863-8503, dhagen@prtel.com; Web: www.dochagencustomknives.com
Specialties: Folders. Autos:bolster release-dual action. Slipjoint folders- **Patterns:** Defense-related straight knives; wide variety of folders. **Technical:** Dual action release, bolster release autos. **Prices:** $300 to $800; some to $3000. **Remarks:** Full-time maker; first knife sold in 1975. Makes his own Damascus. **Mark:** DOC HAGEN in shield, knife, banner logo; or DOC.

HAGGERTY, GEORGE S,
PO Box 88, Jacksonville, VT 05342, Phone: 802-368-7437, swewater@verizon.net
Specialties: Working straight knives and folders. **Patterns:** Hunters, claws, camp and fishing knives, locking folders and backpackers. **Technical:** Forges and grinds W2, 440C and 154CM. **Prices:** $85 to $300. **Remarks:** Part-time maker; first knife sold in 1981. **Mark:** Initials or last name.

HAGUE, GEOFF,
Unit 5, Project Workshops, Laines Farm, Quarley, SP11 8PX, UK, Phone: (+44) 01672-870212, Fax: (+44) 01672 870212, geoff@hagueknives.com; Web: www.hagueknives.com
Specialties: Quality folding knives. **Patterns:** Back lock, locking liner, slip joint, and friction folders. **Technical:** RWL34, D2, titanium, and some gold decoraqtion. Mainly natural handle materials. **Prices:** $900 to $2,000. **Remarks:** Full-time maker. **Mark:** Last name.

HAINES, JEFF HAINES CUSTOM KNIVES,
302 N Mill St, Wauzeka, WI 53826, Phone: 608-875-5325, jeffhaines@centurytel.net
Patterns: Hunters, skinners, camp knives, customer designs welcome. **Technical:** Forges 1095, 5160, and Damascus, grinds A2. **Prices:** $50 and up. **Remarks:** Part-time maker since 1995. **Mark:** Last name.

HALFRICH, JERRY,
340 Briarwood, San Marcos, TX 78666, Phone: 512-353-2582, Fax: 512-392-3659, jerryhalfrich@earthlink.net; Web: www.halfrichknives.com
Specialties: Working knives and specialty utility knives for the professional and serious hunter. Uses proven designs in both straight and folding knives. Plays close attention to fit and finish. Art knives on special request. **Patterns:** Hunters, skinners, lock back liner lock. **Technical:** Grinds both flat and hollow D2, damasteel, BG42 makes high precision folders. **Prices:** $300 to $600, sometimes $1000. **Remarks:** Full-time maker since 2000. DBA Halfrich Custom Knives. **Mark:** Halfrich, San Marcos, TX in a football shape.

HALL, JEFF,
PO Box 435, Los Alamitos, CA 90720, Phone: 562-594- 4740, jhall10176@aol.com
Specialties: Collectible and working folders of his design. Technical: Grinds S30V, ATS-34, and various makers' Damascus. Patterns: Fighters, gentleman's, hunters and utility knives. Prices: $300 to $500; some to $1000. Remarks: Full-time maker. First knife sold 1998. Mark: Last name.

HALLIGAN, ED,
14 Meadow Way, Sharpsburg, GA 30277, Phone: 770- 251-7720, Fax: 770-251-7720
Specialties: Working straight knives and folders, some fancy. **Patterns:** Liner locks, hunters, skinners, boots, fighters and swords. **Technical:** Grinds ATS-34; forges 5160; makes cable and pattern Damascus. **Prices:** $160 to $2500. **Remarks:** Full-time maker; first knife sold in 1985. Doing business as Halligan Knives. **Mark:** Last name, city, state and USA.

HAMLET JR., JOHNNY,
300 Billington, Clute, TX 77531, Phone: 979- 265-6929, nifeman@swbell.net; Web: www.hamlets-handmade- knives.com
Specialties: Working straight knives and folders. **Patterns:** Hunters, fighters, fillet and kitchen knives, locking folders. Likes upswept knives and trailing-points. **Technical:** Grinds 440C, D2, ATS-34. Makes sheaths. **Prices:** $125 and up. **Remarks:** Full-time maker; sold first knife in 1988. **Mark:** Hamlet's Handmade in script.

HAMMOND, HANK,
189 Springlake Dr, Leesburg, GA 31763, Phone: 229-434-1295, godogs57@bellsouth.net
Specialties: Traditional hunting and utility knives of his design. Will also design and produce knives to customer's specifications. **Patterns:** Straight or sheath knives, hunters skinners as well as Bowies and fighters. **Technical:** Grinds (hollow and flat grinds) CPM 154CM, ATS-34. Also uses Damascus and forges 52100. Offers filework on blades. Handle materials include all exotic woods, red stag, sambar stag, deer, elk, oosic, bone, fossil ivory, Micarta, etc. All knives come with sheath handmade for that individual knife. **Prices:** $100 up to $500. **Remarks:** Part- time maker. Sold first knife in 1981. Doing business as Double H Knives. **Mark:** "HH" inside 8 point deer rack.

HAMMOND, JIM,
PO Box 486, Arab, AL 35016, Phone: 256-586-4151, Fax: 256-586-0170, jim@jimhammondknives.com; Web: www.jimhammondkinves.com
Specialties: High-tech fighters and folders. **Patterns:** Proven-design fighters. **Technical:** Grinds 440C, 440V, ATS-34 and other specialty steels. **Prices:** $385 to $1200; some to $9200. **Remarks:** Full-time maker; first knife sold in 1977. Designer for Columbia River Knife and Tool. **Mark:** Full name, city, state in shield logo.

HANCOCK, TIM,
10805 N. 83rd St, Scottsdale, AZ 85260, Phone: 480- 998-8849
Specialties: High-art and working straight knives and folders of his design and to customer preferences. **Patterns:** Bowies, fighters, daggers, tantos, swords, folders. **Technical:** Forges Damascus and 52100; grinds ATS-34. Makes Damascus. Silver-wire inlays; offers carved fittings and file work. **Prices:** $500 to $10,000. **Remarks:** Full-time maker; first knife sold in 1988. Master Smith ABS. **Mark:** Last name or heart.

HAND, BILL,
PO Box 717, 1103 W. 7th St., Spearman, TX 79081, Phone: 806-659-2967, Fax: 806-659-5139, klinker@arn.net
Specialties: Traditional working and using straight knives and folders of his design or to customer specs. **Patterns:** Hunters, Bowies, folders and fighters. **Technical:** Forges 5160, 52100 and Damascus. **Prices:** Start at $150. **Remarks:** Part-time maker; Journeyman Smith. Current delivery time 12 to 16 months. **Mark:** Stylized initials.

HANSEN, LONNIE,
PO Box 4956, Spanaway, WA 98387, Phone: 253- 847-4632, lonniehansen@msn.com; Web: lchansen.com
Specialties: Working straight knives of his design. **Patterns:** Tomahawks, tantos, hunters, fillet. **Technical:** Forges 1086, 52100, grinds 440V, BG-42. **Prices:** Starting at $300. **Remarks:** Part-time maker since 1989. **Mark:** First initial and last name. Also first and last initial.

HANSEN, ROBERT W,
35701 University Ave NE, Cambridge, MN 55008, Phone: 612-689-3242
Specialties: Working straight knives, folders and integrals. **Patterns:** From hunters to minis, camp knives to miniatures; folding lockers and slip-joints in original styles. **Technical:** Grinds O1, 440C and 154CM; likes filework. **Prices:** $75 to $175; some to $550. **Remarks:** Part-time maker; first knife sold in 1983. **Mark:** Fish with last initial inside.

HANSON III, DON L,
PO Box 13, Success, MO 65570-0013, Phone: 573-674-3045, Web: www.sunfishforge.com; Web: www.donhansonknives.com
Specialties: One-of-a-kind Damascus folders and forged fixed blades. **Patterns:** Small, fancy pocket knives, large folding fighters and Bowies. **Technical:** Forges own pattern welded Damascus, file work and carving also carbon steel blades with hamons. **Prices:** $800 and up. **Remarks:** Full-time maker, first knife sold in 1984. ABS mastersmith. **Mark:** Sunfish.

HARA, KOUJI,
292-2 Osugi, Seki-City, Gifu-Pref. 501-3922, JAPAN, Phone: 0575-24-7569, Fax: 0575-24-7569, info@knifehousehara.com; Web: www.knifehousehara.com
Specialties: High-tech and working straight knives of his design; some folders. **Patterns:** Hunters, locking folders and utility/camp knives. **Technical:** Grinds Cowry X, Cowry Y and ATS-34. Prefers high mirror polish; pearl handle inlay. **Prices:** $400 to $2500. **Remarks:** Full-time maker; first knife sold in 1980. Doing business as Knife House "Hara." **Mark:** First initial, last name in fish.

HARDY, DOUGLAS E,
114 Cypress Rd, Franklin, GA 30217, Phone: 706-675-6305

HARDY, SCOTT,
639 Myrtle Ave, Placerville, CA 95667, Phone: 530- 622-5780, Web: www. innercite.com/~shardy
Specialties: Traditional working and using straight knives of his design. **Patterns:** Most anything with an edge. **Technical:** Forges carbon steels. Japanese stone polish. Offers mirror finish; differentially tempers. **Prices:** $100 to $1000. **Remarks:** Part-time maker; first knife sold in 1982. **Mark:** First initial, last name and Handmade with bird logo.

HARKINS, J A,
PO Box 218, Conner, MT 59827, Phone: 406-821-1060, kutter@customknives. net; Web: customknives.net
Specialties: Investment grade folders. **Patterns:** Flush buttons, lockers. **Technical:** Grinds ATS-34. Engraves; offers gem work. **Prices:** Start at $550. **Remarks:** Full-time maker and engraver; first knife sold in 1988. **Mark:** First and middle initials, last name.

HARLEY, LARRY W,
348 Deerfield Dr, Bristol, TN 37620, Phone: 423- 878-5368 (shop)/Cell 423-571-0638, Fax: 276-466-6771, Web: www.lonesomepineknives.com
Specialties: One-of-a-kind Persian in one-of-a-kind Damascus. Working knives, period pieces. **Technical:** Forges and grinds ATS-34, 440c, L6, 15, 20, 1084, and 52100. **Patterns:** Full range of straight knives, tomahawks, razors, buck skinners and hog spears. **Prices:** $200 and up. **Mark:** Pine tree.

HARLEY, RICHARD,
348 Deerfield Dr, Bristol, TN 37620, Phone: 423- 878-5368/423-571-0638
Specialties: Hunting knives, Bowies, friction folders, one-of-a-kind. **Technical:** Forges 1084, S160, 52100, Lg. **Prices:** $150 to $1000. **Mark:** Pine tree with name.

HARM, PAUL W,
818 Young Rd, Attica, MI 48412, Phone: 810-724- 5582, harm@blclinks.net
Specialties: Early American working knives. **Patterns:** Hunters, skinners, patch knives, fighters, folders. **Technical:** Forges and grinds 1084, O1, 52100 and own Damascus. **Prices:** $75 to $1000. **Remarks:** First knife sold in 1990. **Mark:** Connected initials.

HARNER, LLOYD R. "BUTCH",
4865 Hanover Rd., Hanover, PA 17331, harnerknives@gmail.com; Web: www. harnerknives.com
Specialties: Kitchen knives and razors. **Technical:** CPM3V, CPM154, and crucible super-alloy blade steels. **Remarks:** Full-time maker since 2007. **Mark:** Maker's name, "L R Harner."

HARRINGTON, ROGER,
P.O. Box 157, Battle, East Sussex, ENGLAND TN 33 3 DD, Phone: 0854-838-7062, info@bisonbushcraft.co.uk; Web: www.bisonbushcraft.co.uk
Specialties: Working straight knives to his or customer's designs, flat saber Scandinavia-style grinds on full tang knives, also hollow and convex grinds. **Technical:** Grinds O1, D2, Damascus. **Prices:** $200 to $800. **Remarks:** First knife made by hand in 1997 whilst traveling around the world. **Mark:** Bison with bison written under.

HARRIS, CASS,
19855 Fraiser Hill Ln, Bluemont, VA 20135, Phone: 540-554-8774, Web: www. tdogforge.com
Prices: $160 to $500.

HARRIS, JAY,
991 Johnson St, Redwood City, CA 94061, Phone: 415- 366-6077
Specialties: Traditional high-tech straight knives and folders of his design. **Patterns:** Daggers, fighters and locking folders. **Technical:** Uses 440C, ATS-34 and CPM. **Prices:** $250 to $850. **Remarks:** Spare-time maker; first knife sold in 1980.

HARRIS, JEFFERY A,
214 Glen Cove Dr, Chesterfield, MO 63017, Phone: 314-469-6317, Fax: 314-469-6374, jeffro135@aol.com
Remarks: Purveyor and collector of handmade knives.

HARRIS, JOHN,
14131 Calle Vista, Riverside, CA 92508, Phone: 951- 653-2755, johnharrisknives@yahoo.com
Specialties: Hunters, daggers, Bowies, bird and trout, period pieces, Damascus and carbon steel knives, forged and stock removal. **Prices:** $200 to $1000.

HARRIS, RALPH DEWEY,
2607 Bell Shoals Rd, Brandon, FL 33511, Phone: 813-681-5293, Fax: 813-654-8175
Specialties: Collector quality interframe folders. **Patterns:** High tech locking folders of his own design with various mechanisms. **Technical:** Grinds 440C, ATS-34 and commercial Damascus. Offers various frame materials including 416ss, and titanium; file worked frames and his own engraving. **Prices:** $400 to $3000. **Remarks:** Full-time maker; first knife sold in 1978. **Mark:** Last name, or name and city.

HARRISON, BRIAN,
BFH KNIVES, 2359 E Swede Rd, Cedarville, MI 49719, Phone: 906-484-2011, bfhknives@easternup.net; Web: www.bfhknives.com
Specialties: High grade fixed blade knives. **Patterns:** Many sizes & variety of patterns from small pocket carries to large combat and camp knives. Mirror and bead blast finishes. All handles of high grade materials from ivory to highly figured stabilized woods to stag, deer & moose horn and Micarta. Hand sewn fancy sheaths for pocket or belt. **Technical:** Flat & hollow grinds usually ATS-34 but some O1, L6 and stellite 6K. **Prices:** $150 to $1200. **Remarks:** Full-time maker, sole authorship. Made first knife in 1980, sold first knife in 1999. Received much knowledge from the following makers: George Young, Eric Erickson, Webster Wood, Ed Kalfayan who are all generous men. **Mark:** Engraved blade outline w/BFH Knives over the top edge, signature across middle & Cedarville, MI underneath.

HARRISON, JIM (SEAMUS),
721 Fairington View Dr, St. Louis, MO 63129, Phone: 314-894-2525; Cell: 314-791-6350, jrh@seamusknives.com; Web: www.seamusknives.com
Specialties: Gents and fancy tactical locking-liner folders. Compact straight blades for hunting, backpacking and canoeing. **Patterns:** LinerLock® folders. Compact 3 fingered fixed blades often with modified wharncliffes. Survival knife with mortised handles. **Technical:** Grinds talonite, S30V, Mike Norris and Devin Thomas S.S. Damascus, 440-C. Heat treats. **Prices:** Folders $400 to $1,200. Fixed blades $400 to $600. **Remarks:** Full-time maker. **Mark:** Seamus

HARSEY, WILLIAM H,
82710 N. Howe Ln, Creswell, OR 97426, Phone: 519-895-4941, harseyjr@cs.com
Specialties: High-tech kitchen and outdoor knives. **Patterns:** Folding hunters, trout and bird folders; straight hunters, camp knives and axes. **Technical:** Grinds; etches. **Prices:** $125 to $300; some to $1500. Folders start at $350. **Remarks:** Full-time maker; first knife sold in 1979. **Mark:** Full name, state, U.S.A.

HART, BILL,
647 Cedar Dr, Pasadena, MD 21122, Phone: 410-255- 4981
Specialties: Fur-trade era working straight knives and folders. **Patterns:** Springback folders, skinners, Bowies and patch knives. **Technical:** Forges and stock removes 1095 and 5160 wire Damascus. **Prices:** $100 to $600. **Remarks:** Part-time maker; first knife sold in 1986. **Mark:** Name.

HARTMAN, ARLAN (LANNY),
6102 S Hamlin Cir, Baldwin, MI 49304, Phone: 231-745-4029
Specialties: Working straight knives and folders. **Patterns:** Drop-point hunters, coil spring lockers, slip-joints. **Technical:** Flat-grinds D2, 440C and ATS-34. **Prices:** $300 to $2000. **Remarks:** Part-time maker; first knife sold in 1982. **Mark:** Last name.

HARTMAN, TIM,
3812 Pedroncelli Rd NW, Albuquerque, NM 87107, Phone: 505-385-6924, tbonz1@comcast.net
Specialties: Exotic wood scales, sambar stag, filework, hunters. **Patterns:** Fixed blade hunters, skinners, utility and hiking. **Technical:** 154CM, Ats-34 and D2. Mirror finish and contoured scales. **Prices:** Start at $200-$450. **Remarks:** Started making knives in 2004. **Mark:** 3 lines Ti Hartman, Maker, Albuquerque NM

HARTSFIELD, PHILL,
PO Box 1637, Newport Beach, CA 92659-0637, Phone: 949-722-9792 and 714-636-7633, phartsfield@att.net; Web: www.phillhartsfield.com
Specialties: Heavy-duty working and using straight knives. **Patterns:** Fighters, swords and survival knives, most in Japanese profile. **Technical:** Grinds A2. **Prices:** $450 to $20,000. **Remarks:** Full-time maker; first knife sold about 1976. Doing business as A Cut Above. The Hartsfield folder is now available. Color catalog. **Mark:** Initials, chiseled character plus register mark.

HARVEY, HEATHER,
HEAVIN FORGE, PO Box 768, Belfast 1100, SOUTH AFRICA, Phone: 27-13-253-0914, heather@heavinforge.co.za; Web: www.heavinforge.co.za
Specialties: Integral hand forged knives, traditional African weapons, primitive folders and by-gone forged-styles. **Patterns:** All forged knives, war axes, spears, arrows, forks, spoons, and swords. **Technical:** Own carbon Damascus and mokume. Also forges stainless, brass, copper and titanium. Traditional forging and heat-treatment methods used. **Prices:** $300 to $5000, average $1000. **Remarks:** Full-time maker and knifemaking instructor. Master bladesmith with ABS. First Damascus sold in 1995, first knife sold in 1998. Often collaborate with husband, Kevin (ABS MS) using the logo "Heavin." **Mark:** First name and sur name, oval shape with "M S" in middle.

HARVEY, KEVIN,
HEAVIN FORGE, PO Box 768, Belfast 1100, SOUTH AFRICA, Phone: 27-13-253-0914, info@heavinforge.co.za Web: www.heavinforge.co.za
Specialties: Large knives of presentation quality and creative art knives. **Patterns:** Fixed blades of Bowie, dagger and fighter-styles, occasionally folders and swords. **Technical:** Stock removal of stainless and forging of carbon steel and own Damascus. Indigenous African handle materials preferred. Own engraving Often collaborate with wife, Heather (ABS MS) under the logo "Heavin." **Prices:** $500 to $5000 average $1500. **Remarks:**

Full-time maker and knifemaking instructor. Master bladesmith with ABS. First knife sold in 1984. **Mark:** First name and surname, oval with "M S" in the middle.

HARVEY, MAX,
14 Bass Rd, Bull Creek, Perth 6155, Western Australia, AUSTRALIA, Phone: 09-332-7585
Specialties: Daggers, Bowies, fighters and fantasy knives. **Patterns:** Hunters, Bowies, tantos and skinners. **Technical:** Hollow-and flat-grinds 440C, ATS-34, 154CM and Damascus. Offers gem work. **Prices:** $250 to $4000. **Remarks:** Part-time maker; first knife sold in 1981. **Mark:** First and middle initials, last name.

HARVEY, MEL,
P.O. Box 176, Nenana, AK 99760, Phone: 907-832- 5560, tinker1@nenana. net
Specialties: Fixed blade knives for hunting and fishing. **Patterns:** Hunters, skinners. **Technical:** Stock removal on ATS-34, 440C, 01, 1095; Damascus blades using 1095 and 15N20. **Prices:** Starting at $350. **Remarks:** New maker. **Mark:** HARVEY-HOUSE.

HASLINGER, THOMAS,
164 Fairview Dr SE, Calgary, AB, CANADA T2H 1B3, Phone: 403-253-9628, Web: www.haslinger-knives.com
Specialties: One-of-a-kind using, working and art knives HCK signature sweeping grind lines. Maker of New Generation Chef series. Differential heat treated stainless steel. **Patterns:** No fixed patterns, likes to work with customers on design. **Technical:** Grinds various specialty alloys, including Damascus, High end satin finish. Prefers natural handle materials e.g. ancient ivory stag, pearl, abalone, stone and exotic woods. Does inlay work with stone, some sterling silver, niobium and gold wire work. Custom sheaths using matching woods or hand stitched with unique leather like sturgeon, Nile perch or carp. Offers engraving. **Prices:** Starting at $150. **Remarks:** Full-time maker; first knife sold in 1994. Doing business as Haslinger Custom Knives. **Mark:** Two marks used, high end work uses stylized initials, other uses elk antler with Thomas Haslinger, Canada, handcrafted above.

HAWES, CHUCK,
HAWES FORGE, PO Box 176, Weldon, IL 61882, Phone: 217-736-2479
Specialties: 95 percent of all work in own Damascus. **Patterns:** Slip- joints liner locks, hunters, Bowie's, swords, anything in between. **Technical:** Forges everything, uses all high-carbon steels, no stainless. **Prices:** $150 to $4000. **Remarks:** Like to do custom orders, his style or yours. Sells Damascus. Full-time maker since 1995. **Mark:** Small football shape. Chuck Hawes maker Weldon, IL.

HAWK, GRANT AND GAVIN,
Box 401, Idaho City, ID 83631, Phone: 208-392-4911, Web: www.9-hawkknives.com
Specialties: Large folders with unique locking systems D.O.G. lock, toad lock. **Technical:** Grinds ATS-34, titanium folder parts. **Prices:** $450 and up. **Remarks:** Full-time maker. **Mark:** First initials and last names.

HAWKINS, BUDDY,
PO Box 5969, Texarkana, TX 75505-5969, Phone: 903-838-7917, buddyhawkins@cableone.net

HAWKINS, RADE,
110 Buckeye Rd, Fayetteville, GA 30214, Phone: 770-964-1177, Fax: 770-306-2877, radeh@bellsouth.net; Web: wwwhawkinscustomknives.com
Specialties: All styles. **Patterns:** All styles. **Technical:** Grinds and forges. Makes own Damascus **Prices:** Start at $190. **Remarks:** Full-time maker; first knife sold in 1972. Member knifemakers guild, ABS Journeyman Smith. **Mark:** Rade Hawkins Custom Knives.

HAYES, SCOTTY,
Texarkana College, 2500 N Robinson Rd., Tesarkana, TX 75501, Phone: 903-838-4541, ext. 3236, Fax: 903-832-5030, shayes@texakanacollege.edu; Web: www.americanbladesmith.com/ 2005ABSo/o20schedule.htm
Specialties: ABS School of Bladesmithing.

HAYES, WALLY,
9960, 9th Concession, RR#1, Essex, Ont., CANADA K4A-3N2, Phone: 519-776-1284, Web: www.hayesknives.com
Specialties: Classic and fancy straight knives and folders. **Patterns:** Daggers, Bowies, fighters, tantos. **Technical:** Forges own Damascus and O1; engraves. **Prices:** $150 to $14,000. **Mark:** Last name, M.S. and serial number.

HAYNES, JERRY,
260 Forest Meadow Dr, Gunter, TX 75058, Phone: 210-599-2928, jhaynes@ arrow-head.com; Web: http://www.arrow- head.com
Specialties: Working straight knives and folders of his design, also historical blades. **Patterns:** Hunters, skinners, carving knives, fighters, renaissance daggers, locking folders and kitchen knives. **Technical:** Grinds ATS-34, CPM, Stellite 6K, D2 and acquired Damascus. Prefers exotic handle materials. Has B.A. in design. Studied with R. Buckminster Fuller. **Prices:** $200 to $1200. **Remarks:** Part-time maker, will go full- time after retirement in 2007. First knife sold in 1953. **Mark:** Arrowhead and last name.

HAYS, MARK,
HAYS HANDMADE KNIVES, 1008 Kavanagh Dr., Austin, TX 78748, Phone: 512-292-4410, markhays@austin.rr.com
Specialties: Working straight knives and folders. Patterns inspired by

Randall and Stone. **Patterns:** Bowies, hunters and slip-joint folders. **Technical:** 440C stock removal. Repairs and restores Stone knives. **Prices:** Start at $200. **Remarks:** Part-time maker, brochure available, with Stone knives 1974-1983, 1990-1991. **Mark:** First initial, last name, state and serial number.

HAZEN, MARK,
9600 Surrey Rd, Charlotte, NC 28227, Phone: 704-573- 0052, Fax: 704-573-0052, mhazen@carolina.rr.com
Specialties: Working/using straight knives of his design. **Patterns:** Hunters/skinners, fillet, utility/camp, fighters, short swords. **Technical:** Grinds 154 CM, ATS-34, 440C. **Prices:** $75 to $450; some to $1500. **Remarks:** Part-time maker. First knife sold 1982. **Mark:** Name with cross in it, etched in blade.

HEADRICK, GARY,
122 Wilson Blvd, Juane Les Pins, FRANCE 06160, Phone: 033 0610282885, headrick-gary@wanadoo.fr
Specialties: Hi-tech folders with natural furnishings. Back lock & back spring. **Patterns:** Damascus and mokumes. **Technical:** Self made Damascus all steel (no nickel). **Prices:** $500 to $2000. **Remarks:** Full-time maker for last 7 years. German Guild-French Federation. 10 years active. **Mark:** G/P in a circle.

HEANEY, JOHN D,
9 Lefe Court, Haines City, FL 33844, Phone: 863- 422-5823, jdh199@msn. com; Web: www.heaneyknives.com
Specialties: Forged 5160, O1 and Damascus. Prefers using natural handle material such as bone, stag and oosic. Plans on using some of the various ivories on future knives. **Prices:** $250 and up. **Remarks:** ABS member. Received journeyman smith stamp in June. **Mark:** Heaney JS.

HEASMAN, H G,
28 St Mary's Rd, Llandudno, N. Wales, UNITED KINGDOM LL302UB, Phone: (UK)0492-876351
Specialties: Miniatures only. **Patterns:** Bowies, daggers and swords. **Technical:** Files from stock high-carbon and stainless steel. **Prices:** $400 to $600. **Remarks:** Part-time maker; first knife sold in 1975. Doing business as Reduced Reality. **Mark:** NA.

HEATH, WILLIAM,
PO Box 131, Bondville, IL 61815, Phone: 217-863- 2576
Specialties: Classic and working straight knives, folders. **Patterns:** Hunters and Bowies LinerLock® folders. **Technical:** Grinds ATS-34, 440C, 154CM, Damascus, handle materials Micarta, woods to exotic materials snake skins cobra, rattle snake, African flower snake. Does own heat treating. **Prices:** $75 to $300 some $1000. **Remarks:** Full-time maker. First knife sold in 1979. **Mark:** W. D. HEATH.

HEDLUND, ANDERS,
Samstad 400, 454 91, Bradstad, SWEDEN, Phone: 46-523-139 48, anderskniv@passagen.se; Web: http://hem.passagen.se/anderskniv
Specialties: Fancy high-end collectible folders, high-end collectible Nordic hunters with leather carvings on the sheath. Carvings combine traditional designs with own designs. **Patterns:** Own designs. **Technical:** Grinds most steels, but prefers mosaic Damascus and RWL-34. Prefers mother-of-pearl, mammoth, and mosaic steel for folders. Prefers desert ironwood, mammoth, stabilized arctic birch, willow burl, and Damascus steel or RWL-34 for stick tang knives. **Prices:** Starting at $750 for stick tang knives and staring at $1500 for folders. **Remarks:** Part-time maker, first knife sold in 1988. Nordic champion (five countries) several times and Swedish champion 20 times in different classes. **Mark:** Stylized initials or last name.

HEDRICK, DON,
131 Beechwood Hills, Newport News, VA 23608, Phone: 757-877-8100, donaldhedrick@cox.net
Specialties: Working straight knives; period pieces and fantasy knives. **Patterns:** Hunters, boots, Bowies and miniatures. **Technical:** Grinds 440C and commercial Damascus. Also makes micro-mini Randall replicas. **Prices:** $150 to $550; some to $1200. **Remarks:** Part-time maker; first knife sold in 1982. **Mark:** First initial, last name in oval logo.

HEFLIN, CHRISTOPHER M,
6013 Jocely Hollow Rd, Nashville, TN 37205, Phone: 615-352-3909, blix@ bellsouth.net

HEGWALD, J L,
1106 Charles, Humboldt, KS 66748, Phone: 316-473- 3523
Specialties: Working straight knives, some fancy. **Patterns:** Makes Bowies, miniatures. **Technical:** Forges or grinds O1, L6, 440C; mixes materials in handles. **Prices:** $35 to $200; some higher. **Remarks:** Part- time maker; first knife sold in 1983. **Mark:** First and middle initials.

HEHN, RICHARD KARL,
Lehnmuehler Str 1, 55444 Dorrebach, GERMANY, Phone: 06724 3152
Specialties: High-tech, full integral working knives. **Patterns:** Hunters, fighters and daggers. **Technical:** Grinds CPM T-440V, CPM T-420V, forges his own stainless Damascus. **Prices:** $1000 to $10,000. **Remarks:** Full-time maker; first knife sold in 1963. **Mark:** Runic last initial in logo.

HEIMDALE, J E,
7749 E 28 CT, Tulsa, OK 74129, Phone: 918-640-0784, heimdale@sbcglobal.net
Specialties: Art knives **Patterns:** Bowies, daggers **Technical:** Makes allcomponents and handles - exotic woods and sheaths. Uses Damascus blades by other Blademakers, notably R.W. Wilson. **Prices:** $300 and up. **Remarks:** Part-time maker. First knife sold in 1999. **Marks:** JEHCO

HEINZ, JOHN,
611 Cafferty Rd, Upper Black Eddy, PA 18972, Phone: 610-847-8535, Web: www.herugrim.com
Specialties: Historical pieces / copies. **Technical:** Makes his own steel. **Prices:** $150 to $800. **Mark:** "H."

HEITLER, HENRY,
8106 N Albany, Tampa, FL 33604, Phone: 813-933-1645
Specialties: Traditional working and using straight knives of his design and to customer specs. **Patterns:** Fighters, hunters, utility/camp knives and fillet knives. **Technical:** Flat-grinds ATS-34; offers tapered tangs. **Prices:** $135 to $450; some to $600. **Remarks:** Part-time maker; first knife sold in 1990. **Mark:** First initial, last name, city, state circling double H's.

HELSCHER, JOHN W,
2645 Highway 1, Washington, IA 52353, Phone: 319-653-7310

HELTON, ROY,
HELTON KNIVES, 2941 Comstock St., San Diego, CA 92111, Phone: 858-277-5024

HEMBROOK, RON,
HEMBROOK KNIVES, PO Box 201, Neosho, WI 53059, Phone: 920-625-3607, rhembrook3607@charter.net; Web: www.hembrookcustomknives.com
Specialties: Hunters, working knives. **Technical:** Grinds ATS-34, 440C, O1 and Damascus. **Prices:** $125 to $750, some to $1000. **Remarks:** First knife sold in 1980. **Mark:** Hembrook plus a serial number. Part-time maker, makes hunters, daggers, Bowies, folders and miniatures.

HEMPERLEY, GLEN,
13322 Country Run Rd, Willis, TX 77318, Phone: 936-228-5048, hemperley.com
Specialties: Specializes in hunting knives, does fixed and folding knives.

HENDRICKS, SAMUEL J,
2162 Van Buren Rd, Maurertown, VA 22644, Phone: 703-436-3305
Specialties: Integral hunters and skinners of his design. **Patterns:** Boots, hunters and locking folders. **Technical:** Grinds ATS-34, 440C and D2. Integral liners and bolsters of N-S and 7075 T6 aircraft aluminum. Does leatherwork. **Prices:** $50 to $250; some to $500. **Remarks:** Full-time maker; first knife sold in 1992. **Mark:** First and middle initials, last name, city and state in football-style logo.

HENDRICKSON, E JAY,
4204 Ballenger Creek Pike, Frederick, MD 21703, Phone: 301-663-6923, Fax: 301-663-6923, ejayhendrickson@comcast.net
Specialties: Specializes in silver wire inlay. **Patterns:** Bowies, Kukri's, camp, hunters, and fighters. **Technical:** Forges 06, 1084, 5160, 52100, D2, L6 and W2; makes Damascus. Moran-styles on order. **Prices:** $400 to $5000. **Remarks:** Full-time maker; first knife sold in 1975. **Mark:** Last name, M.S.

HENDRICKSON, SHAWN,
2327 Kaetzel Rd, Knoxville, MD 21758, Phone: 301-432-4306
Specialties: Hunting knives. **Patterns:** Clip points, drop points and trailing point hunters. **Technical:** Forges 5160, 1084 and L6. **Prices:** $175 to $400.

HENDRIX, JERRY,
HENDRIX CUSTOM KNIVES, 175 Skyland Dr. Ext., Clinton, SC 29325, Phone: 864-833-2659, jhendrix@backroads.net
Specialties: Traditional working straight knives of all designs. **Patterns:** Hunters, utility, boot, bird and fishing. **Technical:** Grinds ATS-34 and 440C. **Prices:** $85 to $275. **Remarks:** Full-time maker. Hand stitched, waxed leather sheaths. **Mark:** Full name in shape of knife.

HENDRIX, WAYNE,
9636 Burton's Ferry Hwy, Allendale, SC 29810, Phone: 803-584-3825, Fax: 803-584-3825, knives@barnwellsc.com; Web: www.hendrixknives.com
Specialties: Working/using knives of his design. **Patterns:** Hunters and fillet knives. **Technical:** Grinds ATS-34, D2 and 440C. **Prices:** $100 and up. **Remarks:** Full-time maker; first knife sold in 1985. **Mark:** Last name.

HENRIKSEN, HANS J,
Birkegaardsvej 24, DK 3200 Helsinge, DENMARK, Fax: 45 4879 4899
Specialties: Zirconia ceramic blades. **Patterns:** Customer designs. **Technical:** Slip-cast zirconia-water mix in plaster mould; offers hidden or full tang. **Prices:** White blades start at $10cm; colored +50 percent. **Remarks:** Part-time maker; first ceramic blade sold in 1989. **Mark:** Initial logo.

HENSLEY, WAYNE,
PO Box 904, Conyers, GA 30012, Phone: 770-483-8938
Specialties: Period pieces and fancy working knives. **Patterns:** Boots to Bowies, locking folders to miniatures. Large variety of straight knives. **Technical:** Grinds ATS-34, 440C, D2 and commercial Damascus. **Prices:** $85 and up. **Remarks:** Full-time maker; first knife sold in 1974. **Mark:** Last name.

HERB, MARTIN,
2500 Starwood Dr, Richmond, VA 23229

HERBST, PETER,
Komotauer Strasse 26, 91207 Lauf a.d. Pegn., GERMANY, Phone: 09123-13315, Fax: 09123-13379
Specialties: Working/using knives and folders of his design. **Patterns:** Hunters, fighters and daggers; interframe and integral. **Technical:** Grinds CPM-T-440V, UHB-Elmax, ATS-34 and stainless Damascus. **Prices:** $300 to $3000; some to $8000. **Remarks:** Full-time maker; first knife sold in 1981. **Mark:** First initial, last name.

HERBST, THINUS,
PO Box 59158, Karenpark 0118, Akasia, South Africa, Phone: +27 82 254 8016, thinus@herbst.co.za; Web: www.herbst.co.za
Specialties: Plain and fancy working straight knives of own design and liner lock folders. **Patterns:** Hunters, utility knives, art knives, and liner lock folders. **Technical:** Prefer exotic materials for handles. Most knives embellished with file work, carving and scrimshaw. **Prices:** $200 to $2000. **Remarks:** Full-time maker, member of the Knifemakers Guild of South Africa.

HERMAN, TIM,
517 E. 126 Terrace, Olathe, KS 66061-2731, Phone: 913-839-1924, HermanKnives@comcast.net
Specialties: Investment-grade folders of his design; interframes and bolster frames. **Patterns:** Interframes and new designs in carved stainless. **Technical:** Grinds ATS-34 and damasteel Damascus. Engraves and gold inlays with pearl, jade, lapis and Australian opal. **Prices:** $1500 to $20,000 and up. **Remarks:** Full-time maker; first knife sold in 1978. **Mark:** Etched signature.

HERNDON, WM R "BILL",
32520 Michigan St, Acton, CA 93510, Phone: 661-269-5860, bherndons1@earthlink.net
Specialties: Straight knives, plain and fancy. **Technical:** Carbon steel (white and blued), Damascus, stainless steels. **Prices:** Start at $175. **Remarks:** Full-time maker; first knife sold in 1976. American Bladesmith Society journeyman smith. **Mark:** Signature and/or helm logo.

HERRING, MORRIS,
Box 85 721 W Line St, Dyer, AR 72935, Phone: 501-997-8861, morrish@ipa.com

HETHCOAT, DON,
Box 1764, Clovis, NM 88101, Phone: 575-762-5721, dhethcoat@plateautel.net; Web: www.donhethcoat.com
Specialties: Liner lock-locking and multi-blade folders **Patterns:** Hunters, Bowies. **Technical:** Grinds stainless; forges Damascus. **Prices:** Moderate to upscale. **Remarks:** Full-time maker; first knife sold in 1969. **Mark:** Last name on all.

HIBBEN, DARYL,
PO Box 172, LaGrange, KY 40031-0172, Phone: 502-222-0983, dhibben1@bellsouth.net
Specialties: Working straight knives, some fancy to customer specs. **Patterns:** Hunters, fighters, Bowies, short sword, art and fantasy. **Technical:** Grinds 440C, ATS-34, 154CM, Damascus; prefers hollow-grinds. **Prices:** $175 to $3000. **Remarks:** Full-time maker; first knife sold in 1979. Teaches 3- or 5-day knife making classes for beginners or advanced students. **Mark:** Etched full name in script.

HIBBEN, GIL,
PO Box 13, LaGrange, KY 40031, Phone: 502-222-1397, Fax: 502-222-2676, hibbenknives.com; Web: www.gil_hibben@bellsouth.net
Specialties: Working knives and fantasy pieces to customer specs. **Patterns:** Full range of straight knives, including swords, axes and miniatures; some locking folders. **Technical:** Grinds ATS-34, 440C and D2. **Prices:** $300 to $2000; some to $10,000. **Remarks:** Full-time maker; first knife sold in 1957. Maker and designer of Rambo III knife; made swords for movie Marked for Death and throwing knife for movie Under Seige; made belt buckle knife and knives for movie Perfect Weapon; made knives featured in movie Star Trek the Next Generation, Star Trek Nemesis. 1990 inductee Cutlery Hall of Fame; designer for United Cutlery. Official klingon armourer for Star Trek, over 37 movies and TV productions. Celebrating 50 years since first knife sold. Mark: Hibben Knives. City and state, or signature.

HIBBEN, JOLEEN,
PO Box 172, LaGrange, KY 40031, Phone: 502-222-0983, dhibben1@bellsouth.net
Specialties: Miniature straight knives of her design; period pieces. Patterns: Hunters, axes and fantasy knives. Technical: Grinds Damascus, 1095 tool steel and stainless 440C or ATS-34. Uses wood, ivory, bone, feathers and claws on/for handles. Prices: $60 to $600. Remarks: Spare-time maker; first knife sold in 1991. Design knives, make & tool leather sheaths. Produced first inlaid handle in 2005, used by Daryl on a dagger. Mark: Initials or first name.

HIBBEN, WESTLEY G,
14101 Sunview Dr, Anchorage, AK 99515
Specialties: Working straight knives of his design or to customer specs. **Patterns:** Hunters, fighters, daggers, combat knives and some fantasy pieces. **Technical:** Grinds 440C mostly. Filework available. **Prices:** $200 to $400; some to $3000. **Remarks:** Part-time maker; first knife sold in 1988. **Mark:** Signature.

HICKS, GARY,
341 CR 275, Tuscola, TX 79562, Phone: 325-554-9762

HIGH, TOM,
5474 S 1128 Rd, Alamosa, CO 81101, Phone: 719-589- 2108, www. rockymountainscrimshaw.com
Specialties: Hunters, some fancy. **Patterns:** Drop-points in several shapes; some semi-skinners. Knives designed by and for top outfitters and guides. **Technical:** Grinds ATS-34; likes hollow-grinds, mirror finishes; prefers scrimable handles. **Prices:** $300 to $8000.. **Remarks:** Full- time maker; first knife sold in 1965. Limited edition wildlife series knives. **Mark:** Initials connected; arrow through last name.

HILKER, THOMAS N,
PO Box 409, Williams, OR 97544, Phone: 541- 846-6461
Specialties: Traditional working straight knives and folders. **Patterns:** Folding skinner in two sizes, Bowies, fork and knife sets, camp knives and interchangeable. **Technical:** Grinds D2, 440C and ATS-34. Heat- treats. **Prices:** $50 to $350; some to $400. Doing business as Thunderbolt Artisans. Only limited production models available; not currently taking orders. **Remarks:** Full-time maker; first knife sold in 1983. **Mark:** Last name.

HILL, HOWARD E,
111 Mission Lane, Polson, MT 59860, Phone: 406- 883-3405, Fax: 406-883- 3486, knifeman@bigsky.net
Specialties: Autos, complete new design, legal in Montana (with permit). **Patterns:** Bowies, daggers, skinners and lockback folders. **Technical:** Grinds 440C; uses micro and satin finish. **Prices:** $150 to $1000. **Remarks:** Full-time maker; first knife sold in 1981. **Mark:** Persuader.

HILL, RICK,
20 Nassau, Maryville, IL 62062-5618, Phone: 618-288-4370
Specialties: Working knives and period pieces to customer specs. **Patterns:** Hunters, locking folders, fighters and daggers. **Technical:** Grinds D2, 440C and 154CM; forges his own Damascus. **Prices:** $75 to $500; some to $3000. **Remarks:** Part-time maker; first knife sold in 1983. **Mark:** Full name in hill shape logo.

HILL, STEVE E,
40 Rand Pond Rd, Goshen, NH 03752, Phone: 603- 863-4762, Fax: 603-863- 4762, kingpirateboy2@juno.com; Web: www.stevehillknives.com
Specialties: Fancy manual and automatic LinerLock® folders, small fixed blades and classic Bowie knives. **Patterns:** Classic to cool folding and fixed blade designs. **Technical:** Grinds Damascus and occasional 440C, D2. Prefers natural handle materials; offers elaborate filework, carving, and inlays. **Prices:** $400 to $6000, some higher. **Remarks:** Full- time maker; first knife sold in 1978. Google search: Steve Hill custom knives. **Mark:** First initial, last name and handmade. (4400, D2). Damascus folders: mark inside handle.

HILLMAN, CHARLES,
225 Waldoboro Rd, Friendship, ME 04547, Phone: 207-832-4634
Specialties: Working knives of his own or custom design. Heavy Scagel influence. **Patterns:** Hunters, fishing, camp and general utility. Occasional folders. **Technical:** Grinds D2 and 440C. File work, blade and handle carving, engraving. Natural handle materials-antler, bone, leather, wood, horn. Sheaths made to order. **Prices:** $60 to $500. **Remarks:** Part-time maker; first knife sold 1986. **Mark:** Last name in oak leaf.

HINDERER, RICK,
5373 Columbus Rd., Shreve, OH 44676, Phone: 330- 263-0962, Fax: 330- 263-0962, rhind64@earthlink.net; Web: www.rickhindererknives.com
Specialties: Working tactical knives, and some one-of-a kind. **Patterns:** Makes his own. **Technical:** Grinds Duratech 20 CV and CPM S30V. **Prices:** $150 to $4000. **Remarks:** Full-time maker doing business as Rick Hinderer Knives, first knife sold in 1988. **Mark:** R. Hinderer.

HINDMARCH, G,
PO Box 135, Carlyle SK S0C 0R0, CANADA, Phone: 306-453-2568
Specialties: Working and fancy straight knives, Bowies. **Patterns:** Hunters, skinners, Bowies. **Technical:** Grind 440C, ATS-34, some Damascus. **Prices:** $175 - $700. **Remarks:** Part-time maker; first knife sold 1994. All knives satin finish. Does file work, offers engraving, stabilized wood, Giraffe bone, some Micarta. **Mark:** First initial last name, city, province.

HINK III, LES,
1599 Aptos Lane, Stockton, CA 95206, Phone: 209-547- 1292
Specialties: Working straight knives and traditional folders in standard patterns or to customer specs. **Patterns:** Hunting and utility/camp knives; others on request. **Technical:** Grinds carbon and stainless steels. **Prices:** $80 to $200; some higher. **Remarks:** Part-time maker; first knife sold in 1980. **Mark:** Last name, or last name 3.

HINMAN, THEODORE,
186 Petty Plain Road, Greenfield, MA 01301, Phone: 413-773-0448, armenemargosian@verizon.net

HINSON AND SON, R,
2419 Edgewood Rd, Columbus, GA 31906, Phone: 706-327-6801
Specialties: Working straight knives and folders. **Patterns:** Locking folders, liner locks, combat knives and swords. **Technical:** Grinds 440C and commercial Damascus. **Prices:** $200 to $450; some to $1500. **Remarks:** Part-time maker; first knife sold in 1983. Son Bob is co-worker. **Mark:** HINSON, city and state.

HINTZ, GERALD M,
5402 Sahara Ct, Helena, MT 59602, Phone: 406- 458-5412
Specialties: Fancy, high-art, working/using knives of his design. **Patterns:** Bowies, hunters, daggers, fish fillet and utility/camp knives. **Technical:** Forges ATS-34, 440C and D2. Animal art in horn handles or in the blade. **Prices:** $75 to $400; some to $1000. **Remarks:** Part-time maker; first knife sold in 1980. Doing business as Big Joe's Custom Knives. Will take custom orders. **Mark:** F.S. or W.S. with first and middle initials and last name.

HIRAYAMA, HARUMI,
4-5-13 Kitamachi, Warabi City, Saitama Pref. 335-0001, JAPAN, Phone: 048- 443-2248, Fax: 048-443-2248, Web: www.ne.jp/asahi/harumi/knives
Specialties: High-tech working knives of her design. **Patterns:** Locking folders, interframes, straight gents and slip-joints. **Technical:** Grinds 440C or equivalent; uses natural handle materials and gold. **Prices:** Start at $1500. **Remarks:** Part-time maker; first knife sold in 1985. **Mark:** First initial, last name.

HIROTO, FUJIHARA,
, 2-34-7 Koioosako Nishi-ku Hiroshima-city, Hiroshima, JAPAN, Phone: 082- 271-8389, fjhr8363@crest.ocn.ne.jp

HITCHMOUGH, HOWARD,
95 Old Street Rd, Peterborough, NH 03458- 1637, Phone: 603-924-9646, Fax: 603-924-9595, howard@hitchmoughknives.com; Web: www. hitchmoughknives.com
Specialties: High class folding knives. **Patterns:** Lockback folders, liner locks, pocket knives. **Technical:** Uses ATS-34, stainless Damascus, titanium, gold and gemstones. Prefers hand-rubbed finishes and natural handle materials. **Prices:** $1850 - $5000. **Remarks:** Full-time maker; first knife sold in 1967. **Mark:** Last name.

HOBART, GENE,
100 Shedd Rd, Windsor, NY 13865, Phone: 607-655- 1345

HOCKENSMITH, DAN,
12620 WCR 108, Carr, CO 80612, Phone: 970- 897-2884, Web: hockensmithknives.com
Specialties: Traditional working and using straight knives of his design. **Patterns:** Hunters, Bowies, folders and utility/camp knives. **Technical:** Uses his Damascus, 5160, carbon steel, 52100 steel and 1084 steel. Hand forged. **Prices:** $250 to $1500. **Remarks:** Part-time maker; first knife sold in 1987. **Mark:** Last name or stylized "D" with H inside.

HODGE III, JOHN,
422 S 15th St, Palatka, FL 32177, Phone: 904-328- 3897
Specialties: Fancy straight knives and folders. **Patterns:** Various. **Technical:** Pattern-welded Damascus—"Southern-style." **Prices:** To $1000. **Remarks:** Part-time maker; first knife sold in 1981. **Mark:** JH3 logo.

HOEL, STEVE,
PO Box 283, Pine, AZ 85544, Phone: 602-476-4278
Specialties: Investor-class folders, straight knives and period pieces of his design. **Patterns:** Folding interframes lockers and slip-joints; straight Bowies, boots and daggers. **Technical:** Grinds 154CM, ATS-34 and commercial Damascus. **Prices:** $600 to $1200; some to $7500. **Remarks:** Full-time maker. **Mark:** Initial logo with name and address.

HOFER, LOUIS,
Gen Del, Rose Prairie, B.C., CANADA V0C 2H0, Phone: 250-630-2513

HOFFMAN, KEVIN L,
28 Hopeland Dr, Savannah, GA 31419, Phone: 912-920-3579, Fax: 912-920- 3579, kevh052475@aol.com; Web: www.KLHoffman.com
Specialties: Distinctive folders and fixed blades. **Patterns:** Titanium frame lock folders. **Technical:** Sculpted guards and fittings cast in sterling silver and 14k gold. Grinds ATS-34, CPM S30V Damascus. Makes kydex sheaths for his fixed blade working knives. **Prices:** $400 and up. **Remarks:** Full-time maker since 1981. **Mark:** KLH.

HOGAN, THOMAS R,
2802 S. Heritage Ave, Boise, ID 83709, Phone: 208-362-7848

HOGSTROM, ANDERS T,
Granvagen 2, 135 52 Tyreso, SWEDEN, Phone: 46 8 798 5802, andershogstrom@hotmail.com or info@andershogstrom.com; Web: www. andershogstrom.com
Specialties: Short and long daggers, fighters and swords For select pieces makes wooden display stands. **Patterns:** Daggers, fighters, short knives and swords and an occasional sword. **Technical:** Grinds 1050 High Carbon, Damascus and stainless, forges own Damasus on occasion, fossil ivories. Does clay tempering and uses exotic hardwoods. **Prices:** Start at $850. **Marks:** Last name in maker's own signature.

HOKE, THOMAS M,
3103 Smith Ln, LaGrange, KY 40031, Phone: 502- 222-0350
Specialties: Working/using knives, straight knives. Own designs and customer specs. **Patterns:** Daggers, Bowies, hunters, fighters, short swords. **Technical:** Grind 440C, Damascus and ATS-34. Filework on all knives. Tooling on sheaths (custom fit on all knives). Any handle material, mostly exotic. **Prices:** $100 to $700; some to $1500. **Remarks:** Full-time maker, first knife sold in 1986. **Mark:** Dragon on banner which says T.M. Hoke.

custom knifemakers

HOLBROOK, H L,
PO Box 483, Sandy Hook, KY 41171, Phone: 606- 738-9922 home/606-738-6842 Shop, hhknives@mrtc.com
Specialties: Traditional working using straight knives and folders of his design, to customer specs and in standard patterns. Stablized wood. **Patterns:** Hunters, folders. **Technical:** Grinds 440C, ATS-34 and D2. Blades have hand-rubbed satin finish. Uses exotic woods, stag and Micarta. Hand-sewn sheath with each straight knife. **Prices:** $90 to $270; some to $400. **Remarks:** Part-time maker; first knife sold in 1983. Doing business as Holbrook Knives. **Mark:** Name, city, state.

HOLDER, D'ALTON,
7148 W Country Gables Dr, Peoria, AZ 85381, Phone: 623-878-3064, Fax: 623-878-3964, dholderknives@cox.net; Web: d'holder.com
Specialties: Deluxe working knives and high-art hunters. **Patterns:** Drop-point hunters, fighters, Bowies. **Technical:** Grinds ATS-34; uses amber and other materials in combination on stick tangs. **Prices:** $400 to $1000; some to $2000. **Remarks:** Full-time maker; first knife sold in 1966. **Mark:** D'HOLDER, city and state.

HOLLAND, JOHN H,
1580 Nassau St, Titusville, FL 32780, Phone: 321- 267-4378
Specialties: Traditional and fancy working/using straight knives and folders of his design, to customer specs and in standard patterns. **Patterns:** Hunters, and slip-joint folders. **Technical:** Grinds 440V and 440C. Offers engraving. **Prices:** $200 to $500; some to $1000. **Remarks:** Part-time maker; first knife sold in 1988. Doing business as Holland Knives. **Mark:** First and last name, city, state.

HOLLOWAY, PAUL,
714 Burksdale Rd, Norfolk, VA 23518, Phone: 804- 588-7071
Specialties: Working straight knives and folders to customer specs. **Patterns:** Lockers and slip-joints; fighters and boots; fishing and push knives, from swords to miniatures. **Technical:** Grinds A2, D2, 154CM, 440C and ATS-34. **Prices:** $125 to $400; some to $1200. **Remarks:** Part-time maker; first knife sold in 1981. **Mark:** Last name, or last name and city in logo.

HOOK, BOB,
3247 Wyatt Rd, North Pole, AK 99705, Phone: 907-488- 8886, grayling@alaska.net; Web: www.alaskaknifeandforge.com
Specialties: Forged carbon steel. Damascus blades. **Patterns:** Pronghorns, bowies, drop point hunters and knives for the kitchen. **Technical:** 5160, 52100, carbon steel and 1084 and 15N20 pattern welded steel blades are hand forged. Heat treated and ground by maker. Handles are natural materials from Alaska. I favor sole authorship of each piece. **Prices:** $300-$1000. **Remarks:** Apprentice with ABS. I have attended the Bill Moran School of Bladesmithing. Knife maker since 2000. **Mark:** Hook.

HORN, DES,
PO Box 322, Onrusrivier 7201, SOUTH AFRICA, Phone: 27283161795, Fax: 27283161795, deshorn@usa.net
Specialties: Folding knives. **Patterns:** Ball release side lock mechanism and interframe automatics. **Technical:** Prefers working in totally stainless materials. **Prices:** $800 to $7500. **Remarks:** Full-time maker. Enjoys working in gold, titanium, meteorite, pearl and mammoth. **Mark:** Des Horn.

HORN, JESS,
2526 Lansdown Rd, Eugene, OR 97404, Phone: 541-463- 1510, jandahorn@earthlink.net
Specialties: Investor-class working folders; period pieces; collectibles. **Patterns:** High-tech design and finish in folders; liner locks, traditional slip-joints and featherweight models. **Technical:** Grinds ATS-34, 154CM. **Prices:** Start at $1000. **Remarks:** Full-time maker; first knife sold in 1968. **Mark:** Full name or last name.

HORNE, GRACE,
182 Crimicar Ln, Sheffield Britain, UNITED KINGDOM S10 4EJ, gracehorne@hotmail.co.uk
Specialties: Knives of own design including kitchen and utility knives for people with reduced hand use. **Technical:** Working at Sheffield Hallam University researching innovative, contemporary Damascus steels using non-traditional methods of manufacture. **Remarks:** Spare-time maker/full-time researcher. **Mark:** 'gH' and 'Sheffield'.

HORTON, SCOT,
PO Box 451, Buhl, ID 83316, Phone: 208-543-4222
Specialties: Traditional working stiff knives and folders. **Patterns:** Hunters, skinners, utility and show knives. **Technical:** Grinds ATS-34. Uses exotic woods and Micarta. **Prices:** $350 to $2500. **Remarks:** First knife sold in 1990. **Mark:** Full name in arch underlined with arrow, city, state.

HOSSOM, JERRY,
3585 Schilling Ridge, Duluth, GA 30096, Phone: 770-449-7809, jerry@hossom.com; Web: www.hossom.com
Specialties: Working straight knives of his own design. **Patterns:** Fighters, combat knives, modern Bowies and daggers, modern swords, concealment knives for military and LE uses. **Technical:** Grinds 154CM, S30V, CPM-3V, CPM-154 and stainless Damascus. Uses natural and synthetic handle materials. **Prices:** $350-1500, some higher. **Remarks:** Full-time maker since 1997. First knife sold in 1983. **Mark:** First initial and last name, includes city and state since 2002.

HOUSE, GARY,
2851 Pierce Rd, Ephrata, WA 98823, Phone: 509-754- 3272, spindry101@aol.com
Specialties: Mosaic Damascus bar stock. Forged blades. **Patterns:** Unlimited, SW Indian designs, geometric patterns, using 1084, 15N20 and some nickel. Bowies, hunters and daggers. **Technical:** Forge mosaic Damascus. **Prices:** $500 & up. **Remarks:** Some of the finest and most unique patterns available. ABS Journeyman Smith. **Marks:** Initials GTH, G hanging T, H.

HOWARD, DURVYN M,
4220 McLain St S, Hokes Bluff, AL 35903, Phone: 256-492-5720
Specialties: Collectible upscale folders; one-of-a-kind, gentlemen's folders. Multiple patents. **Technical:** Conceptual designs; each unique and different. Uses natural and exotic materials and precious metals. **Prices:** $5000 to $25,000. **Remarks:** Full-time maker; by commission or available work. Work displayed at select shows, K.G. Show etc. **Mark:** Howard: new for 2000; Howard in Garamond Narrow "etched."

HOWE, TORI,
30020 N Stampede Rd, Athol, ID 83801, Phone: 208-449- 1509, wapiti@knifescales.com; Web:www.knifescales.com
Specialties Custom knives, knife scales & Damascus blades. **Remarks:** Carry James Luman polymer clay knife scales.

HOWELL, JASON G,
1112 Sycamore, Lake Jackson, TX 77566, Phone: 979-297-9454, tinyknives@yahoo.com; Web:www.howellbladesmith.com
Specialties: Fixed blades and LinerLock® folders. Makes own Damascus. **Patterns:** Clip and drop point. **Prices:** $150 to $750. **Remarks:** Likes making Mosaic Damascus out of the ordinary stuff. Member of TX Knifemakers and Collectors Association; apprentice in ABS; working towards Journeyman Stamp. **Mark:** Name, city, state.

HOWELL, LEN,
550 Lee Rd 169, Opelika, AL 36804, Phone: 334-749- 1942
Specialties: Traditional and working knives of his design and to customer specs. **Patterns:** Buckskinner, hunters and utility/camp knives. **Technical:** Forges cable Damascus, 1085 and 5160; makes own Damascus. **Mark:** Engraved last name.

HOWELL, TED,
1294 Wilson Rd, Wetumpka, AL 36092, Phone: 205- 569-2281, Fax: 205-569-1764
Specialties: Working/using straight knives and folders of his design; period pieces. **Patterns:** Bowies, fighters, hunters. **Technical:** Forges 5160, 1085 and cable. Offers light engraving and scrimshaw; filework. **Prices:** $75 to $250; some to $450. **Remarks:** Part-time maker; first knife sold in 1991. Doing business as Howell Co. **Mark:** Last name, Slapout AL.

HOWSER, JOHN C,
54 Bell Ln, Frankfort, KY 40601, Phone: 502-875- 3678
Specialties: Slip joint folders (old patterns-multi blades). **Patterns:** Traditional slip joint folders, lockbacks, hunters and fillet knives. **Technical:** Steel S30V, CPM154, ATS-34 and D2. **Prices:** $200 to $600 some to $800. **Remarks:** Full-time maker; first knife sold in 1974. **Mark:** Signature or stamp.

HOY, KEN,
54744 Pinchot Dr, North Fork, CA 93643, Phone: 209-877- 7805

HRISOULAS, JIM,
SALAMANDER ARMOURY, 284-C Lake Mead Pkwy #157, Henderson, NV 89105, Phone: 702-566-8551
Specialties: Working straight knives; period pieces. **Patterns:** Swords, daggers and sgian dubhs. **Technical:** Double-edged differential heat treating. **Prices:** $85 to $175; some to $600 and higher. **Remarks:** Full-time maker; first knife sold in 1973. Author of *The Complete Bladesmith*, *The Pattern Welded Blade* and *The Master Bladesmith*. Doing business as Salamander Armoury. **Mark:** 8R logo and sword and salamander.

HUCKABEE, DALE,
254 Hwy 260, Maylene, AL 35114, Phone: 205- 664-2544, dalehuckabee@hotmail.com
Specialties: Fixed blade hunter and Bowies of his design. **Technical:** Steel used: 5160, 1095, 1084 and some Damascus. **Prices:** Starting at $150 and up, depending on materials used. **Remarks:** Hand forged. Journeyman Smith. Part-time maker. **Mark:** Stamped Huckabee J.S.

HUCKS, JERRY,
KNIVES BY HUCKS, 1807 Perch Road, Moncks Corner, SC 29461, Phone: 843-761-6481, knivesbyhucks@netrockets.com
Specialties: Oyster knives, hunters, Bowies, fillets. Bowies are the maker's favorite with stag & ivory. **Patterns:** Yours and his. **Technical:** ATS-34, BG-42, CPM-154, maker's cable Damascus, also 1084 & 15N20. **Prices:** $125 and up. **Remarks:** Full-time maker, retired as a machinist in 1990. **Mark:** Robin Hood hat with moncke corner, S.C. in oval.

HUDSON, ANTHONY B,
PO Box 368, Amanda, OH 43102, Phone: 740- 969-4200, jjahudson@wmconnect.com
Specialties: Hunting knives, fighters, survival. **Remarks:** ABS Journeyman Smith. **Mark:** A.B. HUDSON.

HUDSON, C ROBBIN,
497 Groton Hollow Rd, Rummney, NH 03266, Phone: 603-786-9944
Specialties: High-art working knives. **Patterns:** Hunters, Bowies, fighters and kitchen knives. **Technical:** Forges W2, nickel steel, pure nickel steel, composite and mosaic Damascus; makes knives one-at-a-time. **Prices:** 500 to $1200; some to $5000. **Remarks:** Full-time maker; first knife sold in 1970. **Mark:** Last name and MS.

HUDSON, ROB,
340 Roush Rd, Northumberland, PA 17857, Phone: 570-473-9588, robscustknives@aol.com Web:www.robscustomknives.com
Specialties: Presentation hunters and Bowies. **Technical:** Hollow grinds CPM-154 stainless and stainless Damascus. **Prices:** $400 to $2000. **Remarks:** Full-time maker. Does business as Rob's Custom Knives. **Mark:** Capital R, Capital H in script.

HUDSON, ROBERT,
3802 Black Cricket Ct, Humble, TX 77396, Phone: 713-454-7207
Specialties: Working straight knives of his design. **Patterns:** Bowies, hunters, skinners, fighters and utility knives. **Technical:** Grinds D2, 440C, 154CM and commercial Damascus. **Prices:** $85 to $350; some to $1500. **Remarks:** Part-time maker; first knife sold in 1980. **Mark:** Full name, handmade, city and state.

HUGHES, BILL,
110 Royale Dr, Texarkana, TX 75503, Phone: 903-838-0134, chughes@tc.cc.tx.us

HUGHES, DAN,
301 Grandview Bluff Rd, Spencer, TN 38585, Phone: 931-946-3044
Specialties: Working straight knives to customer specs. **Patterns:** Hunters, fighters, fillet knives. **Technical:** Grinds 440C and ATS-34. **Prices:** $55 to $175; some to $300. **Remarks:** Part-time maker; first knife sold in 1984. **Mark:** Initials.

HUGHES, DARYLE,
10979 Leonard, Nunica, MI 49448, Phone: 616-837-6623, hughes.builders@verizon.net
Specialties: Working knives. **Patterns:** Buckskinners, hunters, camp knives, kitchen and fishing knives. **Technical:** Forges and grinds 52100 and Damascus. **Prices:** $125 to $1000. **Remarks:** Part-time maker; first knife sold in 1979. **Mark:** Name and city in logo.

HUGHES, ED,
280 1/2 Holly Lane, Grand Junction, CO 81503, Phone: 970-243-8547, edhughes26@msn.com
Specialties: Working and art folders. **Patterns:** Buys Damascus. **Technical:** Grinds stainless steels. Engraves. **Prices:** $300 and up. **Remarks:** Full-time maker; first knife sold in 1978. **Mark:** Name or initials.

HUGHES, LAWRENCE,
207 W Crestway, Plainview, TX 79072, Phone: 806-293-5406
Specialties: Working and display knives. **Patterns:** Bowies, daggers, hunters, buckskinners. **Technical:** Grinds D2, 440C and 154CM. **Prices:** $125 to $300; some to $2000. **Remarks:** Full-time maker; first knife sold in 1979. **Mark:** Name with buffalo skull in center.

HULETT, STEVE,
115 Yellowstone Ave, West Yellowstone, MT 59758-0131, Phone: 406-646-4116, Web: www.seldomseenknives.com
Specialties: Classic, working/using knives, straight knives, folders. Your design, custom specs. **Patterns:** Utility/camp knives, hunters, and LinerLock folders, lock back pocket knives. **Technical:** Grinds 440C stainless steel, O1 Carbon, 1095. Shop is retail and knife shop; people watch their knives being made. We do everything in house: "all but smelt the ore, or tan the hide." **Prices:** Strarting $250 to $7000. **Remarks:** Full- time maker; first knife sold in 1994. **Mark:** Seldom seen knives/West Yellowstone Montana.

HULL, MICHAEL J,
1330 S Hermits Circle, Cottonwood, AZ 86326, Phone: 928-634-2871, mjwhull@earthlink.net
Specialties: Period pieces and working knives. **Patterns:** Hunters, fighters, Bowies, camp and Mediterranean knives, etc. **Technical:** Grinds 440C, ATS-34 and BG42 and S30V. **Prices:** $125 to $750; some to $1000. **Remarks:** Full-time maker; first knife sold in 1983. **Mark:** Name, city, state.

HULSEY, HOYT,
379 Shiloh, Attalla, AL 35954, Phone: 256-538-6765
Specialties: Traditional working straight knives and folders of his design. **Patterns:** Hunters and utility/camp knives. **Technical:** Grinds 440C, ATS-34, O1 and A2. **Prices:** $75 to $250. **Remarks:** Part-time maker; first knife sold in 1989. **Mark:** Hoyt Hulsey Attalla AL.

HUME, DON,
2731 Tramway Circle NE, Albuquerque, NM 87122, Phone: 505-796-9451

HUMENICK, ROY,
PO Box 55, Rescue, CA 95672
Specialties: Multiblade folders. **Patterns:** Original folder and fixed blade designs, also traditional patterns. **Technical:** Grinds premium steels and Damascus. **Prices:** $350 and up; some to $1500. **Remarks:** First knife sold in 1984. **Mark:** Last name in ARC.

HUMPHREYS, JOEL,
90 Boots Rd, Lake Placid, FL 33852, Phone: 863-773-0439
Specialties: Traditional working/using straight knives and folders of his design and in standard patterns. **Patterns:** Hunters, folders and utility/camp knives. **Technical:** Grinds ATS-34, D2, 440C. All knives have tapered tangs, mitered bolster/handle joints, handles of horn or bone fitted sheaths. **Prices:** $135 to $225; some to $350. **Remarks:** Part-time maker; first knife sold in 1990. Doing business as Sovereign Knives. **Mark:** First name or "H" pierced by arrow.

HUNT, MAURICE,
10510 N CR 650 E, Winter: 2925 Argyle Rd. Venice FL 34293, Brownsburg, IN 46112, Phone: 317-892-2982/Winter: 941-493-4027, mdhuntknives@juno.com
Patterns: Bowies, hunters, fighters. **Prices:** $200 to $800. **Remarks:** Part-time maker. Journeyman Smith.

HUNTER, HYRUM,
285 N 300 W, PO Box 179, Aurora, UT 84620, Phone: 435-529-7244
Specialties: Working straight knives of his design or to customer specs. **Patterns:** Drop and clip, fighters dagger, some folders. **Technical:** Forged from two-piece Damascus. **Prices:** Prices are adjusted according to size, complexity and material used. **Remarks:** Will consider any design you have. Part-time maker; first knife sold in 1990. **Mark:** Initials encircled with first initial and last name and city, then state. Some patterns are numbered.

HUNTER, RICHARD D,
7230 NW 200th Ter, Alachua, FL 32615, Phone: 386-462-3150
Specialties: Traditional working/using knives of his design or customer suggestions; filework. **Patterns:** Folders of various types, Bowies, hunters, daggers. **Technical:** Traditional blacksmith; hand forges high-carbon steel (5160, 1084, 52100) and makes own Damascus; grinds 440C and ATS-34. **Prices:** $200 and up. **Remarks:** Part-time maker; first knife sold in 1992. **Mark:** Last name in capital letters.

HURST, COLE,
1583 Tedford, E. Wenatchee, WA 98802, Phone: 509-884-9206
Specialties: Fantasy, high-art and traditional straight knives. **Patterns:** Bowies, daggers and hunters. **Technical:** Blades are made of stone; handles are made of stone, wood or ivory and embellished with fancy woods, ivory or antlers. **Prices:** $100 to $300; some to $2000. **Remarks:** Spare-time maker; first knife sold in 1985. **Mark:** Name and year.

HURST, JEFF,
PO Box 247, Rutledge, TN 37861, Phone: 865-828-5729, jhurst@esper.com
Specialties: Working straight knives and folders of his design. **Patterns:** Tomahawks, hunters, boots, folders and fighters. **Technical:** Forges W2, O1 and his own Damascus. Makes mokume. **Prices:** $250 to $600. **Remarks:** Full-time maker; first knife sold in 1984. Doing business as Buzzard's Knob Forge. **Mark:** Last name; partnered knives are marked with Newman L. Smith, handle artisan, and SH in script.

HURT, WILLIAM R,
9222 Oak Tree Cir, Frederick, MD 21701, Phone: 301-898-7143
Specialties: Traditional and working/using straight knives. **Patterns:** Bowies, hunters, fighters and utility knives. **Technical:** Forges 5160, O1 and O6; makes own Damascus. Offers silver wire inlay. **Prices:** $200 to $600; some higher. **Remarks:** Full-time maker; first knife sold in 1989. **Mark:** First and middle initials, last name.

HUSIAK, MYRON,
PO Box 238, Altona 3018, Victoria, AUSTRALIA, Phone: 03-315-6752
Specialties: Straight knives and folders of his design or to customer specs. **Patterns:** Hunters, fighters, lock-back folders, skinners and boots. **Technical:** Forges and grinds his own Damascus, 440C and ATS-34. **Prices:** $200 to $900. **Remarks:** Part-time maker; first knife sold in 1974. **Mark:** First initial, last name in logo and serial number.

HUTCHESON, JOHN,
SURSUM KNIFE WORKS, 1237 Brown's Ferry Rd., Chattanooga, TN 37419, Phone: 423-667-6193, sursum5071@aol.com; Web: www.sursumknife.com
Specialties: Straight working knives, hunters. **Patterns:** Customer designs, hunting, specialty working knives. **Technical:** Grinds D2, S7, O1 and 5160, ATS-34 on request. **Prices:** $100 to $300, some to $600. **Remarks:** First knife sold 1985, also produces a mid-tech line. Doing business as Sursum Knife Works. **Mark:** Family crest boar's head over 3 arrows.

HYTOVICK, JOE "HY",
14872 SW 111th St, Dunnellon, FL 34432, Phone: 800-749-5339, Fax: 352-489-3732, hyclassknives@aol.com
Specialties: Straight, folder and miniature. **Technical:** Blades from Wootz, Damascus and Alloy steel. **Prices:** To $5000. **Mark:** HY.

I

IAMES, GARY,
PO Box 8493, South Lake, Tahoe, CA 96158, Phone: 530-541-2250, iames@charter.net
Specialties: Working and fancy straight knives and folders. **Patterns:** Bowies, hunters, wedding sets and liner locking folders. **Technical:** Grinds 440C, ATS-34, forges 5160 and 1080, makes Damascus. **Prices:** $300 and up. **Mark:** Initials and last name, city or last name.

IMBODEN II, HOWARD L.,
620 Deauville Dr, Dayton, OH 45429, Phone: 513-439-1536
Specialties: One-of-a-kind hunting, flint, steel and art knives. **Technical:** Forges and grinds stainless, high-carbon and Damascus. Uses obsidian, cast sterling silver, 14K and 18K gold guards. Carves ivory animals and more. **Prices:** $65 to $25,000. **Remarks:** Full-time maker; first knife sold in 1986. Doing business as Hill Originals. **Mark:** First and last initials, II.

IMEL, BILLY MACE,
1616 Bundy Ave, New Castle, IN 47362, Phone: 765-529-1651
Specialties: High-art working knives, period pieces and personal cutlery. **Patterns:** Daggers, fighters, hunters; locking folders and slip-joints with interframes. **Technical:** Grinds D2, 440C and 154CM. **Prices:** $300 to $2000; some to $6000. **Remarks:** Part-time maker; first knife sold in 1973. **Mark:** Name in monogram.

IRIE, MICHAEL L,
MIKE IRIE HANDCRAFT, 1606 Auburn Dr., Colorado Springs, CO 80909, Phone: 719-572-5330, mikeirie@aol.com
Specialties: Working fixed blade knives and handcrafted blades for the do-it-yourselfer. **Patterns:** Twenty standard designs along with custom. **Technical:** Blades are ATS-34, BG-43, 440C with some outside Damascus. **Prices:** Fixed blades $95 and up, blade work $45 and up. **Remarks:** Formerly dba Wood, Irie and Co. with Barry Wood. Full-time maker since 1991. **Mark:** Name.

IRON WOLF FORGE, SEE NELSON KEN,

ISAO, OHBUCHI,
, 702-1 Nouso Yame-City, Fukuoka, JAPAN, Phone: 0943-23-4439, www.5d.biglobe.ne.jp/~ohisao/

ISGRO, JEFFERY,
1516 First St, West Babylon, NY 11704, Phone: 631- 235-1896
Specialties: File work, glass beading, kydex, leather. **Patterns:** Tactical use knives, skinners, capers, Bowies, camp, hunters. **Technical:** ATS- 34, 440C and D2. **Price:** $120 to $600. **Remarks:** Part-time maker. **Mark:** First name, last name, Long Island, NY.

ISHIHARA, HANK,
86-18 Motomachi, Sakura City, Chiba Pref., JAPAN, Phone: 043-485-3208, Fax: 043-485-3208
Specialties: Fantasy working straight knives and folders of his design. **Patterns:** Boots, Bowies, daggers, fighters, hunters, fishing, locking folders and utility camp knives. **Technical:** Grinds ATS-34, 440C, D2, 440V, CV-134, COS25 and Damascus. Engraves. **Prices:** $250 to $1000; some to $10,000. **Remarks:** Full-time maker; first knife sold in 1987. **Mark:** HANK.

J

JACKS, JIM,
344 S. Hollenbeck Ave, Covina, CA 91723-2513, Phone: 626-331-5665
Specialties: Working straight knives in standard patterns. **Patterns:** Bowies, hunters, fighters, fishing and camp knives, miniatures. **Technical:** Grinds Stellite 6K, 440C and ATS-34. **Prices:** Start at $100. **Remarks:** Spare-time maker; first knife sold in 1980. **Mark:** Initials in diamond logo.

JACKSON, CHARLTON R,
6811 Leyland Dr, San Antonio, TX 78239, Phone: 210-601-5112

JACKSON, DAVID,
214 Oleander Ave, Lemoore, CA 93245, Phone: 559-925-8547, jnbcrea@lemoorenet.com
Specialties: Forged steel. **Patterns:** Hunters, camp knives, Bowies. **Prices:** $150 and up. **Mark:** G.D. Jackson - Maker - Lemoore CA.

JACKSON, JIM,
7 Donnington Close, Chapel Row Bucklebury RG7 6PU, ENGLAND, Phone: 011-89-712743, Fax: 011-89-710495, jlandsejackson@aol.com
Specialties: Large Bowies, concentrating on form and balance; collector quality Damascus daggers. **Patterns:** With fancy filework and engraving available. **Technical:** Forges O1, 5160 and CS70 and 15N20 Damascus. **Prices:** From $1000. **Remarks:** Part-time maker. All knives come with a custom tooled leather swivel sheath of exotic material. **Mark:** Jackson England in a circle M.S.

JAKSIK JR., MICHAEL,
427 Marschall Creek Rd, Fredericksburg, TX 78624, Phone: 830-997-1119
Mark: MJ or M. Jaksik.

JANIGA, MATTHEW A,
85 Walden Ct., Fairfield, CA 94533, Phone: 707- 399-8036, mjaniga2003@yahoo.com
Specialties: Period pieces, swords, daggers. **Patterns:** Daggers, fighters and swords. **Technical:** Forges and Damascus. Does own heat treating. Forges own pattern-welded steel. **Prices:** $100 to $1000; some to $5000. **Remarks:** Spare-time maker; first knife sold in 1991. **Mark:** Interwoven initials.

JARVIS, PAUL M,
30 Chalk St, Cambridge, MA 02139, Phone: 617-547- 4355 or 617-666-9090
Specialties: High-art knives and period pieces of his design. **Patterns:** Japanese and Mid-Eastern knives. **Technical:** Grinds Myer Damascus, ATS-34, D2 and O1. Specializes in height-relief Japanese-style carving.

Works with silver, gold and gems. **Prices:** $200 to $17,000. **Remarks:** Part-time maker; first knife sold in 1978.

JEAN, GERRY,
25B Cliffside Dr, Manchester, CT 06040, Phone: 860- 649-6449
Specialties: Historic replicas. **Patterns:** Survival and camp knives. **Technical:** Grinds A2, 440C and 154CM. Handle slabs applied in unique tongue-and-groove method. **Prices:** $125 to $250; some to $1000. **Remarks:** Spare-time maker; first knife sold in 1973. **Mark:** Initials and serial number.

JEFFRIES, ROBERT W,
Route 2 Box 227, Red House, WV 25168, Phone: 304-586-9780, wvknifeman@hotmail.com; Web: www.jeffriesknieswv.tripod.com
Specialties: Hunters, Bowies, daggers, lockback folders and LinerLock push buttons. **Patterns:** Skinning types, drop points, typical working hunters, folders one-of-a-kind. **Technical:** Grinds all types of steel. Makes his own Damascus. **Prices:** $125 to $600. Private collector pieces to $3000. **Remarks:** Starting engraving. Custom folders of his design. Part-time maker since 1988. **Mark:** Name etched or on plate pinned to blade.

JENSEN, JOHN LEWIS,
JENSEN KNIVES, PO Box 50041, Pasadena, CA 91116, Phone: 323-559-7454, Fax: 626-449-1148, john@jensenknives.com; Web: www.jensenknives.com
Specialties: Designer and fabricator of modern, original one-of-a-kind, hand crafted, custom ornamental edged weaponry. Combines skill, precision, distinction and the finest materials, geared toward the discriminating art collector. **Patterns:** Folding knives and fixed blades, daggers, fighters and swords. **Technical:** High embellishment, BFA 96 Rhode Island School of Design: jewelry and metalsmithing. Grinds 440C, ATS-34, Damascus. Works with custom made Damascus to his specs. Uses gold, silver, gemstones, pearl, titanium, fossil mastodon and walrus ivories. Carving, file work, soldering, deep etches Damascus, engraving, layers, bevels, blood grooves. Also forges his own Damascus. **Prices:** Start at $10,000. **Remarks:** Available on a first come basis and via commission based on his designs. Knifemakers Guild voting member and ABS apprenticesmith and member of the Society of North American Goldsmiths. **Mark:** Maltese cross/butterfly shield.

JERNIGAN, STEVE,
3082 Tunnel Rd., Milton, FL 32571, Phone: 850- 994-0802, Fax: 850-994-0802, jerniganknives@mchsi.com
Specialties: Investor-class folders and various theme pieces. **Patterns:** Array of models and sizes in side plate locking interframes and conventional liner construction. **Technical:** Grinds ATS-34, CPM-T-440V and Damascus. Inlays mokume (and minerals) in blades and sculpts marble cases. **Prices:** $650 to $1800; some to $6000. **Remarks:** Full-time maker, first knife sold in 1982. **Mark:** Last name.

JOBIN, JACQUES,
46 St Dominique, Levis Quebec, CANADA G6V 2M7, Phone: 418-833-0283, Fax: 418-833-8378
Specialties: Fancy and working straight knives and folders; miniatures. **Patterns:** Minis, fantasy knives, fighters and some hunters. **Technical:** ATS-34, some Damascus and titanium. Likes native snake wood. Heat-treats. **Prices:** Start at $250. **Remarks:** Full-time maker; first knife sold in 1986. **Mark:** Signature on blade.

JOEHNK, BERND,
Posadowskystrasse 22, 24148 Kiel, GERMANY, Phone: 0431-7297705, Fax: 0431-7297705
Specialties: One-of-a-kind fancy/embellished and traditional straight knives of his design and from customer drawing. **Patterns:** Daggers, fighters, hunters and letter openers. **Technical:** Grinds and file 440C, ATS-34, powder metal orgical, commercial Damascus and various stainless and corrosion-resistant steels. **Prices:** Upscale. **Remarks:** Likes filework. Leather sheaths. Offers engraving. Part-time maker; first knife sold in1990. Doing business as metal design kiel. All knives made by hand. **Mark:** From 2005 full name and city, with certificate.

JOHANNING CUSTOM KNIVES, TOM,
1735 Apex Rd, Sarasota, FL 34240 9386, Phone: 941-371-2104, Fax: 941-378-9427, Web: www.survivalknives.com
Specialties: Survival knives. **Prices:** $375 to $775.

JOHANSSON, ANDERS,
Konstvartarevagen 9, S-772 40 Grangesberg, SWEDEN, Phone: 46 240 23204, Fax: +46 21 358778, www.scrimart.u.se
Specialties: Scandinavian traditional and modern straight knives. **Patterns:** Hunters, fighters and fantasy knives. **Technical:** Grinds stainless steel and makes own Damascus. Prefers water buffalo and mammoth for handle material. **Prices:** Start at $100. **Remarks:** Spare-time maker; first knife sold in 1994. Works together with scrimshander Viveca Sahlin. **Mark:** Stylized initials.

JOHNS, ROB,
1423 S. Second, Enid, OK 73701, Phone: 405-242-2707
Specialties: Classic and fantasy straight knives of his design or to customer specs; fighters for use at Medieval fairs. **Patterns:** Bowies, daggers and swords. **Technical:** Forges and grinds 440C, D2 and 5160. Handles of nylon, walnut or wire-wrap. **Prices:** $150 to $350; some to $2500. **Remarks:** Full-time maker; first knife sold in 1980. **Mark:** Medieval Customs, initials.

JOHNSON, C E GENE,
1240 Coan Street, Chesterton, IN 46304, Phone: 219-787-8324, ddjlady55@aol.com
Specialties: Lock-back folders and springers of his design or to customer specs. **Patterns:** Hunters, Bowies, survival lock-back folders. **Technical:** Grinds D2, 440C, A18, O1, Damascus; likes filework. **Prices:** $100 to $2000. **Remarks:** Full-time maker; first knife sold in 1975. **Mark:** Gene.

JOHNSON, DAVID A,
1791 Defeated Creek Rd, Pleasant Shade, TN 37145, Phone: 615-774-3596, artsmith@mwsi.net

JOHNSON, GORDEN W,
5426 Sweetbriar, Houston, TX 77017, Phone: 713-645-8990
Specialties: Working knives and period pieces. **Patterns:** Hunters, boots and Bowies. **Technical:** Flat-grinds 440C; most knives have narrow tang. **Prices:** $90 to $450. **Remarks:** Full-time maker; first knife sold in 1974. **Mark:** Name, city, state.

JOHNSON, GORDON A.,
981 New Hope Rd, Choudrant, LA 71227, Phone: 318-768-2613
Specialties: Using straight knives and folders of my design, or customers. Offering filework and hand stitched sheaths. **Patterns:** Hunters, bowies, folders and miniatures. **Technical:** Forges 5160, 1084, 52100 and my own Damascus. Some stock removal on working knives and miniatures. **Prices:** Mid range. **Remarks:** First knife sold in 1990. ABS apprentice smith. **Mark:** Interlocking initials G.J. or G. A. J.

JOHNSON, JOHN R,
PO Box 246, New Buffalo, PA 17069, Phone: 717- 834-6265, jrj@jrjknives.com; Web: www.jrjknives.com
Specialties: Working hunting and tactical fixed blade sheath knives. **Patterns:** Hunters, tacticals, Bowies, daggers, neck knives and primitives. **Technical:** Flat, convex and hollow grinds. ATS-34, CPM154CM, L6, O1, D2, 5160, 1095 and Damascus. **Prices:** $60 to $700. **Remarks:** Full-time maker; first knife sold in 1996. Doing business as JRJ Knives. Custom sheath made by maker for every knife, **Mark:** Initials connected.

JOHNSON, JOHN R,
5535 Bob Smith Ave, Plant City, FL 33565, Phone: 813-986-4478, rottyjohn@msn.com
Specialties: Hand forged and stock removal. **Technical:** High tech. Folders. **Mark:** J.R. Johnson Plant City, FL.

JOHNSON, MIKE,
38200 Main Rd, Orient, NY 11957, Phone: 631-323- 3509, mjohnsoncustomknives@hotmail.com
Specialties: Large Bowie knives and cutters, fighters and working knives to customer specs. **Technical:** Forges 5160, O1. **Prices:** $325 to $1200. **Remarks:** Full-time bladesmith. **Mark:** Johnson.

JOHNSON, R B,
Box 11, Clearwater, MN 55320, Phone: 320-558-6128, Fax: 320-558-6128, rbjohnson@mywdo.comorrb@rbjohnsonknives.com;Web:rbjohnsonknives.com
Specialties: Liner locks with titanium, mosaic Damascus. **Patterns:** LinerLock® folders, skeleton hunters, frontier Bowies. **Technical:** Damascus, mosaic Damascus, A-2, O1, 1095. **Prices:** $200 and up. **Remarks:** Full-time maker since 1973. Not accepting orders. **Mark:** R B Johnson (signature).

JOHNSON, RANDY,
2575 E Canal Dr, Turlock, CA 95380, Phone: 209- 632-5401
Specialties: Folders. **Patterns:** Locking folders. **Technical:** Grinds Damascus. **Prices:** $200 to $400. **Remarks:** Spare-time maker; first knife sold in 1989. Doing business as Puedo Knifeworks. **Mark:** PUEDO.

JOHNSON, RICHARD,
W165 N10196 Wagon Trail, Germantown, WI 53022, Phone: 262-251-5772, rlj@execpc.com; Web: http:// www.execpc.com/~rlj/index.html
Specialties: Custom knives and knife repair.

JOHNSON, RUFFIN,
215 LaFonda Dr, Houston, TX 77060, Phone: 281- 448-4407
Specialties: Working straight knives and folders. **Patterns:** Hunters, fighters and locking folders. **Technical:** Grinds 440C and 154CM; hidden tangs and fancy handles. **Prices:** $450 to $650; some to $1350. **Remarks:** Full-time maker; first knife sold in 1972. **Mark:** Wolf head logo and signature.

JOHNSON, RYAN M,
7320 Foster Hixson Cemetery Rd, Hixson, TN 37343, Phone: 615-842-9323
Specialties: Working and using straight knives of his design and to customer specs. **Patterns:** Bowies, hunters and utility/camp knives. **Technical:** Forges 5160, Damascus and files. Prices: $70 to $400; some to $800. **Remarks:** Full-time maker; first knife sold in 1986. **Mark:** Sledge- hammer with halo.

JOHNSON, STEVEN R,
202 E 200 N, PO Box 5, Manti, UT 84642, Phone: 435-835-7941, Fax: 435-835-7941, srj@mail.manti.com; Web: www.srjknives.com
Specialties: Investor-class working knives. **Patterns:** Hunters, fighters, boots. **Technical:** Grinds 154-CM, ATS-34, CPM 154-CM. **Prices:** $800 to $5000. **Remarks:** Full-time maker; first knife sold in 1972. **Mark:** Registered trademark, including name, city, state, and optional signature mark.

JOHNSTON, DR. ROBT,
PO Box 9887 1 Lomb Mem Dr, Rochester, NY 14623

JOKERST, CHARLES,
9312 Spaulding, Omaha, NE 68134, Phone: 402-571-2536
Specialties: Working knives in standard patterns. **Patterns:** Hunters, fighters and pocketknives. **Technical:** Grinds 440C, ATS-34. **Prices:** $90 to $170. **Remarks:** Spare-time maker; first knife sold in 1984. **Mark:** Early work marked RCJ; current work marked with last name and city.

JONES, BARRY M AND PHILLIP G,
221 North Ave, Danville, VA 24540, Phone: 804-793-5282
Specialties: Working and using straight knives and folders of their design and to customer specs; combat and self-defense knives. **Patterns:** Bowies, fighters, daggers, swords, hunters and LinerLock® folders. **Technical:** Grinds 440C, ATS-34 and D2; flat-grinds only. All blades hand polished. **Prices:** $100 to $1000, some higher. **Remarks:** Part-time makers; first knife sold in 1989. **Mark:** Jones Knives, city, state.

JONES, CURTIS J,
210 Springfield Ave, Washington, PA 15301-5244, Phone: 724-225-8829
Specialties: Big Bowies, daggers, his own style of hunters. **Patterns:** Bowies, daggers, hunters, swords, boots and miniatures. **Technical:** Grinds 440C, ATS-34 and D2. Fitted guards only; does not solder. Heat- treats. Custom sheaths: hand-tooled and stitched. **Prices:** $125 to $1500; some to $3000. **Remarks:** Full-time maker; first knife sold in 1975. Mail orders accepted. **Mark:** Stylized initials on either side of three triangles interconnected.

JONES, ENOCH,
7278 Moss Ln, Warrenton, VA 20187, Phone: 540- 341-0292
Specialties: Fancy working straight knives. **Patterns:** Hunters, fighters, boots and Bowies. **Technical:** Forges and grinds O1, W2, 440C and Damascus. **Prices:** $100 to $350; some to $1000. **Remarks:** Part-time maker; first knife sold in 1982. **Mark:** First name.

JONES, FRANKLIN (FRANK) W,
6030 Old Dominion Rd, Columbus, GA 31909, Phone: 706-563-6051, frankscuba@bellsouth.net
Specialties: Traditional/working/tactical/period straight knives of his or your design. **Patterns:** Hunters, skinners, utility/camp, Bowies, fighters, kitchen, neck knives, Harley chains. **Technical:** Forges using 5160, O1, 52100, 1084 1095 and Damascus. Also stock removal of stainless steel. **Prices:** $150 to $1000. **Remarks:** Full-time, American Bladesmith Society Journeyman Smith. **Mark:** F.W. Jones, Columbus, GA.

JONES, JACK P.,
17670 Hwy. 2 East, Ripley, MS 38663, Phone: 662- 837-3882, jacjones@ripleycable.net
Specialties: Working knives in classic design. **Patterns:** Hunters, fighters, and Bowies. **Technical:** Grinds ATS-34, D2, A2, CPM-154 CM. **Prices:** $200 and up. **Remarks:** Full-time maker since retirement in 2005, first knife sold in 1976. **Mark:** J.P. Jones, Ripley, MS.

JONES, JOHN,
62 Sandy Creek Rd, Gympie, Queensland 4570, AUSTRALIA, Phone: 07- 54838731, jaj36@bigpond.com
Specialties: Straight knives, gents folders and folders. **Patterns:** Hunters, Bowies, and art knives. **Technical:** Grinds 440C, AT34, Damasteel. **Prices:** $250 to $2000. **Remarks:** Using knives and collectibles. Prefer natural materials. Full-time maker. **Mark:** Jones in script and year of manufacture.

JONES, JOHN A,
779 SW 131 Hwy, Holden, MO 64040, Phone: 816- 850-4318
Specialties: Working, using knives. Hunters, skinners and fighters. **Technical:** Grinds D2, O1, 440C, 1095. Prefers forging; creates own Damascus. File working on most blades. **Prices:** $50 to $500. **Remarks:** Part-time maker; first knife sold in 1996. Doing business as Old John Knives. **Mark:** OLD JOHN and serial number.

JONES, ROGER MUDBONE,
GREENMAN WORKSHOP, 320 Prussia Rd, Waverly, OH 45690, Phone: 740-739-4562, greenmanworkshop@yahoo.com
Specialties: Working in cutlery to suit working woodsman and fine collector. **Patterns:** Bowies, hunters, folders, hatchets in both period and modern style, scale miniatures a specialty. **Technical:** All cutlery hand forged to shape with traditional methods; multiple quench and draws, limited Damascus production hand carves wildlife and historic themes in stag/antler/ivory, full line of functional and high art leather. All work sole authorship. **Prices:** $50 to $5000 **Remarks:** Full-time maker/first knife sold in 1979. **Mark:** Stamped R. Jones hand made or hand engraved sig. W/Bowie knife mark.

JUSTICE, SHANE,
425 South Brooks St, Sheridan, WY 82801, Phone: 307-673-4432, justicecustomknives@yahoo.com
Specialties: Fixed blade working knives. **Patterns:** Hunters, skinners and camp knives. Other designs produced on a limited basis. **Technical:** Hand forged 5160 and 52100. **Remarks:** Part-time maker. Sole author. **Mark:** Last name.

K

K B S, KNIVES,
RSD 181, North Castlemaine, Vic 3450, AUSTRALIA, Phone: 0011 61 3 54 705864, Fax: 0011 61 3 54 706233
Specialties: Bowies, daggers and miniatures. **Patterns:** Art daggers, traditional Bowies, fancy folders and miniatures. **Technical:** Hollow or flat grind, most steels. **Prices:** $200 to $600+. **Remarks:** Full-time maker; first knife sold in 1983. **Mark:** Initials and address in Southern Cross motif.

KACZOR, TOM,
375 Wharncliffe Rd N, Upper London, Ont., CANADA N6G 1E4, Phone: 519-645-7640

KAGAWA, KOICHI,
1556 Horiyamashita, Hatano-Shi, Kanagawa, JAPAN
Specialties: Fancy high-tech straight knives and folders to customer specs. **Patterns:** Hunters, locking folders and slip-joints. **Technical:** Uses 440C and ATS-34. **Prices:** $500 to $2000; some to $20,000. **Remarks:** Part-time maker; first knife sold in 1986. **Mark:** First initial, last name-YOKOHAMA.

KAIN, CHARLES,
KAIN DESIGNS, 38 South Main St, Indianapolis, IN 46227, Phone: 317-781-8556, Fax: 317-781-8521, charles@kaincustomknives.com; Web: www.kaincustomknives.com
Specialties: Unique Damascus art folders. **Patterns:** Any. **Technical:** Specialized & patented mechanisms. **Remarks:** Unique knife & knife mechanism design. **Mark:** Kain and Signet stamp for unique pieces.

KAJIN, AL,
PO Box 1047, 342 South 6th Ave, Forsyth, MT 59327, Phone: 406-346-2442, kajinknives@cablemt.net
Specialties: Utility/working knives, hunters, kitchen cutlery. Produces own Damascus steel from 15N20 and 1084 and cable. Forges 52100, 5160, 1084, 15N20 and O1. Stock removal ATS-34, D2, O1, and L6. Patterns: All types, especially like to work with customer on their designs. Technical: Maker since 1989. ABS member since 1995. Does own differential heat treating, cryogenic soaking when appropriate. Does all leather work. Prices: Stock removal starts at $250. Forged blades and Damascus starts at $300. Kitchen cutlery starts at $100. Remarks: Likes to use exotic woods. Mark: Interlocked AK on forged blades, etched stylized Kajin in outline of Montana on stock removal knives.

KANDA, MICHIO,
7-32-5 Shinzutumi-cho, Shunan-shi, Yamaguchi 7460033, JAPAN, Phone: 0834-62-1910, Fax: 011-81-83462-1910
Specialties: Fantasy knives of his design. **Patterns:** Animal knives. **Technical:** Grinds ATS-34. **Prices:** $300 to $3000. **Remarks:** Full-time maker; first knife sold in 1985. Doing business as Shusui Kanda. **Mark:** Last name inside "M."

KANKI, IWAO,
14-25 3-Chome Fukui Miki, Hydugo, JAPAN 673-0433, Phone: 07948-3-2555
Specialties: Plane, knife. **Prices:** Not determined yet. **Remarks:** Masters of traditional crafts designated by the Minister of International Trade and Industry (Japan). **Mark:** Chiyozuru Sadahide.

KANSEI, MATSUNO,
109-8 Uenomachi Nishikaiden, Gitu-city, JAPAN 501-1168, Phone: 81-58-234-8643
Specialties: Folders of original design. **Patterns:** LinerLock® folder. **Technical:** Grinds VG-10, Damascus. **Prices:** $350 to $2000. **Remarks:** Full-time maker. First knife sold in 1993. **Mark:** Name.

KANTER, MICHAEL,
ADAM MICHAEL KNIVES, 14550 West Honey Ln., New Berlin, WI 53151, Phone: 262-860-1136, mike@adammichaelknives.com; Web: www.adammichaelknives.com
Specialties: Fixed blades and folders. **Patterns:** Drop point hunters, Bowies and fighters. **Technical:** Jerry Rados Damascus, BG42, CPM, S60V and S30V. **Prices:** $375 and up. **Remarks:** Ivory, mammoth ivory, stabilized woods, and pearl handles. **Mark:** Engraved Adam Michael.

KARP, BOB,
PO Box 47304, Phoenix, AZ 85068, Phone: 602 870-1234 602 870-1234, Fax: 602-331-0283
Remarks: Bob Karp "Master of the Blade."

KATO, SHINICHI,
Rainbow Amalke 402, Ohoragnchi, Nakashidami, Moriyama-ku Nagoya, JAPAN 463-0002, Phone: 81-52-736-6032, skato-402@u0l.gate01.com
Specialties: Flat grind and hand finish. **Patterns:** Bowie, fighter. Hunting and folding knives. **Technical:** Hand forged,flat grind. **Prices:** $100 to $2000. **Remarks:** Part-time maker. **Mark:** Name.

KATSUMARO, SHISHIDO,
, 2-6-11 Kamiseno Aki-ku, Hiroshima, JAPAN, Phone: 090-3634-9054, Fax: 082-227-4438, shishido@d8.dion.ne.jp

KAUFFMAN, DAVE,
4 Clark Creek Loop, Montana City, MT 59634, Phone: 406-442-9328
Specialties: Field grade and exhibition grade hunting knives and ultra light folders. **Patterns:** Fighters, Bowies and drop-point hunters. **Technical:** S30V and SS Damascus. **Prices:** $155 to $1200. **Remarks:** Full- time maker; first knife sold in 1989. On the cover of *Knives '94*. **Mark:** First and last name, city and state.

KAWASAKI, AKIHISA,
11-8-9 Chome Minamiamachi, Suzurandai Kita- Ku, Kobe, JAPAN, Phone: 078-593-0418, Fax: 078-593-0418
Specialties: Working/using knives of his design. **Patterns:** Hunters, kit camp knives. **Technical:** Forges and grinds Molybdenum Panadium. Grinds ATS-34 and stainless steel. Uses Chinese Quince wood, desert ironwood and cow leather. **Prices:** $300 to $800; some to $1000. **Remarks:** Full-time maker. **Mark:** A.K.

KAY, J WALLACE,
332 Slab Bridge Rd, Liberty, SC 29657

KAZSUK, DAVID,
PO Box 39, Perris, CA 92572-0039, Phone: 909-780- 2288, ddkaz@hotmail.com
Specialties: Hand forged. **Prices:** $150+. **Mark:** Last name.

KEARNEY, JAROD,
10 Park St Hamlet, Bordentown, NJ 08505, Phone: 336-656-4617, jarodk@mindspring.com; Web: www.jarodsworkshop.com

KEESLAR, JOSEPH F,
391 Radio Rd, Almo, KY 42020, Phone: 270- 753-7919, Fax: 270-753-7919, sjkees@apex.net
Specialties: Classic and contemporary Bowies, combat, hunters, daggers and folders. **Patterns:** Decorative filework, engraving and custom leather sheaths available. **Technical:** Forges 5160, 52100 and his own Damascus steel. **Prices:** $300 to $3000. **Remarks:** Full-time maker; first knife sold in 1976. ABS Master Smith. **Mark:** First and middle initials, last name in hammer, knife and anvil logo, M.S.

KEESLAR, STEVEN C,
115 Lane 216 Hamilton Lake, Hamilton, IN 46742, Phone: 260-488-3161, sskeeslar@hotmail.com
Specialties: Traditional working/using straight knives of his design and to customer specs. **Patterns:** Bowies, hunters, utility/camp knives. **Technical:** Forges 5160, files 52100 Damascus. **Prices:** $100 to $600; some to $1500. **Remarks:** Part-time maker; first knife sold in 1976. ABS member. **Mark:** Fox head in flames over Steven C. Keeslar.

KEETON, WILLIAM L,
6095 Rehobeth Rd SE, Laconia, IN 47135-9550, Phone: 812-969-2836, wkeeton@epowerc.net; Web: www.keetoncustomknives.com
Specialties: Plain and fancy working knives. **Patterns:** Hunters and fighters; locking folders and slip-joints. Names patterns after Kentucky Derby winners. **Technical:** Grinds any of the popular alloy steels. **Prices:** $175 to $4000. **Remarks:** Full-time maker; first knife sold in 1971. **Mark:** Logo of key.

KEHIAYAN, ALFREDO,
Cuzco 1455 Ing. Maschwitz, CP B1623GXU Buenos Aires, ARGENTINA, Phone: 54-03488-442212, Fax: 54-077-75- 4493-5359, alfredo@kehiayan.com.ar; Web: www.kehiayan.com.ar
Specialties: Functional straight knives. **Patterns:** Utility knives, skinners, hunters and boots. **Technical:** Forges and grinds SAE 52.100, SAE 6180, SAE 9260, SAE 5160, 440C and ATS-34, titanium with nitride. All blades mirror-polished; makes leather sheath and wood cases. **Prices:** $70 to $800; some to $6000. **Remarks:** Full-time maker; first knife sold in 1983. Some knives are satin finish (utility knives). **Mark:** Name.

KEISUKE, GOTOH,
105 Cosumo-City, Otozu 202 Ohita-city, Ohita, JAPAN, Phone: 097-523-0750, k-u-an@ki.rim.or.jp

KELLER, BILL,
12211 Las Nubes, San Antonio, TX 78233, Phone: 210- 653-6609
Specialties: Primarily folders, some fixed blades. **Patterns:** Autos, liner locks and hunters. **Technical:** Grinds stainless and Damascus. **Prices:** $400 to $1000, some to $4000. **Remarks:** Part-time maker, first knife sold 1995. **Mark:** Last name inside outline of Alamo.

KELLEY, GARY,
17485 SW Pheasant Lane, Aloha, OR 97006, Phone: 503-649-7867, Web: www.reproductionblades.com
Specialties: Primitive knives and blades. **Patterns:** Fur trade era rifleman's knives, fur trade, cowboy action, hunting knives. **Technical:** Hand- forges and precision investment casts. **Prices:** $35 to $125. **Remarks:** Family business, reproduction blades. Doing business as Reproduction Blades. **Mark:** Fir tree logo.

KELLY, DAVE,
865 S. Shenandoah St., Los Angeles, CA 90035, Phone: 310-657-7121, dakcon@sbcglobal.net
Specialties: Collector and user one-of-a-kind (his design) fixed blades, liner lock folders, and leather sheaths. **Patterns:** Utility and hunting fixed blade knives with hand-sewn leather sheaths, Gentleman liner lock folders. **Technical:** Grinds carbon steels, hollow, convex, and flat. Offers clay differentially hardened blades, etched and polished. Uses Sambar stag, mammoth ivory, and high-grade burl woods. Hand-sewn leather sheaths for fixed blades and leather pouch sheaths for folders. **Prices:** $250 to $750, some higher. **Remarks:** Full-time maker, first knife made in 2003. **Mark:** First initial, last name with large K.

KELLY, LANCE,
1723 Willow Oak Dr, Edgewater, FL 32132, Phone: 904-423-4933
Specialties: Investor-class straight knives and folders. **Patterns:** Kelly-style in contemporary outlines. **Technical:** Grinds O1, D2 and 440C; engraves; inlays gold and silver. **Prices:** $600 to $3500. **Remarks:** Full-time engraver and knifemaker; first knife sold in 1975. **Mark:** Last name.

KELSEY, NATE,
3401 Cherry St, Anchorage, AK 99504, Phone: 907-360-4469, edgealaska@mac.com; Web: www.edgealaska.com
Specialties: Hand forges or stock removal traditional working knives of own or customer design. Forges own Damascus, makes custom leather sheaths, does fine engraving and scrimshaw. **Technical:** Forges 52100, 1084/15N20, 5160. Grinds ATS-34, 154CM. Prefers natural handle materials. **Prices:** $300 to $1500. **Remarks:** Part-time maker since 1990. Member ABS, Arkansas Knifemakers Assoc. **Mark:** Name and city.

KELSO, JIM,
577 Collar Hill Rd, Worcester, VT 05682, Phone: 802-229-4254, Fax: 802-229-0595, kelsonmaker@gmail.com; Web:www.jimkelso.com
Specialties: Fancy high-art straight knives and folders that mix Eastern and Western influences. Only uses own designs. **Patterns:** Daggers, swords and locking folders. **Technical:** Grinds only custom Damascus. Works with top Damascus bladesmiths. **Prices:** $6000 to $20,000. **Remarks:** Full-time maker; first knife sold in 1980. **Mark:** Stylized initials.

KEMP, LAWRENCE,
8503 Water Tower Rd, Ooletwah, TN 37363, Phone: 423-344-2357, larry@kempknives.com
Specialties: Bowies, hunters and working knives. **Patterns:** Bowies, camp knives, hunters and skinners. **Technical:** Forges carbon steel, and his own Damascus. **Prices:** $150 to $1500. **Remarks:** Part-time maker, first knife sold in 1991. **Mark:** L.A. Kemp.

KENNEDY JR., BILL,
PO Box 850431, Yukon, OK 73085, Phone: 405-354-9150
Specialties: Working straight knives. **Patterns:** Hunters, fighters, minis and fishing knives. **Technical:** Grinds D2, 440C, ATS-34, BG42. **Prices:** $110 and up. **Remarks:** Part-time maker; first knife sold in 1980. **Mark:** Last name and year made.

KERANEN, PAUL,
16 Duncan St., P.O. Box 261, Ahmeek, MI 49901, Phone: 906-337-0774, pkknives@gmail.com
Specialties: Specializes in Japanese style knives and swords. Most clay tempered with hamon. **Patterns:** Does bowies, fighters and hunters. **Technical:** Forges and grinds carbons steel only. Make my own Damascus. **Prices:** $75 to $800. **Mark:** PK etched.

KERN, R W,
20824 Texas Trail W, San Antonio, TX 78257-1602, Phone: 210-698-2549, rkern@ev1.net
Specialties: Damascus, straight and folders. **Patterns:** Hunters, Bowies and folders. **Technical:** Grinds ATS-34, 440C and BG42. Forges own Damascus. **Prices:** $200 and up. **Remarks:** First knives 1980; retired; work as time permits. Member ABS, Texas Knifemaker and Collectors Association. **Mark:** Outline of Alamo with kern over outline.

KEYES, DAN,
6688 King St, Chino, CA 91710, Phone: 909-628-8329

KEYES, GEOFF P.,
13027 Odell Rd NE, Duvall, WA 98019, Phone: 425-844-0758, 5ef@polarisfarm.com; Web: www5elementsforge.com
Specialties: Working grade fixed blades, 19th century style gents knives. **Patterns:** Fixed blades, your design or mine. **Technical:** Hnad-forged 5160, 1084, and own Damascus. **Prices:** $200 and up. **Remarks:** Geoff Keyes DBA 5 Elements Forge, ABS Journeyman Smith. **Mark:** Early mark KEYES etched in script. New mark as of 2009: pressed GPKeyes.

KHALSA, JOT SINGH,
368 Village St, Millis, MA 02054, Phone: 508-376-8162, Fax: 508-532-0517, jotkhalsa@comcast.net; Web: www.khalsakirpans.com, www.lifeknives.com, and www.thekhalsaraj.com
Specialties: Liner locks, one-of-a-kind daggers, swords, and kirpans (Sikh daggers) all original designs. **Technical:** Forges own Damascus, uses others high quality Damascus including stainless, and grinds stainless steels. Uses natural handle materials frequently unusual minerals. Pieces are frequently engraved and more recently carved. **Prices:** Start at $700.

KHARLAMOV, YURI,
Oboronnay 46, 2, Tula, 300007, RUSSIA
Specialties: Classic, fancy and traditional knives of his design. **Patterns:** Daggers and hunters. **Technical:** Forges only Damascus with nickel. Uses natural handle materials; engraves on metal, carves on nut-tree; silver and pearl inlays. **Prices:** $600 to $2380; some to $4000. **Remarks:** Full-time maker; first knife sold in 1988. **Mark:** Initials.

KI, SHIVA,
5222 Ritterman Ave, Baton Rouge, LA 70805, Phone: 225-356-7274, shivakicustomknives@netzero.net; Web: www.shivakicustomknives.com
Specialties: Working straight knives and folders. **Patterns:** Emphasis on personal defense knives, martial arts weapons. **Technical:** Forges and

grinds; makes own Damascus; prefers natural handle materials. **Prices:** $135 to $850; some to $1800. **Remarks:** Full-time maker; first knife sold in 1981. **Mark:** Name with logo.

KIEFER, TONY,
112 Chateaugay Dr, Pataskala, OH 43062, Phone: 740-927-6910
Specialties: Traditional working and using straight knives in standard patterns. **Patterns:** Bowies, fighters and hunters. **Technical:** Grinds 440C and D2; forges D2. Flat-grinds Bowies; hollow-grinds drop-point and trailing-point hunters. **Prices:** $110 to $300; some to $200. **Remarks:** Spare-time maker; first knife sold in 1988. **Mark:** Last name.

KILBY, KEITH,
1902 29th St, Cody, WY 82414, Phone: 307-587-2732
Specialties: Works with all designs. **Patterns:** Mostly Bowies, camp knives and hunters of his design. **Technical:** Forges 52100, 5160, 1095, Damascus and mosaic Damascus. **Prices:** $250 to $3500. **Remarks:** Part-time maker; first knife sold in 1974. Doing business as Foxwood Forge. **Mark:** Name.

KILEY, MIKE AND JANDY,
ROCKING K KNIVES, 1325 Florida, Chino Valley, AZ 86323, Phone: 928-910-2647
Specialties: Period knives for cowboy action shooters and mountain men. **Patterns:** Bowies, drop-point hunters, skinners, sheepsfoot blades and spear points. **Technical:** Steels are 0-1, D2, 1095, ATS 34, 440C and others upon request. Handles include all types of wood, with cocobolo, ironwood, rosewood, maple and bacote being favorites as well as buffalo horn, stag, elk antler, mammoth ivory, giraffe boon, sheep horn and camel bone. **Prices:** $100 to $500 depending on style and materials. Hand-tooled leather sheaths by Jan and Mike.

KILPATRICK, CHRISTIAN A,
6925 Mitchell Ct, Citrus Hieghts, CA 95610, Phone: 916-729-0733, crimsonkil@gmail.com; Web: www.crimsonknives.com
Specialties: All forged weapons (no firearms) from ancient to modern. All blades produced are first and foremost useable tools, and secondly but no less importantly, artistic expressions. **Patterns:** Knives, bowies, daggers, swords, axes, spears, boot knives, bird knives, ethnic blades and historical reproductions. Customer designs welcome. **Technical:** Forges and grinds, makes own Damascus. Does file work. **Prices:** $125 to $3200. **Remarks:** 26 year part time maker. First knife sold in 2002.

KIMBERLEY, RICHARD A,
86-B Arroyo Hondo Rd, Santa Fe, NM 87508, Phone: 505-820-2727
Specialties: Fixed-blade and period knives. **Technical:** O1, 52100, 9260 steels. **Remarks:** Member ABS. Marketed under "Kimberleys of Santa Fe." **Mark:** "By D. KIMBERLEY SANTA FE NM."

KIMSEY, KEVIN,
198 Cass White Rd. NW, Cartersville, GA 30121, Phone: 770-387-0779 and 770-655-8879
Specialties: Tactical fixed blades and folders. **Patterns:** Fighters, folders, hunters and utility knives. **Technical:** Grinds 440C, ATS-34 and D2 carbon. **Prices:** $100 to $400; some to $600. **Remarks:** Three-time *Blade* magazine award winner, knifemaker since 1983. **Mark:** Rafter and stylized KK.

KING, BILL,
14830 Shaw Rd, Tampa, FL 33625, Phone: 813-961-3455
Specialties: Folders, lockbacks, liner locks, automatics and stud openers. **Patterns:** Wide varieties; folders. **Technical:** ATS-34 and some Damascus; single and double grinds. Offers filework and jewel embellishment; nickel-silver Damascus and mokume bolsters. **Prices:** $150 to $475; some to $850. **Remarks:** Full-time maker; first knife sold in 1976. All titanium fitting on liner-locks; screw or rivet construction on lock-backs. **Mark:** Last name in crown.

KING, FRED,
430 Grassdale Rd, Cartersville, GA 30120, Phone: 770-382-8478, Web: http://www.fking83264@aol.com
Specialties: Fancy and embellished working straight knives and folders. **Patterns:** Hunters, Bowies and fighters. **Technical:** Grinds ATS-34 and D2: forges 5160 and Damascus. Offers filework. **Prices:** $100 to $3500. **Remarks:** Spare-time maker; first knife sold in 1984. **Mark:** Kings Edge.

KING, JASON M,
5170 Rockenham Rd, St. George, KS 66423, Phone: 785-494-8377, Web: www.jasonmkingknives.com
Specialties: Working and using straight knives of his design and sometimes to customer specs. Some slip joint and lockback folders. **Patterns:** Hunters, Bowies, tacticals, fighters; some miniatures. **Technical:** Grinds D2, 440C and other Damascus. **Prices:** $75 to $200; some up to $500. **Remarks:** First knife sold in 1998. Likes to use height quality stabilized wood. **Mark:** JMK.

KING JR., HARVEY G,
32266 Hwy K4, Alta Vista, KS 66834, Phone: 785-499-5207, Web: www.harveykingknives.com
Specialties: Traditional working and using straight knives of his design and to customer specs. **Patterns:** Hunters, Bowies and fillet knives. **Technical:** Grinds O1, A2 and D2. Prefers natural handle materials; offers leatherwork. **Prices:** Start at $100. **Remarks:** Part-time maker; first knife sold in 1988. **Mark:** Name, city, state, and serial number.

KINKER, MIKE,
8755 E County Rd 50 N, Greensburg, IN 47240, Phone: 812-663-5277, Fax: 812-662-8131, mokinker@hsonline.net
Specialties: Working/using knives, straight knives. Starting to make folders. Your design. Patterns: Boots, daggers, hunters, skinners, hatchets. Technical: Grind 440C and ATS-34, others if required. Damascus, dovetail bolsters, jeweled blade. Prices: $125 to 375; some to $1000. Remarks: Part-time maker; first knife sold in 1991. Doing business as Kinker Knives. Mark: Kinker and Kinker plus year.

KINNIKIN, TODD,
EUREKA FORGE, 8356 John McKeever Rd., House Springs, MO 63051, Phone: 314-938-6248
Specialties: Mosaic Damascus. Patterns: Hunters, fighters, folders and automatics. Technical: Forges own mosaic Damascus with tool steel Damascus edge. Prefers natural, fossil and artifact handle materials. Prices: $400 to $2400. Remarks: Full-time maker; first knife sold in 1994. Mark: Initials connected.

KIOUS, JOE,
1015 Ridge Pointe Rd, Kerrville, TX 78028, Phone: 830-367-2277, Fax: 830-367-2286, kious@hctc.net
Specialties: Investment-quality interframe and bolstered folders. Patterns: Folder specialist, all types. Technical: Both stainless and non-stainless Damascus. Prices: $1300 to $5000; some to $10,000. Remarks: Full-time maker; first knife sold in 1969. Mark: Last name, city and state or last name only.

KIRK, RAY,
PO Box 1445, Tahlequah, OK 74465, Phone: 918-456-1519, ray@rakerknives.com; Web: www.rakerknives.com
Specialties: Folders skinners fighters, and Bowies. Patterns: Neck knives and small hunters and skinners. Technical: Forges all knives from 52100 and own Damascus. Prices: $65 to $3000. Remarks: Started forging in 1989; makes own Damascus. Does custom steel rolling. Has some 52100 and Damascus in custom flat bar 512E3 for sale Mark: Stamped "Raker" on blade.

KITSMILLER, JERRY,
67277 Las Vegas Dr, Montrose, CO 81401, Phone: 970-249-4290
Specialties: Working straight knives in standard patterns. Patterns: Hunters, boots. Technical: Grinds ATS-34 and 440C only. Prices: $75 to $200; some to $300. Remarks: Spare-time maker; first knife sold in 1984. Mark: JandS Knives.

KLAASEE, TINUS,
PO Box 10221, George 6530, SOUTH AFRICA
Specialties: Hunters, skinners and utility knives. Patterns: Uses own designs and client specs. Technical: N690 stainless steel 440C Damascus. Prices: $700 and up. Remarks: Use only indigenous materials. Hardwood, horns and ivory. Makes his own sheaths and boxes. Mark: Initials and sur name over warthog.

KNAPP, MARK,
The Cutting Edge, 1971 Fox Ave, Fairbanks, AK 99701, Phone: 907-452-7477, cuttingedge@gci.net; Web: www.markknappcustomknives.com
Specialties: Mosaic handles of exotic natural materials from Alaska and around the world. Folders, fixed blades, full and hidden tangs. Patterns: Folders, hunters, skinners, and camp knives. Technical: Forges own Damascus, uses both forging and stock removal with ATS-34, 154CM, stainless Damascus, carbon steel and carbon Damascus. Prices: $800-$3000. Remarks: Full time maker, sold first knife in 2000. Mark: Mark Knapp Custom Knives Fairbanks, AK.

KNICKMEYER, HANK,
6300 Crosscreek, Cedar Hill, MO 63016, Phone: 314-285-3210
Specialties: Complex mosaic Damascus constructions. Patterns: Fixed blades, swords, folders and automatics. Technical: Mosaic Damascus with all tool steel Damascus edges. Prices: $500 to $2000; some $3000 and higher. Remarks: Part-time maker; first knife sold in 1989. Doing business as Dutch Creek Forge and Foundry. Mark: Initials connected.

KNICKMEYER, KURT,
6344 Crosscreek, Cedar Hill, MO 63016, Phone: 314-274-0481

KNIGHT, JASON,
110 Paradise Pond Ln, Harleyville, SC 29448, Phone: 843-452-1163, jasonknightknives.com
Specialties: Bowies. Patterns: Bowies and anything from history or his own design. Technical: 1084, 5160, O1, 52102, Damascus/forged blades. Prices: $200 and up. Remarks: Bladesmith. Mark: KNIGHT.

KNIPSCHIELD, TERRY,
808 12th Ave NE, Rochester, MN 55906, Phone: 507-288-7829, terry@knipknives.com; Web: www.knipknives.com
Specialties: Folders and fixed blades and woodcarving knives. Patterns: Variations of traditional patterns and his own new designs. Technical: Stock removal. Grinds CPM-154CM, ATS-34, stainless Damascus, 01. Prices: $60 to $1200 and higher for upscale folders. Mark: Etchd logo on blade, KNIP with shield image.

KNIPSTEIN, R C (JOE),
731 N Fielder, Arlington, TX 76012, Phone: 817-265-0573;817-265-2021, Fax: 817-265-3410
Specialties: Traditional pattern folders along with custom designs. Patterns: Hunters, Bowies, folders, fighters, utility knives. Technical: Grinds 440C, D2, 154CM and ATS-34. Natural handle materials and full tangs are standard. Prices: Start at $300. Remarks: Part-time maker; first knife sold in 1989. Mark: Last name.

KNOTT, STEVE,
KNOTT KNIVES, 203 Wild Rose, Guyton, GA 31312, Phone: 912-772-7655
Technical: Uses ATS-34/440C and some commercial Damascus, single and double grinds with mirror or satin finishes. Patters: Hunters, boot knives, Bowies, and tantos, slip joint and lock-back folders. Uses a wide variety of handle materials to include ironwood, coca-bola and colored stabilized wood, also horn, bone and ivory upon customer request. Remarks: First knife sold in 1991. Part-time maker.

KNUTH, JOSEPH E,
3307 Lookout Dr, Rockford, IL 61109, Phone: 815-874-9597
Specialties: High-art working straight knives of his design or to customer specs. Patterns: Daggers, fighters and swords. Technical: Grinds 440C, ATS-34 and D2. Prices: $150 to $1500; some to $15,000. Remarks: Full-time maker; first knife sold in 1989. Mark: Initials on bolster face.

KOHLS, JERRY,
N4725 Oak Rd, Princeton, WI 54968, Phone: 920-295-3648
Specialties: Working knives and period pieces. Patterns: Hunters-boots and Bowies, your designs or his. Technical: Grinds, ATS-34 440c 154CM and 1095 and commercial Damascus. Remarks: Part-time maker. Mark: Last name.

KOJETIN, W,
20 Bapaume Rd Delville, Germiston 1401, SOUTH AFRICA, Phone: 27118733305/mobile 27836256208
Specialties: High-art and working straight knives of all designs. Patterns: Daggers, hunters and his own Man hunter Bowie. Technical: Grinds D2 and ATS-34; forges and grinds 440B/C. Offers "wrap-around" pava and abalone handles, scrolled wood or ivory, stacked filework and setting of faceted semi-precious stones. Prices: $185 to $600; some to $11,000. Remarks: Spare-time maker; first knife sold in 1962. Mark: Billy K.

KOLITZ, ROBERT,
W9342 Canary Rd, Beaver Dam, WI 53916, Phone: 920-887-1287
Specialties: Working straight knives to customer specs. Patterns: Bowies, hunters, bird and trout knives, boots. Technical: Grinds O1, 440C; commercial Damascus. Prices: $50 to $100; some to $500. Remarks: Spare-time maker; first knife sold in 1979. Mark: Last initial.

KOMMER, RUSS,
4609 35th Ave N, Fargo, NC 58102, Phone: 907-346-3339
Specialties: Working straight knives with the outdoorsman in mind. Patterns: Hunters, semi-skinners, fighters, folders and utility knives, art knives. Technical: Hollow-grinds ATS-34, 440C and 440V. Prices: $125 to $850; some to $3000. Remarks: Full-time maker; first knife sold in 1995. Mark: Bear paw—full name, city and state or full name and state.

KOPP, TODD M,
PO Box 3474, Apache Jct., AZ 85217, Phone: 480-983-6143, tmkopp@msn.com
Specialties: Classic and traditional straight knives. Fluted handled daggers. Patterns: Bowies, boots, daggers, fighters, hunters, swords and folders. Technical: Grinds 5160, 440C, ATS-34. All Damascus steels, or customers choice. Some engraving and filework. Prices: $200 to $1200; some to $4000. Remarks: Part-time maker; first knife sold in 1989. Mark: Last name in Old English, some others name, city and state.

KOSTER, STEVEN C,
16261 Gentry Ln, Huntington Beach, CA 92647, Phone: 714-840-8621, hbkosters@verizon.net
Specialties: Bowies, daggers, skinners, camp knives. Technical: Use 5160, 52100, 1084, 1095 steels. Prices: $200 to $1000. Remarks: Wood and leather sheaths with silver furniture. ABS Journeyman 2003. Mark: Koster squeezed between lines.

KOVACIK, ROBERT,
Erenburgova 23, Lucenec 98407, SLOVAKIA, Phone: 00421474332566 Mobil:00421470907644800, Fax: 00421470907644800, robert.kovacik@post.sk Web: www.robertkovacik.com
Specialties: Engraved hunting knives, guns engraved; Knifemakers. Technical: Fixed blades, folder knives, miniatures. Prices: $350 to $20,000 U.S. Mark: R.

KOVAR, EUGENE,
2626 W 98th St., Evergreen Park, IL 60642, Phone: 708-636-3724/708-790-4115, baldemaster333@aol.com
Specialties: One-of-a-kind miniature knives only. Patterns: Fancy to fantasy miniature knives; knife pendants and tie tacks. Technical: Files and grinds nails, nickel-silver and sterling silver. Prices: $5 to $35; some to $100. Mark: GK.

KOYAMA, CAPTAIN BUNSHICHI,
3-23 Shirako-cho, Nakamura-ku, Nagoya City 453-0817, JAPAN, Phone: 052-461-7070, Fax: 052-461-7070
Specialties: Innovative folding knife. Patterns: General purpose one hand. Technical: Grinds ATS-34 and Damascus. Prices: $400 to $900; some to $1500. Remarks: Part-time maker; first knife sold in 1994. Mark: Captain B. Koyama and the shoulder straps of CAPTAIN.

KRAFT, STEVE,
408 NE 11th St, Abilene, KS 67410, Phone: 785-263-1411
Specialties: Folders, lockbacks, scale release auto, push button auto. Patterns: Hunters, boot knives and fighters. Technical: Grinds ATS-34, Damascus; uses titanium, pearl, ivory etc. Prices: $500 to $2500. Remarks: Part-time maker; first knife sold in 1984. Mark: Kraft.

KRAPP, DENNY,
1826 Windsor Oak Dr, Apopka, FL 32703, Phone: 407-880-7115
Specialties: Fantasy and working straight knives of his design. Patterns: Hunters, fighters and utility/camp knives. Technical: Grinds ATS-34 and 440C. Prices: $85 to $300; some to $800. Remarks: Spare-time maker; first knife sold in 1988. Mark: Last name.

KRAUSE, ROY W,
22412 Corteville, St. Clair Shores, MI 48081, Phone: 810-296-3995, Fax: 810-296-2663
Specialties: Military and law enforcement/Japanese-style knives and swords. Patterns: Combat and back-up, Bowies, fighters, boot knives, daggers, tantos, wakazashis and katanas. Technical: Grinds ATS-34, A2, D2, 1045, O1 and commercial Damascus; differentially hardened Japanese-style blades. Prices: Moderate to upscale. Remarks: Full-time maker. Mark: Last name on traditional knives; initials in Japanese characters on Japanese-style knives.

KREGER, THOMAS,
1996 Dry Branch Rd., Lugoff, SC 29078, Phone: 803-438-4221, tdkreger@bellsouth.net
Specialties: South Carolina/George Herron style working/using knives. Customer designs considered. Patterns: Hunters, skinners, fillet, liner lock folders, kitchen, and camp knives. Technical: Hollow and flat grinds of ATS-34, CPM154CM, and 5160. Prices: $100 and up. Remarks: Full-time maker. President of the South Carolina Association of Knifemakers 2002-06. Mark: TDKreger.

KREH, LEFTY,
210 Wichersham Way, "Cockeysville", MD 21030

KREIBICH, DONALD L.,
1638 Commonwealth Circle, Reno, NV 89503, Phone: 775-746-0533, dmkreno@sbcglobal.net
Specialties: Working straight knives in standard patterns. Patterns: Bowies, boots and daggers; camp and fishing knives. Technical: Grinds 440C, 154CM and ATS-34; likes integrals. Prices: $100 to $200; some to $500. Remarks: Part-time maker; first knife sold in 1980. Mark: First and middle initials, last name.

KRESSLER, D F,
Mittelweg 31 i, D-28832 Achim, GERMANY, Phone: 49-4202765742, Fax: 49-042 02/7657 41, info@kresslerknives.com; Web: www.kresslerknives.com
Specialties: High-tech integral and interframe knives. Patterns: Hunters, fighters, daggers. Technical: Grinds new state-of-the-art steels; prefers natural handle materials. Prices: Upscale. Mark: Name in logo.

KRETSINGER JR., PHILIP W,
17536 Bakersville Rd, Boonsboro, MD 21713, Phone: 301-432-6771
Specialties: Fancy and traditional period pieces. Patterns: Hunters, Bowies, camp knives, daggers, carvers, fighters. Technical: Forges W2, 5160 and his own Damascus. Prices: Start at $200. Remarks: Full-time knifemaker. Mark: Name.

KUBASEK, JOHN A,
74 Northhampton St, Easthampton, MA 01027, Phone: 413-527-7917, jaknife01@verizon.net
Specialties: Left- and right-handed LinerLock® folders of his design or to customer specs. Also new knives made with Ripcord patent. Patterns: Fighters, tantos, drop points, survival knives, neck knives and belt buckle knives. Technical: Grinds 154CM, S30 and Damascus. Prices: $395 to $1500. Remarks: Part-time maker; first knife sold in 1985. Mark: Name and address etched.

L

LADD, JIM S,
1120 Helen, Deer Park, TX 77536, Phone: 713-479-7286
Specialties: Working knives and period pieces. Patterns: Hunters, boots and Bowies plus other straight knives. Technical: Grinds D2, 440C and 154CM. Prices: $125 to $225; some to $550. Remarks: Part-time maker; first knife sold in 1965. Doing business as The Tinker. Mark: First and middle initials, last name.

LADD, JIMMIE LEE,
1120 Helen, Deer Park, TX 77536, Phone: 713-479-7186
Specialties: Working straight knives. Patterns: Hunters, skinners and utility knives. Technical: Grinds 440C and D2. Prices: $75 to $225. Remarks: First knife sold in 1979. Mark: First and middle initials, last name.

LAGRANGE, FANIE,
12 Canary Crescent, Table View 7441, SOUTH AFRICA, Phone: 27 21 55 76 805
Specialties: African-influenced styles in folders and fixed blades. Patterns: All original patterns with many one-of-a-kind. Technical: Mostly stock removal in 12C27, ATS-34, stainless Damascus. Prices: $350 to $3000. Remarks: Professional maker. SA Guild member. Mark: Name over spear.

LAINSON, TONY,
114 Park Ave, Council Bluffs, IA 51503, Phone: 712-322-5222
Specialties: Working straight knives, liner locking folders. Technical: Grinds 154CM, ATS-34, 440C buys Damascus. Handle materials include Micarta, carbon fiber G-10 ivory pearl and bone. Prices: $95 to $600. Remarks: Part-time maker; first knife sold in 1987. Mark: Name and state.

LAIRSON SR., JERRY,
H C 68 Box 970, Ringold, OK 74754, Phone: 580-876-3426, bladesmt@brightok.net; Web: www.lairson-custom-knives.net
Specialties: Damascus collector grade knives & high performance field grade hunters & cutting competition knives. Patterns: Damascus, random, raindrop, ladder, twist and others. Technical: All knives hammer forged. Mar Tempering Prices: Field grade knives $300. Collector grade $400 & up. Mark: Lairson. Remarks: Makes any style knife but prefer fighters and hunters. ABS Mastersmith, AKA member, KGA member. Cutting competition competitor.

LAKE, RON,
3360 Bendix Ave, Eugene, OR 97401, Phone: 541-484-2683
Specialties: High-tech working knives; inventor of the modern interframe folder. Patterns: Hunters, boots, etc.; locking folders. Technical: Grinds 154CM and ATS-34. Patented interframe with special lock release tab. Prices: $2200 to $3000; some higher. Remarks: Full-time maker; first knife sold in 1966. Mark: Last name.

LALA, PAULO RICARDO P AND LALA, ROBERTO P.,
R Daniel Martins 636, Centro, Presidente Prudente, SP-19031-260, BRAZIL, Phone: 0182-210125, Web: http://www.orbita.starmedia/~korth
Specialties: Straight knives and folders of all designs to customer specs. Patterns: Bowies, daggers fighters, hunters and utility knives. Technical: Grinds and forges D6, 440C, high-carbon steels and Damascus. Prices: $60 to $400; some higher. Remarks: Full-time makers; first knife sold in 1991. All stainless steel blades are ultra sub-zero quenched. Mark: Sword carved on top of anvil under KORTH.

LAMB, CURTIS J,
3336 Louisiana Ter, Ottawa, KS 66067-8996, Phone: 785-242-6657

LAMBERT, JARRELL D,
2321 FM 2982, Granado, TX 77962, Phone: 512-771-3744
Specialties: Traditional working and using straight knives of his design and to customer specs. Patterns: Bowies, hunters, tantos and utility/ camp knives. Technical: Grinds ATS-34; forges W2 and his own Damascus. Makes own sheaths. Prices: $80 to $600; some to $1000. Remarks: Part-time maker; first knife sold in 1982. Mark: Etched first and middle initials, last name; or stamped last name.

LAMBERT, KIRBY,
536 College Ave, Regina Saskatchewan S4N X3, CANADA, kirby@lambertknives.com; Web: www.lambertknives.com
Specialties: Tactical/utility folders. Tactical/utility Japanese style fixed blades. Prices: $200 to $1500 U.S. Remarks: Full-time maker since 2002. Mark: Black widow spider and last name Lambert.

LAMEY, ROBERT M,
15800 Lamey Dr, Biloxi, MS 39532, Phone: 228-396-9066, Fax: 228-396-9022, rmlamey@ametro.net; Web: www.lameyknives.com
Specialties: Bowies, fighters, hard use knives. Patterns: Bowies, fighters, hunters and camp knives. Technical: Forged and stock removal. Prices: $125 to $350. Remarks: Lifetime reconditioning; will build to customer designs, specializing in hard use, affordable knives. Mark: LAMEY.

LAMPSON, FRANK G,
3215 Saddle Bag Circle, Rimrock, AZ 86335, Phone: 928-567-7395, fglampson@yahoo.com
Specialties: Working folders; one-of-a-kinds. Patterns: Folders, hunters, utility knives, fillet knives and Bowies. Technical: Grinds ATS-34, 440C and 154CM. Prices: $100 to $750; some to $3500. Remarks: Full-time maker; first knife sold in 1971. Mark: Name in fish logo.

LANCASTER, C G,
No 2 Schoonwinkel St, Parys, Free State, SOUTH AFRICA, Phone: 0568112090
Specialties: High-tech working and using knives of his design and to customer specs. Patterns: Hunters, locking folders and utility/camp knives. Technical: Grinds Sandvik 12C27, 440C and D2. Offers anodized titanium bolsters. Prices: $450 to $750; some to $1500. Remarks: Part-time maker; first knife sold in 1990. Mark: Etched logo.

LANCE, BILL,
PO Box 4427, Eagle River, AK 99577, Phone: 907-694-1487
Specialties: Ooloos and working straight knives; limited issue sets. Patterns: Several ulu patterns, drop-point skinners. Technical: Uses ATS-34, Vascomax 350; ivory, horn and high-class wood handles. Prices: $85 to $300; art sets to $3000. Remarks: First knife sold in 1981. Mark: Last name over a lance.

LANDERS, JOHN,
758 Welcome Rd, Newnan, GA 30263, Phone: 404- 253-5719
Specialties: High-art working straight knives and folders of his design. **Patterns:** Hunters, fighters and slip-joint folders. **Technical:** Grinds 440C, ATS-34, 154CM and commercial Damascus. **Prices:** $85 to $250; some to $500. **Remarks:** Part-time maker; first knife sold in 1989. **Mark:** Last name.

LANE, BEN,
4802 Massie St, North Little Rock, AR 72218, Phone: 501- 753-8238
Specialties: Fancy straight knives of his design and to customer specs; period pieces. **Patterns:** Bowies, hunters, utility/camp knives. **Technical:** Grinds D2 and 154CM; forges and grinds 1095. Offers intricate handle work including inlays and spacers. **Prices:** $120 to $450; some to $5000. **Remarks:** Part-time maker; first knife sold in 1989. **Mark:** Full name, city, state.

LANER, DEAN,
1480 Fourth St, Susanville, CA 96130, Phone: 530-310- 1917, laner54knives@yahoo.com
Specialties: Fancy working fixed blades, of his design, will do custom orders. **Patterns:** Hunters, fighters, combat, fishing, Bowies, utility, and kitchen knives. **Technical:** Grinds 154CM, ATS-34, D2, buys Damascus. Does mostly hollow grinding, some flat grinds. Uses Micarta, mastodon ivory, hippo ivory, exotic woods. Loves doing spacer work on stick tang knives. A leather or kydes sheath comes with every knife. Life-time warrantee and free sharpening also. **Remarks:** Part-time maker, first knife sold in 1993. **Prices:** $150 to $1000. **Mark:** LANER CUSTOM KNIVES over D next to a tree.

LANGLEY, GENE H,
1022 N. Price Rd, Florence, SC 29506, Phone: 843-669-3150
Specialties: Working knives in standard patterns. **Patterns:** Hunters, boots, fighters, locking folders and slip-joints. **Technical:** Grinds 440C, 154CM and ATS-34. **Prices:** $125 to $450; some to $1000. **Remarks:** Part-time maker; first knife sold in 1979. **Mark:** Name.

LANGLEY, MICK,
1015 Centre Crescent, Qualicum Beach, B.C., CANADA V9K 2G6, Phone: 250-752-4261
Specialties: Period pieces and working knives. **Patterns:** Bowies, push daggers, fighters, boots. Some folding lockers. **Technical:** Forges 5160, 1084, W2 and his own Damascus. **Prices:** $250 to $2500; some to $4500. **Remarks:** Full-time maker, first knife sold in 1977. **Mark:** Langley with M.S. (for ABS Master Smith)

LANKTON, SCOTT,
8065 Jackson Rd. R-11, Ann Arbor, MI 48103, Phone: 313-426-3735
Specialties: Pattern welded swords, krisses and Viking period pieces. **Patterns:** One-of-a-kind. **Technical:** Forges W2, L6 nickel and other steels. **Prices:** $600 to $12,000. **Remarks:** Part-time bladesmith, full- time smith; first knife sold in 1976. **Mark:** Last name logo.

LAOISLAV, SANTA-LASKY,
Tatranska 32 97401 Banska, Bystrica, SLOVAKIA, santa.ladislav@pobox.sk; Web: www.lasky.sk
Specialties: Damascus hunters, daggers and swords. **Patterns:** Carious Damascus patterns. **Prices:** $300 to 6000 U.S. **Mark:** L or Lasky.

LAPEN, CHARLES,
Box 529, W. Brookfield, MA 01585
Specialties: Chef's knives for the culinary artist. **Patterns:** Camp knives, Japanese-style swords and wood working tools, hunters. **Technical:** Forges 1075, car spring and his own Damascus. Favors narrow and Japanese tangs. **Prices:** $200 to $400; some to $2000. **Remarks:** Part-time maker; first knife sold in 1972. **Mark:** Last name.

LAPLANTE, BRETT,
4545 CR412, McKinney, TX 75071, Phone: 972- 838-9191, blap007@aol.com
Specialties: Working straight knives and folders to customer specs. **Patterns:** Survival knives, Bowies, skinners, hunters. **Technical:** Grinds D2 and 440C. Heat-treats. **Prices:** $200 to $800. **Remarks:** Part-time maker; first knife sold in 1987. **Mark:** Last name in Canadian maple leaf logo.

LARAMIE, MARK,
301 McCain St., Raeford, NC 28376, Phone: 978- 502-2726, mark@malknives.com; Web: www.malknives.com
Specialties: Traditional fancy & art knives. **Patterns:** Slips, back-lock L/ L, automatics, single and multi blades. **Technical:** Free hand ground blades of D2, 440, and Damascus. **Mark:** M.A.L. Knives w/fish logo.

LARGIN,
KELGIN KNIVES, 104 Knife Works Ln, Sevierville, TN 37876, Phone: 765-969-5012, kelginfinecutlery@hotmail.com; Web: wwwkelgin.com
Specialties: Retired from general knife making. Only take limited orders in meteorite Damascus or solid meteorite blades. **Patterns:** Any. **Technical:** Stock removal or forged. **Prices:** $500 & up. **Remarks:** Run the Kelgin Knife Makers Co-op at Smoky Mtn. Knife Works. **Mark:** K.C. Largin - Kelgin mark retired in 2004.

LARSON, RICHARD,
549EHawkeyeAve,Turlock,CA95380,Phone:209-668-1615,lebatardknives@aol.com
Specialties: Sound working knives, lightweight folders, practical tactical

knives. **Patterns:** Hunters, trout and bird knives, fish fillet knives, Bowies, tactical sheath knives, one- and two-blade folders. **Technical:** Grinds ATS-34, A2, D2, CPM 3V and commercial. Damascus; forges and grinds 52100, O1 and 1095. Machines folder frames from aircraft aluminum. **Prices:** $40 to $650. **Remarks:** Full-time maker. First knife made in 1974. Offers knife repair, restoration and sharpening. All knives are serial numbered and registered in the name of original purchaser. **Mark:** Stamped last name or etched logo of last name, city, and state.

LARY, ED,
951 Rangeline Rd, Mosinee, WI 54476, Phone: 715-693- 3940, laryblades@hotmail.com
Specialties: Upscale hunters and art knives with display presentations. **Patterns:** Hunters, period pieces. **Technical:** Grinds all steels, heat treats, fancy file work and engraving. **Prices:** Upscale. **Remarks:** Full- time maker since 1974. **Mark:** Hand engraved "Ed Lary" in script.

LAURENT, KERMIT,
1812 Acadia Dr, LaPlace, LA 70068, Phone: 504- 652-5629
Specialties: Traditional and working straight knives and folders of his design. **Patterns:** Bowies, hunters, utilities and folders. **Technical:** Forges own Damascus, plus uses most tool steels and stainless. Specializes in altering cable patterns. Uses stabilized handle materials, especially select exotic woods. **Prices:** $100 to $2500; some to $50,000. **Remarks:** Full-time maker; first knife sold in 1982. Doing business as Kermit's Knife Works. Favorite material is meteorite Damascus. **Mark:** First name.

LAWRENCE, ALTON,
201 W Stillwell, De Queen, AR 71832, Phone: 870-642-7643, Fax: 870-642-4023, uncle21@riversidemachine.net; Web: riversidemachine.net
Specialties: Classic straight knives and folders to customer specs. **Patterns:** Bowies, hunters, folders and utility/camp knives. **Technical:** Forges 5160, 1095, 1084, Damascus and railroad spikes. **Prices:** Start at $100. **Remarks:** Part-time maker; first knife sold in 1988. **Mark:** Last name inside fish symbol.

LAY, L J,
602 Mimosa Dr, Burkburnett, TX 76354, Phone: 940-569-1329
Specialties: Working straight knives in standard patterns; some period pieces. **Patterns:** Drop-point hunters, Bowies and fighters. **Technical:** Grinds ATS-34 to mirror finish; likes Micarta handles. **Prices:** Moderate. **Remarks:** Full-time maker; first knife sold in 1985. **Mark:** Name or name with ram head and city or stamp L J Lay.

LAY, R J (BOB),
Box 1225, Logan Lake, B.C., CANADA V0K 1W0, Phone: 250-523-9923, Fax: SAME, rjlay@telus.net
Specialties: Traditional-styled, fancy straight knifes of his design. Specializing in hunters. **Patterns:** Bowies, fighters and hunters. **Technical:** Grinds 440C, ATS-34, S30V, CPM-154CM. Uses exotic handle and spacer material. File cut, prefers narrow tang. Sheaths available. **Price:** $200 to $500, some to $5000. **Remarks:** Full-time maker, first knife sold in 1976. Doing business as Lay's Custom Knives. **Mark:** Signature acid etched.

LEACH, MIKE J,
5377 W Grand Blanc Rd., Swartz Creek, MI 48473, Phone: 810-655-4850
Specialties: Fancy working knives. **Patterns:** Hunters, fighters, Bowies and heavy-duty knives; slip-joint folders and integral straight patterns. **Technical:** Grinds D2, 440C and 154CM; buys Damascus. **Prices:** Start at $300. **Remarks:** Full-time maker; first knife sold in 1952. **Mark:** First initial, last name.

LEAVITT JR., EARL F,
Pleasant Cove Rd Box 306, E. Boothbay, ME 04544, Phone: 207-633-3210
Specialties: 1500-1870 working straight knives and fighters; pole arms. **Patterns:** Historically significant knives, classic/modern custom designs. **Technical:** Flat-grinds O1; heat-treats. Filework available. **Prices:** $90 to $350; some to $1000. **Remarks:** Full-time maker; first knife sold in 1981. Doing business as Old Colony Manufactory. **Mark:** Initials in oval.

LEBATARD, PAUL M,
14700 Old River Rd, Vancleave, MS 39565, Phone: 228-826-4137, Fax: 228-826-2933, lebatardknives@aol.com
Specialties: Sound working hunting and fillet knives, lightweight folders, practical tactical knives. **Patterns:** Hunters, trout and bird knives, fish fillet knives, kitchen knives, Bowies, tactical sheath knives, lock back folders, one- and two-blade slip joint folders. **Remarks:** Full-time maker, first knife made in 1974. Offers knife repair, restoration and sharpening.

LEBER, HEINZ,
Box 446, Hudson's Hope, B.C., CANADA V0C 1V0, Phone: 250-783-5304
Specialties: Working straight knives of his design. **Patterns:** 20 models, from capers to Bowies. **Technical:** Hollow-grinds D2 and M2 steel; mirror-finishes and full tang only. Likes moose, elk, stone sheep for handles. **Prices:** $175 to $1000. **Remarks:** Full-time maker; first knife sold in 1975. **Mark:** Initials connected.

LECK, DAL,
Box 1054, Hayden, CO 81639, Phone: 970-276-3663
Specialties: Classic, traditional and working knives of his design and in standard patterns; period pieces. **Patterns:** Boots, hunters, fighters and push daggers. **Technical:** Forges O1 and 5160; makes his own Damascus. **Prices:** $175 to $700; some to $1500. **Remarks:** Part- time

maker; first knife sold in 1990. Doing business as The Moonlight Smithy. **Mark:** Stamped: hammer and anvil with initials.

LEE, RANDY,
PO Box 1873, St. Johns, AZ 85936, Phone: 928-337- 2594, Fax: 928-337-5002, randyleeknives@yahoo.com; Web.www.randyleeknives.com
Specialties: Traditional working and using straight knives of his design. **Patterns:** Bowies, fighters, hunters, daggers. **Technical:** Grinds ATS-34, 440C Damascus, and 154CPM. Offers sheaths. **Prices:** $325 to $2500. **Remarks:** Part-time maker; first knife sold in 1979. **Mark:** Full name, city, state.

LELAND, STEVE,
2300 Sir Francis Drake Blvd, Fairfax, CA 94930-1118, Phone: 415-457-0318, Fax: 415-457-0995, Web: www.stephenleland@comcast.net
Specialties: Traditional and working straight knives and folders of his design. **Patterns:** Hunters, fighters, Bowies, chefs. **Technical:** Grinds O1, ATS-34 and 440C. Does own heat treat. Makes nickel silver sheaths. **Prices:** $150 to $750; some to $1500. **Remarks:** Part-time maker; first knife sold in 1987. Doing business as Leland Handmade Knives. **Mark:** Last name.

LEMCKE, JIM L,
10649 Haddington Ste 180, Houston, TX 77043, Phone: 888-461-8632, Fax: 713-461-8221, jimll@hal-pc.org; Web: www.texasknife.com
Specialties: Large supply of custom ground and factory finished blades; knife kits; leather sheaths; in-house heat treating and cryogenic tempering; exotic handle material (wood, ivory, oosik, horn, stabilized woods); machines and supplies for knifemaking; polishing and finishing supplies; heat treat ovens; etching equipment; bar, sheet and rod material (brass, stainless steel, nickel silver); titanium sheet material. Catalog. $4.

LENNON, DALE,
459 County Rd 1554, Alba, TX 75410, Phone: 903- 765-2392, devildaddy1@netzero.net
Specialties: Working / using knives. **Patterns:** Hunters, fighters and Bowies. **Technical:** Grinds high carbon steels, ATS-34, forges some. **Prices:** Starts at $120. **Remarks:** Part-time maker, first knife sold in 2000. **Mark:** Last name.

LEONARD, RANDY JOE,
188 Newton Rd, Sarepta, LA 71071, Phone: 318-994-2712

LEONE, NICK,
9 Georgetown, Pontoon Beach, IL 62040, Phone: 618- 797-1179, nickleone@sbcglobal.net
Specialties: 18th century period straight knives. **Patterns:** Skinners, hunters, neck, leg and friction folders. **Technical:** Forges 5160, W2, O1, 1098, 52100 and his own Damascus. **Prices:** $100 to $1000; some to $3500. **Remarks:** Full-time maker; first knife sold in 1987. Doing business as Anvil Head Forge. **Mark:** Last name, NL, AHF.

LEPORE, MICHAEL J,
66 Woodcutters Dr, Bethany, CT 06524, Phone: 203-393-3823
Specialties: One-of-a-kind designs to customer specs; mostly handmade. **Patterns:** Fancy working straight knives and folders. **Technical:** Forges and grinds W2, W1 and O1; prefers natural handle materials. **Prices:** Start at $350. **Remarks:** Spare-time maker; first knife sold in 1984. **Mark:** Last name.

LERCH, MATTHEW,
N88 W23462 North Lisbon Rd, Sussex, WI 53089, Phone: 262-246-6362, Web: www.lerchcustomknives.com
Specialties: Folders and folders with special mechanisms. **Patterns:** Interframe and integral folders; lock backs, assisted openers, side locks, button locks and liner locks. **Technical:** Grinds ATS-34, 1095, 440 and Damascus. Offers filework and embellished bolsters. **Prices:** $900 and up. **Remarks:** Part-time maker; first knife sold in 1995. **Mark:** Last name.

LEVENGOOD, BILL,
15011 Otto Rd, Tampa, FL 33624, Phone: 813- 961-5688, bill.levengood@verison.net; Web: www.levengoodknives.com
Specialties: Working straight knives and folders. **Patterns:** Hunters, Bowies, folders and collector pieces. **Technical:** Grinds ATS-34, 530V and Damascus. **Prices:** $175 to $1500. **Remarks:** Full time maker; first knife sold in 1983. **Mark:** Last name, city, state.

LEVIN, JACK,
7216 Bay Pkwy, Brooklyn, NY 11204, Phone: 718-232- 8574, jacklevin1@yahoo.com
Specialties: Folders with mechanisms.

LEVINE, BOB,
101 Westwood Dr, Tullahoma, TN 37388, Phone: 931-454-9943, levineknives@msn.com
Specialties: Working left- and right-handed LinerLock® folders. **Patterns:** Hunters and folders. **Technical:** Grinds ATS-34, 440C, D2, O1 and some Damascus; hollow and some flat grinds. Uses sheep horn, fossil ivory, Micarta and exotic woods. Provides custom leather sheath with each fixed knife. **Prices:** Starting at $275. **Remarks:** Full-time maker; first knife sold in 1984. Voting member Knifemakers Guild, German Messermaker Guild. **Mark:** Name and logo.

LEWIS, BILL,
PO Box 63, Riverside, IA 52327, Phone: 319-629-5574, wildbill37@geticonnect.com
Specialties: Folders of all kinds including those made from one-piece of white tail antler with or without the crown. **Patterns:** Hunters, folding hunters, fillet, Bowies, push daggers, etc. **Prices:** $20 to $200. **Remarks:** Full-time maker; first knife sold in 1978. **Mark:** W.E.L.

LEWIS, MIKE,
21 Pleasant Hill Dr, DeBary, FL 32713, Phone: 386-753- 0936, dragonsteel@prodigy.net
Specialties: Traditional straight knives. **Patterns:** Swords and daggers. **Technical:** Grinds 440C, ATS-34 and 5160. Frequently uses cast bronze and cast nickel guards and pommels. **Prices:** $100 to $750. **Remarks:** Part-time maker; first knife sold in 1988. **Mark:** Dragon Steel and serial number.

LEWIS, TOM R,
1613 Standpipe Rd, Carlsbad, NM 88220, Phone: 585-885-3616, lewisknives@carlsbadnm.com; Web: www.cavemen.net/ lewisknives/
Specialties: Traditional working straight knives. **Patterns:** Outdoor knives, hunting knives and Bowies. **Technical:** Grinds ATS-34 forges 5168 and O1. Makes wire, pattern welded and chainsaw Damascus. **Prices:** $140 to $1500. **Remarks:** Part-time maker; first knife sold in 1980. Doing business as TR Lewis Handmade Knives. **Mark:** Lewis family crest.

LICATA, STEVEN,
LICATA CUSTOM KNIVES, 844 Boonton Ave., Boonton, NJ 07005, Phone: 973-588-4909, steven.licata@att.net; Web: steven.licata.home.att.net
Specialties: Fantasy swords and knives. One-of-a-kind sculptures in steel. **Prices:** $200 to $25,000.

LIEBENBERG, ANDRE,
8 Hilma Rd, Bordeauxrandburg 2196, SOUTH AFRICA, Phone: 011-787-2303
Specialties: High-art straight knives of his design. **Patterns:** Daggers, fighters and swords. **Technical:** Grinds 440C and 12C27. **Prices:** $250 to $500; some $4000 and higher. Giraffe bone handles with semi-precious stones. **Remarks:** Spare-time maker; first knife sold in 1990. **Mark:** Initials.

LIEGEY, KENNETH R,
132 Carney Dr, Millwood, WV 25262, Phone: 304-273-9545
Specialties: Traditional working/using straight knives of his design and to customer specs. **Patterns:** Hunters, utility/camp knives, miniatures. **Technical:** Grinds 440C. **Prices:** $75 to $150; some to $300. **Remarks:** Spare-time maker; first knife sold in 1977. **Mark:** First and middle initials, last name.

LIGHTFOOT, GREG,
RR #2, Kitscoty, AB, CANADA T0B 2P0, Phone: 780-846-2812, Pitbull@lightfootknives.com; Web: www.lightfootknives.com
Specialties: Stainless steel and Damascus. **Patterns:** Boots, fighters and locking folders. **Technical:** Grinds BG-42, 440C, D2, CPM steels, Stellite 6K. Offers engraving. **Prices:** $500 to $2000. **Remarks:** Full-time maker; first knife sold in 1988. Doing business as Lightfoot Knives. **Mark:** Shark with Lightfoot Knives below.

LIKARICH, STEVE,
PO Box 961, Colfax, CA 95713, Phone: 530-346- 8480
Specialties: Fancy working knives; art knives of his design. **Patterns:** Hunters, fighters and art knives of his design. **Technical:** Grinds ATS-34, 154CM and 440C; likes high polishes and filework. **Prices:** $200 to $2000; some higher. **Remarks:** Full-time maker; first knife sold in 1987. **Mark:** Name.

LINKLATER, STEVE,
8 Cossar Dr, Aurora, Ont., CANADA L4G 3N8, Phone: 905-727-8929, knifman@sympatico.ca
Specialties: Traditional working/using straight knives and folders of his design. **Patterns:** Fighters, hunters and locking folders. **Technical:** Grinds ATS-34, 440V and D2. **Prices:** $125 to $350; some to $600. **Remarks:** Part-time maker; first knife sold in 1987. Doing business as Links Knives. **Mark:** LINKS.

LISCH, DAVID K,
9239 8th Ave. SW, Seattle, WA 98106, Phone: 206- 919-5431, Web: www.davidlisch.com
Specialties: One-of-a-kind collectibles, straight knives of own design and to customer specs. **Patterns:** Hunters, skinners, Bowies, and fighters. **Technical:** Forges all his own Damascus under 360-pound air hammer. Forges and chisels wrought iron, pure iron, and bronze butt caps. **Prices:** Starting at $350. **Remarks:** Full-time blacksmith, part-time bladesmith. **Mark:** D Lisch.

LISTER JR., WELDON E,
9140 Sailfish Dr, Boerne, TX 78006, Phone: 210-981-2210
Specialties: One-of-a-kind fancy and embellished folders. **Patterns:** Locking and slip-joint folders. **Technical:** Commercial Damascus and O1. All knives embellished. Engraves, inlays, carves and scrimshaws. **Prices:** Upscale. **Remarks:** Spare-time maker; first knife sold in 1991. **Mark:** Last name.

LITTLE, GARY M,
HC84 Box 10301, PO Box 156, Broadbent, OR 97414, Phone: 503-572-2656 **Specialties:** Fancy working knives. **Patterns:** Hunters, tantos, Bowies, axes and buckskinners; locking folders and interframes. **Technical:** Forges and grinds O1, L6, 1095; makes his own Damascus; bronze fittings. **Prices:** $85 to $300; some to $2500. **Remarks:** Full-time maker; first knife sold in 1979. Doing business as Conklin Meadows Forge. **Mark:** Name, city and state.

LITTLE, LARRY,
1A Cranberry Ln, Spencer, MA 01562, Phone: 508- 885-2301 **Specialties:** Working straight knives of his design or to customer specs. Likes Scagel-style. **Patterns:** Hunters, fighters, Bowies, folders. **Technical:** Grinds and forges L6, O1, 5160, 1095, 1080. Prefers natural handle material especially antler. Uses nickel silver. Makes own heavy duty leather sheath. **Prices:** Start at $125. **Remarks:** Part-time maker. First knife sold in 1985. Offers knife repairs. **Mark:** Little on one side, LL brand on the other.

LIVELY, TIM AND MARIAN,
PO Box 1172, Marble Falls, TX 78654, Web: www.livelyknives.com **Specialties:** Multi-cultural primitive knives of their design on speculation. **Patterns:** Old world designs. **Technical:** Hand forges using ancient techniques without electricity; hammer finish. **Prices:** High. **Remarks:** Full-time makers; first knife sold in 1974. Offers knifemaking DVD online. **Mark:** Last name.

LIVESAY, NEWT,
3306 S. Dogwood St, Siloam Springs, AR 72761, Phone: 479-549-3356, Fax: 479-549-3357, newt@newtlivesay.com; Web:www.newtlivesay.com **Specialties:** Combat utility knives, hunting knives, titanium knives, swords, axes, KYDWX sheaths for knives and pistols, custom orders.

LIVINGSTON, ROBERT C,
PO Box 6, Murphy, NC 28906, Phone: 704- 837-4155 **Specialties:** Art letter openers to working straight knives. **Patterns:** Minis to machetes. **Technical:** Forges and grinds most steels. **Prices:** Start at $20. **Remarks:** Full-time maker; first knife sold in 1988. Doing business as Mystik Knifeworks. **Mark:** MYSTIK.

LOCKETT, STERLING,
527 E Amherst Dr, Burbank, CA 91504, Phone: 818-846-5799 **Specialties:** Working straight knives and folders to customer specs. **Patterns:** Hunters and fighters. **Technical:** Grinds. **Prices:** Moderate. **Remarks:** Spare-time maker. **Mark:** Name, city with hearts.

LOERCHNER, WOLFGANG,
WOLFE FINE KNIVES, PO Box 255, Bayfield, Ont., CANADA N0M 1G0, Phone: 519-565-2196 **Specialties:** Traditional straight knives, mostly ornate. **Patterns:** Small swords, daggers and stilettos; locking folders and miniatures. **Technical:** Grinds D2, 440C and 154CM; all knives hand-filed and flat-ground. **Prices:** $300 to $5000; some to $10,000. **Remarks:** Part-time maker; first knife sold in 1983. Doing business as Wolfe Fine Knives. **Mark:** WOLFE.

LONEWOLF, J AGUIRRE,
481 Hwy 105, Demorest, GA 30535, Phone: 706-754-4660, Fax: 706-754-8470, Web: http://hemc.net/~lonewolf **Specialties:** High-art working and using straight knives of his design. **Patterns:** Bowies, hunters, utility/camp knives and fine steel blades. **Technical:** Forges Damascus and high-carbon steel. Most knives have hand-carved moose antler handles. **Prices:** $55 to $500; some to $2000. **Remarks:** Full-time maker; first knife sold in 1980. Doing business as Lonewolf Trading Post. **Mark:** Stamp.

LONG, GLENN A,
10090 SW 186th Ave, Dunnellon, FL 34432, Phone: 352-489-4272, galong99@att.net **Specialties:** Classic working and using straight knives of his design and to customer specs. **Patterns:** Hunters, Bowies, utility. **Technical:** Grinds 440C D2 and 440V. **Prices:** $85 to $300; some to $800. **Remarks:** Part-time maker; first knife sold in 1990. **Mark:** Last name inside diamond.

LONGWORTH, DAVE,
PO Box 222, Neville, OH 45156, Phone: 513- 876-2372 **Specialties:** High-tech working knives. **Patterns:** Locking folders, hunters, fighters and elaborate daggers. **Technical:** Grinds O1, ATS-34, 440C; buys Damascus. **Prices:** $125 to $600; some higher. **Remarks:** Part-time maker; first knife sold in 1980. **Mark:** Last name.

LOOS, HENRY C,
210 Ingraham, New Hyde Park, NY 11040, Phone: 516-354-1943, hcloos@optonline.net **Specialties:** Miniature fancy knives and period pieces of his design. **Patterns:** Bowies, daggers and swords. **Technical:** Grinds O1 and 440C. Uses sterling, 18K, rubies and emeralds. All knives come with handmade hardwood cases. **Prices:** $90 to $195; some to $250. **Remarks:** Spare-time maker; first knife sold in 1990. **Mark:** Script last initial.

LORO, GENE,
2457 State Route 93 NE, Crooksville, OH 43731, Phone: 740-982-4521, Fax: 740-982-1249, geney@aol.com **Specialties:** Hand forged knives. **Patterns:** Damascus, Random, Ladder, Twist, etc. **Technical:** ABS Journeyman Smith. **Prices:** $200 and up. **Remarks:** Loro and hand forged by Gene Loro. **Mark:** Loro. Retired engineer.

LOTT, SHERRY,
1100 Legion Park Rd, Greensburg, KY 42743, Phone: 270-932-2212, sherrylott@alltel.net **Specialties:** One-of-a-kind, usually carved handles. **Patterns:** Art. **Technical:** Carbon steel, stock removal. **Prices:** Moderate. **Mark:** Sherry Lott. **Remarks:** First knife sold in 1994.

LOVE, ED,
19443 Mill Oak, San Antonio, TX 78258, Phone: 210-497- 1021, Fax: 210-497-1021, annaedlove@sbcglobal.net **Specialties:** Hunting, working knives and some art pieces. **Technical:** Grinds ATS-34, and 440C. **Prices:** $150 and up. **Remarks:** Part-time maker. First knife sold in 1980. **Mark:** Name in a weeping heart.

LOVELESS, R W,
PO Box 7836, Riverside, CA 92503, Phone: 951-689- 7800 **Specialties:** Working knives, fighters and hunters of his design. **Patterns:** Contemporary hunters, fighters and boots. **Technical:** Grinds 154CM and ATS-34. **Prices:** $850 to $4950. **Remarks:** Full-time maker since 1969. **Mark:** Name in logo.

LOVESTRAND, SCHUYLER,
1136 19th St SW, Vero Beach, FL 32962, Phone: 772-778-0282, Fax: 772-466-1126, lovestranded@aol.com **Specialties:** Fancy working straight knives of his design and to customer specs; unusual fossil ivories. **Patterns:** Hunters, fighters, Bowies and fishing knives. **Technical:** Grinds stainless steel. **Prices:** $275 and up. **Remarks:** Part-time maker; first knife sold in 1982. **Mark:** Name in logo.

LOVETT, MICHAEL,
PO Box 691551, Killeen, TX 76549, Phone: 254- 554-0956, michaellovett@embarqmail.com **Specialties:** Maker of the authorized Loveless Connection Knives. **Patterns:** Over 40 original R. W. Loveless patterns. **Technical:** ATS-34 ground to Loveless specs. **Prices:** $695 to $5000. **Remarks:** R. W. Loveless - mentor; Jim Merritt - mentor; exact Loveless designs. These renditions of the Loveless Knives are closest money can buy. The intent is for more people to be able to enjoy a true Loveless design. **Mark:** Loveless Authorized Double Nude or football logo

LOZIER, DON,
5394 SE 168th Ave, Ocklawaha, FL 32179, Phone: 352- 625-3576 **Specialties:** Fancy and working straight knives of his design and in standard patterns. **Patterns:** Daggers, fighters, boot knives, and hunters. **Technical:** Grinds ATS-34, 440C and Damascus. Most pieces are highly embellished by notable artisans. Taking limited number of orders per annum. **Prices:** Start at $250; most are $1250 to $3000; some to $12,000. **Remarks:** Full-time maker. **Mark:** Name.

LUCHAK, BOB,
15705 Woodforest Blvd, Channelview, TX 77530, Phone: 281-452-1779 **Specialties:** Presentation knives; start of The Survivor series. **Patterns:** Skinners, Bowies, camp axes, steak knife sets and fillet knives. **Technical:** Grinds 440C. Offers electronic etching; filework. **Prices:** $50 to $1500. **Remarks:** Full-time maker; first knife sold in 1983. Doing business as Teddybear Knives. **Mark:** Full name, city and state with Teddybear logo.

LUCHINI, BOB,
1220 Dana Ave, Palo Alto, CA 94301, Phone: 650-321- 8095, rwluchin@bechtel.com

LUCIE, JAMES R,
4191 E. Fruitport R, Fruitport, MI 49415, Phone: 231- 865-6390, Fax: 231-865-3170, scagel@netonecom.net **Specialties:** Hand-forges William Scagel-style knives. **Patterns:** Authentic scagel-style knives and miniatures. **Technical:** Forges 5160, 52100 and 1084 and forges his own pattern welded Damascus steel. **Prices:** Start at $750. **Remarks:** Full-time maker; first knife sold in 1975. Believes in sole authorship of his work. ABS Journeyman Smith. **Mark:** Scagel Kris with maker's name and address.

LUCKETT, BILL,
108 Amantes Ln, Weatherford, TX 76088, Phone: 817- 594-9288, bill_luckett@hotmail.com **Specialties:** Uniquely patterned robust straight knives. **Patterns:** Fighters, Bowies, hunters. **Technical:** 154CM stainless. **Prices:** $550 to $1500. **Remarks:** Part-time maker; first knife sold in 1975. **Mark:** Last name over Bowie logo.

LUDWIG, RICHARD O,
57-63 65 St, Maspeth, NY 11378, Phone: 718- 497-5969 **Specialties:** Traditional working/using knives. **Patterns:** Boots, hunters and utility/camp knives folders. **Technical:** Grinds 440C, ATS-34 and BG42. File work on guards and handles; silver spacers. Offers scrimshaw. **Prices:** $325 to $400; some to $2000. **Remarks:** Full-time maker. **Mark:** Stamped first initial, last name, state.

LUI, RONALD M,
4042 Harding Ave, Honolulu, HI 96816, Phone: 808- 734-7746 **Specialties:** Working straight knives and folders in standard patterns. **Patterns:** Hunters, boots and liner locks. **Technical:** Grinds 440C and ATS-34. **Prices:** $100 to $700. **Remarks:** Spare-time maker; first knife sold in 1988. **Mark:** Initials connected.

LUM, MITCH,
4616 25th Ave NE #563, Seattle, WA 98105, Phone: 206- 356-6813, mitch@mitchlum.com; Web:www.mitchlum.com

LUM, ROBERT W,
901 Travis Ave, Eugene, OR 97404, Phone: 541- 688-2737
Specialties: High-art working knives of his design. Patterns: Hunters, fighters, tantos and folders. Technical: Grinds 440C, 154CM and ATS- 34; plans to forge soon. Prices: $175 to $500; some to $800. Remarks: Full-time maker; first knife sold in 1976. Mark: Chop with last name underneath.

LUMAN, JAMES R,
Clear Creek Trail, Anaconda, MT 59711, Phone: 406-560-1461
Specialties: San Mai and composite end patterns. Patterns: Pool and eye Spirograph southwest composite patterns. Technical: All patterns with blued steel; all made by him. Prices: $200 to $800. Mark: Stock blade removal. Pattern welded steel. Bottom ricasso JRL.

LUNDSTROM, JAN-AKE,
Mastmostigen 8, 66010 Dals-Langed, SWEDEN, Phone: 0531-40270
Specialties: Viking swords, axes and knives in cooperation with handle makers. Patterns: All traditional-styles, especially swords and inlaid blades. Technical: Forges his own Damascus and laminated steel. Prices: $200 to $1000. Remarks: Full-time maker; first knife sold in 1985; collaborates with museums. Mark: Runic.

LUNN, GAIL,
434 CR 1422, Mountain Home, AR 72653, Phone: 870- 424-2662, gail@lunnknives.com; Web: www.lunnknives.com
Specialties: Fancy folders and double action autos, some straight blades. Patterns: One-of-a-kind, all types. Technical: Stock removal, hand made. Prices: $300 and up. Remarks: Fancy file work, exotic materials, inlays, stone etc. Mark: Name in script.

LUNN, LARRY A,
434 CR 1422, Mountain Home, AR 72653, Phone: 870-424-2662, larry@lunnknives.com; Web: www.lunnknives.com
Specialties: Fancy folders and double action autos; some straight blades. Patterns: All types; his own designs. Technical: Stock removal; commercial Damascus. Prices: $125 and up. Remarks: File work inlays and exotic materials. Mark: Name in script.

LUPOLE, JAMIE G,
KUMA KNIVES, 285 Main St., Kirkwood, NY 13795, Phone: 607-775-9368, jlupole@stny.rr.com
Specialties: Working and collector grade fixed blades, ethnic-styled blades. Patterns: Fighters, Bowies, tacticals, hunters, camp, utility, personal carry knives, some swords. Technical: Forges and grinds 10XX series and other high-carbon steels, grinds ATS-34 and 440C, will use just about every handle material available. Prices: $80 to $500 and up. Remarks: Part-time maker since 1999. Marks: "KUMA" hot stamped, name, city and state-etched, or "Daiguma saku" in kanji.

LUTZ, GREG,
127 Crescent Rd, Greenwood, SC 29646, Phone: 864- 229-7340
Specialties: Working and using knives and period pieces of his design and to customer specs. Patterns: Fighters, hunters and swords. Technical: Forges 1095 and O1; grinds ATS-34. Differentially heat-treats forged blades; uses cryogenic treatment on ATS-34. Prices: $50 to $350; some to $1200. Remarks: Part-time maker; first knife sold in 1986. Doing business as Scorpion Forge. Mark: First initial, last name.

LYLE III, ERNEST L,
LYLE KNIVES, PO Box 1755, Chiefland, FL 32644, Phone: 352-490-6693, ernestlyle@msn.com
Specialties: Fancy period pieces; one-of-a-kind and limited editions. Patterns: Arabian/Persian influenced fighters, military knives, Bowies and Roman short swords; several styles of hunters. Technical: Grinds 440C, D2 and 154 CM. Engraves. Prices: Upscale. Remarks: Full-time maker; first knife sold in 1974. Mark: Last name in capital letters - LYLE over a much smaller Chief land.

LYNCH, TAD,
140 Timberline Dr., Beene, AR 72012, Phone: 501-626- 1647, lynchknives@yahoo.com
Specialties: Forged fixed blades of original design and Bowies based on 19th century examples. Patterns: Hunters, skinners, Bowies, tomahawks, neck knives. Technical: Hand-forged 1084, 1095, clay/edge quenched; 52100; Damascus, san mai. Prices: Starting at $250. Remarks: Part-time maker, also offers custom leather work via wife Amy Lynch. Mark: T.D. Lynch over anvil.

LYNN, ARTHUR,
29 Camino San Cristobal, Galisteo, NM 87540, Phone: 505-466-3541, lynnknives@aol.com
Specialties: Handforged Damascus knives. Patterns: Folders, hunters, Bowies, fighters, kitchen. Technical: Forges own Damascus. Prices: Moderate.

LYTTLE, BRIAN,
Box 5697, High River, AB, CANADA T1V 1M7, Phone: 403-558-3638, brian@lyttleknives.com; Web: www.lyttleknives.com
Specialties: Fancy working straight knives and folders; art knives. Patterns: Bowies, daggers, dirks, sgian dubhs, folders, dress knives, tantos, short swords. Technical: Forges Damascus steel; engraving; scrimshaw; heat-treating; classes. Prices: $450 to $15,000. Remarks: Full-time maker; first knife sold in 1983. Mark: Last name, country.

M

MACDONALD, DAVID,
2824 Hwy 47, Los Lunas, NM 87031, Phone: 505-866-5866

MACDONALD, JOHN,
9 David Dr, Raymond, NH 03077, Phone: 603- 895-0918
Specialties: Working/using straight knives of his design and to customer specs. Patterns: Japanese cutlery, Bowies, hunters and working knives. Technical: Grinds O1, L6 and ATS-34. Swords have matching handles and scabbards with Japanese flair. Prices: $70 to $250; some to $500. Remarks: Part-time maker; first knife sold in 1988. Wood/glass-topped custom cases. Doing business as Mac the Knife. Mark: Initials.

MACKIE, JOHN,
13653 Lanning, Whittier, CA 90605, Phone: 562-945- 6104
Specialties: Forged. Patterns: Bowie and camp knives. Technical: Attended ABS Bladesmith School. Prices: $75 to $500. Mark: JSM in a triangle.

MACKRILL, STEPHEN,
PO Box 1580, Pinegowrie, JHB 2123, SOUTH AFRICA, Phone: 27-11-474-7139, Fax: 27-11-474-7139, info@mackrill.co.za; Web: www.mackrill.net
Specialties: Art fancy, historical, collectors and corporate gifts cutlery. Patterns: Fighters, hunters, camp, custom lock back and LinerLock® folders. Technical: N690, 12C27, ATS-34, silver and gold inlay on handles; wooden and silver sheaths. Prices: $330 and upwards. Remarks: First knife sold in 1978. Mark: Mackrill fish with country of origin.

MADRULLI, MME JOELLE,
Residence Ste Catherine B1, Salon De Provence, FRANCE 13330

MAE, TAKAO,
1-119 1-4 Uenohigashi, Toyonaka, Osaka, JAPAN 560- 0013, Phone: 81-6-6852-2758, Fax: 81-6-6481-1649, takamae@nifty.com
Remarks: Distinction stylish in art-forged blades, with lacquered ergonomic handles.

MAESTRI, PETER A,
S11251 Fairview Rd, Spring Green, WI 53588, Phone: 608-546-4481
Specialties: Working straight knives in standard patterns. Patterns: Camp and fishing knives, utility green-river-styled. Technical: Grinds 440C, 154CM and 440A. Prices: $15 to $45; some to $150. Remarks: Full-time maker; first knife sold in 1981. Provides professional cutler service to professional cutters. Mark: CARISOLO, MAESTRI BROS., or signature.

MAGEE, JIM,
748 S Front #3, Salina, KS 67401, Phone: 785-820-6928, jimmagee@cox.net
Specialties: Working and fancy folding knives. Patterns: Liner locking folders, favorite is his Persian. Technical: Grinds ATS-34, Devin Thomas & Eggerling Damascus, titanium. Liners Prefer mother-of-pearl handles. Prices: Start at $225 to $1200. Remarks: Part-time maker, first knife sold in 2001. Purveyor since 1982. Past president of the Professional Knifemakers Association Mark: Last name.

MAGRUDER, JASON,
10W Saint Elmo Ave, Colorado Springs, CO 80906, Phone: 719-210-1579, belstain@hotmail.com
Specialties: Fancy/embellished and working/using knives of his own design or to customer specs. Fancy filework and carving. Patterns: Tactical straight knives, hunters, Bowies and lockback folders. Technical: Flats grinds S30V, CPM3V, and 1080. Forges own Damascus. Prices: $150 and up. Remarks: Part-time maker; first knife sold in 2000. Mark: Magruder, or initials J M.

MAHOMEDY, A R,
PO Box 76280, Marble Ray KZN, 4035, SOUTH AFRICA, Phone: +27 31 577 1451, arm-koknives@mweb.co.za; Web: www.arm-koknives.co.za
Specialties: Daggers, elegant folders, hunters & utilities. Prefers to work to commissions, collections & presentations. With handles of mother-of-pearl, fossil & local ivories. Exotic dyed/stablized burls, giraffe bone and horns. Technical: Via stock removal grinds Damasteel, carbon and mosaic Damascus, ATS-34, N690, 440A, 440B, 12 C 27 and RWL 34. Prices: $500 and up. Remarks: Part-time maker. First knife sold in 1995. Member knifemakers guild of SA. Mark: Logo of initials A R M crowned with a "Minaret."

MAIENKNECHT, STANLEY,
38648 S R 800, Sardis, OH 43946

MAINES, JAY,
SUNRISE RIVER CUSTOM KNIVES, 5584 266th St., Wyoming, MN 55092, Phone: 651-462-5301, jaymaines@fronternet.net; Web: http://www.sunrisecustomknives.com
Specialties: Heavy duty working, classic and traditional fixed blades. Some high-tech and fancy embellished knives available. Patterns: Hunters, skinners, fillet, bowies tantos, boot daggers etc. etc. Technical: Hollow ground, stock removal blades of 440C, ATS-34 and CPM S-90V. Prefers natural handle materials, exotic hard woods, and stag, rams and buffalo horns. Offers dovetailed bolsters in brass, stainless steel and nickel silver. Custom sheaths from matching wood or hand-stitched from heavy duty

water buffalo hide. **Prices:** Moderate to up-scale. **Remarks:** Part-time maker; first knife sold in 1992. Doing business as Sunrise River Custom Knives. Offers fixed blade knives repair and handle conversions. **Mark:** Full name under a Rising Sun logo.

MAISEY, ALAN,
PO Box 197, Vincentia 2540, NSW, AUSTRALIA, Phone: 2-4443 7829, tosanaji@excite.com
Specialties: Daggers, especially krisses; period pieces. **Technical:** Offers knives and finished blades in Damascus and nickel Damascus. **Prices:** $75 to $2000; some higher. **Remarks:** Part-time maker; provides complete restoration service for krisses. Trained by a Japanese Kris smith. **Mark:** None, triangle in a box, or three peaks.

MAJER, MIKE,
50 Palmetto Bay Rd, Hilton Head, SC 29928, Phone: 843-681-3483

MAKOTO, KUNITOMO,
3-3-18 Imazu-cho, Fukuyama-city, Hiroshima, JAPAN, Phone: 084-933-5874, kunitomo@po.iijnet.or.jp

MALABY, RAYMOND J,
835 Calhoun Ave, Juneau, AK 99801, Phone: 907-586-6981, Fax: 907-523-8031, malaby@gci.net
Specialties: Straight working knives. **Patterns:** Hunters, skiners, Bowies, and camp knives. **Technical:** Hand forged 1084, 5160, O1 and grinds ATS-34 stainless. **Prices:** $195 to $400. **Remarks:** First knife sold in 1994. **Mark:** First initial, last name, city, and state.

MALLOY, JOE,
1039 Schwabe St, Freeland, PA 18224, Phone: 570- 636-2781, jdmalloy@msn.com
Specialties: Working straight knives and lock back folders—plain and fancy—of his design. **Patterns:** Hunters, utility, Bowie, survival knives, folders. **Technical:** Grinds ATS-34, 440C, D2 and A2 and Damascus. Makes own leather and kydex sheaths. **Prices:** $100 to $1800. **Remarks:** Part-time maker; first knife sold in 1982. **Mark:** First and middle initials, last name, city and state.

MANDT, JOE,
3735 Overlook Dr. NE, St. Petersburg, FL 33703, Phone: 813-244-3816, jmforge@mac.com
Specialties: Forged Bowies, camp knives, hunters, skinners, fighters, boot knives, military style field knives. **Technical:** Forges plain carbon steel and high carbon tool steels, including W2, 1084, 5160, O1, 9260, 15N20, cable Damascus, pattern welded Damascus, flat and convex grinds. Prefers natural handle materials, hand-rubbed finishes, and stainless low carbon steel, Damascus and wright iron fittings. Does own heat treat. **Prices:** $150 to $750. **Remarks:** Part-time maker, first knife sold in 206. **Mark:** "MANDT".

MANEKER, KENNETH,
RR 2, Galiano Island, B.C., CANADA V0N 1P0, Phone: 604-539-2084
Specialties: Working straight knives; period pieces. **Patterns:** Camp knives and hunters; French chef knives. **Technical:** Grinds 440C, 154CM and Vascowear. **Prices:** $50 to $200; some to $300. **Remarks:** Part-time maker; first knife sold in 1981. Doing business as Water Mountain Knives. **Mark:** Japanese Kanji of initials, plus glyph.

MANKEL, KENNETH,
7836 Cannonsburg Rd, PO Box 35, Cannonsburg, MI 49317, Phone: 616-874-6955, Fax: 616-8744-4053

MANLEY, DAVID W,
3270 Six Mile Hwy, Central, SC 29630, Phone: 864-654-1125, dmanleyknives@wmconnect.com
Specialties: Working straight knives of his design or to custom specs. **Patterns:** Hunters, boot and fighters. **Technical:** Grinds 440C and ATS- 34. **Prices:** $60 to $250. **Remarks:** Part-time maker; first knife sold in 1994. **Mark:** First initial, last name, year and serial number.

MANN, MICHAEL L,
IDAHO KNIFE WORKS, PO Box 144, Spirit Lake, ID 83869, Phone: 509 994-9394, Web: www.idahoknifeworks.com
Specialties: Good working blades-historical reproduction, modern or custom design. **Patterns:** Cowboy Bowies, Mountain Man period blades, old-style folders, designer and maker of "The Cliff Knife", hunter knives, hand ax and fish fillet. **Technical:** High-carbon steel blades-hand forged 5160. Stock removed 15N20 steel. Also Damascus. **Prices:** $130 to $670+. **Remarks:** Made first knife in 1965. Full-time making knives as Idaho Knife Works since 1986. Functional as well as collectible. Each knife truly unique! **Mark:** Four mountain peaks are his initials MM.

MANN, TIM,
BLADEWORKS, PO Box 1196, Honokaa, HI 96727, Phone: 808-775-0949, Fax: 808-775-0949, birdman@shaka.com
Specialties: Hand-forged knives and swords. **Patterns:** Bowies, tantos, pesh kabz, daggers. **Technical:** Use 5160, 1050, 1075, 1095 and ATS- 34 steels, cable Damascus. **Prices:** $200 to $800. **Remarks:** Just learning to forge Damascus. **Mark:** None yet.

MARAGNI, DAN,
RD 1 Box 106, Georgetown, NY 13072, Phone: 315- 662-7490
Specialties: Heavy-duty working knives, some investor class. **Patterns:** Hunters, fighters and camp knives, some Scottish types. **Technical:** Forges

W2 and his own Damascus; toughness and edge-holding a high priority. **Prices:** $125 to $500; some to $1000. **Remarks:** Full-time maker; first knife sold in 1975. **Mark:** Celtic initials in circle.

MARINGER, TOM,
2692 Powell St., Springdale, AR 72764, maringer@arkansas.net; Web: shirepost.com/cutlery.
Specialties: Working straight and curved blades with stainless steel furniture and wire-wrapped handles. **Patterns:** Subhilts, daggers, boots, swords. **Technical:** Grinds D-2, A-2, ATS-34. May be safely disassembled by the owner via pommel screw or pegged construction. **Prices:** $2000 to $3000, some to $20,000. **Remarks:** Former full-time maker, now part-time. First knife sold in 1975. **Mark:** Full name, year, and serial number etched on tang under handle.

MARKLEY, KEN,
7651 Cabin Creek Lane, Sparta, IL 62286, Phone: 618-443-5284
Specialties: Traditional working and using knives of his design and to customer specs. **Patterns:** Fighters, hunters and utility/camp knives. **Technical:** Forges 5160, 1095 and L6; makes his own Damascus; does file work. **Prices:** $150 to $800; some to $2000. **Remarks:** Part-time maker; first knife sold in 1991. Doing business as Cabin Creek Forge. **Mark:** Last name, JS.

MARLOWE, CHARLES,
10822 Poppleton Ave, Omaha, NE 68144, Phone: 402-933-5065, cmarlowe1@cox.net; Web: www.marloweknives.com
Specialties: Folding knives and balisong. **Patterns:** Tactical pattern folders. **Technical:** Grind ATS-34, S30V, CPM154, 154CM, Damasteel, others on request. Forges/grinds 1095 on occasion. **Prices:** Start at $450. **Remarks:** First knife sold in 1993. Full-time since 1999. **Mark:** Turtle logo with Marlowe above, year below.

MARLOWE, DONALD,
2554 Oakland Rd, Dover, PA 17315, Phone: 717-764-6055
Specialties: Working straight knives in standard patterns. **Patterns:** Bowies, fighters, boots and utility knives. **Technical:** Grinds D2 and 440C. Integral design hunter models. **Prices:** $130 to $850. **Remarks:** Spare-time maker; first knife sold in 1977. **Mark:** Last name.

MARSH, JEREMY,
6169 3 Mile NE, Ada, MI 49301, Phone: 616-889- 1945, steelbean@hotmail.com; Web: www.marshcustomknives.com
Specialties: Locking liner folders, dressed-up gents knives, tactical knives, and dress tacticals. **Technical:** CPM S30V stainless and Damascus blade steels using the stock-removal method of bladesmithing. **Prices:** $450 to $1500. **Remarks:** Self-taught, part-time knifemaker; first knife sold in 2004. **Mark:** Maker's last name and large, stylized M.

MARSHALL, GLENN,
PO Box 1099, 305 Hoffmann St., Mason, TX 76856, Phone: 325-347-6207
Specialties: Working knives, hunting knives, special folders, period pieces, and commemmorative knives. **Patterns:** Straight and folding hunters, fighters and camp knives. **Technical:** Steel used 440C, D2, CPM and 440V. **Prices:** $200 and up according to options. **Remarks:** Full-time maker; first knife sold in 1930. Sold #1 in 1932. **Mark:** First initial, last name, city and state with anvil logo.

MARSHALL, STEPHEN R,
975 Harkreader Rd, Mt. Juliet, TN 37122

MARTIN, BRUCE E,
Rt. 6, Box 164-B, Prescott, AR 71857, Phone: 501- 887-2023
Specialties: Fancy working straight knives of his design. **Patterns:** Bowies, camp knives, skinners and fighters. **Technical:** Forges 5160, 1095 and his own Damascus. Uses natural handle materials; filework available. **Prices:** $75 to $350; some to $500. **Remarks:** Full-time maker; first knife sold in 1979. **Mark:** Name in arch.

MARTIN, GENE,
PO Box 396, Williams, OR 97544, Phone: 541-846- 6755, bladesmith@customknife.com
Specialties: Straight knives and folders. **Patterns:** Fighters, hunters, skinners, boot knives, spring back and lock back folders. **Technical:** Grinds ATS-34, 440C, Damascus and 154CM. Forges; makes own Damascus; scrimshaws. **Prices:** $150 to $2500. **Remarks:** Full-time maker; first knife sold in 1993. Doing business as Provision Forge. **Mark:** Name and/or crossed staff and sword.

MARTIN, HAL W,
781 Hwy 95, Morrilton, AR 72110, Phone: 501-354- 1682, hal.martin@sbcglobal.net
Specialties: Hunters, Bowies and fighters. **Prices:** $250 and up. **Mark:** MARTIN.

MARTIN, HERB,
2500 Starwood Dr, Richmond, VA 23229, Phone: 804- 747-1675, hamjlm@earthlink.net
Specialties: Working straight knives. **Patterns:** Skinners, hunters and utility. **Technical:** Hollow grinds ATS-34, and Micarta handles. **Prices:** $85 to $125. **Remarks:** Part-time Maker. First knife sold in 2001. **Mark:** HA MARTIN.

MARTIN, MICHAEL W,
Box 572, Jefferson St, Beckville, TX 75631, Phone: 903-678-2161
Specialties: Classic working/using straight knives of his design and in standard patterns. **Patterns:** Hunters. **Technical:** Grinds ATS-34, 440C, O1 and A2. Bead blasted, Parkerized, high polish and satin finishes. Sheaths are handmade. Also hand forges cable Damascus. **Prices:** $185 to $280 some higher. **Remarks:** Part-time maker; first knife sold in 1995. Doing business as Michael W. Martin Knives. **Mark:** Name and city, state in arch.

MARTIN, PETER,
28220 N. Lake Dr, Waterford, WI 53185, Phone: 262- 706-3076, Web: www.petermartinknives.com
Specialties: Fancy, fantasy and working straight knives and folders of his design and in standard patterns. **Patterns:** Bowies, fighters, hunters, locking folders and liner locks. **Technical:** Forges own Mosaic Damascus, powdered steel and his own Damascus. Prefers natural handle material; offers file work and carved handles. **Prices:** Moderate. **Remarks:** Full-time maker; first knife sold in 1988. Doing business as Martin Custom Products. Uses only natural handle materials. **Mark:** Martin Knives.

MARTIN, RANDALL J,
51 Bramblewood St, Bridgewater, MA 02324, Phone: 508-279-0682
Specialties: High tech folding and fixed blade tactical knives employing the latest blade steels and exotic materials. Employs a unique combination of 3d-CNC machining and hand work on both blades and handles. All knives are designed for hard use. Clean, radical grinds and ergonomic handles are hallmarks of RJ's work, as is his reputation for producing "Scary Sharp" knives. **Technical:** Grinds CPM30V, CPM 3V, CPM154CM, A2 and stainless Damascus. Other CPM alloys used on request. Performs all heat treating and cryogenic processing in-house. **Remarks:** Full-time maker since 2001 and materials engineer. Former helicopter designer. First knife sold in 1976.

MARTIN, TONY,
108 S. Main St., PO Box 324, Arcadia, MO 63621, Phone: 573-546-2254, arcadian@charter.net; Web: www.arcadianforge.com
Specialties: Specializes in historical designs, esp. puukko, skean dhu. **Remarks:** Premium quality blades, exotic wood handles, unmatched fit and finish. **Mark:** AF.

MARTIN, WALTER E,
570 Cedar Flat Rd, Williams, OR 97544, Phone: 541-846-6755
MARTIN

MARTIN, JOHN ALEXANDER,
821 N Grand Ave, Okmulgee, OK 74447, Phone: 918-758-1099, jam@jamblades.com; Web: www.jamblades.com
Specialties: Inlaid and engraved handles. **Patterns:** Bowies, fighters, hunters and traditional patterns. Swords, fixed blade knives, folders and axes. **Technical:** Forges 5160, 1084, 10XX, O1, L6 and his own Damascus. **Prices:** Start at $300. **Remarks:** Part-time maker. **Mark:** Two initials with last name and MS or 5 pointed star.

MARZITELLI, PETER,
19929 35A Ave, Langley, B.C., CANADA V3A 2R1, Phone: 604-532-8899, marzitelli@shaw.ca
Specialties: Specializes in unique functional knife shapes and designs using natural and synthetic handle materials. **Patterns:** Mostly folders, some daggers and art knives. **Technical:** Grinds ATS-34, S/S Damascus and others. **Prices:** $220 to $1000 (average $375). **Remarks:** Full-time maker; first knife sold in 1984. **Mark:** Stylized logo reads "Marz."

MASON, BILL,
1114 St Louis #33, Excelsior Springs, MO 64024, Phone: 816-637-7335
Specialties: Combat knives; some folders. **Patterns:** Fighters to match knife types in book *Cold Steel*. **Technical:** Grinds O1, 440C and ATS-34. **Prices:** $115 to $250; some to $350. **Remarks:** Spare-time maker; first knife sold in 1979. **Mark:** Initials connected.

MASSEY, AL,
Box 14 Site 15 RR#2, Mount Uniacke, Nova Scotia, CANADA B0N 1Z0, Phone: 902-866-4754, armjan@attcanada.ca
Specialties: Working knives and period pieces. **Patterns:** Swords and daggers of Celtic to medieval design, Bowies. **Technical:** Forges 5160, 1084 and 1095. Makes own Damascus. **Prices:** $100 to $400, some to $900. **Remarks:** Part-time maker, first blade sold in 1988. **Mark:** Initials and JS on Ricasso.

MASSEY, ROGER,
4928 Union Rd, Texarkana, AR 71854, Phone: 870- 779-1018
Specialties: Traditional and working straight knives and folders of his design and to customer specs. **Patterns:** Bowies, hunters, daggers and utility knives. **Technical:** Forges 1084 and 52100, makes his own Damascus. Offers filework and silver wire inlay in handles. **Prices:** $200 to $1500; some to $2500. **Remarks:** Part-time maker; first knife sold in 1991. **Mark:** Last name, M.S.

MASSEY, RON,
61638 El Reposo St., Joshua Tree, CA 92252, Phone: 760-366-9239 after 5 p.m., Fax: 763-366-4620
Specialties: Classic, traditional, fancy/embellished, high art, period pieces, working/using knives, straight knives, folders, and automatics. Your design, customer specs, about 175 standard patterns. **Patterns:** Automatics, hunt-

ers and fighters. All folders are side-locking folders. Unless requested as lock books slip joint he specializes or custom designs. **Technical:** ATS-34, 440C, D-2 upon request. Engraving, filework, scrimshaw, most of the exotic handle materials. All aspects are performed by him: inlay work in pearls or stone, handmade Pem' work. **Prices:** $110 to $2500; some to $6000. **Remarks:** Part-time maker; first knife sold in 1976.

MATA, LEONARD,
3583 Arruza St, San Diego, CA 92154, Phone: 619- 690-6935

MATHEWS, CHARLIE AND HARRY,
TWIN BLADES, 121 Mt Pisgah Church Rd., Statesboro, GA 30458, Phone: 912-865-9098, twinblades@bulloch.net; Web: www.twinxblades.com
Specialties: Working straight knives, carved stag knives. **Patterns:** Hunters, fighters, Bowies and period pieces. **Technical:** Grinds D2, CPMS30V, CPM3V, ATS-34 and commercial Damascus; handmade sheaths some with exotic leather, file work. Forges 1095, 1084, and 5160. **Prices:** Starting at $125. **Remarks:** Twin brothers making knives full-time under the label of Twin Blades. Charter members Georgia Custom Knifemakers Guild. Members of The Knifemakers Guild. **Mark:** Twin Blades over crossed knives, reverse side steel type.

MATSUNO, KANSEI,
109-8 Uenomachi Nishikaiden, Gifu-City 501- 1168, JAPAN, Phone: 81 58 234 8643

MATSUOKA, SCOT,
94-415 Ukalialii Place, Mililani, HI 96789, Phone: 808-625-6658, Fax: 808-625-6658, scottym@hawaii.rr.com; Web: www.matsuokaknives.com
Specialties: Folders, fixed blades with custom hand-stitched sheaths. **Patterns:** Gentleman's knives, hunters, tactical folders. **Technical:** CPM 154CM, 440C, 154, BG42, bolsters, file work, and engraving. **Prices:** Starting price $350. **Remarks:** Part-time maker, first knife sold in 2002. **Mark:** Logo, name and state.

MATSUSAKI, TAKESHI,
MATSUSAKI KNIVES, 151 Ono-Cho Sasebo- shi, Nagasaki, JAPAN, Phone: 0956-47-2938, Fax: 0956-47-2938
Specialties: Working and collector grade front look and slip joint. **Patterns:** Sheffield type folders. **Technical:** Grinds ATS-34 k-120. **Price:** $250 to $1000, some to $8000. **Remarks:** Part-time maker, first knife sold in 1990. **Mark:** Name and initials.

MAXEN, MICK,
2 Huggins Welham Green, "Hatfield, Herts", UNITED KINGDOM AL97LR, Phone: 01707 261213, mmaxen@aol.com
Specialties: Damascus and Mosaic. **Patterns:** Medieval-style daggers and Bowies. **Technical:** Forges CS75 and 15N20 / nickel Damascus. **Mark:** Last name with axe above.

MAXFIELD, LYNN,
382 Colonial Ave, Layton, UT 84041, Phone: 801- 544-4176, maxfieldknives@q.com
Specialties: Sporting knives, some fancy. **Patterns:** Hunters, fishing, fillet, special purpose; some locking folders. **Technical:** Grinds 440-C, 154-CM, CPM154, D2, CPM S30V, and Damascus. **Prices:** $125 to $400; some to $900. **Remarks:** Part-time maker; first knife sold in 1979. **Mark:** Name, city and state.

MAXWELL, DON,
1484 Celeste Ave, Clovis, CA 93611, Phone: 559- 299-2197, maxwellknives@aol.com; Web: maxwellknives.com
Specialties: Fancy folding knives and fixed blades of his design. **Patterns:** Hunters, fighters, utility/camp knives, LinerLock® folders, flippers and fantasy knives. **Technical:** Grinds 440C, ATS-34, D2, CPM 154, and commercial Damascus. **Prices:** $250 to $1000; some to $2500. **Remarks:** Full-time maker; first knife sold in 1987. **Mark:** Last name only.

MAY, CHARLES,
10024 McDonald Rd., Aberdeen, MS 39730, Phone: 662-369-0404, charlesmayknives@yahoo.com; Web: charlesmayknives.blademakers.com
Specialties: Fixed-blade sheath knives. **Patterns:** Hunters and fillet knives. **Technical:** Scandinavian-ground D2 and S30V blades, black micarta and wood handles, nickel steel pins with maker's own pocket carry or belt-loop pouches. **Prices:** $215 to $495. **Mark:** "Charles May Knives" and a knife in a circle.

MAYNARD, LARRY JOE,
PO Box 493, Crab Orchard, WV 25827
Specialties: Fancy and fantasy straight knives. **Patterns:** Big knives; a Bowie with a full false edge; fighting knives. **Technical:** Grinds standard steels. **Prices:** $350 to $500; some to $1000. **Remarks:** Full-time maker; first knife sold in 1986. **Mark:** Middle and last initials.

MAYNARD, WILLIAM N.,
2677 John Smith Rd, Fayetteville, NC 28306, Phone: 910-425-1615
Specialties: Traditional and working straight knives of all designs. **Patterns:** Combat, Bowies, fighters, hunters and utility knives. **Technical:** Grinds 440C, ATS-34 and commercial Damascus. Offers fancy filework; handmade sheaths. **Prices:** $100 to $300; some to $750. **Remarks:** Full-time maker; first knife sold in 1988. **Mark:** Last name.

MAYO JR., HOWARD ALTON,
18036 Three Rivers Rd., Biloxi, MS 39532, Phone: 228-326-8298
Specialties: Traditional working straight knives, folders and tactical. **Patterns:** Hunters, fighters, tactical, bird, Bowies, fish fillet knives and lightweight folders. **Technical:** Grinds 440C, ATS-34, D-2, Damascus, forges and grinds 52100 and custom makes sheaths. **Prices:** $100 to $1000. **Remarks:** Part-time maker **Mark:** All knives are serial number and registered in the name of the original purchaser, stamped last name or etched.

MAYO JR., TOM,
67 412 Alahaka St, Waialua, HI 96791, Phone: 808- 637-6560, mayot001@hawaii.rr.com; Web: www.mayoknives.com
Specialties: Framelocks/tactical knives. **Patterns:** Combat knives, hunters, Bowies and folders. **Technical:** Titanium/stellite/S30V. **Prices:** $500 to $1000. **Remarks:** Full-time maker; first knife sold in 1982. **Mark:** Volcano logo with name and state.

MAYVILLE, OSCAR L,
2130 E. County Rd 910S, Marengo, IN 47140, Phone: 812-338-4159
Specialties: Working straight knives; period pieces. **Patterns:** Kitchen cutlery, Bowies, camp knives and hunters. **Technical:** Grinds A2, O1 and 440C. **Prices:** $50 to $350; some to $500. **Remarks:** Full-time maker; first knife sold in 1984. **Mark:** Initials over knife logo.

MCABEE, WILLIAM,
27275 Norton Grade, Colfax, CA 95713, Phone: 530-389-8163
Specialties: Working/using knives. **Patterns:** Fighters, Bowies, Hunters. **Technical:** Grinds ATS-34. **Prices:** $75 to $200; some to $350. **Remarks:** Part-time maker; first knife sold in 1990. **Mark:** Stylized WM stamped.

MCCALLEN JR., HOWARD H,
110 Anchor Dr, So Seaside Park, NJ 08752

MCCARLEY, JOHN,
4165 Harney Rd, Taneytown, MD 21787
Specialties: Working straight knives; period pieces. **Patterns:** Hunters, Bowies, camp knives, miniatures, throwing knives. **Technical:** Forges W2, O1 and his own Damascus. **Prices:** $150 to $300; some to $1000. **Remarks:** Part-time maker; first knife sold in 1977. **Mark:** Initials in script.

MCCARTY, HARRY,
1479 Indian Ridge Rd, Blaine, TN 37709
Specialties: Period pieces. **Patterns:** Trade knives, Bowies, 18th and 19th century folders and hunting swords. **Technical:** Forges and grinds high-carbon steel. **Prices:** $75 to $1300. **Remarks:** Full-time maker; first knife sold in 1977. Doing business as Indian Ridge Forge.**Mark:** Stylized initials inside a shamrock.

MCCLURE, JERRY,
3052 Isim Rd, Norman, OK 73026, Phone: 405- 321-3614, jerry@jmcclureknives.net; Web: www.jmcclureknives.net
Specialties: Gentleman's folder, linerlock with my jeweled pivot system of 10 rubies, forged one-of-a kind Damascus Bowies, and a line of hunting/camp knives. **Patterns:** Folders, Bowie, and hunting/camp **Technical** Forges own Damascus, also uses Damasteel and does own heat treating. **Prices** $500 to $3,000 and up **Remarks** Full-time maker, made first knife in 1965. **Mark** J.MCCLURE

MCCLURE, MICHAEL,
803 17th Ave, Menlo Park, CA 94025, Phone: 650-323-2596, mikesknives@comcast.net
Specialties: Working/using straight knives of his design and to customer specs. **Patterns:** Bowies, hunters, skinners, utility/camp, tantos, fillets and boot knives. **Technical:** Forges high-carbon and Damascus; also grinds stainless, all grades. **Prices:** Start at $200. **Remarks:** Part-time maker; first knife sold in 1991. ABS Journeyman Smith. **Mark:** Mike McClure.

MCCONNELL JR., LOYD A,
1710 Rosewood, Odessa, TX 79761, Phone: 915-363-8344, ccknives@ccknives.com; Web: www.ccknives.com
Specialties: Working straight knives and folders, some fancy. **Patterns:** Hunters, boots, Bowies, locking folders and slip-joints. **Technical:** Grinds CPM Steels, ATS-34 and BG-42 and commercial Damascus. **Prices:** $175 to $900; some to $10,000. **Remarks:** Full-time maker; first knife sold in 1975. Doing business as Cactus Custom Knives. Markets product knives under name: Lone Star Knives. **Mark:** Name, city and state in cactus logo.

MCCORNOCK, CRAIG,
MCC MTN OUTFITTERS, 4775 Rt. 212/PO 162, Willow, NY 12495, Phone: 845-679-9758, Mccmtn@aol.com; Web: www.mccmtn.com
Specialties: Carry, utility, hunters, defense type knives and functional swords. **Patterns:** Drop points, hawkbills, tantos, wakIzashis, katanas **Technical:** Stock removal, forged and Damascus, (yes, he still flints knap). **Prices:** $200 to $2000. **Mark:** McM.

MCCOUN, MARK,
14212 Pine Dr, DeWitt, VA 23840, Phone: 804-469- 7631, markmccoun@aol.com
Specialties: Working/using straight knives of his design and in standard patterns; custom miniatures. **Patterns:** Locking liners, integrals. **Technical:** Grinds Damascus, ATS-34 and 440C. **Prices:** $150 to $500. **Remarks:** Part-time maker; first knife sold in 1989. **Mark:** Name, city and state.

MCCRACKIN, KEVIN,
3720 Hess Rd, House Springs, MO 63051, Phone: 636-677-6066

MCCRACKIN AND SON, V J,
3720 Hess Rd, House Springs, MO 63051, Phone: 636-677-6066
Specialties: Working straight knives in standard patterns. **Patterns:** Hunters, Bowies and camp knives. **Technical:** Forges L6, 5160, his own Damascus, cable Damascus. **Prices:** $125 to $700; some to $1500. **Remarks:** Part-time maker; first knife sold in 1983. Son Kevin helps make the knives. **Mark:** Last name, M.S.

MCCULLOUGH, JERRY,
274 West Pettibone Rd, Georgiana, AL 36033, Phone: 334-382-7644, ke4er@alaweb.com
Specialties: Standard patterns or custom designs. **Technical:** Forge and grind scrap-tool and Damascus steels. Use natural handle materials and turquoise trim on some. Filework on others. **Prices:** $65 to $250 and up. **Remarks:** Part-time maker. **Mark:** Initials (JM) combined.

MCDONALD, RICH,
4590 Kirk Rd, Columbiana, OH 44408, Phone: 330- 482-0007, Fax: 330-482-0007
Specialties: Traditional working/using and art knives of his design. **Patterns:** Bowies, hunters, folders, primitives and tomahawks. **Technical:** Forges 5160, 1084, 1095, 52100 and his own Damascus. Fancy filework. **Prices:** $200 to $1500. **Remarks:** Full-time maker; first knife sold in 1994. **Mark:** First and last initials connected.

MCDONALD, ROBERT J,
14730 61 Court N, Loxahatchee, FL 33470, Phone: 561-790-1470
Specialties: Traditional working straight knives to customer specs. **Patterns:** Fighters, swords and folders. **Technical:** Grinds 440C, ATS-34 and forges own Damascus. **Prices:** $150 to $1000. **Remarks:** Part-time maker; first knife sold in 1988. **Mark:** Electro-etched name.

MCDONALD, ROBIN J,
7300 Tolleson Ave NW, Albuquerque, NM 87114-3546
Specialties: Working knives of maker's design. **Patterns:** Bowies, hunters, camp knives and fighters. **Technical:** Forges primarily 5160. **Prices:** $100 to $500. **Remarks:** Part-time maker; first knife sold in 1999. **Mark:** Initials RJM.

MCDONALD, W J "JERRY",
7173 Wickshire Cove E, Germantown, TN 38138, Phone: 901-756-9924, wjmcdonaldknives@email.msn.com; Web: www.mcdonaldknives.com
Specialties: Classic and working/using straight knives of his design and in standard patterns. **Patterns:** Bowies, hunters kitchen and traditional spring back pocket knives. **Technical:** Grinds ATS-34, 154CM, D2, 440V, BG42 and 440C. **Prices:** $125 to $1000. **Remarks:** Full-time maker; first knife sold in 1989. **Mark:** First and middle initials, last name, maker, city and state. Some of his knives are stamped McDonald in script.

MCFALL, KEN,
PO Box 458, Lakeside, AZ 85929, Phone: 928-537- 2026, Fax: 928-537-8066, knives@citlink.net
Specialties: Fancy working straight knives and some folders. **Patterns:** Daggers, boots, tantos, Bowies; some miniatures. **Technical:** Grinds D2, ATS-34 and 440C. Forges his own Damascus. **Prices:** $200 to $1200. **Remarks:** Part-time maker; first knife sold in 1984. **Mark:** Name, city and state.

MCFARLIN, ERIC E,
PO Box 2188, Kodiak, AK 99615, Phone: 907-486- 4799
Specialties: Working knives of his design. **Patterns:** Bowies, skinners, camp knives and hunters. **Technical:** Flat and convex grinds 440C, A2 and AEB-L. **Prices:** Start at $200. **Remarks:** Part-time maker; first knife sold in 1989. **Mark:** Name and city in rectangular logo.

MCFARLIN, J W,
3331 Pocohantas Dr, Lake Havasu City, AZ 86404, Phone: 928-453-7612, Fax: 928-453-7612, aztheedge@NPGcable.com
Technical: Flat grinds, D2, ATS-34, 440C, Thomas and Peterson Damascus. **Remarks:** From working knives to investment. Customer designs always welcome. 100 percent handmade. Made first knife in 1972. **Prices:** $150 to $3000. **Mark:** Hand written in the blade.

MCGILL, JOHN,
PO Box 302, Blairsville, GA 30512, Phone: 404-745- 4686
Specialties: Working knives. **Patterns:** Traditional patterns; camp knives. **Technical:** Forges L6 and 9260; makes Damascus. **Prices:** $50 to $250; some to $500. **Remarks:** Full-time maker; first knife sold in 1982. **Mark:** XYLO.

MCGOWAN, FRANK E,
12629 Howard Lodge Dr, Summer address, Sykesvile, MD 21784, Phone: 443-285-3815, fmcgowan1@comcast.net
Specialties: Fancy working knives and folders to customer specs. **Patterns:** Survivor knives, fighters, fishing knives, folders and hunters. **Technical:** Grinds and forges O1, 440C, 5160, ATS-34, 52100, or customer choice. **Prices:** $100 to $1000; some more. **Remarks:** Full-time maker; first knife sold in 1986. **Mark:** Last name.

MCGOWAN, FRANK E,
2023 Robin Ct, Winter address, Sebring, FL 33870, Phone: 443-285-3815, fmcgowan1@comcast.net

Specialties: Fancy working knives and folders to customer specs. **Patterns:** Survivor knives, fighters, fishing knives, folders and hunters. **Technical:** Grinds and forges O1, 440C, 5160, ATS-34, 52100 or customer choice. **Prices:** $100 to $1000, some more. **Remarks:** Full-time maker. First knife sold in 1986. **Mark:** Last name.

MCGRATH, PATRICK T,
8343 Kenyon Ave, Westchester, CA 90045, Phone: 310-338-8764, hidinginLA@excite.com

MCGRODER, PATRICK J,
5725 Chapin Rd, Madison, OH 44057, Phone: 216-298-3405, Fax: 216-298-3405

Specialties: Traditional working/using knives of his design. **Patterns:** Bowies, hunters and utility/camp knives. **Technical:** Grinds ATS-34, D2 and customer requests. Does reverse etching; heat-treats; prefers natural handle materials; custom made sheath with each knife. **Prices:** $125 to $250. **Remarks:** Part-time maker. **Mark:** First and middle initials, last name, maker, city and state.

MCGUANE IV, THOMAS F,
410 South 3rd Ave, Bozeman, MT 59715, Phone: 406-586-0248, Web: http://www.thomasmcguane.com

Specialties: Multi metal inlaid knives of handmade steel. **Patterns:** Lock back and LinerLock® folders, fancy straight knives. **Technical:** 1084/1SN20 Damascus and Mosaic steel by maker. **Prices:** $1000 and up. **Mark:** Surname or name and city, state.

MCHENRY, WILLIAM JAMES,
Box 67, Wyoming, RI 02898, Phone: 401-539-8353

Specialties: Fancy high-tech folders of his design. **Patterns:** Locking folders with various mechanisms. **Technical:** One-of-a-kind only, no duplicates. Inventor of the Axis Lock. Most pieces disassemble and feature top-shelf materials including gold, silver and gems. **Prices:** Upscale. **Remarks:** Full-time maker; first knife sold in 1988. Former goldsmith. **Mark:** Last name or first and last initials.

MCINTYRE, SHAWN,
71 Leura Grove, Hawthorn East Victoria, AUSTRALIA 3123, Phone: 61 3 9813 2049/Cell 61 412 041 062, macpower@netspace.net.au; Web: www.mcintyreknives.com

Specialties: Damascus & CS fixed blades and art knives. **Patterns:** Bowies, hunters, fighters, kukris, integrals. **Technical:** Forges, makes own Damascus including pattern weld, mosaic, and composite multi-bars form O1 & 15N20 Also uses 1084, W2, and 52100. **Prices:** $275 to $2000. **Remarks:** Full-time maker since 1999. **Mark:** Mcintyre in script.

MCKEE, NEIL,
674 Porter Hill Rd., Stevensville, MT 59870, Phone: 406-777-3507, mckeenh@peoplepc.com

Specialties: Early American. **Patterns:** Nessmuk, DeWeese, French folders, art pieces. **Technical:** Engraver. **Prices:** $150 to $1000. **Mark:** Oval with initials.

MCKENZIE, DAVID BRIAN,
2311 B Ida Rd, Campbell River B, CANADA V9W-4V7

MCKIERNAN, STAN,
11751 300th St, Lamoni, IA 50140, Phone: 641-784-6873/641-781-0368, slmck@hotmailc.com

Specialties: Self-sheathed knives and miniatures. **Patterns:** Daggers, ethnic designs and individual styles. **Technical:** Grinds Damascus and 440C. **Prices:** $200 to $500, some to $1500. **Mark:** "River's Bend" inside two concentric circles.

MCLENDON, HUBERT W,
125 Thomas Rd, Waco, GA 30182, Phone: 770-574-9796

Specialties: Using knives; his design or customer's. **Patterns:** Bowies and hunters. **Technical:** Hand ground or forged ATS-34, 440C and D2. **Prices:** $100 to $300. **Remarks:** First knife sold in 1978. **Mark:** McLendon or Mc.

MCLUIN, TOM,
36 Fourth St, Dracut, MA 01826, Phone: 978-957-4899, tmcluin@comcast.net; Web: www.mcluinknives.com

Specialties: Working straight knives and folders of his design. **Patterns:** Boots, hunters and folders. **Technical:** Grinds ATS-34, 440C, O1 and Damascus; makes his own mokume. **Prices:** $100 to $400; some to $700. **Remarks:** Part-time maker; first knife sold in 1991. **Mark:** Last name.

MCLURKIN, ANDREW,
2112 Windy Woods Dr, Raleigh, NC 27607, Phone: 919-834-4693, mclurkincustomknives.com

Specialties: Collector grade folders, working folders, fixed blades, and miniatures. Knives made to order and to his design. **Patterns:** Locking liner and lock back folders, hunter, working and tactical designs. **Technical:** Using patterned Damascus, Mosaic Damascus, ATS-34, BG-42, and CPM steels. Prefers natural handle materials such as pearl, ancient ivory and stabilized wood. Also using synthetic materials such as carbon fiber, titanium, and G10. **Prices:** $250 and up. **Mark:** Last name. Mark is often on inside of folders.

MCMANUS, DANNY,
413 Fairhaven Drive, Taylors, SC 29687, Phone: 864-268-9849, Fax: 864-268-9699, DannyMcManus@bigfoot.com

Specialties: High-tech and traditional working/using straight knives of his design, to customer specs and in standard patterns. **Patterns:** Boots, Bowies, fighters, hunters and utility/camp knives. **Technical:** Forges stainless steel Damascus; grinds ATS-34. Offers engraving and scrimshaw. **Prices:** $300 to $2000; some to $3000. **Remarks:** Full-time maker; first knife sold in 1997. Doing business as Stamascus KnifeWorks Corp. **Mark:** Stamascus.

MCNABB, TOMMY,
CAROLINA CUSTOM KNIVES, PO Box 327, Bethania, NC 27010, Phone: 336-924-6053, Fax: 336-924-4854, tommy@tmcnabb.com; Web: carolinaknives.com

Specialties: Classic and working knives of his own design or to customer's specs. **Patterns:** Traditional bowies. Tomahawks, hunters and customer designs. **Technical:** Forges his own Damascus steel, hand forges or grinds ATS-34 and other hi-tech steels. Prefers mirror finish or satin finish on working knives. Uses exotic or natural handle material and stabilized woods. **Price:** $300-$3500. **Remarks:** Full time maker. Made first knife in 1982. **Mark:** "Carolina Custom Knives" on stock removal blades "T. McNabb" on custom orders and Damascus knives.

MCRAE, J MICHAEL,
6100 Lake Rd, Mint Hill, NC 28227, Phone: 704-545-2929, scotia@carolina.rr.com; Web: www.scotiametalwork.com

Specialties: Scottish dirks, sgian dubhs, broadswords. **Patterns:** Traditional blade styles with traditional and slightly non-traditional handle treatments. **Technical:** Forges 5160 and his own Damascus. Prefers stag and exotic hardwoods for handles, many intricately carved. **Prices:** Starting at $125, some to $3500. **Remarks:** Journeyman Smith in ABS, member of North Carolina Custom Knifemakers Guild and ABANA. Full-time maker, first knife sold in 1982. Doing business as Scotia Metalwork. **Mark:** Last name underlined with a claymore.

MEERDINK, KURT,
248 Yulan Barryville Rd., Barryville, NY 12719-5305, Phone: 845-557-0783

Specialties: Working straight knives. **Patterns:** Hunters, Bowies, tactical and neck knives. **Technical:** Grinds ATS-34, 440C, D2, Damascus. **Prices:** $95 to $1100. **Remarks:** Full-time maker, first knife sold in 1994. **Mark:** Meerdink Maker, Rio NY.

MEIER, DARYL,
75 Forge Rd, Carbondale, IL 62901, Phone: 618-549-3234, Web: www.meiersteel.com

Specialties: One-of-a-kind knives and swords. **Patterns:** Collaborates on blades. **Technical:** Forges his own Damascus, W1 and A203E, 440C, 431, nickel 200 and clad steel. **Prices:** $250 to $450; some to $6000. **Remarks:** Full-time smith and researcher since 1974; first knife sold in 1974. **Mark:** Name or circle/arrow symbol or SHAWNEE.

MELIN, GORDON C,
14207 Coolbank Dr, La Mirada, CA 90638, Phone: 562-946-5753

MELLARD, J R,
17006 Highland Canyon Dr., Houston, TX 77095, Phone: 281-550-9464

MELOY, SEAN,
7148 Rosemary Lane, Lemon Grove, CA 91945-2105, Phone: 619-465-7173

Specialties: Traditional working straight knives of his design. **Patterns:** Bowies, fighters and utility/camp knives. **Technical:** Grinds 440C, ATS-34 and D2. **Prices:** $125 to $300. **Remarks:** Part-time maker; first knife sold in 1985. **Mark:** Broz Knives.

MENEFEE, RICKY BOB,
2440 County Road 1322, Blawchard, OK 73010, rmenefee@pldi.net

Specialties: Working straight knives and pocket knives. **Patterns:** Hunters, fighters, minis & Bowies. **Technical:** Grinds ATS-34, 440C, D2, BG42 and S30V. **Price:** $130 to $1000. **Remarks:** Part-time maker, first knife sold in 2001. Member of KGA of Oklahoma, also Knifemakers Guild. **Mark:** Menefee made or Menefee stamped in blade.

MENSCH, LARRY C,
Larry's Knife Shop, 578 Madison Ave, Milton, PA 17847, Phone: 570-742-9554

Specialties: Custom orders. **Patterns:** Bowies, daggers, hunters, tantos, short swords and miniatures. **Technical:** Grinds ATS-34, stainless steel Damascus; blade grinds hollow, flat and slack. Filework; bending guards and fluting handles with finger grooves. Offers engraving and scrimshaw. **Prices:** $200 and up. **Remarks:** Full-time maker; first knife sold in 1993. Doing business as Larry's Knife Shop. **Mark:** Connected capital "L" and small "m" in script.

MERCER, MIKE,
149 N. Waynesville Rd, Lebanon, OH 45036, Phone: 513-932-2837, mmercer08445@roadrunner.com

Specialties: Miniatures and autos. **Patterns:** All folder patterns. **Technical:** Diamonds and gold, one-of-a-kind, Damascus, O1, stainless steel blades. **Prices:** $500 to $5000. **Remarks:** Carved wax - lost wax casting. **Mark:** Stamp - Mercer.

MERCHANT, TED,
7 Old Garrett Ct, White Hall, MD 21161, Phone: 410- 343-0380
Specialties: Traditional and classic working knives. **Patterns:** Bowies, hunters, camp knives, fighters, daggers and skinners. **Technical:** Forges W2 and 5160; makes own Damascus. Makes handles with wood, stag, horn, silver and gem stone inlay; fancy filework. **Prices:** $125 to $600; some to $1500. **Remarks:** Full-time maker; first knife sold in 1985. **Mark:** Last name.

MERZ III, ROBERT L,
1447 Winding Canyon, Katy, TX 77493, Phone: 281-391-2897, bobmerz@consolidated.net; Web: www.merzknives.com
Specialties: Folders. **Prices:** $250 to $700. **Remarks:** Full time maker; first knife sold in 1974. **Mark:** MERZ.

MESHEJIAN, MARDI,
5 Bisbee Court 109 PMB 230, Santa Fe, NM 87508, Phone: 505-310-7441, toothandnail13@yahoo.com
Specialties: One-of-a-kind fantasy and high art straight knives & folders. **Patterns:** Swords, daggers, folders and other weapons. **Technical:** Forged steel Damascus and titanium Damascus. **Prices:** $300 to $5000 some to $7000. **Mark:** Stamped stylized "M."

MESSER, DAVID T,
134 S Torrence St, Dayton, OH 45403-2044, Phone: 513-228-6561
Specialties: Fantasy period pieces, straight and folding, of his design. **Patterns:** Bowies, daggers and swords. **Technical:** Grinds 440C, O1, 06 and commercial Damascus. Likes fancy guards and exotic handle materials. **Prices:** $100 to $225; some to $375. **Remarks:** Spare-time maker; first knife sold in 1991. **Mark:** Name stamp.

METHENY, H A "WHITEY",
7750 Waterford Dr, Spotsylvania, VA 22553, Phone: 540-582-3095, Fax: 540-582-3095, hametheny@aol.com; Web: www.methenyknives.com
Specialties: Working and using straight knives of his design and to customer specs. **Patterns:** Hunters and kitchen knives. **Technical:** Grinds 440C and ATS-34. Offers filework; tooled custom sheaths. **Prices:** $200 to $350. **Remarks:** Spare-time maker; first knife sold in 1990. **Mark:** Initials/full name football logo.

METSALA, ANTHONY,
30557 103rd St. NW, Princeton, MN 55371, Phone: 763-389-2628, acmetsala@izoom.net; Web: www.metsalacustomknives.com
Specialties: Sole authorship one-off mosaic Damascus liner locking folders, sales of makers finished one-off mosaic Damascus blades. **Patterns:** Except for a couple EDC folding knives, maker does not use patterns. **Technical:** Forges own mosaic Damascus carbon blade and bolster material. All stainless steel blades are heat treated by Paul Bos. **Prices:** $250 to $1500. **Remarks:** Full-time knifemaker and Damascus steel maker, first knife sold in 2005. **Mark:** A.C. Metsala or Metsala.

METZ, GREG T,
c/o James Ranch HC 83, Cascade, ID 83611, Phone: 208-382-4336, metzenterprise@yahoo.com
Specialties: Hunting and utility knives. **Prices:** $350 and up. **Remarks:** Natural handle materials; hand forged blades; 1084 and 1095. **Mark:** METZ (last name).

MEYER, CHRISTOPHER J,
737 Shenipsit Lake Rd, Tolland, CT 06084, Phone: 860-875-1826, shenipsitforge.cjm@gmail.com
Specialties: Hand forged tool steels. **Patterns:** Bowies, fighters, hunters, and camp knives. **Technical:** Forges O1, 1084, W2, Grinds ATS-34, O1, D2, CPM154CM. **Remarks:** Spare-time maker, sold first knife in 2003. **Mark:** Name or "Shenipsit forge, Meyer".

MICHINAKA, TOSHIAKI,
I-679 Koyamacho-nishi Tottori-shi, Tottori 680- 0947, JAPAN, Phone: 0857-28-5911
Specialties: Art miniature knives. **Patterns:** Bowies, hunters, fishing, camp knives & miniatures. **Technical:** Grinds ATS-34 and 440C. **Prices:** $300 to $900 some higher. **Remarks:** Part-time maker. First knife sold in 1982. **Mark:** First initial, last name.

MICHO, KANDA,
7-32-5 Shinzutsumi-cho, Shinnanyo-city, Yamaguchi, JAPAN, Phone: 0834-62-1910

MICKLEY, TRACY,
42112 Kerns Dr, North Mankato, MN 56003, Phone: 507-947-3760, tracy@mickleyknives.com; Web: www.mickleyknives.com
Specialties: Working and collectable straight knives using mammoth ivory or burl woods, LinerLock® folders. **Patterns:** Custom and classic hunters, utility, fighters and Bowies. **Technical:** Grinding 154-CM, BG-42 forging O1 and 52100. **Prices:** Starting at $325 **Remarks:** Part-time since 1999. **Mark:** Last name.

MILES JR., C R "IRON DOCTOR",
1541 Porter Crossroad, Lugoff, SC 29078, Phone: 803-438-5816
Specialties: Traditional working straight knives of his design or made to custom specs. **Patterns:** Hunters, fighters, utility camp knives and hatches. **Technical:** Grinds O1, D2, ATS-34, 440C, and 1095. Forges 18th century style cutlery of high carbon steels. Also forges and grinds old files to make knives. Custom leather sheaths. **Prices:** $100 and up. **Remarks:** Part-time maker, first knife sold in 1997. Member of South Carolina Association of Knifemakers since 1997. **Mark:** Iron doctor plus name and serial number.

MILITANO, TOM,
CUSTOM KNIVES, 77 Jason Rd., Jacksonville, AL 36265-6655, Phone: 256-435-7132, jeffkin57@aol.com
Specialties: Fixed blade, one-of-a-kind knives. **Patterns:** Bowies, fighters, hunters and tactical knives. **Technical:** Grinds 440C, ATS-34, A2, and Damascus. Hollow grinds, flat grinds, and decorative filework. **Prices:** $150 plus. **Remarks:** Part-time maker. Sold first knives in the mid to late 1980s. Memberships: Founding member of New England Custom Knife Association. **Mark:** Name engraved in ricasso area - type of steel on reverse side.

MILLARD, FRED G,
27627 Kopezyk Ln, Richland Center, WI 53581, Phone: 608-647-5376
Specialties: Working/using straight knives of his design or to customer specs. **Patterns:** Bowies, hunters, utility/camp knives, kitchen/steak knives. **Technical:** Grinds ATS-34, O1, D2 and 440C. Makes sheaths. **Prices:** $110 to $300. **Remarks:** Full-time maker; first knife sold in 1993. Doing business as Millard Knives. **Mark:** Mallard duck in flight with serial number.

MILLER, BOB,
7659 Fine Oaks Pl, Oakville, MO 63129, Phone: 314- 846-8934
Specialties: Mosaic Damascus; collector using straight knives and folders. **Patterns:** Hunters, Bowies, utility/camp knives, daggers. **Technical:** Forges own Damascus, mosaic-Damascus and 52100. **Prices:** $125 to $500. **Remarks:** Part-time maker; first knife sold in 1983. **Mark:** First and middle initials and last name, or initials.

MILLER, DON,
1604 Harrodsburg Rd, Lexington, KY 40503, Phone: 606-276-3299

MILLER, HANFORD J,
Box 97, Cowdrey, CO 80434, Phone: 970-723- 4708
Specialties: Working knives in Moran styles, Bowie, period pieces, Cinquedea. **Patterns:** Daggers, Bowies, working knives. **Technical:** All work forged: W2, 1095, 5160 and Damascus. ABS methods; offers fine silver repousse, scabboard mountings and wire inlay, oak presentation cases. **Prices:** $400 to $1000; some to $3000 and up. **Remarks:** Full- time maker; first knife sold in 1968. **Mark:** Initials or name within Bowie logo.

MILLER, JAMES P,
9024 Goeller Rd, RR 2, Box 28, Fairbank, IA 50629, Phone: 319-635-2294, Web: www.damascusknives.biz
Specialties: All tool steel Damascus; working knives and period pieces. **Patterns:** Hunters, Bowies, camp knives and daggers. **Technical:** Forges and grinds 1095, 52100, 440C and his own Damascus. **Prices:** $175 to $500; some to $1500. **Remarks:** Full-time maker; first knife sold in 1970. **Mark:** First and middle initials, last name with knife logo.

MILLER, M A,
11625 Community Center Dr, Unit #1531, Northglenn, CO 80233, Phone: 303-280-3816
Specialties: Using knives for hunting. 3-1/2"-4" Loveless drop-point. Made to customer specs. **Patterns:** Skinners and camp knives. **Technical:** Grinds 440C, D2, O1 and ATS-34 Damascus miniatures. **Prices:** $225 to $350; miniatures $75 to $150. **Remarks:** Part-time maker; first knife sold in 1988. **Mark:** Last name stamped in block letters or first and middle initials, last name, maker, city and state with triangles on either side etched.

MILLER, MICHAEL,
3030 E Calle Cedral, Kingman, AZ 86401, Phone: 928-757-1359, mike@mmilleroriginals.com
Specialties: Hunters, Bowies, and skinners with exotic burl wood, stag, ivory and gemstone handles. **Patterns:** High carbon steel knives. **Technical:** High carbon and nickel alloy Damascus and high carbon and meteorite Damascus. Also mosaic Damascus. **Prices:** $235 to $4500. **Remarks:** Full-time maker since 2002, first knife sold 2000; doing business as M Miller Originals. **Mark:** First initial and last name with 'handmade' underneath.

MILLER, MICHAEL E,
1400 Skyview Dr, El Reno, OK 73036, Phone: 405-422-3602
Specialties: Traditional working/using knives of his design. **Patterns:** Bowies, hunters and kitchen knives. **Technical:** Grinds ATS-34, CPM 440V; forges Damascus and cable Damascus and 52100. Prefers scrimshaw, fancy pins, basket weave and embellished sheaths. **Prices:** $80 to $300; some to $500. **Remarks:** Part-time maker; first knife sold in 1984. Doing business as Miller Custom Knives. Member of KGA of Oklahoma and Salt Fork Blacksmith Association. **Mark:** First and middle initials, last name, maker.

MILLER, MICHAEL K,
28510 Santiam Hwy, Sweet Home, OR 97386, Phone: 541-367-4927, miller@ptlnet.net
Specialties: Specializes in kitchen cutlery of his design or made to customer specs. **Patterns:** Hunters, utility/camp knives and kitchen cutlery. **Technical:** Grinds ATS-34, AEBL and 440-C. Wife does scrimshaw as well. Makes custom sheaths and holsters. **Prices:** $200. **Remarks:** Full- time maker; first knife sold in 1989. **Mark:** MandM Kustom Krafts.

MILLER, NATE,
Sportsman's Edge, 1075 Old Steese Hwy N, Fairbanks, AK 99712, Phone: 907-479-4774, sportsmansedge@gci.net
Specialties: Fixed blade knives for hunting, fishing, kitchen and collector pieces. **Patterns:** Hunters, skinners, utility, tactical, fishing, camp knives-your pattern or mine. **Technical:** Stock removal maker, ATS-34, 154CM, D2, 1095, other steels on request. Handle material includes micarta, horn, antler, fossilized ivory and bone, wide selection of woods. **Prices:** $225-$800. **Remarks:** Full time maker since 2002. **Mark:** Nate Miller, Fairbanks, AK.

MILLER, R D,
10526 Estate Lane, Dallas, TX 75238, Phone: 214-348-3496
Specialties: One-of-a-kind collector-grade knives. **Patterns:** Boots, hunters, Bowies, camp and utility knives, fishing and bird knives, miniatures. **Technical:** Grinds a variety of steels to include O1, D2, 440C, 154CM and 1095. **Prices:** $65 to $300; some to $900. **Remarks:** Full- time maker; first knife sold in 1984. **Mark:** R.D. Custom Knives with date or bow and arrow logo.

MILLER, RICK,
516 Kanaul Rd, Rockwood, PA 15557, Phone: 814-926- 2059
Specialties: Working/using straight knives of his design and in standard patterns. **Patterns:** Bowies, daggers, hunters and friction folders. **Technical:** Grinds L6. Forges 5160, L6 and Damascus. Patterns for Damascus are random, twist, rose or ladder. **Prices:** $75 to $250; some to $400. **Remarks:** Part-time maker; first knife sold in 1982. **Mark:** Script stamp "R.D.M."

MILLER, RON,
NORTH POLE KNIVES, PO BOX 55301, NORTH POLE, AK 99705, Phone: 907-488-5902, JTMRON@NESCAPE.NET
<Specialties: Custom handmade hunting knives built for the extreme conditions of Alaska. Custom fillet blades, tactical fighting knives, custom kitchen knives. Handles are made from mammoth ivory, musk ox, fossilized walrus tusk. Hunters have micarta handles. **Patterns:** Hunters, skinners, fillets, fighters. **Technical:** Stock removal for D2, ATS-34, 109HR, 154CM, and Damascus. **Prices:** $180 and up. **Remarks:** Makes custom sheaths for the above knives. **Mark:** Ron Miller, circle with North Pole Knives with bowie style blade through circle.

MILLER, RONALD T,
12922 127th Ave N, Largo, FL 34644, Phone: 813- 595-0378 (after 5 p.m.)
Specialties: Working/using straight knives in standard patterns. **Patterns:** Combat knives, camp knives, kitchen cutlery, fillet knives, locking folders and butterflies. **Technical:** Grinds D2, 440C and ATS-34; offers brass inlays and scrimshaw. **Prices:** $45 to $325; some to $750. **Remarks:** Part-time maker; first knife sold in 1984. **Mark:** Name, city and state in palm tree logo.

MILLER, TERRY,
P.O. Box 262, Healy, AK 99743, Phone: 907-683-1239, terry@denalidomehome.com
Specialties: Alaskan ulas with wood or horn. **Remarks:** New to knifemaking (3 years).

MILLS, LOUIS G,
9450 Waters Rd, Ann Arbor, MI 48103, Phone: 734- 668-1839
Specialties: High-art Japanese-style period pieces. **Patterns:** Traditional tantos, daggers and swords. **Technical:** Makes steel from iron; makes his own Damascus by traditional Japanese techniques. **Prices:** $900 to $2000; some to $8000. **Remarks:** Spare-time maker. **Mark:** Yasutomo in Japanese Kanji.

MILLS, MICHAEL,
151 Blackwell Rd, Colonial Beach, VA 22443-5054, Phone: 804-224-0265
Specialties: Working knives, hunters, skinners, utility and Bowies. **Technical:** Forge 5160 differential heat-treats. **Prices:** $300 and up. **Remarks:** Part-time maker, ABS Journeyman. **Mark:** Last name in script.

MINK, DAN,
PO Box 861, 196 Sage Circle, Crystal Beach, FL 34681, Phone: 727-786-5408, blademkr@gmail.com
Specialties: Traditional and working knives of his design. **Patterns:** Bowies, fighters, folders and hunters. **Technical:** Grinds ATS-34, 440C and D2. Blades and tanges embellished with fancy filework. Uses natural and rare handle materials. **Prices:** $125 to $450. **Remarks:** Part-time maker; first knife sold in 1985. **Mark:** Name and star encircled by custom made, city, state.

MINNICK, JIM,
144 North 7th St, Middletown, IN 47356, Phone: 765- 354-4108
Specialties: Lever-lock folding art knives, liner-locks. **Patterns:** Stilettos, Persian and one-of-a-kind folders. **Technical:** Grinds and carves Damascus, stainless, and high-carbon. **Prices:** $950 to $7000. **Remarks:** Part-time maker; first knife sold in 1976. Husband and wife team. **Mark:** Minnick and JMJ.

MIRABILE, DAVID,
1715 Glacier Ave, Juneau, AK 99801, Phone: 907- 463-3404
Specialties: Elegant edged weapons. **Patterns:** Fighters, Bowies, claws, tklinget daggers, executive desk knives. **Technical:** Forged high-carbon steels, his own Damascus; uses ancient walrus ivory and prehistoric bone extensively, very rarely uses wood. **Prices:** $350 to $7000. **Remarks:** Full-time maker. Knives sold through art gallery in Juneau, AK. **Mark:** Last name etched or engraved.

MITCHELL, JAMES A,
PO Box 4646, Columbus, GA 31904, Phone: 404-322-8582
Specialties: Fancy working knives. **Patterns:** Hunters, fighters, Bowies and locking folders. **Technical:** Grinds D2, 440C and commercial Damascus. **Prices:** $100 to $400; some to $900. **Remarks:** Part-time maker; first knife sold in 1976. Sells knives in sets. **Mark:** Signature and city.

MITCHELL, MAX DEAN AND BEN,
3803 VFW Rd, Leesville, LA 71440, Phone: 318-239-6416
Specialties: Hatchet and knife sets with folder and belt and holster all match. **Patterns:** Hunters, 200 L6 steel. **Technical:** L6 steel; soft back, hand edge. **Prices:** $300 to $500. **Remarks:** Part-time makers; first knife sold in 1965. Custom orders only; no stock. **Mark:** First names.

MITCHELL, WM DEAN,
PO Box 2, Warren, TX 77664, Phone: 409-547- 2213
Specialties: Functional and collectable cutlery. **Patterns:** Personal and collector's designs. **Technical:** Forges own Damascus and carbon steels. **Prices:** Determined by the buyer. **Remarks:** Gentleman knifemaker. ABS Master Smith 1994. **Mark:** Full name with anvil and MS or WDM and MS.

MITSUYUKI, ROSS,
PO Box 29577, Honolulu, HI 96820, Phone: 808-671-3335, Fax: 808-671-3335, rossman@hawaiiantel.net; Web: www.picturetrail.com/homepage/mrbing
Specialties: Working straight knives and folders/engraving titanium & 416 S.S. **Patterns:** Hunting, fighters, utility knives and boot knives. **Technical:** 440C, BG42, ATS-34, 530V, and Damascus. **Prices:** $100 and up. **Remarks:** Spare-time maker, first knife sold in 1998. **Mark:** (Honu) Hawaiian sea turtle.

MIVILLE-DESCHENES, ALAIN,
1952 Charles A Parent, Quebec, CANADA G2B 4B2, Phone: 418-845-0950, Fax: 418-845-0950, amd@miville- deschenes.com; Web: www.miville-deschenes.com
Specialties: Working knives of his design or to customer specs and art knives. **Patterns:** Bowies, skinner, hunter, utility, camp knives, fighters, art knives. **Technical:** Grinds ATS-34, CPMS30V, 0-1, D2, and sometime forge carbon steel. **Prices:** $250 to $700; some higher. **Remarks:** Part-time maker; first knife sold in 2001. **Mark:** Logo (small hand) and initials (AMD).

MIZE, RICHARD,
FOX CREEK FORGE, 2038 Fox Creek Rd., Lawrenceburg, KY 40342, Phone: 502-859-0602, foxcreek@kih.net; Web: www.foxcreekforge.com
Specialties: Forges spring steel, 5160, 10xx steels, natural handle materials. **Patterns:** Traditional working knives, period flavor Bowies, rifle knives. **Technical:** Does own heat treating, differential temper. **Prices:** $100 to $400. **Remarks:** Strongly advocates sole authorship. **Mark:** Initial M hot stamped.

MOJZIS, JULIUS,
B S Timravy 6, 98511 Halic, SLOVAKIA, mojzisj@stoneline.sk; Web: www.juliusmojzis.com
Specialties: Art Knives. **Prices:** USD $2000. **Mark:** MOJZIS.

MONCUS, MICHAEL STEVEN,
1803 US 19 N, Smithville, GA 31787, Phone: 912-846-2408

MONTANO, GUS A,
11217 Westonhill Dr, San Diego, CA 92126-1447, Phone: 619-273-5357
Specialties: Traditional working/using straight knives of his design. **Patterns:** Boots, Bowies and fighters. **Technical:** Grinds 1095 and 5160; grinds and forges cable. Double or triple hardened and triple drawn; hand-rubbed finish. Prefers natural handle materials. **Prices:** $200 to $400; some to $600. **Remarks:** Spare-time maker; first knife sold in 1997. **Mark:** First initial and last name.

MONTEIRO, VICTOR,
31 Rue D'Opprebais, 1360 Maleves Ste Marie, BELGIUM, Phone: 010 88 0441, victor.monteiro@skynet.be
Specialties: Working and fancy straight knives, folders and integrals of his design. **Patterns:** Fighters, hunters and kitchen knives. **Technical:** Grinds ATS-34, 440C, D2, Damasteel and other commercial Damascus, embellishment, filework and domed pins. **Prices:** $300 to $1000, some higher. **Remarks:** Part-time maker; first knife sold in 1989. **Mark:** Logo with initials connected.

MONTJOY, CLAUDE,
706 Indian Creek Rd, Clinton, SC 29325, Phone: 864-697-6160
Specialties: Folders, slip joint, lock, lock liner and interframe. **Patterns:** Hunters, boots, fighters, some art knives and folders. **Technical:** Grinds ATS-34 and Damascus. Offers inlaid handle scales. **Prices:** $100 to $500. **Remarks:** Full-time maker; first knife sold in 1982. Custom orders, no catalog. **Mark:** Montjoy.

MOONEY, MIKE,
19432 E Cloud Rd, Queen Creek, AZ 85242, Phone: 480-987-3576, mike@moonblades.com; Web: www.moonblades.com
Specialties: Fancy working straight knives of his design or customers. **Patterns:** Fighters, Bowies, daggers, hunters, kitchen, camp. **Technical:** Flat-grind, hand-rubbed finish, S30V, commercial Damascus, CPM154. **Prices:** $250 to $2000. **Remarks:** Doing business as moonblades.com. **Mark:** M. Mooney followed by crescent moon.

MOORE, JAMES B,
1707 N Gillis, Ft. Stockton, TX 79735, Phone: 915- 336-2113
Specialties: Classic working straight knives and folders of his design. **Patterns:** Hunters, Bowies, daggers, fighters, boots, utility/camp knives, locking folders and slip-joint folders. **Technical:** Grinds 440C, ATS-34, D2, L6, CPM and commercial Damascus. **Prices:** $85 to $700; exceptional knives to $1500. **Remarks:** Full-time maker; first knife sold in 1972. **Mark:** Name, city and state.

MOORE, JON P,
304 South N Rd, Aurora, NE 68818, Phone: 402-849- 2616, Web: www.sharpdecisionknives.com
Specialties: Working and fancy straight knives using antler, exotic bone, wood and Micarta. Will use customers antlers on request. **Patterns:** Hunters, skinners, camp Bowies. **Technical:** Hand forged high carbon steel. Makes his own Damascus. **Remarks:** Part-time maker, sold first knife in 2003, member of ABS - apprentice. Does on location knife forging demonstrations. **Mark:** Signature.

MOORE, MARVE,
HC 89 Box 393, Willow, AK 99688, Phone: 907-232- 0478, marvemoore@aol.com
Specialties: Fixed blades forged and stock removal. **Patterns:** Hunter, skinners, fighter, short swords. **Technical:** 100 percent of his work is done by hand. **Prices:** $100 to $500. **Remarks:** Also makes his own sheaths. **Mark:** -MM-.

MOORE, MICHAEL ROBERT,
70 Beauliew St, Lowell, MA 01850, Phone: 978-479-0589, Fax: 978-441-1819

MOORE, TED,
340 E Willow St, Elizabethtown, PA 17022, Phone: 717- 367-3939, tedmoore@supernet.com; Web: www.tedmooreknives.com
Specialties: Damascus folders, cigar cutters. **Patterns:** Locking folders and slip joint. **Technical:** Grinds Damascus, high-carbon and stainless; also ATS-34 and D2. **Prices:** $250 to $1500. **Remarks:** Part-time maker; first knife sold 1993. Knife and gun leather also. **Mark:** Moore U.S.A.

MORETT, DONALD,
116 Woodcrest Dr, Lancaster, PA 17602-1300, Phone: 717-746-4888

MORGAN, JEFF,
9200 Arnaz Way, Santee, CA 92071, Phone: 619-448- 8430
Specialties: Fancy working straight knives. **Patterns:** Hunters, fighters, boots, old west designs. **Technical:** Grinds D2, 440C, ATS-34, 5160 and 1095; likes exotic handles. **Prices:** $60 to $300; some to $800. **Remarks:** Full-time maker; first knife sold in 1977, Knifemakers Guild Member since 1984. **Mark:** Initials connected.

MORGAN, TOM,
14689 Ellett Rd, Beloit, OH 44609, Phone: 330-537- 2023
Specialties: Working straight knives and period pieces. **Patterns:** Hunters, boots and presentation tomahawks. **Technical:** Grinds O1, 440C and 154CM. **Prices:** Knives, $65 to $200; tomahawks, $100 to $325. **Remarks:** Full-time maker; first knife sold in 1977. **Mark:** Last name and type of steel used.

MORRIS, C H,
1590 Old Salem Rd, Frisco City, AL 36445, Phone: 334- 575-7425
Specialties: LinerLock® folders. **Patterns:** Interframe liner locks. **Technical:** Grinds 440C and ATS-34. **Prices:** Start at $350. **Remarks:** Full- time maker; first knife sold in 1973. Doing business as Custom Knives. **Mark:** First and middle initials, last name.

MORRIS, DARRELL PRICE,
92 Union, St. Plymouth, Devon, ENGLAND PL1 3EZ, Phone: 0752 223546
Specialties: Traditional Japanese knives, Bowies and high-art knives. **Technical:** Nickel Damascus and mokume. **Prices:** $1000 to $4000. **Remarks:** Part-time maker; first knife sold in 1990. **Mark:** Initials and Japanese name—Kuni Shigae.

MORRIS, ERIC,
306 Ewart Ave, Beckley, WV 25801, Phone: 304-255- 3951

MOSES, STEVEN,
1610 W Hemlock Way, Santa Ana, CA 92704

MOSIER, JOSHUA J,
SPRING CREEK KNIFE WORKS, PO Box 476/ 608 7th St, Deshler, NE 68340, Phone: 402-365-4386, joshm@sl- kw.com; Web:www.sc-kw.com
Specialties: Working straight and folding knives of his designs with customer specs. **Patterns:** Hunter/utility LinerLock® folders. **Technical:** Forges random pattern Damascus, 01, and 5160. **Prices:** $85 and up. **Remarks:** Part-time maker, sold first knife in 1986. **Mark:** SCKW.

MOULTON, DUSTY,
135 Hillview Lane, Loudon, TN 37774, Phone: 865- 408-9779, Web: www.moultonknives.com
Specialties: Fancy and working straight knives. **Patterns:** Hunters, fighters, fantasy and miniatures. **Technical:** Grinds ATS-34 and Damascus. **Prices:** $300 to $2000. **Remarks:** Full-time maker; first knife sold in 1991. Now doing engraving on own knives as well as other makers. **Mark:** Last name.

MOUNT, DON,
4574 Little Finch Ln, Las Vegas, NV 89115, Phone: 702- 531-2925
Specialties: High-tech working and using straight knives of his design. **Patterns:** Bowies, fighters and utility/camp knives. **Technical:** Uses 440C and ATS-34. **Prices:** $150 to $300; some to $1000. **Remarks:** Part-time maker; first knife sold in 1985. **Mark:** Name below a woodpecker.

MOYER, RUSS,
1266 RD 425 So, Havre, MT 59501, Phone: 406-395- 4423
Specialties: Working knives to customer specs. **Patterns:** Hunters, Bowies and survival knives. **Technical:** Forges W2 & 5160. **Prices:** $150 to $350. **Remarks:** Part-time maker; first knife sold in 1976. **Mark:** Initials in logo.

MULKEY, GARY,
533 Breckenridge Rd, Branson, MO 65616, Phone: 417-335-0123, gary@mulkeyknives.com; Web: www.mulkeyknives.com
Specialties: Working and fancy fixed blades and folders of his design and to customer's specs. **Patterns:** Hunters, Bowies, fighters and folders. Lock back and single action autos. **Technical:** Prefers 1095 or D2 with Damascus, filework, inlets or clay coated blades available on order. **Prices:** $200 to $1000 plus. **Remarks:** Full-time maker since 1997. Shop/showroom open to public. **Mark:** MUL above skeleton key.

MULLER, JODY,
3359 S. 225th Rd., Goodson, MO 65663, Phone: 417- 852-4306/417-752-3260, mullerforge2@hotmail.com; Web: www.mullerforge.com
Specialties: Hand engraving, carving and inlays, fancy folders and oriental styles. **Patterns:** One-of-a-kind fixed blades and folders in all styles. **Technical:** Forges own Damascus and high carbon steel. **Prices:** $300 and up. **Remarks:** Full-time Journeyman Smith, knifemaker, does hand engraving, carving and inlay. All work done by maker. **Mark:** Muller J.S.

MUNROE, DERYK C,
PO Box 3454, Bozeman, MT 59772

MURSKI, RAY,
12129 Captiva Ct, Reston, VA 22091-1204, Phone: 703- 264-1102, murski@vtisp.com
Specialties: Fancy working/using folders of his design. **Patterns:** Hunters, slip-joint folders and utility/camp knives. **Technical:** Grinds CPM-3V **Prices:** $125 to $500. **Remarks:** Spare-time maker; first knife sold in 1996. **Mark:** Engraved name with serial number under name.

MUTZ, JEFF,
8210 Rancheria Dr. Unit 7, Rancho Cucamonga, CA 91730, Phone: 909-931-9829, jmutzknives@hotmail.com; Web: www.jmutzknives.com
Specialties: Traditional working/using fixed blade and slip-jointed knives of own design and customer specs. **Patterns:** Hunters, skinners, and folders. **Technical:** Grinds 440C. Offers scrimshaw. **Prices:** $145 to $500. **Remarks:** Full-time maker, first knife sold in 1998. **Mark:** First initial, last name over "maker."

MYERS, PAUL,
644 Maurice St, Wood River, IL 62095, Phone: 618-258- 1707
Specialties: Fancy working straight knives and folders. **Patterns:** Full range of folders, straight hunters and Bowies; tie tacks; knife and fork sets. **Technical:** Grinds D2, 440C, ATS-34 and 154CM. **Prices:** $100 to $350; some to $3000. **Remarks:** Full-time maker; first knife sold in 1974. **Mark:** Initials with setting sun on front; name and number on back.

MYERS, STEVE,
903 Hickory Rd., Virginia, IL 62691-8716, Phone: 217- 452-3157, Web: www.myersknives.net
Specialties: Working straight knives and integrals. **Patterns:** Camp knives, hunters, skinners, Bowies, and boot knives. **Technical:** Forges own Damascus and high carbon steels. **Prices:** $250 to $1,000. **Remarks:** Full-time maker, first knife sold in 1985. **Mark:** Last name in logo.

N

NATEN, GREG,
1804 Shamrock Way, Bakersfield, CA 93304-3921
Specialties: Fancy and working/using folders of his design. **Patterns:** Fighters, hunters and locking folders. **Technical:** Grinds 440C, ATS-34 and CPM440V. Heat-treats; prefers desert ironwood, stag and mother-of- pearl. Designs and sews leather sheaths for straight knives. **Prices:** $175 to $600; some to $950. **Remarks:** Spare-time maker; first knife sold in 1992. **Mark:** Last name above battle-ax, handmade.

NAUDE, LOUIS,
3 Flamingo, Protea Heights, Cape Town, Western Cape 7560, www.louisnaude.co.za

NEALY, BUD,
RR1, Box 1439, Stroudsburg, PA 18360, Phone: 570-402- 1018, Fax: 570-402-1018, budnealy@ptd.net; Web: www.budnealyknifemaker.com
Specialties: Original design concealment knives with designer multi-concealment sheath system. **Patterns:** Concealment knives, boots, combat and collector pieces. **Technical:** Grinds CPM 154, S30V & Damascus. **Prices:** $200 to $2500. **Remarks:** Full-time maker; first knife sold in 1980. **Mark:** Name, city, state or signature.

NEDVED, DAN,
206 Park Dr, Kalispell, MT 59901, Phone: 406-752-5060
Specialties: Slip joint folders, liner locks, straight knives. **Patterns:** Mostly

traditional or modern blend with traditional lines. **Technical:** Grinds ATS-34, 440C, 1095 and uses other makers Damascus. **Prices:** $95 and up. Mostly in the $150 to $200 range. **Remarks:** Part-time maker, averages 2 a month. **Mark:** Dan Nedved or Nedved with serial # on opposite side.

NEELY, GREG,
5419 Pine St, Bellaire, TX 77401, Phone: 713-991-2677, ediiorio@houston.rr.com
    Specialties: Traditional patterns and his own patterns for work and/or collecting. **Patterns:** Hunters, Bowies and utility/camp knives. **Technical:** Forges own Damascus, 1084, 5160 and some tool steels. Differentially tempers. **Prices:** $225 to $5000. **Remarks:** Part-time maker; first knife sold in 1987. **Mark:** Last name or interlocked initials, MS.

NEILSON, J,
RR 2 Box 16, Wyalusing, PA 18853, Phone: 570-746-4944, mountainhollow@epix.net; Web: www.mountainhollow.net
    Specialties: Working and collectable fixed blade knives. **Patterns:** Hunter/fighters, Bowies, neck knives and daggers. **Technical:** 1084, 1095, 5160, W-2, 52100, maker's own Damascus. **Prices:** $175 to $2500. **Remarks:** ABS Master Smith, full-time maker, first knife sold in 2000, doing business as Neilson's Mountain Hollow. Each knife comes with a sheath by Tess. **Mark:** J. Neilson MS.

NELSON, DR CARL,
2500 N Robison Rd, Texarkana, TX 75501

NELSON, KEN,
11059 Hwy 73, Pittsville, WI 54466, Phone: 715-323-0538 or 715-884-6448, Email:dwarveniron@yahoo.com
    Specialties: Working straight knives, period pieces. **Patterns:** Utility, hunters, dirks, daggers, throwers, hawks, axes, swords, pole arms and blade blanks as well. **Technical:** Forges 5160, 52100, W2, 10xx, L6, carbon steels and own Damascus. Does his own heat treating. **Prices:** $50 to $350, some to $3000. **Remarks:** Part-time maker. First knife sold in 1995. Doing business as Iron Wolf Forge. **Mark:** Stylized wolf paw print.

NELSON, TOM,
PO Box 2298, Wilropark 1731, Gauteng, SOUTH AFRICA, Phone: 27 11 7663991, Fax: 27 11 7687161, tom.nelson@telkomsa.net
    Specialties: Own Damascus (Hosaic etc.) **Patterns:** One-of-a-kind art knives, swords and axes. **Prices:** $500 to $1000.

NETO JR., NELSON AND DE CARVALHO, HENRIQUE M.,
R. Joao Margarido No 20-V, Guerra, Braganca Paulista, SP-12900-000, BRAZIL, Phone: 011-7843-6889, Fax: 011-7843-6889
    Specialties: Straight knives and folders. **Patterns:** Bowies, katanas, jambyias and others. **Technical:** Forges high-carbon steels. **Prices:** $70 to $3000. **Remarks:** Full-time makers; first knife sold in 1990. **Mark:** HandN.

NEUHAEUSLER, ERWIN,
Heiligenangerstrasse 15, 86179 Augsburg, GERMANY, Phone: 0821/81 49 97, ERWIN@AUASBURGKNIVES.DE
    Specialties: Using straight knives of his design. **Patterns:** Hunters, boots, Bowies and folders. **Technical:** Grinds ATS-34, RWL-34 and Damascus. **Prices:** $200 to $750. **Remarks:** Spare-time maker; first knife sold in 1991. **Mark:** Etched logo, last name and city.

NEVLING, MARK,
BURR OAK KNIVES, PO Box 9, Hume, IL 61932, Phone: 217-887-2522, burroakknives@aol.com; Web: www.burroakknives.com
    Specialties: Straight knives and folders of his own design. **Patterns:** Hunters, fighters, Bowies, folders, and small executive knives. **Technical:** Convex grinds, Forges, uses only high-carbon and Damascus. **Prices:** $200 to $2000. **Remarks:** Full-time maker, first knife sold 1988. Apprentice Damascus smith to George Werth.

NEWCOMB, CORBIN,
628 Woodland Ave, Moberly, MO 65270, Phone: 660-263-4639
    Specialties: Working straight knives and folders; period pieces. **Patterns:** Hunters, axes, Bowies, folders, buckskinned blades and boots. **Technical:** Hollow-grinds D2, 440C and 154CM; prefers natural handle materials. Makes own Damascus; offers cable Damascus. **Prices:** $100 to $500. **Remarks:** Full-time maker; first knife sold in 1982. Doing business as Corbin Knives. **Mark:** First name and serial number.

NEWHALL, TOM,
3602 E 42nd Stravenue, Tucson, AZ 85713, Phone: 520-721-0562, gggaz@aol.com

NEWTON, LARRY,
1758 Pronghorn Ct, Jacksonville, FL 32225, Phone: 904-221-2340, Fax: 904-220-4098, CNewton1234@aol.com
    Specialties: Traditional and slender high-grade gentlemen's automatic folders, locking liner type tactical, and working straight knives. **Patterns:** Front release locking folders, interframes, hunters, and skinners. **Technical:** Grinds Damascus, ATS-34, 440C and D2. **Prices:** Folders start at $350, straights start at $150. **Remarks:** Retired teacher. Full-time maker. First knife sold in 1989. **Mark:** Last name.

NEWTON, RON,
223 Ridge Ln, London, AR 72847, Phone: 479-293-3001, rnewton@cei.net
    Specialties: Mosaic Damascus folders with accelerated actions. **Patterns:** One-of-a-kind. **Technical:** 1084-15N20 steels used in his mosaic Damascus steels. **Prices:** $1000 to $5000. **Remarks:** Also making antique Bowie repros and various fixed blades. **Mark:** All capital letters in NEWTON "Western Invitation" font.

NICHOLSON, R. KENT,
PO Box 204, Phoenix, MD 21131, Phone: 410-323-6925
    Specialties: Large using knives. **Patterns:** Bowies and camp knives in the Moran-style. **Technical:** Forges W2, 9260, 5160; makes Damascus. **Prices:** $150 to $995. **Remarks:** Part-time maker; first knife sold in 1984. **Mark:** Name.

NIELSON, JEFF V,
1060 S Jones Rd, Monroe, UT 84754, Phone: 435-527-4242, jvn1u205@hotmail.com
    Specialties: Classic knives of his design and to customer specs. **Patterns:** Fighters, hunters; miniatures. **Technical:** Grinds 440C stainless and Damascus. **Prices:** $100 to $1200. **Remarks:** Part-time maker; first knife sold in 1991. **Mark:** Name, location.

NIEMUTH, TROY,
3143 North Ave, Sheboygan, WI 53083, Phone: 414-452-2927
    Specialties: Period pieces and working/using straight knives of his design and to customer specs. **Patterns:** Hunters and utility/camp knives. **Technical:** Grinds 440C, 1095 and A2. **Prices:** $85 to $350; some to $500. **Remarks:** Full-time maker; first knife sold in 1995. **Mark:** Etched last name.

NILSSON, JONNY WALKER,
Tingsstigen 11, SE-933 33 Arvidsjaur, SWEDEN, Phone: (46) 960-13048, 0960.1304@telia.com; Web: www.jwnknives.com
    Specialties: High-end collectible Nordic hunters, engraved reindeer antler. World class freehand engravings. Matching engraved sheaths in leather, bone and Arctic wood with inlays. Combines traditional techniques and design with his own innovations. Master Bladesmith who specializes in forging mosaic Damascus. Sells unique mosaic Damascus bar stock to folder makers. **Patterns:** Own designs and traditional Sami designs. **Technical:** Mosaic Damascus of UHB 20 C 15N20 with pure nickel, hardness HRC 58-60. **Prices:** $1500 to $6000. **Remarks:** Full-time maker since 1988. Nordic Champion (5 countries) numerous times, 50 first prizes in Scandinavian shows. Yearly award in his name in Nordic Championship. Knives inspired by 10,000 year old indigenous Sami culture. **Mark:** JN on sheath, handle, custom wood box. JWN on blade.

NIRO, FRANK,
2469 Waverly Dr., Blind Bay, B.C. Canada V0E1H1, Phone: 250-675-4234
    Specialties: Liner locking folding knives in his designs in what might be called standard patterns. **Technical:** Enjoys grinding mainly mosaic Damascus with pure nickel of the make up for blades that are often double ground; as well as meteorite for bolsters which are then etched and heat colored. Uses 416 stainless for spacers with inlays of natural materials, gem stones with also file work. Liners are made from titanium are most often fully file worked and anodized. Only uses natural materials particularly mammoth ivory for scales. **Prices:** $500 to $1500 **Remarks:** Full time maker. Has been selling knives for over thirty years. **Mark:** Last name on the inside of the spacer.

NISHIUCHI, MELVIN S,
6121 Forest Park Dr, Las Vegas, NV 89156, Phone: 702-438-2327
    Specialties: Collectable quality using/working knives. **Patterns:** Locking liner folders, fighters, hunters and fancy personal knives. **Technical:** Grinds ATS-34 and Devin Thomas Damascus; prefers semi-precious stone and exotic natural handle materials. **Prices:** $375 to $2000. **Remarks:** Part-time maker; first knife sold in 1985. **Mark:** Circle with a line above it.

NOLEN, R D AND STEVE,
105 Flowingwells Rd, Pottsboro, TX 75076, Phone: 903-786-2454, blademaster@nolenknives.com; Web: www.nolenknives.com
    Specialties: Working knives; display pieces. **Patterns:** Wide variety of straight knives, butterflies and buckles. **Technical:** Grind D2, 440C and 154CM. Offer filework; make exotic handles. **Prices:** $150 to $800; some higher. **Remarks:** Full-time makers; first knife sold in1958. Steve is third generation maker. **Mark:** NK in oval logo.

NORDELL, INGEMAR,
Skarpå 2103, 82041 Färila, SWEDEN, Phone: 0651-23347
    Specialties: Classic working and using straight knives. **Patterns:** Hunters, Bowies and fighters. **Technical:** Forges and grinds ATS-34, D2 and Sandvik. **Prices:** $120 to $1500. **Remarks:** Part-time maker; first knife sold in 1985. **Mark:** Initials or name.

NOREN, DOUGLAS E,
14676 Boom Rd, Springlake, MI 49456, Phone: 616-842-4247, gnoren@icsdata.com
    Specialties: Hand forged blades, custom built and made to order. Hand file work, carving and casting. Stag and stacked handles. Replicas of Scagel and Joseph Rogers. Hand tooled custom made sheaths. **Technical:** Master smith, 5160, 52100 and 1084 steel. **Prices:** Start at $250. **Remarks:** Sole authorship, works in all mediums, ABS Mastersmith, all knives come with a custom hand-tooled sheath. Also makes anvils. Enjoys the challenge and meeting people.

NORFLEET, ROSS W,
4110 N Courthouse Rd, Providence Forge, VA 23140-3420, Phone: 804-966-2596, rossknife@aol.com
 Specialties: Classic, traditional and working/using knives of his design or in standard patterns. **Patterns:** Hunters and folders. **Technical:** Hollow-grinds 440C and ATS-34. **Prices:** $150 to $550. **Remarks:** Part-time maker; first knife sold in 1992. **Mark:** Last name.

NORTON, DON,
95N Wilkison Ave, Port Townsend, WA 98368-2534, Phone: 306-385-1978
 Specialties: Fancy and plain straight knives. **Patterns:** Hunters, small Bowies, tantos, boot knives, fillets. **Technical:** Prefers 440C, Micarta, exotic woods and other natural handle materials. Hollow-grinds all knives except fillet knives. **Prices:** $185 to $2800; average is $200. **Remarks:** Full-time maker; first knife sold in 1980. **Mark:** Full name, Hsi Shuai, city, state.

NOTT, RON P,
PO Box 281, Summerdale, PA 17093, Phone: 717-732- 2763, neitznott@aol.com
 Specialties: High-art folders and some straight knives. **Patterns:** Scale release folders. **Technical:** Grinds ATS-34, 416 and nickel-silver. Engraves, inlays gold. **Prices:** $250 to $3000. **Remarks:** Full-time maker; first knife sold in 1993. Doing business as Knives By Nott, customer engraving. **Mark:** First initial, last name and serial number.

NOWLAND, RICK,
3677 E Bonnie Rd, Waltonville, IL 62894, Phone: 618-279-3170, ricknowland@frontiernet.net
 Specialties: Slip joint folders in traditional patterns. **Patterns:** Trapper, whittler, sowbelly, toothpick and copperhead. **Technical:** Uses ATS-34, bolsters and liners have integral construction. **Prices:** $225 to $1000. **Remarks:** Part-time maker. **Mark:** Last name.

NUNN, GREGORY,
HC64 Box 2107, Castle Valley, UT 84532, Phone: 435-259-8607
 Specialties: High-art working and using knives of his design; new edition knife with handle made from anatomized dinosaur bone, first ever made. **Patterns:** Flaked stone knives. **Technical:** Uses gem-quality agates, jaspers and obsidians for blades. **Prices:** $250 to $2300. **Remarks:** Full- time maker; first knife sold in 1989. **Mark:** Name, knife and edition numbers, year made.

O

OCHS, CHARLES F,
124 Emerald Lane, Largo, FL 33771, Phone: 727- 536-3827, Fax: 727-536-3827, chuckandbelle@juno.com
 Specialties: Working knives; period pieces. **Patterns:** Hunters, fighters, Bowies, buck skinners and folders. **Technical:** Forges 52100, 5160 and his own Damascus. **Prices:** $150 to $1800; some to $2500. **Remarks:** Full-time maker; first knife sold in 1978. **Mark:** OX Forge.

O'DELL, CLYDE,
176 Ouachita 404, Camden, AR 71701, Phone: 870- 574-2754, abcodell@arkansas.net
 Specialties: Working knives. **Patterns:** Hunters, camp knives, Bowies, daggers, tomahawks. **Technical:** Forges 5160 and 1084. **Prices:** Starting at $125. **Remarks:** Spare-time maker. **Mark:** Last name.

ODGEN, RANDY W,
10822 Sage Orchard, Houston, TX 77089, Phone: 713-481-3601

ODOM JR., VICTOR L.,
PO Box 572, North, SC 29112, Phone: 803-247- 2749, cell 803-608-0829, vlodom3@tds.net
 Specialties: Forged knives and tomahawks; stock removal knives. **Patterns:** Hunters, Bowies and folders. **Technical:** Use 1095, 5160, 52100 high carbon and alloy steels, ATS-34, and 55. **Prices:** Straight knives $60 and up. Folders @$250 and up. **Remarks:** Student of Mr. George Henron. SCAK.ORG. Secretary of the Couth Carolina Association of Knifemakers. **Mark:** Steel stamp "ODOM" and etched "Odom Forge North, SC" plus a serial number.

OGDEN, BILL,
OGDEN KNIVES, PO Box 52, Avis
AVIS, PA 17721, Phone: 570-974-9114
 Specialties: One-of-a-kind, liner-lock folders, hunters, skinners, minis. **Technical:** Grinds ATS-34, 440-C, D2, 52100, Damascus, natural and unnatural handle materials, hand-stitched custom sheaths. **Prices:** $50 and up. **Remarks:** Part-time maker since 1992. **Marks:** Last name or "OK" stamp (Ogden Knives).

OGLETREE JR., BEN R,
2815 Israel Rd, Livingston, TX 77351, Phone: 409-327-8315
 Specialties: Working/using straight knives of his design. **Patterns:** Hunters, kitchen and utility/camp knives. **Technical:** Grinds ATS-34, W1 and 1075; heat-treats. **Prices:** $200 to $400. **Remarks:** Part-time maker; first knife sold in 1955. **Mark:** Last name, city and state in oval with a tree on either side.

O'HARE, SEAN,
1831 Rte. 776, Grand Manan, NB, CANADA E5G 2H9, Phone: 506-662-8524, sean@ohareknives.com; Web: www.ohareknives.com
 Specialties: Fixed blade hunters and tactical knives. **Patterns:** Neck knives to larger hunter and tactical knives. **Technical:** Stock removal, full and hidden tang knives. **Prices:** $125 USD to $800 USD. **Remarks:** Strives to balance aesthetics, functionality and durability. **Mark:** 1st is "OHARE KNIVES", 2nd is "NWT CANADA."

OLIVE, MICHAEL E,
6388 Angora Mt Rd, Leslie, AR 72645, Phone: 870- 363-4668
 Specialties: Fixed blades. **Patterns:** Bowies, camp knives, fighters and hunters. **Technical:** Forged blades of 1084, W2, 5160, Damascus of 1084, and1572. **Prices:** $250 and up. **Remarks:** Received J.S. stamp in 2005. **Mark:** Olive.

OLIVER, TODD D,
894 Beaver Hollow, Spencer, IN 47460, Phone: 812- 829-1762
 Specialties: Damascus hunters and daggers. High-carbon as well. **Patterns:** Ladder, twist random. **Technical:** Sole author of all his blades. **Prices:** $350 and up. **Remarks:** Learned bladesmithing from Jim Batson at the ABS school and Damascus from Billy Merritt in Indiana. **Mark:** T.D. Oliver Spencer IN. Two crossed swords and a battle ax.

OLOFSON, CHRIS,
29 KNIVES, 1 Kendall SQ Bldg. 600, Cambridge, MA 02139, Phone: 617-492-0451, artistacie@earthlink.net

OLSON, DARROLD E,
PO Box 1539, Springfield, OR 97477, Phone: 541-285-1412
 Specialties: Straight knives and folders of his design and to customer specs. **Patterns:** Hunters, liner locks and locking folders. **Technical:** Grinds 440C, ATS-34 and 154CM. Uses anodized titanium; sheaths wet-molded. **Prices:** $250 to $550. **Remarks:** Part-time maker; first knife sold in 1989. **Mark:** Etched logo, year, type of steel and name.

OLSON, ROD,
Box 5973, High River, AB, CANADA T1V 1P6, Phone: 403-652-2744, Fax: 403-646-5838
 Specialties: Lockback folders with gold toothpicks. **Patterns:** Locking folders. **Technical:** Grinds ATS-34 blades and spring, filework-14kt bolsters and liners. **Prices:** Mid range. **Remarks:** Part-time maker; first knife sold in 1979. **Mark:** Last name on blade.

OLSON, WAYNE C,
890 Royal Ridge Dr, Bailey, CO 80421, Phone: 303-816-9486
 Specialties: High-tech working knives. **Patterns:** Hunters to folding lockers; some integral designs. **Technical:** Grinds 440C, 154CM and ATS- 34; likes hand-finishes; precision-fits stainless steel fittings—no solder, no nickel silver. **Prices:** $275 to $600; some to $3000. **Remarks:** Part- time maker; first knife sold in 1979. **Mark:** Name, maker.

OLSZEWSKI, STEPHEN,
1820 Harkney Hill Rd, Coventry, RI 02816, Phone: 401-397-4774, blade5377@yahoo.com; Web: www.olszewskiknives.com
 Specialties: Lock back, liner locks, automatics (art knives). **Patterns:** One-of-a-kind art knives specializing in figurals. **Technical:** Damascus steel, titanium file worked liners, fossil ivory and pearl. Double actions. **Prices:** $1750 to $20,000. **Remarks:** Will custom build to your specifications. Quality work with guarantee. **Mark:** SCO inside fish symbol. Also "Olszewski."

O'MALLEY, DANIEL,
4338 Evanston Ave N, Seattle, WA 98103, Phone: 206-527-0315
 Specialties: Custom chef's knives. **Remarks:** Making knives since 1997.

O'MARCHEARLEY, MICHAEL,
129 Lawnview Dr., Wilmington, OH 45177, Phone: 937-728-2818, omachearleycustomknives@yahoo.com
 Specialties: Forged and Stock removal; hunters, skinners, bowies, plain to fancy. **Technical:** ATS-34 and 5160, forges own Damascus. **Prices:** $180-$1000 and up. **Remarks:** Full-time maker, first knife made in 1999. **Mark:** Last name and shamrock.

ONION, KENNETH J,
47-501 Hui Kelu St, Kaneohe, HI 96744, Phone: 808-239-1300, Fax: 808-289-1301, shopjunky@aol.com; Web: www.kenonionknives.com
 Specialties: Folders featuring speed safe as well as other invention gadgets. **Patterns:** Hybrid, art, fighter, utility. **Technical:** S30V, CPM 154V, Cowry Y, SQ-2 and Damascus. **Prices:** $500 to $20,000. **Remarks:** Full-time maker; designer and inventor. First knife sold in 1991. **Mark:** Name and state.

ORTEGA, BEN M,
165 Dug Rd, Wyoming, PA 18644, Phone: 717-696- 3234

ORTON, RICH,
3625 Fleming St, Riverside, CA 92509, Phone: 951-685-3019, ortonknifeworks@earthlink.net
 Specialties: Straight knives only. **Patterns:** Bird, trout and bowies. **Technical:** Grinds ATS-34, CPM154. Heat treats by Paul Bos. **Prices:** $100 to $1000. **Remarks:** Full-time maker; first knife sold in 1992. Doing business as Orton Knife Works. **Mark:** Last name, city state (maker)

OSBORNE, DONALD H,
5840 N McCall, Clovis, CA 93611, Phone: 559- 299-9483, Fax: 559-298-1751, oforge@sbcglobal.net
 Specialties: Traditional working using straight knives and folder of his design. **Patterns:** Working straight knives, Bowies, hunters, camp knives and folders. **Technical:** Forges carbon steels and makes Damascus. Grinds

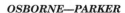
ATS-34, 154CM, and 440C. **Prices:** $150 and up. **Remarks:** Part-time maker. **Mark:** Last name logo and J.S.

OSBORNE, WARREN,
#2-412 Alysa Ln, Waxahachie, TX 75167, Phone: 972-935-0899, Fax: 972-937-9004, ossie1@worldnet.att.net; Web: www.osborneknives.com
Specialties: Investment grade collectible, interframes, one-of-a-kinds; unique locking mechanisms and cutting competition knives. **Patterns:** Folders; bolstered and interframes; conventional lockers, front lockers and back lockers; some slip-joints; some high-art pieces. **Technical:** Grinds CPM M4, BG42, CPM S30V, Damascus - some forged and stock removed cutting competition knives. **Prices:** $1200 to $3500; some to $5000. Interframes $1250 to $3000. **Remarks:** Full-time maker; first knife sold in 1980. **Mark:** Last name in boomerang logo.

OTT, FRED,
1257 Rancho Durango Rd, Durango, CO 81303, Phone: 970-375-9669
Patterns: Bowies, hunters tantos and daggers. **Technical:** Forges 1086M, W2 and Damascus. **Prices:** $250 to $1000. **Remarks:** Full-time maker. **Mark:** Last name.

OUYE, KEITH,
PO Box 25307, Honolulu, HI 96825, Phone: 808-395-7000, keithouyeknives@yahoo.com; Web: www.keithouyeknives.com
Specialties: Folders with 1/8 blades and titanium handles. **Patterns:** Tactical design with liner lock and flipper. **Technical:** Blades are stainless steel ATS 34, CPM154 stainless steel and S30V. Titanium liners (.071) and scales 3/16 pivots and stop pin, titanium pocket clip. Heat treat by Paul Bos.**Prices:** $450-$600 with engraved knives starting at $995 and up. **Remarks:** Engraving done by C.J. Cal (www.caiengraving.com) and Bruce Shaw Retired, so basically a full time knifemaker. Sold first fixed blade in 2004 and first folder in 2005. **Mark:** Ouye/Hawaii with steel type on back side **Other:** Selected by Blade Magazine (March 2006 issue) as one of five makers to watch in 2006.

OVEREYNDER, T R,
1800 S. Davis Dr, Arlington, TX 76013, Phone: 817-277-4812, Fax: 817-277-4812, trovereynderknives@sbcglobal.net; Web: www.overeynderknives.com
Specialties: Highly finished collector-grade knives. Multi-blades. **Patterns:** Fighters, Bowies, daggers, locking folders, 70 percent collector-grade multi blade slip joints, 25 percent interframe, 5 percent fixed blade **Technical:** Grinds CPM-D2, BG-42, S60V, S30V, CPM154, CPM M4, RWL-34 vendor supplied Damascus. Has been making titanium-frame folders since 1977. **Prices:** $750 to $2000, some to $7000. **Remarks:** Full-time maker; first knife sold in 1977. Doing business as TRO Knives. **Mark:** T.R. OVEREYNDER KNIVES, city and state.

OWENS, DONALD,
2274 Lucille Ln, Melbourne, FL 32935, Phone: 321-254-9765

OWENS, JOHN,
14500 CR 270, Nathrop, CO 81236, Phone: 719-395-0870
Specialties: Hunters. **Prices:** $200 to $375 some to $650. **Remarks:** Spare-time maker. **Mark:** Last name.

OWNBY, JOHN C,
3316 Springbridge Ln, Plano, TX 75025, john@johnownby.com; Web: www.johnownby.com
Specialties: Hunters, utility/camp knives. **Patterns:** Hunters, locking folders and utility/camp knives. **Technical:** 440C, D2 and ATS-34. All blades are flat ground. Prefers natural materials for handles—exotic woods, horn and antler. **Prices:** $150 to $350; some to $500. **Remarks:** Part-time maker; first knife sold in 1993. Doing business as John C. Ownby Handmade Knives. **Mark:** Name, city, state.

OYSTER, LOWELL R,
543 Grant Rd, Corinth, ME 04427, Phone: 207-884-8663
Specialties: Traditional and original designed multi-blade slip-joint folders. **Patterns:** Hunters, minis, camp and fishing knives. **Technical:** Grinds O1; heat-treats. **Prices:** $55 to $450; some to $750. **Remarks:** Full-time maker; first knife sold in 1981. **Mark:** A scallop shell.

P

PACHI, FRANCESCO,
Via Pometta 1, 17046 Sassello (SV), ITALY, Phone: 019 720086, Fax: 019 720086, Web: www.pachi-knives.com
Specialties: Folders and straight knives of his design. **Patterns:** Utility, hunters and skinners. **Technical:** Grinds RWL-34, CPM S30V and Damascus. **Prices:** $800 to $3500. **Remarks:** Full-time maker; first knife sold in 1991. **Mark:** Logo with last name.

PACKARD, BOB,
PO Box 311, Elverta, CA 95626, Phone: 916-991-5218
Specialties: Traditional working/using straight knives of his design and to customer specs. **Patterns:** Hunters, fishing knives, utility/camp knives. **Technical:** Grinds ATS-34, 440C; Forges 52100, 5168 and cable Damascus. **Prices:** $75 to $225. **Mark:** Engraved name and year.

PADGETT JR., EDWIN L,
340 Vauxhall St, New London, CT 06320-3838, Phone: 860-443-2938
Specialties: Skinners and working knives of any design. **Patterns:** Straight and folding knives. **Technical:** Grinds ATS-34 or any tool steel upon request. **Prices:** $50 to $300. **Mark:** Name.

PADILLA, GARY,
PO Box 5706, Bellingham, WA 98227, Phone: 360-756-7573, gkpadilla@yahoo.com
Specialties: Unique knives of all designs and uses. **Patterns:** Hunters, kitchen knives, utility/camp knives and obsidian ceremonial knives. **Technical:** Grinds 440C, ATS-34, O1 and Damascus. **Prices:** Generally $100 to $200. **Remarks:** Part-time maker; first knife sold in 1977. **Mark:** Stylized name.

PAGE, LARRY,
1200 Mackey Scott Rd, Aiken, SC 29801-7620, Phone: 803-648-0001
Specialties: Working knives of his design. **Patterns:** Hunters, boots and fighters. **Technical:** Grinds ATS-34. **Prices:** Start at $85. **Remarks:** Part-time maker; first knife sold in 1983. **Mark:** Name, city and state in oval.

PAGE, REGINALD,
6587 Groveland Hill Rd, Groveland, NY 14462, Phone: 716-243-1643
Specialties: High-art straight knives and one-of-a-kind folders of his design. **Patterns:** Hunters, locking folders and slip-joint folders. **Technical:** Forges O1, 5160 and his own Damascus. Prefers natural handle materials but will work with Micarta. **Remarks:** Spare-time maker; first knife sold in 1985. **Mark:** First initial, last name.

PAINTER, TONY,
87 Fireweed Dr, Whitehorse Yukon, CANADA Y1A 5T8, Phone: 867-633-3323, jimmies@klondiker.com; Web: www.tonypainterdesigns.com
Specialties: One-of-a-kind using knives, some fancy, fixed and folders. **Patterns:** No fixed patterns. **Technical:** Grinds ATS-34, D2, O1, S30V, Damascus satin finish. Prefers to use exotic woods and other natural materials. Micarta and G10 on working knives. **Prices:** Starting at $200. **Remarks:** Full-time knifemaker and carver. First knife sold in 1996. **Mark:** Two stamps used: initials TP in a circle and painter.

PALM, RIK,
10901 Scripps Ranch Blvd, San Diego, CA 92131, Phone: 858-530-0407, rikpalm@knifesmith.com; Web: www.knifesmith.com
Specialties: Sole authorship of one-of-a-kind unique art pieces, working/using knives and sheaths. **Patterns:** Carved nature themed knives, camp, hunters, friction folders, tomahawks, and small special pocket knives. **Technical:** Makes own Damascus, forges 5160H, 1084, 1095, W2, O1. Does his own heat treating including clay hardening. **Prices:** $80 and up. **Remarks:** American Bladesmith Society Journeyman Smith. First blade sold in 2000. **Mark:** Stamped, hand signed, etched last name signature.

PALMER, TAYLOR,
TAYLOR-MADE SCENIC KNIVES INC., Box 97, Blanding, UT 84511, Phone: 435-678-2523, taylormadewoodeu@citlink.net
Specialties: Bronze carvings inside of blade area. **Prices:** $250 and up. **Mark:** Taylor Palmer Utah.

PANAK, PAUL S,
9128 Stanhope-Kellogsville Rd, Kinsman, OH 44428, Phone: 330-876-2210, burn@burnknives.com; Web: www.burnknives.com
Specialties: Italian-styled knives. DA OTF's, Italian style stilettos. **Patterns:** Vintage-styled Italians, fighting folders and high art gothic-styles all with various mechanisms. **Technical:** Grinds ATS-34, 154 CM, 440C and Damascus. **Prices:** $800 to $3000. **Remarks:** Full-time maker, first knife sold in 1998. **Mark:** "Burn."

PARDUE, JOE,
PO Box 693, Spurger, TX 77660, Phone: 409-429-7074, Fax: 409-429-5657

PARDUE, MELVIN M,
4461 Jerkins Rd., Repton, AL 36475, Phone: 251-248-2686, mpardue@frontiernet.net; Web: www.pardueknives.com
Specialties: Folders, collectable, combat, utility and tactical. **Patterns:** Lockback, liner lock, push button; all blade and handle patterns. **Technical:** Grinds 154CM, 440C, 12C27. Forges mokume and Damascus. Uses titanium. **Prices:** $400 to $1600. **Remarks:** Full-time maker, Guild member, ABS member, AFC member. First knife made in 1957; first knife sold professionally in 1974. **Mark:** Mel Pardue.

PARKER, CLIFF,
6350 Tulip Dr, Zephyrhills, FL 33544, Phone: 813-973-1682
Specialties: Damascus gent knives. **Patterns:** Locking liners, some straight knives. **Technical:** Mostly use 1095, 1084, 15N20, 203E and powdered steel. **Prices:** $700 to $1800. **Remarks:** Making own Damascus and specializing in mosaics; first knife sold in 1996. Full-time beginning in 2000. **Mark:** CP.

PARKER, J E,
11 Domenica Cir, Clarion, PA 16214, Phone: 814-226-4837, jimparkerknives@hotmail.com Web:www.jimparkerknives.com
Specialties: Fancy/embellished, traditional and working straight knives of his design and to customer specs. Engraving and scrimshaw by the best in the business. **Patterns:** Bowies, hunters and LinerLock® folders. **Technical:** Grinds 440C, 440V, ATS-34 and nickel Damascus. Prefers mastodon, oosik, amber and malachite handle material. **Prices:** $75 to $5200. **Remarks:** Full-time maker; first knife sold in 1991. Doing business as Custom Knife. **Mark:** J E Parker and Clarion PA stamped or etched in blade.

PARKER, ROBERT NELSON,
1527 E Fourth St, Royal Oak, MI 48067, Phone: 248-545-8211, rnparkerknives@ wowway.com; Web: classicknifedesign@wowway.com
Specialties: Traditional working and using straight knives of his design. **Patterns:** Chutes, subhilts, hunters, and fighters. **Technical:** Grinds ATS-34; GB-42, S-30V, BG-42, ATS, 34-D-Z, no forging, hollow and flat grinds, full and hidden tangs. Hand-stitched leather sheaths. **Prices:** $400 to $1400; some to $2000. **Remarks:** Full-time maker; first knife sold in 1986. **Mark:** Full name.

PARKS, BLANE C,
15908 Crest Dr, Woodbridge, VA 22191, Phone: 703-221-4680
Specialties: Knives of his design. **Patterns:** Boots, Bowies, daggers, fighters, hunters, kitchen knives, locking and slip-joint folders, utility/camp knives, letter openers and friction folders. **Technical:** Grinds ATS-34, 440C, D2 and other carbon steels. Offers filework, silver wire inlay and wooden sheaths. **Prices:** Start at $250 to $650; some to $1000. **Remarks:** Part-time maker; first knife sold in 1993. Doing business as B.C. Parks Knives. **Mark:** First and middle initials, last name.

PARKS, JOHN,
3539 Galilee Church Rd, Jefferson, GA 30549, Phone: 706-367-4916
Specialties: Traditional working and using straight knives of his design. **Patterns:** Hunters, integral bolsters, and personal knives. **Technical:** Forges 1095 and 5168. **Prices:** $275 to $600; some to $800. **Remarks:** Part-time maker; first knife sold in 1989. **Mark:** Initials.

PARLER, THOMAS O,
11 Franklin St, Charleston, SC 29401, Phone: 803-723-9433

PARRISH, ROBERT,
271 Allman Hill Rd, Weaverville, NC 28787, Phone: 828-645-2864
Specialties: Heavy-duty working knives of his design or to customer specs. **Patterns:** Survival and duty knives; hunters and fighters. **Technical:** Grinds 440C, D2, O1 and commercial Damascus. **Prices:** $200 to $300; some to $6000. **Remarks:** Part-time maker; first knife sold in 1970. **Mark:** Initials connected, sometimes with city and state.

PARRISH III, GORDON A,
940 Lakloey Dr, North Pole, AK 99705, Phone: 907-488-0357, ga-parrish@ gci.net
Specialties: Classic and high-art straight knives of his design and to customer specs; working and using knives. **Patterns:** Bowies and hunters. **Technical:** Grinds tool steel and ATS-34. Uses mostly Alaskan handle materials. **Prices:** $200 to $1000. **Remarks:** Spare-time maker; first knife sold in 1980. **Mark:** Last name, state.

PARSONS, LARRY,
1038 W Kyle Way, Mustang, OK 73064, Phone: 405-376-9408, l.j.parsons@ sbcglobal.net
Specialties: Variety of sheaths from plain leather, geometric stamped, also inlays of various types. **Prices:** Starting at $35 and up

PARSONS, MICHAEL R,
MCKEE KNIVES, 7042 McFarland Rd., Indianapolis, IN 46227, Phone: 317-784-7943, mparsons@comcast.net
Specialties: Hand-forged fixed-blade and folding knives, all fancy but all are useable knives. **Patterns:** Engraves, carves, wire inlay, and leather work. All knives one-of-a-kind. **Technical:** Blades forged from files, all work hand done. Doing business as McKee Knives. **Prices:** $350 to $2000. **Mark:** McKee.

PARSONS, PETE,
5905 High Country Dr., Helena, MT 59602, Phone: 406-202-0181, Parsons14@ MT.net; Web: www.ParsonsMontanaKnives.com
Specialties: Forged utility blades in straight steel or Damascus (will grind stainless on customer request). Folding knives of my own design. **Patterns:** Hunters, fighters, Bowies, hikers, camp knives, everyday carry folders, tactical folders, gentleman's folders. Some customer designed pieces. **Technical:** Forges carbon steel, grinds carbon steel and some stainless. Forges own Damascus. **Mark:** Left side of blade PARSONS stamp or Parsons Helena, MT etch.

PARTRIDGE, JERRY D.,
P.O. Box 977, DeFuniak Springs, FL 32435, Phone: 850-585-0458, jerry@ partridgeknives.com; Web: www.partridgeknives.com
Specialties: Various-sized skinners and fighting knives of carbon Damascus and 440C stainless (both plain and fileworked). I primarily use mammoth tooth, exotic woods (such as ebonywood, cocobolo, kingwood, blackwood, rosewood, and bloodwood) and giraffe bone. **Prices:** $250 and up, depending on materials used. **Remarks:** First knife sold in 2007. **Mark:** Partridge Knives logo on the blade.

PASSMORE, JIMMY D,
316 SE Elm, Hoxie, AR 72433, Phone: 870-886-1922

PATRICK, BOB,
12642 24A Ave, S. Surrey, B.C., CANADA V4A 8H9, Phone: 604-538-6214, Fax: 604-888-2683, bob@knivesonnet.com; Web: www.knivesonnet.com
Specialties: Maker's designs only, No orders. **Patterns:** Bowies, hunters, daggers, throwing knives. **Technical:** D2, 5160, Damascus. **Prices:** Good value for the money. **Remarks:** Full-time maker; first knife sold in 1987. Doing business as Crescent Knife Works. **Mark:** Logo with name and province or Crescent Knife Works.

PATRICK, CHUCK,
PO Box 127, Brasstown, NC 28902, Phone: 828-837-7627
Specialties: Period pieces. **Patterns:** Hunters, daggers, tomahawks, pre-Civil War folders. **Technical:** Forges hardware, his own cable and Damascus, available in fancy pattern and mosaic. **Prices:** $150 to $1000; some higher. **Remarks:** Full-time maker. **Mark:** Hand-engraved name or flying owl.

PATRICK, PEGGY,
PO Box 127, Brasstown, NC 28902, Phone: 828-837-7627
Specialties: Authentic period and Indian sheaths, braintan, rawhide, beads and quill work. **Technical:** Does own braintan, rawhide; uses only natural dyes for quills, old color beads.

PATRICK, WILLARD C,
PO Box 5716, Helena, MT 59604, Phone: 406-458-6552, Fax: 406-458-7068, wkamar2@onewest.net
Specialties: Working straight knives and one-of-a-kind art knives of his design or to customer specs. **Patterns:** Hunters, Bowies, fish, patch and kitchen knives. **Technical:** Grinds ATS-34, 1095, O1, A2 and Damascus. **Prices:** $100 to $2000. **Remarks:** Full-time maker; first knife sold in 1989. Doing business as Wil-A-Mar Cutlery. **Mark:** Shield with last name and a dagger.

PATTAY, RUDY,
510 E. Harrison St, Long Beach, NY 11561, Phone: 516-431-0847, dolphinp@ optonline.net; Web: www.pattayknives.com
Specialties: Fancy and working straight knives of his design. **Patterns:** Bowies, hunters, utility/camp knives, drop point, skinners. **Technical:** Hollow-grinds ATS-34, 440C, O1. Offers commercial Damascus, stainless steel soldered guards; fabricates guard and butt cap on lathe and milling machine. Heat-treats. Prefers synthetic handle materials. Offers hand-sewn sheaths. **Prices:** $100 to $350; some to $500. **Remarks:** Full-time maker; first knife sold in 1990. **Mark:** First initial, last name in sorcerer logo.

PATTERSON, PAT,
Box 246, Barksdale, TX 78828, Phone: 830-234-3586, pat@pattersonknives.com
Specialties: Traditional fixed blades and LinerLock® folders. **Patterns:** Hunters and folders. **Technical:** Grinds 440C, ATS-34, D2, O1 and Damascus. **Prices:** $250 to $1000. **Remarks:** Full-time maker. First knife sold in 1991. **Mark:** Name and city.

PATTON, DICK AND ROB,
6803 View Ln, Nampa, ID 83687, Phone: 208-468-4123, grpatton@ pattonknives.com; Web: www.pattonknives.com
Specialties: Custom Damascus, hand forged, fighting knives, Bowie and tactical. **Patterns:** Mini Bowie, Merlin Fighter, Mandrita Fighting Bowie. **Prices:** $100 to $2000.

PAULO, FERNANDES R,
Raposo Tavares No 213, Lencois Paulista, 18680, Sao Paulo, BRAZIL, Phone: 014-263-4281
Specialties: An apprentice of Jose Alberto Paschoarelli, his designs are heavily based on the later designs. **Technical:** Grinds tool steels and stainless steels. Part-time knifemaker. **Prices:** Start from $100. **Mark:** P.R.F.

PAWLOWSKI, JOHN R,
111 Herman Melville Ave, Newport News, VA 23606, Phone: 757-870-4284, Fax: 757-223-5935, www.virginiacustomcutlery.com
Specialties: Traditional working and using straight knives and folders. **Patterns:** Hunters, Bowies, fighters and camp knives. **Technical:** Stock removal, grinds 440C, ATS-34, 154CM and buys Damascus. **Prices:** $150 to $500; some higher. **Remarks:** Part-time maker, first knife sold in 1983, Knifemaker Guild Member. **Mark:** Name with attacking eagle.

PEAGLER, RUSS,
PO Box 1314, Moncks Corner, SC 29461, Phone: 803-761-1008
Specialties: Traditional working straight knives of his design and to customer specs. **Patterns:** Hunters, fighters, boots. **Technical:** Hollow-grinds 440C, ATS-34 and O1; uses Damascus steel. Prefers bone handles. **Prices:** $85 to $300; some to $500. **Remarks:** Spare-time maker; first knife sold in 1983. **Mark:** Initials.

PEASE, W D,
657 Cassidy Pike, Ewing, KY 41039, Phone: 606-845-0387, Web: www.wdpeaseknives.com
Specialties: Display-quality working folders. **Patterns:** Fighters, tantos and boots; locking folders and interframes. **Technical:** Grinds ATS-34 and commercial Damascus; has own side-release lock system. **Prices:** $500 to $1000; some to $3000. **Remarks:** Full-time maker; first knife sold in 1970. **Mark:** First and middle initials, last name and state. W. D. Pease Kentucky.

PEELE, BRYAN,
219 Ferry St, PO Box 1363, Thompson Falls, MT 59873, Phone: 406-827-4633, banana_peele@yahoo.com
Specialties: Fancy working and using knives of his design. **Patterns:** Hunters, Bowies and fighters. **Technical:** Grinds 440C, ATS-34, D2, O1 and commercial Damascus. **Prices:** $110 to $300; some to $900. **Remarks:** Part-time maker; first knife sold in 1985. **Mark:** The Elk Rack, full name, city, state.

PENDLETON, LLOYD,
24581 Shake Ridge Rd, Volcano, CA 95689, Phone: 209-296-3353, Fax: 209-296-3353
Specialties: Contemporary working knives in standard patterns. **Patterns:** Hunters, fighters and boots. **Technical:** Grinds and ATS-34; mirror finishes. **Prices:** $400 to $900. **Remarks:** Full-time maker; first knife sold in 1973. **Mark:** First initial, last name logo, city and state.

PENDRAY, ALFRED H,
13950 NE 20th St, Williston, FL 32696, Phone: 352-528-6124
Specialties: Working straight knives and folders; period pieces. **Patterns:** Fighters and hunters, axes, camp knives and tomahawks. **Technical:** Forges Wootz steel; makes his own Damascus; makes traditional knives from old files and rasps. **Prices:** $125 to $1000; some to $3500. **Remarks:** Part-time maker; first knife sold in 1954. **Mark:** Last initial in horseshoe logo.

PENFOLD, MICK,
PENFOLD KNIVES, 5 Highview Close, Tremar, Cornwall PL14 5SJ, ENGLAND, Phone: 01579-345783, Fax: 01579-345783, mickpenfold@btinternet.com; Web: www.penfoldknives.com
Specialties: Hunters, fighters, Bowies. **Technical:** Grinds 440C, ATS- 34, and Damascus. **Prices:** $200 to $1800. **Remarks:** Part-time maker. First knives sold in 1999. **Mark:** Last name.

PENNINGTON, C A,
163 Kainga Rd, Kainga Christchurch 8009, NEW ZEALAND, Phone: 03-3237292, capennington@xtra.co.nz
Specialties: Classic working and collectors knives. Folders a specialty. **Patterns:** Classical styling for hunters and collectors. **Technical:** Forges his own all tool steel Damascus. Grinds D2 when requested. **Prices:** $240 to $2000. **Remarks:** Full-time maker; first knife sold in 1988. Color brochure $3. **Mark:** Name, country.

PEPIOT, STEPHAN,
73 Cornwall Blvd, Winnipeg, Man., CANADA R3J- 1E9, Phone: 204-888-1499
Specialties: Working straight knives in standard patterns. **Patterns:** Hunters and camp knives. **Technical:** Grinds 440C and industrial hack- saw blades. **Prices:** $75 to $125. **Remarks:** Spare-time maker; first knife sold in 1982. Not currently taking orders. **Mark:** PEP.

PERRY, CHRIS,
1654 W. Birch, Fresno, CA 93711, Phone: 559-246- 7446, chris.perry4@comcast.net
Specialties: Traditional working/using straight knives of his design. **Patterns:** Boots, hunters and utility/camp knives. **Technical:** Grinds ATS- 34, Damascus, 416ss fittings, silver and gold fittings, hand-rubbed finishes. **Prices:** Starting at $250. **Remarks:** Part-time maker, first knife sold in 1995. **Mark:** Name above city and state.

PERRY, JIM,
Hope Star PO Box 648, Hope, AR 71801, jenn@comfabinc.com

PERRY, JOHN,
9 South Harrell Rd, Mayflower, AR 72106, Phone: 501- 470-3043, jpknives@cyberback.com
Specialties: Investment grade and working folders; Antique Bowies and slip joints. **Patterns:** Front and rear lock folders, liner locks, hunters and Bowies. **Technical:** Grinds CPM440V, D2 and making own Damascus. Offers filework. **Prices:** $375 to $1200; some to $3500. **Remarks:** Part- time maker; first knife sold in 1991. Doing business as Perry Custom Knives. **Mark:** Initials or last name in high relief set in a diamond shape.

PERRY, JOHNNY,
PO Box 35, Inman, SC 29349, Phone: 864-431-6390, perr3838@bellsouth.net
Mark: High Ridge Forge.

PERSSON, CONNY,
PL 588, 820 50 Loos, SWEDEN, Phone: +46 657 10305, Fax: +46 657 413 435, connyknives@swipnet.se; Web: www.connyknives.com
Specialties: Mosaic Damascus. **Patterns:** Mosaic Damascus. **Technical:** Straight knives and folders. **Prices:** $1000 and up. **Mark:** C. Persson.

PETEAN, FRANCISCO AND MAURICIO,
R. Dr. Carlos de Carvalho Rosa 52, Centro, Birigui, SP-16200-000, BRAZIL, Phone: 0186-424786
Specialties: Classic knives to customer specs. **Patterns:** Bowies, boots, fighters, hunters and utility knives. **Technical:** Grinds D6, 440C and high- carbon steels. Prefers natural handle material. **Prices:** $70 to $500. **Remarks:** Full-time maker; first knife sold in 1985. **Mark:** Last name, hand made.

PETERSEN, DAN L,
10610 SW 81st, Auburn, KS 66402, Phone: 785- 256-2640, dan@petersenknives.com; Web: www.petersenknives.com
Specialties: Period pieces and forged integral hilts on hunters and fighters. **Patterns:** Texas-style Bowies, boots and hunters in high-carbon and Damascus steel. **Technical:** Austempers forged high-carbon sword blades. Precision heat treating using salt tanks. **Prices:** $400 to $5000. **Remarks:** First knife sold in 1978. ABS Master Smith. **Mark:** Stylized initials, MS.

PETERSON, CHRIS,
Box 143, 2175 W Rockyford, Salina, UT 84654, Phone: 435-529-7194
Specialties: Working straight knives of his design. **Patterns:** Large fighters, boots, hunters and some display pieces. **Technical:** Forges O1 and meteor. Makes and sells his own Damascus. Engraves, scrimshaws and inlays. **Prices:** $150 to $600; some to $1500. **Remarks:** Full-time maker; first knife sold in 1986. **Mark:** A drop in a circle with a line through it.

PETERSON, ELDON G,
368 Antelope Trl, Whitefish, MT 59937, Phone: 406-862-2204, draino@digisys.net; Web: http://www.kmg.org/egpeterson
Specialties: Fancy and working folders, any size. **Patterns:** Lockback interframes, integral bolster folders, liner locks, and two-blades. **Technical:** Grinds 440C and ATS-34. Offers gold inlay work, gem stone inlays and engraving. **Prices:** $285 to $5000. **Remarks:** Full-time maker; first knife sold in 1974. **Mark:** Name, city and state.

PETERSON, KAREN,
THE PEN AND THE SWORD LTD., PO Box 290741, Brooklyn, NY 11229-0741, Phone: 718-382-4847, Fax: 718-376- 5745, info@pensword.com; Web: www.pensword.com

PETERSON, LLOYD (PETE) C,
64 Halbrook Rd, Clinton, AR 72031, Phone: 501-893-0000, wmblade@cyberback.com
Specialties: Miniatures and mosaic folders. **Prices:** $250 and up. **Remarks:** Lead time is 6-8 months. **Mark:** Pete.

PFANENSTIEL, DAN,
1824 Lafayette Ave, Modesto, CA 95355, Phone: 209-575-5937, dpfan@sbcglobal.net
Specialties: Japanese tanto, swords. One-of-a-kind knives. **Technical:** Forges simple carbon steels, some Damascus. **Prices:** $200 to $1000. **Mark:** Circle with wave inside.

PHILIPPE, D A,
PO Box 306, Cornish, NH 03746, Phone: 603-543-0662
Specialties: Traditional working straight knives. **Patterns:** Hunters, trout and bird, camp knives etc. **Technical:** Grinds ATS-34, 440C, A-2, Damascus, flat and hollow ground. Exotic woods and antler handles. Brass, nickel silver and stainless components. **Prices:** $125 to $800. **Remarks:** Full-time maker, first knife sold in 1984. **Mark:** First initial, last name.

PHILLIPS, ALISTAIR,
Amaroo, ACT, 2914, AUSTRALIA, alistair.phillips@knives.mutantdiscovery.com; Web: http://knives.mutantdiscovery.com
Specialties: Slipjoint folders, forged or stock removal fixed blades. **Patterns:** Single blade slipjoints, smaller neck knives, and hunters. **Technical:** Flat grnds O1, ATS-34, and forged 1055. **Prices:** $800 to $400. **Remarks:** Part-time maker, first knife made in 2005. **Mark:** Stamped signature.

PHILLIPS, DENNIS,
16411 West Bennet Rd, Independence, LA 70443, Phone: 985-878-8275
Specialties: Specializes in fixed blade military combat tacticals.

PHILLIPS, JIM,
PO Box 168, Williamstown, NJ 08094, Phone: 609-567- 0695

PHILLIPS, RANDY,
759 E. Francis St, Ontario, CA 91761, Phone: 909- 923-4381
Specialties: Hunters, collector-grade liner locks and high-art daggers. **Technical:** Grinds D2, 440C and 154CM; embellishes. **Prices:** Start at $200. **Remarks:** Part-time maker; first knife sold in 1981. Not currently taking orders. **Mark:** Name, city and state in eagle head.

PHILLIPS, SCOTT C,
671 California Rd, Gouverneur, NY 13642, Phone: 315-287-1280, Web: www.mangusknives.com
Specialties: Sheaths in leather. Fixed blade hunters, boot knives, Bowies, buck skinners (hand forged and stock removal). **Technical:** 440C, 5160, 1095 and 52100. **Prices:** Start at $125. **Remarks:** Part-time maker; first knife sold in 1993. **Mark:** Before "2000" as above after S Mangus.

PICKENS, SELBERT,
2295 Roxalana Rd, Dunbar, WV 25064, Phone: 304-744-4048
Specialties: Using knives. **Patterns:** Standard sporting knives. **Technical:** Stainless steels; stock removal method. **Prices:** Moderate. **Remarks:** Part-time maker. **Mark:** Name.

PICKETT, TERRELL,
66 Pickett Ln, Lumberton, MS 39455, Phone: 601- 794-6125, pickettfence66@bellsouth.net
Specialties: Fix blades, camp knives, Bowies, hunters, & skinners. Forge and stock removal and some firework. **Technical:** 5160, 1095, 52100, 440C and ATS-34. **Prices:** Range from $150 to $550. **Mark:** Logo on stock removal T.W. Pickett and on forged knives Terrell Pickett's Forge.

PIENAAR, CONRAD,
19A Milner Rd, Bloemfontein 9300, SOUTH AFRICA, Phone: 027 514364180, Fax: 027 514364180
Specialties: Fancy working and using straight knives and folders of his design, to customer specs and in standard patterns. **Patterns:** Hunters, locking folders, cleavers, kitchen and utility/camp knives. **Technical:** Grinds 12C27, D2 and ATS-34. Uses some Damascus. Scrimshaws; inlays gold. Knives come with wooden box and custom-made leather sheath.

PIENAAR—PRESSBURGER

Prices: $300 to $1000. **Remarks:** Part-time maker; first knife sold in 1981. Doing business as C.P. Knifemaker. Makes slip joint folders and liner locking folders. **Mark:** Initials and serial number.

PIERCE, HAROLD L,
106 Lyndon Lane, Louisville, KY 40222, Phone: 502-429-5136
Specialties: Working straight knives, some fancy. **Patterns:** Big fighters and Bowies. **Technical:** Grinds D2, 440C, 154CM; likes sub-hilts. **Prices:** $150 to $450; some to $1200. **Remarks:** Full-time maker; first knife sold in 1982. **Mark:** Last name with knife through the last initial.

PIERCE, RANDALL,
903 Wyndam, Arlington, TX 76017, Phone: 817- 468-0138

PIERGALLINI, DANIEL E,
4011 N. Forbes Rd, Plant City, FL 33565, Phone: 813-754-3908, Fax: 8137543908, coolnifedad@earthlink.net
Specialties: Traditional and fancy straight knives and folders of his design or to customer's specs. **Patterns:** Hunters, fighters, skinners, working and camp knives. **Technical:** Grinds 440C, O1, D2, ATS-34, some Damascus; forges his own mokume. Uses natural handle material. **Prices:** $450 to $800; some to $1800. **Remarks:** Part-time maker; sold first knife in 1994. **Mark:** Last name, city, state or last name in script.

PIESNER, DEAN,
1786 Sawmill Rd, Conestogo, Ont., CANADA N0B 1N0, Phone: 519-664-3648, dean47@rogers.com
Specialties: Classic and period pieces of his design and to customer specs. **Patterns:** Bowies, skinners, fighters and swords. **Technical:** Forges 5160, 52100, steel Damascus and nickel-steel Damascus. Makes own mokume gane with copper, brass and nickel silver. Silver wire inlays in wood. **Prices:** Start at $150. **Remarks:** Full-time maker; first knife sold in 1990. **Mark:** First initial, last name, JS.

PITMAN, DAVID,
PO Drawer 2566, Williston, ND 58802, Phone: 701- 572-3325

PITT, DAVID F,
6812 Digger Pine Ln, Anderson, CA 96007, Phone: 530- 357-2393
Specialties: Fixed blade, hunters and hatchets. Flat ground mirror finish. **Patterns:** Hatchets with gut hook, small gut hooks, guards, bolsters or guard less. **Technical:** Grinds A2, 440C, 154CM, ATS-34, D2. **Prices:** $150 to $750. **Remarks:** Guild member since 1982. **Mark:** Bear paw with name David F. Pitt.

PLUNKETT, RICHARD,
29 Kirk Rd, West Cornwall, CT 06796, Phone: 860-672-3419; Toll free: 888-KNIVES-8
Specialties: Traditional, fancy folders and straight knives of his design. **Patterns:** Slip-joint folders and small straight knives. **Technical:** Grinds O1 and stainless steel. Offers many different file patterns. **Prices:** $150 to $450. **Remarks:** Full-time maker; first knife sold in 1994. **Mark:** Signature and date under handle scales.

POLK, CLIFTON,
4625 Webber Creek Rd, Van Buren, AR 72956, Phone: 479-474-3828, cliffpolkknives1@aol.com; Web: www.polkknives.com
Specialties: Fancy working folders. **Patterns:** One blades spring backs in five sizes, LinerLock®, automatics, double blades spring back folder with standard drop & clip blade or bird knife with drop and vent hook or cowboy's knives with drop and hoof pick and straight knives. **Technical:** Uses D2 & ATS-34. Makes all own Damascus using 1084, 1095, O1, 15N20, 5160. Using all kinds of exotic woods. Stag, pearls, ivory, mastodon ivory and other bone and horns. **Prices:** $200 to $3000. **Remarks:** Retired fire fighter, made knives since 1974. **Mark:** Polk.

POLK, RUSTY,
5900 Wildwood Dr, Van Buren, AR 72956, Phone: 479-410-3661, polkknives@aol.com; Web: www.polkknives.com
Specialties: Skinners, hunters, Bowies, fighters and forging working knives fancy Damascus, daggers, boot knives and survival knives. **Patterns:** Drop point, and forge to shape. **Technical:** ATS-34, 440C, Damascus, D2, 51/60, 1084, 15N20, does all his forging. **Prices:** $200 to $1500. **Mark:** R. Polk all hand made. RP on miniatures.

POLKOWSKI, AL,
8 Cathy Lane, Chester, NJ 07930, Phone: 908-879- 6030, Web: polkowskiknives.com
Specialties: High-tech straight knives and folders for adventurers and professionals. **Patterns:** Fighters, side-lock folders, boots and concealment knives. **Technical:** Grinds 154CM and S30V, satin and beadblast finishes; Kydex sheaths. **Prices:** Start at $100. **Remarks:** Full-time maker; first knife sold in 1985. **Mark:** Last name with lightning bolts.

POLLOCK, WALLACE J,
806 Russet Vly Dr, Cedar Park, TX 78613, wally@pollocknives.com
Specialties: Using knives, skinner, hunter, fighting, camp knives. **Patterns:** Use his own patterns or yours. Traditional hunters, daggers, fighters, camp knives. **Technical:** Grinds ATS-34, D-2, BG-42, makes own Damascus, D-2, O-1, ATS-34, prefer D-2, handles exotic wood, horn, bone, ivory. **Remarks:** Full-time maker, sold first knife 1973. **Prices:** $250 to $2500. **Mark:** Last name, maker, city/state.

POLZIEN, DON,
1912 Inler Suite-L, Lubbock, TX 79407, Phone: 806- 791-0766, blindinglightknives.net
Specialties: Traditional Japanese-style blades; restores antique Japanese swords, scabbards and fittings. **Patterns:** Hunters, fighters, one-of- a-kind art knives. **Technical:** 1045-1050 carbon steels, 440C, D2, ATS- 34, standard and cable Damascus. **Prices:** $150 to $2500. **Remarks:** Full-time maker. First knife sold in 1990. **Mark:** Oriental characters inside square border.

PONZIO, DOUG,
10219 W State Rd 81, Beloit, WI 53511, Phone: 608- 313-3223, prfgdoug@hughes.net; Web: www.ponziodamascus.com
Specialties: Mosaic Damascus, stainless Damascus. **Mark:** P.F.

POOLE, MARVIN O,
PO Box 552, Commerce, GA 30529, Phone: 803- 225-5970
Specialties: Traditional working/using straight knives and folders of his design and in standard patterns. **Patterns:** Bowies, fighters, hunters, locking folders, bird and trout knives. **Technical:** Grinds 440C, D2, ATS- 34. **Prices:** $50 to $150; some to $750. **Remarks:** Part-time maker; first knife sold in 1980. **Mark:** First initial, last name, year, serial number.

POSKOCIL, HELMUT,
Oskar Czeijastrasse 2, A-3340 Waidhofen/Ybbs, AUSTRIA, Phone: 0043-7442-54519, Fax: 0043-7442-54519
Specialties: High-art and classic straight knives and folders of his design. **Patterns:** Bowies, daggers, hunters and locking folders. **Technical:** Grinds ATS-34 and stainless and carbon Damascus. Hardwoods, fossil ivory, horn and amber for handle material; silver wire and gold inlays; silver butt caps. Offers engraving and scrimshaw. **Prices:** $350 to $850; some to $3500. **Remarks:** Part-time maker; first knife sold in 1991. **Mark:** Name.

POSNER, BARRY E,
12501 Chandler Blvd Suite 104, N. Hollywood, CA 91607, Phone: 818-752-8005, Fax: 818-752-8006
Specialties: Working/using straight knives. **Patterns:** Hunters, kitchen and utility/camp knives. **Technical:** Grinds ATS-34; forges 1095 and nickel. **Prices:** $95 to $400. **Remarks:** Part-time maker; first knife sold in 1987. Doing business as Posner Knives. Supplier of finished mosaic handle pin stock. **Mark:** First and middle initials, last name.

POTIER, TIMOTHY F,
PO Box 711, Oberlin, LA 70655, Phone: 337-639- 2229, tpotier@hotmail.com
Specialties: Classic working and using straight knives to customer specs; some collectible. **Patterns:** Hunters, Bowies, utility/camp knives and belt axes. **Technical:** Forges carbon steel and his own Damascus; offers filework. **Prices:** $300 to $1800; some to $4000. **Remarks:** Part- time maker; first knife sold in 1981. **Mark:** Last name, MS.

POTOCKI, ROGER,
Route 1 Box 333A, Goreville, IL 62939, Phone: 618- 995-9502

POTTER, BILLY,
6323 Hyland Dr., Dublin, OH 43017, Phone: 614-766- 6845, potterknives@yahoo.com; Web: www.potterknives.com
Specialties: Working straight knives; his design or to customers patterns. **Patterns:** Bowie, fighters, utilities, skinners, hunters, folding lock blade, miniatures and tomahawks. **Technical:** Grinds and forges, carbon steel, L6, 0-1, 1095, 5160, 1084 and 52000. Grinds 440C stainless. Forges own Damascus. Handles: prefers exotic hardwood, curly and birdseye maples. Bone, ivory, antler, pearl and horn. Some scrimshaw. **Prices:** Start at $100 up to $800. **Remarks:** Part-time maker; first knife sold 1996. **Mark:** First and last name Nashport OH.

POWELL, JAMES,
2500 North Robinson Rd, Texarkana, TX 75501

POWELL, ROBERT CLARK,
PO Box 321, 93 Gose Rd., Smarr, GA 31086, Phone: 478-994-5418
Specialties: Composite bar Damascus blades. **Patterns:** Art knives, hunters, combat, tomahawks. **Patterns:** Hand forges all blades. **Prices:** $300 and up. **Remarks:** ABS Journeyman Smith. **Mark:** Powell.

PRATER, MIKE,
PRATER AND COMPANY, 81 Sanford Ln., Flintstone, GA 30725, cmprater@aol.com; Web: www.casecustomknives.com
Specialties: Customizing factory knives. **Patterns:** Buck knives, case knives, hen and rooster knives. **Technical:** Manufacture of mica pearl. **Prices:** Varied. **Remarks:** First knife sold in 1980. **Mark:** Mica pearl.

PRESSBURGER, RAMON,
59 Driftway Rd, Howell, NJ 07731, Phone: 732-363-0816
Specialties: BG-42. Only knifemaker in U.S.A. that has complete line of affordable hunting knives made from BG-42. **Patterns:** All types hunting styles. **Technical:** Uses all steels; main steels are D-2 and BG-42. **Prices:** $75 to $500. **Remarks:** Full-time maker; has been making hunting knives for 30 years. Makes knives to your patterning. **Mark:** NA.

PRICE, TIMMY,
PO Box 906, Blairsville, GA 30514, Phone: 706-745- 5111

PRIMOS, TERRY,
932 Francis Dr, Shreveport, LA 71118, Phone: 318- 686-6625, tprimos@sport.rr.com or terry@primosknives.com; Web: www.primosknives.com
Specialties: Traditional forged straight knives. **Patterns:** Hunters, Bowies, camp knives, and fighters. **Technical:** Forges primarily 1084 and 5160; also forges Damascus. **Prices:** $250 to $600. **Remarks:** Full-time maker; first knife sold in 1993. **Mark:** Last name.

PRINSLOO, THEUNS,
PO Box 2263, Bethlehem, 9700, SOUTH AFRICA, Phone: 27824663885, theunmesa@telkomsa.net; Web: www.theunsprinsloo.com
Specialties: Fancy folders. **Technical:** Own Damascus and mokume. **Prices:** $450 to $1500.

PRITCHARD, RON,
613 Crawford Ave, Dixon, IL 61021, Phone: 815- 284-6005
Specialties: Plain and fancy working knives. **Patterns:** Variety of straight knives, locking folders, interframes and miniatures. **Technical:** Grinds 440C, 154CM and commercial Damascus. **Prices:** $100 to $200; some to $1500. **Remarks:** Part-time maker; first knife sold in 1979. **Mark:** Name and city.

PROVENZANO, JOSEPH D,
39043 Dutch Lane, Ponchatoula, LA 70454, Phone: 225-615-4846
Specialties: Working straight knives and folders in standard patterns. **Patterns:** Hunters, Bowies, folders, camp and fishing knives. **Technical:** Grinds ATS-34, 440C, 154CM, CPM 4400V, CPM420V and Damascus. Hollow-grinds hunters. **Prices:** $110 to $300; some to $1000. **Remarks:** Part-time maker; first knife sold in 1980. **Mark:** Joe-Pro.

PRYOR, STEPHEN L,
HC Rt 1, Box 1445, Boss, MO 65440, Phone: 573-626-4838, Fax: same, Knives4U3@juno.com; Web: www.stevescutler.com
Specialties: Working and fancy straight knives, some to customer specs. **Patterns:** Bowies, hunting/fishing, utility/camp, fantasy/art. **Technical:** Grinds 440C, ATS-34, 1085, some Damascus, and does filework. Stag and exotic hardwood handles. **Prices:** $250 and up. **Remarks:** Full-time maker; first knife sold in 1991. **Mark:** Stylized first initial and last name over city and state.

PUGH, JIM,
PO Box 711, Azle, TX 76020, Phone: 817-444-2679, Fax: 817-444-5455
Specialties: Fancy/embellished limited editions by request. **Patterns:** 5- to 7-inch Bowies, wildlife art pieces, hunters, daggers and fighters; some commemoratives. **Technical:** Multi color transplanting in solid 18K gold, fine gems; grinds 440C and ATS-34. Offers engraving, fancy file etching and leather sheaths for wildlife art pieces. Ivory and coco bolo handle material on limited editions. Designs animal head butt caps and paws or bear claw guards; sterling silver heads and guards. **Prices:** $60,000 to $80,000 each in the Big Five 2000 edition. **Remarks:** Full-time maker; first knife sold in 1970. **Mark:** Pugh (Old English).

PULIS, VLADIMIR,
CSA 230-95, SL Republic, 96701 Kremnica, SLOVAKIA, Phone: 00421 903 340076, Fax: 00427 903 390076, vpulis@host.sk; Web: www.vpulis.host.sk
Specialties: Fancy and high-art straight knives of his design. **Patterns:** Daggers and hunters. **Technical:** Forges Damascus steel. All work done by hand. **Prices:** $250 to $3000; some to $10,000. **Remarks:** Full-time maker; first knife sold in 1990. **Mark:** Initials in sixtagon.

PULLIAM, MORRIS C,
560 Jeptha Knob Rd, Shelbyville, KY 40065, Phone: 502-633-2261, mcpulliam@fastballinternet.com
Specialties: Working knives, Cherokee River pattern Damascus. **Patterns:** Hunters and tomahawks. **Technical:** Forges L6, W2, 1095, Damascus and bar 320 layer Damascus. **Prices:** $165 to $1200. **Remarks:** Full-time maker; first knife sold in 1974. Makes knives for Native American festivals. Doing business as Knob Hill Forge. Member of Piqua Sept Shawnee of Ohio. Indian name Waapiti NI-Paw-1 Elk Standing. As a member of a state tribe, is an American Indian artist and craftsman by federal law. **Mark:** Small and large - Pulliam.

PURSLEY, AARON,
8885 Coal Mine Rd, Big Sandy, MT 59520, Phone: 406-378-3200
Specialties: Fancy working knives. **Patterns:** Locking folders, straight hunters and daggers, personal wedding knives and letter openers. **Technical:** Grinds O1 and 440C; engraves. **Prices:** $900 to $2500. **Remarks:** Full-time maker; first knife sold in 1975. **Mark:** Initials connected with year.

PURVIS, BOB AND ELLEN,
2416 N Loretta Dr, Tucson, AZ 85716, Phone: 520-795-8290, repknives2@cox.net
Specialties: Hunter, skinners, Bowies, using knives, gentlemen folders and collectible knives. **Technical:** Grinds ATS-34, 440C, Damascus, Dama steel, heat-treats and cryogenically quenches. We do gold-plating, salt bluing, scrimshawing, filework and fashion handmade leather sheaths. Materials used for handles include exotic woods, mammoth ivory, mother-of-pearl, G-10 and Micarta. **Prices:** $165 to $800. **Remarks:** Knifemaker since retirement in 1984. Selling them since 1993. **Mark:** Script or print R.E. Purvis ~ Tucson, AZ or last name only.

PUTNAM, DONALD S,
590 Wolcott Hill Rd, Wethersfield, CT 06109, Phone: 860-563-9718, Fax: 860-563-9718, dpknives@cox.net
Specialties: Working knives for the hunter and fisherman. **Patterns:** His design or to customer specs. **Technical:** Uses stock removal method, O1, W2, D2, ATS-34, 154CM, 440C and CPM REX 20; stainless steel Damascus on request. **Prices:** $250 and up. **Remarks:** Full-time maker; first knife sold in 1985. **Mark:** Last name with a knife outline.

Q

QUAKENBUSH, THOMAS C,
2426 Butler Rd, Ft Wayne, IN 46808, Phone: 219-483-0749

QUARTON, BARR,
PO Box 4335, McCall, ID 83638, Phone: 208-634- 3641
Specialties: Plain and fancy working knives; period pieces. **Patterns:** Hunters, tantos and swords. **Technical:** Forges and grinds 154CM, ATS- 34 and his own Damascus. **Prices:** $180 to $450; some to $4500. **Remarks:** Part-time maker; first knife sold in 1978. Doing business as Barr Custom Knives. **Mark:** First name with bear logo.

QUATTLEBAUM, CRAIG,
18855 Andreanof Lp, Eagle River, AK 99577, Phone: 907-622-3919, mustang376@gci.net
Specialties: Traditional straight knives and one-of-a-kind knives of his design; period pieces. **Patterns:** Bowies and fighters. **Technical:** Forges 5168, 1095 and own Damascus. **Prices:** $300 to $2000. **Remarks:** Part-time maker; first knife sold in 1988. **Mark:** Stylized initials.

QUESENBERRY, MIKE,
110 Evergreen Cricle, Blairsden, CA 96103, Phone: 530-836-4606, quesenberry@psln.com; Web: www.quesenberryknives.com
Specialties: Hunters, daggers, Bowies, and integrals. **Technical:** Forges 52100, 1095, 1084, 5160. Makes own Damascus. Will use stainless on customer requests. Does own heat-treating and own leather work. **Prices:** Starting at $300. **Remarks:** Parttime maker. ABS member since 2006. **Mark:** Last name.

R

RACHLIN, LESLIE S,
1200 W Church St, Elmira, NY 14905, Phone: 607-733-6889, lrachlin@stry.rr.com
Specialties: Classic and working/using straight knives and folders of his design. **Patterns:** Hunters and utility/camp knives. **Technical:** Grinds 440C. **Prices:** $50 to $700. **Remarks:** Spare-time maker; first knife sold in 1989. Doing business as Tinkermade Knives. **Mark:** LSR

RADER, MICHAEL,
P.O. Box 393, Wilkeson, WA 98396, Phone: 253- 255-7064, michael@raderblade.com; Web: www.raderblade.com
Specialties: Swords, kitchen knives, integrals. **Patterns:** Non traditional designs. Inspired by various cultures. **Technical:** Most blades in forged 51200 + 200-600 layer Damascus in ISN-20 + 8660. **Prices:** $350 - $5,000. **Remarks:** ABS Journeyman Smith **Mark:** "Rader" on one side, "J.S." on other

RADOS, JERRY F,
7523 E 5000 N Rd, Grant Park, IL 60940, Phone: 815-472-3350, Fax: 815-472-3944
Specialties: Deluxe period pieces. **Patterns:** Hunters, fighters, locking folders, daggers and camp knives. **Technical:** Forges and grinds his own Damascus which he sells commercially; makes pattern-welded Turkish Damascus. **Prices:** Start at $900. **Remarks:** Full-time maker; first knife sold in 1981. **Mark:** Last name.

RAGSDALE, JAMES D,
3002 Arabian Woods Dr, Lithonia, GA 30038, Phone: 770-482-6739
Specialties: Fancy and embellished working knives of his design or to customer specs. **Patterns:** Hunters, folders and fighters. **Technical:** Grinds 440C, ATS-34 and A2. **Prices:** $150 and up. **Remarks:** Full-time maker; first knife sold in 1984. **Mark:** Fish symbol with name above, town below.

RAINVILLE, RICHARD,
126 Cockle Hill Rd, Salem, CT 06420, Phone: 860-859-2776, w1jo@snet.net
Specialties: Traditional working straight knives. **Patterns:** Outdoor knives, including fishing knives. **Technical:** L6, 400C, ATS-34. **Prices:** $100 to $800. **Remarks:** Full-time maker; first knife sold in 1982. **Mark:** Name, city, state in oval logo.

RALEY, R. WAYNE,
825 Poplar Acres Rd, Collierville, TN 38017, Phone: 901-853-2026

RALPH, DARREL,
BRIAR KNIVES, 4185 S St Rt 605, Galena, OH 43021, Phone: 740-965-9970, dr@darrelralph.com; Web: www.darrelralph.com
Specialties: Fancy, high-art, high-tech, collectible straight knives and folders of his design and to customer specs; unique mechanisms, some disassemble. **Patterns:** Daggers, fighters and swords. **Technical:** Forges his own Damascus, nickel and high-carbon. Uses mokume and Damascus; mosaics and special patterns. Engraves and heat-treats. Prefers pearl, ivory and abalone handle material; uses stones and jewels. **Prices:** $250 to six figures. **Remarks:** Full-time maker; first knife sold in 1987. Doing business as Briar Knives. **Mark:** DDR.

RAMEY, LARRY,
1315 Porter Morris Rd, Chapmansboro, TN 37035- 5120, Phone: 615-307-4233, larryrameyknives@hotmail.com; Web: www.larryrameyknives.com
Specialties: Titanium knives. Technical: Pictures taken by Hawkinson Photography.

RAMONDETTI, SERGIO,
VIA MARCONI N 24, 12013 CHIUSA DI PESIO (CN), ITALY, Phone: 0171 734490, Fax: 0171 734490, s.ramon@tin.it
Specialties: Folders and straight knives of his design. Patterns: Utility, hunters and skinners. Technical: Grinds RWL-34 and Damascus. Prices: $500 to $2000. Remarks: Part-time maker; first knife sold in 1999. Mark: Logo (S.Ramon) with last name.

RAMSEY, RICHARD A,
8525 Trout Farm Rd, Neosho, MO 64850, Phone: 417-451-1493, rams@direcway.com; Web: www.ramseyknives.com
Specialties: Drop point hunters. Patterns: Various Damascus. Prices: $125 to $1500. Mark: RR double R also last name-RAMSEY.

RANDALL, PATRICK,
160 Mesa Ave., Newbury Park, CA 91320, Phone: 805-754-8093, pat@patrickknives.com; Web: www.patrickknives.com
Specialties: EDC slipjoint folders, drop point hunters, and dive knives of own design. Technical: Materials are mostly O1, A2, and ATS-34. Wood, stag, jigged bone, and micarta handles. Prices: $125 to $225. Remarks: Part-time maker, 4 years of experience, makes about 50 knives per year.

RANDALL JR., JAMES W,
11606 Keith Hall Rd, Keithville, LA 71047, Phone: 318-925-6480, Fax: 318-925-1709, jw@jwrandall.com; Web: www.jwrandall.com
Specialties: Collectible and functional knives. Patterns: Bowies, hunters, daggers, swords, folders and combat knives. Technical: Forges 5160, 1084, O1 and his Damascus. Prices: $400 to $8000. Remarks: Part-time. First knife sold in 1998. Mark: JW Randall, MS.

RANDALL MADE KNIVES,
4857 South Orange Blossom Trail, Orlando, FL 32839, Phone: 407-855-8075, Fax: 407-855-9054, Web: http:// www.randallknives.com
Specialties: Working straight knives. Patterns: Hunters, fighters and Bowies. Technical: Forges and grinds O1 and 440B. Prices: $170 to $550; some to $450. Remarks: Full-time maker; first knife sold in 1937. Mark: Randall made, city and state in scimitar logo.

RANDOW, RALPH,
4214 Blalock Rd, Pineville, LA 71360, Phone: 318- 640-3369

RANKL, CHRISTIAN,
Possenhofenerstr 33, 81476 Munchen, GERMANY, Phone: 0049 01 71 3 66 26 79, Fax: 0049 8975967265, christian@crankl.de.
Specialties: Tail-lock knives. Patterns: Fighters, hunters and locking folders. Technical: Grinds ATS-34, D2, CPM1440V, RWL 34 also stainless Damascus. Prices: $450 to $950; some to $2000. Remarks: Full- time maker; first knife sold in 1989. Mark: Electrochemical etching on blade.

RAPP, STEVEN J,
8033 US Hwy 25-70, Marshall, NC 28753, Phone: 828-649-1092
Specialties: Gold quartz; mosaic handles. Patterns: Daggers, Bowies, fighters and San Francisco knives. Technical: Hollow- and flat-grinds 440C and Damascus. Prices: Start at $500. Remarks: Full-time maker; first knife sold in 1981. Mark: Name and state.

RAPPAZZO, RICHARD,
142 Dunsbach Ferry Rd, Cohoes, NY 12047, Phone: 518-783-6843
Specialties: Damascus locking folders and straight knives. Patterns: Folders, dirks, fighters and tantos in original and traditional designs. Technical: Hand-forges all blades; specializes in Damascus; uses only natural handle materials. Prices: $400 to $1500. Remarks: Part-time maker; first knife sold in 1985. Mark: Name, date, serial number.

RARDON, A D,
1589 SE Price Dr, Polo, MO 64671, Phone: 660-354- 2544
Specialties: Folders, miniatures. Patterns: Hunters, buck skinners, Bowies, miniatures and daggers. Technical: Grinds O1, D2, 440C and ATS-34. Prices: $150 to $2000; some higher. Remarks: Full-time maker; first knife sold in 1954. Mark: Fox logo.

RARDON, ARCHIE F,
1589 SE Price Dr, Polo, MO 64671, Phone: 660- 354-2330
Specialties: Working knives. Patterns: Hunters, Bowies and miniatures. Technical: Grinds O1, D2, 440C, ATS-34, cable and Damascus. Prices: $50 to $500. Remarks: Part-time maker. Mark: Boar hog.

RAY, ALAN W,
1287 FM 1280 E, Lovelady, TX 75851, Phone: 936-544- 6611, Fax: 936-636-2931, awray@rayzblades.com; Web: www.rayzblades.com
Specialties: Working straight knives of his design. Patterns: Hunters. Technical: Forges 01, L6 and 5160 for straight knives. Prices: $200 to $1000. Remarks: Full-time maker; first knife sold in 1979. Mark: Stylized initials.

REBELLO, INDIAN GEORGE,
358 Elm St, New Bedford, MA 02740- 3837, Phone: 508-951-2719, indgeo@juno.com; Web: www.indiangeorgesknives.com
Specialties: One-of-a-kind fighters and Bowies. Patterns: To customer's specs, hunters and utilities. Technical: Forges his own Damascus, 5160, 52100, 1084, 1095, cable and O1. Grinds S30V, ATS-34, 154CM, 440C, D2 and A2. Prices: Starting at $250. Remarks: Full-time maker, first knife sold in 1991. Doing business as Indian George's Knives. Founding father of the New England Knife Guild. Member of the N.C.C.A. and A.B.S. Mark: Indian George's Knives.

RED, VERNON,
2020 Benton Cove, Conway, AR 72034, Phone: 501- 450-7284, knivesvr@conwaycorp.net
Specialties: Custom design straight knives or folders of own design or customer's. Patterns: Hunters, fighters, Bowies, folders. Technical: Hollow grind, flat grind, stock removal and forged blades. Uses 440C, D-2, ATS-34, 1084, 1095, and Damascus.Prices: $150 and up. Remarks: Made first knife in 1982, first folder in 1992. Member of (AKA) Arkansas Knives Association. Doing business as Custom Made Knives by Vernon Red. Mark: Last name.

REDDIEX, BILL,
27 Galway Ave, Palmerston North, NEW ZEALAND, Phone: 06-357-0383, Fax: 06-358-2910
Specialties: Collector-grade working straight knives. Patterns: Traditional-style Bowies and drop-point hunters. Technical: Grinds 440C, D2 and O1; offers variety of grinds and finishes. Prices: $130 to $750. Remarks: Full-time maker; first knife sold in 1980. Mark: Last name around kiwi bird logo.

REED, DAVE,
Box 132, Brimfield, MA 01010, Phone: 413-245-3661
Specialties: Traditional styles. Makes knives from chains, rasps, gears, etc. Patterns: Bush swords, hunters, working minis, camp and utility knives. Technical: Forges 1075 and his own Damascus. Prices: Start at $50. Remarks: Part-time maker; first knife sold in 1970. Mark: Initials.

REED, JOHN M,
257 Navajo Dr, Oak Hill, FL 32759, Phone: 386-345- 4763
Specialties: Hunter, utility, some survival knives. Patterns: Trailing Point, and drop point sheath knives. Technical: ATS-34, Rockwell 60 exotic wood or natural material handles. Prices: $135 to $300. Depending on handle material. Remarks: Likes the stock removal method. "Old Fashioned trainling point blades." Handmade and sewn leather sheaths. Mark: "Reed" acid etched on left side of blade.

REEVE, CHRIS,
2949 Victory View Way, Boise, ID 83709-2946, Phone: 208-375-0367, Fax: 208-375-0368, crkinfo@chrisreeve.com; Web: www.chrisreeve.com
Specialties: Originator and designer of the One Piece range of fixed blade utility knives and of the Sebenza Integral Lock folding knives made by Chris Reeve Knives. Currently makes only one or two pieces per year himself. Patterns: Art folders and fixed blades; one-of-a-kind. Technical: Grinds specialty stainless steels, Damascus and other materials to his own design. Prices: $1000 and upwards. Remarks: Full-time in knife business; first knife sold in 1982. Mark: Signature and date.

REGGIO JR., SIDNEY J,
PO Box 851, Sun, LA 70463, Phone: 504-886- 5886
Specialties: Miniature classic and fancy straight knives of his design or in standard patterns. Patterns: Fighters, hunters and utility/camp knives. Technical: Grinds 440C, ATS-34 and commercial Damascus. Engraves; scrimshaws; offers filework. Hollow grinds most blades. Prefers natural handle material. Offers handmade sheaths. Prices: $85 to $250; some to $500. Remarks: Part-time maker; first knife sold in 1988. Doing business as Sterling Workshop. Mark: Initials.

REPKE, MIKE,
4191 N. Euclid Ave., Bay City, MI 48706, Phone: 517- 684-3111
Specialties: Traditional working and using straight knives of his design or to customer specs; classic knives; display knives. Patterns: Hunters, Bowies, skinners, fighters boots, axes and swords. Technical: Grind 440C. Offer variety of handle materials. Prices: $99 to $1500. Remarks: Full-time makers. Doing business as Black Forest Blades. Mark: Knife logo.

REVERDY, NICOLE AND PIERRE,
5 Rue de L'egalite', 26100 Romans, FRANCE, Phone: 334 75 05 10 15, Web: http://www.reverdy.com
Specialties: Art knives; legend pieces. Pierre and Nicole, his wife, are creating knives of art with combination of enamel on pure silver (Nicole) and poetic Damascus (Pierre) such as the "La dague a la licorne." Patterns: Daggers, folding knives Damascus and enamel, Bowies, hunters and other large patterns. Technical: Forges his Damascus and "poetic Damascus"; where animals such as unicorns, stags, dragons or star crystals appear, works with his own EDM machine to create any kind of pattern inside the steel with his own touch. Prices: $2000 and up. Remarks: Full-time maker since 1989; first knife sold in 1986. Nicole (wife) collaborates with enamels. Mark: Reverdy.

REVISHVILI, ZAZA,
2102 Linden Ave, Madison, WI 53704, Phone: 608- 243-7927
Specialties: Fancy/embellished and high-art straight knives and folders of his design. Patterns: Daggers, swords and locking folders. Technical: Uses Damascus; silver filigree, silver inlay in wood; enameling. Prices: $1000 to $9000; some to $15,000. Remarks: Full-time maker; first knife sold in 1987. Mark: Initials, city.

REXROAT, KIRK,
527 Sweetwater Circle Box 224, Wright, WY 82732, Phone: 307-464-0166, rexknives@vcn.com; Web: www.rexroatknives.com
Specialties: Using and collectible straight knives and folders of his design or to customer specs. **Patterns:** Bowies, hunters, folders. **Technical:** Forges Damascus patterns, mosaic and 52100. **Prices:** $400 and up. **Remarks:** Part-time maker, Master Smith in the ABS; first knife sold in 1984. Doing business as Rexroat Knives. **Mark:** Last name.

REYNOLDS, DAVE,
Rt 2 Box 36, Harrisville, WV 26362, Phone: 304- 643-2889, wvreynolds@zoomintevnet.net
Specialties: Working straight knives of his design. **Patterns:** Bowies, kitchen and utility knives. **Technical:** Grinds and forges L6, 1095 and 440C. Heat-treats. **Prices:** $50 to $85; some to $175. **Remarks:** Full- time maker; first knife sold in 1980. Doing business as Terra-Gladius Knives. **Mark:** Mark on special orders only; serial number on all knives.

REYNOLDS, JOHN C,
#2 Andover HC77, Gillette, WY 82716, Phone: 307-682-6076
Specialties: Working knives, some fancy. **Patterns:** Hunters, Bowies, tomahawks and buck skinners; some folders. **Technical:** Grinds D2, ATS-34, 440C and forges own Damascus and knives. Scrimshaws. **Prices:** $200 to $3000. **Remarks:** Spare-time maker; first knife sold in 1969. **Mark:** On ground blades JC Reynolds Gillette, WY, on forged blades, initials make the mark-JCR.

RHEA, LIN,
413 Grant 291020, Prattsville, AR 72129, Phone: 870-699- 5095, lwrhea1@windstream.net; Web: www.rheaknives.com
Specialties: Traditional and early American styled Bowies in high carbon steel or Damascus. **Patterns:** Bowies, hunters and fighters. **Technical:** Filework wire inlay. Sole authorship of construction, Damascus and embellishment. **Prices:** $280 to $1500. **Remarks:** Serious part-time maker and rated as a Journeyman Bladesmith in the ABS.

RHO, NESTOR LORENZO,
Primera Junta 589, (6000) Junin, Buenos Aires, ARGENTINA, Phone: (02362) 15670686
Specialties: Classic and fancy straight knives of his design. **Patterns:** Bowies, fighters and hunters. **Technical:** Grinds 420C, 440C, 1084, 51- 60, 52100, L6, and W1. Offers semi-precious stones on handles, acid etching on blades and blade engraving. **Prices:** $90 to $500, some to $1500. **Remarks:** Full-time maker; first knife sold in 1975. **Mark:** Name.

RIBONI, CLAUDIO,
Via L Da Vinci, Truccazzano (MI), ITALY, Phone: 02 95309010, Web: www.riboni-knives.com

RICARDO ROMANO, BERNARDES,
Ruai Coronel Rennò 1261, Itajuba MG, BRAZIL 37500, Phone: 0055-2135-622-5896
Specialties: Hunters, fighters, Bowies. **Technical:** Grinds blades of stainless and tools steels. **Patterns:** Hunters. **Prices:** $100 to $700. **Mark:** Romano.

RICHARD, RAYMOND,
31047 SE Jackson Rd., Gresham, OR 97080, Phone: 503-663-1219, rayskee13@hotmail.com; Web: www.hawknknives.com
Specialties: Hand-forged knives, tomahawks, and axes, all one-of-a- kind. **Prices:** $200 and up, some to $3000. **Remarks:** Full-time maker since 1994. **Mark:** Name on spine of blades.

RICHARDS, CHUCK,
7243 Maple Tree Lane SE, Salem, OR 97317, Phone: 503-569-5549, chuck@woodforge.com; Web: www.woodchuckforge.com
Specialties: Fixed blade Damascus. One-of-a-kind. **Patterns:** Hunters, fighters. **Prices:** $200 to $1200. **Remarks:** Likes to work with customers on a truly custom knife. **Mark:** A C Richards or ACR.

RICHARDS, RALPH (BUD),
6413 Beech St, Bauxite, AR 72011, Phone: 501-602-5367, DoubleR042@aol.com; Web: SwampPoodleCreations.com
Specialties: Forges 55160, 1084, and 15N20 for Damascus. S30V, 440C, and others. Wood, mammoth, giraffe and mother of pearl handles.

RICHARDSON JR., PERCY,
1117 Kettler St., Navasota, TX 77868, Phone: 936-288-1690, Web: www.richardsonknives@yahoo.com
Specialties: Working straight knives and folders. **Patterns:** Hunters, skinners, bowies, fighters and folders. **Technical:** Grinds 154CM, ATS- 34, and D2. **Prices:** $175 - $750 some bowies to $1200. **Remarks:** Part time maker, first knife sold in 1990. Doing business as Richardsons Handmade Knives. **Mark:** Texas star with last name across it.

RICHERSON, RON,
P.O. Box 51, Greenburg, KY 42743, Phone: 270- 405-0491, Fax: 270-299-2471, rricherson@windstream.net
Specialties: Collectible and functional fixed blades, locking liners, and autos of his design. **Technical:** Grinds ATS-34, S30V, S60V, CPM-154, D2, 440, high carbon steel, and his and others' Damascus. Prefers natural materials for handles and does both stock removal and forged work, some with embellishments. **Prices:** $160 to $850, some higher. **Remarks:** Full-time

maker. Probationary member Knifemakers' Guild and apprentice member American Bladesmith Society. Made first knife in September 2006, sold first knife in December 2006. **Mark:** Name in oval with city and state. Also name in center of oval Green River Custom Knives.

RICKE, DAVE,
1209 Adams St, West Bend, WI 53090, Phone: 262-334- 5739, R.L5710@sbcglobal.net
Specialties: Working knives; period pieces. **Patterns:** Hunters, boots, Bowies; locking folders and slip joints. **Technical:** Grinds ATS-34, A2, 440C and 154CM. **Prices:** $145 and up. **Remarks:** Full-time maker; first knife sold in 1976. Knifemakers Guild voting member. **Mark:** Last name.

RIDEN, DOUG,
12 Weeks Rd, Box 945, Eastford, CT 06242, Phone: 860-974-0518, Web: www.darkwaterforge.com
Specialties: Hard working, high performance knives. **Patterns:** Hunters, fighters, choppers, kitchen knives. **Technical:** Forged 5160, 1084, W2, L6. **Prices:** $100 to $600. **Remarks:** Full-time maker, first knife sold 2006.

RIDER, DAVID M,
PO Box 5946, Eugene, OR 97405-0911, Phone: 541- 343-8747

RIEPE, RICHARD A,
17604 E 296 St, Harrisonville, MO 64701

RIETVELD, BERTIE,
PO Box 53, Magaliesburg 1791, SOUTH AFRICA, Phone: 2783 232 8766, bertie@rietveldknives.com; Web: www.rietveldknives.com
Specialties: Art daggers, Bolster lock folders, Persian designs, embraces elegant designs. **Patterns:** Mostly one-of-a-kind. **Technical:** Sole authorship, work only in own Damascus, gold inlay, blued stainless fittings. **Prices:** $500 - $8,000 **Remarks:** First knife made in 1979. Annual shows attended: ECCKS, Blade Show, Milan Show, South African Guild Show. **Marks:** Logo is elephant in half circle with name, enclosed in Stanhope lens

RIGNEY JR., WILLIE,
191 Colson Dr, Bronston, KY 42518, Phone: 606- 679-4227
Specialties: High-tech period pieces and fancy working knives. **Patterns:** Fighters, boots, daggers and push knives. **Technical:** Grinds 440C and 154CM; buys Damascus. Most knives are embellished. **Prices:** $150 to $1500; some to $10,000. **Remarks:** Full-time maker; first knife sold in 1978. **Mark:** First initial, last name.

RINKES, SIEGFRIED,
Am Sportpl 2, D 91459, Markterlbach, GERMANY

RIZZI, RUSSELL J,
37 March Rd, Ashfield, MA 01330, Phone: 413-625- 2842
Specialties: Fancy working and using straight knives and folders of his design or to customer specs. **Patterns:** Hunters, locking folders and fighters. **Technical:** Grinds 440C, D2 and commercial Damascus. **Prices:** $150 to $750; some to $2500. **Remarks:** Part-time maker; first knife sold in 1990. **Mark:** Last name, Ashfield, MA.

ROBBINS, BILL,
299 Fairview St, Globe, AZ 85501, Phone: 928-402- 0052, billrknifemaker@aol.com
Specialties: Plain and fancy working straight knives. Makes to his designs and most anything you can draw. **Patterns:** Hunting knives, utility knives, and Bowies. **Technical:** Grinds ATS-34, 440C, tool steel, high carbon, buys Damascus. **Prices:** $70 to $450. **Remarks:** Part-time maker, first knife sold in 2001. **Mark:** Last name or desert scene with name.

ROBBINS, HOWARD P,
1407 S 217th Ave, Elkhorn, NE 68022, Phone: 402-289-4121, ARobb1407@aol.com
Specialties: High-tech working knives with clean designs, some fancy. **Patterns:** Folders, hunters and camp knives. **Technical:** Grinds 440C. Heat-treats; likes mirror finishes. Offers leatherwork. **Prices:** $100 to $500; some to $1000. **Remarks:** Full-time maker; first knife sold in 1982. **Mark:** Name, city and state.

ROBERTS, CHUCK,
PO Box 7174, Golden, CO 80403, Phone: 303-642-2388, chuck@crobertsart.com; Web: www.crobertsart.com
Specialties: Price daggers, large Bowies, hand-rubbed satin finish. **Patterns:** Bowies and California knives. **Technical:** Grinds 440C, 5160 and ATS-34. Handles made of stag, ivory or mother-of-pearl. **Prices:** $1250. **Remarks:** Full-time maker. Company name is C. Roberts - Art that emulates the past. **Mark:** Last initial or last name.

ROBERTS, GEORGE A,
PO Box 31228, 211 Main St., Whitehorse, YT, CANADA Y1A 5P7, Phone: 867-667-7099, Fax: 867-667-7099, Web: www.yuk-biz.com/bandit blades
Specialties: Mastadon ivory, fossil walrus ivory handled knives, scrimshawed or carved. **Patterns:** Side lockers, fancy bird and trout knives, hunters, fillet blades. **Technical:** Grinds stainless Damascus, all surgical steels. **Prices:** Up to $3500 U.S. **Remarks:** Full-time maker; first knives sold in 1986. Doing business as Bandit Blades. Most recent works have gold nuggets in fossilized Mastodon ivory. Something new using mosaic pins in mokume bolster and in mosaic Damascus, it creates a new look. **Mark:** Bandit Yukon with pick and shovel crossed.

ROBERTS, JACK,
10811 Sagebluff Dr, Houston, TX 77089, Phone: 281-481-1784, jroberts59@houston.rr.com
Specialties: Hunting knives and folders, offers scrimshaw by wife Barbara. **Patterns:** Drop point hunters and LinerLock® folders. **Technical:** Grinds 440-C, offers file work, texturing, natural handle materials and Micarta. **Prices:** $200 to $800 some higher. **Remarks:** Part-time maker, sold first knife in 1965. **Mark:** Name, city, state.

ROBERTS, MICHAEL,
601 Oakwood Dr, Clinton, MS 39056, Phone: 601-540-6222, Fax: 601-213-4891
Specialties: Working and using knives in standard patterns and to customer specs. **Patterns:** Hunters, Bowies, tomahawks and fighters. **Technical:** Forges 5160, O1, 1095 and his own Damascus. Uses only natural handle materials. **Prices:** $145 to $500; some to $1100. **Remarks:** Part-time maker; first knife sold in 1988. **Mark:** Last name or first and last name in Celtic script.

ROBERTSON, LEO D,
3728 Pleasant Lake Dr, Indianapolis, IN 46227, Phone: 317-882-9899, ldr52@juno.com
Specialties: Hunting and folders. **Patterns:** Hunting, fillet, Bowie, utility, folders and tantos. **Technical:** Uses ATS-34, 154CM, 440C, 1095, D2 and Damascus steels. **Prices:** Fixed knives $75 to $350, folders $350 to $600. **Remarks:** Handles made with stag, wildwoods, laminates, mother-of-pearl. Made first knife in 1990. Member of American Bladesmith Society. **Mark:** Logo with full name in oval around logo.

ROBINSON, CALVIN,
5501 Twin Creek Circle, Pace, FL 32571, Phone: 850 572 1504, calvinshandmadeknives@yahoo.com
Specialties: Working knives of my own design. **Patterns:** Hunters, fishing, folding and kitchen and purse knives. **Technical:** Grinds D-2, A-2, O1, high carbon and stainless damascus. **Prices:** $215.00 to $600.00. **Remarks:** Full-time maker. **Mark:** Calvin Robinson Pace, Florida.

ROBINSON, CHARLES (DICKIE),
PO Box 221, Vega, TX 79092, Phone: 806-676-6428, dickie@amaonline.com; Web: www.robinsonknives.com
Specialties: Classic and working/using knives. Does his own engraving. **Patterns:** Bowies, daggers, fighters, hunters and camp knives. **Technical:** Forges O1, 5160, 52100 and his own Damascus. **Prices:** $350 to $850; some to $5000. **Remarks:** Part-time maker; first knife sold in 1988. Doing business as Robinson Knives. ABS Master Smith. **Mark:** Robinson MS.

ROBINSON, CHUCK,
SEA ROBIN FORGE, 1423 Third Ave., Picayune, MS 39466, Phone: 601-798-0060, robi5515@bellsouth.net
Specialties: Deluxe period pieces and working / using knives of his design and to customer specs. **Patterns:** Bowies, fighters, hunters, utility knives and original designs. **Technical:** Forges own Damascus, 52100, O1, L6 and 1070 thru 1095. **Prices:** Start at $225. **Remarks:** First knife 1958. **Mark:** Fish logo, anchor and initials C.R.

ROBINSON, ROBERT W,
1569 N. Finley Pt, Polson, MT 59860, Phone: 406-887-2259, Fax: 406-887-2259
Specialties: High-art straight knives, folders and automatics of his design. **Patterns:** Hunters and locking folders. **Technical:** Grinds ATS-34, 154CM and 440V. Inlays pearl and gold; engraves sheep horn and ivory. **Prices:** $150 to $500; some to $2000. **Remarks:** Full-time maker; first knife sold in 1983. Doing business as Robbie Knife. **Mark:** Name on left side of blade.

ROBINSON III, REX R,
10531 Poe St, Leesburg, FL 34788, Phone: 352- 787-4587
Specialties: One-of-a-kind high-art automatics of his design. **Patterns:** Automatics, liner locks and lock back folders. **Technical:** Uses tool steel and stainless Damascus and mokume; flat grinds. Hand carves folders. **Prices:** $1800 to $7500. **Remarks:** First knife sold in 1988. **Mark:** First name inside oval.

ROCHFORD, MICHAEL R,
PO Box 577, Dresser, WI 54009, Phone: 715-755-3520, mrrochford@centurytel.net
Specialties: Working straight knives and folders. Classic Bowies and Moran traditional. **Patterns:** Bowies, fighters, hunters: slip-joint, locking and liner locking folders. **Technical:** Grinds ATS-34, 440C, 154CM and D-2; forges W2, 5160, and his own Damascus. Offers metal and metal and leather sheaths. Filework and wire inlay. **Prices:** $150 to $1000; some to $2000. **Remarks:** Part-time maker; first knife sold in 1984. **Mark:** Name.

RODEBAUGH, JAMES L,
4875 County Rd, Carpenter, WY 82054

RODEWALD, GARY,
447 Grouse Ct, Hamilton, MT 59840, Phone: 406- 363-2192
Specialties: Bowies of his design as inspired from historical pieces. **Patterns:** Hunters, Bowies and camp/combat. Forges 5160 1084 and his own Damascus of 1084, 15N20, field grade hunters AT-34-440C, 440V, and BG42. **Prices:** $200 to $1500. **Remarks:** Sole author on knives, sheaths done by saddle maker. **Mark:** Rodewald.

RODKEY, DAN,
18336 Ozark Dr, Hudson, FL 34667, Phone: 727-863- 8264
Specialties: Traditional straight knives of his design and in standard patterns. **Patterns:** Boots, fighters and hunters. **Technical:** Grinds 440C, D2 and ATS-34. **Prices:** Start at $200. **Remarks:** Full-time maker; first knife sold in 1985. Doing business as Rodkey Knives. **Mark:** Etched logo on blade.

ROE JR., FRED D,
4005 Granada Dr, Huntsville, AL 35802, Phone: 205- 881-6847
Specialties: Highly finished working knives of his design; period pieces. **Patterns:** Hunters, fighters and survival knives; locking folders; specialty designs like diver's knives. **Technical:** Grinds 154CM, ATS-34 and Damascus. Field-tests all blades. **Prices:** $125 to $250; some to $2000. **Remarks:** Part-time maker; first knife sold in 1980. **Mark:** Last name.

ROGERS, RAY,
PO Box 126, Wauconda, WA 98859, Phone: 509-486- 8069, knives @ rayrogers.com; Web: www.rayrogers.com
Specialties: LinerLock® folders. Asian and European professional chef's knives. **Patterns:** Rayzor folders, chef's knives and cleavers of his own and traditional designs, drop point hunters and fillet knives. **Technical:** Stock removal S30V, 440, 1095, O1 Damascus and other steels. Does all own heat treating, clay tempering, some forging G-10, Micarta, carbon fiber on folders, stabilized burl woods on fixed blades. **Prices:** $200 to $450. **Remarks:** Knives are made one-at-a-time to the customer's order. Happy to consider customizing knife designs to suit your preferences and sometimes create entirely new knives when necessary. As a full-time knifemaker is willing to spend as much time as it takes (usually through email) discussing the options and refining details of a knife's design to insure that you get the knife you really want.

ROGERS, RICHARD,
PO Box 769, Magdalena, NM 87825, Phone: 575- 838-7237, r.s.rogers@hotmail.com
Specialties: Sheffield-style folders and multi-blade folders. **Patterns:** Folders: various traditional patterns. One-of-a-kind fixed blades: Bowies, daggers, hunters, utility knives. **Technical:** Mainly uses ATS-34 and prefer natural handle materials. **Prices:** $400 and up. **Mark:** Last name.

ROGHMANS, MARK,
607 Virginia Ave, LaGrange, GA 30240, Phone: 706-885-1273
Specialties: Classic and traditional knives of his design. **Patterns:** Bowies, daggers and fighters. **Technical:** Grinds ATS-34, D2 and 440C. **Prices:** $250 to $500. **Remarks:** Part-time maker; first knife sold in 1984. Doing business as LaGrange Knife. **Mark:** Last name and/or LaGrange Knife.

ROHN, FRED,
7675 W Happy Hill Rd, Coeur d'Alene, ID 83814, Phone: 208-667-0774
Specialties: Hunters, boot knives, custom patterns. **Patterns:** Drop points, double edge, etc. **Technical:** Grinds 440 or 154CM. **Prices:** $85 and up. **Remarks:** Part-time maker. **Mark:** Logo on blade; serial numbered.

ROLLERT, STEVE,
PO Box 65, Keenesburg, CO 80643-0065, Phone: 303-732-4858, steve@doveknives.com; Web: www.doveknives.com
Specialties: Highly finished working knives. **Patterns:** Variety of straight knives; locking folders and slip-joints. **Technical:** Forges and grinds W2, 1095, ATS-34 and his pattern-welded, cable Damascus and nickel Damascus. **Prices:** $300 to $1000; some to $3000. **Remarks:** Full-time maker; first knife sold in 1980. Doing business as Dove Knives. **Mark:** Last name in script.

RONZIO, N. JACK,
PO Box 248, Fruita, CO 81521, Phone: 970-858- 0921

ROOT, GARY,
644 East 14th St, Erie, PA 16503, Phone: 814-459-0196
Specialties: Damascus Bowies with hand carved eagles, hawks and snakes for handles. Few folders made. **Patterns:** Daggers, fighters, hunter/field knives. **Technical:** Using handforged Damascus from Ray Bybar Jr (M.S.) and Robert Eggerling. Grinds D2, 440C, 1095 and 5160. Some 5160 is hand forged. **Prices:** $80 to $300 some to $1000. **Remarks:** Full time maker, first knife sold in 1976. **Mark:** Name over Erie, PA.

ROSE, DEREK W,
14 Willow Wood Rd, Gallipolis, OH 45631, Phone: 740-446-4627

ROSE II, DOUN T,
Ltc US Special Operations Command (ret), 1795/96 W Sharon Rd SW, Fife Lake, MI 49633, Phone: 231-645-1369, Web: www.epicureanclassic.com
Specialties: Straight working, collector and presentation knives to a high level of fit and finish. Design in collaboration with customer. **Patterns:** Field knives, Scagel, Bowies, period pieces, axes and tomahawks, fishing and hunting spears. Fine cutlery under "Epicurean Classic" name. **Technical:** Forged and billet ground, high carbon and stainless steel appropriate to end use. Sourced from: Crucible, Frye, Admiral and Starret. Some period pieces from recovered stock. Makes own damascus and mokume gane. **Remarks:** Full-time maker, ABS since 2000, William Scagel Memorial Scholarship 2002, Bill Moran School of Blade Smithing 2003, Apprentice under Master Blacksmith Dan Nickels at Black Rock Forge current. **Mark:** Last name ROSE in block letters with five petal "wild rose" in place of O. Doing business as Rose Cutlery.

ROSENBAUGH, RON,
2806 Stonegate Dr, Crystal Lake, IL 60012, Phone: 815-477-0027, rgr@rosenbaughcustomknives.com; Web: www.rosenbaughcustomknives.com
Specialties: Fancy and plain working knives using own designs, collaborations, and traditional patterns. **Patterns:** Bird, trout, boots, hunters, fighters, some Bowies. **Technical:** Grinds high alloy stainless, tool steels, and Damascus; forges 1084,5160, 52100, and spring steels. **Prices:** $150 to $1000. **Remarks:** Part-time maker, first knife sold in 1004. **Mark:** Last name, logo, city.

ROSENFELD, BOB,
955 Freeman Johnson Rd, Hoschton, GA 30548, Phone: 770-867-2647, www.1bladesmith@msn.com
Specialties: Fancy and embellished working/using straight knives of his design and in standard patterns. **Patterns:** Daggers, hunters and utility/camp knives. **Technical:** Forges 52100, A203E, 1095 and L6 Damascus. Offers engraving. **Prices:** $125 to $650; some to $1000. **Remarks:** Full-time maker; first knife sold in 1984. Also makes folders; ABS Journeyman. **Mark:** Last name or full name, Knifemaker.

ROSS, D L,
27 Kinsman St, Dunedin, NEW ZEALAND, Phone: 64 3 464 0239, Fax: 64 3 464 0239
Specialties: Working straight knives of his design. **Patterns:** Hunters, various others. **Technical:** Grinds 440C. **Prices:** $100 to $450; some to $700 NZ (not U.S. $). **Remarks:** Part-time maker; first knife sold in 1988. **Mark:** Dave Ross, Maker, city and country.

ROSS, GREGG,
4556 Wenhart Rd, Lake Worth, FL 33463, Phone: 407-439-4681
Specialties: Working/using straight knives. **Patterns:** Bowies, hunters and utility/camp knives. **Technical:** Forges and grinds ATS-34, Damascus and cable Damascus. Uses decorative pins. **Prices:** $125 to $250; some to $400. **Remarks:** Part-time maker; first knife sold in 1992. **Mark:** Name, city and state.

ROSS, STEPHEN,
534 Remington Dr, Evanston, WY 82930, Phone: 307-789-7104
Specialties: One-of-a-kind collector-grade classic and contemporary straight knives and folders of his design and to customer specs; some fantasy pieces. **Patterns:** Combat and survival knives, hunters, boots and folders. **Technical:** Grinds stainless; forges spring and tool steel. Engraves, scrimshaws. Makes leather sheaths. **Prices:** $160 to $3000. **Remarks:** Part-time-time maker; first knife sold in 1971. **Mark:** Last name in modified Roman; sometimes in script.

ROSS, TIM,
3239 Oliver Rd, Thunder Bay, Ont., CANADA P7G 1S9, Phone: 807-935-2667, Fax: 807-935-3179
Specialties: Fixed blades. **Patterns:** Hunting, fishing, collector. **Technical:** Uses D2, Stellite, 440C, Forges 52100, Damascus cable. **Prices:** $150 to $750 some to $5000. **Mark:** Tang stamps Ross custom knives.

ROSSDEUTSCHER, ROBERT N,
133 S Vail Ave, Arlington Heights, IL 60005, Phone: 847-577-0404, Web: www.rnrknives.com
Specialties: Frontier-style and historically inspired knives. **Patterns:** Trade knives, Bowies, camp knives and hunting knives, tomahawks and lances. **Technical:** Most knives are hand forged, a few are stock removal. **Prices:** $135 to $1500. **Remarks:** Journeyman Smith of the American Bladesmith Society. **Mark:** Back-to-back "R's", one upside down and backwards, one right side up and forward in an oval. Sometimes with name, town and state; depending on knife style.

ROTELLA, RICHARD A,
643 75th St, Niagara Falls, NY 14304
Specialties: Working knives of his design. **Patterns:** Various fishing, hunting and utility knives; folders. **Technical:** Grinds ATS-34. Prefers hand-rubbed finishes. **Prices:** $65 to $450; some to $900. **Remarks:** Spare-time maker; first knife sold in 1977. Not taking orders at this time; only sells locally. **Mark:** Name and city in stylized waterfall logo.

ROULIN, CHARLES,
113 B Rt. de Soral, 1233 Geneva, SWITZERLAND, Phone: 022-757-4479, Fax: 022-757-4479, coutelier@coutelier-Roulin.com; Web: www.coutelier-roulin.com
Specialties: Fancy high-art straight knives and folders of his design. **Patterns:** Bowies, locking folders, slip-joint folders and miniatures. **Technical:** Grinds 440C, ATS-34 and D2. Engraves; carves nature scenes and detailed animals in steel, ivory, on handles and blades. **Prices:** $500 to $3000; some to $10,000. **Remarks:** Full-time maker; first knife sold in 1988. **Mark:** Symbol of fish with name or name engraved.

ROWE, FRED,
BETHEL RIDGE FORGE, 3199 Roberts Rd, Amesville, OH 45711, Phone: 866-325-2164, fred.rowe@bethelridgeforge.com; Web: www.bethelridgeforge.com
Specialties: Damascus and carbon steel sheath knives. **Patterns:** Bowies, hunters, fillet small kokris. **Technical:** His own Damascus, 52100, O1, L6, 1095 carbon steels, mosaics. **Prices:** $200 to $2000. **Remarks:** All blades are clay hardened. **Mark:** Bethel Ridge Forge.

ROZAS, CLARK D,
1436 W "G" St, Wilmington, CA 90744, Phone: 310-518-0488
Specialties: Hand forged blades. **Patterns:** Pig stickers, toad stabbers, whackers, choppers. **Technical:** Damascus, 52100, 1095, 1084, 5160. **Prices:** $200 to $600. **Remarks:** A.B.S. member; part-time maker since 1995. **Mark:** Name over dagger.

RUANA KNIFE WORKS,
Box 520, Bonner, MT 59823, Phone: 406-258-5368, Fax: 406-258-2895, info@ruanaknives.com; Web: www.ruanaknives.com
Specialties: Working knives and period pieces. **Patterns:** Variety of straight knives. **Technical:** Forges 5160 chrome alloy for Bowies and 1095. **Prices:** $200 and up. **Remarks:** Full-time maker; first knife sold in 1938. Brand new non catalog knives available on ebay under seller name ruanaknives. For free catalog email regular mailing address to info@ruanaknives.com **Mark:** Name.

RUPERT, BOB,
301 Harshaville Rd, Clinton, PA 15026, Phone: 724-573-4569, rbrupert@aol.com
Specialties: Wrought period pieces with natural elements. **Patterns:** Elegant straight blades, friction folders. **Technical:** Forges colonial 7; 1095; 5160; diffuse mokume-gane and Damascus. **Prices:** $150 to $1500; some higher. **Remarks:** Part-time maker; first knife sold in 1980. Evening hours studio since 1980. Likes simplicity that disassembles. **Mark:** R etched in Old English.

RUPLE, WILLIAM H,
201 Brian Dr., Pleasanton, TX 78064, Phone: 830-569-0007, bknives@devtex.net
Specialties: Multi-blade folders, slip joints, some lock backs. **Patterns:** Like to reproduce old patterns. Offers filework and engraving. **Technical:** Grinds CPM-154 and other carbon and stainless steel and commercial Damascus. **Prices:** $950 to $2500. **Remarks:** Full-time maker; first knife sold in 1988. **Mark:** Ruple.

RUSS, RON,
5351 NE 160th Ave, Williston, FL 32696, Phone: 352-528-2603, RussRs@aol.com
Specialties: Damascus and mokume. **Patterns:** Ladder, rain drop and butterfly. **Technical:** Most knives, including Damascus, are forged from 52100-E. **Prices:** $65 to $2500. **Mark:** Russ.

RUSSELL, MICK,
4 Rossini Rd, Pari Park, Port Elizabeth 6070, SOUTH AFRICA
Specialties: Art knives. **Patterns:** Working and collectible bird, trout and hunting knives, defense knives and folders. **Technical:** Grinds D2, 440C, ATS-34 and Damascus. Offers mirror or satin finishes. **Prices:** Start at $100. **Remarks:** Full-time maker; first knife sold in 1986. **Mark:** Stylized rhino incorporating initials.

RUSSELL, TOM,
6500 New Liberty Rd, Jacksonville, AL 36265, Phone: 205-492-7866
Specialties: Straight working knives of his design or to customer specs. **Patterns:** Hunters, folders, fighters, skinners, Bowies and utility knives. **Technical:** Grinds D2, 440C and ATS-34; offers filework. **Prices:** $75 to $225. **Remarks:** Part-time maker; first knife sold in 1987. Full-time tool and die maker. **Mark:** Last name with tulip stamp.

RUTH, MICHAEL G,
3101 New Boston Rd, Texarkana, TX 75501, Phone: 903-832-7166/cell:903-277-3663, Fax: 903-832-4710, mike@ruthknives.com; Web: www.ruthknives.com
Specialties: Hunters, bowies & fighters. Damascus & carbon steel. **Prices:** $375 & up. **Mark:** Last name.

RYBAR JR., RAYMOND B,
2328 South Sunset Dr., Came Verde, AZ 86322, Phone: 928-567-6372, ray@rybarknives.com; Web: www.rybarknives.com
Specialties: Straight knives or folders with customers name, logo, etc. in mosaic pattern. **Patterns:** Common patterns plus mosaics of all types. **Technical:** Forges own Damascus. Primary forging of self smelted steel - smelting classes. **Prices:** $200 to $1200; Bible blades to $10,000. **Remarks:** Master Smith (A.B.S.) Primary focus toward Biblically themed blades **Mark:** Rybar or stone church forge or Rev. 1:3 or R.B.R. between diamonds.

RYBERG, GOTE,
Faltgatan 2, S-562 00 Norrahammar, SWEDEN, Phone: 4636-61678

RYDBOM, JEFF,
PO Box 548, Annandale, MN 55302, Phone: 320-274-9639, jry1890@hotmail.com
Specialties: Ring knives. **Patterns:** Hunters, fighters, Bowie and camp knives. **Technical:** Straight grinds O1, A2, 1566 and 5150 steels. **Prices:** $150 to $1000. **Remarks:** No pinning of guards or pommels. All silver brazed. **Mark:** Capital "C" with J R inside.

RYUICHI, KUKI,
504-7 Tokorozawa-Shinmachi, Tokorozawa-city, Saitama, JAPAN, Phone: 042-943-3451

RZEWNICKI, GERALD,
8833 S Massbach Rd, Elizabeth, IL 61028-9714, Phone: 815-598-3239

S

SAINDON, R BILL,
233 Rand Pond Rd, Goshen, NH 03752, Phone: 603-863-1874, dayskiev71@aol.com
Specialties: Collector-quality folders of his design or to customer specs. **Patterns:** Latch release, LinerLock® and lockback folders. **Technical:** Offers limited amount of own Damascus; also uses Damas makers steel. Prefers natural handle material, gold and gems. **Prices:** $500 to $4000. **Remarks:** Full-time maker; first knife sold in 1981. Doing business as Daynia Forge. **Mark:** Sun logo or engraved surname.

SAKAKIBARA, MASAKI,
20-8 Sakuragaoka, 2-Chome Setagaya-ku, Tokyo 156-0054, JAPAN, Phone: 81-3-3420-0375

SAKMAR, MIKE,
903 S. Latson Rd. #257, Howell, MI 48843, Phone: 517-546-6388, Fax: 517-546-6399, sakmarent@yahoo.com; Web: www.sakmarenterprises.com
Specialties: Mokume in various patterns and alloy combinations. **Patterns:** Bowies, fighters, hunters and integrals. **Technical:** Grinds ATS-34, Damascus and high-carbon tool steels. Uses mostly natural handle materials—elephant ivory, walrus ivory, stag, wildwood, oosic, etc. Makes mokume for resale. **Prices:** $250 to $2500; some to $4000. **Remarks:** Part-time maker; first knife sold in 1990. Supplier of mokume. **Mark:** Last name.

SALLEY, JOHN D,
3965 Frederick-Ginghamsburg Rd., Tipp City, OH 45371, Phone: 937-698-4588, Fax: 937-698-4131
Specialties: Fancy working knives and art pieces. **Patterns:** Hunters, fighters, daggers and some swords. **Technical:** Grinds ATS-34, 12C27 and W2; buys Damascus. **Prices:** $85 to $1000; some to $6000. **Remarks:** Part-time maker; first knife sold in 1979. **Mark:** First initial, last name.

SAMPSON, LYNN,
381 Deakins Rd, Jonesborough, TN 37659, Phone: 423-348-8373
Specialties: Highly finished working knives, mostly folders. **Patterns:** Locking folders, slip-joints, interframes and two-blades. **Technical:** Grinds D2, 440C and ATS-34; offers extensive filework. **Prices:** Start at $300. **Remarks:** Full-time maker; first knife sold in 1982. **Mark:** Name and city in logo.

SANDBERG, RONALD B,
24784 Shadowwood Ln, Browntown, MI 48134, Phone: 734-671-6866, msc@ili.net
Specialties: Good looking and functional hunting knives, filework, mixing of handle materials. **Patterns:** Hunters, skinners and Bowies. **Prices:** $120 and up. **Remarks:** Doing business as Mighty Sharp Cuts. **Mark:** R.B. Sandberg.

SANDERS, A.A.,
3850 72 Ave NE, Norman, OK 73071, Phone: 405-364-8660
Specialties: Working straight knives and folders. **Patterns:** Hunters, fighters, daggers and Bowies. **Technical:** Forges his own Damascus; offers stock removal with ATS-34, 440C, A2, D2, O1, 5160 and 1095. **Prices:** $85 to $1500. **Remarks:** Full-time maker; first knife sold in 1985. Formerly known as Athern Forge. **Mark:** Name.

SANDERS, BILL,
335 Bauer Ave, PO Box 957, Mancos, CO 81328, Phone: 970-533-7223, Fax: 970-533-7390, billsand@frontier.net; Web: www.billsandershandmadeknives.com
Specialties: Survival knives, working straight knives, some fancy and some fantasy, of his design. **Patterns:** Hunters, boots, utility knives, using belt knives. **Technical:** Grinds 440C, ATS-34 and commercial Damascus. Provides wide variety of handle materials. **Prices:** $170 to $800. **Remarks:** Full-time maker. Formerly of Timberline Knives. **Mark:** Name, city and state.

SANDERS, MICHAEL M,
PO Box 1106, Ponchatoula, LA 70454, Phone: 225-294-3601, sanders@bellsouth.net
Specialties: Working straight knives and folders, some deluxe. **Patterns:** Hunters, fighters, Bowies, daggers, large folders and deluxe Damascus miniatures. **Technical:** Grinds O1, D2, 440C, ATS-34 and Damascus. **Prices:** $75 to $650; some higher. **Remarks:** Full-time maker; first knife sold in 1967. **Mark:** Name and state.

SANDLIN, LARRY,
4580 Sunday Dr, Adamsville, AL 35005, Phone: 205-674-1816
Specialties: High-art straight knives of his design. **Patterns:** Boots, daggers, hunters and fighters. **Technical:** Forges 1095, L6, O1, carbon steel and Damascus. **Prices:** $200 to $1500; some to $5000. **Remarks:** Part-time maker; first knife sold in 1990. **Mark:** Chiseled last name in Japanese.

SANDOW, NORMAN E,
63 B Moore St, Howick, Auckland, NEW ZEALAND, Phone: 095328912, sanknife@ezysurf.co.nz
Specialties: Quality LinerLock® folders. Working and fancy straight knives. Some one-of-a-kind. Embellishments available. **Patterns:** Most patterns, hunters, boot, bird and trout, etc., and to customer's specs. **Technical:** Predominate knife steel ATS-34. Also in use 12C27, D2 and Damascus. High class handle material used on both folders and straight knives. All blades made via the stock removal method. **Prices:** $350 to $2500. **Remarks:** Full-time maker. **Mark:** Norman E Sandow in semi-circular design.

SANDS, SCOTT,
2 Lindis Ln, New Brighton, Christchurch 9, NEW ZEALAND
Specialties: Classic working and fantasy swords. **Patterns:** Fantasy, medieval, celtic, viking, katana, some daggers. **Technical:** Forges own Damascus; 1080 and L6; 5160 and L6; O1 and L6. All hand-polished, does own heat-treating, forges non-Damascus on request. **Prices:** $1500 to $15,000+. **Remarks:** Full-time maker; first blade sold in 1996. **Mark:** Stylized Moon.

SANTIAGO, ABUD,
Av Gaona 3676 PB A, Buenos Aires 1416, ARGENTINA, Phone: 5411 4612 8396, info@phi-sabud.com; Web: www.phi-sabud.com/blades.html

SARGANIS, PAUL,
2215 Upper Applegate Rd, Jacksonville, OR 97530, Phone: 541-899-2831, paulsarganis@hotmail.com; Web: www.sarganis.50megs.com
Specialties: Hunters, folders, Bowies. **Technical:** Forges 5160, 1084. Grinds ATS-34 and 440C. **Prices:** $120 to $500. **Remarks:** Spare-time maker, first knife sold in 1987. **Mark:** Last name.

SARVIS, RANDALL J,
110 West Park Ave, Fort Pierre, SD 57532, Phone: 605-223-2772, rsarvis@sdln.net

SASS, GARY N,
2048 Buckeye Dr, Sharpsville, PA 16150, Phone: 724-866-6165, gnsass@yahoo.com
Specialties: Working straight knives of his design or to customer specifications. **Patterns:** Hunters, fighters, utility knives, push daggers. **Technical:** Grinds 440C, ATS-34 and Damascus. Uses exotic wood, buffalo horn, warthog tusk and semi-precious stones. **Prices:** $50 to $250, some higher. **Remarks:** Part-time maker. First knife sold in 2003. **Mark:** Initials G.S. formed into a diamond shape.

SAVIANO, JAMES,
124 Wallis St., Douglas, MA 01516, Phone: 508-476-7644, jimsaviano@gmail.com
Specialties: Straight knives. **Patterns:** Hunters, bowies, fighters, daggers, short swords. **Technical:** Hand-forged high-carbon and my own damascus steel. **Prices:** Starting at $300. **Remarks:** ABS mastersmith, maker since 2000, sole authorship. **Mark:** Last name or stylized JPS initials.

SAWBY, SCOTT,
480 Snowberry Ln, Sandpoint, ID 83864, Phone: 208-263-4171, scotmar@imbris.net; Web: www.sawbycustomknives.com
Specialties: Folders, working and fancy. **Patterns:** Locking folders, patent locking systems and interframes. **Technical:** Grinds D2, 440C, CPM154, ATS-34, S30V, and Damascus. **Prices:** $700 to $3000. **Remarks:** Full-time maker; first knife sold in 1974. Engraving by wife Marian. **Mark:** Last name, city and state.

SCARROW, WIL,
c/o LandW Mail Service, PO Box 1036, Gold Hill, OR 97525, Phone: 541-855-1236, willsknife@earthlink.net
Specialties: Carving knives, also working straight knives in standard patterns or to customer specs. **Patterns:** Carving, fishing, hunting, skinning, utility, swords and Bowies. **Technical:** Forges and grinds: A2, L6, W1, D2, 5160, 1095, 440C, AEB-L, ATS-34 and others on request. Offers some filework. **Prices:** $40 to $850; some higher. Prices include sheath (carver's $40 and up). **Remarks:** Spare-time maker; first knife sold in 1983. Two to eight month construction time on custom orders. Doing business as Scarrow's Custom Stuff and Gold Hill Knife works (in Oregon). Carving knives available at Raven Dog Enterprises. Contact at Ravedog@aol.com. Carving knives available at the 'Wild Duck' Woodcarvers Supply. Contact at duckstore@aol.com. **Mark:** SC with arrow and date/year made.

SCHALLER, ANTHONY BRETT,
5609 Flint Ct. NW, Albuquerque, NM 87120, Phone: 505-899-0155, brett@schallerknives.com; Web: www.schallerknives.com
Specialties: Straight knives and locking-liner folders of his design and in standard patterns. **Patterns:** Boots, fighters, utility knives and folders. **Technical:** Grinds CPM154, S30V, and stainless Damascus. Offers filework, hand-rubbed finishes and full and narrow tangs. Prefers exotic woods or Micarta for handle materials, G-10 and carbon fiber to handle materials. **Prices:** $100 to $350; some to $500. **Remarks:** Part-time maker; first knife sold in 1990. **Mark:** A.B. Schaller - Albuquerque NM - handmade.

SCHEID, MAGGIE,
124 Van Stallen St, Rochester, NY 14621-3557
Specialties: Simple working straight knives. **Patterns:** Kitchen and utility knives; some miniatures. **Technical:** Forges 5160 high-carbon steel. **Prices:** $100 to $200. **Remarks:** Part-time maker; first knife sold in 1986. **Mark:** Full name.

SCHEMPP, ED,
PO Box 1181, Ephrata, WA 98823, Phone: 509-754-2963, Fax: 509-754-3212
Specialties: Mosaic Damascus and unique folder designs. **Patterns:** Primarily folders. **Technical:** Grinds CPM440V; forges many patterns of mosaic using powdered steel. **Prices:** $100 to $400; some to $2000. **Remarks:** Part-time maker; first knife sold in 1991. Doing business as Ed Schempp Knives. **Mark:** Ed Schempp Knives over five heads of wheat, city and state.

SCHEMPP, MARTIN,
PO Box 1181, 5430 Baird Springs Rd NW, Ephrata, WA 98823, Phone: 509-754-2963, Fax: 509-754-3212
Specialties: Fantasy and traditional straight knives of his design, to customer specs and in standard patterns; Paleolithic-styles. **Patterns:** Fighters and Paleolithic designs. **Technical:** Uses opal, Mexican rainbow and obsidian. Offers scrimshaw. **Prices:** $15 to $100; some to $250. **Remarks:** Spare-time maker; first knife sold in 1995. **Mark:** Initials and date.

SCHEPERS, GEORGE B,
PO Box 395, Shelton, NE 68876-0395
Specialties: Fancy period pieces of his design. **Patterns:** Bowies, swords, tomahawks; locking folders and miniatures. **Technical:** Grinds W1, W2 and his own Damascus; etches. **Prices:** $125 to $600; some higher. **Remarks:** Full-time maker; first knife sold in 1981. **Mark:** Schep.

SCHEURER, ALFREDO E FAES,
Av Rincon de los Arcos 104, Col Bosque Res del Sur, C.P. 16010, MEXICO, Phone: 5676 47 63
Specialties: Fancy and fantasy knives of his design. **Patterns:** Daggers. **Technical:** Grinds stainless steel; casts and grinds silver. Sets stones in silver. **Prices:** $2000 to $3000. **Remarks:** Spare-time maker; first knife sold in 1989. **Mark:** Symbol.

SCHILLING, ELLEN,
95 Line Rd, Hamilton Square, NJ 08690, Phone: 609-448-0483

SCHIPPNICK, JIM,
PO Box 326, Sanborn, NY 14132, Phone: 716-731-3715, ragnar@ragweedforge.com; Web: www.ragweedforge.com
Specialties: Nordic, early American, rustic. **Mark:** Runic R. **Remarks:** Also imports Nordic knives from Norway, Sweden and Finland.

SCHIRMER, MIKE,
34 Highway HH, Cherryville, MO 65446-3062, Phone: 573-743-3407, schirmer@3rivers.net
Specialties: Working straight knives of his design or to customer specs; mostly hunters and personal knives. **Patterns:** Hunters, camp, kitchen, Bowies and fighters. **Technical:** Grinds O1, D2, A2 and Damascus and Talonoite. **Prices:** Start at $150. **Remarks:** Full-time maker; first knife sold in 1992. Doing business as Ruby Mountain Knives. **Mark:** Name or name and location.

SCHLUETER, DAVID,
2136 Cedar Gate Rd., Madison Heights, VA 24572, Phone: 434-384-8642, drschlueter@hotmail.com
Specialties: Japanese-style swords. **Patterns:** Larger blades. O-tanto to Tachi, with focus on less common shapes. **Technical:** Forges and grinds carbon steels, heat-treats and polishes own blades, makes all fittings, does own mounting and finishing. **Prices:** Start at $3000. **Remarks:** Sells fully mounted pieces only, doing business as Odd Frog Forge. **Mark:** Full name and date.

SCHMITZ, RAYMOND E,
PO Box 1787, Valley Center, CA 92082, Phone: 760-749-4318

SCHNEIDER, CRAIG M,
5380 N Amity Rd, Claremont, IL 62421, Phone: 618-869-2094/217-377-5715
Specialties: Straight knives of his own design. **Patterns:** Bowies, hunters, tactical, bird & trout. **Technical:** Forged high-carbon steel and Damascus. Flat grind and differential heat treatment use a wide selection of handle, guard and bolster material, also offers leather sheaths. **Prices:** $100 to $3000. **Remarks:** Part-time maker; first knife sold in 1985. **Mark:** Stylized initials.

SCHNEIDER, HERMAN,
14084 Apple Valley Rd, Apple Valley, CA 92307, Phone: 760-946-9096
Specialties: Presentation pieces, Fighters, Hunters. **Prices:** Starting at $900. **Mark:** H.J. Schneider-Maker.

SCHNEIDER, KARL A,
209 N. Brownleaf Rd, Newark, DE 19713, Phone: 302-737-0277, dmatj@msn.com
Specialties: Traditional working and using straight knives of his design. **Patterns:** Hunters, kitchen and fillet knives. **Technical:** Grinds ATS-34, CM154, 52100, AUS8 - AUS6. Shapes handles to fit hands; uses Micarta, Pakkawood and exotic woods. Makes hand-stitched leather cases. **Prices:** $100 to $300. **Remarks:** Part-time maker; first knife sold in 1974. **Mark:** Name, address; also name in shape of fish.

SCHOEMAN, CORRIE,
Box 28596, Danhof 9310, SOUTH AFRICA, Phone: 027 51 4363528 Cell: 027 82-3750789, corries@intekom.co.za
Specialties: High-tech folders of his design or to customer's specs. **Patterns:** Linerlock folders and automatics. **Technical:** ATS-34, Damascus or stainless Damascus with titanium frames; prefers exotic materials for handles. **Prices:** $650 to $2000. **Remarks:** Full-time maker; first knife sold in 1984. All folders come with filed liners and back and jeweled inserts. **Mark:** Logo in knife shape engraved on inside of back bar.

SCHOENFELD, MATTHEW A,
RR #1, Galiano Island, B.C., CANADA V0N 1P0, Phone: 250-539-2806
Specialties: Working knives of his design. **Patterns:** Kitchen cutlery, camp knives, hunters. **Technical:** Grinds 440C. **Prices:** $85 to $500. **Remarks:** Part-time maker; first knife sold in 1978. **Mark:** Signature, Galiano Is. B.C., and date.

SCHOENINGH, MIKE,
49850 Miller Rd, North Powder, OR 97867, Phone: 541-856-3239

SCHOLL, TIM,
1389 Langdon Rd, Angier, NC 27501, Phone: 910-897-2051, tscholl@charter.net
Specialties: Fancy and working/using straight knives and folders of his design and to customer specs. **Patterns:** Bowies, hunters, tomahawks, daggers & fantasy knives. **Technical:** Forges high carbon and tool steel makes Damascus, grinds ATS-34 and D2 on request. **Prices:** $150 to $6000. **Remarks:** Part-time maker; first knife sold in 1990. Doing business as Tim Scholl Custom Knives. **Mark:** S pierced by arrow.

SCHRADER, ROBERT,
55532 Gross De, Bend, OR 97707, Phone: 541-598-7301
Specialties: Hunting, utility, Bowie. **Patterns:** Fixed blade. **Prices:** $150 to $600.

SCHRAP, ROBERT G,
CUSTOM LEATHER KNIFE SHEATH CO., 7024 W Wells St, Wauwatosa, WI 53213-3717, Phone: 414-771-6472, Fax: 414-479-9765, knifesheaths@aol.com; Web: www.customsheaths.com
Specialties: Leatherwork. **Prices:** $35 to $100. **Mark:** Schrap in oval.

SCHROEN, KARL,
4042 Bones Rd, Sebastopol, CA 95472, Phone: 707-823-4057, Fax: 707-823-2914
Specialties: Using knives made to fit. **Patterns:** Sgian dubhs, carving sets, wood-carving knives, fishing knives, kitchen knives and new cleaver design. **Technical:** Forges A2, ATS-34, D2 and L6 cruwear S30V 590V. **Prices:** $150 to $6000. **Remarks:** Full-time maker; first knife sold in 1968. Author of *The Hand Forged Knife*. **Mark:** Last name.

SCHUCHMANN, RICK,
3975 Hamblen Dr, Cincinnati, OH 45255, Phone: 513-553-4316
Specialties: Replicas of antique and out-of-production Scagels and Randalls, primarily miniatures. **Patterns:** All sheath knives, mostly miniatures, hunting and fighting knives, some daggers and hatchets. **Technical:** Stock removal, 440C and O1 steel. Most knives are flat ground, some convex. **Prices:** $175 to $600 and custom to $4000. **Remarks:** Part-time maker, sold first knife in 1997. Knives on display in the Randall Museum. Sheaths are made exclusively at Sullivan's Holster Shop, Tampa, FL **Mark:** SCAR.

SCHULTZ, ROBERT W,
PO Box 70, Cocolalla, ID 83813-0070

SCHWARZER, STEPHEN,
119-2 Shoreside Trail, Crescent City, FL 32112, Phone: 386-698-2840, Fax: 386-649-8585, steveschwarzer@gbso.net; Web: www.steveschwarzer.com
Specialties: Mosaic Damascus and picture mosaic in folding knives. All Japanese blades are finished working with Wally Hostetter considered the top Japanese lacquer specialist in the U.S.A. Also produces a line of carbon steel skinning knives at $300. **Patterns:** Folders, axes and buckskinner knives. **Technical:** Specializes in picture mosaic Damascus and powder metal mosaic work. Sole authorship; all work including carving done in-house. Most knives have file work and carving. Hand carved steel and precious metal guards. **Prices:** $1500 to $5000, some higher; carbon steel and primitive knives much less. **Remarks:** Full-time maker; first knife sold in 1976, considered by many to be one of the top mosaic Damascus specialists in the world. Mosaic Master level work. **Mark:** Schwarzer + anvil.

SCIMIO, BILL,
HC 01 Box 24A, Spruce Creek, PA 16683, Phone: 814-632-3751, blackcrowforge@aol.com

SCOFIELD, EVERETT,
2873 Glass Mill Rd, Chickamauga, GA 30707, Phone: 706-375-2790
Specialties: Historic and fantasy miniatures. **Patterns:** All patterns. **Technical:** Uses only the finest tool steels and other materials. Uses only natural, precious and semi-precious materials. **Prices:** $100 to $1500. **Remarks:** Full-time maker; first knife sold in 1971. Doing business as Three Crowns Cutlery. **Mark:** Three Crowns logo.

SCORDIA, PAOLO,
Via Terralba 143, 00050 Torrimpietra, Roma, ITALY, Phone: 06-61697231, pands@mail.nexus.it; Web: www.scordia-knives.com
Specialties: Working and fantasy knives of his own design. **Patterns:** Any pattern. **Technical:** Forges own Damascus, welds own mokume and grinds ATS-34, etc. use hardwoods and Micarta for handles, brass and nickel-silver for fittings. Makes sheaths. **Prices:** $100 to $1000. **Remarks:** Part-time maker; first knife sold in 1988. **Mark:** Initials with sun and moon logo.

SCOTT, AL,
2245 Harper Valley Rd, Harper, TX 78631, Phone: 830-864- 4182
Specialties: High-art straight knives of his design. **Patterns:** Daggers, swords, early European, Middle East and Japanese knives. **Technical:** Uses ATS-34, 440C and Damascus. Hand engraves; does file work; cuts filigree in the blade; offers ivory carving and precious metal inlay. **Remarks:** Full-time maker; first knife sold in 1994. Doing business as Al Scott Maker of Fine Blade Art. **Mark:** Name engraved in Old English, sometime inlaid in 24K gold.

SCROGGS, JAMES A,
108 Murray Hill Dr, Warrensburg, MO 64093, Phone: 660-747-2568, jscroggsknives@embarqmail.com
Specialties: Straight knives, prefers light weight. **Patterns:** Hunters, hideouts, and fighters. **Technical:** Grinds L6, O1, 1095, plus experiments in steels. Prefers handles of walnut in English, bastonge, American black. Also uses myrtle, maple, Osage orange. **Prices:** $200 to $1000. **Remarks:** 1st knife sold in 1985. Part-time maker, no orders taken. **Mark:** SCROGGS in block or script.

SCULLEY, PETER E,
340 Sunset Dr, Rising Fawn, GA 30738, Phone: 706-398-0169

SEARS, MICK,
4473 Ernest Scott Rd., Kershaw, SC 29067, Phone: 803- 475-4937
Specialties: Scots and confederate reproductions; Bowies and fighters. **Patterns:** Bowies, fighters. **Technical:** Grinds 440C and 1095. **Prices:** $50 to $150; some to $300. **Remarks:** Part-time maker; first knife sold in 1975. Doing business as Mick's Custom Knives. **Mark:** First name.

SEIB, STEVE,
7914 Old State Road, Evansville, IN 47710, Phone: 812- 867-2231, sseib@insightbb.com
Specialties: Working straight knives. **Pattern:** Skinners, hunters, bowies and camp knives. **Technical:** Forges high-carbon and makes own damascus. **Remarks:** Part-time maker. ABS member. **Mark:** Last name.

SELENT, CHUCK,
PO Box 1207, Bonners Ferry, ID 83805-1207, Phone: 208-267-5807
Specialties: Period, art and fantasy miniatures; exotics; one-of-a-kinds. **Patterns:** Swords, daggers and others. **Technical:** Works in Damascus, meteorite, 440C and tool steel. Offers scrimshaw. Offers his own casting and leatherwork; uses jewelry techniques. Makes display cases for miniatures. **Prices:** $75 to $400. **Remarks:** Part-time maker; first knife sold in 1990. **Mark:** Last name and bear paw print logo scrimshawed on handles or leatherwork.

SELF, ERNIE,
950 O'Neill Ranch Rd, Dripping Springs, TX 78620-9760, Phone: 512-940-7134, ernieself@hillcountrytx.net
Specialties: Traditional and working straight knives and folders of his design and in standard patterns. **Patterns:** Hunters, locking folders and slipjoints. **Technical:** Grinds 440C, D2, 440V, ATS-34 and Damascus. Offers fancy filework. **Prices:** $250 to $1000; some to $2500. **Remarks:** Full-time maker; first knife sold in 1982. Also customizes Buck 110's and 112's folding hunters. **Mark:** In oval shape - Ernie Self Maker Dripping Springs TX.

SELLEVOLD, HARALD,
S Kleivesmau:2, PO Box 4134, N5835 Bergen, NORWAY, Phone: 47 55-310682, haraldsellevold@c2i.net; Web:knivmakeren.com
Specialties: Norwegian-styles; collaborates with other Norse craftsmen. **Patterns:** Distinctive ferrules and other mild modifications of traditional patterns; Bowies and friction folders. **Technical:** Buys Damascus blades; blacksmiths his own blades. Semi-gemstones used in handles; gemstone inlay. **Prices:** $350 to $2000. **Remarks:** Full-time maker; first knife sold in 1980. **Mark:** Name and country in logo.

SELZAM, FRANK,
Martin Reinhard Str 23 97631, Bad Koenigshofen, GERMANY, Phone: 09761-5980
Specialties: Hunters, working knives to customers specs, hand tooled and stitched leather sheaths large stock of wood and German stag horn. **Patterns:** Mostly own design. **Technical:** Forged blades, own Damascus, also stock removal stainless. **Prices:** $250 to $1500. **Remark:** First knife sold in 1978. **Mark:** Last name stamped.

SENTZ, MARK C,
4084 Baptist Rd, Taneytown, MD 21787, Phone: 410- 756-2018
Specialties: Fancy straight working knives of his design. **Patterns:** Hunters, fighters, folders and utility/camp knives. **Technical:** Forges 1085, 1095, 5160, 5155 and his Damascus. Most knives come with wood-lined leather sheath or wooden presentation sheath. **Prices:** Start at $275. **Remarks:** Full-time maker; first knife sold in 1989. Doing business as M. Charles Sentz Gunsmithing, Inc. **Mark:** Last name.

SERAFEN, STEVEN E,
24 Genesee St, New Berlin, NY 13411, Phone: 607-847-6903
Specialties: Traditional working/using straight knives of his design and to customer specs. **Patterns:** Bowies, fighters, hunters. **Technical:** Grinds ATS-34, 440C, high-carbon steel. **Prices:** $175 to $600; some to $1200. **Remarks:** Part-time maker; first knife sold in 1990. **Mark:** First and middle initial, last name in script.

SERVEN, JIM,
PO Box 1, Fostoria, MI 48435, Phone: 517-795-2255
Specialties: Highly finished unique folders. **Patterns:** Fancy working folders, axes, miniatures and razors; some straight knives. **Technical:** Grinds 440C; forges his own Damascus. **Prices:** $150 to $800; some to $1500. **Remarks:** Full-time maker; first knife sold in 1971. **Mark:** Name in map logo.

SEVEY CUSTOM KNIFE,
94595 Chandler Rd, Gold Beach, OR 97444, Phone: 541-247-2649, sevey@charter.net; Web: www.seveyknives.com
Specialties: Fixed blade hunters. **Patterns:** Drop point, trailing paint, clip paint, full tang, hidden tang. **Technical:** D-2, and ATS-34 blades, stock removal. Heat treatment by Paul Bos. **Prices:** $225 and up depending on overall length and grip material. **Mark:** Sevey Custom Knife.

SFREDDO, RODRIGO MENEZES,
Rua 15 De Setembro 66, Centro Nova Petropolis RS, cep g5 150-000, BRAZIL 95150-000, Phone: 011- 55-54-303-303-90, www.brazilianbladesmiths.com.br; www.sbccutelaria.org.br
Specialties: Integrals, Bowies, hunters, dirks & swords. **Patterns:** Forges his own Damascus and 52100 steel. **Technical:** Specialized in integral knives and Damascus. **Prices:** From $350 and up. **Remarks:** Considered by many to be the Brazil's best bladesmith. ABS SBC Member. **Mark:** S. Sfreddo on the left side of the blade.

SHADLEY, EUGENE W,
26315 Norway Dr, Bovey, MN 55709, Phone: 218-245-1639, Fax: call first, bses@uslink.net
Specialties: Gold frames are available on some models. **Patterns:** Whittlers, stockman, sowbelly, congress, trapper, etc. **Technical:** Grinds ATS-34, 416 frames. **Prices:** Starts at $600. **Remarks:** Full-time maker; first knife sold in 1985. Doing business as Shadley Knives. **Mark:** Last name.

SHADMOT, BOAZ,
MOSHAV PARAN D N, Arava, ISRAEL 86835, srb@arava.co.il

SHARRIGAN, MUDD,
111 Bradford Rd, Wiscasset, ME 04578-4457, Phone: 207-882-9820, Fax: 207-882-9835
Specialties: Custom designs; repair straight knives, custom leather sheaths. **Patterns:** Daggers, fighters, hunters, buckskinner, Indian crooked knives and seamen working knives; traditional Scandinavian- styles. **Technical:** Forges 1095, 52100, 5160, W2, O1. Laminates 1095 and mild steel. **Prices:** $50 to $325; some to $1200. **Remarks:** Full-time maker; first knife sold in 1982. **Mark:** First name and swallow tail carving.

SHAVER II, JAMES R,
1529 Spider Ridge Rd, Parkersburg, WV 26104, Phone: 304-422-2692, admin@spiderridgeforge.com Web:www.spiderridgeforge.com
Specialties: Hunting and working straight knives in carbon and Damascus steel. **Patterns:** Bowies and daggers in Damascus and carbon steels. **Technical:** Forges 5160 carbon and Damascus in 01 pure nickel 1018. **Prices:** $85 to $125; some to $750. Some to $1000 **Remarks:** Part-time maker; sold first knife in 1998. Believes in sole authorship. **Mark:** Last name.

SHEEHY, THOMAS J,
4131 NE 24th Ave, Portland, OR 97211-6411, Phone: 503-493-2843
Specialties: Hunting knives and ulus. **Patterns:** Own or customer designs. **Technical:** 1095/O1 and ATS-34 steel. **Prices:** $35 to $200. **Remarks:** Do own heat treating; forged or ground blades. **Mark:** Name.

SHEETS, STEVEN WILLIAM,
6 Stonehouse Rd, Mendham, NJ 07945, Phone: 201-543-5882

SHIFFER, STEVE,
PO Box 582, Leakesville, MS 39451, Phone: 601- 394-4425, aiifish2@yahoo.com; Web: wwwchoctawplantationforge.com
Specialties: Bowies, fighters, hard use knives. **Patterns:** Fighters, hunters, combat/utility knives. Walker pattern LinerLock® folders. Allen pattern scale and bolster release autos. **Technical:** Most work forged, stainless stock removal. Makes own Damascus. O1 and 5160 most used also 1084, 440c, 154cm, s30v. **Prices:** $125 to $1000. **Remarks:** First knife sold in 2000, all heat treatment done by maker. Doing business as Choctaw Plantation Forge. **Mark:** Hot mark sunrise over creek.

SHINOSKY, ANDY,
3117 Meanderwood Dr, Canfield, OH 44406, Phone: 330-702-0299, andrew@shinosky.com; Web: www.shinosky.com
Specialties: Collectable folders and interframes. **Patterns:** Drop point, spear point, trailing point, daggers. **Technical:** Grinds ATS-34 and Damascus. Prefers natural handle materials. Most knives are engraved by Andy himself. **Prices:** Start at $800. **Remarks:** Part-time maker/ engraver. First knife sold in 1992. **Mark:** Name.

SHIPLEY, STEVEN A,
800 Campbell Rd Ste 137, Richardson, TX 75081, Phone: 972-644-7981, Fax: 972-644-7985, steve@shipleysphotography
Specialties: Hunters, skinners and traditional straight knives. **Technical:** Hand grinds ATS-34, 440C and Damascus steels. Each knife is custom sheathed by his son, Dan. **Prices:** $175 to $2000. **Remarks:** Part-time maker; like smooth lines and unusual handle materials. **Mark:** S A Shipley.

SHOEMAKER, CARROLL,
380 Yellowtown Rd, Northup, OH 45658, Phone: 740-446-6695
Specialties: Working/using straight knives of his design. **Patterns:** Hunters, utility/camp and early American backwoodsmen knives. **Technical:** Grinds ATS-34; forges old files, O1 and 1095. Uses some Damascus; offers scrimshaw and engraving. **Prices:** $100 to $175; some to $350. **Remarks:** Spare-time maker; first knife sold in 1977. **Mark:** Name and city or connected initials.

SHOEMAKER, SCOTT,
316 S Main St, Miamisburg, OH 45342, Phone: 513-859-1935
Specialties: Twisted, wire-wrapped handles on swords, fighters and fantasy blades; new line of seven models with quick-draw, multi-carry Kydex sheaths. **Patterns:** Bowies, boots and one-of-a-kinds in his design or to customer specs. **Technical:** Grinds A6 and ATS-34; buys Damascus. Hand satin finish is standard. **Prices:** $100 to $1500; swords to $8000. **Remarks:** Part-time maker; first knife sold in 1984. **Mark:** Angel wings with last initial, or last name.

SHOGER, MARK O,
14780 SW Osprey Dr Suite 345, Beaverton, OR 97007, Phone: 503-579-2495, mosdds@msn.com
Specialties: Working and using straight knives and folders of his design; fancy and embellished knives. **Patterns:** Hunters, Bowies, daggers and folders. **Technical:** Forges O1, W2, 1084, 5160, 52100 and 1084/15n20 pattern weld. **Remarks:** Spare-time maker. **Mark:** Last name or stamped last initial over anvil.

SHORE, JOHN I,
2901 Sheldon Jackson St., Anchorage, AK 99508, Phone: 907-272-2253, akknife@acsalaska.net; Web: www.akknife.com
Specialties: Working straight knives, hatchets, and folders. **Patterns:** Hunters, skinners, Bowies, fighters, working using knives. **Technical:** Prefer using exotic steels, grinds most CPM's, Damasteel, RWL34, BG42, D2 and some ATS-34. Prefers exotic hardwoods, stabilized materials, Micarta, and pearl. **Prices:** Comparable to other top makers. **Remarks:** Full-time maker; first knife sold in 1985. Voting member Knifemakers Guild & Dertche Messermacker Guild. Doing business as Alaska Knifemaker. **Mark:** Name in script, Kenai, AK.

SHULL, JAMES,
5146 N US 231 W, Rensselaer, IN 47978, Phone: 219-866-0436, nbjs@netnitco.net
Specialties: Working knives of hunting, fillet, Bowie patterns. **Technical:** Forges or uses 1095, 5160, 52100 & O1. **Prices:** $100 to $300. **Remarks:** DBA Shull Handforged Knives. **Mark:** Last name in arc.

SIBRIAN, AARON,
4308 Dean Dr, Ventura, CA 93003, Phone: 805-642-6950
Specialties: Tough working knives of his design and in standard patterns. **Patterns:** Makes a "Viper utility"—a kukri derivative and a variety of straight using knives. **Technical:** Grinds 440C and ATS-34. Offers traditional Japanese blades; soft backs, hard edges, temper lines. **Prices:** $60 to $100; some to $250. **Remarks:** Spare-time maker; first knife sold in 1989. **Mark:** Initials in diagonal line.

SIMMONS, H R,
1100 Bay City Rd, Aurora, NC 27806, Phone: 252-322-5969
Specialties: Working/using straight knives of his design. **Patterns:** Fighters, hunters and utility/camp knives. **Technical:** Forges and grinds Damascus and L6; grinds ATS-34. **Prices:** $150 to $250; some to $400. **Remarks:** Part-time maker; first knife sold in 1987. Doing business as HRS Custom Knives, Royal Forge and Trading Company. **Mark:** Initials.

SIMONELLA, GIANLUIGI,
Via Battiferri 33, 33085 Maniago, ITALY, Phone: 01139-427-730350
Specialties: Traditional and classic folding and working/using knives of his design and to customer specs. **Patterns:** Bowies, fighters, hunters, utility/camp knives. **Technical:** Forges ATS-34, D2, 440C. **Prices:** $250 to $400; some to $1000. **Remarks:** Full-time maker; first knife sold in 1988. **Mark:** Wilson.

SIMS, BOB,
PO Box 772, Meridian, TX 76665, Phone: 254-435-6240
Specialties: Traditional working straight knives and folders in standard patterns. **Patterns:** Locking folders, slip-joint folders and hunters. **Technical:** Grinds D2, ATS-34 and O1. Offers filework on some knives. **Prices:** $150 to $275; some to $600. **Remarks:** Full-time maker; first knife sold in 1975. **Mark:** The division sign.

SINCLAIR, J E,
520 Francis Rd, Pittsburgh, PA 15239, Phone: 412-793-5778
Specialties: Fancy hunters and fighters, liner locking folders. **Patterns:** Fighters, hunters and folders. **Technical:** Flat-grinds and hollow grind, prefers hand rubbed satin finish. Uses natural handle materials. **Prices:** $185 to $800. **Remarks:** Part-time maker; first knife sold in 1995. **Mark:** First and middle initials, last name and maker.

SINYARD, CLESTON S,
27522 Burkhardt Dr, Elberta, AL 36530, Phone: 334-987-1361, nimoforge1@gulftel.com; Web: www.knifemakersguild
Specialties: Working straight knives and folders of his design. **Patterns:** Hunters, buckskinners, Bowies, daggers, fighters and all-Damascus folders. **Technical:** Makes Damascus from 440C, stainless steel, D2 and regular high-carbon steel; forges "forefinger pad" into hunters and skinners. **Prices:** In Damascus $450 to $1500; some $2500. **Remarks:** Full-time maker; first knife sold in 1980. Doing business as Nimo Forge. **Mark:** Last name, U.S.A. in anvil.

SISEMORE, CHARLES RUSSEL,
RR 2 Box 329AL, Mena, AR 71953, Phone: 918-383-1360

SISKA, JIM,
48 South Maple St, Westfield, MA 01085, Phone: 413-642-3059, siskaknives@comcast.net
Specialties: Traditional working straight knives, no folders. **Patterns:** Hunters, fighters, Bowies and one-of-a-kinds; folders. **Technical:** Grinds D2, A2, 54CM and ATS-34; buys Damascus. Likes exotic woods. **Prices:** $300 and up. **Remarks:** Part-time. **Mark:** Siska in Old English.

SJOSTRAND, KEVIN,
1541 S Cain St, Visalia, CA 93292, Phone: 209-625-5254
Specialties: Traditional and working/using straight knives and folders of his design or to customer specs. **Patterns:** Bowies, hunters, utility/camp knives, lockback, springbuck and LinerLock® folders. **Technical:** Grinds ATS-34, 440C and 1095. Prefers high polished blades and full tang. Natural and stabilized hardwoods, Micarta and stag handle material. **Prices:** $75 to $300. **Remarks:** Part-time maker; first knife sold in 1992. Doing business as Black Oak Blades. **Mark:** Oak tree, Black Oak Blades, name, or just last name.

SKIFF, STEVEN,
SKIFF MADE BLADES, PO Box 537, Broadalbin, NY 12025, Phone: 518-883-4875, skiffmadeblades@hotmail.com; Web: www.skiffmadeblades.com
Specialties: Custom using/collector grade straight blades and LinerLock® folders of maker's design or customer specifications. **Patterns:** Hunters, utility/camp knives, tactical/fancy art folders. **Prices:** Straight blades $225 and up. Folders $450 and up. **Technical:** Stock removal hollow ground ATS-34, 154 CM, S30V, and tool steel. Damascus-Devon Thomas, Robert Eggerling, Mike Norris and Delbert Ealy. Nickel silver and stainless in-house heat treating. Handle materials: man made and natural woods (stablilized). Horn shells sheaths for straight blades, sews own leather and uses sheaths by "Tree-Stump Leather." **Remarks:** First knife sold 1997. Started making folders in 2000. **Mark:** SKIFF on blade of straight blades and in inside of backspacer on folders.

SKOW, H.A. "TEX",
TEX KNIVES, 3534 Gravel Springs Rd, Senatobia, MS 38668, Phone: 662-301-1568, texknives@bellsouth.net; Web: www.texknives.com
Specialties: One-of-a-kind daggers, Bowies, boot knives and hunters. **Patterns:** Different Damascus patterns (by Bob Eggerling). **Technical:** 440C, 58, 60 Rockwell hardness. Engraving by Joe Mason. **Prices:** Negotiable. **Mark:** TEX.

SLEE, FRED,
9 John St, Morganville, NJ 07751, Phone: 732-591-9047
Specialties: Working straight knives, some fancy, to customer specs. **Patterns:** Hunters, fighters, fancy daggers and folders. **Technical:** Grinds D2, 440C and ATS-34. **Prices:** $285 to $1100. **Remarks:** Part-time maker; first knife sold in 1980. **Mark:** Letter "S" in Old English.

SLOAN, SHANE,
4226 FM 61, Newcastle, TX 76372, Phone: 940-846-3290
Specialties: Collector-grade straight knives and folders. **Patterns:** Uses stainless Damascus, ATS-34 and 12C27. Bowies, lockers, slip-joints, fancy folders, fighters and period pieces. **Technical:** Grinds D2 and ATS-34. Uses hand-rubbed satin finish. Prefers rare natural handle materials. **Prices:** $250 to $6500. **Remarks:** Full-time maker; first knife sold in 1985. **Mark:** Name and city.

SLOBODIAN, SCOTT,
4101 River Ridge Dr, PO Box 1498, San Andreas, CA 95249, Phone: 209-286-1980, Fax: 209-286-1982, scott@slobodianswords.com; Web: www.slobodianswords.com
Specialties: Japanese-style knives and swords, period pieces, fantasy pieces and miniatures. **Patterns:** Small kweikens, tantos, wakazashis, katanas, traditional samurai swords. **Technical:** Flat-grinds 1050, commercial Damascus. **Prices:** $800 to $3500; some to $7500. **Remarks:** Full-time maker; first knife sold in 1987. **Mark:** Blade signed in Japanese characters and various scripts.

SMALE, CHARLES J,
509 Grove Ave, Waukegan, IL 60085, Phone: 847-244-8013

custom knifemakers

SMALL, ED,
Rt 1 Box 178-A, Keyser, WV 26726, Phone: 304-298-4254
Specialties: Working knives of his design; period pieces. **Patterns:** Hunters, daggers, buckskinners and camp knives; likes one-of-a-kinds. **Technical:** Forges and grinds W2, L6 and his own Damascus. **Prices:** $150 to $1500. **Remarks:** Full-time maker; first knife sold in 1978. Doing business as Iron Mountain Forge Works. **Mark:** Script initials connected.

SMART, STEVE,
907 Park Row Cir, McKinney, TX 75070-3847, Phone: 214-837-4216, Fax: 214-837-4111
Specialties: Working/using straight knives and folders of his design, to customer specs and in standard patterns. **Patterns:** Bowies, hunters, kitchen knives, locking folders, utility/camp, fishing and bird knives. **Technical:** Grinds ATS-34, D2, 440C and O1. Prefers mirror polish or satin finish; hollow-grinds all blades. All knives come with sheath. Offers some filework. **Prices:** $95 to $225; some to $500. **Remarks:** Spare-time maker; first knife sold in 1983. **Mark:** Name, Custom, city and state in oval.

SMIT, GLENN,
627 Cindy Ct, Aberdeen, MD 21001, Phone: 410-272- 2959, wolfsknives@comcast.net
Specialties: Working and using straight and folding knives of his design or to customer specs. Customizes and repairs all types of cutlery. Exclusive maker of Dave Murphy Style knives. **Patterns:** Hunters, Bowies, daggers, fighters, utility/camp, folders, kitchen knives and miniatures, Murphy combat, C.H.A.I.K., Little 88 and Tiny 90-styles. **Technical:** Grinds 440C, ATS-34, O1, A2 also grinds 6AL4V titanium allox for blades. Reforges commercial Damascus and makes own Damascus, cast aluminum handles. **Prices:** Miniatures start at $30; full-size knives start at $50. **Remarks:** Spare-time maker; first knife sold in 1986. Doing business as Wolf's Knives. **Mark:** G.P. SMIT, with year on reverse side, Wolf's Knives-Murphy's way with date.

SMITH, J D,
69 Highland, Roxbury, MA 02119, Phone: 617-989-0723, jdsmith02119@yahoo.com
Specialties: Fighters, Bowies, Persian, locking folders and swords. **Patterns:** Bowies, fighters and locking folders. **Technical:** Forges and grinds D2, his Damascus, O1, 52100 etc. and wootz-pattern hammer steel. **Prices:** $500 to $2000; some to $5000. **Remarks:** Full-time maker; first knife sold in 1987. Doing business as Hammersmith. **Mark:** Last initial alone or in cartouche.

SMITH, J.B.,
21 Copeland Rd., Perkinston, MS 39573, Phone: 228-380- 1851
Specialties: Traditional working knives for the hunter and fisherman. **Patterns:** Hunters, Bowies, and fishing knives; copies of 1800 period knives. **Technical:** Grinds ATS-34, 440C. **Prices:** $100 to $800. **Remarks:** Full-time maker, first knife sold in 1972. **Mark:** J.B. Smith MAKER PERKINSTON, MS.

SMITH, JOHN M,
3450 E Beguelin Rd, Centralia, IL 62801, Phone: 618- 249-6444, jknife@frontiernet.net
Specialties: Folders. **Patterns:** Folders. **Prices:** $250 to $2500. **Remarks:** First knife sold in 1980. Not taking orders at this time on fixed blade knives. Part-time maker. **Mark:** Etched signature or logo.

SMITH, JOHN W,
1322 Cow Branch Rd, West Liberty, KY 41472, Phone: 606-743-3599, jwsknive@mrtc.com; Web: www.jwsmithknives.com
Specialties: Fancy and working locking folders of his design or to customer specs. **Patterns:** Interframes, traditional and daggers. **Technical:** Grinds 530V and his own Damascus. Offers gold inlay, engraving with gold inlay, hand-fitted mosaic pearl inlay and filework. Prefers hand- rubbed finish. Pearl and ivory available. **Prices:** Utility pieces $375 to $650. Art knives $1200 to $10,000. **Remarks:** Full-time maker. **Mark:** Initials engraved inside diamond.

SMITH, JOSH,
Box 753, Frenchtown, MT 59834, Phone: 406-626-5775, josh@joshsmithknives.com; Web: www.joshsmithknives.com
Specialties: Mosaic, Damascus, LinerLock® folders, automatics, Bowies, fighters, etc. **Patterns:** All kinds. **Technical:** Advanced Mosaic and Damascus. **Prices:** $450 and up. **Remarks:** A.B.S. Master Smith. **Mark:** Josh Smith with year (Josh08Smith).

SMITH, LENARD C,
PO Box D68, Valley Cottage, NY 10989, Phone: 914-268-7359

SMITH, MICHAEL J,
1418 Saddle Gold Ct, Brandon, FL 33511, Phone: 813-431-3790, smithknife@hotmail.com; Web: www.smithknife.com
Specialties: Fancy high art folders of his design. **Patterns:** Locking locks and automatics. **Technical:** Uses ATS-34, non-stainless and stainless Damascus; hand carves folders, prefers ivory and pearl. Hand-rubbed satin finish. Liners are 6AL4V titanium. **Prices:** $500 to $3000. **Remarks:** Full-time maker; first knife sold in 1989. **Mark:** Name, city, state.

SMITH, NEWMAN L.,
865 Glades Rd Shop #3, Gatlinburg, TN 37738, Phone: 423-436-3322, thesmithshop@aol.com; Web: www.thesmithsshop.com
Specialties: Collector-grade and working knives. **Patterns:** Hunters, slip-joint and lock-back folders, some miniatures. **Technical:** Grinds O1 and ATS-34; makes fancy sheaths. **Prices:** $165 to $750; some to $1000. **Remarks:** Full-time maker; first knife sold in 1984. Partners part- time to handle Damascus blades by Jeff Hurst; marks these with SH connected. **Mark:** First and middle initials, last name.

SMITH, RALPH L,
525 Groce Meadow Rd, Taylors, SC 29687, Phone: 864-444-0819, ralph_smith1@charter.net; Web: www.smithhandcraftedknives.com
Specialties: Working knives: straight and folding knives. Hunters, skinners, fighters, bird, boot, Bowie and kitchen knives. **Technical:** Concave Grind D2, ATS 34, 440C, steel hand finish or polished. **Prices:** $125 to $350 for standard models. **Remarks:** First knife sold in 1976. KMG member since 1981. SCAK founding member and past president. **Mark:** SMITH hand-crafted knives in SC state outline.

SMITH, RAYMOND L,
217 Red Chalk Rd, Erin, NY 14838, Phone: 607- 795-5257, Bladesmith@earthlink.net; Web: www.theanvilsedge.com
Specialties: Working/using straight knives and folders to customer specs and in standard patterns; period pieces. **Patterns:** Bowies, hunters, skip-joints. **Technical:** Forges 5160, 52100, 1018, 15N20, 1084 Damascus and wire cable Damascus. Filework. **Prices:** $100 to $1500; estimates for custom orders. **Remarks:** Full-time maker; first knife sold in 1991. ABS Master Smith. Doing business as The Anvils Edge. **Mark:** Ellipse with RL Smith, Erin NY MS in center.

SMITH, RICK,
BEAR BONE KNIVES, 1843 W Evans Creek Rd., Rogue River, OR 97537, Phone: 541-582-4144, BearBoneSmith@msn.com; Web: www.bearbone.com
Specialties: Classic, historical style Bowie knives, hunting knives and various contemporary knife styles. **Technical:** Blades are either forged or made by stock removal method depending on steel used. Also forge weld wire Damascus. Does own heat treating and tempering using digital even heat kiln. Stainless blades are sent out for cryogenic "freeze treat." Preferred steels are O1, tool, 5160, 1095, 1084, ATS-34, 154CM, 440C and various high carbon Damascus. **Prices:** $350 to $1500. Custom leather sheaths available for knives. **Remarks:** Full-time maker since 1997. Serial numbers no longer put on knives. Official business name is "Bear Bone Knives." **Mark:** Early maker's mark was "Bear Bone" over capital letters "RS" with downward arrow between letters and "Hand Made" underneath letters. Mark on small knives is 3/8 circle containing "RS" with downward arrow between letters. Current mark since 2003 is "R Bear Bone Smith" arching over image of coffin Bowie knife with two shooting stars and "Rogue River, Oregon" underneath.

SMITH, SHAWN,
2644 Gibson Ave, Clouis, CA 93611, Phone: 559-323- 6234, kslc@sbcglobal.net
Specialties:<BN Working and fancy straight knives. Patterns: Hunting, trout, fighters, skinners. Technical:<BN Hollow grinds ATS-34, 154CM, A-2. Prices: $150.00 and up. Remarks: Part time maker. Mark: Shawn Smith handmade.

SMITH JR., JAMES B "RED",
Rt 2 Box 1525, Morven, GA 31638, Phone: 912-775-2844
Specialties: Folders. **Patterns:** Rotating rear-lock folders. **Technical:** Grinds ATS-34, D2 and Vascomax 350. **Prices:** Start at $350. **Remarks:** Full-time maker; first knife sold in 1985. **Mark:** GA RED in cowboy hat.

SMOCK, TIMOTHY E,
1105 N Sherwood Dr, Marion, IN 46952, Phone: 765-664-0123

SMOKER, RAY,
113 Church Rd, Searcy, AR 72143, Phone: 501-796- 2712
Specialties: Rugged, no nonsense working knives of his design only. **Patterns:** Hunters, skinners, utility/camp and flat-ground knives. **Technical:** Forges his own Damascus and 52100; makes sheaths. Uses improved multiple edge quench he developed. **Prices:** $450 and up; price includes sheath. **Remarks:** Semi-retired; first knife sold in 1992. **Mark:** Last name.

SNARE, MICHAEL,
3352 E Mescal St, Phoenix, AZ 85028

SNELL, JERRY L,
539 Turkey Trl, Fortson, GA 31808, Phone: 706-324- 4922
Specialties: Working straight knives of his design and in standard patterns. **Patterns:** Hunters, boots, fighters, daggers and a few folders. **Technical:** Grinds 440C, ATS-34; buys Damascus. **Prices:** $175 to $1000. **Remarks:** Part-time maker.

SNODY, MIKE,
135 Triple Creek Rd, Fredericksburg, TX 78624, Phone: 361-443-0161, info@snodyknives.com; Web: www.snodyknives.com
Specialties: High performance straight knives in traditional and Japanese-styles. **Patterns:** Skinners, hunters, tactical, Kwaiken and tantos. **Technical:** Grinds BG42, ATS-34, 440C and A2. Offers full or tapered tangs, upgraded handle materials such as fossil ivory, coral and exotic woods. Traditional diamond wrap over stingray on Japanese-style knives. Sheaths available in leather or Kydex. **Prices:** $100 to $1000. **Remarks:** Part-time maker; first knife sold in 1999. **Mark:** Name over knife maker.

SNOW, BILL,
4824 18th Ave, Columbus, GA 31904, Phone: 706-576-4390, tipikw@knology.net
Specialties: Traditional working/using straight knives and folders of his design and to customer specs. Offers engraving and scrimshaw. **Patterns:** Bowies, fighters, hunters and folders. **Technical:** Grinds ATS-34, 440V, 440C, 420V, CPM350, BG42, A2, D2, 5160, 52100 and O1; forges if needed. Cryogenically quenches all steels; inlaid handles; some integrals; leather or Kydex sheaths. **Prices:** $125 to $700; some to $3500. **Remarks:** Now also have 530V, 10V and 3V steels in use. Full-time maker; first knife sold in 1958. Doing business as Tipi Knife works. **Mark:** Old English scroll "S" inside a tipi.

SNYDER, MICHAEL TOM,
PO Box 522, Zionsville, IN 46077-0522, Phone: 317-873-6807, wildcatcreek@indy.pr.com

SOAPER, MAX H.,
2375 Zion Rd, Henderson, KY 42420, Phone: 270-827-8143
Specialties: Primitive Longhunter knives, scalpers, camp knives, coboy Bowies, neck knives, working knives, period pieces from the 18th century. **Technical:** Forges 5160, 1084, 1095; all blades differentially head treated. **Prices:** $80 to $500. **Remarks:** Part-time maker since 1989. **Mark:** Initials in script.

SOLOMON, MARVIN,
23750 Cold Springs Rd, Paron, AR 72122, Phone: 501-821-3170, Fax: 501-821-6541, mardot@swbell.net; Web: www.coldspringsforge.com
Specialties: Traditional working and using straight knives of his design and to customer specs, also lock back 7 LinerLock® folders. **Patterns:** Single blade folders. **Technical:** Forges 5160, 1095, O1 and random Damascus. **Prices:** $125 to $1000. **Remarks:** Part-time maker; first knife sold in 1990. Doing business as Cold Springs Forge. **Mark:** Last name.

SONNTAG, DOUGLAS W,
902 N 39th St, Nixa, MO 65714, Phone: 417-693-1640, Fax: 417-582-1392, dougsonntag@gmail.com
Specialties: Working knives; art knives. **Patterns:** Hunters, boots, straight working knives; Bowies, some folders, camp/axe sets. **Technical:** Grinds D2, ATS-34, forges own Damascus; does own heat treating. **Prices:** $225 and up. **Remarks:** Full-time maker; first knife sold in 1986. **Mark:** Etched name in arch.

SONTHEIMER, G DOUGLAS,
12604 Bridgeton Dr, Potomac, MD 20854, Phone: 301-948-5227
Specialties: Fixed blade knives. **Patterns:** Whitetail deer, backpackers, camp, claws, fillet, fighters. **Technical:** Hollow Grinds. **Price:** $500 and up. **Remarks:** Spare-time maker; first knife sold in 1976. **Mark:** LORD.

SOPPERA, ARTHUR,
"Pilatusblick", Oberer Schmidberg, CH-9631 Ulisbach, SWITZERLAND, Phone: 71-988 23 27, Fax: 71-988 47 57, doublelock@hotmail.com; Web: www.sopperaknifeart.ch
Specialties: High-art, high-tech knives of his design. **Patterns:** Locking folders, and fixed blade knives. **Technical:** Grinds ATS-34 and commercial Damascus. Folders have button lock of his own design; some are fancy folders in jeweler's fashion. Also makes jewelry with integrated small knives. **Prices:** $300 to $1500, some $2500 and higher. **Remarks:** Full-time maker; first knife sold in 1986. **Mark:** Stylized initials, name, country.

SORNBERGER, JIM,
25126 Overland Dr, Volcano, CA 95689, Phone: 209-295-7819
Specialties: Classic San Francisco-style knives. Collectible straight knives. **Patterns:** 1095-1084/15W2. Makes own Damascus and powder metal. Fighters, daggers, Bowies; miniatures; hunters, custom canes, liner locks folders. **Technical:** Grinds 440C, 154CM and ATS-34; engraves, carves and embellishes. **Prices:** $500 to $20,000 in gold with gold quartz inlays. **Remarks:** Full-time maker; first knife sold in 1970. **Mark:** First initial, last name, city and state.

SOWELL, BILL,
100 Loraine Forest Ct, Macon, GA 31210, Phone: 478-994-9863, billsowell@reynoldscable.net
Specialties: Antique reproduction Bowies, forging Bowies, hunters, fighters, and most others. Also folders. **Technical:** Makes own Damascus, using 1084/15N20, also making own designs in powder metals, forges 5160-1095-1084, and other carbon steels, grinds ATS-34. **Prices:** Starting at $150 and up. **Remarks:** Part-time maker. Sold first knife in 1998. Does own leather work. **Mark:** Iron Horse Knives; Iron Horse Forge.

SPARKS, BERNARD,
PO Box 73, Dingle, ID 83233, Phone: 208-847-1883, dogknifeii@juno.com; Web: www.sparksknives.com
Specialties: Maker engraved, working and art knives. Straight knives and folders of his own design. **Patterns:** Locking inner-frame folders, hunters, fighters, one-of-a-kind art knives. **Technical:** Grinds 530V steel, 440-C, 154CM, ATS-34, D-2 and forges by special order; triple temper, cryogenic soak. Mirror or hand finish. New Liquid metal steel. **Prices:** $300 to $2000. **Remarks:** Full-time maker, first knife sold in 1967. **Mark:** Last name over state with a knife logo on each end of name. Prior 1980, stamp of last name.

SPENCER, KEITH,
PO Box 149, Chidlow Western Australia, AUSTRALIA 6556, Phone: 61 8 95727255, Fax: 61 8 95727266, spencer@knivesaustralia.com.au
Specialties: Survival & bushcraft bladeware. **Patterns:** Best known for Kakadu Bushcraft knife (since 1989). Leilira mini survival knife (since 1993). **Prices:** $100 to $400 AV. **Mark:** Spencer Australia.

SPICKLER, GREGORY NOBLE,
5614 Mose Cir, Sharpsburg, MD 21782, Phone: 301-432-2746

SPINALE, RICHARD,
4021 Canterbury Ct, Lorain, OH 44053, Phone: 440-282-1565
Specialties: High-art working knives of his design. **Patterns:** Hunters, fighters, daggers and locking folders. **Technical:** Grinds 440C, ATS-34 and 07; engraves. Offers gold bolsters and other deluxe treatments. **Prices:** $300 to $1000; some to $3000. **Remarks:** Spare-time maker; first knife sold in 1976. **Mark:** Name, address, year and model number.

SPIVEY, JEFFERSON,
9244 W Wilshire, Yukon, OK 73099, Phone: 405-721-4442
Specialties: The Saber tooth: a combination hatchet, saw and knife. **Patterns:** Built for the wilderness, all are one-of-a-kind. **Technical:** Grinds chromemoly steel. The saw tooth spine curves with a double row of biangular teeth. **Prices:** Start at $275. **Remarks:** First knife sold in 1977. As of September 2006 Spivey knives has resumed production of the sabertooth knife. **Mark:** Name and serial number.

SPRAGG, WAYNE E,
252 Oregon Ave, Lovell, WY 82431, Phone: 307-548-7212
Specialties: Working straight knives, some fancy. **Patterns:** Folders. **Technical:** Forges carbon steel and makes Damascus. **Prices:** $200 and up. **Remarks:** All stainless heat-treated by Paul Bos. Carbon steel in shop heat treat. **Mark:** Last name front side w/s initials on reverse side.

SPROKHOLT, ROB,
GATHERWOOD, Burgerweg 5, Netherlands, EUROPE 1754 KB Burgerbrug, Phone: 0031 6 51230225, Fax: 0031 84 2238446, info@gatherwood.nl; Web: www.gatherwood.nl
Specialties: One-of-a-kind knives. Top materials collector grade, made to use. **Patterns:** Outdoor knives (hunting, sailing, hiking), Bowies, man's surviving companions MSC, big tantos, folding knives. **Technical:** Handles mostly stabilized or oiled wood, ivory, Micarta, carbon fibre, G10. Stiff knives are full tang. Characteristic one row of massive silver pins or tubes. Folding knives have a LinerLock® with titanium or Damascus powdersteel liner thumb can have any stone you like. Stock removal grinder: flat or convex. Steel 440-C, RWL-34, ATS-34, PM damascener steel. **Prices:** Start at 320 euro. **Remarks:** Writer of the first Dutch knifemaking book, supply shop for knife enthusiastic. First knife sold in 2000. **Mark:** Gatherwood in an eclipse etched blade or stamped in an intarsia of silver in the spine.

ST. AMOUR, MURRAY,
RR 3, 222 Dicks Rd, Pembroke ON, CANADA K8A 6W4, Phone: 613-735-1061, knives@webhart.net; Web: www.stamourknives.com
Specialties: Working fixed blades. **Patterns:** Hunters, fish, fighters, Bowies and utility knives. **Technical:** Grinds ATS-34, 154CM, CPM-S-30-Y-60-Y-904 and Damascus. **Prices:** $75 and up. **Remarks:** Full-time maker; sold first knife in 1992. **Mark:** Last name over Canada.

ST. CLAIR, THOMAS K,
12608 Fingerboard Rd, Monrovia, MD 21770, Phone: 301-482-0264

ST. CYR, H RED,
1218 N Cary Ave, Wilmington, CA 90744, Phone: 310-518-9525

STAFFORD, RICHARD,
104 Marcia Ct, Warner Robins, GA 31088, Phone: 912-923-6372
Specialties: High-tech straight knives and some folders. **Patterns:** Hunters in several patterns, fighters, boots, camp knives, combat knives and period pieces. **Technical:** Grinds ATS-34 and 440C; satin finish is standard. **Prices:** Starting at $75. **Remarks:** Part-time maker; first knife sold in 1983. **Mark:** Last name.

STALCUP, EDDIE,
PO Box 2200, Gallup, NM 87305, Phone: 505-863-3107, sstalcup@cnetco.com
Specialties: Working and fancy hunters, bird and trout. Special custom orders. **Patterns:** Drop point hunters, locking liner and multi blade folders. **Technical:** ATS-34, 154 CM, 440C, CPM 154 and S30V. **Prices:** $150 to $1500. **Remarks:** Scrimshaw, exotic handle material, wet formed sheaths. Membership Arizona Knife Collectors Association. Southern California

blades collectors & professional knife makers assoc. **Mark:** E.F. Stalcup, Gallup, NM.

STANCER, CHUCK,
62 Hidden Ranch Rd NW, Calgary, AB, CANADA T3A 5S5, Phone: 403-295-7370, stancerc@telusplanet.net
Specialties: Traditional and working straight knives. **Patterns:** Bowies, hunters and utility knives. **Technical:** Forges and grinds most steels. **Prices:** $175 and up. **Remarks:** Part-time maker. **Mark:** Last name.

STANFORD, PERRY,
405N Walnut #9, Broken Arrow, OK 74012, Phone: 918-251-7983 or 866-305-5690, stanfordoutdoors@valornet; Web: www.stanfordoutdoors.homestead.com
Specialties: Drop point, hunting and skinning knives, handmade sheaths. **Patterns:** Stright, hunting, and skinners. **Technical:** Grinds 440C, ATS-34 and Damascus. **Prices:** $65 to $275. **Remarks:** Part-time maker, first knife sold in 2007. Knifemaker supplier, manufacturer of paper sharpening systems. Doing business as Stanford Outdoors. **Mark:** Company name and nickname.

STANLEY, JOHN,
604 Elm St, Crossett, AR 71635, Phone: 970-304-3005
Specialties: Hand forged fixed blades with engraving and carving. **Patterns:** Scottish dirks, skeans and fantasy blades. **Technical:** Forge high-carbon steel, own Damascus. Prices $70 to $500. **Remarks:** All work is sole authorship. Offers engraving and carving services on other knives and handles. **Mark:** Varies.

STAPEL, CHUCK,
Box 1617, Glendale, CA 91209, Phone: 213-66- KNIFE, Fax: 213-669-1577, www.stapelknives.com
Specialties: Working knives of his design. **Patterns:** Variety of straight knives, tantos, hunters, folders and utility knives. **Technical:** Grinds D2, 440C and AEB-L. **Prices:** $185 to $12,000. **Remarks:** Full-time maker; first knife sold in 1974. **Mark:** Last name or last name, U.S.A.

STAPLETON, WILLIAM E,
BUFFALO 'B' FORGE, 5425 Country Ln, Merritt Island, FL 32953
Specialties: Classic and traditional knives of his design and customer spec. **Patterns:** Hunters and using knives. **Technical:** Forges, O1 and L6 Damascus, cable Damascus and 5160; stock removal on request. **Prices:** $150 to $1000. **Remarks:** Part-time maker, first knife sold 1990. Doing business as Buffalo "B" Forge. **Mark:** Anvil with S initial in center of anvil.

STECK, VAN R,
260 W Dogwood Ave, Orange City, FL 32763, Phone: 407-416-1723, Web: www.van@thudknives.com
Specialties: Frame lock folders with his own lock design. Fighters, hunting & fillet, spike hawks and Asian influence on swords, sickles, spears, also traditional Bowies. **Technical:** Stock removal ATS-34, D2, forges 5160, 1095 & 1084. **Prices:** $75 to $750. **Remarks:** Free hand grinds, distal taper, hollow and chisel. Specialize in filework and Japanese handle wrapping. Voting member of the Knifemakers' Guild. **Mark:** GEISHA with sword & initials and T.H.U.D. knives.

STEFFEN, CHUCK,
504 Dogwood Ave NW, St. Michael, MN, Phone: 763-497-3615
Specialties: Custom hunting knives, fixed blades folders. Specializing in exotic materials. Damascus excellent fit form and finishes.

STEGALL, KEITH,
701 Outlet View Dr, Wasilla, AK 99654, Phone: 907- 376-0703, kas5200@yahoo.com
Specialties: Traditional working straight knives. **Patterns:** Most patterns. **Technical:** Grinds 440C and 154CM. **Prices:** $100 to $300. **Remarks:** Spare-time maker; first knife sold in 1987. **Mark:** Name and state with anchor.

STEGNER, WILBUR G,
9242 173rd Ave SW, Rochester, WA 98579, Phone: 360-273-0937, wilbur@wgsk.net; Web: www.wgsk.net
Specialties: Working/using straight knives and folders of his design. **Patterns:** Hunters and locking folders. **Technical:** Grinds ATS-34 and other tool steels. Quenches, tempers and hardness tests each blade. **Prices:** $100 to $1000; some to $5000. **Remarks:** Full-time maker; first knife sold in 1979. Google search key words-"STEGNER KNIVES." **Mark:** First and middle initials, last name in bar over shield logo.

STEIER, DAVID,
7722 Zenith Way, Louisville, KY 40219, Web: www.steierknives.com
Specialties: Folding LinerLocks, Bowies, slipjoints, lockbacks, and straight hunters. **Technical:** Stock removal blades of 440C, ATS-34, and Damascus from outside sources like Robert Eggerling and Mike Norris. **Prices:** $150 for straight hunters to $1400 for fully decked-out folders. **Remarks:** First knife sold in 1979. **Mark:** Last name STEIER.

STEIGER, MONTE L,
Box 186, Genesee, ID 83832, Phone: 208-285-1769, montesharon@genesee-id.com
Specialties: Traditional working/using straight knives of all designs. **Patterns:** Hunters, utility/camp knives, fillet and chefs. Carving sets and steak knives. **Technical:** Grinds 1095, O1, 440C, ATS-34. Handles of stacked leather, natural wood, Micarta or pakkawood. Each knife comes with right-

or left-handed sheath. **Prices:** $110 to $600. **Remarks:** Spare- time maker; first knife sold in 1988. Retired librarian **Mark:** First initial, last name, city and state.

STEIGERWALT, KEN,
507 Savagehill Rd, Orangeville, PA 17859, Phone: 570-683-5156, Web: www.steigerwaltknives.com
Specialties: Carving on bolsters and handle material. **Patterns:** Folders, button locks and rear locks. **Technical:** Grinds ATS-34, 440C and commercial Damascus. Experiments with unique filework. **Prices:** $500 to $5000. **Remarks:** Full-time maker; first knife sold in 1981. **Mark:** Kasteigerwalt

STEINAU, JURGEN,
Julius-Hart Strasse 44, Berlin 0-1162, GERMANY, Phone: 372-6452512, Fax: 372-645-2512
Specialties: Fantasy and high-art straight knives of his design. **Patterns:** Boots, daggers and switch-blade folders. **Technical:** Grinds 440B, 2379 and X90 Cr.Mo.V. 78. **Prices:** $1500 to $2500; some to $3500. **Remarks:** Full-time maker; first knife sold in 1984. **Mark:** Symbol, plus year, month day and serial number.

STEINBERG, AL,
5244 Duenas, Laguna Woods, CA 92653, Phone: 949-951-2889, lagknife@fea.net
Specialties: Fancy working straight knives to customer specs. **Patterns:** Hunters, Bowies, fishing, camp knives, push knives and high end kitchen knives. **Technical:** Grinds O1, 440C and 154CM. **Prices:** $60 to $2500. **Remarks:** Full-time maker; first knife sold in 1972. **Mark:** Signature, city and state.

STEINBRECHER, MARK W,
1122 92nd Place, Pleasant Prairie, WI 53158-4939
Specialties: Working and fancy folders. **Patterns:** Daggers, pocket knives, fighters and gents of his own design or to customer specs. **Technical:** Hollow grinds ATS-34, O1 and makes Damascus. Uses natural handle materials: stag, ivories, mother-of-pearl. File work and some inlays. **Prices:** $500 to $1200, some to $2500. **Remarks:** Part-time maker, first folder sold in 1989. **Mark:** Name etched or handwritten on ATS-34; stamped on Damascus.

STEKETEE, CRAIG A,
871 N Hwy 60, Billings, MO 65610, Phone: 417- 744-2770, stekknives@earthlink.net
Specialties: Classic and working straight knives and swords of his design. **Patterns:** Bowies, hunters, and Japanese-style swords. **Technical:** Forges his own Damascus; bronze, silver and Damascus fittings, offers filework. Prefers exotic and natural handle materials. **Prices:** $200 to $4000. **Remarks:** Full-time maker. **Mark:** STEK.

STEPHAN, DANIEL,
2201 S Miller Rd, Valrico, FL 33594, Phone: 727- 580-8617, knifemaker@verizon.net
Specialties: Art knives, one-of-a-kind.

STERLING, MURRAY,
693 Round Peak Church Rd, Mount Airy, NC 27030, Phone: 336-352-5110, Fax: Fax: 336-352-5105, sterck@surry.net; Web: www.sterlingcustomknives.com
Specialties: Single and dual blade folders. Interframes and integral dovetail frames. **Technical:** Grinds ATS-34 or Damascus by Mike Norris and/or Devin Thomas. **Prices:** $300 and up. **Remarks:** Full-time maker; first knife sold in 1991. **Mark:** Last name stamped.

STERLING, THOMAS J,
ART KNIVES BY, 120 N Pheasant Run, Coupeville, WA 98239, Phone: 360-678-9269, Fax: 360-678-9269, netsuke@comcast.net; Web: www.bladegallery.com or www.sterlingsculptures.com
Specialties: Since 2003 Tom Sterling and Dr. J.P. Higgins have created a unique collaboration of one-of-a-kind, ultra-quality art knives with percussion or pressured flaked stone blades and creatively sculpted handles. Their knives are often highly influenced by the traditions of Japanese netsuke and unique fusions of cultures, reflecting stylistically integrated choices of exotic hardwoods, fossil ivories and semi-precious materials, contrasting inlays and polychromed and pyrographed details. **Prices:** $300 to $900. **Remarks:** Limited output ensures highest quality artwork and exceptional levels of craftsmanship. **Mark:** Signatures Sterling and Higgins.

STETTER, J. C.,
115 E College Blvd PMB 180, Roswell, NM 88201, Phone: 505-627-0978
Specialties: Fixed and folding. **Patterns:** Traditional and yours. **Technical:** Forged and ground of varied materials including his own pattern welded steel. **Prices:** Start at $250. **Remarks:** Full-time maker, first knife sold 1989. **Mark:** Currently "J.C. Stetter."

STEWART, EDWARD L,
4297 Audrain Rd 335, Mexico, MO 65265, Phone: 573-581-3883
Specialties: Fixed blades, working knives some art. **Patterns:** Hunters, Bowies, utility/camp knives. **Technical:** Forging 1095-W-2-I-6-52100 makes own Damascus. **Prices:** $85 to $500. **Remarks:** Part-time maker first knife sold in 1993. **Mark:** First and last initials-last name.

STEYN, PETER,
PO Box 76, Welkom 9460, Freestate, SOUTH AFRICA, Phone: 27573525201, Fax: 27573523566, Web:www.petersteynknives.com email:info@ petersteynknives.com
Specialties: Fixed blade working knives of own design, tendency toward tactical creative & artistic styles all with hand stitched leather sheaths. **Patterns:**Hunters, skinners, fighters & wedge ground daggers. **Technical:** Grinds 12C27, D2, N690. Blades are bead-blasted in plain or camo patterns & own exclusive crator finish. Prefers synthetic handle materials also uses cocobolo & ironwood. **Prices:** $200-$600. **Remarks:**Full time maker, first knife sold 2005, member of South African Guild.**Mark:** Letter 'S' in shape of pyramid with full name above & 'Handcrafted' below.

STIMPS, JASON M,
374 S Shaffer St, Orange, CA 92866, Phone: 714- 744-5866

STIPES, DWIGHT,
2651 SW Buena Vista Dr, Palm City, FL 34990, Phone: 772-597-0550, dwightstipes@adelphia.net
Specialties: Traditional and working straight knives in standard patterns. **Patterns:** Boots, Bowies, daggers, hunters and fighters. **Technical:** Grinds 440C, D2 and D3 tool steel. Handles of natural materials, animal, bone or horn. **Prices:** $75 to $150. **Remarks:** Full-time maker; first knife sold in 1972. **Mark:** Stipes.

STOCKWELL, WALTER,
368 San Carlos Ave, Redwood City, CA 94061, Phone: 650-363-6069, walter@ stockwellknives.com; Web: www.stockwellknives.com
Specialties: Scottish dirks, sgian dubhs. **Patterns:** All knives one-of-a-kind. **Technical:** Grinds ATS-34, forges 5160, 52100, L6. **Prices:** $125 to $500.**Remarks:**Part-time maker since 1992; graduate of ABS bladesmithing school. **Mark:** Shooting star over "STOCKWELL." Pre-2000, "WKS."

STODDART, W B BILL,
2357 Mack Rd #105, Fairfield, OH 45014, Phone: 513-851-1543
Specialties: Sportsmen's working knives and multi-blade folders. **Patterns:** Hunters, camp and fish knives; multi-blade reproductions of old standards. **Technical:** Grinds A2, 440C and ATS-34; makes sheaths to match handle materials. **Prices:** $80 to $300; some to $850. **Remarks:** Part-time maker; first knife sold in 1976. **Mark:** Name, Cincinnati, state.

STOKES, ED,
22614 Cardinal Dr, Hockley, TX 77447, Phone: 713-351- 1319
Specialties: Working straight knives and folders of all designs. **Patterns:** Boots, Bowies, daggers, fighters, hunters and miniatures. **Technical:** Grinds ATS-34, 440C and D2. Offers decorative butt caps, tapered spacers on handles and finger grooves, nickel-silver inlays, handmade sheaths. **Prices:** $185 to $290; some to $350. **Remarks:** Full-time maker; first knife sold in 1973. **Mark:** First and last name, Custom Knives with Apache logo.

STONE, JERRY,
PO Box 1027, Lytle, TX 78052, Phone: 830-709-3042
Specialties: Traditional working and using folders of his design and to customer specs; fancy knives. **Patterns:** Fighters, hunters, locking folders and slip joints. Also make automatics. **Technical:** Grinds 440C and ATS-34. Offers filework. **Prices:** $175 to $1000. **Remarks:** Full-time maker; first knife sold in 1973. **Mark:** Name over Texas star/town and state underneath.

STORCH, ED,
RR 4 Mannville, Alberta T0B 2W0, CANADA, Phone: 780- 763-2214, storchkn@ agt.net; Web: www.storchknives.com
Specialties: Working knives, fancy fighting knives, kitchen cutlery and art knives. Knifemaking classes. **Patterns:** Working patterns, Bowies and folders. **Technical:** Forges his own Damascus. Grinds ATS-34. Builds friction folders. Salt heat treating. **Prices:** $45 to $750 (U.S.). **Remarks:** Part-time maker; first knife sold in 1984. Hosts annual Northwest Canadian Knifemakers Symposium; 60 to 80 knifemakers and families. **Mark:** Last name.

STORMER, BOB,
10 Karabair Rd, St. Peters, MO 63376, Phone: 636- 441-6807, bobstormer@ sbcglobal.net
Specialties: Straight knives, using collector grade. **Patterns:** Bowies, skinners, hunters, camp knives. **Technical:** Forges 5160, 1095. **Prices:** $150 to $400. **Remarks:** Part-time maker, ABS Journeyman Smith 2001. **Mark:** Setting sun/fall trees/initials.

STOUT, CHARLES,
RT3 178 Stout Rd, Gillham, AR 71841, Phone: 870- 386-5521

STOUT, JOHNNY,
1205 Forest Trail, New Braunfels, TX 78132, Phone: 830-606-4067, johnny@ stoutknives.com; Web: www.stoutknives.com
Specialties: Folders, some fixed blades. Working knives, some fancy. **Patterns:** Hunters, tactical, Bowies, automatics, liner locks and slip- joints. **Technical:** Grinds stainless and carbon steels; forges own Damascus. **Prices:** $450 to $895; some to $3500. **Remarks:** Full-time maker; first knife sold in 1983. Hosts semi-annual Guadalupe Forge Hammer-in and Knifemakers Rendezvous. **Mark:** Name and city in logo with serial number.

STOVER, HOWARD,
100 Palmetto Dr Apt 7, Pasadena, CA 91105, Phone: 765-452-3928

STOVER, TERRY "LEE",
1809 N 300 E, Kokomo, IN 46901, Phone: 765-452-3928
Specialties: Damascus folders with filework; Damascus Bowies of his design or to customer specs. **Patterns:** Lockback folders and Sheffield- style Bowies. **Technical:** Forges 1095, Damascus using O2, 203E or O2, pure nickel. Makes mokume. Uses only natural handle material. **Prices:** $300 to $1700; some to $2000. **Remarks:** Part-time maker; first knife sold in 1984. **Mark:** First and middle initials, last name in knife logo; Damascus blades marked in Old English.

STRAIGHT, KENNETH J,
11311 103 Lane N, Largo, FL 33773, Phone: 813-397-9817

STRANDE, POUL,
Soster Svenstrup Byvej 16, Dastrup 4130 Viby Sj., DENMARK, Phone: 46 19 43 05, Fax: 46 19 53 19, Web: www.poulstrande.com
Specialties: Classic fantasy working knives; Damasceret blade, Nikkel Damasceret blade, Lamineret: Lamineret blade with Nikkel. **Patterns:** Bowies, daggers, fighters, hunters and swords. **Technical:** Uses carbon steel and 15C20 steel. **Prices:** NA. **Remarks:** Full-time maker; first knife sold in 1985. **Mark:** First and last initials.

STRICKLAND, DALE,
1440 E Thompson View, Monroe, UT 84754, Phone: 435-896-8362
Specialties: Traditional and working straight knives and folders of his design and to customer specs. **Patterns:** Hunters, folders, miniatures and utility knives. **Technical:** Grinds Damascus and 440C. **Prices:** $120 to $350; some to $500. **Remarks:** Part-time maker; first knife sold in 1991. **Mark:** Oval stamp of name, Maker.

STRIDER, MICK,
STRIDER KNIVES, 120 N Pacific Unit L-7, San Marcos, CA 92069, Phone: 760-471-8275, Fax: 503-218-7069, striderguys@striderknives.com; Web: www.striderknives.com

STRONG, SCOTT,
1599 Beaver Valley Rd, Beavercreek, OH 45434, Phone: 937-426-9290
Specialties: Working knives, some deluxe. **Patterns:** Hunters, fighters, survival and military-style knives, art knives. **Technical:** Forges and grinds O1, A2, D2, 440C and ATS-34. Uses no solder; most knives disassemble. **Prices:** $75 to $450; some to $1500. **Remarks:** Spare-time maker; first knife sold in 1983. **Mark:** Strong Knives.

STROYAN, ERIC,
Box 218, Dalton, PA 18414, Phone: 717-563-2603
Specialties: Classic and working/using straight knives and folders of his design. **Patterns:** Hunters, locking folders, slip-joints. **Technical:** Forges Damascus; grinds ATS-34, D2. **Prices:** $200 to $600; some to $2000. **Remarks:** Part-time maker; first knife sold in 1968. **Mark:** Signature or initials stamp.

STUART, STEVE,
Box 168, Gores Landing, Ont., CANADA K0K 2E0, Phone: 905-440-6910, stevestuart@xplornet.com
Specialties: Straight knives. **Patterns:** Tantos, fighters, skinners, file and rasp knives. **Technical:** Uses 440C, CPM154, CPMS30V, Micarta and natural handle materials. **Prices:** $60 to $400. **Remarks:** Part-time maker. **Mark:** SS.

STYREFORS, MATTIAS,
Unbyn 23, SE-96193 Boden, SWEDEN, infor@styrefors.com
Specialties: Damascus and mosaic Damascus. Fixed blade Nordic hunters, folders and swords. **Technical:** Forges, shapes and grinds Damascus and mosaic Damascus from mostly UHB 15N20 and 20C with contrasts in nickel and 15N20. Hardness HR 58. **Prices:** $800 to $3000. **Remarks:** Full-time maker since 1999. International reputation for high end Damascus blades. Uses stabilized Arctic birch and willow burl, horn, fossils, exotic materials, and scrimshaw by Viveca Sahlin for knife handles. Hand tools and hand stitches leather sheaths in cow raw hide. Works in well equipped former military forgery in northern Sweden. **Mark:** MS.

SUEDMEIER, HARLAN,
762 N 60th Rd, Nebraska City, NE 68410, Phone: 402-873-4372
Patterns: Straight knives. **Technical:** Forging hi carbon Damascus. **Prices:** Starting at $175. **Mark:** First initials & last name.

SUGIHARA, KEIDOH,
4-16-1 Kamori-Cho, Kishiwada City, Osaka, F596-0042, JAPAN, Fax: 0724- 44-2677
Specialties: High-tech working straight knives and folders of his design. **Patterns:** Bowies, hunters, fighters, fishing, boots, some pocket knives and liner-lock folders. **Technical:** Grinds ATS-34, COS-25, buys Damascus and high-carbon steels. **Prices** $60 to $4000. **Remarks:** Full-time maker, first knife sold in 1980. **Mark:** Initial logo with fish design.

SUGIYAMA, EDDY K,
2361 Nagayu, Naoirimachi Naoirigun, Ohita, JAPAN, Phone: 0974-75-2050
Specialties: One-of-a-kind, exotic-style knives. **Patterns:** Working, utility and miniatures. **Technical:** CT rind, ATS-34 and D2. **Prices:** $400 to $1200. **Remarks:** Full-time maker. **Mark:** Name or cedar mark.

SUMMERLIN, DANNY,
7058 Howe, Groves, TX 77619, Phone: 409- 344-3190
Specialties: Hunters and skinners. **Patterns:** Makes only hunters and skinners full tang. **Technical:** Grinds ATS-34 & 154 CM. **Prices:** $125- $250

SUMMERS, ARTHUR L,
1310 Hess Rd, Concord, NC 28025, Phone: 704-644-0018, arthursummers88@hotmail.com
Specialties: Drop points, clip points, straight blades. **Patterns:** Hunters, Bowies and personal knives. **Technical:** Grinds 440C, ATS-34, D2 and Damascus. **Prices:** $250 to $1000. **Remarks:** Full-time maker; first knife sold in 1987. **Mark:** Serial number is the date.

SUMMERS, DAN,
2675 NY Rt. 11, Whitney Pt., NY 13862, Phone: 607- 692-2391, dansumm11@msn.com
Specialties: Period knives and tomahawks. **Technical:** All hand forging. **Prices:** Most $100 to $400.

SUMMERS, DENNIS K,
827 E. Cecil St, Springfield, OH 45503, Phone: 513-324-0624
Specialties: Working/using knives. **Patterns:** Fighters and personal knives. **Technical:** Grinds 440C, A2 and D2. Makes drop and clip point. **Prices:** $75 to $200. **Remarks:** Part-time maker; first knife sold in 1995. **Mark:** First and middle initials, last name, serial number.

SUNDERLAND, RICHARD,
Av Infraganti 23, Col Lazaro Cardenas, Puerto Escondido Oaxaca, MEXICO 71980, Phone: 011 52 94 582 1451, sunamerica@prodigy.net.mx7
Specialties: Personal and hunting knives with carved handles in oosic and ivory. **Patterns:** Hunters, Bowies, daggers, camp and personal knives. **Technical:** Grinds 440C, ATS-34 and O1. Handle materials of rosewoods, fossil mammoth ivory and oosic. **Prices:** $150 to $1000. **Remarks:** Part-time maker; first knife sold in 1983. Doing business as Sun Knife Co. **Mark:** SUN.

SUTTON, S RUSSELL,
4900 Cypress Shores Dr, New Bern, NC 28562, Phone: 252-637-3963, srsutton@suddenlink.net; Web: www.suttoncustomknives.com
Specialties: Straight knives and folders to customer specs and in standard patterns. **Patterns:** Boots, hunters, interframes, slip joints and locking liners. **Technical:** Grinds ATS-34, 440C and stainless Damascus. **Prices:** $220 to $950; some to $1250. **Remarks:** Full-time maker; first knife sold in 1992. **Mark:** Etched last name. **Other:** Engraved bolsters and guards available on some knives by maker.

SWEAZA, DENNIS,
4052 Hwy 321 E, Austin, AR 72007, Phone: 501- 941-1886, knives4den@aol.com

SWEENEY, COLTIN D,
1216 S 3 St W, Missoula, MT 59801, Phone: 406-721-6782

SWYHART, ART,
509 Main St, PO Box 267, Klickitat, WA 98628, Phone: 509-369-3451, swyhart@gorge.net; Web: www.knifeoutlet.com/swyhart.htm
Specialties: Traditional working and using knives of his design. **Patterns:** Bowies, hunters and utility/camp knives. **Technical:** Forges 52100, 5160 and Damascus 1084 mixed with either 15N20 or O186. Blades differentially heat-treated with visible temper line. **Prices:** $75 to $250; some to $350. **Remarks:** Part-time maker; first knife sold in 1983. **Mark:** First name, last initial in script.

SYMONDS, ALBERTO E,
Rambla M Gandhi 485, Apt 901, Montevideo 11300, URUGUAY, Phone: 011 598 5608207, Fax: 011 598 2 7103201, albertosymonds@hotmail.com
Specialties: All kinds including puukos, nice sheaths, leather and wood. **Prices:** $300 to $2200. **Mark:** AESH and current year.

SYSLO, CHUCK,
3418 South 116 Ave, Omaha, NE 68144, Phone: 402- 333-0647, ciscoknives@cox.net
Specialties: Hunters, working knives, daggers & misc. **Patterns:** Hunters, daggers and survival knives; locking folders. **Technical:** Flat-grinds D2, 440C and 154CM; hand polishes only. **Prices:** $250 to $1000; some to $3000. **Remarks:** Part-time maker; first knife sold in 1978. Uses many natural materials. **Mark:** CISCO in logo.

SZAREK, MARK G,
94 Oakwood Ave, Revere, MA 02151, Phone: 781- 289-7102
Specialties: Classic period working and using straight knives and tools. **Patterns:** Hunting knives, American and Japanese woodworking tools. **Technical:** Forges 5160, 1050, Damascus; differentially hardens blades with fireclay. **Prices:** $50 to $750. **Remarks:** Part-time maker; first knife sold in 1989. Produces Japanese alloys for sword fittings and accessories. Custom builds knife presentation boxes and cabinets. **Mark:** Last name.

SZILASKI, JOSEPH,
52 Woods Dr, Pine Plains, NY 12567, Phone: 518- 398-0309, Web: www.szilaski.com
Specialties: Straight knives, folders and tomahawks of his design, to customer specs and in standard patterns. Many pieces are one-of-a-kind. **Patterns:** Bowies, daggers, fighters, hunters, art knives and early American-styles. **Technical:** Forges A2, D2, O1 and Damascus. **Prices:** $450 to $4000; some to $10,000. **Remarks:** Full-time maker; first knife sold in 1990. ABS Master Smith and voting member KMG. **Mark:** Snake logo.

T

TABOR, TIM,
18925 Crooked Lane, Lutz, FL 33548, Phone: 813-948- 6141, taborknives.com
Specialties: Fancy folders, Damascus Bowies and hunters. **Patterns:** My own design folders & customer requests. **Technical:** ATS-34, hand forged Damascus, 1084, 15N20 mosaic Damascus, 1095, 5160 high carbon blades, flat grind, file work & jewel embellishments. **Prices:** $175 to $1500. **Remarks:** Part-time maker, sold first knife in 2003. **Mark:** Last name

TAKACH, ANDREW,
504 Church St., Herminie, PA 15637, Phone: 724- 446-1926, a-takach@takachforge.com; Web: www.takachforge.com
Specialties: One-of-a-kind fixed blade working knives (own design or customer's). Mostly all fileworked. **Patterns:** Hunters, skinners, caping, fighters, and designs of own style. **Technical:** Forges mostly 5160, 1090, 01, an down pattern welded Damascus, nickle Damascus, and cable and various chain Damascus. Also do some San Mai. **Prices:** $100 to $350, some over $550. **Remarks:** Doing business as Takach Forge. First knife sold in 2004. **Mark:** Takach (stamped).

TAKAHASHI, MASAO,
39-3 Sekine-machi, Maebashi-shi, Gunma 371 0047, JAPAN, Phone: 81 27 234 2223, Fax: 81 27 234 2223
Specialties: Working straight knives. **Patterns:** Daggers, fighters, hunters, fishing knives, boots. **Technical:** Grinds ATS-34 and Damascus. **Prices:** $350 to $1000 and up. **Remarks:** Full-time maker; first knife sold in 1982. **Mark:** M. Takahashi.

TALLY, GRANT,
26961 James Ave, Flat Rock, MI 48134, Phone: 734- 789-8961
Specialties: Straight knives and folders of his design. **Patterns:** Bowies, daggers, fighters. **Technical:** Grinds ATS-34, 440C and D2. Offers filework. **Prices:** $250 to $1000. **Remarks:** Part-time maker; first knife sold in 1985. Doing business as Tally Knives. **Mark:** Tally (last name).

TAMBOLI, MICHAEL,
12447 N 49 Ave, Glendale, AZ 85304, Phone: 602-978-4308, mnbtamboli@gmail.com
Specialties: Miniatures, some full size. **Patterns:** Miniature hunting knives to fantasy art knives. **Technical:** Grinds ATS-34 & Damascus. **Prices:** $75 to $500; some to $2000. **Remarks:** Full time maker; first knife sold in 1978. **Mark:** Initials, last name, last name city and state, MT Custom Knives or Mike Tamboli in Japanese script.

TASMAN, KERLEY,
9 Avignon Retreat, Pt Kennedy 6172, Western Australia, AUSTRALIA, Phone: 61 8 9593 0554, Fax: 61 8 9593 0554, taskerley@optusnet.com.au
Specialties: Knife/harness/sheath systems for elite military personnel and body guards. **Patterns:** Utility/tactical knives, hunters small game and presentation grade knives. **Technical:** ATS-34 and 440C, Damascus, flat and hollow grids. **Prices:** $200 to $1800 U.S. **Remarks:** Will take presentation grade commissions. Multi award winning maker and custom jeweler. **Mark:** Maker's initials.

TAYLOR, BILLY,
10 Temple Rd, Petal, MS 39465, Phone: 601-544- 0041
Specialties: Straight knives of his design. **Patterns:** Bowies, skinners, hunters and utility knives. **Technical:** Flat-grinds 440C, ATS-34 and 154CM. **Prices:** $60 to $300. **Remarks:** Part-time maker; first knife sold in 1991. **Mark:** Full name, city and state.

TAYLOR, C GRAY,
560 Poteat Ln, Fall Branch, TN 37656, Phone: 423- 348-8304, graysknives@aol.com or graysknives@hotmail.com; Web: www.cgraytaylor.net
Specialties: Traditonal multi-blade lobster folders, also art display Bowies and daggers. **Patterns:** Orange Blossom, sleeveboard and gunstocks. **Technical:** Grinds. **Prices:** Upscale. **Remarks:** Full-time maker; first knife sold in 1975. **Mark:** Name, city and state.

TAYLOR, DAVID,
113 Stewart Hill Dr, Rogersville, TN 37857, Phone: 423-921-0733, dtaylor0730@charter.net; Web: www.dtguitars.com
Patterns: Multi-blade folders, traditional patterns. **Technical:** Grinds ATS-34. **Prices:** $400 and up. **Remarks:** First sold knife in 1981 at age 14. Became a member of Knifemakers Guild at age 14. Made first folder in 1983. Full-time pastor of Baptist Church and part-time knifemaker.

TAYLOR, SHANE,
18 Broken Bow Ln, Miles City, MT 59301, Phone: 406-234-7175, shane@taylorknives.com; Web: www.taylorknives.com
Specialties: One-of-a-kind fancy Damascus straight knives and folders. **Patterns:** Bowies, folders and fighters. **Technical:** Forges own mosaic and pattern welded Damascus. **Prices:** $450 and up. **Remarks:** ABS Master Smith, full-time maker; first knife sold in 1982. **Mark:** First name.

TERAUCHI, TOSHIYUKI,
7649-13 219-11 Yoshida, Fujita-Cho Gobo- Shi, JAPAN

TERRILL, STEPHEN,
16357 Goat Ranch Rd, Springville, CA 93265, Phone: 559-539-3116, slterrill@yahoo.com
Specialties: Deluxe working straight knives and folders. **Patterns:** Fighters, tantos, boots, locking folders and axes; traditional oriental patterns. **Technical:** Forges 1095, 5160, Damascus, stock removal ATS-34. **Prices:** $300+. **Remarks:** Full-time maker; first knife sold in 1972. **Mark:** Name, city, state in logo.

TERZUOLA, ROBERT,
10121 Eagle Rock NE, Albuquerque, NM 87122, Phone: 505-473-1002, Fax: 505-438-8018, terzuola@earthlink.net
Specialties: Working folders of his design; period pieces. **Patterns:** High-tech utility, defense and gentleman's folders. **Technical:** Grinds CPM154, Damascus, and CPM S30V. Offers titanium, carbon fiber and G10 composite for side-lock folders and tactical folders. **Prices:** $550 to $2000. **Remarks:** Full-time maker; first knife sold in 1980. **Mark:** Mayan dragon head, name.

THAYER, DANNY O,
8908S 100W, Romney, IN 47981, Phone: 765- 538-3105, dot61h@juno.com
Specialties: Hunters, fighters, Bowies. **Prices:** $250 and up.

THEIS, TERRY,
21452 FM 2093, Harper, TX 78631, Phone: 830-864- 4438
Specialties: All European and American engraving styles. **Prices:** $200 to $2000. **Remarks:** Engraver only.

THEVENOT, JEAN-PAUL,
16 Rue De La Prefecture, Dijon, FRANCE 21000
Specialties: Traditional European knives and daggers. **Patterns:** Hunters, utility-camp knives, daggers, historical or modern style. **Technical:** Forges own Damascus, 5160, 1084. **Remarks:** Part-time maker. ABS Master Smith. **Mark:** Interlocked initials in square.

THIE, BRIAN,
13250 150th St, Burlington, IA 52601, Phone: 319-985- 2276, bkthie@mepotelco.net; Web: www.mepotelco.net/web/tknives
Specialties: Working using knives from basic to fancy. **Patterns:** Hunters, fighters, camp and folders. **Technical:** Forges blades and own Damascus. **Prices:** $100 and up. **Remarks:** ABS Journeyman Smith, part- time maker. Sole author of blades including forging, heat treat, engraving and sheath making. **Mark:** Last name hand engraved into the blade, JS stamped into blade.

THILL, JIM,
10242 Bear Run, Missoula, MT 59803, Phone: 406-251- 5475
Specialties: Traditional and working/using knives of his design. **Patterns:** Fighters, hunters and utility/camp knives. **Technical:** Grinds D2 and ATS-34; forges 10-95-85, 52100, 5160, 10 series, reg. Damascus- mosaic. Offers hand cut sheaths with rawhide lace. **Prices:** $145 to $350; some to $1250. **Remarks:** Full-time maker; first knife sold in 1962. **Mark:** Running bear in triangle.

THOMAS, BOB G,
RR 1 Box 121, Thebes, IL 62990-9718

THOMAS, DAVID E,
8502 Hwy 91, Lillian, AL 36549, Phone: 251-961- 7574, redbluff@gulftel.com
Specialties: Bowies and hunters. **Technical:** Hand forged blades in 5160, 1095 and own Damascus. **Prices:** $400 and up. **Mark:** Stylized DT, maker's last name, serial number.

THOMAS, DEVIN,
PO Box 568, Panaca, NV 89042, Phone: 775-728- 4363, hoss@devinthomas.com; Web: www.devinthomas.com
Specialties: Traditional straight knives and folders in standard patterns. **Patterns:** Bowies, folders, hunters. **Technical:** Forges stainless Damascus, nickel and 1095. Uses, makes and sells mokume with brass, copper and nickel-silver. **Prices:** $300 to $1200. **Remarks:** Full-time maker; first knife sold in 1979. **Mark:** First and last name, city and state with anvil, or first name only.

THOMAS, KIM,
PO Box 531, Seville, OH 44273, Phone: 330-769-9906
Specialties: Fancy and traditional straight knives of his design and to customer specs; period pieces. **Patterns:** Boots, daggers, fighters, swords. **Technical:** Forges own Damascus from 5160, 1010 and nickel. **Prices:** $135 to $1500; some to $3000. **Remarks:** Part-time maker; first knife sold in 1986. Doing business as Thomas Iron Works. **Mark:** KT.

THOMAS, ROCKY,
1716 Waterside Blvd, Moncks Corner, SC 29461, Phone: 843-761-7761
Specialties: Traditional working knives in standard patterns. **Patterns:** Hunters and utility/camp knives. **Technical:** ATS-34 and commercial Damascus. **Prices:** $130 to $350. **Remarks:** Spare-time maker; first knife sold in 1986. **Mark:** First name in script and/or block.

THOMPSON, KENNETH,
4887 Glenwhite Dr, Duluth, GA 30136, Phone: 770-446-6730
Specialties: Traditional working and using knives of his design. **Patterns:** Hunters, Bowies and utility/camp knives. **Technical:** Forges 5168, O1, 1095 and 52100. **Prices:** $75 to $1500; some to $2500. **Remarks:** Part-time maker; first knife sold in 1990. **Mark:** P/W; or name, P/W, city and state.

THOMPSON, LEON,
45723 SW Saddleback Dr, Gaston, OR 97119, Phone: 503-357-2573
Specialties: Working knives. **Patterns:** Locking folders, slip-joints and liner locks. **Technical:** Grinds ATS-34, D2 and 440C. **Prices:** $200 to $600. **Remarks:** Full-time maker; first knife sold in 1976. **Mark:** First and middle initials, last name, city and state.

THOMPSON, LLOYD,
PO Box 1664, Pagosa Springs, CO 81147, Phone: 970-264-5837
Specialties: Working and collectible straight knives and folders of his design. **Patterns:** Straight blades, lock back folders and slip joint folders. **Technical:** Hollow-grinds ATS-34, D2 and O1. Uses sambar stag and exotic woods. **Prices:** $150 to upscale. **Remarks:** Full-time maker; first knife sold in 1985. Doing business as Trapper Creek Knife Co. **Remarks:** Offers three-day knife-making classes. **Mark:** Name.

THOMPSON, TOMMY,
4015 NE Hassalo, Portland, OR 97232-2607, Phone: 503-235-5762
Specialties: Fancy and working knives; mostly liner-lock folders. **Patterns:** Fighters, hunters and liner locks. **Technical:** Grinds D2, ATS-34, CPM440V and T15. Handles are either hardwood inlaid with wood banding and stone or shell, or made of agate, jasper, petrified woods, etc. **Prices:** $75 to $500; some to $1000. **Remarks:** Part-time maker; first knife sold in 1987. Doing business as Stone Birds. Knife making temporarily stopped due to family obligations. **Mark:** First and last name, city and state.

THOMSEN, LOYD W,
30173 Black Banks Rd, Oelrichs, SD 57763, Phone: 605-535-6162, loydt@yahoo.com; Web: horseheadcreekknives.com
Specialties: High-art and traditional working/using straight knives and presentation pieces of his design and to customer specs; period pieces. Hand carved animals in crown of stag on handles and carved display stands. **Patterns:** Bowies, hunters, daggers and utility/camp knives. **Technical:** Forges and grinds 1095HC, 1084, L6, 15N20, 440C stainless steel, nickel 200; special restoration process on period pieces. Makes sheaths. Uses natural materials for handles. **Prices:** $350 to $1000. **Remarks:** Full-time maker; first knife sold in 1995. Doing business as Horsehead Creek Knives. **Mark:** Initials and last name over a horse's head.

THORBURN, ANDRE E.,
P.O. Box 1748, Bela Bela, Warmbaths 0480, SOUTH AFRICA, Phone: 27-82-650-1441, thorburn@icon.co.za; Web: www.thorburnknives.com
Specialties: Working and fancy folders of own design to customer specs. **Technical:** Uses RWL34, 12C27, 19C27, D2, Carbon and stainless Damascus. **Prices:** Starting at $350. **Remarks:** Full-time maker since 1996, first knife sold in 1990. Member of American Knifemakers Guild and South African, Italian, and German guilds; chairman of Knifemakers Guild of South Africa. **Mark:** Initials and name in a double circle.

THOUROT, MICHAEL W,
T-814 Co Rd 11, Napoleon, OH 43545, Phone: 419-533-6832, Fax: 419-533-3516, mike2row@henry-net.com; Web: wwwsafariknives.com
Specialties: Working straight knives to customer specs. Designed two-handled skinning ax and limited edition engraved knife and art print set. **Patterns:** Fishing and fillet knives, Bowies, tantos and hunters. **Technical:** Grinds O1, D2, 440C and Damascus. **Prices:** $200 to $5000. **Remarks:** Part-time maker; first knife sold in 1968. **Mark:** Initials.

THUESEN, ED,
21211 Knolle Rd, Damon, TX 77430, Phone: 979-553- 1211, Fax: 979-553-1211
Specialties: Working straight knives. **Patterns:** Hunters, fighters and survival knives. **Technical:** Grinds D2, 440C, ATS-34 and Vascowear. **Prices:** $150 to $275; some to $600. **Remarks:** Part-time maker; first knife sold in 1979. Runs knifemaker supply business. **Mark:** Last name in script.

TICHBOURNE, GEORGE,
7035 Maxwell Rd #5, Mississauga, Ont., CANADA L5S 1R5, Phone: 905-670-0200, sales @tichbourneknives.com; Web: www.tichbourneknives.com
Specialties: Traditional working and using knives as well as unique collectibles. **Patterns:** Bowies, hunters, outdoor, kitchen, integrals, art, military, Scottish dirks, folders, kosher knives. **Technical:** Stock removal 440C, Stellite 6K, stainless Damascus. Handle materials include mammoth, meteorite, mother-of-pearl, precious gems, mosiac, abalone, stag, Micarta, exotic high resin woods and corian scrimshawed by George. Leather sheaths are hand stitched and tooled by George as well as the silver adornments for the dirk sheaths. **Prices:** $60 up to $5000 U.S. **Remarks:** Full-time maker with his OWN STORE. First knife sold in 1990. **Mark:** Full name over maple leaf.

TIENSVOLD, ALAN L,
PO Box 355, Rushville, NE 69360, Phone: 308- 327-2046
Specialties: Working knives, tomahawks and period pieces, high end Damascus knives. **Patterns:** Random, ladder, twist and many more. **Technical:** Hand forged blades, forges own Damascus. **Prices:** Working knives start at $300. **Remarks:** Received Journeyman rating with the ABS in 2002. Does own engraving and fine work. **Mark:** Tiensvold hand made U.S.A. on left side, JS on right.

TIENSVOLD, JASON,
PO Box 795, Rushville, NE 69360, Phone: 308- 327-2046, ironprik@gpcom.net
Specialties: Working and using straight knives of his design; period pieces. Gentlemen folders, art folders. Single action automatics. **Patterns:** Hunters, skinners, Bowies, fighters, daggers, liner locks. **Technical:** Forges own Damascus using 15N20 and 1084, 1095, nickel, custom file work. **Prices:** $200 to $4000. **Remarks:** Full-time maker, first knife sold in 1994; doing business under Tiensvold Custom Knives. **Mark:** J. Tiensvold.

TIGHE, BRIAN,
12-111 Fourth Ave, Suite 376 Ridley Square, St. Catharines, Ont., CANADA L0S 1M0, Phone: 905-892-2734, Fax: 905- 892-2734, Web: www.tigheknives.com
Specialties: High tech tactical folders. **Patterns:** Boots, daggers, locking and slip-joint folders. **Technical:** CPM 440V and CPM 420V. Prefers natural handle material inlay; hand finishes. **Prices:** $450 to $2000. **Remarks:** Part-time maker; first knife sold in 1989. **Mark:** Etched signature.

TILL, CALVIN E AND RUTH,
211 Chaping, Chadron, NE 69337
Specialties: Straight knives, hunters, Bowies; no folders **Patterns:** Training point, drop point hunters, Bowies. **Technical:** ATS-34 sub zero quench RC59, 61. **Prices:** $700 to $1200. **Remarks:** Sells only the absolute best knives they can make. Manufactures every part in their knives. **Mark:** RC Till. The R is for Ruth.

TILTON, JOHN,
24041 Hwy 383, Iowa, LA 70647, Phone: 337-582-6785, john@jetknives.com
Specialties: Bowies, camp knives, skinners and folders. **Technical:** All forged blades. Makes own Damascus. **Prices:** $150 and up. **Remarks:** ABS Journeyman Smith. **Mark:** Initials J.E.T.

TINDERA, GEORGE,
BURNING RIVER FORGE, 751 Hadcock Rd, Brunswick, OH 44212-2648, Phone: 330-220-6212
Specialties: Straight knives; his designs. **Patterns:** Personal knives; classic Bowies and fighters. **Technical:** Hand-forged high-carbon; his own cable and pattern welded Damascus. **Prices:** $100 to $400. **Remarks:** Spare-time maker; sold first knife in 1995. Natural handle materials.

TINGLE, DENNIS P,
19390 E Clinton Rd, Jackson, CA 95642, Phone: 209-223-4586, dtknives@earthlink.net
Specialties: Swords, fixed blades: small to medium, tomahawks. **Technical:** All blades forged. **Remarks:** ABS, JS. **Mark:** D. Tingle over JS.

TIPPETTS, COLTEN,
4068 W Miners Farm Dr, Hidden Springs, ID 83714, Phone: 208-229-7772, colten@interstate-electric.com
Specialties: Fancy and working straight knives and fancy locking folders of his own design or to customer specifications. **Patterns:** Hunters and skinners, fighters and utility. **Technical:** Grinds BG-42, high-carbon 1095 and Damascus. **Prices:** $200 to $1000. **Remarks:** Part-time maker; first knife sold in 1996. **Mark:** Fused initials.

TKOMA, FLAVIO,
R Manoel Rainho Teixeira 108-Pres, Prudonte SP19031-220, BRAZIL, Phone: 0182-22-0115, fikoma@itelesonica.com.br
Specialties: Tactical fixed blade knives, LinerLock® folders and balisongs. **Patterns:** Utility and defense tactical knives built with hi-tech materials. **Technical:** Grinds S30V and Damasteel. **Prices:** $500 to $1000. **Mark:** Ikoma hand made beside Samurai.

TODD, RICHARD C,
375th LN 4600, Chambersburg, IL 62323, Phone: 217-327-4380, ktodd45@yahoo.com
Specialties: Multi blade folders and silver sheaths. **Patterns:** Jewel selling and hard engraving. **Mark:** RT with letter R crossing the T or R Todd.

TOICH, NEVIO,
Via Pisacane 9, Rettorgole di Caldogna, Vincenza, ITALY 36030, Phone: 0444-985065, Fax: 0444-301254
Specialties: Working/using straight knives of his design or to customer specs. **Patterns:** Bowies, hunters, skinners and utility/camp knives. **Technical:** Grinds 440C, D2 and ATS-34. Hollow-grinds all blades and uses mirror polish. Offers hand-sewn sheaths. Uses wood and horn. **Prices:** $120 to $300; some to $450. **Remarks:** Spare-time maker; first knife sold in 1989. Doing business as Custom Toich. **Mark:** Initials and model number punched.

TOKAR, DANIEL,
Box 1776, Shepherdstown, WV 25443
Specialties: Working knives; period pieces. **Patterns:** Hunters, camp knives, buckskinners, axes, swords and battle gear. **Technical:** Forges L6, 1095 and his Damascus; makes mokume, Japanese alloys and bronze daggers; restores old edged weapons. **Prices:** $25 to $800; some to $3000. **Remarks:** Part-time maker; first knife sold in 1979. Doing business as The Willow Forge. **Mark:** Arrow over rune and date.

TOLLEFSON, BARRY A,
104 Sutter Pl, PO Box 4198, Tubac, AZ 85646, Phone: 520-398-9327
Specialties: Working straight knives, some fancy. **Patterns:** Hunters, skinners, fighters and camp knives. **Technical:** Grinds 440C, ATS-34 and D2. Likes mirror-finishes; offers some fancy filework. Handles made from elk, deer and exotic hardwoods. **Prices:** $75 to $300; some higher. **Remarks:** Part-time maker; first knife sold in 1990. **Mark:** Stylized initials.

TOMBERLIN, BRION R,
ANVIL TOP CUSTOM KNIVES, 825 W Timberdell, Norman, OK 73072, Phone: 405-202-6832, anviltopp@aol.com
Specialties: Hand forged blades, working pieces, standard classic patterns, some swords, and customer designs. **Patterns:** Bowies, hunters, fighters, Persian and eastern-styles. Likes Japanese blades. **Technical:** Forge 1050, 1075, 1084, 1095, 5160, some forged stainless, also do some stock removal in stainless. **Prices:** Start at $150 up to $800 or higher for swords and custom pieces. **Remarks:** Part-time maker, member America Bladesmith Society, Journeyman Smith. Prefers natural handle materials, hand rubbed finishes. Likes temperlines. **Mark:** "BRION" on forged blades, "ATCK" on stock removal, stainless and early forged blades.

TOMES, P J,
594 High Peak Ln, Shipman, VA 22971, Phone: 434-263- 8662, tomgsknives@juno.com; Web: www.tomesknives.com
Specialties: Scagel reproductions. **Patterns:** Front-lock folders. **Technical:** Forges 52100. **Prices:** $150 to $750. **Mark:** Last name, USA, MS, stamped in forged blades.

TOMEY, KATHLEEN,
146 Buford Pl, Macon, GA 31204, Phone: 478- 746-8454, ktomey@tomeycustomknives.com; Web: www.tomeycustomknives.com
Specialties: Working hunters, skinners, daily users in fixed blades, plain and embellished. Tactical neck and belt carry. Japanese influenced. Bowies. **Technical:** Grinds O1, ATS-34, flat or hollow grind, filework, satin and mirror polish finishes. High quality leather sheaths with tooling. Kydex with tactical. **Prices:** $150 to $500. **Remarks:** Almost full-time maker. **Mark:** Last name in diamond.

TOMPKINS, DAN,
PO Box 398, Peotone, IL 60468, Phone: 708-258- 3620
Specialties: Working knives, some deluxe, some folders. **Patterns:** Hunters, boots, daggers and push knives. **Technical:** Grinds D2, 440C, ATS-34 and 154CM. **Prices:** $85 to $150; some to $400. **Remarks:** Part- time maker; first knife sold in 1975. **Mark:** Last name, city, state.

TONER, ROGER,
531 Lightfoot Pl, Pickering, Ont., CANADA L1V 5Z8, Phone: 905-420-5555
Specialties: Exotic sword canes. **Patterns:** Bowies, daggers and fighters. **Technical:** Grinds 440C, D2 and Damascus. Scrimshaws and engraves. Silver cast pommels and guards in animal shapes; twisted silver wire inlays. Uses semi-precious stones. **Prices:** $200 to $2000; some to $3000. **Remarks:** Part-time maker; first knife sold in 1982. **Mark:** Last name.

TORGESON, SAMUEL L,
25 Alpine Ln, Sedona, AZ 86336-6809

TORRES, HENRY,
2329 Moody Ave., Clovis, CA 93619, Phone: 559- 297-9154, Web: www.htknives.com
Specialties: Forged high-performance hunters and working knives, Bowies, and fighters. **Technical:** 52100 and 5160 and makes own Damascus. **Prices:** $350 to $3000. **Remarks:** Started forging in 2004. Has mastersmith with American Bladesmith Association.

TOSHIFUMI, KURAMOTO,
3435 Higashioda, Asakura-gun, Fukuoka, JAPAN, Phone: 0946-42-4470

TOWELL, DWIGHT L,
2375 Towell Rd, Midvale, ID 83645, Phone: 208- 355-2419
Specialties: Solid, elegant working knives; art knives, high quality hand engraving and gold inlay. **Patterns:** Hunters, Bowies, daggers and folders. **Technical:** Grinds 154CM, ATS-34, 440C and other maker's Damascus. **Prices:** Upscale. **Remarks:** Full-time maker. First knife sold in 1970. Member of AKI. **Mark:** Towell, sometimes hand engraved.

TOWNSEND, ALLEN MARK,
6 Pine Trail, Texarkana, AR 71854, Phone: 870-772-8945
TRACE RINALDI CUSTOM BLADES,
28305 California Ave, Hemet, CA 92545, Phone: 951-926-5422, Trace@thrblades.com; Web: www.thrblades.com
Technical: Grinds S30V, 3V, A2 and talonite fixed blades. **Prices:** $300-$1000. **Remarks:** Tactical and utility for the most part. **Mark:** Diamond with THR inside.
TRACY, BUD,
495 Flanders Rd, Reno, NV 8951-4784
TREIBER, LEON,
PO Box 342, Ingram, TX 78025, Phone: 830-367- 2246, treiberknives@hotmail.com; Web: www.treiberknives.com
Specialties: Folders of his design and to customer specs. **Patterns:** Fixed blades. **Technical:** Grinds CPM-T-440V, D2, 440C, Damascus, 420V and ATS-34. **Prices:** $350 to $3500. **Remarks:** Part-time maker; first knife sold in 1992. Doing business as Treiber Knives. **Mark:** First initial, last name, city, state.
TREML, GLENN,
RR #14 Site 12-10, Thunder Bay, Ont., CANADA P7B 5E5, Phone: 807-767-1977
Specialties: Working straight knives of his design and to customer specs. **Patterns:** Hunters, kitchen knives and double-edged survival knives. **Technical:** Grinds 440C, ATS-34 and O1; stock removal method. Uses various woods and Micarta for handle material. **Prices:** $150 and up. **Mark:** Stamped last name.
TRINDLE, BARRY,
1660 Ironwood Trail, Earlham, IA 50072-8611, Phone: 515-462-1237
Specialties: Engraved folders. **Patterns:** Mostly small folders, classical-styles and pocket knives. **Technical:** 440 only. Engraves. Handles of wood or mineral material. **Prices:** Start at $1000. **Mark:** Name on tang.
TRISLER, KENNETH W,
6256 Federal 80, Rayville, LA 71269, Phone: 318-728-5541
TRITZ, JEAN JOSE,
Schopstrasse 23, 20255 Hamburg, GERMANY, Phone: 040-49 78 21
Specialties: Scandinavian knives, Japanese kitchen knives, friction folders, swords. **Patterns:** Puukkos, Tollekniven, Hocho, friction folders, swords. **Technical:** Forges tool steels, carbon steels, 52100 Damascus, mokume, San Maj. **Prices:** $200 to $2000; some higher. **Remarks:** Full-time maker; first knife sold in 1989. Does own leatherwork, prefers natural materials. Sole authorship. Speaks French, German, English, Norwegian. **Mark:** Initials in monogram.
TRUJILLO, ALBERT M B,
2035 Wasmer Cir, Bosque Farms, NM 87068, Phone: 505-869-0428, cutups@surfmk.com
Specialties: Working/using straight knives of his design or to customer specs. **Patterns:** Hunters, skinners, fighters, working/using knives. File work offered. **Technical:** Grinds ATS-34, D2, 440C, S30V. Tapers tangs, all blades cryogenically treated. **Prices:** $75 to $500. **Remarks:** Part- time maker; first knife sold in 1997. **Mark:** First and last name under logo.
TRUNCALI, PETE,
2914 Anatole Court, Garland, TX 75043, Phone: 214- 763-7127, Web:www.truncalikniives.com
Specialties: Lockback folders, locking liner folders, automatics and fixed blades. Does business as Truncali Custom Knives.
TSCHAGER, REINHARD,
Piazza Parrocchia 7, I-39100 Bolzano, ITALY, Phone: 0471-970642, Fax: 0471-970642, goldtschager@dnet.it
Specialties: Classic, high-art, collector-grade straight knives of his design. **Patterns:** Jewel knife, daggers, and hunters. **Technical:** Grinds ATS-34, D2 and Damascus. Oval pins. Gold inlay. Offers engraving. **Prices:** $900 to $2000; some to $3000. **Remarks:** Spare-time maker; first knife sold in 1979. **Mark:** Gold inlay stamped with initials.
TUOMINEN, PEKKA,
Pohjois-Keiteleentie 20, 72930 Tossavanlahti, FINLAND, Phone: 358405167853, puukkopekka@luukku.com; Web: www.puukkopekka.com
Specialties: Puukko knives. **Patterns:** Puukkos, hunters, leukus, and folders. **Technical:** Forges silversteel, 1085, 52100, and makes own Damascus 15N20 and 1095. Grinds RWL-34 and ATS-34. **Prices:** Starting at $170. **Remarks:** Part-time maker. **Mark:** Name.
TURCOTTE, LARRY,
1707 Evergreen, Pampa, TX 79065, Phone: 806- 665-9369, 806-669-0435
Specialties: Fancy and working/using knives of his design and to customer specs. **Patterns:** Hunters, kitchen knives, utility/camp knives. **Technical:** Grinds 440C, D2, ATS-34. Engraves, scrimshaws, silver inlays. **Prices:** $150 to $350; some to $1000. **Remarks:** Part-time maker; first knife sold in 1977. Doing business as Knives by Turcotte. **Mark:** Last name.

TURECEK, JIM,
12 Elliott Rd, Ansonia, CT 06401, Phone: 203-734-8406
Specialties: Exotic folders, art knives and some miniatures. **Patterns:** Trout and bird knives with split bamboo handles and one-of-a-kind folders. **Technical:** Grinds and forges stainless and carbon Damascus. **Prices:** $750 to $1500; some to $3000. **Remarks:** Full-time maker; first knife sold in 1983. **Mark:** Last initial in script, or last name.
TURNBULL, RALPH A,
14464 Linden Dr, Spring Hill, FL 34609, Phone: 352-688-7089, tbull2000@bellsouth.net; Web: www.turnbullknives.com
Specialties: Fancy folders. **Patterns:** Primarily gents pocket knives. **Technical:** Wire EDM work on bolsters. **Prices:** $300 and up. **Remarks:** Full-time maker; first knife sold in 1973. **Mark:** Signature or initials.
TURNER, KEVIN,
17 Hunt Ave, Montrose, NY 10548, Phone: 914-739- 0535
Specialties: Working straight knives of his design and to customer specs; period pieces. **Patterns:** Daggers, fighters and utility knives. **Technical:** Forges 5160 and 52100. **Prices:** $90 to $500. **Remarks:** Part-time maker; first knife sold in 1991. **Mark:** Acid-etched signed last name and year.
TYCER, ART,
23820 N Cold Springs Rd, Paron, AR 72122, Phone: 501- 821-4487, blades1@tycerknives.com; Web: www.tycerknives.com
Specialties: Fancy working/using straight knives of his design, to customer specs and standard patterns. **Patterns:** Boots, Bowies, daggers, fighters, hunters, kitchen and utility knives. **Technical:** Grinds ATS-34, 440C and a variety of carbon steels. Uses exotic woods with spacer material, stag and water buffalo. Offers filework. **Prices:** $175 and up depending on size and embellishments or Damascus. **Remarks:** Now making folders (liner locks). Making and using his own Damascus and other Damascus also. Full-time maker. **Mark:** Flying "T" over first initial inside an oval.
TYRE, MICHAEL A,
1219 Easy St, Wickenburg, AZ 85390, Phone: 928- 684-9601/602-377-8432, michaeltyre@msn.com
Specialties: Quality folding knives upscale gents folders one-of-a-kind collectable models. **Patterns:** Working fixed blades for hunting, kitchen and fancy Bowies. **Technical:** Grinds prefer hand rubbed satin finishes and use natural handle materials. **Prices:** $250 to $1300.
TYSER, ROSS,
1015 Hardee Court, Spartanburg, SC 29303, Phone: 864-585-7616
Specialties: Traditional working and using straight knives and folders of his design and in standard patterns. **Patterns:** Bowies, hunters and slip- joint folders. **Technical:** Grinds 440C and commercial Damascus. Mosaic pins; stone inlay. Does filework and scrimshaw. Offers engraving and cut-work and some inlay on sheaths. **Prices:** $45 to $125; some to $400. **Remarks:** Part-time maker; first knife sold in 1995. Doing business as RT Custom Knives. **Mark:** Stylized initials.

U

UCHIDA, CHIMATA,
977-2 Oaza Naga Shisui Ki, Kumamoto, JAPAN 861-1204

V

VAGNINO, MICHAEL,
PO Box 67, Visalia, CA 93279, Phone: 559-636- 2800, mvknives@lightspeed.net; Web: www.mvknives.com
Specialties: Working and fancy straight knives and folders of his design and to customer specs. **Patterns:** Hunters, Bowies, camp, kitchen and folders: locking liners, slip-joint, lock-back and double-action autos. **Technical:** Forges 52100, A2, 1084 and 15N20 Damascus and grinds stainless. **Prices:** $275 to $2000 plus. **Remarks:** Full-time maker, ABS Master Smith. **Mark:** Logo, last name.
VAIL, DAVE,
554 Sloop Point Rd, Hampstead, NC 28443, Phone: 910- 270-4456
Specialties: Working/using straight knives of his own design or to the customer's specs. **Patterns:** Hunters/skinners, camp/utility, fillet, Bowies. **Technical:** Grinds ATS-34, 440c, 154 CM and 1095 carbon steel. **Prices:** $90 to $450. **Remarks:** Part-time maker. Member of NC Custom Knifemakers Guild. **Mark:** Etched oval with "Dave Vail Hampstead NC" inside.
VALLOTTON, BUTCH AND AREY,
621 Fawn Ridge Dr, Oakland, OR 97462, Phone: 541-459-2216, Fax: 541-459-7473
Specialties: Quick opening knives w/complicated mechanisms. **Patterns:** Tactical, fancy, working, and some art knives. **Technical:** Grinds all steels, uses others' Damascus. Uses Spectrum Metal. **Prices:** From $350 to $4500. **Remarks:** Full-time maker since 1984; first knife sold in 1981. Co/designer, Appelgate Fairbarn folding w/Bill Harsey. **Mark:** Name w/viper head in the "V."
VALLOTTON, RAINY D,
1295 Wolf Valley Dr, Umpqua, OR 97486, Phone: 541-459-0465
Specialties: Folders, one-handed openers and art pieces. **Patterns:** All patterns. **Technical:** Stock removal all steels; uses titanium liners and bolsters; uses all finishes. **Prices:** $350 to $3500. **Remarks:** Full-time maker. **Mark:** Name.

VALLOTTON, SHAWN,
621 Fawn Ridge Dr, Oakland, OR 97462, Phone: 503-459-2216
Specialties: Left-hand knives. **Patterns:** All styles. **Technical:** Grinds 440C, ATS-34 and Damascus. Uses titanium. Prefers bead-blasted or anodized finishes. **Prices:** $250 to $1400. **Remarks:** Full-time maker. **Mark:** Name and specialty.

VALLOTTON, THOMAS,
621 Fawn Ridge Dr, Oakland, OR 97462, Phone: 541-459-2216
Specialties: Custom autos. **Patterns:** Tactical, fancy. **Technical:** File work, uses Damascus, uses Spectrum Metal. **Prices:** From $350 to $700. **Remarks:** Full-time maker. Maker of Protégé 3 canoe. **Mark:** T and a V mingled.

VALOIS, A. DANIEL,
3552 W Lizard Ck Rd, Lehighton, PA 18235, Phone: 717-386-3636
Specialties: Big working knives; various sized lock-back folders with new safety releases. **Patterns:** Fighters in survival packs, sturdy working knives, belt buckle knives, military-style knives, swords. **Technical:** Forges and grinds A2, O1 and 440C; likes full tangs. **Prices:** $65 to $240; some to $600. **Remarks:** Full-time maker; first knife sold in 1969. **Mark:** Anvil logo with last name inside.

VAN CLEVE, STEVE,
Box 372, Sutton, AK 99674, Phone: 907-745-3038

VAN DE MANAKKER, THIJS,
Koolweg 34, 5759 px Helenaveen, HOLLAND, Phone: 0493539369
Specialties: Classic high-art knives. **Patterns:** Swords, utility/camp knives and period pieces. **Technical:** Forges soft iron, carbon steel and Bloomery Iron. Makes own Damascus, Bloomery Iron and patterns. **Prices:** $20 to $2000; some higher. **Remarks:** Full-time maker; first knife sold in 1969. **Mark:** Stylized "V."

VAN DEN ELSEN, GERT,
Purcelldreef 83, 5012 AJ Tilburg, NETHERLANDS, Phone: 013-4563200, gvdelsen@home.nl; Web: www.7knifedwarfs.com
Specialties: Fancy, working/using, miniatures and integral straight knives of the maker's design or to customer specs. **Patterns:** Bowies, fighters, hunters and Japanese-style blades. **Technical:** Grinds ATS-34 and 440C; forges Damascus. Offers filework, differentially tempered blades and some mokume-gane fittings. **Prices:** $350 to $1000; some to $4000. **Remarks:** Part-time maker; first knife sold in 1982. Doing business as G-E Knives. **Mark:** Initials GE in lozenge shape.

VAN DER WESTHUIZEN, PETER,
PO Box 1698, Mossel Bay 6500, SOUTH AFRICA, Phone: 27 446952388
Specialties: Working knives, folders, daggers and art knives. **Patterns:** Hunters, skinners, bird, trout and sidelock folders. **Technical:** Sandvik, 12627. Damascus indigenous wood and ivory. **Prices:** From $450 to $5500. **Remarks:** First knife sold in 1987. Full-time since 1996. **Mark:** Initial & surname. Handmade RSA.

VAN DIJK, RICHARD,
76 Stepney Ave Rd 2, Harwood Dunedin, NEW ZEALAND, Phone: 0064-3-4780401, Web: www.hoihoknives.com
Specialties: Damascus, Fantasy knives, sgiandubhs, dirks, swords, and hunting knives. **Patterns:** Mostly one-ofs, anything from bird and trout to swords, no folders. **Technical:** Forges mainly own Damascus, some 5160, O1, 1095, L6. Prefers natural handle materials, over 35 years experience as goldsmith, handle fittings are often made from sterling silver and sometimes gold, manufactured to cap the handle, use gemstones if required. Makes own sheaths. **Prices:** $300 and up. **Remarks:** Full-time maker, first knife sold in 1980. Doing business as HOIHO KNIVES. **Mark:** Stylized initials RvD in triangle.

VAN EIZENGA, JERRY W,
14281 Cleveland, Nunica, MI 49448, Phone: 616-638-2275
Specialties: Hand forged blades, Scagel patterns and other styles. **Patterns:** Camp, hunting, bird, trout, folders, axes, miniatures. **Technical:** 5160, 52100, 1084. **Prices:** Start at $250. **Remarks:** Part-time maker, sole author of knife and sheath. First knife made 1970s. ABS member who believes in the beauty of simplicity. **Mark:** J.S. stamp.

VAN ELDIK, FRANS,
Ho Flaan 3, 3632BT Loenen, NETHERLANDS, Phone: 0031 294 233 095, Fax: 0031 294 233 095
Specialties: Fancy collector-grade straight knives and folders of his design. **Patterns:** Hunters, fighters, boots and folders. **Technical:** Forges and grinds D2, 154CM, ATS-34 and stainless Damascus. **Prices:** Start at $450. **Remarks:** Spare-time maker; first knife sold in 1979. Knifemaker 30 years, 25 year member of Knifemakers Guild. **Mark:** Lion with name and Amsterdam.

VAN HEERDEN, ANDRE,
P.O. Box 905-417, Garsfontein, Pretoria, SOUTH AFRICA 0042, Phone: 27 82 566 6030, andrevh@iafrica.com; Web: www.andrevanheerden.com
Specialties: Fancy and working folders of his design to customer specs. **Technical:** Grinds RWL34, 19C27, D2, carbon and stainless Damascus. **Prices:** Starting at $350. **Remarks:** Part-time maker, first knife sold in 2003. **Mark:** Initials and name in a double circle.

VAN REENEN, IAN,
6003 Harvard St, Amarillo, TX 79109, Phone: 806-236-8333, ianvanreenen@suddenlink.net Web:www.ianvanreenenknives.com
Specialties: Safari pocketknife sold over 700 in Amarillo alone. **Patterns:** Folders and fixed blades. **Technical:** ATS-34 and 440C blade steels, or the maker forges 5160 and 1084 carbon steel. **Prices:** $330 for fixed blades to $600 for folders. **Remarks:** First knife sold in 1998. **Mark:** "IVR" with "Texas" underneath. Forged blades and slip joints marked with last name Van Reenen only.

VAN RIJSWIJK, AAD,
AVR KNIVES, Arij Koplaan 16B, 3132 AA Vlaardingen, NETHERLANDS, Phone: +31 10 2343227, Fax: +31 10 2343648, info@avrknives.com; Web: www.avrknives.com
Specialties: High-art interframe folders of his design and in shaving sets. **Patterns:** Hunters and locking folders. **Technical:** Uses semi-precious stones, mammoth, ivory, walrus ivory, iron wood. **Prices:** $550 to $3800. **Remarks:** Full-time maker; first knife sold in 1993. **Mark:** NA.

VAN RIPER, JAMES N,
PO Box 7045, Citrus Heights, CA 95621-7045, Phone: 916-721-0892

VANDERFORD, CARL G,
2290 Knob Creek Rd, Columbia, TN 38401, Phone: 931-381-1488
Specialties: Traditional working straight knives and folders of his design. **Patterns:** Hunters, Bowies and locking folders. **Technical:** Forges and grinds 440C, O1 and wire Damascus. **Prices:** $60 to $125. **Remarks:** Part-time maker; first knife sold in 1987. **Mark:** Last name.

VANDERKOLFF, STEPHEN,
5 Jonathan Crescent, Mildmay Ontario, CANADA N0g 2JO, Phone: 519-367-3401, steve@vanderkolffknives.com; Web: www.vanderkolffknives.com
Specialties: Fixed blades from gent's pocketknives and drop hunters to full sized Bowies and art knives. **Technical:** Primary blade steel 440C, Damasteel or custom made Damascus. All heat treat done by maker and all blades hardness tested. Handle material: stag, stabilized woods or MOP. **Prices:** $150 to $1200. **Remarks:** Started making knives in 1998 and sold first knife in 2000. Winner of the best of show art knife 2005 Wolverine Knife Show.

VANDEVENTER, TERRY L,
3274 Davis Rd, Terry, MS 39170-8719, Phone: 601-371-7414, tvandeventer@comcast.net
Specialties: Bowies, hunters, camp knives, friction folders. **Technical:** 1084, 1095, 15N20 and L6 steels. Damascus and mokume. Natural handle materials. **Prices:** $350 to $2500. **Remarks:** Sole author; makes everything here. First ABS MS from the state of Mississippi. **Mark:** T.L. Vandeventer (silhouette of snake underneath). MS on ricasso.

VANHOY, ED AND TANYA,
24255 N Fork River Rd, Abingdon, VA 24210, Phone: 276-944-4885, vanhoyknives@hughes.net
Specialties: Traditional and working/using straight knives of his design, make folders. **Patterns:** Fighters, straight knives, folders, hunters and art knives. **Technical:** Grinds ATS-34 and 440V; forges D2. Offers filework, engraves, acid etching, mosaic pins, decorative bolsters and custom fitted English bridle leather sheaths. **Prices:** $250 to $3000. **Remarks:** Full-time maker; first knife sold in 1977. Wife also engraves. Doing business as Van Hoy Custom Knives. **Mark:** Acid etched last name.

VARDAMAN, ROBERT,
2406 Mimosa Lane, Hattiesburg, MS 39402, Phone: 601-268-3889, rv7x@comcast.net
Specialties: Working straight knives of his design or to customer specs. **Patterns:** Bowies, hunters, skinners, utility and camp knives. **Technical:** Forges 52100, 5160, 1084 and 1095. Filework. **Prices:** $100 to $500. **Remarks:** Part-time maker. First knife sold in 2004. **Mark:** Last name, last name with Mississippi state logo.

VASQUEZ, JOHNNY DAVID,
1552 7th St, Wyandotte, MI 48192, Phone: 734-281-2455

VAUGHAN, IAN,
351 Doe Run Rd, Manheim, PA 17545-9368, Phone: 717-665-6949

VECERA, J R,
213 Douglas, Thrall, TX 76578, Phone: 512-365-8627
Specialties: Own and customers designs. Fighters, folders, exotic skinners. **Technical:** Flat, hollow and convex grinds. As of now some forging with more in the future. O1, D2, 440C, ATS-34 steels. **Prices:** $125 to $1400. **Remarks:** Love to do unique & one-of-a-kind designs. **Mark:** Native TX Vecera in oval or Vecera

VEIT, MICHAEL,
3289 E Fifth Rd, LaSalle, IL 61301, Phone: 815-223-3538, whitebear@starband.net
Specialties: Damascus folders. **Technical:** Engraver, sole author. **Prices:** $2500 to $6500. **Remarks:** Part-time maker; first knife sold in 1985. **Mark:** Name in script.

VELARDE, RICARDO,
7240 N Greenfield Dr, Park City, UT 84098, Phone: 435-901-1773, velardeknives.com
Specialties: Investment grade integrals and interframs. **Patterns:** Boots, fighters and hunters; hollow grind. **Technical:** BG on Integrals. **Prices:** $950 to $4800. **Remarks:** First knife sold in 1992. **Mark:** First initial, last name on blade; city, state, U.S.A. at bottom of tang.

VELICK, SAMMY,
3457 Maplewood Ave, Los Angeles, CA 90066, Phone: 310-663-6170, metaltamer@gmail.com
Specialties: Working knives and art pieces. **Patterns:** Hunter, utility and fantasy. **Technical:** Stock removal and forges. **Prices:** $100 and up. **Mark:** Last name.

VENSILD, HENRIK,
GI Estrup, Randersvei 4, DK-8963 Auning, DENMARK, Phone: +45 86 48 44 48
Specialties: Classic and traditional working and using knives of his design; Scandinavian influence. **Patterns:** Hunters and using knives. **Technical:** Forges Damascus. Hand makes handles, sheaths and blades. **Prices:** $350 to $1000. **Remarks:** Part-time maker; first knife sold in 1967. **Mark:** Initials.

VESTAL, CHARLES,
26662 Shortsville Rd., Abingdon, VA 24210, Phone: 276-492-3262, charles@vestalknives.com; Web: www.vestalknives.com
Specialties: Hunters and double ground fighters in traditional designs and own designs. **Technical:** Grinds CPM-154, ATS-134, 154-CM and other steels. **Prices:** $300 to $1000, some higher. **Remarks:** First knife sold in 1995.

VIALLON, HENRI,
Les Belins, 63300 Thiers, FRANCE, Phone: 04-73- 80-24-03, Fax: 04 73-51-02-02
Specialties: Folders and complex Damascus **Patterns:** His draws. **Technical:** Forge. **Prices:** $1000 to $5000. **Mark:** H. Viallon.

VIELE, H J,
88 Lexington Ave, Westwood, NJ 07675, Phone: 201-666- 2906, h.viele@verizon.net
Specialties: Folding knives of distinctive shapes. **Patterns:** High-tech folders and one-of-a-kind. **Technical:** Grinds ATS-34 and S30V. **Prices:** Start at $575. **Remarks:** Full-time maker; first knife sold in 1973. **Mark:** Japanese design for the god of war.

VIKING KNIVES (SEE JAMES THORLIEF ERIKSEN),

VILAR, RICARDO AUGUSTO FERREIRA,
Rua Alemada Dos Jasmins NO 243, Parque Petropolis, Mairipora Sao Paulo, BRAZIL 07600-000, Phone: 011-55-11-44-85-43-46, ricardovilar@ig.com.br.
Specialties: Traditional Brazilian-style working knives of the Sao Paulo state. **Patterns:** Fighters, hunters, utility, and camp knives, welcome customer design. Specialize in the "true" Brazilian camp knife "Soracabana". **Technical:** Forges only with sledge hammer to 100 percent shape in 5160 and 52100 and his own Damascus steels. Makes own sheaths in the "true" traditional "Paulista"-style of the state of Sao Paulo. **Remark:** Full-time maker. **Prices:** $250 to $600. Uses only natural handle materials. **Mark:** Special designed signature styled name R. Vilar.

VILLA, LUIZ,
R. Com. Miguel Calfat, 398 Itaim Bibi, Sao Paulo, SP- 04537-081, BRAZIL, Phone: 011-8290649
Specialties: One-of-a-kind straight knives and jewel knives of all designs. **Patterns:** Bowies, hunters, utility/camp knives and jewel knives. **Technical:** Grinds D6, Damascus and 440C; forges 5160. Prefers natural handle material. **Prices:** $70 to $200. **Remarks:** Part-time maker; first knife sold in 1990. **Mark:** Last name and serial number.

VILLAR, RICARDO,
Al. dos Jasmins 243 Mairipora, S.P. 07600-000, BRAZIL, Phone: 011-4851649
Specialties: Straight working knives to customer specs. **Patterns:** Bowies, fighters and utility/camp knives. **Technical:** Grinds D6, ATS-34 and 440C stainless. **Prices:** $80 to $200. **Remarks:** Part-time maker; first knife sold in 1993. **Mark:** Percor over sword and circle.

VINING, BILL,
9 Penny Lane, Methuen, MA 01844, Phone: 978-688- 4729, billv@medawebs.com; Web: www.medawebs.com/knives
Specialties Liner locking folders. Slip joints & lockbacks. **Patterns:** Likes to make patterns of his own design. **Technical:** S30V, 440C, ATS-34. Damascus from various makers. **Prices:** $450 and up. **Remarks:** Part- time maker. **Mark:** VINING or B. Vining.

VISTE, JAMES,
EDGE WISE FORGE, 13401 Mt Elliot, Detroit, MI 48212, Phone: 313-664-7455, grumblejunky@hotmail.com
Mark: EWF touch mark.

VISTNES, TOR,
N-6930 Svelgen, NORWAY, Phone: 047-57795572
Specialties: Traditional and working knives of his design. **Patterns:** Hunters and utility knives. **Technical:** Grinds Uddeholm Elmax. Handles made of rear burls of different Nordic stabilized woods. **Prices:** $300 to $1100. **Remarks:** Part-time maker; first knife sold in 1988. **Mark:** Etched name and deer head.

VITALE, MACE,
925 Rt 80, Guilford, CT 06437, Phone: 203-457-5591, Web: www.laurelrockforge.com
Specialties: Hand forged blades. **Patterns:** Hunters, utility, chef, Bowies and fighters. **Technical:** W2, 1095, 1084, L6. Hand forged and finished. **Prices:** $100 to $1000. **Remarks:** American Bladesmith Society, Journeyman Smith. Full-time maker; first knife sold 2001. **Mark:** MACE.

VOGT, DONALD J,
9007 Hogans Bend, Tampa, FL 33647, Phone: 813 973-3245, vogtknives@verizon.net
Specialties: Art knives, folders, automatics. **Technical:** Uses Damascus steels for blade and bolsters, filework, hand carving on blade bolsters and handles. Other materials used: jewels, gold, stainless steel. Prefers to use natural handle materials. **Prices:** $400 to $10,000. **Remarks:** Part- time maker; first knife sold in 1997. **Mark:** Last name.

VOGT, PATRIK,
Kungsvagen 83, S-30270 Halmstad, SWEDEN, Phone: 46-35-30977
Specialties: Working straight knives. **Patterns:** Bowies, hunters and fighters. **Technical:** Forges carbon steel and own Damascus. **Prices:** From $100. **Remarks:** Not currently making knives. **Mark:** Initials or last name.

VOORHIES, LES,
14511 Lk Mazaska Tr, Faribault, MN 55021, Phone: 507-332-0736, lesvor@msn.com; Web: www.lesvoorhiesknives.com
Specialties: Steels. **Patterns:** Liner locks & autos. **Technical:** ATS-34 Damascus. **Prices:** $250 to $1200. **Mark:** L. Voorhies.

VOSS, BEN,
362 Clark St, Galesburg, IL 61401, Phone: 309-342-6994
Specialties: Fancy working knives of his design. **Patterns:** Bowies, fighters, hunters, boots and folders. **Technical:** Grinds 440C, ATS-34 and D2. **Prices:** $35 to $1200. **Remarks:** Part-time maker; first knife sold in 1986. **Mark:** Name, city and state.

VOTAW, DAVID P,
305 S State St, Pioneer, OH 43554, Phone: 419-737- 2774
Specialties: Working knives; period pieces. **Patterns:** Hunters, Bowies, camp knives, buckskinners and tomahawks. **Technical:** Grinds O1 and D2. **Prices:** $100 to $200; some to $500. **Remarks:** Part-time maker; took over for the late W.K. Kneubuhler. Doing business as W-K Knives. **Mark:** WK with V inside anvil.

W

WADA, YASUTAKA,
2-6-22 Fujinokidai, Nara City, Nara prefect 631- 0044, JAPAN, Phone: 0742 46-0689
Specialties: Fancy and embellished one-of-a-kind straight knives of his design. **Patterns:** Bowies, daggers and hunters. **Technical:** Grinds ATS-34. **Prices:** $400 to $2500; some higher. **Remarks:** Part-time maker; first knife sold in 1990. **Mark:** Owl eyes with initial and last name underneath or last name.

WAGAMAN, JOHN K,
107 E Railroad St, Selma, NC 27576, Phone: 919-965-9659, Fax: 919-965-9901
Specialties: Fancy working knives. **Patterns:** Bowies, miniatures, hunters, fighters and boots. **Technical:** Grinds D2, 440C, 154CM and commercial Damascus; inlays mother-of-pearl. **Prices:** $110 to $2000. **Remarks:** Part-time maker; first knife sold in 1975. **Mark:** Last name.

WAITES, RICHARD L,
PO Box 188, Broomfield, CO 80038, Phone: 303- 465-9970, Fax: 303-465-9971, dickknives@aol.com
Specialties: Working fixed blade knives of all kinds including "paddle blade" skinners. Hand crafted sheaths, some upscale and unusual. **Technical:** Grinds 440C, ATS 34, D2. **Prices:** $100 to $500. **Remarks:** Part-time maker. First knife sold in 1998. Doing business as R.L. Waites Knives. **Mark:** Oval etch with first and middle initial and last name on top and city and state on bottom. Memberships; Professional Knifemakers Association and Rocky Mountain Blade Collectors Club.

WALKER—WATERS

WALKER, DON,
2850 Halls Chapel Rd, Burnsville, NC 28714, Phone: 828-675-9716, dlwalkernc@aol.com

WALKER, JIM,
22 Walker Ln, Morrilton, AR 72110, Phone: 501-354- 3175, jwalker46@att.net **Specialties:** Period pieces and working/using knives of his design and to customer specs. **Patterns:** Bowies, fighters, hunters, camp knives. **Technical:** Forges 5160, O1, L6, 52100, 1084, 1095. **Prices:** Start at $450. **Remarks:** Full-time maker; first knife sold in 1993. **Mark:** Three arrows with last name/MS.

WALKER, JOHN W,
10620 Moss Branch Rd, Bon Aqua, TN 37025, Phone: 931-670-4754 **Specialties:** Straight knives, daggers and folders; sterling rings, 14K gold wire wrap; some stone setting. **Patterns:** Hunters, boot knives, others. **Technical:** Grinds 440C, ATS-34, L6, etc. Buys Damascus. **Prices:** $150 to $500 some to $1500. **Remarks:** Knifemakers Guild member, part-time maker; first knife sold in 1982. **Mark:** Hohenzollern Eagle with name, or last name.

WALKER, MICHAEL L,
925-A Paseo del, Pueblo Sur Taos, NM 87571, Phone: 505-751-3409, Fax: 505-751-3417, metalwerkr@msn.com **Specialties:** Innovative knife designs and locking systems; titanium and SS furniture and art. **Patterns:** Folders from utility grade to museum quality art; others upon request. **Technical:** State-of-the-art materials: titanium, stainless Damascus, gold, etc. **Prices:** $3500 and above. **Remarks:** Designer/MetalCrafts; full-time professional knifemaker since 1980; four U.S. patents; invented LinerLock® and was awarded registered U.S. trademark no. 1,585,333. **Mark:** Early mark MW, Walker's Lockers by M.L. Walker; current M.L. Walker or Michael Walker.

WALLINGFORD JR., CHARLES W,
9024 Old Union Rd, Union, KY 41091, Phone: 859-384-4141, Web: www.cwknives.com **Specialties:** 18th and 19th century styles, patch knives, rifleman knives. **Technical:** 1084 and 5160 forged blades. **Prices:** $125 to $300. **Mark:** CW.

WALTERS, A F,
PO Box 523, 275 Crawley Rd., TyTy, GA 31795, Phone: 229-528-6207 **Specialties:** Working knives, some to customer specs. **Patterns:** Locking folders, straight hunters, fishing and survival knives. **Technical:** Grinds D2, 154CM and 13C26. **Prices:** Start at $200. **Remarks:** Part- time maker. Label: "The jewel knife." **Mark:** "J" in diamond and knife logo.

WARD, CHUCK,
PO Box 2272, 1010 E North St, Benton, AR 72018- 2272, Phone: 501-778-4329, chuckbop@aol.com **Specialties:** Traditional working and using straight knives and folders of his design. **Technical:** Grinds 440C, D2, A2, ATS-34 and O1; uses natural and composite handle materials. **Prices:** $90 to $400, some higher. **Remarks:** Part-time maker; first knife sold in 1990. **Mark:** First initial, last name.

WARD, J J,
7501 S R 220, Waverly, OH 45690, Phone: 614-947-5328 **Specialties:** Traditional and working/using straight knives and folders of his design. **Patterns:** Hunters and locking folders. **Technical:** Grinds ATS-34, 440C and Damascus. Offers handmade sheaths. **Prices:** $125 to $250; some to $500. **Remarks:** Spare-time maker; first knife sold in 1980. **Mark:** Etched name.

WARD, KEN,
1125 Lee Roze Ln, Grants Pass, OR 97527, Phone: 541- 956-8864 **Specialties:** Working knives, some to customer specs. **Patterns:** Straight, axes, Bowies, buckskinners and miniatures. **Technical:** Grinds ATS-34, Damascus. **Prices:** $100 to $700. **Remarks:** Part-time maker; first knife sold in 1977. **Mark:** Name.

WARD, RON,
1363 Nicholas Dr, Loveland, OH 45140, Phone: 513-722- 0602 **Specialties:** Classic working and using straight knives, fantasy knives. **Patterns:** Bowies, hunter, fighters, and utility/camp knives. **Technical:** Grinds 440C, 154CM, ATS-34, uses composite and natural handle materials. **Prices:** $50 to $750. **Remarks:** Part-time maker, first knife sold in 1992. Doing business as Ron Ward Blades. **Mark:** Ron Ward Blades, Loveland OH.

WARD, W C,
817 Glenn St, Clinton, TN 37716, Phone: 615-457-3568 **Specialties:** Working straight knives; period pieces. **Patterns:** Hunters, Bowies, swords and kitchen cutlery. **Technical:** Grinds O1. **Prices:** $85 to $150; some to $500. **Remarks:** Part-time maker; first knife sold in 1969. He styled the Tennessee Knife Maker. **Mark:** TKM.

WARDELL, MICK,
20 Clovelly Rd, Bideford, N Devon EX39 3BU, ENGLAND, Phone: 01237 475312, wardellknives@hotmail.co.uk Web: www.wardellscustomknives.com **Specialties:** Folders of his design. **Patterns:** Locking and slip-joint folders, Bowies. **Technical:** Grinds stainless Damascus, S30V and RWL34. Heat-treats. **Prices:** $300 to $2500. **Remarks:** Full-time maker; first knife sold in 1986. **Mark:** M. Wardell - England.

WARDEN, ROY A,
275 Tanglewood Rd, Union, MO 63084, Phone: 314- 583-8813, rwarden@yhti.net **Specialties:** Complex mosaic designs of "EDM wired figures" and "stack up" patterns and "lazer cut" and "torch cut" and "sawed" patterns combined. **Patterns:** Mostly "all mosaic" folders, automatics, fixed blades. **Technical:** Mosaic Damascus with all tool steel edges. **Prices:** $500 to $2000 and up. **Remarks:** Part-time maker; first knife sold in 1987. **Mark:** WARDEN stamped or initials connected.

WARE, TOMMY,
158 Idlewilde, Onalaska, TX 77360, Phone: 936-646- 4649 **Specialties:** Traditional working and using straight knives, folders and automatics of his design and to customer specs. **Patterns:** Hunters, automatics and locking folders. **Technical:** Grinds ATS-34, 440C and D2. Offers engraving and scrimshaw. **Prices:** $425 to $650; some to $1500. **Remarks:** Full-time maker; first knife sold in 1990. Doing business as Wano Knives. **Mark:** Last name inside oval, business name above, city and state below, year on side.

WARREN, AL,
1423 Sante Fe Circle, Roseville, CA 95678, Phone: 916- 784-3217/Cell phone 916-257-5904, Fax: 215-318-2945, al@warrenknives.com; Web: www.warrenknives.com **Specialties:** Working straight knives and folders, some fancy. **Patterns:** Hunters, Bowies, fillets, lockback, folders & multi blade. **Technical:** Grinds ATS-34 and S30V.440V. **Prices:** $135 to $3200.**Remarks:** Part- time maker; first knife sold in 1978. **Mark:** First and middle initials, last name.

WARREN, DANIEL,
571 Lovejoy Rd, Canton, NC 28716, Phone: 828- 648-7351 **Specialties:** Using knives. **Patterns:** Drop point hunters. **Prices:** $200 to $500. **Mark:** Warren-Bethel NC.

WARREN (SEE DELLANA), DELLANA,

WARTHER, DALE,
331 Karl Ave, Dover, OH 44622, Phone: 216-343- 7513, dalew@warthers.com **Specialties:** Working knives; period pieces. **Patterns:** Kitchen cutlery, daggers, hunters and some folders. **Technical:** Forges and grinds O1, D2 and 440C. **Prices:** $350 to $15,000. **Remarks:** Full-time maker; first knife sold in 1967. Takes orders only at shows or by personal interviews at his shop. **Mark:** Dale Warther.

WASHBURN, ARTHUR D,
ADW CUSTOM KNIVES, 10 Hinman St/POB 625, Pioche, NV 89043, Phone: 775-962-5463, awashburn@adwcustomknives.com; Web: www.adwcustomknives.com **Specialties:** Locking liner folders. **Patterns:** Slip joint folders (single and multiplied), lock-back folders, some fixed blades. Do own heat-treating; Rockwell test each blade. **Technical:** Carbon and stainless Damascus, some 1084, 1095, ATS-34, 154CM and S30V. Makes own two color Mokum. **Prices:** $200 to $1000 and up. **Remarks:** Sold first knife in 1997. Part-time maker. **Mark:** ADW enclosed in an oval or ADW.

WASHBURN JR., ROBERT LEE,
1162 West Diamond Valley Drive, St George, UT 847700, Phone: 435-619-4432, Fax: 435-574-8554, rlwashburn@excite.com; Web:www.washburnknives.com **Specialties:** Hand-forged period, Bowies, tactical, boot and hunters. **Patterns:** Bowies, tantos, loot hunters, tactical and folders. **Prices:** $100 to $2500. **Remarks:** All hand forged. 52100 being his favorite steel. **Mark:** Washburn Knives W.

WATANABE, WAYNE,
PO Box 3563, Montebello, CA 90640, wwknives@gmail.com; Web: www.geocities.com/ww-knives **Specialties:** Straight knives in Japanese-styles. One-of-a-kind designs; welcomes customer designs. **Patterns:** Tantos to katanas, Bowies. **Technical:** Flat grinds A2, O1 and ATS-34. Offers hand-rubbed finishes and wrapped handles. **Prices:** Start at $200. **Remarks:** Part-time maker. **Mark:** Name in characters with flower.

WATERS, BILL,
431 Walker Rd, Stevensville, MD 21666, Phone: 410- 643-5041

WATERS, GLENN,
11 Shinakawa Machi, Hirosaki City 036-8183, JAPAN, Phone: 172-33-8881, gwaters@luck.ocn.ne.jp; Web: www.glennwaters.com **Specialties:** One-of-a-kind collector-grade highly embellished art knives. Folders, fixed blades, and automatics. **Patterns:** Locking liner folders, automatics and fixed art knives. **Technical:** Grinds blades from Damasteel, and selected Damascus makers, mostly stainless. Does own engraving,

gold inlaying and stone setting, filework, and carving. Gold and Japanese precious metal fabrication. Prefers exotic material, high karat gold, silver, Shyaku Dou, Shibu Ichi Gin, precious gemstones. **Prices:** Upscale. **Remarks:** Designs and makes some-of-a-kind highly embellished art knives often with fully engraved handles and blades. A jeweler by trade for 20 years before starting to make knives. Full-time since 1999, first knife sold in 1994. **Mark:** Glenn Waters maker Japan, G. Waters or Glen in Japanese writing.

WATERS, HERMAN HAROLD,
2516 Regency, Magnolia, AR 71753, Phone: 870-234-5409

WATERS, LU,
2516 Regency, Magnolia, AR 71753, Phone: 870-234- 5409

WATSON, BERT,
PO Box 26, Westminster, CO 80036-0026, Phone: 303-587-3064, watsonlock@aol.com
    Specialties: Working/using straight knives of his design and to customer specs. **Patterns:** Hunters, utility/camp knives. **Technical:** Grinds O1, ATS-34, 440C, D2, A2 and others. **Prices:** $150 to $800. **Remarks:** Part- time maker; first knife sold in 1974. Doing business as Game Trail Knives. **Mark:** GTK or Bert or Watson.

WATSON, BILLY,
440 Forge Rd, Deatsville, AL 36022, Phone: 334-365- 1482, billy@watsonknives.com; Web: www.watsonknives.com
    Specialties: Working and using straight knives and folders of his design; period pieces. **Patterns:** Hunters, Bowies and utility/camp knives. **Technical:** Forges and grinds his own Damascus, 1095, 5160 and 52100. **Prices:** $40 to $1500. **Remarks:** Full-time maker; first knife sold in 1970. Doing business as Billy's Blacksmith Shop. **Mark:** Last name.

WATSON, DANIEL,
350 Jennifer Ln, Driftwood, TX 78619, Phone: 512-847-9679, info@angelsword.com; Web: http://www.angelsword.com
    Specialties: One-of-a-kind knives and swords. **Patterns:** Hunters, daggers, swords. **Technical:** Hand-purify and carbonize his own high-carbon steel, pattern-welded Damascus, cable and carbon-induced crystalline Damascus. Teehno-Wootz™ Damascus steel, heat treats including cryogenic processing. European and Japanese tempering. **Prices:** $125 to $25,000. **Remarks:** Full-time maker; first knife sold in 1979. **Mark:** "Angel Sword" on forged pieces; "Bright Knight" for stock removal. Avatar on Techno-Wootz™ Damascus. Bumon on traditional Japanese blades.

WATSON, PETER,
66 Kielblock St, La Hoff 2570, SOUTH AFRICA, Phone: 018-84942
    Specialties: Traditional working and using straight knives and folders of his design. **Patterns:** Hunters, locking folders and utility/camp knives. **Technical:** Sandvik and 440C. **Prices:** $120 to $250; some to $1500. **Remarks:** Part-time maker; first knife sold in 1989. **Mark:** Buffalo head with name.

WATSON, TOM,
1103 Brenau Terrace, Panama City, FL 32405, Phone: 850-785-9209, tomwatsonknives@aol.com; Web: www.tomwatsonknives.com
    Specialties: Utility/tactical linerlocks. **Patterns:** Tactical, utility and art investment pieces. **Technical:** Flat grinds satin finished D2 and Damascus. **Prices:** Starting at $375. **Remarks:** Full time maker. In business since 1978. **Mark:** Name and city.

WATTELET, MICHAEL A,
PO Box 649, 125 Front, Minocqua, WI 54548, Phone: 715-356-3069, redtroll@verizon.net
    Specialties: Working and using straight knives of his design and to customer specs; fantasy knives. **Patterns:** Daggers, fighters and swords. **Technical:** Grinds 440C and L6; forges and grinds O1. Silversmith. **Prices:** $75 to $1000; some to $5000. **Remarks:** Full-time maker; first knife sold in 1966. Doing business as M and N Arts Ltd. **Mark:** First initial, last name.

WATTS, JOHNATHAN,
9560 S Hwy 36, Gatesville, TX 76528, Phone: 254-487-2866
    Specialties: Traditional folders. **Patterns:** One and two blade folders in various blade shapes. **Technical:** Grinds ATS-34 and Damascus on request. **Prices:** $120 to $400. **Remarks:** Part-time maker; first knife sold in 1997. **Mark:** J Watts.

WATTS, WALLY,
9560 S Hwy 36, Gatesville, TX 76528, Phone: 254- 487-2866
    Specialties: Unique traditional folders of his design. **Patterns:** One- to five-blade folders and single-blade gents in various blade shapes. **Technical:** Grinds ATS-34; Damascus on request. **Prices:** $165 to $500. **Remarks:** Full-time maker; first knife sold in 1986. **Mark:** Last name.

WEBSTER, BILL,
58144 West Clear Lake Rd, Three Rivers, MI 49093, Phone: 269-244-2873, Web: www.websterknifeworks.com
    Specialties: Working and using straight knives, especially for hunters. His patterns are custom designed. **Patterns:** Hunters, skinners, camp knives, Bowies and daggers. **Technical:** Hand-filed blades made of D2 steel only, unless other steel is requested. Preferred handle material is stabilized and exotic wood and stag. Sheaths are made by Green River Leather in Kentucky. Hand-sewn sheaths by Bill Dehn in Three Rivers, MI. **Prices:** $75 to $500. **Remarks:** Part-time maker, first knife sold in 1978. **Mark:** Originally WEB stamped on blade, at present, Webster Knifeworks Three Rivers, MI laser etched on blade.

WEHNER, RUDY,
297 William Warren Rd, Collins, MS 39428, Phone: 601-765-4997
    Specialties: Reproduction antique Bowies and contemporary Bowies in full and miniature. **Patterns:** Skinners, camp knives, fighters, axes and Bowies. **Technical:** Grinds 440C, ATS-34, 154CM and Damascus. **Prices:** $100 to $500; some to $850. **Remarks:** Full-time maker; first knife sold in 1975. **Mark:** Last name on Bowies and antiques; full name, city and state on skinners.

WEILAND JR., J REESE,
PO Box 2337, Riverview, FL 33568, Phone: 813-671-0661, RWPHIL413@earthlink.net; Web: www.rwcustomknive.som
    Specialties: Hawk bills; tactical to fancy folders. **Patterns:** Hunters, tantos, Bowies, fantasy knives, spears and some swords. **Technical:** Grinds ATS-34, 154CM, 440C, D2, O1, A2, Damascus. Titanium hardware on locking liners and button locks. **Prices:** $150 to $4000. **Remarks:** Full- time maker, first knife sold in 1978. Knifemakers Guild member since 1988.

WEINAND, GEROME M,
14440 Harpers Bridge Rd, Missoula, MT 59808, Phone: 406-543-0845
    Specialties: Working straight knives. **Patterns:** Bowies, fishing and camp knives, large special hunters. **Technical:** Grinds O1, 440C, ATS- 34, 1084, L6, also stainless Damascus, Aebl and 304; makes all-tool steel Damascus; Dendritic D2 from powdered steel. Heat-treats. **Prices:** $30 to $100; some to $500. **Remarks:** Full-time maker; first knife sold in 1982. **Mark:** Last name.

WEINSTOCK, ROBERT,
PO Box 170028, San Francisco, CA 94117- 0028, Phone: 415-731-5968, robertweinstock@att.net
    Specialties: Folders, slip joins, lockbacks, autos. **Patterns:** Daggers, folders. **Technical:** Grinds A2, O1 and 440C. Chased and hand-carved blades and handles. Also using various Damascus steels from other makers. **Prices:** $3000 to 7000. **Remarks:** Full-time maker; first knife sold in 1994. **Mark:** Last name carved in steel.

WEISS, CHARLES L,
18847 N 13th Ave, Phoenix, AZ 85027, Phone: 623-582-6147, weissknife@juno.com; Web: www.weissknives.com
    Specialties: High-art straight knives and folders; deluxe period pieces. **Patterns:** Daggers, fighters, boots, push knives and miniatures. **Technical:** Grinds 440C, 154CM and ATS-34. **Prices:** $300 to $1200; some to $2000. **Remarks:** Full-time maker; first knife sold in 1975. **Mark:** Name and city.

WELLING, RONALD L,
15446 Lake Ave, Grand Haven, MI 49417, Phone: 616-846-2274
    Specialties: Scagel knives of his design or to customer specs. **Patterns:** Hunters, camp knives, miniatures, bird, trout, folders, double edged, hatchets, skinners and some art pieces. **Technical:** Forges Damascus 1084 and 1095. Antler, ivory and horn. **Prices:** $250 to $3000. **Remarks:** Full-time maker. ABS Journeyman maker. **Mark:** First initials and or name and last name. City and state. Various scagel kris (1 or 2).

WERTH, GEORGE W,
5223 Woodstock Rd, Poplar Grove, IL 61065, Phone: 815-544-4408
    Specialties: Period pieces, some fancy. **Patterns:** Straight fighters, daggers and Bowies. **Technical:** Forges and grinds O1, 1095 and his Damascus, including mosaic patterns. **Prices:** $200 to $650; some higher. **Remarks:** Full-time maker. Doing business as Fox Valley Forge. **Mark:** Name in logo or initials connected.

WESCOTT, CODY,
5330 White Wing Rd, Las Cruces, NM 88012, Phone: 505-382-5008
    Specialties: Fancy and presentation grade working knives. **Patterns:** Hunters, locking folders and Bowies. **Technical:** Hollow-grinds D2 and ATS-34; all knives file worked. Offers some engraving. Makes sheaths. **Prices:** $80 to $300; some to $950. **Remarks:** Full-time maker; first knife sold in 1982. **Mark:** First initial, last name.

WEST, CHARLES A,
1315 S Pine St, Centralia, IL 62801, Phone: 618- 532-2777
    Specialties: Classic, fancy, high tech, period pieces, traditional and working/using straight knives and folders. **Patterns:** Bowies, fighters and locking folders. **Technical:** Grinds ATS-34, O1 and Damascus. Prefers hot blued finishes. **Prices:** $100 to $1000; some to $2000. **Remarks:** Full-time maker; first knife sold in 1963. Doing business as West Custom Knives. **Mark:** Name or name, city and state.

WEST, PAT,
PO Box 9, Charlotte, TX 78011, Phone: 830-277-1290
    Specialties: Classic working and using straight knives and folders. **Patterns:** Hunters, slip-joint folders. **Technical:** Grinds ATS-34, D2. Offers filework and decorates liners on folders. **Prices:** $400 to $700. **Remarks:** Spare-time maker; first knife sold in 1984. **Mark:** Name.

WESTBERG, LARRY,
305 S Western Hills Dr, Algona, IA 50511, Phone: 515-295-9276
    Specialties: Traditional and working straight knives of his design and in standard patterns. **Patterns:** Bowies, hunters, fillets and folders. **Technical:** Grinds 440C, D2 and 1095. Heat-treats. Uses natural handle materials. **Prices:** $85 to $600; some to $1000. **Remarks:** Part-time maker; first knife sold in 1987. **Mark:** Last name-town and state.

WHEELER, GARY,
351 Old Hwy 48, Clarksville, TN 37040, Phone: 931- 552-3092, ir22shtr@charter.net
Specialties: Working to high end fixed blades. **Patterns:** Bowies, Hunters, combat knives, daggers and a few folders. **Technical:** Forges 5160, 1080, 52100 and his own Damascus, will use stainless steel on request. **Prices:** $125 to $2000. **Remarks:** Full-time maker since 2001, first knife sold in 1985 collaborates/works at B&W Blade Works. **Mark:** Stamped last name.

WHEELER, ROBERT,
289 S Jefferson, Bradley, IL 60915, Phone: 815- 932-5854, b2btaz@brmemc.net

WHETSELL, ALEX,
1600 Palmetto Tyrone Rd, Sharpsburg, GA 30277, Phone: 770-463-4881
Specialties: Knifekits.com, a source for fold locking liner type and straight knife kits. These kits are industry standard for folding knife kits. **Technical:** Many selections of colored G10 carbon fiber and wood handle material for kits, as well as bulk sizes for the custom knifemaker, heat treated folding knife pivots, screws, bushings, etc.

WHIPPLE, WESLEY A,
PO Box 3771, Kodiak, AK 99615, Phone: 907- 486-6737, wildernessknife@yahoo.com
Specialties: Working straight knives, some fancy. **Patterns:** Hunters, Bowies, camp knives, fighters. **Technical:** Forges high-carbon steels, Damascus, offers relief carving and silver wire inlay checkering. **Prices:** $300 to $1400; some higher. **Remarks:** Full-time maker; first knife sold in 1989. A.K.A. Wilderness Knife and Forge. **Mark:** Last name/JS.

WHITE, BRYCE,
1415 W Col Glenn Rd, Little Rock, AR 72210, Phone: 501-821-2956
Specialties: Hunters, fighters, makes Damascus, file work, handmade only. **Technical:** L6, 1075, 1095, O1 steels used most. **Patterns:** Will do any pattern or use his own. **Prices:** $200 to $300. Sold first knife in 1995. **Mark:** White.

WHITE, DALE,
525 CR 212, Sweetwater, TX 79556, Phone: 325-798- 4178, dalew@taylortel.net
Specialties: Working and using knives. **Patterns:** Hunters, skinners, utilities and Bowies. **Technical:** Grinds 440C, offers file work, fancy pins and scrimshaw by Sherry Sellers. **Prices:** From $45 to $300. **Remarks:** Sold first knife in 1975. **Mark:** Full name, city and state.

WHITE, GARRETT,
871 Sarijon Rd, Hartwell, GA 30643, Phone: 706- 376-5944
Specialties: Gentlemen folders, fancy straight knives. **Patterns:** Locking liners and hunting fixed blades. **Technical:** Grinds 440C, S30V, and stainless Damascus. **Prices:** $150 to $1000. **Remarks:** Part-time maker. **Mark:** Name.

WHITE, GENE E,
9005 Ewing Dr, Bethesda, MD 20817-3357, Phone: 301-564-3164
Specialties: Small utility/gents knives. **Patterns:** Eight standard hunters; most other patterns on commission basis. Currently no swords, axes and fantasy knives. **Technical:** Stock removal 440C and D2; others on request. Mostly hollow grinds; some flat grinds. Prefers natural handle materials. Makes own sheaths. **Prices:** Start at $85. **Remarks:** Part-time maker; first knife sold in 1971. **Mark:** First and middle initials, last name.

WHITE, JOHN PAUL,
231 S Bayshore, Valparaiso, FL 32580, Phone: 850-729-9174, johnwhiteknives@gmail.com
Specialties: Forged hunters, fighters, traditional Bowies and personal carry knives with handles of natural materials and fittings with detailed file work. **Technical:** Forges carbon steel and own Damascus. **Prices:** $400 to $2000. **Remarks:** Master Smith, American Bladesmith Society. **Mark:** First initial, last name.

WHITE, LOU,
7385 Red Bud Rd NE, Ranger, GA 30734, Phone: 706- 334-2273

WHITE, RICHARD T,
359 Carver St, Grosse Pointe Farms, MI 48236, Phone: 313-881-4690

WHITE, ROBERT J,
RR 1 641 Knox Rd 900 N, Gilson, IL 61436, Phone: 309-289-4487
Specialties: Working knives, some deluxe. **Patterns:** Bird and trout knives, hunters, survival knives and locking folders. **Technical:** Grinds A2, D2 and 440C; commercial Damascus. Heat-treats. **Prices:** $125 to $250; some to $600. **Remarks:** Full-time maker; first knife sold in 1976. **Mark:** Last name in script.

WHITE JR., ROBERT J BUTCH,
RR 1, Gilson, IL 61436, Phone: 309- 289-4487
Specialties: Folders of all sizes. **Patterns:** Hunters, fighters, boots and folders. **Technical:** Forges Damascus; grinds tool and stainless steel. **Prices:** $500 to $1800. **Remarks:** Spare-time maker; first knife sold in 1980. **Mark:** Last name in block letters.

WHITENECT, JODY,
Elderbank, Halifax County, Nova Scotia, CANADA B0N 1K0, Phone: 902-384-2511
Specialties: Fancy and embellished working/using straight knives of his design and to customer specs. **Patterns:** Bowies, fighters and hunters. **Technical:** Forges 1095 and O1; forges and grinds ATS-34. Various filework on blades and bolsters. **Prices:** $200 to $400; some to $800. **Remarks:** Part-time maker; first knife sold in 1996. **Mark:** Longhorn stamp or engraved.

WHITESELL, J. DALE,
P.O. Box 455, Stover, MO 65078, Phone: 573- 372-5182, dwknives@heroesonline.us
Specialties: Fixed blade working knives, a nd some collector pieces. **Patterns:** Hunting and skinner knives and camp knives. **Technical:** Blades ground from O1, 1095, and 440C in hollow, flat and saber grinds. Wood, bone, deer antler, and G10 are basic handle materials. **Prices:** $100 to $250. **Remarks:** Part-time maker, first knife sold in 2003. Doing business as Dale's Knives. **Mark:** Whitesell on the left side of the blade.

WHITLEY, L WAYNE,
1675 Carrow Rd, Chocowinity, NC 27817-9495, Phone: 252-946-5648

WHITLEY, WELDON G,
4308 N Robin Ave, Odessa, TX 79764, Phone: 432-530-0448, Fax: 432-530-0048, wgwhitley@juno.com
Specialties: Working knives of his design or to customer specs. **Patterns:** Hunters, folders and various double-edged knives. **Technical:** Grinds 440C, 154CM and ATS-34. **Prices:** $150 to $1250. **Mark:** Name, address, road-runner logo.

WHITMAN, JIM,
21044 Salem St, Chugiak, AK 99567, Phone: 907-688- 4575, Fax: 907-688-4278, Web: www.whitmanknives.com
Specialties: Working straight knives and folders; some art pieces. **Patterns:** Hunters, skinners, Bowies, camp knives, working fighters, swords and hatchets. **Technical:** Grinds AEB-L Swedish, 440C, 154CM, ATS- 34, and Damascus in full convex. Prefers exotic hardwoods, natural and native handle materials: whale bone, antler, ivory and horn. **Prices:** Start at $150. **Remarks:** Full-time maker; first knife sold in 1983. **Mark:** Name, city, state.

WHITTAKER, ROBERT E,
PO Box 204, Mill Creek, PA 17060
Specialties: Using straight knives. Has a line of knives for buckskinners. **Patterns:** Hunters, skinners and Bowies. **Technical:** Grinds O1, A2 and D2. Offers filework. **Prices:** $35 to $100. **Remarks:** Part-time maker; first knife sold in 1980. **Mark:** Last initial or full initials.

WHITTAKER, WAYNE,
2900 Woodland Ct, Metamore, MI 48455, Phone: 810-797-5315, lindorwayne@yahoo.com
Specialties: Liner lock folders-lock backs-autos. **Patterns:** Bowies, daggers and hunters. **Technical:** Damascus **Prices:** $300 to $500; some to $2000. **Remarks:** Full-time maker; first knife sold in 1985. **Mark:** Initials on inside of backbar.

WHITTEMORE, RYAN A,
725 Alder St, Montomery, AL 36113-6123, ryan.whittemore@us.army.mil
Specialties: Working using straight knives of his design or to customer specs. **Patterns:** Hunters, fighters, and Bowies. **Technical:** Forges 5160, 1084, 52100, O1. Flat grinds D2, A2, 440C. **Prices:** $100 to $200. **Remarks:** Part-time maker, first knife sold in 1994. Active duty military, frequent moves and/or deployments may affect deliver times. Due to frequent moves, email is the best contact method. **Mark:** Last name.

WHITWORTH, KEN J,
41667 Tetley Ave, Sterling Heights, MI 48078, Phone: 313-739-5720
Specialties: Working straight knives and folders. **Patterns:** Locking folders, slip joints and boot knives. **Technical:** Grinds 440C, 154CM and D2. **Prices:** $100 to $225; some to $450. **Remarks:** Part-time maker; first knife sold in 1976. **Mark:** Last name.

WICKER, DONNIE R,
2544 E 40th Ct, Panama City, FL 32405, Phone: 904-785-9158
Specialties: Traditional working and using straight knives of his design or to customer specs. **Patterns:** Hunters, fighters and slip-joint folders. **Technical:** Grinds 440C, ATS-34, D2 and 154CM. Heat-treats and does hardness testing. **Prices:** $90 to $200; some to $400. **Remarks:** Part- time maker; first knife sold in 1975. **Mark:** First and middle initials, last name.

WIGGINS, HORACE,
203 Herndon Box 152, Mansfield, LA 71502, Phone: 318-872-4471
Specialties: Fancy working knives. **Patterns:** Straight and folding hunters. **Technical:** Grinds O1, D2 and 440C. **Prices:** $90 to $275. **Remarks:** Part-time maker; first knife sold in 1970. **Mark:** Name, city and state in diamond logo.

WILCHER, WENDELL L,
RR 6 Box 6573, Palestine, TX 75801, Phone: 903-549-2530
Specialties: Fantasy, miniatures and working/using straight knives and folders of his design and to customer specs. Patterns: Fighters, hunters, locking folders. Technical: Hand works (hand file and hand sand knives), not grind. Prices: $75 to $250; some to $600. Remarks: Part-time maker; first knife sold in 1987. Mark: Initials, year, serial number.

WILE, PETER,
RR 3, Bridgewater, Nova Scotia, CANADA B4V 2W2, Phone: 902-543-1373, peterwile@ns.sympatico.ca
Specialties: Collector-grade one-of-a-kind file-worked folders. Patterns: Folders or fixed blades of his design or to customers specs. Technical: Grinds ATS-34, carbon and stainless Damascus. Does intricate filework on blades, spines and liners. Carves. Prefers natural handle materials. Does own heat treating. Prices: $350 to $2000; some to $4000. Remarks: Part-time maker; sold first knife in 1985; doing business as Wile Knives. Mark: Wile.

WILKINS, MITCHELL,
15523 Rabon Chapel Rd, Montgomery, TX 77316, Phone: 936-588-2696, mwilkins@consolidated.net

WILLEY, WG,
14210 Sugar Hill Rd, Greenwood, DE 19950, Phone: 302-349-4070, Web: www.willeyknives.com
Specialties: Fancy working straight knives. Patterns: Small game knives, Bowies and throwing knives. Technical: Grinds 440C and 154CM. Prices: $350 to $600; some to $1500. Remarks: Part-time maker; first knife sold in 1975. Owns retail store. Mark: Last name inside map logo.

WILLIAMS, JASON L,
PO Box 67, Wyoming, RI 02898, Phone: 401-539-8353, Fax: 401-539-0252
Specialties: Fancy and high tech folders of his design, co-inventor of the Axis Lock. Patterns: Fighters, locking folders, automatics and fancy pocket knives. Technical: Forges Damascus and other steels by request. Uses exotic handle materials and precious metals. Offers inlaid spines and gemstone thumb knobs. Prices: $1000 and up. Remarks: Full-time maker; first knife sold in 1989. Mark: First and last initials on pivot.

WILLIAMS JR., RICHARD,
1440 Nancy Circle, Morristown, TN 37814, Phone: 615-581-0059
Specialties: Working and using straight knives of his design or to customer specs. Patterns: Hunters, dirks and utility/camp knives. Technical: Forges 5160 and uses file steel. Hand-finish is standard; offers filework. Prices: $80 to $180; some to $250. Remarks: Spare-time maker; first knife sold in 1985. Mark: Last initial or full initials.

WILLIAMSON, TONY,
Rt 3 Box 503, Siler City, NC 27344, Phone: 919-663-3551
Specialties: Flint knapping: knives made of obsidian flakes and flint with wood, antler or bone for handles. Patterns: Skinners, daggers and flake knives. Technical: Blades have width/thickness ratio of at least 4 to 1. Hafts with methods available to prehistoric man. Prices: $58 to $160. Remarks: Student of Errett Callahan. Mark: Initials and number code to identify year and number of knives made.

WILLIS, BILL,
RT 7 Box 7549, Ava, MO 65608, Phone: 417-683-4326
Specialties: Forged blades, Damascus and carbon steel. Patterns: Cable, random or ladder lamented. Technical: Professionally heat treated blades. Prices: $75 to $600. Remarks: Lifetime guarantee on all blades against breakage. All work done by maker; including leather work. Mark: WF.

WILSON, CURTIS M,
PO Box 383, Burleson, TX 76097, Phone: 817-295-3732, cwknifeman2026@att.net; Web: www.cwilsonknives.com
Specialties: Traditional working/using knives, fixed blade, folders, slip joint, LinerLock® and lock back knives. Art knives, presentation grade Bowies, folder repair, heat treating services. Sub-zero quench. Patterns: Hunters, camp knives, military combat, single and multi-blade folders. Dr's knives large or small or custom design knives. Technical: Grinds ATS-34, 440C 52100, D2, S30V, CPM 154, mokume gane, engraves, scrimshaw, sheaths leather of kykex heat treating and file work. Prices: $150-750. Remarks: Part-time maker since 1984. Sold first knife in 1993. Mark: Curtis Wilson in ribbon or Curtis Wilson with hand made in a half moon.

WILSON, JAMES G,
PO Box 4024, Estes Park, CO 80517, Phone: 303-586-3944
Specialties: Bronze Age knives; Medieval and Scottish-styles; tomahawks. Patterns: Bronze knives, daggers, swords, spears and battle axes; 12-inch steel Misericorde daggers, sgian dubhs, "his and her" skinners, bird and fish knives, capers, boots and daggers. Technical: Casts bronze; grinds D2, 440C and ATS-34. Prices: $49 to $400; some to $1300. Remarks: Part-time maker; first knife sold in 1975. Mark: WilsonHawk.

WILSON, JON J,
1826 Ruby St, Johnstown, PA 15902, Phone: 814-266-6410
Specialties: Miniatures and full size. Patterns: Bowies, daggers and hunters. Technical: Grinds Damascus, 440C and O1. Scrimshaws and carves. Prices: $75 to $500; some higher. Remarks: Full-time maker; first knife sold in 1988. Mark: First and middle initials, last name.

WILSON, MIKE,
1416 McDonald Rd, Hayesville, NC 28904, Phone: 828-389-8145
Specialties: Fancy working and using straight knives of his design or to customer specs, folders. Patterns: Hunters, Bowies, utility knives, gut hooks, skinners, fighters and miniatures. Technical: Hollow grinds 440C, L6, O1 and D2. Mirror finishes are standard. Offers filework. Prices: $50 to $600. Remarks: Full-time maker; first knife sold in 1985. Mark: Last name.

WILSON, PHILIP C,
SEAMOUNT KNIFEWORKS, PO Box 846, Mountain Ranch, CA 95246, Phone: 209-754-1990, seamount@bigplanet.com; Web: www.seamountknifeworks.com
Specialties: Working knives; emphasis on salt water fillet knives and utility hunters of his design. Patterns: Fishing knives, hunters, kitchen knives. Technical: Grinds CPM S-30V, CPM10V, S-90V and CPM154. Heat-treats and Rockwell tests all blades. Prices: Start at $320. Remarks: First knife sold in 1985. Doing business as Sea-Mount Knife Works. Mark: Signature.

WILSON, RON,
2639 Greenwood Ave, Morro Bay, CA 93442, Phone: 805-772-3381
Specialties: Classic and fantasy straight knives of his design. Patterns: Daggers, fighters, swords and axes, mostly all miniatures. Technical: Forges and grinds Damascus and various tool steels; grinds meteorite. Uses gold, precious stones and exotic wood. Prices: Vary. Remarks: Part-time maker; first knives sold in 1995. Mark: Stamped first and last initials.

WILSON, RW,
PO Box 2012, Weirton, WV 26062, Phone: 304-723-2771
Specialties: Working straight knives; period pieces. Patterns: Bowies, tomahawks and patch knives. Technical: Grinds 440C; scrimshaws. Prices: $85 to $175; some to $1000. Remarks: Part-time maker; first knife sold in 1966. Knifemaker supplier. Offers free knife-making lessons. Mark: Name in tomahawk.

WILSON, STAN,
8931 Pritcher Rd, Lithia, FL 33547, Phone: 727-461-1992, swilson@stanwilsonknives.com; Web: www.stanwilsonknives.com
Specialties: Fancy folders and automatics of his own design. Patterns: Locking liner folders, single and dual action autos, daggers. Technical: Stock removal, uses Damascus, stainless and high carbon steels, prefers ivory and pearl, Damascus with blued finishes and filework. Prices: $400 and up. Remarks: Member of Knifemakers Guild and Florida Knifemakers Association. Full-time maker will do custom orders. Mark: Name in script.

WILSON (SEE SIMONELLA, GIANLUIGI),

WINGO, GARY,
240 Ogeechee, Ramona, OK 74061, Phone: 918-536-1067, wingg_2000@yahoo.com; Web: www.geocities.com/wingg_2000/gary.html
Specialties: Folder specialist. Steel 44OC, D2, others on request. Handle bone-stag, others on request. Patterns: Trapper three-blade stockman, four-blade congress, single- and two-blade barlows. Prices: 150 to $400. Mark: First knife sold 1994. Steer head with Wingo Knives or Straight line Wingo Knives.

WINGO, PERRY,
22 55th St, Gulfport, MS 39507, Phone: 228-863-3193
Specialties: Traditional working straight knives. Patterns: Hunters, skinners, Bowies and fishing knives. Technical: Grinds 440C. Prices: $75 to $1000. Remarks: Full-time maker; first knife sold in 1988. Mark: Last name.

WINKLER, DANIEL,
PO Box 2166, Blowing Rock, NC 28605, Phone: 828-295-9156, danielwinkler@bellsouth.net; Web: www.winklerknives.com
Specialties: Forged cutlery styled in the tradition of an era past as well as producing a contemporary mid-tech line. Patterns: Fixed blades, friction folders, lock back folders, and axes/tomahawks. Technical: Forges, grinds, and heat treats carbon steels, specialty steels, and his own Damascus steel. Prices: $400 to $4000+. Remarks: Full-time maker since 1988. Exclusively offers leatherwork by Karen Shook. ABS Master Smith; Knifemakers Guild voting member. Mark: Before 2008: initials connected. 2008 and after: handmade marked Dwinkler; mid-tech marked WinklerKnives II

WINN, TRAVIS A.,
558 E 3065 S, Salt Lake City, UT 84106, Phone: 801- 467-5957
Specialties: Fancy working knives and knives to customer specs. **Patterns:** Hunters, fighters, boots, Bowies and fancy daggers, some miniatures, tantos and fantasy knives. **Technical:** Grinds D2 and 440C. Embellishes. **Prices:** $125 to $500; some higher. **Remarks:** Part-time maker; first knife sold in 1976. **Mark:** TRAV stylized.

WINSTON, DAVID,
1671 Red Holly St, Starkville, MS 39759, Phone: 601-323-1028
Specialties: Fancy and traditional knives of his design and to customer specs. **Patterns:** Bowies, daggers, hunters, boot knives and folders. **Technical:** Grinds 440C, ATS-34 and D2. Offers filework; heat-treats. **Prices:** $40 to $750; some higher. **Remarks:** Part-time maker; first knife sold in 1984. Offers lifetime sharpening for original owner. **Mark:** Last name.

WINTER, GEORGE,
5940 Martin Hwy, Union City, TN 38261

WIRTZ, ACHIM,
Mittelstrasse 58, Wuerselen, D-52146, GERMANY, Phone: 0049-2405-462-486, wootz@web.de; Web: www.7knifedwarfs.com
Specialties: Medieval, Scandinavian and Middle East-style knives. **Technical:** Forged blades only, Damascus steel, Woots, Mokume. **Prices:** Start at $200. **Remarks:** Part-time maker. First knife sold in 1997. **Mark:** Stylized initials.

WISE, DONALD,
304 Bexhill Rd, St Leonardo-On-Sea, East Sussex, TN3 8AL, ENGLAND
Specialties: Fancy and embellished working straight knives to customer specs. **Patterns:** Hunters, Bowies and daggers. **Technical:** Grinds Sandvik 12C27, D2 D3 and O1. Scrimshaws. **Prices:** $110 to $300; some to $500. **Remarks:** Full-time maker; first knife sold in 1983. **Mark:** KNIFECRAFT.

WITSAMAN, EARL,
3957 Redwing Circle, Stow, OH 44224, Phone: 330- 688-4208, eawits@aol.com; Web: http://hometown.aol.com//eawits/ index.html
Specialties: Straight and fantasy miniatures. **Patterns:** Wide variety—Randalls to D-guard Bowies. **Technical:** Grinds O1, 440C and 300 stainless; buys Damascus; highly detailed work. **Prices:** $85 to $300. **Remarks:** Part-time maker; first knife sold in 1974. **Mark:** Initials.

WOLF, BILL,
4618 N 79th Ave, Phoenix, AZ 85033, Phone: 623-846- 3585, Fax: 623-846-3585, wolfknives@yahoo.com
Specialties: Investor-grade folders and straight knives. **Patterns:** Lockback, slip joint and side lock interframes. **Technical:** Grinds ATS-34 and 440C. **Prices:** $400 to $10,000. **Remarks:** Full-time maker; first knife sold in 1989. **Mark:** Name.

WOLF JR., WILLIAM LYNN,
4006 Frank Rd, Lagrange, TX 78945, Phone: 409-247-4626

WOOD, ALAN,
Greenfield Villa, Greenhead, Brampton CA8 7HH, ENGLAND, a.wood@knivesfreeserve.co.uk; Web: www.alanwoodknives.co.uk
Specialties: High-tech working straight knives of his design. **Patterns:** Hunters, utility/camp and bushcraft knives. **Technical:** Grinds 12027, RWL-34, stainless Damascus and O1. Blades are cryogenic treated. **Prices:** $200 to $800; some to $750. **Remarks:** Full-time maker; first knife sold in 1979. Not currently taking orders. **Mark:** Full name with stag tree logo.

WOOD, LARRY B,
6945 Fishburg Rd, Huber Heights, OH 45424, Phone: 513-233-6751
Specialties: Fancy working knives of his design. **Patterns:** Hunters, buckskinners, Bowies, tomahawks, locking folders and Damascus miniatures. **Technical:** Forges 1095, file steel and his own Damascus. **Prices:** $125 to $500; some to $2000. **Remarks:** Full-time maker; first knife sold in 1974. Doing business as Wood's Metal Studios. **Mark:** Variations of last name, sometimes with blacksmith logo.

WOOD, OWEN DALE,
6492 Garrison St, Arvada, CO 80004-3157, Phone: 303-456-2748, wood.owen@gmail.com; Web: www.owenwoodcustomknives.com
Specialties: Folding knives and daggers. **Patterns:** Own Damascus, specialties in 456 composite blades. **Technical:** Materials: Damascus stainless steel, exotic metals, gold, rare handle materials. **Prices:** $1000 to $9000. **Remarks:** Folding knives in art deco and art noveau themes. Full-time maker from 1981. **Mark:** OWEN WOOD.

WOOD, WEBSTER,
22041 Shelton Trail, Atlanta, MI 49709, Phone: 989- 785-2996, littlewolf@racc2000.com
Specialties: Works mainly in stainless; art knives, Bowies, hunters and folders. **Remarks:** Full-time maker; first knife sold in 1980. Guild member since 1984. All engraving done by maker. **Mark:** Initials inside shield and name.

WRIGHT, KEVIN,
671 Leland Valley Rd W, Quilcene, WA 98376-9517, Phone: 360-765-3589, kevinw@ptpc.com
Specialties: Fancy working or collector knives to customer specs. **Patterns:** Hunters, boots, buckskinners, miniatures. **Technical:** Forges and grinds L6, 1095, 440C and his own Damascus. **Prices:** $75 to $500; some to $2000. **Remarks:** Part-time maker; first knife sold in 1978. **Mark:** Last initial in anvil.

WRIGHT, L T,
1523 Pershing Ave, Steubenville, OH 43952, Phone: 740-282-4947, knifemkr@sbcglobal.net; Web: www.ltwrightknives.com
Specialties: Hunting and tactical knives. **Patterns:** Drop point hunters, bird, trout and tactical. **Technical:** Grinds D2, 440C and O1. **Remarks:** Full-time maker.

WRIGHT, RICHARD S,
PO Box 201, 111 Hilltop Dr, Carolina, RI 02812, Phone: 401-364-3579, rswswitchblades@hotmail.com; Web: www.richardswright.com
Specialties: Bolster release switchblades. **Patterns:** Folding fighters, gents pocket knives, one-of-a-kind high-grade automatics. **Technical:** Reforges and grinds various makers Damascus. Uses a variety of tool steels. Uses natural handle material such as ivory and pearl, extensive file-work on most knives. **Prices:** $2000 and up. **Remarks:** Full-time knifemaker with background as a gunsmith. Made first folder in 1991. **Mark:** RSW on blade, all folders are serial numbered.

WRIGHT, TIMOTHY,
PO Box 3746, Sedona, AZ 86340, Phone: 928- 282-4180
Specialties: High-tech folders and working knives. **Patterns:** Interframe locking folders, non-inlaid folders, straight hunters and kitchen knives. **Technical:** Grinds BG-42, AEB-L, K190 and Cowry X; works with new steels. All folders can disassemble and are furnished with tools. **Prices:** $150 to $1800; some to $3000. **Remarks:** Full-time maker; first knife sold in 1975. **Mark:** Last name and type of steel used.

WUERTZ, TRAVIS,
2487 E Hwy 287, Casa Grande, AZ 85222, Phone: 520-723-4432

WYATT, WILLIAM R,
Box 237, Rainelle, WV 25962, Phone: 304-438- 5494
Specialties: Classic and working knives of all designs. **Patterns:** Hunters and utility knives. **Technical:** Forges and grinds saw blades, files and rasps. Prefers stag handles. **Prices:** $45 to $95; some to $350. **Remarks:** Part-time maker; first knife sold in 1990. **Mark:** Last name in star with knife logo.

Y

YASHINSKI, JOHN L,
207 N Platt, PO Box 1284, Red Lodge, MT 59068, Phone: 406-446-3916
Specialties: Native American Beaded sheaths. **Prices:** Vary.

YEATES, JOE A,
730 Saddlewood Circle, Spring, TX 77381, Phone: 281-367-2765, joeyeates291@cs.com; Web: www.yeatesBowies.com
Specialties: Bowies, toothpicks and combat knives. **Technical:** Grinds 440C, D2 and ATS-34. **Prices:** $600 to $2500. **Remarks:** Full-time maker; first knife sold in 1975. **Mark:** Last initial within outline of Texas; or last initial.

YESKOO, RICHARD C,
76 Beekman Rd, Summit, NJ 07901

YORK, DAVID C,
PO Box 3166, Chino Valley, AZ 86323, Phone: 928- 636-1709
Specialties: Working straight knives and folders. **Patterns:** Prefers small hunters and skinners; locking folders. **Technical:** Grinds D2 and 440C; buys Damascus. **Prices:** $75 to $300; some to $600. **Remarks:** Part- time maker; first knife sold in 1975. **Mark:** Last name.

YOSHIHARA, YOSHINDO,
8-17-11 Takasago Katsushi, Tokyo, JAPAN

YOSHIKAZU, KAMADA,
, 540-3 Kaisaki Niuta-cho, Tokushima, JAPAN, Phone: 0886-44-2319

YOSHIO, MAEDA,
, 3-12-11 Chuo-cho tamashima Kurashiki-city, Okayama, JAPAN, Phone: 086-525-2375

YOUNG, BUD,
Box 336, Port Hardy, BC, CANADA V0N 2P0, Phone: 250-949-6478
Specialties: Fixed blade, working knives, some fancy. **Patterns:** Drop-points to skinners. **Technical:** Hollow or flat grind, 5160, 440C, mostly ATS-34, satin finish. **Prices:** $150 to $500 CDN. **Remarks:** Spare-time maker; making knives since 1962; first knife sold in 1985. Not taking orders at this time, sell as produced. **Mark:** Name.

YOUNG, CLIFF,
Fuente De La Cibeles No 5, Atascadero, San Miguel De Allende, GTO., MEXICO, Phone: 37700, Fax: 011-52-415-2-57-11
Specialties: Working knives. **Patterns:** Hunters, fighters and fishing knives. **Technical:** Grinds all; offers D2, 440C and 154CM. **Prices:** Start at $250. **Remarks:** Part-time maker; first knife sold in 1980. **Mark:** Name.

YOUNG, ERROL,
4826 Storey Land, Alton, IL 62002, Phone: 618-466- 4707
  Specialties: Traditional working straight knives and folders. **Patterns:** Wide range, including tantos, Bowies, miniatures and multi-blade folders. **Technical:** Grinds D2, 440C and ATS-34. **Prices:** $75 to $650; some to $800. **Remarks:** Part-time maker; first knife sold in 1987. **Mark:** Last name with arrow.

YOUNG, GEORGE,
713 Pinoak Dr, Kokomo, IN 46901, Phone: 765-457- 8893
  Specialties: Fancy/embellished and traditional straight knives and folders of his design and to customer specs. **Patterns:** Hunters, fillet/camp knives and locking folders. **Technical:** Grinds 440C, CPM440V, and stellite 6K. Fancy ivory, black pearl and stag for handles. Filework: all stellite construction (6K and 25 alloys). Offers engraving. **Prices:** $350 to $750; some $1500 to $3000. **Remarks:** Full-time maker; first knife sold in 1954. Doing business as Young's Knives. **Mark:** Last name integral inside Bowie.

YOUNG, RAYMOND L,
CUTLER/BLADESMITH, 2922 Hwy 188E, Mt. Ida, AR 71957, Phone: 870-867-3947
  Specialties: Cutler-Bladesmith, sharpening service. **Patterns:** Hunter, skinners, fighters, no guard, no ricasso, chef tools. **Technical:** Edge tempered 1095, 516C, mosiac handles, water buffalo and exotic woods. **Prices:** $100 and up. **Remarks:** Federal contractor since 1995. Surgical steel sharpening. **Mark:** R.

YURCO, MIKE,
PO Box 712, Canfield, OH 44406, Phone: 330-533-4928, shorinki@aol.com
  Specialties: Working straight knives. **Patterns:** Hunters, utility knives, Bowies and fighters, push knives, claws and other hideouts. **Technical:** Grinds 440C, ATS-34 and 154CM; likes mirror and satin finishes. **Prices:** $20 to $500. **Remarks:** Part-time maker; first knife sold in 1983. **Mark:** Name, steel, serial number.

Z

ZACCAGNINO JR., DON,
2256 Bacom Point Rd, Pahokee, FL 33476- 2622, Phone: 561-924-7032, zackknife@aol.com
  Specialties: Working knives and some period pieces of their designs. **Patterns:** Heavy-duty hunters, axes and Bowies; a line of light-weight hunters, fillets and personal knives. **Technical:** Grinds 440C and 17-4 PH; highly finished in complex handle and blade treatments. **Prices:** $165 to $500; some to $2500. **Remarks:** Part-time maker; first knife sold in 1969 by Don Zaccagnino Sr. **Mark:** ZACK, city and state inside oval.

ZAHM, KURT,
488 Rio Casa, Indialantic, FL 32903, Phone: 407-777- 4860
  Specialties: Working straight knives of his design or to customer specs. **Patterns:** Daggers, fancy fighters, Bowies, hunters and utility knives. **Technical:** Grinds D2, 440C; likes filework. **Prices:** $75 to $1000. **Remarks:** Part-time maker; first knife sold in 1985. **Mark:** Last name.

ZAKABI, CARL S,
PO Box 893161, Mililani Town, HI 96789-0161, Phone: 808-626-2181
  Specialties: User-grade straight knives of his design, cord wrapped and bare steel handles exclusively. **Patterns:** Fighters, hunters and utility/camp knives. **Technical:** Grinds 440C and ATS-34. **Prices:** $90 to $400. **Remarks:** Spare-time maker; first knife sold in 1988. Doing business as Zakabi's Knifeworks LLC. **Mark:** Last name and state inside a Hawaiian sharktooth dagger.

ZAKHAROV, GLADISTON,
Bairro Rio Comprido, Rio Comprido Jacarei, Jacaret SP, BRAZIL 12302-070, Phone: 55 12 3958 4021, Fax: 55 12 3958 4103, arkhip@terra.com.br; Web: www.arkhip.com.br
  Specialties: Using straight knives of his design. **Patterns:** Hunters, kitchen, utility/camp and barbecue knives. **Technical:** Grinds his own "secret steel." **Prices:** $30 to $200. **Remarks:** Full-time maker. **Mark:** Arkhip Special Knives.

ZBORIL, TERRY,
5320 CR 130, Caldwell, TX 77836, Phone: 979-535- 4157, terry.zboril@worldnet.att.net
  Specialties: ABS Journeyman Smith.

ZEMBKO III, JOHN,
140 Wilks Pond Rd, Berlin, CT 06037, Phone: 860- 828-3503, johnzembko@hotmail.com
  Specialties: Working knives of his design or to customer specs. **Patterns:** Likes to use stabilized high-figured woods. **Technical:** Grinds ATS-34, A2, D2; forges O1, 1095; grinds Damasteel. **Prices:** $50 to $400; some higher. **Remarks:** First knife sold in 1987. **Mark:** Name.

ZEMITIS, JOE,
14 Currawong Rd, Cardiff Hts, 2285 Newcastle, AUSTRALIA, Phone: 0249549907, jjvzem@networksmm.com.au
  Specialties: Traditional working straight knives. **Patterns:** Hunters, Bowies, tantos, fighters and camp knives. **Technical:** Grinds O1, D2, W2 and 440C; makes his own Damascus. Embellishes; offers engraving and scrimshaw. **Prices:** $150 to $3000. **Remarks:** Full-time maker; first knife sold in 1983. **Mark:** First initial, last name and country, or last name.

ZIMA, MICHAEL F,
732 State St, Ft. Morgan, CO 80701, Phone: 970- 867-6078, Web: http://www.zimaknives.com
  Specialties: Working and collector quality straight knives and folders. **Patterns:** Hunters, lock backs, LinerLock®, slip joint and automatic folders. **Technical:** Grinds Damascus, 440C, ATS-34 and 154CM. **Prices:** $200 and up. **Remarks:** Full-time maker; first knife sold in 1982. **Mark:** Last name.

ZINKER, BRAD,
BZ KNIVES, 1591 NW 17 St, Homestead, FL 33030, Phone: 305-216-0404, bzknives@aol.com
  Specialties: Fillets, folders and hunters. Technical: Uses ATS-34 and stainless Damascus. Prices: $200 to $600. Remarks: Voting member of Knifemakers Guild and Florida Knifemakers Association. Mark: Offset connected initials BZ.

ZIRBES, RICHARD,
Neustrasse 15, D-54526 Niederkail, GERMANY, Phone: 0049 6575 1371
  Specialties: Fancy embellished knives with engraving and self-made scrimshaw (scrimshaw made by maker). High-tech working knives and high-tech hunters, boots, fighters and folders. All knives made by hand. **Patterns:** Boots, fighters, folders, hunters. **Technical:** Uses only the best steels for blade material like CPM-T 440V, CPM-T 420V, ATS-34, D2, C440, stainless Damascus or steel according to customer's desire. **Prices:** Working knives and hunters: $200 to $600. Fancy embellished knives with engraving and/or scrimshaw: $800 to $3000. **Remarks:** Part- time maker; first knife sold in 1991. Member of the German Knifemaker Guild. **Mark:** Zirbes or R. Zirbes.

ZOWADA, TIM,
4509 E Bear River Rd, Boyne Falls, MI 49713, Phone: 231-348-5446, knifeguy@nmo.net
  Specialties: Working knives, some fancy. **Patterns:** Hunters, camp knives, boots, swords, fighters, tantos and locking folders. **Technical:** Forges O2, L6, W2 and his own Damascus. **Prices:** $150 to $1000; some to $5000. **Remarks:** Full-time maker; first knife sold in 1980.

ZSCHERNY, MICHAEL,
1840 Rock Island Dr, Ely, IA 52227, Phone: 319-848-3629, zschernyknives@aol.com
  Specialties: Quality folding knives. **Patterns:** Liner-lock and lock-back folders in titanium, working straight knives. **Technical:** Grinds ATS-34 and commercial Damascus, prefers natural materials such as pearls and ivory. **Prices:** Starting at $500. **Remarks:** Full-time maker, first knife sold in 1978. **Mark:** Last name, city and state; folders, last name with stars inside folding knife.

Carolina Custom Knives,
  See Tommy Mcnabb
Iron Wolf Forge, See Nelson Ken
Viking Knives (See James Thorlief
  Eriksen),
Warren (See Dellana), Dellana
Wilson (See Simonella, Gianluigi),

AK

Barlow, Jana Poirier	Anchorage
Brennan, Judson	Delta Junction
Breuer, Lonnie	Wasilla
Broome, Thomas A	Kenai
Cannon, Raymond W	Homer
Cawthorne, Christopher A	Wrangell
Chamberlin, John A	Anchorage
Cutting Edge, The, Mark	Fairbanks
Dempsey, Gordon S	N. Kenai
Dufour, Arthur J	Anchorage
England, Virgil	Anchorage
Flint, Robert	Anchorage
Gouker, Gary B	Sitka
Grebe, Gordon S	Anchor Point
Harvey, Mel	Nenana
Hibben, Westley G	Anchorage
Hook, Bob	North Pole
Kelsey, Nate	Anchorage
Knapp, Mark	Fairbanks
Lance, Bill	Eagle River
Malaby, Raymond J	Juneau
Mcfarlin, Eric E	Kodiak
Miller, Nate	Fairbanks
Miller, Ron	North Pole
Miller, Terry	Healy
Mirabile, David	Juneau
Moore, Marve	Willow
Parrish Iii, Gordon A	North Pole
Quattlebaum, Craig	Eagle River
Shore, John I	Anchorage
Stegall, Keith	Wasilla
Van Cleve, Steve	Sutton
Whipple, Wesley A	Kodiak
Whitman, Jim	Chugiak

AL

Batson, James	Madison
Baxter, Dale	Trinity
Bell, Tony	Woodland
Bowles, Chris	Reform
Brend, Walter	Vinemont
Bullard, Bill	Andalusia
Coffman, Danny	Jacksonville
Conn Jr., C T	Attalla
Daniels, Alex	Town Creek
Dark, Robert	Oxford
Di Marzo, Richard	Birmingham
Durham, Kenneth	Cherokee
Elrod, Roger R	Enterprise
Fikes, Jimmy L	Jasper
Fogg, Don	Jasper
Fowler, Ricky And Susan	Robertsdale
Gilbreath, Randall	Dora
Golden, Randy	Montgomery
Hammond, Jim	Arab
Howard, Durvyn M	Hokes Bluff
Howell, Len	Opelika
Howell, Ted	Wetumpka
Huckabee, Dale	Maylene
Hulsey, Hoyt	Attalla
Mccullough, Jerry	Georgiana
Militano, Tom	Jacksonville
Morris, C H	Frisco City
Pardue, Melvin M	Repton
Roe Jr., Fred D	Huntsville

Russell, Tom	Jacksonville
Sandlin, Larry	Adamsville
Sinyard, Cleston S	Elberta
Thomas, David E	Lillian
Watson, Billy	Deatsville
Whittemore, Ryan A	Montomery

AR

Anders, David	Center Ridge
Ardwin, Corey	North Little Rock
Barnes Jr., Cecil C.	Center Ridge
Brown, Jim	Little Rock
Browning, Steven W	Benton
Bullard, Tom	Flippin
Cabe, Jerry (Buddy)	Hattieville
Cook, James R	Nashville
Copeland, Thom	Nashville
Crawford, Pat And Wes	West Memphis
Crowell, James L	Mtn. View
Dozier, Bob	Springdale
Duvall, Fred	Benton
Echols, Roger	Nashville
Edge, Tommy	Cash
Ferguson, Lee	Hindsville
Ferguson, Linda	Hindsville
Fisk, Jerry	Nashville
Fitch, John S	Clinton
Flournoy, Joe	El Dorado
Foster, Ronnie E	Morrilton
Foster, Timothy L	El Dorado
Frizzell, Ted	West Fork
Gadberry, Emmet	Hattieville
Greenaway, Don	Fayetteville
Herring, Morris	Dyer
Lane, Ben	North Little Rock
Lawrence, Alton	De Queen
Livesay, Newt	Siloam Springs
Lunn, Gail	Mountain Home
Lunn, Larry A	Mountain Home
Lynch, Tad	Beene
Maringer, Tom	Springdale
Martin, Bruce E	Prescott
Martin, Hal W	Morrilton
Massey, Roger	Texarkana
Newton, Ron	London
O'Dell, Clyde	Camden
Olive, Michael E	Leslie
Passmore, Jimmy D	Hoxie
Perry, Jim	Hope
Perry, John	Mayflower
Peterson, Lloyd (Pete) C	Clinton
Polk, Clifton	Van Buren
Polk, Rusty	Van Buren
Red, Vernon	Conway
Rhea, Lin	Prattsville
Richards, Ralph (Bud)	Bauxite
Sisemore, Charles Russel	Mena
Smoker, Ray	Searcy
Solomon, Marvin	Paron
Stanley, John	Crossett
Stout, Charles	Gillham
Sweaza, Dennis	Austin
Townsend, Allen Mark	Texarkana
Tycer, Art	Paron
Walker, Jim	Morrilton
Ward, Chuck	Benton
Waters, Herman Harold	Magnolia
Waters, Lu	Magnolia
White, Bryce	Little Rock
Young, Raymond L	Mt. Ida

ARGENTINA

Ayarragaray, Cristian L.
    (3100) Parana-Entre Rios

Bertolami, Juan Carlos	Neuquen
Gibert, Pedro	San Rafael Mendoza
Kehiayan, Alfredo	
	CP B1623GXU Buenos Aires
Rho, Nestor Lorenzo	Buenos Aires
Santiago, Abud	Buenos Aires 1416

AUSTRALIA

Bennett, Peter	Engadine N.S.W. 2233
Brodziak, David	
	Albany, Western Australia
Crawley, Bruce R	Croydon 3136 Victoria
Cross, Robert	Tamworth 2340, NSW
Del Raso, Peter	
	Mt. Waverly, Victoria, 3149
Gerner, Thomas	Western Australia
Giljevic, Branko	N.S.W.
Green, William (Bill)	View Bank Vic.
Harvey, Max	
	Perth 6155, Western Australia
Husiak, Myron	Victoria
Jones, John	Gympie, Queensland 4570
K B S, Knives	Vic 3450
Maisey, Alan	Vincentia 2540, NSW
Mcintyre, Shawn	Hawthorn East Victoria
Phillips, Alistair	ACT, 2914
Spencer, KeithChidlow	Western Australia
Tasman, Kerley	Western Australia
Zemitis, Joe	2285 Newcastle

AUSTRIA

Poskocil, Helmut	A-3340
Waidhofen/Ybbs	

AZ

Ammons, David C	Tucson
Bennett, Glen C	Tucson
Birdwell, Ira Lee	Congress
Boye, David	Dolan Springs
Bryan, Tom	Gilbert
Cheatham, Bill	Laveen
Choate, Milton	Somerton
Clark, R W	Surprise
Dawson, Lynn	Prescott Valley
Deubel, Chester J.	Tucson
Dodd, Robert F	Camp Verde
Fuegen, Larry	Prescott
Goo, Tai	Tucson
Hancock, Tim	Scottsdale
Hoel, Steve	Pine
Holder, D'Alton	Peoria
Hull, Michael J	Cottonwood
Karp, Bob	Phoenix
Kiley, Mike And Jandy	Chino Valley
Kopp, Todd M	Apache Jct.
Lampson, Frank G	Rimrock
Lee, Randy	St. Johns
Mcfall, Ken	Lakeside
Mcfarlin, J W	Lake Havasu City
Miller, Michael	Kingman
Mooney, Mike	Queen Creek
Newhall, Tom	Tucson
Purvis, Bob And Ellen	Tucson
Robbins, Bill	Globe
Rybar Jr., Raymond B	Came Verde
Snare, Michael	Phoenix
Tamboli, Michael	Glendale
Tollefson, Barry A	Tubac
Torgeson, Samuel L	Sedona
Tyre, Michael A	Wickenburg
Weiss, Charles L	Phoenix
Wolf, Bill	Phoenix
Wright, Timothy	Sedona

Wuertz, Travis	Casa Grande
York, David C	Chino Valley

B.C. Canada

Niro, Frank	Blind Bay

BELGIUM

Dox, Jan	B 2900 Schoten
Monteiro, Victor	1360 Maleves Ste Marie

BRAZIL

Bodolay, Antal	
	Belo Horizonte MG-31730-700
Bossaerts, Carl	
	14051-110, Ribeirao Preto, S.P.
Campos, Ivan	Tatui, SP
Dorneles, Luciano Oliverira	
	Nova Petropolis, RS
Gaeta, Angelo	SP-17201-310
Gaeta, Roberto	Sao Paulo
Garcia, Mario Eiras	
	Sao Paulo SP-05516-070
Lala, Paulo Ricardo P And	
Lala, Roberto P.	SP- 19031-260
Neto Jr., Nelson And De Carvalho,	
Henrique M.	SP-12900-000
Paulo, Fernandes R	Sao Paulo
Petean, Francisco And Mauricio	
SP-16200-000	
Ricardo Romano, Bernardes	Itajuba MG
Sfreddo, Rodrigo Menezes	
	cep g5 150-000
Tkoma, Flavio	Prudonte SP19031-220
Vilar, Ricardo Augusto Ferreira	Mairipora
Sao Paulo	
Villa, Luiz	Sao Paulo, SP.-04537-081
Villar, Ricardo	S.P. 07600-000
Zakharov, Gladiston	Jacaret SP

CA

Abegg, Arnie	Huntington Beach
Abernathy, Paul J	Eureka
Adkins, Richard L	Mission Viejo
Aldrete, Bob	Lomita
Athey, Steve	Riverside
Barnes, Gregory	Altadena
Barron, Brian	San Mateo
Benson, Don	Escalon
Berger, Max A.	Carmichael
Biggers, Gary	Ventura
Blum, Chuck	Brea
Bost, Roger E	Palos Verdes
Boyd, Francis	Berkeley
Brack, Douglas D	Ventura
Breshears, Clint	Manhattan Beach
Brooks, Buzz	Los Angles
Browne, Rick	Upland
Brunetta, David	Laguna Beach
Butler, Bart	Ramona
Cabrera, Sergio B	Wilmington
Cantrell, Kitty D	Ramona
Caston, Darriel	Sacramento
Caswell, Joe	Newbury
Coffey, Bill	Clovis
Cohen, Terry A	Laytonville
Coleman, John A	Citrus Heightss
Connolly, James	Oroville
Davis, Charlie	Santee
De Maria Jr., Angelo	Carmel Valley
Dion, Greg	Oxnard
Dixon Jr., Ira E	Ventura
Doolittle, Mike	Novato

Driscoll, Mark	La Mesa
Ellis, Dave/Abs Mastersmith	Vista
Ellis, William Dean	Sanger
Emerson, Ernest R	Torrance
English, Jim	Jamul
English, Jim	Jamul
Ernest, Phil (Pj)	Whittier
Essegian, Richard	Fresno
Felix, Alexander	Torrance
Ferguson, Jim	Temecula
Fisher, Theo (Ted)	Montague
Forrest, Brian	Descanso
Fraley, D B	Dixon
Fred, Reed Wyle	Sacramento
Freer, Ralph	Seal Beach
Fulton, Mickey	Willows
Girtner, Joe	Brea
Gofourth, Jim	Santa Paula
Guarnera, Anthony R	Quartzhill
Guidry, Bruce	Murrieta
Hall, Jeff	Los Alamitos
Hardy, Scott	Placerville
Harris, Jay	Redwood City
Harris, John	Riverside
Hartsfield, Phill	Newport Beach
Helton, Roy	San Diego
Herndon, Wm R "Bill"	Acton
Hink Iii, Les	Stockton
Hoy, Ken	North Fork
Humenick, Roy	Rescue
Iames, Gary	Tahoe
Jacks, Jim	Covina
Jackson, David	Lemoore
Janiga, Matthew A	Fairfield
Jensen, John Lewis	Pasadena
Johnson, Randy	Turlock
Kazsuk, David	Perris
Kelly, Dave	Los Angeles
Keyes, Dan	Chino
Kilpatrick, Christian A	Citrus Hieghts
Koster, Steven C	Huntington Beach
Laner, Dean	Susanville
Larson, Richard	Turlock
Leland, Steve	Fairfax
Likarich, Steve	Colfax
Lockett, Sterling	Burbank
Loveless, R W	Riverside
Luchini, Bob	Palo Alto
Mackie, John	Whittier
Massey, Ron	Joshua Tree
Mata, Leonard	San Diego
Maxwell, Don	Clovis
Mcabee, William	Colfax
Mcclure, Michael	Menlo Park
Mcgrath, Patrick T	Westchester
Melin, Gordon C	La Mirada
Meloy, Sean	Lemon Grove
Montano, Gus A	San Diego
Morgan, Jeff	Santee
Moses, Steven	Santa Ana
Mutz, Jeff	Rancho Cucamonga
Naten, Greg	Bakersfield
Orton, Rich	Riverside
Osborne, Donald H	Clovis
Packard, Bob	Elverta
Palm, Rik	San Diego
Pendleton, Lloyd	Volcano
Perry, Chris	Fresno
Pfanenstiel, Dan	Modesto
Phillips, Randy	Ontario
Pitt, David F	Anderson
Posner, Barry E	N. Hollywood
Quesenberry, Mike	Blairsden
Randall, Patrick	Newbury Park
Rozas, Clark D	Wilmington

Schmitz, Raymond E	Valley Center
Schneider, Herman	Apple Valley
Schroen, Karl	Sebastopol
Sibrian, Aaron	Ventura
Sjostrand, Kevin	Visalia
Slobodian, Scott	San Andreas
Smith, Shawn	Clouis
Sornberger, Jim	Volcano
St. Cyr, H Red	Wilmington
Stapel, Chuck	Glendale
Steinberg, Al	Laguna Woods
Stimps, Jason M	Orange
Stockwell, Walter	Redwood City
Stover, Howard	Pasadena
Strider, Mick	San Marcos
Terrill, Stephen	Springville
Tingle, Dennis P	Jackson
Torres, Henry	Clovis
Trace Rinaldi Custom Blades,	Hemet
Vagnino, Michael	Visalia
Van Riper, James N	Citrus Heights
Velick, Sammy	Los Angeles
Warren, Al	Roseville
Watanabe, Wayne	Montebello
Weinstock, Robert	San Francisco
Wilson, Philip C	Mountain Ranch
Wilson, Ron	Morro Bay

CANADA

Arnold, Joe	London, Ont.
Beauchamp, Gaetan	Stoneham, PQ
Beets, Marty	Williams Lake, BC
Bell, Donald	Bedford, Nova Scotia
Berg, Lothar	Kitchener ON
Beshara, Brent (Besh)	Stayner, Ont.
Boos, Ralph	Edmonton, Alberta
Bourbeau, Jean Yves	Ile Perrot, Quebec
Bradford, Garrick	Kitchener ON
Dallyn, Kelly	Calgary, AB
Debraga, Jose C	Aux Lievres, Quebec
Debraga, Jovan	Quebec
Deringer, Christoph	Cookshire, Quebec
Diotte, Jeff	LaSalle Ontario
Doiron, Donald	Messines, PQ
Doucette, R	Brantford, Ont.
Doussot, Laurent	St. Bruno, Quebec
Downie, James T	Port Franks, Ont.
Dublin, Dennis	Enderby, B.C.
Frigault, Rick	Niagara Falls, Ont.
Ganshorn, Cal	Regina, Saskatchewan
Garvock, Mark W	Balderson, Ont.
Gilbert, Chantal	Quebec City Quebec
Haslinger, Thomas	Calgary, AB
Hayes, Wally	Essex, Ont.
Hindmarch, G	Carlyle SK S0C 0R0
Hofer, Louis	Rose Prairie, B.C.
Jobin, Jacques	Levis Quebec
Kaczor, Tom	Upper London, Ont.
Lambert, Kirby	
	Regina Saskatchewan S4N X3
Langley, Mick	Qualicum Beach, B.C.
Lay, R J (Bob)	Logan Lake, B.C.
Leber, Heinz	Hudson's Hope, B.C.
Lightfoot, Greg	Kitscoty, AB
Linklater, Steve	Aurora, Ont.
Loerchner, Wolfgang	Bayfield, Ont.
Lyttle, Brian	High River, AB
Maneker, Kenneth	Galiano Island, B.C.
Marzitelli, Peter	Langley, B.C.
Massey, Al	Mount Uniacke, Nova Scotia
Mckenzie, David Brian	Campbell River B
Miville-Deschenes, Alain	Quebec
O'Hare, Sean	Grand Manan, NB
Olson, Rod	High River, AB

Painter, Tony — Whitehorse Yukon
Patrick, Bob — S. Surrey, B.C.
Pepiot, Stephan — Winnipeg, Man.
Piesner, Dean — Conestogo, Ont.
Roberts, George A — Whitehorse, YT
Ross, Tim — Thunder Bay, Ont.
Schoenfeld, Matthew A — Galiano Island, B.C.
St. Amour, Murray — Pembroke ON
Stancer, Chuck — Calgary, AB
Storch, Ed — Alberta T0B 2W0
Stuart, Steve — Gores Landing, Ont.
Tichbourne, George — Mississauga, Ont.
Tighe, Brian — St. Catharines, Ont.
Toner, Roger — Pickering, Ont.
Treml, Glenn — Thunder Bay, Ont.
Vanderkolff, Stephen — Mildmay Ontario
Whitenect, Jody — Nova Scotia
Wile, Peter — Bridgewater, Nova Scotia
Young, Bud — Port Hardy, BC

CO

Anderson, Mark Alan — Denver
Anderson, Mel — Hotchkiss
Barrett, Cecil Terry — Colorado Springs
Booco, Gordon — Hayden
Brandon, Matthew — Denver
Brock, Kenneth L — Allenspark
Burrows, Chuck — Durango
Dannemann, Randy — Hotchkiss
Davis, Don — Loveland
Dawson, Barry — Durango
Delong, Dick — Aurora
Dennehy, Dan — Del Norte
Dennehy, John D — Wellington
Dill, Robert — Loveland
Fronefield, Daniel — Peyton
High, Tom — Alamosa
Hockensmith, Dan — Carr
Hughes, Ed — Grand Junction
Irie, Michael L — Colorado Springs
Kitsmiller, Jerry — Montrose
Leck, Dal — Hayden
Magruder, Jason — Colorado Springs
Miller, Hanford J — Cowdrey
Miller, M A — Northglenn
Olson, Wayne C — Bailey
Ott, Fred — Durango
Owens, John — Nathrop
Roberts, Chuck — Golden
Rollert, Steve — Keenesburg
Ronzio, N. Jack — Fruita
Sanders, Bill — Mancos
Thompson, Lloyd — Pagosa Springs
Waites, Richard L — Broomfield
Watson, Bert — Westminster
Wilson, James G — Estes Park
Wood, Owen Dale — Arvada
Zima, Michael F — Ft. Morgan

CT

Barnes, William — Wallingford
Buebendorf, Robert E — Monroe
Chapo, William G — Wilton
Framski, Walter P — Prospect
Jean, Gerry — Manchester
Lepore, Michael J — Bethany
Meyer, Christopher J — Tolland
Padgett Jr., Edwin L — New London
Plunkett, Richard — West Cornwall
Putnam, Donald S — Wethersfield
Rainville, Richard — Salem
Riden, Doug — Eastford
Turecek, Jim — Ansonia

Vitale, Mace — Guilford
Zembko Iii, John — Berlin

DE

Antonio Jr., William J — Newark
Schneider, Karl A — Newark
Willey, Wg — Greenwood

DENMARK

Andersen, Henrik Lefolii — 3480, Fredensborg
Anso, Jens — 116, 8472 Sporup
Bentzen, Leif —
Dyrnoe, Per — DK 3400 Hilleroed
Henriksen, Hans J — DK 3200 Helsinge
Strande, Poul — Dastrup 4130 Viby Sj.
Vensild, Henrik — DK-8963 Auning

ENGLAND

Bailey, I.R. — Norfolk
Boden, Harry — Derbyshire DE4 2AJ
Farid R, Mehr — Kent
Harrington, Roger — East Sussex
Jackson, Jim — Chapel Row Bucklebury RG7 6PU
Morris, Darrell Price — Devon
Penfold, Mick Tremar, Cornwall PL14 5SJ
Wardell, Mick — N Devon EX39 3BU
Wise, Donald — East Sussex, TN3 8AL
Wood, Alan — Brampton CA8 7HH

EUROPE

Sprokholt, Rob — Netherlands

FINLAND

Tuominen, Pekka — 72930 Tossavanlahti

FL

Adams, Les — Hialeah
Alexander, Oleg, Cossack Blades — Wellington
Anders, Jerome — Miramar
Angell, Jon — Hawthorne
Atkinson, Dick — Wausau
Bacon, David R. — Bradenton
Barry Iii, James J. — West Palm Beach
Bartrug, Hugh E. — St. Petersburg
Beers, Ray — Lake Wales
Benjamin Jr., George — Kissimmee
Birnbaum, Edwin — Miami
Blackwood, Neil — Lakeland
Bosworth, Dean — Key Largo
Bradley, John — Pomona Park
Bray Jr., W Lowell — New Port Richey
Brown, Harold E — Arcadia
Burris, Patrick R — Jacksonville
Butler, John — Havana
Chase, Alex — DeLand
Cole, Dave — Satellite Beach
D'Andrea, John — Citrus Springs
Davis Jr., Jim — Zephyrhills
Dietzel, Bill — Middleburg
Doggett, Bob — Brandon
Dotson, Tracy — Baker
Ellerbe, W B — Geneva
Ellis, Willy B — Palm Harbor
Enos Iii, Thomas M — Orlando
Ferrara, Thomas — Naples
Ferris, Bill — Palm Beach Garden
Fowler, Charles R — Ft McCoy

Gamble, Roger — St. Petersburg
Garner Jr., William O — Pensacola
Gibson Sr., James Hoot — Bunnell
Goers, Bruce — Lakeland
Granger, Paul J — Largo
Griffin Jr., Howard A — Davie
Grospitch, Ernie — Orlando
Harris, Ralph Dewey — Brandon
Heaney, John D — Haines City
Heitler, Henry — Tampa
Hodge Iii, John — Palatka
Holland, John H — Titusville
Humphreys, Joel — Lake Placid
Hunter, Richard D — Alachua
Hytovick, Joe "Hy" — Dunnellon
Jernigan, Steve — Milton
Johanning Custom Knives, Tom — Sarasota
Johnson, John R — Plant City
Kelly, Lance — Edgewater
King, Bill — Tampa
Krapp, Denny — Apopka
Levengood, Bill — Tampa
Lewis, Mike — DeBary
Long, Glenn A — Dunnellon
Lovestrand, Schuyler — Vero Beach
Lozier, Don — Ocklawaha
Lyle Iii, Ernest L — Chiefland
Mandt, Joe — St. Petersburg
Mcdonald, Robert J — Loxahatchee
Mcgowan, Frank E — Sebring
Miller, Ronald T — Largo
Mink, Dan — Crystal Beach
Newton, Larry — Jacksonville
Ochs, Charles F — Largo
Owens, Donald — Melbourne
Parker, Cliff — Zephyrhills
Partridge, Jerry D. — DeFuniak Springs
Pendray, Alfred H — Williston
Piergallini, Daniel E — Plant City
Randall Made Knives, — Orlando
Reed, John M — Oak Hill
Robinson, Calvin — Pace
Robinson Iii, Rex R — Leesburg
Rodkey, Dan — Hudson
Ross, Gregg — Lake Worth
Russ, Ron — Williston
Schwarzer, Stephen — Crescent City
Smith, Michael J — Brandon
Stapleton, William E — Merritt Island
Steck, Van R — Orange City
Stephan, Daniel — Valrico
Stipes, Dwight — Palm City
Straight, Kenneth J — Largo
Tabor, Tim — Lutz
Turnbull, Ralph A — Spring Hill
Vogt, Donald J — Tampa
Watson, Tom — Panama City
Weiland Jr., J Reese — Riverview
White, John Paul — Valparaiso
Wicker, Donnie R — Panama City
Wilson, Stan — Lithia
Zaccagnino Jr., Don — Pahokee
Zahm, Kurt — Indialantic
Zinker, Brad — Homestead

FRANCE

Bennica, Charles — 34190 Moules et Baucels
Chauzy, Alain — 21140 Seur-en-Auxios
Doursin, Gerard — Pernes les Fontaines
Ganster, Jean-Pierre — F-67000 Strasbourg
Graveline, Pascal And Isabelle — 29350 Moelan- sur-Mer
Headrick, Gary — Juane Les Pins

Madrulli, Mme Joelle Salon De Provence
Reverdy, Nicole And Pierre
Thevenot, Jean-Paul   Dijon
Viallon, Henri

GA

Arrowood, Dale	Sharpsburg
Ashworth, Boyd	Powder Springs
Barker, Robert G.	Bishop
Bentley, C L	Albany
Bish, Hal	Jonesboro
Black, Scott	Covington
Bradley, Dennis	Blairsville
Buckner, Jimmie H	Putney
Chamblin, Joel	Concord
Cole, Welborn I	Athens
Crockford, Jack	Chamblee
Davis, Steve	Powder Springs
Dempsey, David	Macon
Dunn, Charles K	Shiloh
Frost, Dewayne	Barnesville
Gaines, Buddy	Commerce
Glover, Warren D	Cleveland
Greene, David	Covington
Halligan, Ed	Sharpsburg
Hammond, Hank	Leesburg
Hardy, Douglas E	Franklin
Hawkins, Rade	Fayetteville
Hensley, Wayne	Conyers
Hinson And Son, R	Columbus
Hoffman, Kevin L	Savannah
Hossom, Jerry	Duluth
Jones, Franklin (Frank) W	Columbus
Kimsey, Kevin	Cartersville
King, Fred	Cartersville
Knott, Steve	Guyton
Landers, John	Newnan
Lonewolf, J Aguirre	Demorest
Mathews, Charlie And Harry	Statesboro
Mcgill, John	Blairsville
Mclendon, Hubert W	Waco
Mitchell, James A	Columbus
Moncus, Michael Steven	Smithville
Parks, John	Jefferson
Poole, Marvin O	Commerce
Powell, Robert Clark	Smarr
Prater, Mike	Flintstone
Price, Timmy	Blairsville
Ragsdale, James D	Lithonia
Roghmans, Mark	LaGrange
Rosenfeld, Bob	Hoschton
Scofield, Everett	Chickamauga
Sculley, Peter E	Rising Fawn
Smith Jr., James B "Red"	Morven
Snell, Jerry L	Fortson
Snow, Bill	Columbus
Sowell, Bill	Macon
Stafford, Richard	Warner Robins
Thompson, Kenneth	Duluth
Tomey, Kathleen	Macon
Walters, A F	TyTy
Whetsell, Alex	Sharpsburg
White, Garrett	Hartwell
White, Lou	Ranger

GERMANY

Balbach, Markus	35789 Weilmunster-Laubuseschbach/Ts.
Becker, Franz	84533, Marktl/Inn
Boehlke, Guenter	56412 Grossholbach
Borger, Wolf	76676 Graben-Neudorf
Dell, Wolfgang	D-73277 Owen-Teck
Drumm, Armin	D-89160 Dornstadt
Faust, Joachim	95497 Goldkronach
Fruhmann, Ludwig	84489 Burghausen
Greiss, Jockl	D 77773 Schenkenzell
Hehn, Richard Karl	55444 Dorrebach
Herbst, Peter	91207 Lauf a.d. Pegn.
Joehnk, Bernd	24148 Kiel
Kressler, D F	D-28832 Achim
Neuhaeusler, Erwin	86179 Augsburg
Rankl, Christian	81476 Munchen
Rinkes, Siegfried	Markterlbach
Selzam, Frank	Bad Koenigshofen
Steinau, Jurgen	Berlin 0-1162
Tritz, Jean Jose	20255 Hamburg
Wirtz, Achim	D-52146
Zirbes, Richard	D-54526 Niederkail

GREECE

Filippou, Ioannis-Minas	Athens 17122

HI

Bucholz, Mark A	Holualoa
Dolan, Robert L.	Kula
Fujisaka, Stanley	Kaneohe
Gibo, George	Hilo
Lui, Ronald M	Honolulu
Mann, Tim	Honokaa
Matsuoka, Scot	Mililani
Mayo Jr., Tom	Waialua
Mitsuyuki, Ross	Honolulu
Onion, Kenneth J	Kaneohe
Ouye, Keith	Honolulu
Zakabi, Carl S	Mililani Town

HOLLAND

Van De Manakker, Thijs	5759 px Helenaveen

IA

Brooker, Dennis	Derby
Brower, Max	Boone
Clark, Howard F	Runnells
Cockerham, Lloyd	Denham Springs
Helscher, John W	Washington
Lainson, Tony	Council Bluffs
Lewis, Bill	Riverside
Mckiernan, Stan	Lamoni
Miller, James P	Fairbank
Thie, Brian	Burlington
Trindle, Barry	Earlham
Westberg, Larry	Algona
Zscherny, Michael	Ely

ID

Alderman, Robert	Sagle
Alverson, Tim (R.V.)	Moscow
Burke, Bill	Boise
Eddy, Hugh E	Caldwell
Hawk, Grant And Gavin	Idaho City
Hogan, Thomas R	Boise
Horton, Scot	Buhl
Howe, Tori	Athol
Mann, Michael L	Spirit Lake
Metz, Greg T	Cascade
Patton, Dick And Rob	Nampa
Quarton, Barr	McCall
Reeve, Chris	Boise
Rohn, Fred	Coeur d'Alene
Sawby, Scott	Sandpoint
Schultz, Robert W	Cocolalla
Selent, Chuck	Bonners Ferry
Sparks, Bernard	Dingle
Steiger, Monte L	Genesee

Tippetts, Colten	Hidden Springs
Towell, Dwight L	Midvale

IL

Bloomer, Alan T	Maquon
Camerer, Craig	Chesterfield
Cook, Louise	Ozark
Cook, Mike	Ozark
Detmer, Phillip	Breese
Dicristofano, Anthony P	Northlake
Eaker, Allen L	Paris
Hawes, Chuck	Weldon
Heath, William	Bondville
Hill, Rick	Maryville
Knuth, Joseph E	Rockford
Kovar, Eugene	Evergreen Park
Leone, Nick	Pontoon Beach
Markley, Ken	Sparta
Meier, Daryl	Carbondale
Myers, Paul	Wood River
Myers, Steve	Virginia
Nevling, Mark	Hume
Nowland, Rick	Waltonville
Potocki, Roger	Goreville
Pritchard, Ron	Dixon
Rados, Jerry F	Grant Park
Rosenbaugh, Ron	Crystal Lake
Rossdeutscher, Robert N	Arlington Heights
Rzewnicki, Gerald	Elizabeth
Schneider, Craig M	Claremont
Smale, Charles J	Waukegan
Smith, John M	Centralia
Thomas, Bob G	Thebes
Todd, Richard C	Chambersburg
Tompkins, Dan	Peotone
Veit, Michael	LaSalle
Voss, Ben	Galesburg
Werth, George W	Poplar Grove
West, Charles A	Centralia
Wheeler, Robert	Bradley
White, Robert J	Gilson
White Jr., Robert J Butch	Gilson
Young, Errol	Alton

IN

Adkins, Larry	Indianapolis
Ball, Ken	Mooresville
Barkes, Terry	Edinburgh
Barrett, Rick L. (Toshi Hisa)	Goshen
Bose, Reese	Shelburn
Bose, Tony	Shelburn
Chaffee, Jeff L	Morris
Claiborne, Jeff	Franklin
Crowl, Peter	Waterloo
Damlovac, Sava	Indianapolis
Darby, Jed	Greensburg
Fitzgerald, Dennis M	Fort Wayne
Fraps, John R	Indianpolis
Hunt, Maurice	Brownsburg
Imel, Billy Mace	New Castle
Johnson, C E Gene	Chesterton
Kain, Charles	Indianapolis
Keeslar, Steven C	Hamilton
Keeton, William L	Laconia
Kinker, Mike	Greensburg
Mayville, Oscar L	Marengo
Minnick, Jim	Middletown
Oliver, Todd D	Spencer
Parsons, Michael R	Indianapolis
Quakenbush, Thomas C	Ft Wayne
Robertson, Leo D	Indianapolis
Seib, Steve	Evansville
Shull, James	Rensselaer

Smock, Timothy E	Marion
Snyder, Michael Tom	Zionsville
Stover, Terry "Lee"	Kokomo
Thayer, Danny O	Romney
Young, George	Kokomo

ISRAEL

Shadmot, Boaz	Arava

ITALY

Albericci, Emilio	24100, Bergamo
Ameri, Mauro	16010 Genova
Ballestra, Santino	18039 Ventimiglia (IM)
Bertuzzi, Ettore	24068 Seriate (Bergamo)
Bonassi, Franco	Pordenone 33170
Fogarizzu, Boiteddu	07016 Pattada
Giagu, Salvatore And Deroma Maria Rosaria	07016 Pattada (SS)
Pachi, Francesco	17046 Sassello (SV)
Ramondetti, Sergio	12013 CHIUSA DI PESIO (CN)
Riboni, Claudio	Truccazzano (MI)
Scordia, Paolo	Roma
Simonella, Gianluigi	33085 Maniago
Toich, Nevio	Vincenza
Tschager, Reinhard	I-39100 Bolzano

JAPAN

Aida, Yoshihito	Itabashi-ku, Tokyo 175-0094
Ebisu, Hidesaku	Hiroshima City
Fujikawa, Shun	Osaka 597 0062
Fukuta, Tak	Seki-City, Gifu-Pref
Hara, Kouji	Gifu-Pref. 501-3922
Hirayama, Harumi	Saitama Pref. 335-0001
Hiroto, Fujihara	Hiroshima
Isao, Ohbuchi	Fukuoka
Ishihara, Hank	Chiba Pref.
Kagawa, Koichi	Kanagawa
Kanda, Michio	Yamaguchi 7460033
Kanki, Iwao	Hydugo
Kansei, Matsuno	Gitu-city
Kato, Shinichi	Moriyama-ku Nagoya
Katsumaro, Shishido	Hiroshima
Kawasaki, Akihisa	Kobe
Keisuke, Gotoh	Ohita
Koyama, Captain Bunshichi	Nagoya City 453- 0817
Mae, Takao	Toyonaka, Osaka
Makoto, Kunitomo	Hiroshima
Matsuno, Kansei	Gifu-City 501-1168
Matsusaki, Takeshi	Nagasaki
Michinaka, Toshiaki	Tottori 680-0947
Micho, Kanda	Yamaguchi
Ryuichi, Kuki	Saitama
Sakakibara, Masaki	Tokyo 156-0054
Sugihara, Keidoh	Osaka, F596-0042
Sugiyama, Eddy K	Ohita
Takahashi, Masao	Gunma 371 0047
Terauchi, Toshiyuki	Fujita-Cho Gobo-Shi
Toshifumi, Kuramoto	Fukuoka
Uchida, Chimata	Kumamoto
Wada, Yasutaka	Nara prefect 631-0044
Waters, Glenn	Hirosaki City 036-8183
Yoshihara, Yoshindo	Tokyo
Yoshikazu, Kamada	Tokushima
Yoshio, Maeda	Okayama

KS

Bradburn, Gary	Wichita
Burrows, Stephen R	Humboldt
Chard, Gordon R	Iola
Courtney, Eldon	Wichita
Craig, Roger L	Topeka
Culver, Steve	Meriden
Darpinian, Dave	Olathe
Davison, Todd A.	Lyons
Dawkins, Dudley L	Topeka
Dick, Dan	Hutchinson
Dugger, Dave	Westwood
Greene, Steve	Rossville
Hegwald, J L	Humboldt
Herman, Tim	Olathe
King, Jason M	St. George
King Jr., Harvey G	Alta Vista
Kraft, Steve	Abilene
Lamb, Curtis J	Ottawa
Magee, Jim	Salina
Petersen, Dan L	Auburn

KY

Adams, Jim	Scottsville
Addison, Kyle A	Hazel
Barbara Baskett Custom Knives,	Eastview
Barr, A.T.	Nicholasville
Baskett, Barbara	Eastview
Baumgardner, Ed	Glendale
Bodner, Gerald "Jerry"	Louisville
Bybee, Barry J	Cadiz
Carson, Harold J "Kit"	Vine Grove
Coil, Jimmie J	Owensboro
Downing, Larry	Bremen
Dunn, Steve	Smiths Grove
Edwards, Mitch	Glasgow
Finch, Ricky D	West Liberty
Fister, Jim	Simpsonville
France, Dan	Cawood
Frederick, Aaron	West Liberty
Gevedon, Hanners (Hank)	Crab Orchard
Greco, John	Greensburg
Hibben, Daryl	LaGrange
Hibben, Gil	LaGrange
Hibben, Joleen	LaGrange
Hoke, Thomas M	LaGrange
Holbrook, H L	Sandy Hook
Howser, John C	Frankfort
Keeslar, Joseph F	Almo
Lott, Sherry	Greensburg
Miller, Don	Lexington
Mize, Richard	Lawrenceburg
Pease, W D	Ewing
Pierce, Harold L	Louisville
Pulliam, Morris C	Shelbyville
Richerson, Ron	Greenburg
Rigney Jr., Willie	Bronston
Smith, John W	West Liberty
Soaper, Max H.	Henderson
Steier, David	Louisville
Wallingford Jr., Charles W	Union

LA

Barker, Reggie	Springhill
Blaum, Roy	Covington
Caldwell, Bill	West Monroe
Calvert Jr., Robert W (Bob)	Rayville
Capdepon, Randy	Carencro
Capdepon, Robert	Carencro
Chauvin, John	Scott
Culpepper, John	Monroe
Dake, C M	New Orleans
Dake, Mary H	New Orleans
Durio, Fred	Opelousas
Elkins, Van	Bastrop
Faucheaux, Howard J	Loreauville
Fontenot, Gerald J	Mamou
Gorenflo, Gabe	Baton Rouge
Gorenflo, James T (Jt)	Baton Rouge
Graves, Dan	Shreveport
Johnson, Gordon A.	Choudrant
Ki, Shiva	Baton Rouge
Laurent, Kermit	LaPlace
Leonard, Randy Joe	Sarepta
Mitchell, Max Dean And Ben	Leesville
Phillips, Dennis	Independence
Potier, Timothy F	Oberlin
Primos, Terry	Shreveport
Provenzano, Joseph D	Ponchatoula
Randall Jr., James W	Keithville
Randow, Ralph	Pineville
Reggio Jr., Sidney J	Sun
Sanders, Michael M	Ponchatoula
Tilton, John	Iowa
Trisler, Kenneth W	Rayville
Wiggins, Horace	Mansfield

MA

Dailey, G E	Seekonk
Dugdale, Daniel J.	Walpole
Entin, Robert	Boston
Gaudette, Linden L	Wilbraham
Gedraitis, Charles J	Holden
Grossman, Stewart	Clinton
Hinman, Theodore	Greenfield
Jarvis, Paul M	Cambridge
Khalsa, Jot Singh	Millis
Kubasek, John A	Easthampton
Lapen, Charles	W. Brookfield
Little, Larry	Spencer
Martin, Randall J	Bridgewater
Mcluin, Tom	Dracut
Moore, Michael Robert	Lowell
Olofson, Chris	Cambridge
Rebello, Indian George	New Bedford
Reed, Dave	Brimfield
Rizzi, Russell J	Ashfield
Saviano, James	Douglas
Siska, Jim	Westfield
Smith, J D	Roxbury
Szarek, Mark G	Revere
Vining, Bill	Methuen

MD

Bagley, R. Keith	White Plains
Barnes, Aubrey G.	Hagerstown
Barnes, Gary L.	New Windsor
Beers, Ray	Monkton
Bouse, D. Michael	Waldorf
Cohen, N J (Norm)	Baltimore
Dement, Larry	Prince Fredrick
Freiling, Albert J	Finksburg
Fuller, Jack A	New Market
Gossman, Scott	Forest Hill
Hart, Bill	Pasadena
Hendrickson, E Jay	Frederick
Hendrickson, Shawn	Knoxville
Hurt, William R	Frederick
Kreh, Lefty	"Cockeysville"
Kretsinger Jr., Philip W	Boonsboro
Mccarley, John	Taneytown
Mcgowan, Frank E	Sykesvile
Merchant, Ted	White Hall
Nicholson, R. Kent	Phoenix
Sentz, Mark C	Taneytown
Smit, Glenn	Aberdeen
Sontheimer, G Douglas	Potomac
Spickler, Gregory Noble	Sharpsburg
St. Clair, Thomas K	Monrovia
Walker, Bill	Stevensville
White, Gene E	Bethesda

ME

Ceprano, Peter J.	Auburn
Coombs Jr., Lamont	Bucksport
Courtois, Bryan	Saco
Gray, Daniel	Brownville
Hillman, Charles	Friendship
Leavitt Jr., Earl F	E. Boothbay
Oyster, Lowell R	Corinth
Sharrigan, Mudd	Wiscasset

MEXICO

Scheurer, Alfredo E Faes	C.P. 16010
Sunderland, Richard	
	Puerto Escondido Oaxaca
Young, Cliff San Miguel De Allende, GTO.	

MI

Ackerson, Robin E	Buchanan
Andrews, Eric	Grand Ledge
Arms, Eric	Tustin
Behnke, William	Kingsley
Bethke, Lora Sue	Grand Haven
Booth, Philip W	Ithaca
Buckbee, Donald M	Grayling
Canoy, Andrew B	Hubbard Lake
Carr, Tim	Muskegon
Carroll, Chad	Grant
Casey, Kevin	Hickory Corners
Cashen, Kevin R	Hubbardston
Cook, Mike A	Portland
Cousino, George	Onsted
Cowles, Don	Royal Oak
Dilluvio, Frank J	Warren
Ealy, Delbert	Indian River
Erickson, Walter E.	Atlanta
Gordon, Larry B	Farmington Hills
Gottage, Dante	Clinton Twp.
Gottage, Judy	Clinton Twp.
Harm, Paul W	Attica
Harrison, Brian	Cedarville
Hartman, Arlan (Lanny)	Baldwin
Hughes, Daryle	Nunica
Keranen, Paul	Ahmeek
Krause, Roy W	St. Clair Shores
Lankton, Scott	Ann Arbor
Leach, Mike J	Swartz Creek
Lucie, James R	Fruitport
Mankel, Kenneth	Cannonsburg
Marsh, Jeremy	Ada
Mills, Louis G	Ann Arbor
Noren, Douglas E	Springlake
Parker, Robert Nelson	Royal Oak
Repke, Mike	Bay City
Rose Ii, Doun T	Fife Lake
Sakmar, Mike	Howell
Sandberg, Ronald B	Browntown
Serven, Jim	Fostoria
Tally, Grant	Flat Rock
Van Eizenga, Jerry W	Nunica
Vasquez, Johnny David	Wyandotte
Viste, James	Detroit
Webster, Bill	Three Rivers
Welling, Ronald L	Grand Haven
White, Richard T	Grosse Pointe Farms
Whittaker, Wayne	Metamore
Whitworth, Ken J	Sterling Heights
Wood, Webster	Atlanta
Zowada, Tim	Boyne Falls

MN

Davis, Joel	Albert Lea
Goltz, Warren L	Ada
Griffin, Thomas J	Windom
Hagen, Doc	Pelican Rapids
Hansen, Robert W	Cambridge
Johnson, R B	Clearwater
Knipschield, Terry	Rochester
Maines, Jay	Wyoming
Metsala, Anthony	Princeton
Mickley, Tracy	North Mankato
Rydbom, Jeff	Annandale
Shadley, Eugene W	Bovey
Steffen, Chuck	St. Michael
Voorhies, Les	Faribault

MO

Allred, Elvan	St. Charles
Andrews, Russ	Sugar Creek
Betancourt, Antonio L.	St. Louis
Braschler, Craig W.	Doniphan
Buxton, Bill	Kaiser
Cover, Raymond A	Festus
Cox, Colin J	Raymore
Davis, W C	El Dorado Springs
Dippold, Al	Perryville
Ehrenberger, Daniel Robert	Mexico
Engle, William	Boonville
Hanson Iii, Don L.	Success
Harris, Jeffery A	Chesterfield
Harrison, Jim (Seamus)	St. Louis
Jones, John A	Holden
Kinnikin, Todd	House Springs
Knickmeyer, Hank	Cedar Hill
Knickmeyer, Kurt	Cedar Hill
Martin, Tony	Arcadia
Mason, Bill	Excelsior Springs
Mccrackin, Kevin	House Spings
Mccrackin And Son, V J	House Springs
Miller, Bob	Oakville
Mulkey, Gary	Branson
Muller, Jody	Goodson
Newcomb, Corbin	Moberly
Pryor, Stephen L	Boss
Ramsey, Richard A	Neosho
Rardon, A D	Polo
Rardon, Archie F	Polo
Riepe, Richard A	Harrisonville
Schirmer, Mike	Cherryville
Scroggs, James A	Warrensburg
Sonntag, Douglas W	Nixa
Steketee, Craig A	Billings
Stewart, Edward L	Mexico
Stormer, Bob	St. Peters
Warden, Roy A	Union
Whitesell, J. Dale	Stover
Willis, Bill	Ava

MS

Black, Scott	Picayune
Boleware, David	Carson
Davis, Jesse W	Sarah
Dickerson, Gordon S	New Augusta
Evans, Bruce A	Booneville
Flynt, Robert G	Gulfport
Jones, Jack P.	Ripley
Lamey, Robert M	Biloxi
Lebatard, Paul M	Vancleave
May, Charles	Aberdeen
Mayo Jr., Howard Alton	Biloxi
Pickett, Terrell	Lumberton
Roberts, Michael	Clinton
Robinson, Chuck	Picayune
Shiffer, Steve	Leakesville
Skow, H.A. "Tex"	Senatobia
Smith, J.B.	Perkinston
Taylor, Billy	Petal

Vandeventer, Terry L	Terry
Vardaman, Robert	Hattiesburg
Wehner, Rudy	Collins
Wingo, Perry	Gulfport
Winston, David	Starkville

MT

Barnes, Jack	Whitefish
Barnes, Wendell	Clinton
Barth, J.D.	Alberton
Beam, John R.	Kalispell
Beaty, Robert B.	Missoula
Bell, Don	Lincoln
Bizzell, Robert	Butte
Boxer, Bo	Whitefish
Brooks, Steve R	Walkerville
Caffrey, Edward J	Great Falls
Carlisle, Jeff	Simms
Christensen, Jon P	Shepherd
Colter, Wade	Colstrip
Conklin, George L	Ft. Benton
Crowder, Robert	Thompson Falls
Curtiss, Steve L	Eureka
Dunkerley, Rick	Seeley Lake
Eaton, Rick	Broadview
Ellefson, Joel	Manhattan
Fassio, Melvin G	Lolo
Forthofer, Pete	Whitefish
Fritz, Erik L	Forsyth
Gallagher, Barry	Lewistown
Harkins, J A	Conner
Hill, Howard E	Polson
Hintz, Gerald M	Helena
Hulett, Steve	West Yellowstone
Kajin, Al	Forsyth
Kauffman, Dave	Montana City
Luman, James R	Anaconda
Mcguane Iv, Thomas F	Bozeman
Mckee, Neil	Stevensville
Moyer, Russ	Havre
Munroe, Deryk C	Bozeman
Nedved, Dan	Kalispell
Parsons, Pete	Helena
Patrick, Willard C	Helena
Peele, Bryan	Thompson Falls
Peterson, Eldon G	Whitefish
Pursley, Aaron	Big Sandy
Robinson, Robert W	Polson
Rodewald, Gary	Hamilton
Ruana Knife Works,	Bonner
Smith, Josh	Frenchtown
Sweeney, Coltin D	Missoula
Taylor, Shane	Miles City
Thill, Jim	Missoula
Weinand, Gerome M	Missoula
Yashinski, John L	Red Lodge

NC

Baker, Herb	Eden
Barefoot, Joe W.	Wilmington
Best, Ron	Stokes
Britton, Tim	Bethania
Busfield, John	Roanoke Rapids
Coltrain, Larry D	Buxton
Daniel, Travis E	Chocowinity
Drew, Gerald	Mill Spring
Edwards, Fain E	Topton
Fox, Paul	Claremont
Gaddy, Gary Lee	Washington
Goguen, Scott	Newport
Goode, Brian	Shelby
Greene, Chris	Shelby
Gross, W W	Archdale
Gurganus, Carol	Colerain

Gurganus, Melvin H — Colerain
Guthrie, George B — Bassemer City
Hazen, Mark — Charlotte
Kommer, Russ — Fargo
Laramie, Mark — Raeford
Livingston, Robert C — Murphy
Maynard, William N. — Fayetteville
Mclurkin, Andrew — Raleigh
Mcnabb, Tommy — Bethania
Mcrae, J Michael — Mint Hill
Parrish, Robert — Weaverville
Patrick, Chuck — Brasstown
Patrick, Peggy — Brasstown
Rapp, Steven J — Marshall
Scholl, Tim — Angier
Simmons, H R — Aurora
Sterling, Murray — Mount Airy
Summers, Arthur L — Concord
Sutton, S Russell — New Bern
Vail, Dave — Hampstead
Wagaman, John K — Selma
Walker, Don — Burnsville
Warren, Daniel — Canton
Whitley, L Wayne — Chocowinity
Williamson, Tony — Siler City
Wilson, Mike — Hayesville
Winkler, Daniel — Blowing Rock

ND

Pitman, David — Williston

NE

Archer, Ray And Terri — Omaha
Jokerst, Charles — Omaha
Marlowe, Charles — Omaha
Moore, Jon P — Aurora
Mosier, Joshua J — Deshler
Robbins, Howard P — Elkhorn
Schepers, George B — Shelton
Suedmeier, Harlan — Nebraska City
Syslo, Chuck — Omaha
Tiensvold, Alan L — Rushville
Tiensvold, Jason — Rushville
Till, Calvin E And Ruth — Chadron

NETHERLANDS

Van Den Elsen, Gert — 5012 AJ Tilburg
Van Eldik, Frans — 3632BT Loenen
Van Rijswijk, Aad — 3132 AA Vlaardingen

NEW ZEALAND

Bassett, David J. — Glendene, Auckland 0645
Gunther, Eddie — 2013 Auckland
Pennington, C A — Kainga Christchurch 8009
Reddiex, Bill — Palmerston North
Ross, D L — Dunedin
Sandow, Norman E — Howick, Auckland
Sands, Scott — Christchurch 9
Van Dijk, Richard — Harwood Dunedin

NH

Carlson, Kelly — Antrim
Hill, Steve E — Goshen
Hitchmough, Howard — Peterborough
Hudson, C Robbin — Rummney
Macdonald, John — Raymond
Philippe, D A — Cornish
Saindon, R Bill — Goshen

NJ

Eden, Thomas — Cranbury
Grussenmeyer, Paul G — Cherry Hill
Kearney, Jarod — Bordentown
Licata, Steven — Boonton
Mccallen Jr., Howard H — So Seaside Park
Phillips, Jim — Williamstown
Polkowski, Al — Chester
Pressburger, Ramon — Howell
Schilling, Ellen — Hamilton Square
Sheets, Steven William — Mendham
Slee, Fred — Morganville
Viele, H J — Westwood
Yeskoo, Richard C — Summit

NM

Black, Tom — Albuquerque
Cherry, Frank J — Albuquerque
Cordova, Joseph G — Peralta
Cumming, Bob — Cedar Crest
Digangi, Joseph M — Santa Cruz
Duran, Jerry T — Albuquerque
Dyess, Eddie — Roswell
Fisher, Jay — Clovis
Goode, Bear — Navajo Dam
Gunter, Brad — Tijeras
Hartman, Tim — Albuquerque
Hethcoat, Don — Clovis
Hume, Don — Albuquerque
Kimberley, Richard L. — Santa Fe
Lewis, Tom R — Carlsbad
Lynn, Arthur — Galisteo
Macdonald, David — Los Lunas
Mcdonald, Robin J — Albuquerque
Meshejian, Mardi — Santa Fe
Rogers, Richard — Magdalena
Schaller, Anthony Brett — Albuquerque
Stalcup, Eddie — Gallup
Stetter, J. C. — Roswell
Terzuola, Robert — Albuquerque
Trujillo, Albert M B — Bosque Farms
Walker, Michael L — Pueblo Sur Taos
Wescott, Cody — Las Cruces

NORWAY

Bache-Wiig, Tom — Eivindvik
Sellevold, Harald — N5835 Bergen
Vistnes, Tor

NV

Barnett, Van — Reno
Beasley, Geneo — Wadsworth
Cameron, Ron G — Logandale
Dellana, — Reno
George, Tom — Henderson
Hrisoulas, Jim — Henderson
Kreibich, Donald L. — Reno
Mount, Don — Las Vegas
Nishiuchi, Melvin S — Las Vegas
Thomas, Devin — Panaca
Tracy, Bud — Reno
Washburn, Arthur D — Pioche

NY

Baker, Wild Bill — Boiceville
Castellucio, Rich — Amsterdam
Cute, Thomas — Cortland
Davis, Barry L — Castleton
Farr, Dan — Rochester
Faust, Dick — Rochester
Hobart, Gene — Windsor
Isgro, Jeffery — West Babylon
Johnson, Mike — Orient
Johnston, Dr. Robt — Rochester
Levin, Jack — Brooklyn
Loos, Henry C — New Hyde Park
Ludwig, Richard O — Maspeth
Lupole, Jamie G — Kirkwood
Maragni, Dan — Georgetown
Mccornock, Craig — Willow
Meerdink, Kurt — Barryville
Page, Reginald — Groveland
Pattay, Rudy — Long Beach
Peterson, Karen — Brooklyn
Phillips, Scott C — Gouverneur
Rachlin, Leslie S — Elmira
Rappazzo, Richard — Cohoes
Rotella, Richard A — Niagara Falls
Scheid, Maggie — Rochester
Schippnick, Jim — Sanborn
Serafen, Steven E — New Berlin
Skiff, Steven — Broadalbin
Smith, Lenard C — Valley Cottage
Smith, Raymond L — Erin
Summers, Dan — Whitney Pt.
Szilaski, Joseph — Pine Plains
Turner, Kevin — Montrose

OH

Bailey, Ryan — Galena
Bendik, John — Olmsted Falls
Busse, Jerry — Wauseon
Collins, Lynn M — Elyria
Coppins, Daniel — Cambridge
Cottrill, James I — Columbus
Downing, Tom — Cuyahoga Falls
Downs, James F — Powell
Etzler, John — Grafton
Foster, R L (Bob) — Mansfield
Francis, John D — Ft. Loramie
Franklin, Mike — Aberdeen
Geisler, Gary R — Clarksville
Gittinger, Raymond — Tiffin
Glover, Ron — Mason
Greiner, Richard — Green Springs
Hinderer, Rick — Shreve
Hudson, Anthony B — Amanda
Imboden Ii, Howard L. — Dayton
Jones, Roger Mudbone — Waverly
Kiefer, Tony — Pataskala
Longworth, Dave — Neville
Loro, Gene — Crooksville
Maienknecht, Stanley — Sardis
Mcdonald, Rich — Columbiana
Mcgroder, Patrick J — Madison
Mercer, Mike — Lebanon
Messer, David T — Dayton
Morgan, Tom — Beloit
O'Marchearley, Michael — Wilmington
Panak, Paul S — Kinsman
Potter, Billy — Dublin
Ralph, Darrel — Galena
Rose, Derek W — Gallipolis
Rowe, Fred — Amesville
Salley, John D — Tipp City
Schuchmann, Rick — Cincinnati
Shinosky, Andy — Canfield
Shoemaker, Carroll — Northup
Shoemaker, Scott — Miamisburg
Spinale, Richard — Lorain
Stoddart, W B Bill — Fairfield
Strong, Scott — Beavercreek
Summers, Dennis K — Springfield
Thomas, Kim — Seville
Thourot, Michael W — Napoleon

Tindera, George	Brunswick
Votaw, David P	Pioneer
Ward, J J	Waverly
Ward, Ron	Loveland
Warther, Dale	Dover
Witsaman, Earl	Stow
Wood, Larry B	Huber Heights
Wright, L T	Steubenville
Yurco, Mike	Canfield

OK

Baker, Ray	Sapulpa
Burke, Dan	Edmond
Carrillo, Dwaine	Moore
Crenshaw, Al	Eufaula
Damasteel Stainless Damascus, Norman	
Darby, David T	Cookson
Dill, Dave	Bethany
Duff, Bill	Poteau
Englebretson, George	Oklahoma City
Gepner, Don	Norman
Giraffebone Inc.,	Norman
Heimdale, J E	Tulsa
Johns, Rob	Enid
Kennedy Jr., Bill	Yukon
Kirk, Ray	Tahlequah
Lairson Sr., Jerry	Ringold
Martin, John Alexander	Okmulgee
Mcclure, Jerry	Norman
Menefee, Ricky Bob	Blawchard
Miller, Michael E	El Reno
Parsons, Larry	Mustang
Sanders, A.A.	Norman
Spivey, Jefferson	Yukon
Stanford, Perry	Broken Arrow
Tomberlin, Brion R	Norman
Wingo, Gary	Ramona

OR

Bell, Michael	Coquille
Bochman, Bruce	Grants Pass
Brandt, Martin W	Springfield
Buchanan, Thad	Prineville
Buchman, Bill	Bend
Buchner, Bill	Idleyld Park
Busch, Steve	Oakland
Cameron House,	Salem
Carter, Murray M	Vernonia
Clark, Nate	Yoncalla
Coon, Raymond C	Gresham
Davis, Terry	Sumpter
Dowell, T M	Bend
Frank, Heinrich H	Dallas
Gamble, Frank	Salem
Goddard, Wayne	Eugene
Harsey, William H	Creswell
Hilker, Thomas N	Williams
Horn, Jess	Eugene
Kelley, Gary	Aloha
Lake, Ron	Eugene
Little, Gary M	Broadbent
Lum, Robert W	Eugene
Martin, Gene	Williams
Martin, Walter E	Williams
Miller, Michael K	Sweet Home
Olson, Darrold E	Springfield
Richard, Raymond	Gresham
Richards, Chuck	Salem
Rider, David M	Eugene
Sarganis, Paul	Jacksonville
Scarrow, Wil	Gold Hill
Schoeningh, Mike	North Powder
Schrader, Robert	Bend
Sevey Custom Knife,	Gold Beach

Sheehy, Thomas J	Portland
Shoger, Mark O	Beaverton
Smith, Rick	Rogue River
Thompson, Leon	Gaston
Thompson, Tommy	Portland
Vallotton, Butch And Arey	Oakland
Vallotton, Rainy D	Umpqua
Vallotton, Shawn	Oakland
Vallotton, Thomas	Oakland
Ward, Ken	Grants Pass

PA

Anderson, Gary D	Spring Grove
Appleby, Robert	Shickshinny
Besedick, Frank E	Ruffsdale
Candrella, Joe	Warminster
Clark, D E (Lucky)	Johnstown
Corkum, Steve	Littlestown
Darby, Rick	Levittown
Evans, Ronald B	Middleton
Frey Jr., W Frederick	Milton
Godlesky, Bruce F.	Apollo
Goldberg, David	Ft Washington
Gottschalk, Gregory J	Carnegie
Harner, Lloyd R. "Butch"	Hanover
Heinz, John	Upper Black Eddy
Hudson, Rob	Northumberland
Johnson, John R	New Buffalo
Jones, Curtis J	Washington
Malloy, Joe	Freeland
Marlowe, Donald	Dover
Mensch, Larry C	Milton
Miller, Rick	Rockwood
Moore, Ted	Elizabethtown
Morett, Donald	Lancaster
Nealy, Bud	Stroudsburg
Neilson, J	Wyalusing
Nott, Ron P	Summerdale
Ogden, Bill	Avis
AVIS	
Ortega, Ben M	Wyoming
Parker, J E	Clarion
Root, Gary	Erie
Rupert, Bob	Clinton
Sass, Gary N	Sharpsville
Scimio, Bill	Spruce Creek
Sinclair, J E	Pittsburgh
Steigerwalt, Ken	Orangeville
Stroyan, Eric	Dalton
Takach, Andrew	Herminie
Valois, A. Daniel	Lehighton
Vaughan, Ian	Manheim
Whittaker, Robert E	Mill Creek
Wilson, Jon J	Johnstown

RI

Bardsley, Norman P.	Pawtucket
Dickison, Scott S	Portsmouth
Mchenry, William James	Wyoming
Olszewski, Stephen	Coventry
Williams, Jason L	Wyoming
Wright, Richard S	Carolina

RUSSIA

Kharlamov, Yuri	300007

SC

Beatty, Gordon H.	Seneca
Branton, Robert	Awendaw
Campbell, Courtnay M	Columbia
Cannady, Daniel L	Allendale
Cox, Sam	Gaffney

Denning, Geno	Gaston
Fecas, Stephen J	Anderson
Gainey, Hal	Greenwood
George, Harry	Aiken
Gregory, Michael	Belton
Hendrix, Jerry	Clinton
Hendrix, Wayne	Allendale
Hucks, Jerry	Moncks Corner
Kay, J Wallace	Liberty
Knight, Jason	Harleyville
Kreger, Thomas	Lugoff
Langley, Gene H	Florence
Lutz, Greg	Greenwood
Majer, Mike	Hilton Head
Manley, David W	Central
Mcmanus, Danny	Taylors
Miles Jr., C R "Iron Doctor"	Lugoff
Montjoy, Claude	Clinton
Odom Jr., Victor L.	North
Page, Larry	Aiken
Parler, Thomas O	Charleston
Peagler, Russ	Moncks Corner
Perry, Johnny	Inman
Sears, Mick	Kershaw
Smith, Ralph L	Taylors
Thomas, Rocky	Moncks Corner
Tyser, Ross	Spartanburg

SD

Boley, Jamie	Parker
Boysen, Raymond A	Rapid Ciy
Ferrier, Gregory K	Rapid City
Sarvis, Randall J	Fort Pierre
Thomsen, Loyd W	Oelrichs

SLOVAK REPUBLIC

Albert, Stefan	Filakovo 98604

SLOVAKIA

Bojtos, Arpad	98403 Lucenec
Kovacik, Robert	Lucenec 98407
Laoislav, Santa-Lasky	Bystrica
Mojzis, Julius	
Pulis, Vladimir	96701 Kremnica

SOUTH AFRICA

Arm-Ko Knives,	Marble Ray 4035 KZN
Baartman, George	Limpopo
Bauchop, Robert	Kwazulu-Natal 4278
Beukes, Tinus	Vereeniging 1939
Bezuidenhout, Buzz	
	Malvern, Queensburgh, Natal 4093
Boardman, Guy	New Germany 3619
Brown, Rob E	Port Elizabeth
Burger, Fred	Kwa-Zulu Natal
Dickerson, Gavin	Petit 1512
Fellows, Mike	Mosselbay 6500
Grey, Piet	Naboomspruit 0560
Harvey, Heather	Belfast 1100
Harvey, Kevin	Belfast 1100

South Africa

Herbst, Thinus	Karenpark 0118, Akasia

SOUTH AFRICA

Horn, Des	
Klaasee, Tinus	George 6530
Kojetin, W	Germiston 1401
Lagrange, Fanie	Table View 7441
Lancaster, C G	Free State

Liebenberg, Andre
Bordeauxrandburg 2196
Mackrill, Stephen JHB 2123
Mahomedy, A R Marble Ray KZN, 4035
Nelson, Tom Gauteng
Pienaar, Conrad Bloemfontein 9300
Prinsloo, Theuns Bethlehem, 9700
Rietveld, Bertie Magaliesburg 1791
Russell, Mick Port Elizabeth 6070
Schoeman, Corrie Danhof 9310
Steyn, Peter Freestate
Thorburn, Andre E.
Bela Bela, Warmbaths 0480
Van Der Westhuizen, Peter
Mossel Bay 6500
Van Heerden, AndreGarsfontein, Pretoria
Watson, Peter La Hoff 2570

SWEDEN

Bergh, Roger 91598 Bygdea
Billgren, Per
Eklund, Maihkel S-820 41 Farila
Embretsen, Kaj S-82830 Edsbyn
Hedlund, Anders Bradstad
Hogstrom, Anders T
Johansson, Anders
S-772 40 Grangesberg
Lundstrom, Jan-Ake 66010 Dals-Langed
Nilsson, Jonny Walker
SE-933 33 Arvidsjaur
Nordell, Ingemar 82041 Färila
Persson, Conny 820 50 Loos
Ryberg, Gote S-562 00 Norrahammar
Styrefors, Mattias
Vogt, Patrik S-30270 Halmstad

SWITZERLAND

Roulin, Charles 1233 Geneva
Soppera, Arthur CH-9631 Ulisbach

TN

Accawi, Fuad Clinton
Bailey, Joseph D. Nashville
Baker, Vance Riceville
Blanchard, G R (Gary) Pigeon Forge
Breed, Kim Clarksville
Byrd, Wesley L Evensville
Canter, Ronald E Jackson
Casteel, Dianna Monteagle
Casteel, Douglas Monteagle
Centofante, Frank Madisonville
Claiborne, Ron Knox
Clay, Wayne Pelham
Conley, Bob Jonesboro
Coogan, Robert Smithville
Corby, Harold Johnson City
Elder Jr., Perry B Clarksville
Ewing, John H Clinton
Harley, Larry W Bristol
Harley, Richard Bristol
Heflin, Christopher M Nashville
Hughes, Dan Spencer
Hurst, Jeff Rutledge
Hutcheson, John Chattanooga
Johnson, David A Pleasant Shade
Johnson, Ryan M Hixson
Kemp, Lawrence Ooletwah
Largin, Sevierville
Levine, Bob Tullahoma
Marshall, Stephen R Mt. Juliet
Mccarty, Harry Blaine
Mcdonald, W J "Jerry" Germantown
Moulton, Dusty Loudon

Raley, R. Wayne Collierville
Ramey, Larry Chapmansboro
Sampson, Lynn Jonesborough
Smith, Newman L. Gatlinburg
Taylor, C Gray Fall Branch
Taylor, David Rogersville
Vanderford, Carl G Columbia
Walker, John W Bon Aqua
Ward, W C Clinton
Wheeler, Gary Clarksville
Williams Jr., Richard Morristown
Winter, George Union City

TX

Adams, William D Burton
Alexander, Eugene Ganado
Allen, Mike "Whiskers" Malakoff
Appleton, Ron Bluff Dale
Ashby, Douglas Dallas
Barnes, Marlen R. Atlanta
Barr, Judson C. Irving
Batts, Keith Hooks
Blasingame, Robert Kilgore
Blum, Kenneth Brenham
Bradshaw, Bailey Diana
Bratcher, Brett Plantersville
Broadwell, David Wichita Falls
Brooks, Michael Lubbock
Bullard, Randall Canyon
Burden, James Burkburnett
Callahan, F Terry Boerne
Carey, Peter Lago Vista
Carpenter, Ronald W Jasper
Carter, Fred Wichita Falls
Champion, Robert Amarillo
Chase, John E Aledo
Chew, Larry Granbury
Churchman, T W (Tim) Bandera
Cole, James M Bartonville
Connor, John W Odessa
Connor, Michael Winters
Cosgrove, Charles G Arlington
Costa, Scott Spicewood
Crain, Jack W Granbury
Darcey, Chester L College Station
Davey, Kevin Boerne
Davidson, Jeff Haltom City
Davidson, Larry Cedar Hill
Davis, Vernon M Waco
Dean, Harvey J Rockdale
Dietz, Howard New Braunfels
Dominy, Chuck Colleyville
Dyer, David Granbury
Eldridge, Allan Ft. Worth
Elishewitz, Allen New Braunfels
Epting, Richard College Station
Eriksen, James Thorlief Garland
Evans, Carlton Fort Davis
Fant Jr., George Atlanta
Ferguson, Jim San Angelo
Fortune Products, Inc., Marble Falls
Foster, Al Magnolia
Foster, Norvell C Marion
Fowler, Jerry Hutto
Fritz, Jesse Slaton
Fuller, Bruce A Baytown
Gann, Tommy Canton
Garner, Larry W Tyler
Gault, Clay Lexington
George, Les Corpus Christi
Graham, Gordon New Boston
Green, Bill Sachse
Griffin, Rendon And Mark Houston
Guinn, Terry Seymour

Halfrich, Jerry San Marcos
Hamlet Jr., Johnny Clute
Hand, Bill Spearman
Hawkins, Buddy Texarkana
Hayes, Scotty Tesarkana
Haynes, Jerry Gunter
Hays, Mark Austin
Hemperley, Glen Willis
Hicks, Gary Tuscola
Howell, Jason G Lake Jackson
Hudson, Robert Humble
Hughes, Bill Texarkana
Hughes, Lawrence Plainview
Jackson, Charlton R San Antonio
Jaksik Jr., Michael Fredericksburg
Johnson, Gorden W Houston
Johnson, Ruffin Houston
Keller, Bill San Antonio
Kern, R W San Antonio
Kious, Joe Kerrville
Knipstein, R C (Joe) Arlington
Ladd, Jim S Deer Park
Ladd, Jimmie Lee Deer Park
Lambert, Jarrell D Granado
Laplante, Brett McKinney
Lay, L J Burkburnett
Lemcke, Jim L Houston
Lennon, Dale Alba
Lister Jr., Weldon E Boerne
Lively, Tim And Marian Marble Falls
Love, Ed San Antonio
Lovett, Michael Killeen
Luchak, Bob Channelview
Luckett, Bill Weatherford
Marshall, Glenn Mason
Martin, Michael W Beckville
Mcconnell Jr., Loyd A Odessa
Mellard, J R Houston
Merz Iii, Robert L Katy
Miller, R D Dallas
Mitchell, Wm Dean Warren
Moore, James B Ft. Stockton
Neely, Greg Bellaire
Nelson, Dr Carl Texarkana
Nolen, R D And Steve Pottsboro
Odgen, Randy W Houston
Ogletree Jr., Ben R Livingston
Osborne, Warren Waxahachie
Overeynder, T R Arlington
Ownby, John C Plano
Pardue, Joe Spurger
Patterson, Pat Barksdale
Pierce, Randall Arlington
Pollock, Wallace J Cedar Park
Polzien, Don Lubbock
Powell, James Texarkana
Pugh, Jim Azle
Ray, Alan W Lovelady
Richardson Jr., Percy Navasota
Roberts, Jack Houston
Robinson, Charles (Dickie) Vega
Ruple, William H Pleasanton
Ruth, Michael G Texarkana
Scott, Al Harper
Self, Ernie Dripping Springs
Shipley, Steven A Richardson
Sims, Bob Meridian
Sloan, Shane Newcastle
Smart, Steve McKinney
Snody, Mike Fredericksburg
Stokes, Ed Hockley
Stone, Jerry Lytle
Stout, Johnny New Braunfels
Summerlin, Danny Groves
Theis, Terry Harper

Thuesen, Ed	Damon
Treiber, Leon	Ingram
Truncali, Pete	Garland
Turcotte, Larry	Pampa
Van Reenen, Ian	Amarillo
Vecera, J R	Thrall
Ware, Tommy	Onalaska
Watson, Daniel	Driftwood
Watts, Johnathan	Gatesville
Watts, Wally	Gatesville
West, Pat	Charlotte
White, Dale	Sweetwater
Whitley, Weldon G	Odessa
Wilcher, Wendell L	Palestine
Wilkins, Mitchell	Montgomery
Wilson, Curtis M	Burleson
Wolf Jr., William Lynn	Lagrange
Yeates, Joe A	Spring
Zboril, Terry	Caldwell

UK

Hague, Geoff	Quarley, SP11 8PX

UNITED KINGDOM

Heasman, H G	Llandudno, N. Wales
Horne, Grace	Sheffield Britain
Maxen, Mick	"Hatfield, Herts"

URUGUAY

Gonzalez, Leonardo Williams	CP 20000
Symonds, Alberto E	Montevideo 11300

UT

Allred, Bruce F	Layton
Black, Earl	Salt Lake City
Ence, Jim	Richfield
Ennis, Ray	Ogden
Erickson, L.M.	Ogden
Hunter, Hyrum	Aurora
Johnson, Steven R	Manti
Maxfield, Lynn	Layton
Nielson, Jeff V	Monroe
Nunn, Gregory	Castle Valley
Palmer, Taylor	Blanding
Peterson, Chris	Salina
Strickland, Dale	Monroe
Velarde, Ricardo	Park City
Washburn Jr., Robert Lee	St George
Winn, Travis A.	Salt Lake City

VA

Apelt, Stacy E	Norfolk
Arbuckle, James M	Yorktown
Ballew, Dale	Bowling Green
Batley, Mark S.	Wake
Batson, Richard G.	Rixeyville
Beverly Ii, Larry H	Spotsylvania
Catoe, David R	Norfolk
Chamberlain, Charles R	Barren Springs
Davidson, Edmund	Goshen
Douglas, John J	Lynch Station
Eaton, Frank L Jr	Stafford
Foster, Burt	Bristol
Frazier, Ron	Powhatan
Harris, Cass	Bluemont
Hedrick, Don	Newport News
Hendricks, Samuel J	Maurertown
Herb, Martin	Richmond
Holloway, Paul	Norfolk
Jones, Barry M And Phillip G	Danville
Jones, Enoch	Warrenton

Martin, Herb	Richmond
Mccoun, Mark	DeWitt
Metheny, H A "Whitey"	Spotsylvania
Mills, Michael	Colonial Beach
Murski, Ray	Reston
Norfleet, Ross W	Providence Forge
Parks, Blane C	Woodbridge
Pawlowski, John R	Newport News
Schlueter, David	Madison Heights
Tomes, P J	Shipman
Vanhoy, Ed And Tanya	Abingdon
Vestal, Charles	Abingdon

VT

Haggerty, George S	Jacksonville
Kelso, Jim	Worcester

WA

Amoureux, A W	Northport
Begg, Todd M.	Spanaway
Ber, Dave	San Juan Island
Berglin, Bruce D	Mount Vernon
Boguszewski, Phil	Lakewood
Boyer, Mark	Bothell
Bromley, Peter	Spokane
Brothers, Robert L	Colville
Brown, Dennis G	Shoreline
Brunckhorst, Lyle	Bothell
Bump, Bruce D.	Walla Walla
Butler, John R	Shoreline
Campbell, Dick	Colville
Chamberlain, Jon A	E. Wenatchee
Conti, Jeffrey D	Bonney Lake
Conway, John	Kirkland
Crowthers, Mark F	Rolling Bay
D'Angelo, Laurence	Vancouver
Davis, John	Selah
Diskin, Matt	Freeland
Dole, Roger	Buckley
Evans, Vincent K And Grace	Cathlamet
Ferry, Tom	Auburn
Frey, Steve	Snohomish
Gray, Bob	Spokane
Greenfield, G O	Everett
Hansen, Lonnie	Spanaway
House, Gary	Ephrata
Hurst, Cole	E. Wenatchee
Keyes, Geoff P.	Duvall
Lisch, David K	Seattle
Lum, Mitch	Seattle
Norton, Don	Port Townsend
O'Malley, Daniel	Seattle
Padilla, Gary	Bellingham
Rader, Michael	Wilkeson
Rogers, Ray	Wauconda
Schempp, Ed	Ephrata
Schempp, Martin	Ephrata
Stegner, Wilbur G	Rochester
Sterling, Thomas J	Coupeville
Swyhart, Art	Klickitat
Wright, Kevin	Quilcene

Western Cape

Naude, Louis	Cape Town

WI

Boyes, Tom	Addison
Brandsey, Edward P	Janesville
Bruner Jr., Fred Bruner Blades	Fall Creek
Carr, Joseph E.	Menomonee Falls
Coats, Ken	Stevens Point
Delarosa, Jim	Janesville

Fiorini, Bill	DeSoto
Genske, Jay	Fond du Lac
Haines, Jeff Haines Custom Knives	
	Wauzeka
Hembrook, Ron	Neosho
Johnson, Richard	Germantown
Kanter, Michael	New Berlin
Kohls, Jerry	Princeton
Kolitz, Robert	Beaver Dam
Lary, Ed	Mosinee
Lerch, Matthew	Sussex
Maestri, Peter A	Spring Green
Martin, Peter	Waterford
Millard, Fred G	Richland Center
Nelson, Ken	Pittsville
Niemuth, Troy	Sheboygan
Ponzio, Doug	Beloit
Revishvili, Zaza	Madison
Ricke, Dave	West Bend
Rochford, Michael R	Dresser
Schrap, Robert G	Wauwatosa
Steinbrecher, Mark W	Pleasant Prairie
Wattelet, Michael A	Minocqua

WV

Bowen, Tilton	Baker
Derr, Herbert	St. Albans
Drost, Jason D	French Creek
Drost, Michael B	French Creek
Elliott, Jerry	Charleston
Jeffries, Robert W	Red House
Liegey, Kenneth R	Millwood
Maynard, Larry Joe	Crab Orchard
Morris, Eric	Beckley
Pickens, Selbert	Dunbar
Reynolds, Dave	Harrisville
Shaver Ii, James R	Parkersburg
Small, Ed	Keyser
Tokar, Daniel	Shepherdstown
Wilson, Rw	Weirton
Wyatt, William R	Rainelle

WY

Alexander, Darrel	Ten Sleep
Ankrom, W.E.	Cody
Banks, David L.	Riverton
Barry, Scott	Laramie
Bartlow, John	Sheridan
Bennett, Brett C	Cheyenne
Draper, Audra	Riverton
Draper, Mike	Riverton
Fowler, Ed A.	Riverton
Friedly, Dennis E	Cody
Justice, Shane	Sheridan
Kilby, Keith	Cody
Rexroat, Kirk	Wright
Reynolds, John C	Gillette
Rodebaugh, James L	Carpenter
Ross, Stephen	Evanston
Spragg, Wayne E	Lovell

ZIMBABWE

Burger, Pon	Bulawayo

Not all knifemakers are organization-types, but those listed here are in good standing with these organizations.

the knifemakers' guild

2009 voting membership

a Les Adams, Douglas A. Alcorn, Mike "Whiskers" Allen, Tom Anderson, W. E. Ankrom, Santino e Arlete Ballestra

b Norman P. Bardsley, A. T. Barr, James J. Barry, III, John Bartlow, Gene Baskett, Donald I. Bell, Tom Black, Gary Blanchard, Arpad Bojtos, Philip W. Booth, Tony Bose, Dennis Bradley, Gordon Gayle Bradley, Edward Brandsey, W. Lowell Bray, Jr., George Clint Breshears, Rick Browne, Fred Bruner, Jr., Jimmie H. Buckner, R. D. "Dan" Burke, Patrick R. Burris, John Busfield, Robert K. Bagley

c Ron G. Cameron, Daniel Cannady, Robert Capdepon, Harold J. "Kit" Carson, Casteel Custom Knives, Frank Centofante, Joel Chamblin, William Chapo, Alex W. Chase, Edward V. Chavar, William Cheatham, Howard F. Clark, Wayne Clay, Vernon W. Coleman, Blackie Collins, Bob F. Conley, Gerald Corbit, George Cousino, Colin J. Cox, Pat Crawford, Dan Cruze, Roy D. Cutchin

d Charles Dake, Alex K. Daniels, Jack Davenport, Edmund Davidson, Jim Davis, Kenneth D. Davis, Terry A. Davis, Vernon M. Davis, William C. Davis, Dan Dennehy, Herbert K. Derr, Joseph R. DeWitt, William J. Dietzel, Frank Dilluvio, Dippold Forge, David Dodds, Bob Doggett, Tracy Dotson, T. M. Dowell, Larry Downing, Tom Downing, James F. Downs, William Duff, Richard J. Dunkerley, Fred Durio, Ralph . D'Elia, Jr

e Easler Knives, Allen Elishewitz, Jim Elliott, David Ellis, William B. Ellis, William E. Engle, Viking Knives - James T. Eriksen, Carlton R. Evans

f Howard Faucheaux, Stephen J. Fecas, Lee Ferguson, Linda Ferguson, Jay Fisher, Derek B. Fraley, Franklin Custom Knives, John R Fraps, Ronald A. Frazier, Aaron Frederick, Dennis E. Friedly, Lynx Mountain View Estates - Larry Fuegen, Shun Fujikawa, Stanley Fujisaka, Tak Fukuta, Bruce A. Fuller, Shiro Furukawa

g Frank Gamble, Roger Gamble, Clay Gault, Charles Gedraitis, James "Hoot" Gibson,Sr., Warren Glover, Stefan Gobec, Warren L. Goltz, Gregory J. Gottschalk, Jockl Greiss, Kenneth W. Guth

h Philip (Doc) L. Hagen, The Malt House - Geoff Hague, Gerald Halfrich, Jeff Hall, Jim Hammond, Koji Hara, Larry Harley, Ralph Dewey Harris, Rade Hawkins, Henry Heitler, Glenn Hemperley, Earl Jay Hendrickson, Wayne Hendrix, Wayne G. Hensley, Don D. Hethcoat, Gil Hibben, Steven E. Hill, Harumi Hirayama, Steven W. Hoel, Kevin Hoffman, Miles (Jerry) G. Hossom, Durvyn Howard, Rob Hudson, Roy Humenick, Joseph Hytovick

i Billy Mace Imel, Michael Irie

j James T. Jacks, Paul Jarvis, Steve Jernigan, Brad Johnson, Ronald B. Johnson, Steven R. Johnson, William "Bill" C. Johnson, Enoch D. Jones

k William L. Keeton, Bill Kennedy, Jr., Jot Singh Khalsa, Harvey King, Jr., Bill King, Joe Kious, Roy W. Krause,

Dietmar Dietmar Kressler, John Kubasek

l Kermit Laurent, Gary E. Le Blanc, William L. Levengood, Bob Levine, Yakov Levin, Steve Linklater, Ken Linton, Wolfgang Loerchner, R. W. Loveless, Schuyler Lovestrand, Don Lozier, Gail Lunn, Larry Lunn, Ernest Lyle

m Stephen Mackrill, Joe Malloy, Jerry McClure, Loyd A. McConnell, Jr., Charles R. McConnell, Robert J. McDonald, W. J. McDonald, Frank McGowan, Mike Mercer, Ted Merchant, Robert L. Merz, III, Toshiaki Michinaka, Stephen C. Miller, Daniel J. Mink, Sidney "Pete" Moon, James B. Moore, Jeff Morgan

n Bud Nealy, Corbin Newcomb, Larry Newton, R. D. Nolen, Ingemar Nordell, Ross W Norfleet

o Charles F. Ochs, III, Ben R. Ogletree, Jr., Raymond Frank Oldham, Stephen C. Olszewski, Warren Osborne, T. R. Overeynder, John E. Owens, Jr.

p Larry Page, Joseph Pardue, Mel Pardue, Cliff Parker, Larry D. Patterson, John R. Pawlowski, W. D. Pease, Alfred Pendray, John W. Permar, John L. Perry, Daniel Piergallini, David F. Pitt, Leon M. Pittman, Otakar Pok, Alvin J. Polkowski, Joseph R. Prince, Theunis C. Prinsloo, Jim Pugh, Morris C. Pulliam

r James D. Ragsdale, Steven Rapp, John Reynolds, Ronald F. Richard, Dave Ricke, Michael Rochford, A. G. Russell

s Masaki Sakakibara, Michael A. Sakmar, Hiroyuki Sakurai, Scott W. Sawby, Juergen Schanz, Maurice & Alan Schrock, Steve Schwarzer, Mark C. Sentz, Yoshinori Seto, Eugene W. Shadley, James R. Shaver, II, Brad Shepherd, John I. Shore, Bill Simons, R. J. Sims, James E. Sinclair, Cleston S. Sinyard, Jim Siska, Scott Slobodian, J. D. Smith, John W. Smith, Ralph Smith, Marvin Solomon, James Sornberger, W. C. Sowell, David Steier, Kenneth A. Steigerwalt, Jurgen Steinau, Daniel L. Stephan, Murray Sterling, Johnny Stout, Keidoh Sugihara, Russ Sutton, Charles C. Syslo, Joseph Szilaski

t Grant Tally, Robert Terzuola, Leon Thompson, Dan Tompkins, John Toner, Bobby L. Toole, Dwight Towell, Leon Treiber, Reinhard Tschager, Ralph Turnbull, Arthur Tycer

v Louis Van De Walt, Frans Van Eldik, Aas van Rijswijk, Edward T. VanHoy, Ricardo Velarde, Donald Vogt

w George A. Walker, John W. Walker, Charles B. Ward, Dale E. Warther, Charles G. Weeber, John S. Weever, Weldon G. Whitley, Wayne Whittaker, Donnie R. Wicker, R. W. Wilson, Stan Wilson, Daniel Winkler, Richard S. Wright, Timothy Wright

y Yoshindo Yoshihara, George L. Young, John Young, Mike Yurco

z Brad Zinker, Michael Zschemy

abs mastersmith listing

a David Anders, Jerome Anders, Gary D. Anderson

b Bailey Bradshaw, Gary Barnes, Aubrey G. Barnes Sr., James L. Batson, Jimmie H. Buckner, Bruce Bump

c Ed Caffrey, Murray Carter, Kevin R. Cashen, Jon Christensen, Howard F. Clark, Wade Colter, Michael Connor, James R. Cook, Joseph G. Cordova, Jim Crowell

d Sava Damlovac, Harvey J. Dean, Christoph Deringer, Bill Dietzel, Audra L. Draper, Rick Dunkerley, Steve Dunn, Ken Durham

e Dave Ellise

f Robert Ferry, William Fiorini, Jerry Fisk, James O. Fister, John S. Fitch, Joe Flournoy, Don Fogg, Burt Foster, Ronnie Foster, Tim Foster, Ed Fowler, Larry Fuegen, Bruce A. Fuller, Jack A. Fuller

g Bert Gaston, Thomas Gerner, Wayne Goddard, Greg Gottschalk

h Ed Halligan, Timothy J. Hancock, Kevin Harvey, Heather Harvey, Wally Hayes, Charlie E. Haynes, E. Jay Hendrickson, Don Hethcoat, John Horrigan, C. Robbin Hudson

j Jim L. Jackson

k Joseph F. Keelsar, Keith Kilby, Ray Kirk, Hank Knickmeyer, Bob Kramer, Phil Kretsinger

l J.D. Lambert, Mick Langley, Jerry Lairson Sr.

m Dan Maragni, Chris J. Marks, John Martin, Roger D. Massey, Victor J. McCrackin, Hanford Miller, William Dean Mitchell

n Gregory T. Neely, Ron Newton, Doug Noren

o Charles F. Ochs III

p Alfred Pendray, John Perry, Dan L. Petersen, Timothy Potier

r James W. Randall Jr., Kirk Rexroat, Charles R. Robinson, James Rodebaugh, Raymond B. Rybar Jr.

s Stephen C. Schwarzer, Mark C. Sentz, J.D. Smith, Jousha J. Smith, Raymond L. Smith, H. Red St. Cry, Joseph Szilaski

t Shane Taylor, Jason Tiensvold, P.J. Tomes

v Michael V. Vagnino Jr., Terry Vandeventer

w James L. Walker, Michael L. Williams, Daniel Winkler

miniature knifemaker's society

Paul Abernathy, Gerald Bodner, Fred Cadwell, Barry Carithers, Kenneth Corey, Don Cowles, David J. Davis, Allen Eldridge, Linda Ferguson, Buddy Gaines, Larry Greenburg, Tom & Gwenn Guinn, Karl Hallberg, Bob Hergert, Laura Holmes, Brian Jacobson, Gary Kelley, R. F. Koebeman, Sterling Kopke, Gary E. Lack, Les Levinson, Henry C. Loos, Howard Maxwell, Mal Mele, Ray Mende, Toshiaki Michinaka, Paul Myer, Noriaki Narushima, Carol A. Olmsted, Allen R. Olsen, Charles Ostendorf, David Perkins, John Rakusan, Mark Rogers, Mary Ann Schultz, Jack Taylor, Valentin V. Timofeyev, Mike Viehman, Michael A. Wattelet, Kenneth P. Whitchard Jr., James D. Whitehead, Steve Williams, Carol A. Winold, Earl and Sue Witsaman, John Yashinski

professional knifemaker's association

Mike Allen, James Agnew, Usef Arie, Ray Archer, Eddie J. Baca, John Bartlow, Donald Bell, Brett C. Bennett, Tom Black, James E. Bliss, Philip Booth, Douglas Brack, Kenneth L. Brock, Ron Burke, Lucas Burnley, Ward Byrd, Craig Camerer, Tim S. Cameron, Ken Cardwell, Rod S. Carter, Del Corsi, Roger L. Craig, Joel Davis, John D. Dennehy, Dan Dennehy, Chester Deubel, Audra L. Draper, Mike J. Draper, Jim English, Ray W. Ennis, James T. Eriksen, Kirby Evers, Lee Ferguson, John Fraps, Scott Gere, Bob Glassman, Sal Glesser, Marge Hartman, Mike Henry, Don Hethcoat, Gary Hicks, Guy E. Hielscher, Alan Hodges, Mike L. Irie, David Johansen, Donald Jones, Jack Jones, Jot Singh Khalsa, Harvey King, Steve Kraft, Jim R. Largent, Ken Linton, Mike A. Lundemann, Jim Magee, Daniel May, Jerry & Sandy McClure, Clayton Miller, Skip Miller, Mark S. Molnar, Tyree L. Montell, Mike Mooney, Gary Moore, Steve Nolen, Rick Nowland, Fred A. Ott, Rob Patton, Dick Patton, James L. Poplin, Bill Redd, Dennis Riley, Terry Roberts, Steve Rollert, Charles R. Sauer, Jerry Schroeder, James Scroggs, Pete Semich, Eddie F. Stalcup, Craig Steketee, J.C. Stetter, Troy Taylor, Robert Terzuola, Roy Thompson, Loyd W. Thomsen, Jim D. Thrash, Ed Thuesen, Dick Waites, Mark Waites, Bill Waldrup, Tommy Ware, David Wattenberg, Hans Weinmueller, Dan Westlind, Harold J. Wheeler, RW Wilson, Denise Wolford, Michael C. Young, Monte Zavatta, Michael F. Zima, Daniel F. Zvonek

state/regional associations

alaska interior knifemakers association
Frank Ownby, Fred DeCicco, Bob Hook, Jenny Day, Kent Setzer, Kevin Busk, Loren Wellnite, Mark Knapp, Matthew Hanson, Mel Harvey, Nate Miller, Richard Kacsur, Ron Miller, Terry Miller, Bob LaFrance, Randy Olsen

alaska knifemakers association
A.W. Amoureux, John Arnold, Bud Aufdermauer, Robert Ball, J.D. Biggs, Lonnie Breuer, Tom Broome, Mark Bucholz, Irvin Campbell, Virgil Campbell, Raymond Cannon, Christopher Cawthorne, John Chamberlin, Bill Chatwood, George Cubic, Bob Cunningham, Gordon S. Dempsey, J.L. Devoll, James Dick, Art Dufour, Alan Eaker, Norm Grant, Gordon Grebe, Dave Highers, Alex Hunt, Dwight Jenkins, Hank Kubaiko, Bill Lance, Bob Levine, Michael Miller, John Palowski, Gordon Parrish, Mark W. Phillips, Frank Pratt, Guy Recknagle, Ron Robertson, Steve Robertson, Red Rowell, Dave Smith, Roger E. Smith, Gary R. Stafford, Keith Stegall, Wilbur Stegner, Norm Story, Robert D. Shaw, Thomas Trujillo, Ulys Whalen, Jim Whitman, Bob Willis

arizona knifemakers association
D. "Butch" Beaver, Bill Cheatham, Dan Dagget, Tom Edwards, Anthony Goddard, Steve Hoel, Ken McFall, Milford Oliver, Jerry Poletis, Merle Poteet, Mike Quinn, Elmer Sams, Jim Sornberger, Glen Stockton, Bruce Thompson, Sandy Tudor, Charles Weiss

arkansas knifemakers association
David Anders, Auston Baggs, Don Bailey, Reggie Barker, Marlen R. Barnes, Paul Charles Basch, Lora Sue Bethke, James Black, R.P. Black, Joel Bradford, Gary Braswell, Paul Brown, Shawn Brown, Troy L. Brown, Jim Butler, Buddy Cabe, Allen Conner, James Cook, Thom Copeland, Gary L. Crowder, Jim Crowell, David T. Darby, Fred Duvall, Rodger Echols, David Etchieson, Lee Ferguson, Jerry Fisk, John Fitch, Joe & Gwen Flournoy, Dewayne Forrester, John Fortenbury, Ronnie Foster, Tim Foster, Emmet Gadberry, Larry Garner, Ed Gentis, Paul Giller, James T. Gilmore, Terry Glassco, D.R. (Rick) Gregg, Lynn Griffith, Arthur J. Gunn, Jr., David Gunnell, Morris Herring, Don "Possum" Hicks, Jim Howington, B. R. Hughes, Ray Kirk, Douglas Knight, Lile Handmade Knives, Jerry Lairson Sr., Claude Lambert, Alton Lawrence, Jim Lemcke, Michael H. Lewis, Willard Long, Dr. Jim Lucie, Hal W. Martin, Tony Martin, Roger D. Massey, Douglas Mays, Howard McCallen Jr., Jerry McClure, John McKeehan, Joe McVay, Bart Messina, Thomas V. Militano, Jim Moore, Jody Muller, Greg Neely, Ron Newton, Douglas Noren, Keith Page, Jimmy Passmore,

John Perry, Lloyd "Pete" Peterson, Cliff Polk, Terry Primos, Paul E. Pyle Jr., Ted Quandt, Vernon Red, Tim Richardson, Dennis Riley, Terry Roberts, Charles R. Robinson, Kenny Rowe, Mike Ruth, Ken Sharp, Terry Shurtleff, Roy Slaughter, Joe D. Smith, Marvin Solomon, Hoy Spear, Charles Stout, Arthur Tycer, Ross Tyser, James Walker, Chuck Ward, Herman Waters, Bryce White, Tillmon T. Whitley III, Mike Williams, Rick Wilson, Terry Wright, Ray Young

australian knifemakers guild inc.

Peter Bald, Col Barn, Wayne Barrett, Alistair Bastian, David Brodziak, Stuart Burdett, Terry Cox, John Creedy, Malcolm Day, John Deering, Peter Del Raso, Glen Drane, Michael Fechner, John Foxwell, Keith Fludder, Adam Fromholtz, Thomas Gerner, Peter Gordon, Stephen Gregory-Jones, Barry Gunston, Karim Haddad, Frank Heine, Glen Henke, Michael Hint, Douglas Jarrett, Dean Johnson, John Jones, Wolf Kahrau, Peter Kandavnieks, Peter Kenney, Tasman Kerley, John Kilby, Robert Klitscher, Greg Lyell, Maurice McCarthy, Shawn McIntyre, Alex Mead, Ray Mende, Richard Moase, Dave Myhill, Adam Parker, Mike Petersen, Murray Shanaughan, Gary Siemer, Peter Spann, Rod Stines, Jim Steele, David Strickland, Doug Timbs, Hardy Wangemann, Brendon Ware, Bob Wilhelm, Kwong Yeang, Ross Yeats

california knifemakers association

Arnie Abegg, George J. Antinarelli, Elmer Art, Gregory Barnes, Mary Michael Barnes, Hunter Baskins, Gary Biggers, Roger Bost, Clint Breshears, Buzz Brooks, Steven E. Bunyea, Peter Carey, Joe Caswell, Frank Clay, Richard Clow, T.C. Collins, Richard Corbaley, Stephanie Engnath, Alex Felix, Jim Ferguson, Dave Flowers, Logwood Gion, Peter Gion, Joseph Girtner, Tony Gonzales, Russ Green, Tony Guarnera, Bruce Guidry, Dolores Hayes, Bill Herndon, Neal A. Hodges, Richard Hull, Jim Jacks, Lawrence Johnson, David Kazsuk, James P. Kelley, Richard D. Keyes, Michael P. Klein, Steven Koster, John Kray, Bud Lang, Tomas N. Lewis, R.W. Loveless, John Mackie, Thomas Markey, James K. Mattis, Toni S. Mattis, Patrick T. McGrath, Larry McLean, Jim Merritt, Greg Miller, Walt Modest, Russ Moody, Emil Morgan, Gerald Morgan, Mike Murphy, Thomas Orth, Tom Paar, Daniel Pearlman, Mel Peters, Barry Evan Posner, John Radovich, James L. Rodebaugh, Clark D. Rozas, Ron Ruppe, Brian Saffran, Red St. Cyr, James Stankovich, Bill Stroman, Tony Swatton, Gary Tamms, James P. Tarozon, Scott Taylor, Tru-Grit Inc., Tommy Voss, Jessie C. Ward, Wayne Watanabe, Charles Weiss, Steven A. Williams, Harlan M. Willson, Steve Wolf, Barry B. Wood

canadian knifemakers guild

Gaetan Beauchamp, Shawn Belanger, Don Bell, Brent Beshara, Dave Bolton, Conrad Bondu, Darren Chard, Garry Churchill, Guillaume J. Cote, Christoph Deringer, Jeff Diotte, Randy Doucette, Jim Downie, John Dorrell, Eric Elson, Lloyd Fairbairn, Paul-Aime Fortier, Rick Frigault, John Freeman, Mark Garvock, Brian Gilbert, Murray Haday, Tom Hart, Thomas Haslinger, Ian Hubel, Paul Johnston (London, Ont.), Paul Johnston (Smith Falls, Ont.), Jason Kilcup, Kirby Lambert, Greg Lightfoot, Jodi Link, Wolfgang Loerchner, Mel Long, Brian Lyttle, David Macdonald, Michael Mason, Alan Massey, Leigh Maulson, James McGowan, Edward McRae, Mike Mossington, Sean O'Hare, Rod Olson, Neil Ostroff, Ron Post, George Roberts, Brian Russell, Murray St. Armour, Michael Sheppard, Corey Smith, David Smith, Jerry Smith, Walt Stockdale, Matt Stocker, Ed Storch, Steve Stuart, George Tichbourne, Brian Tighe, Robert Tremblay, Glenn Treml, Steve Vanderkloff, James Wade, Bud Weston, Peter Wile

florida knifemaker's association

Dick Atkinson, Barney Barnett, James J. Barry III, Dawayne Batten, Howard Bishop, Andy Blackton, Dennis Blaine, Dennis Blankenhem, Dr. Stephen A. Bloom, Dean Bosworth, John Boyce, Bill Brantley, W. Lowell Bray Jr., Patrick Burris, Norman J. Caesar, Steve Christian, Mark Clark, Lowell Cobb, William Cody, David Cole, Steve Corn, David Cross, Jack Davenport, Kevin Davey, J.D. Davis, Kenny Davis, Ralph D'Elia, Bob Doggett, Jim Elliot, William Ellis, Tom M. Enos, Jon Feazell, Mike Fisher, Todd Fisher, Roger Gamble, James "Hoot" Gibson, Pedro Gonzalez, Ernie Grospitch, Fred Harrington, Dewey Harris, Henry Heitler, Kevin Hoffman, Edward O. Holloway, Stewart Holloway, Joe Hytovick, Tom Johanning, Raymond C. Johnson II, Richard Johnson, Roy Kelleher, Paul S. Kent, Bill King, F.D. Kingery, John E. Klingensmith, William S. Letcher, Bill Levengood, Glenn Long, Gail Lunn, Larry Lunn, Ernie Lyle, Bob Mancuso, Joe Mandt, Kevin A. Manley, Michael Matthews, Jim McNeil, Faustina Mead,

Steve Miller, Dan Mink, Steven Morefield, Martin L. "Les" Murphy, Gary Nelson, Larry Newton, Toby Nipper, Praddep Singh Parihar, Cliff Parker, Larry Patterson, Dan Piergallini, Martin Prudente, Bud Pruitt, John "Mickey" Reed, Terry Lee Renner, Roberto Sanchez, Rusty Sauls, Dennis J. Savage, David Semones, Ann Sheffield, Brad Shepherd, Bill Simons, Stephen J. Smith, Kent Swicegood, Tim Tabor, Michael Tison, Ralph Turnbull, Louis M. Vallet, Donald Vogt, Reese Weiland Jr., Travis Williamson, Stan Wilson, Denny & Maggie Young, Brad Zinker

georgia custom knifemakers' guild

Don Adams, Aaron Brewer, Henry Cambron, Frank Chikey, John Costa, Scott Davison, Steve Davis, Carroll Dutton, Emory Fennell, Brent Fisher, Dewayne Frost, Buddy Gaines, Dean Gates, Warren Glover, George Hancox, Wayne Hensley, Franklin Jones, Alvin Kinsey, Charlie Mathews, Harry Mathews, Leroy Mathews, Dan Mink, James Mitchell, Sandy Morrissey, Joan Poythress, Carey Quinn, Carl Rechsteiner, Joe Sangster, Jamey Saunders, Ken Simmons, Brad Singley, Jim Small, Bill Snow, Pat Steadman, Kathleen Tomey, Don Tommey, David Turner, Alex Whetsel, Garrett White, Gerald White, Ryan Whittemore, Richard Wittman

knife group association of oklahoma

David Anders, Rocky Anderson, Wally Armstrong, Jerry Barlow, Troy Brown, Tom Buchanan, Jayson H. Bucy, Tony Cable, Dawnavan Crawford, Gary Crowder, Steve Culver, David Darby, Lynn Drury, Bill Duff, David Etchieson, Harry Fentress, Lee Ferguson, Linda Ferguson, Randy Folks, Daniel Fulk, Michael Gibbons, Darren Gower, Paul Happy, Bob Hathaway, Billy Helton, Ed Hites, David Horton, Ed Jones, Les Jones, Jim Keen, Bill Kennedy, Barbara Kirk, Ray Kirk, Reese Lane, Jerry Lairson, Sr., Al Lawrence, Jerry Ligon, Aidan Martin, Barbara Martin, Duncan Martin, John Martin, Jerry McClure, Sandy McClure, Rick Menefee, Michael E. Miller, Ray Milligan, Duane Morganflash, Gary Mulkey, Jerald Nickels, Darrel Parent, Jerry Parkhurst, Chris Parson, Larry Parsons, Jerry Paul, Larry Paulen, Paul Piccola, Cliff Polk, Rusty Polk, Roland Quimby, Ron Reeves, Justin Reichert, Lin Rhea, Dan Schneringer, Terry Schreiner, Allen Shafer, Charlie Smith, Clifford Smith, Doug Sonntag, Mike Stegall, Gary Steinmetz, Bob Tidwell, Brian Tomberlin, Chuck Ward, Jesse Webb, Rob Weber, Joe Wheeler, Joe Wilkie, Larry Winegar, Gary Wingo

knifemakers' guild of southern africa

Jeff Angelo, John Arnold, George Baartman, Francois Basson, Rob Bauchop, George Beechey, Arno Bernard, Buzz Bezuidenhout, Harucus Blomerus, Chris Booysen, Thinus Bothma, Ian Bottomley, Peet Bronkhorst, Rob Brown, Fred Burger, Sharon Burger, Trevor Burger, William Burger, Brian Coetzee, Larry Connelly, Andre de Beer, André de Villiers, Melodie de Witt, Gavin Dickerson, Roy Dunseith, Mike Fellows, Leigh Fogarty, Werner Fourie, Andrew Frankland, Brian Geyer, Ettoré Gianferrari, Dale Goldschmidt, Stan Gordon, Nick Grabe, John Grey, Piet Gray, Heather Harvey, Kevin Harvey, Dries Hattingh, Gawie Herbst, Thinus Herbst, Greg Hesslewood, Des Horn, Nkosi Jubane, Billy Kojetin, Mark Kretschmer, Steven Lewis, Garry Lombard, Steve Lombard, Ken Madden, Abdur-Rasheed Mahomedy, Peter Mason, Edward Mitchell, George Muller, Günther Muller, Tom Nelson, Andries Olivier, Jan Olivier, Christo Oosthuizen, Cedric Pannell, Willie Paulsen, Nico Pelzer, Conrad Pienaar, David Pienaar, Jan Potgieter, Lourens Prinsloo, Theuns Prinsloo, Hilton Purvis, Derek Rausch, Chris Reeve, Bertie Rietveld, Melinda Rietveld, Dean Riley, John Robertson, Corrie Schoeman, Eddie Scott, Harvey Silk, Mike Skellern, Toi Skellern, Carel Smith, Ken Smythe, Graham Sparks, Peter Steyn, André Thorburn, Hennie Van Brakel, Fanie Van Der Linde, Johan van der Merwe, Van van der Merwe, Marius Van der Vyver, Louis Van der Walt, Cor Van Ellinckhuijzen, Andre van Heerden, Danie Van Wyk, Ben Venter, Willie Venter, Gert Vermaak, René Vermeulen, Erich Vosloo, Desmond Waldeck, Albie Wantenaar, Henning Wilkinson, John Wilmot, Wollie Wolfaardt, Owen Wood

midwest knifemakers association

E.R. Andrews III, Frank Berlin, Charles Bolton, Tony Cates, Mike Chesterman, Ron Duncan, Larry Duvall, Bobby Eades, Jackie Emanuel, James Haynes, John Jones, Mickey Koval, Ron Lichlyter, George Martoncik, Gene Millard, William Miller, Corbin Newcomb, Chris Owen, A.D. Rardon, Archie Rardon, Max Smith, Ed Stewart, Charles Syslo, Melvin Williams

montana knifemaker's association
Peter C. Albert, Chet Allinson, Marvin Allinson, Tim & Sharyl Alverson, Bill Amoureux, Jan Anderson, Wendell Barnes, Jim & Kay Barth, Bob & Marian Beaty, Don Bell, Brett Bennett, Robert Bizzell, BladeGallery, Paul Bos, Daryl & Anna May Boyd, Chuck Bragg, Frederick Branch, Peter Bromley, Bruce Brown, Emil Bucharksky, Bruce & Kay Bump, Bill Burke, Alpha Knife Supply Bybee, Ed Caffrey, Jim & Kate Carroll, Murray Carter, Jon & Brenda Christensen, Norm Cotterman, Seith Coughlin, Bob Crowder, Mike Dalimata, John Davis, Maria DesJardins, Rich & Jacque Duxbury, Dan Erickson, Mel & Darlene Fassio, E.V. Ford, Eric Fritz, Dana & Sandy Hackney, Doc & Lil Hagen, Gary & Betsy Hannon, Eli Hansen, J.A. Harkins, Tedd Harris, Sam & Joy Hensen, Loren Higgins, Mickey Hines, Gerald & Pamela Hintz, Gary House, Tori Howe, Kevin Hutchins, Al Inman, Frank & Shelley Jacobs, Karl Jermunson, Keith Johnson, Don Kaschmitter, Steven Kelly, Dan & Penny Kendrick, Monte Koppes, Donald Kreuger, David Lisch, James Luman, Robert Martin, Max McCarter, Neil McKee, Larry McLaughlin, Mac & Nancy McLaughlin, Phillip Moen, Gerald Morgan, Randy Morgan, Dan & Andrea Nedved, Daniel O'Malley, Joe Olson, Collin Paterson, Willard & Mark Patrick, Jeffrey & Tyler Pearson, Brian Pender, James Poling, Chance & Kerri Priest, Richard Prusz, Greg Rabatin, Jim Raymond, Jim Rayner, Darren Reeves, John Reynolds, Ryan Robison, Gary Rodewald, Buster Ross, Ruana Knifeworks, Charles Sauer, Dean Schroeder, Michael Sheperes, Mike Smith, Gordon St. Clair, Terry Steigers, George Stemple, Dan & Judy Stucky, Art & Linda Swyhart, Jim Thill, Cary Thomas, James & Tammy Venne, Bill & Lori Waldrup, Jonathan & Doris Walther, Kenneth Ward, Michael Wattelet, Darlene Weinand, Gerome & Darlene Weinand, Daniel & Donna Westlind, Matt & Michelle Whitmus, Dave Wilkes, Mike & Sean Young

national independent cutlery association
Ron & Patsy Beck, Bob Bennett, Dave Bishop, Steve Corn, Dave Harvey, C.J. McKay, Mike Murray, Gary Parker, Rachel Schindler, Joe Tarbell

new england bladesmiths guild
Phillip Baldwin, Gary Barnes, Paul Champagne, Jimmy Fikes, Don Fogg, Larry Fuegen, Rob Hudson, Midk Langley, Louis Mills, Dan Maragni, Jim Schmidt, Wayne Valachovic and Tim Zowada

north carolina custom knifemakers' guild
Douglas M. Bailey, Lester "Red" Banks, Robert E. Barber, Dr. James Batson, Wayne Bernauer, William M. Bisher, Tim Britton, Richard Brown, E. Gene Calloway, Joe Corbin, Gary W. Cunningham, Travis Daniel, Rob Davis, Jim A. Decoster, Geno Denning, David W. Diggs, Charles F. Fogarty, Alan Folts, Phillip L. Gaddy, Jim L. Gardner, Norman A. Gervais, Ed Halligan, Robert R. Ham, Koji Hara, Cap Hayes, John B. Hege, Mark Hazen, Mark R. Henry, Terrill Hoffman, Jesse Houser, Jr., B.R. Hughes, Dan Johnson, Tommy Johnson, Barry & Phillip Jones, Frank Joyce, Jacob Kelly, Tony Kelly, Robert Knight, Dr. Jim Lucie, Gerry McGinnis, Dave McKeithan, Andrew McLurkin, Tommy McNabb, Michael McRae, William T. Morris, Ron Newton, Calvin Nichols, Victor L. Odom Jr., Charles Ostendorf, Cory Owens, Avery Parker, Howard Peacock, James Poplin, Murphy G. Ragsdale, William B. Roberson, Henry Clay Runion, Bruce M. Ryan, Steve Sallee, Tim Scholl, Danks Seel, Andy D. Sharpe, J. Wayne Short, Harland & Karen Simmons, Ken Simmons, Richard M. Snelling, Johnnie Sorrell, Chuck Staples Jr., Murray Sterling, Russ Sutton, Kathleen Tomey, Bruce Turner, Dave Vail, Ed & Tanya VanHoy, Wayne Whitley, James A. Williams, L.E. Wilson, Daniel Winkler, Rob Wotzak

ohio knifemakers association
Raymond Babcock, Van Barnett, Harold A. Collins, Larry Detty, Tom Downing, Jim Downs, Patty Ferrier, Jeff Flannery, James Fray, Bob Foster, Raymond Guess, Scott Hamrie, Rick Hinderer, Curtis Hurley, Ed Kalfayan, Michael Koval, Judy Koval, Larry Lunn, Stanley Maienknecht, Dave Marlott, Mike Mercer, David Morton, Patrick McGroder, Charles Pratt, Darrel Ralph, Roy Roddy, Carroll Shoemaker, John Smith, Clifton Smith, Art Summers, Jan Summers, Donald Tess, Dale Warther, John Wallingford, Earl Witsaman, Joanne Yurco, Mike Yurco

saskatchewan knifemakers guild
Marty Beets, Art Benson, Doug Binns, Darren Breitkrenz, Clarence Broeksma, Irv Brunas, Emil Bucharsky, Ernie Cardinal, Raymond Caron, Faron Comaniuk, Murray Cook, Sanford Crickett, Jim Dahlin, Herb Davison, Kevin Donald, Brian Drayton, Dallas Dreger, Roger Eagles, Brian Easton, Marvin Engel, Ray Fehler, Rob Fehler, Ken Friedrick, Calvin Granshorn, Vernon Ganshorn, Dale Garling, Alan Goode, Dave Goertz, Darren Greenfield, Gary Greer, Jay Hale, Wayne Hamilton, Phil Haughian, Robert Hazell, Bryan Hebb, Daug Heuer, Garth Hindmarch, John R. Hopkins, Lavern Ilg, Clifford Kaufmann, Meryl Klassen, Bob Kowalke, Todd Kreics, Donald Krueger, Paul Laronge, Patricia Leahy, Ron Lockhart, Pat Macnamara, Benjamin Manton, Ed Mcrac, Len Meeres, Randy Merkley, Arnold Miller, Robert Minnes, Ron Nelson, Brian Obrigewitsch, Bryan Olafson, Blaine Parrry, Doug Peltier, Darryl Perlett, Dean Pickrell, Barry Popick, Jim Quickfall, Bob Robson, Gerry Rush, Geoff Rutledge, Carl Sali, Kim Senft, Eugene Schreiner, Curtis Silzer, Christopher Silzer, David Silzer, Kent Silzer, Don Spasoff, Bob Stewart, Dan Stinnen, Lorne Stadyk, Eugene R. Thompson, Ron Wall, Ken Watt, Trevor, Whitfield, David Wilkes, Merle Williams, Gerry Wozencroft, Ed Zelter, Al Zerr, Brian Zerr, Ronald Zinkhan

south carolina association of knifemakers
Douglas Bailey, Ken Black, Bobby Branton, Gordo Brooks, Richard Bridwell, Daniel Cannaday, Rodger F. Casey, Thomas H. Clegg, John Conn, Allen Corbett, Bill Dauksch, Geno Denning, Charlie Douan, Perry B. Elder Jr., Gene Ellison, Eddy T. Elsmore, Robbie D. Estabrook Jr., Lewis A. Fowler, Jim Frazier, Tally Grant, Jerry G. Hendrix, Wayne Hendrix, George Herron (in memory), Jerry T. Hucks, Johnny Johnson, Lonnie L. Jones, John Keaton, Thomas D. Kreger, Gene Langley, Tommy B. Lee, David Manley, Bill M. Massey, C.R. Miles, Gene Miller, Claude Montjoy, Patrick H. Morgan, Barry L. Myers, Paul G. Nystrom Jr., Lee O'Quinn, Victor L. Odom Jr., Larry Page, James C. Rabb, Ricky Rankin, Rick Rockwood, John M. Sarratt, Gene Scaffe, Mick Sears, David Stroud, Robert Stuckey, Rocky Thomas, Allen Timmons, Justin Walker, Mickey Walker, Woody Walker, H. Syd Willis Jr.

tennessee knifemakers association
John Bartlow, Doug Casteel, Harold Crisp, Larry Harley, John W. Walker, Harold Woodward, Harold Wright

texas knifemakers & collectors association
Dwyane A. Bandy, Ed Barker, Zane W. Blackwell, Robert Blassingame, Tim Bradberry, Gayle Bradley, Craig Brewer, Stanley G. Buzek, Daniel J. Cassidy, David Childers, Emil R. Colmenares, Stephen J. Conway, Ed Crater, Steward P. Crawford, Chester L. Darcey, Wesley W. Davis, Harvey J. Dean, James E. Drouillard II, Allen Elishewitz, Richard G. Eptin, Carlton R. Evans, Jesse H. Everett Jr., Jeffrey Feller, Christopher Flo, Bill Fotte, Norvell C. Foster, Theodore G. Freisenhahn, Emiliano Garcia, Mark Grimes, Don Halter, Johnny Hamlet, Bill Hand, Glenn Hemperley, Robert Hensarling, Roy Hinds, Jason Howell, Karl Jakubik, Jose Jalomo, Jr., Bill Keller, Greg Ledet, Jim Lemcke, Dale Lennon, Ken Linton, Charlie O. Majors, Glenn Marshall, Roger McBee, Jerry McClure, Sandy McClure, Larry A. Meyers, Bill Middlebrook, Perry W. Miller, Richard G. Morgan, Don Morrow, Guy W. Nelson, Mike O'Brien, Warren Osborne, Ed Osorio, Tom R. Overeynder, John Ownby, Glenn Parks, Pat Patterson, William P. Petersen III, Benjamin Paul, Piccola, Wallace J. Pollock, Rusty Presgon, Don Robinson, Michael J. Rudolph, Bill Ruple, Merle L. Rush, James A. Schiller, Richard Self, Scott K. Stevens, Johnny L. Stout, Gene Tedford, John Thompson, Jason C. Tippy, Turner E. Touchton Jr., Don Townsend, Leon Treiber, Larry Turcotte, Carlos R. Valenzuela, Ian Van Reenen, John Venier, Jeffery A. Vesley, Ray R. Villarreal, Bruce Voyles, Harold A. Waddle, Harold Wheeler, Weldon Whitley, Steve Woods, John Woody, Forrest M. Young

photo index

The firms listed here are special in the sense that they make or market special kinds of knives made in facilities they own or control either in the U.S. or overseas. Or they are special because they make knives of unique design or function. The second phone number listed is the fax number.

sporting cutlers

A.G. RUSSELL KNIVES
2900 S. 26th Street
Rogers, AR 72758-8571
479-631-0055;
fax 479-631-8734
lynnd@agrussell.com; www.agrussell.com
The oldest knife mail-order company, highest quality. Free catalog available. In these catalogs you will find the newest and the best. If you like knives, this catalog is a must

AL MAR KNIVES
PO Box 2295
Tualatin, OR 97062-2295
503-670-9080; 503-639-4789
www.almarknives.com
Featuring our Ultralight™ series of knives. Sere 2000™ Shrike, Sere™, Operator™, Nomad™ and Ultraligh series™

ALCAS CORPORATION
1116 E State St
Olean, NY 14760
716-372-3111; 716-373-6155
www.cutco.com
Household cutlery / sport knives

ANZA KNIVES
C Davis
Dept BL 12 PO Box 710806
Santee, CA 92072-0806
619-561-9445; 619-390-6283
sales@anzaknives.com;
www.anzaknives.com

B&D TRADING CO.
3935 Fair Hill Rd
Fair Oaks, CA 95628

BARTEAUX MACHETES, INC.
1916 SE 50th St
Portland, OR 97215
503-233-5880
barteaux@machete.com; www.machete.com
Manufacture of machetes, saws, garden tools

BEAR & SON CUTLERY
(FORMERLY BEAR MGC CUTLERY)
PO Box 600
5111 Berwyn Rd Suite 110
College Park, MD 20740 USA
800-338-6799; 301-486-0901
www.knifecenter.com
Folding pocket knives, fixed blades, specialty products

BECK'S CUTLERY & SPECIALTIES
McGregor Village Center
107 Edinburgh South Dr
Cary, NC 27511
919-460-0203; 919-460-7772
beckscutlery@mindspring.com;
www.beckscutlery.com

BENCHMADE KNIFE CO. INC.
300 Beavercreek Rd
Oregon City, OR 97045
800-800-7427
info@benchmade.com;
www.benchmade.com
Sports, utility, law enforcement, military, gift and semi custom

BERETTA U.S.A. CORP.
17601 Beretta Dr
Accokeek, MD 20607
800-636-3420 Customer Service
www.berettausa.com
Full range of hunting & specialty knives

BEST KNIVES / GT KNIVES
PO Box 151048
Fort Myers, FL 33914
800-956-5696; fax 941-240-1756
info@bestknives.com;
www.bestknives.com/gtknives.com
Law enforcement & military automatic knives

BLACKJACK KNIVES
PO Box 3
Greenville, WV 24945
304-832-6878; Fax 304-832-6550
knifeware@verizon.net;
www.knifeware.com

BLUE GRASS CUTLERY CORP.
20 E Seventh St PO Box 156
Manchester, OH 45144
937-549-2602; 937-549-2709 or 2603
sales @bluegrasscutlery.com;
www.bluegrasscutlery.com
Manufacturer of Winchester Knives, John Primble Knives and many contract lines

BOB'S TRADING POST
308 N Main St
Hutchinson, KS 67501
620-669-9441
www.gunshopfinder.com
Tad custom knives with Reichert custom sheaths one at a time, one-of-a-kind

BOKER USA INC
1550 Balsam St
Lakewood, CO 80214-5917
303-462-0662; 303-462-0668
sales@bokerusa.com; www.bokerusa.com
Wide range of fixed blade and folding knives for hunting, military, tactical and general use

BROWNING
One Browning Place
Morgan, UT 84050
800-333-3504; Customer Service:
801-876-2711 or 800-333-3288
www.browning.com
Outdoor hunting & shooting products

BUCK KNIVES INC.
660 S Lochsa St
Post Falls, ID 83854-5200
800-326-2825; Fax: 208-262-0555
www.buckknives.com
Sports cutlery

BULLDOG BRAND KNIVES
6715 Heritage Business Ct
Chattanooga, TN 37421
423-894-5102; 423-892-9165
Fixed blade and folding knives for hunting and general use

BUSSE COMBAT KNIFE CO.
11651 Co Rd 12
Wauseon, OH 43567
419-923-6471; 419-923-2337
www.bussecombat.com
Simple & very strong straight knife designs for tactical & expedition use

CAMILLUS CUTLERY CO.
54 W Main St.
Camillus, NY 13031
315-672-8111; 315-672-8832
customerservice@camillusknives.com

CAS IBERIA INC.
650 Industrial Blvd
Sale Creek, TN 37373
423-332-4700
www.casiberia.com
Extensive variety of fixed-blade and folding knives for hunting, diving, camping, military and general use.

CASE CUTLERY
W R & Sons
PO Box 4000
Owens Way
Bradford, PA 16701
800-523-6350; Fax: 814-368-1736
consumer-relations@wrcase.com
www.wrcase.com
Folding pocket knives

CHICAGO CUTLERY CO.
5500 Pearl St.
Rosemont, IL 60018
847-678-8600
www.chicagocutlery.com
Sport & utility knives.

CHRIS REEVE KNIVES
2949 S. Victory View Way
Boise, ID 83709-2946
208-375-0367; Fax: 208-375-0368
crknifo@chrisreeve.com;
www.chrisreeve.com
Makers of the award winning Yarborough/ Green Beret Knife; the One Piece Range; and the Sebenza and Mnandi folding knives

COAST CUTLERY CO
PO Box 5821
Portland, OR 97288
800-426-5858
www.coastcutlery.com
Variety of fixed-blade and folding knives and multi-tools for hunting, camping and general use

COLD STEEL INC
3036-A Seaborg Ave.
Ventura, CA 93003
800-255-4716 or 805-650-8481
customerservice@coldsteel.com;
www.coldsteel.com
Wide variety of folding lockbacks and fixed-blade hunting, fishing and neck knives, as well as bowies, kukris, tantos, throwing knives, kitchen knives and swords

COLONIAL KNIFE COMPANY DIVISION OF COLONIAL CUTLERY INTERNATIONAL
PO Box 960
North Scituate, RI 02857
866-421-6500; Fax: 401-737-0054
colonialcutlery@aol.com;
www.colonialcutlery@aol.com or
www.colonialknifecompany.com
Collectors edition specialty knives. Special promotions. Old cutler, barion, trappers, military knives. Industrial knives-electrician.

COLUMBIA RIVER KNIFE & TOOL
18348 SW 126th Place
Tualatin, OR 97026
800-891-3100; 503-685-5015
info@crkt.com; www.crkt.com
Complete line of sport, work and tactical knives

CONDOR™ TOOL & KNIFE
Rick Jones, Natl. Sales Manager
6309 Marina Dr
Orlando, FL 32819
407-876-0886
rtj@earthlink.net

CRAWFORD KNIVES, LLC
205 N Center Drive
West Memphis, AR 72301
870-732-2452
www.crawfordknives.com
Folding knives for tactical and general use

DAVID BOYE KNIVES
PO Box 1238
Dolan Springs, AZ 86441-1238
800-853-1617 or 928-767-4273
boye@ctaz.com; www.boyeknives.com
Boye Dendritic Cobalt boat knives

DUNN KNIVES
Steve Greene
PO Box 204; 5830 NW Carlson Rd
Rossville KS 66533
800-245-6483
steve.greene@dunnknives.com;
www.dunnknives.com
Custom knives

EMERSON KNIVES, INC.
PO Box 4180
Torrance, CA 90510-4180
310-212-7455; Fax: 310-212-7289
www.emersonknives.com
Hard use tactical knives; folding & fixed blades

EXTREMA RATIO SAS
Mauro Chiostri/Maurizio Castrati
Via Tourcoing 40/p
59100 Prato
ITALY
0039 0574 584639; Fax: 0039 0574 581312
info@extremaratio.com
Tactical/military knives and sheaths, blades and sheaths to customers specs

FALLKNIVEN AB
Havrevägen 10
S-961 42 Boden
SWEDEN
46-921 544 22; Fax: 46-921 544 33
info@fallkniven.se; www.fallkniven.com
High quality stainless knives

FROST CUTLERY CO
PO Box 22636
Chattanooga, Tn 37422
800-251-7768; Fax: 423-894-9576
www.frostcutleryco.com
Wide range of fixed-blade and folding knives with a multitude of handle materials

GATCO SHARPENERS
PO Box 600
Getzville, NY 14068
716-877-2200; Fax: 716-877-2591
gatco@buffnet.net;
www.gatcosharpeners.com
Precision sharpening systems, diamond sharpening systems, ceramic sharpening systems, carbide sharpening systems, natural Arkansas stones

GERBER LEGENDARY BLADES
14200 SW 72nd Ave
Portland, OR 97224
503-639-6161; Fax: 503-684-7008
www.gerberblades.com
Knives, multi-tools, axes, saws, outdoor products

GROHMANN KNIVES LTD.
PO Box 40
116 Water St
Pictou, Nova Scotia B0K 1H0
CANADA
888-756-4837; Fax: 902-485-5872
www.grohmannknives.com
Fixed-blade belt knives for hunting and fishing, folding pocketknives for hunting and general use

H&B FORGE CO.
235 Geisinger Rd
Shiloh, OH 44878
419-895-1856
hbforge@direcway.com; www.hbforge.com
Special order hawks, camp stoves, fireplace accessories, muzzleloading accroutements

HISTORIC EDGED WEAPONRY
1021 Saddlebrook Dr
Hendersonville, NC 28739
828-692-0323; 828-692-0600
histwpn@bellsouth.net
Antique knives from around the world; importer of puukko and other knives from Norway, Sweden, Finland and Lapland; also edged weaponry book "Travels for Daggers" by Eiler R. Cook

JOY ENTERPRISES-FURY CUTLERY
Port Commerce Center III
1862 M.L. King Jr. Blvd
Riviera Beach, FL 33404
800-500-3879; Fax: 561-863-3277
mail@joyenterprises.com;
www.joyenterprises.com;
www.furycutlery.com
Fury™ Mustang™ extensive variety of fixed-blade and folding knives for hunting, fishing, diving, camping, military and general use; novelty key-ring knives. Muela Sporting Knives

KA-BAR KNIVES INC
200 Homer St
Olean, NY 14760
800-282-0130; Fax: 716-790-7188
info@ka-bar.com; www.ka-bar.com

KATZ KNIVES, INC.
10924 Mukilteo Speedway #287
Mukilteo, WA 98275
480-786-9334; 480-786-9338
katzkn@aol.com; www.katzknives.com

KELLAM KNIVES CO.
902 S Dixie Hwy
Lantana, FL 33462
800-390-6918; Fax: 561-588-3186
info@kellamknives.com;
www.kellamknives.com
Largest selection of Finnish knives; handmade & production

KERSHAW/KAI CUTLERY CO.
7939 SW Burns Way
Wilsonville, OR 97070

KLOTZLI (MESSER KLOTZLI)
Hohengasse 3 CH 3400
Burgdorf
SWITZERLAND
(34) 422-23 78; Fax: (34) 422-76 93
info@klotzli.com; www.klotzli.com
High-tech folding knives for tactical and general use

KNIFEWARE INC
PO Box 3
Greenville, WV 24945
304-832-6878; Fax: 304-832-6550
knifeware@verizon.net; www.knifeware.com
Blackjack and Big Country Cross reference Big Country Knives see Knifeware Inc.

KNIGHTS EDGE LTD.
5696 N Northwest Highway
Chicago, IL 60646-6136
773-775-3888; Fax: 773-775-3339
sales@knightsedge.com;
www.knightsedge.com
Medieval weaponry, swords, suits of armor, katanas, daggers

KNIVES OF ALASKA, INC.
Charles or Jody Allen
3100 Airport Dr
Denison, TX 75020
800-572-0980; 903-786-7371
info@knivesofalaska.com;
www.knivesofalaska.com
High quality hunting & outdoorsmen's knives

KNIVES OF ALASKA, INC.
Charles or Jody Allen
3100 Airport Dr
Denison, TX 75020
800-572-0980; 903-786-7371
info@knivesofalaska.com;
www.knivesofalaska.com
High quality hunting & outdoorsmen's knives

KNIVES PLUS
2467 40 West
Amarillo, TX 79109
800-687-6202
www.knivesplus.com
Retail cutlery and cutlery accessories since 1987; free catalog available

LAKOTA (BRUNTON CO.)
620 E Monroe Ave
Riverton, WY 82501
307-856-6559
AUS 8-A high-carbon stainless steel blades

LEATHERMAN TOOL GROUP, INC.
PO Box 20595
Portland, OR 97294-059 0595 5
800-847-8665; Fax: 503-253-7830
mktg@leatherman.com;
www.leatherman.com
Multi-tools

LONE WOLF KNIVES
Doug Hutchens, Marketing Manager
9373 SW Barber Street, Suite A
Wilsonville, OR 97070
503-431-6777
customerservice@lonewolfknives.com;
www.lonewolfknives.com

LONE STAR WHOLESALE
P.O. Box 587
Amarillo, TX 79105
806-356-9540; Fax 806-359-1603
knivesplus@knivesplus.com
Great prices, dealers only, most major brands

MARBLE'S OUTDOORS
420 Industrial Park
Gladstone, MI 49837
906-428-3710; Fax: 906-428-3711
info@marblescutlery.com;
www.marblesoutdoors.com

MASTER CUTLERY INC
701 Penhorn Ave
Secaucus, NJ 07094
888-271-7229; Fax: 201-271-7666
www.mastercutlery.com
Largest variety in the knife industry

MASTERS OF DEFENSE KNIFE CO.
   (BLACKHAWK PRODUCTS GROUP)
4850 Brookside Court
Norfolk, VA 23502
800-694-5263; 888-830-2013
cs@blackhawk.com; www.modknives.com
Fixed-blade and folding knives for tactical and general use

MCCANN INDUSTRIES
132 S 162nd PO Box 641
Spanaway, WA 98387
253-537-6919; Fax: 253-537-6993
mccann.machine@worldnet.att.net;
www.mccannindustries.com

MEYERCO MANUFACTURING
4481 Exchange Service Dr
Dallas, TX 75236
214-467-8949; 214-467-9241
www.meyercousa.com
Folding tactical,rescue and speed-assisted pocketknives; fixed-blade hunting and fishing designs; multi-function camping tools and machetes

MICROTECH KNIVES
300 Chestnut Street Ext.
Bradford, PA 16701
814-363-9260; Fax: 814-363-9284
mssweeney@microtechknives.com;
www.microtechknives.com
Manufacturers of the highest quality production knives

MORTY THE KNIFE MAN, INC.
80 Smith St
Farmingdale, NY 11735
631-249-2072
clkiff@mtkm.com;
www.mortytheknifeman.com

MUSEUM REPLICAS LTD.
P.O. Box 840
2147 Gees Mill Rd
Conyers, GA 30012
800-883-8838; Fax: 770-388-0246
www.museumreplicas.com
Historically accurate & battle-ready swords & daggers

MYERCHIN, INC.
14765 Nova Scotia Dr
Fontana, CA 92336
909-463-6741; 909-463-6751
myerchin@myerchin.com;
www.myerchin.com
Rigging/ Police knives

NATIONAL KNIFE DISTRIBUTORS
125 Depot St
Forest City, NC 28043
800-447-4342; 828-245-5121
nkdi@nkdi.com; www.nkdi.com
Benchmark pocketknives from Solingen, Germany

NORMARK CORP.
10395 Yellow Circle Dr
Minnetonka, MN 55343-9101
800-874-4451; 612-933-0046
www.rapala.com
Hunting knives, game shears and skinning ax

ONTARIO KNIFE CO.
PO Box 145
Franklinville, NY 14737
800-222-5233; 800-299-2618
sales@ontarioknife.com;
www.ontarioknife.com
Fixed blades, tactical folders, military & hunting knives, machetes

OUTDOOR EDGE CUTLERY CORP.
4699 Nautilus Ct. S #503
Boulder, CO 80301
800-447-3343; 303-530-7667
info@outdooredge.com;
www.outdooredge.com

PILTDOWN PRODUCTIONS
Errett Callahan
2 Fredonia Ave
Lynchburg, VA 24503
434-528-3444
www.errettcallahan.com

QUEEN CUTLERY COMPANY
PO Box 500
Franklinville, NY 14737
800-222-5233; 800-299-2618
sales@ontarioknife.com;
www.queencutlery.com
Pocket knives, collectibles, Schatt & Morgan, Robeson, club knives

QUIKUT
118 East Douglas Road
Walnut Ridge, AR 72476
800-338-7012; Fax: 870-886-9162
www.quikut.com

RANDALL MADE KNIVES
4857 South Orange Blossom Trail
Orlando, FL 32839
407-855-8075; Fax: 407-855-9054
grandall@randallknives.com;
www.randallknives.com
Handmade fixed-blade knives for hunting, fishing, diving, military and general use

REMINGTON ARMS CO., INC.
PO Box 700
870 Remington Drive
Madison, NC 27025-0700
800-243-9700; Fax: 336-548-7801
www.remington.com

SANTA FE STONEWORKS
3790 Cerrillos Rd.
Santa Fe, NM 87507
800-257-7625; Fax: 505-471-0036
knives@rt66.com;
www.santafestoneworks.com
Gem stone handles

SARCO CUTLERY LLC
449 Lane Dr
Florence AL 35630
256-766-8099
www.sarcoknives.com
Etching and engraving services, club knives, etc. New knives, antique-collectible knives

SOG SPECIALTY KNIVES & TOOLS, INC.
6521 212th St SW
Lynnwood, WA 98036
425-771-6230; Fax: 425-771-7689
info@sogknives.com; www.sogknives.com
SOG assisted technology, Arc-Lock, folding knives, specialized fixed blades, multi-tools

SPYDERCO, INC.
820 Spyderco Way
Golden, CO 80403
800-525-7770; 303-278-2229
sales@spyderco.com;
www.spyderco.com
Knives and sharpeners

SWISS ARMY BRANDS INC.
Service Center
65 Trap Falls Road
Shelton, CT 06484
800-442-2706; Fax: 800-243-4006
www.swissarmy.com
Folding multi-blade designs and multi-tools for hunting, fishing, camping, hiking, golfing and general use. One of the original brands (Victorinox) of Swiss Army Knives

TAYLOR BRANDS LLC
1043 Fordtown Road
Kingsport, TN 37662-1638
800-251-0254; Fax: 423-247-5371
info@taylorbrandsllc.com;
www.taylorcutlery.com
Fixed-blade and folding knives for tactical, rescue, hunting and general use

TIGERSHARP TECHNOLOGIES
1002 N Central Expwy Suite 499
Richardson TX 75080
888-711-8437; Fax: 972-907-0716
www.tigersharp.com

TIMBERLINE KNIVES
PO Box 600
Getzville, NY 14068-0600
800-548-7427; Fax: 716-877-2591
www.timberlineknives.com
High technology production knives for professionals, sporting, tradesmen & kitchen use

TINIVES
1725 Smith Rd
Fortson, GA 31808
888-537-9991; 706-322-9892
info@tinives.com; www.tinives.com
High-tech folding knives for tactical, law enforcement and general use

TRU-BALANCE KNIFE CO.
6869 Lake Bluff Dr
Comstock Park, MI 49321
(616) 647-1215

TURNER, P.J., KNIFE MFG., INC.
P.O. Box 1549
164 Allred Rd
Afton, WY 83110
307-885-0611
pjtkm@silverstar.com;
www2.silverstar.com/turnermfg

UTICA CUTLERY CO
820 Noyes St
PO Box 10527
Utica, NY 13503-1527
800-879-2526; Fax: 315-733-6602
info@uticacutlery.com; www.uticacutlery.com
Wide range of folding and fixed-blade designs, multi-tools and steak knives

WARNER, KEN
PO Box 3
Greenville, WV 24945
304-832-6878; 304-832-6550
www.knifeware.com

WENGER NORTH AMERICA
15 Corporate Dr
Orangeburg, NY 10962
800-267-3577 or 800-447-7422
www.wengerna.com
One of the official makers of folding multi-blade Swiss Army knives

WILD BOAR BLADES / KOPROMED USA
1701 Broadway PMB 282
Vancouver, WA 98663
360-735-0570; Fax: 360-735-0390
info@wildboarblades.com;
wildboarblades@aol.com;
www.wildboarblade.com
Wild Boar Blades is pleased to carry a full line of Kopromed knives and kitchenware imported from Poland

WORLD CLASS EXHIBITION KNIVES
Cary Desmon
941-504-2279
www.withoutequal.com
Carries an extensive line of Pius Lang knives

WILLIAM HENRY FINE KNIVES
3200 NE Rivergate St
McMinnville, OR 97128
888-563-4500; Fax: 503-434-9704

www.williamhenryknives.com
Semi-custom folding knives for hunting and general use; some limited editions

WUU JAU CO. INC
2600 S Kelly Ave
Edmond, OK 73013
800-722-5760; Fax: 877-256-4337
mail@wuujau.com; www.wuujau.com
Wide variety of imported fixed-blade and folding knives for hunting, fishing, camping, and general use. Wholesale to knife dealers only

WYOMING KNIFE CORP.
101 Commerce Dr
Ft. Collins, CO 80524
970-224-3454; Fax: 970-226-0778
wyoknife@hotmail.com;
www.wyomingknife.com

XIKAR INC
PO Box 025757
Kansas City MO 64102
888-676-7380; 816-474-7555
info@xikar.com; www.xikar.com
Gentlemen's cutlery and accessories

importers

A.G. RUSSELL KNIVES INC
2900 S. 26th St.
Rogers, AR 72758-8571
800-255-9034 or 479-631-0055;
fax 479-631-8734
lynnd@agrussell.com; www.agrussell.com
The oldest knife mail-order company, highest quality. Free catalog available. In these catalogs you will find the newest and the best. If you like knives, this catalog is a must. Celebrating 40 years in the industry

ADAMS INTERNATIONAL KNIFEWORKS
8710 Rosewood Hills
Edwardsville, IL 62025
Importers & foreign cutlers

AITOR-BERRIZARGO S.L.
P.I. Eitua PO Box 26
48240 Berriz Vizcaya
SPAIN
946826599; 94602250226
info@aitor.com; www.aitor.com
Sporting knives

ATLANTA CUTLERY CORP.
P.O.Box 839
Conyers, Ga 30012
800-883-0300; Fax: 770-388-0246
custserve@atlantacutlery.com;
www.atlantacutlery.com
Exotic knives from around the world

BAILEY'S
PO Box 550
Laytonville, CA 95454
800-322-4539; 707-984-8115
baileys@baileys-online.com;
www.baileys-online.com

BELTRAME, FRANCESCO
Fratelli Beltrame F&C snc Via dei Fabbri
15/B-33085 MANIAGO (PN)
ITALY
39 0427 701859
www.italianstiletto.com

BOKER USA, INC.
1550 Balsam St
Lakewood, CO 80214-5917
303-462-0662; 303-462-0668
sales@bokerusa.com; www.bokerusa.com
Ceramic blades

CAMPOS, IVAN DE ALMEIDA
R. Stelio M. Loureiro, 205
Centro, Tatui
BRAZIL
00-55-15-33056867
www.ivancampos.com

C.A.S. IBERIA, INC.
650 Industrial Blvd
Sale Creek, TN 37373
423-332-4700; 423-332-7248
info@casiberia.com; www.casiberia.com

CAS/HANWEI, MUELA
Catoctin Cutlery
PO Box 188
Smithsburg, MD 21783

CLASSIC INDUSTRIES
1325 Howard Ave, Suite 408
Burlingame, CA 94010

COAST CUTLERY CO.
8033 NE Holman St.
Portland, OR 97218
800-426-5858
staff@coastcutlery.com;
www.coastcutlery.com

COLUMBIA PRODUCTS CO.
PO Box 1333
Sialkot 51310
PAKISTAN

COLUMBIA PRODUCTS INT'L
PO Box 8243
New York, NY 10116-8243
201-854-3054; Fax: 201-854-7058
nycolumbia@aol.com;
http://www.columbiaproducts.homestead.
com/cat.html
Pocket, hunting knives and swords of all kinds

COMPASS INDUSTRIES, INC.
104 E. 25th St
New York, NY 10010
800-221-9904; Fax: 212-353-0826
jeff@compassindustries.com;
www.compassindustries.com
Imported pocket knives

CONAZ COLTELLERIE
Dei F.Lli Consigli-Scarperia
Via G. Giordani, 20
50038 Scarperia (Firenze)
ITALY
36 55 846187; 39 55 846603
conaz@dada.it; www.consigliscarpeia.com
Handicraft workmanship of knives of the ancient Italian tradition. Historical and collection knives

CONSOLIDATED CUTLERY CO., INC.
696 NW Sharpe St
Port St. Lucie, FL 34983
772-878-6139

CRAZY CROW TRADING POST
PO Box 847
Pottsboro, TX 75076
800-786-6210; Fax: 903-786-9059
info@crazycrow.com; www.crazycrow.com
Solingen blades, knife making parts & supplies

DER FLEISSIGEN BEAVER
(The Busy Beaver)
Harvey Silk
PO Box 1166
64343 Griesheim
GERMANY
49 61552231; 49 6155 2433
Der.Biber@t-online.de
Retail custom knives. Knife shows in Germany & UK

EXTREMA RATIO SAS
Mauro Chiostri; Mavrizio Castrati
Via Tourcoing 40/p
59100 Prato (PO)
ITALY
0039 0574 58 4639; 0039 0574 581312
info@extremarazio.com;
www.extremaratio.com
Tactical & military knives manufacturing

FALLKNIVEN AB
Havrevagen 10
S-96142 Boden
SWEDEN
46 92154422; 46 92154433
info@fallkniven.se
www.fallkniven.com
High quality knives

FREDIANI COLTELLI FINLANDESI
Via Lago Maggiore 41
I-21038 Leggiuno
ITALY

GIESSER MESSERFABRIK GMBH, JOHANNES
Raiffeisenstr 15
D-71349 Winnenden
GERMANY
49-7195-1808-29
info@giesser.de; www.giesser.de
Professional butchers and chef's knives

HIMALAYAN IMPORTS
3495 Lakeside Dr
Reno, NV 89509
775-825-2279
unclebill@himalayan-imports.com; www.
himilayan-imports.com

IVAN DE ALMEIDA CAMPOS-KNIFE DEALER
R. Xi De Agosto
107, Centro, Tatui, Sp 18270
BRAZIL
55-15-251-8092; 55-15-251-4896
campos@bitweb.com.br
Custom knives from all Brazilian knifemakers

JOY ENTERPRISES
1862 M.L. King Blvd
Riviera Beach, FL 33404
800-500-3879; 561-863-3277
mail@joyenterprises.com;
www.joyenterprises.com
Fury™, Mustang™, Hawg Knives, Muela

KELLAM KNIVES CO.
902 S Dixie Hwy
Lantana, FL 33462
800-390-6918; 561-588-3186
info@kellamknives.com;
www.kellamknives.com
Knives from Finland; own line of knives

KNIFE IMPORTERS, INC.
11307 Conroy Ln
Manchaca, TX 78652
512-282-6860, Fax: 512-282-7504
Wholesale only

KNIGHTS EDGE
5696 N Northwest Hwy
Chicago, IL 60646
773-775-3888; 773-775-3339
www.knightsedge.com
Exclusive designers of our Rittersteel, Stagesteel and Valiant Arms and knightedge lines of weapon

LEISURE PRODUCTS CORP.
PO Box 1171
Sialkot-51310
PAKISTAN

L. C. RISTINEN
Suomi Shop
17533 Co Hwy 38
Frazee MN 56544
218-538-6633; 218-538-6633
icrist@wcta.net
Scandinavian cutlery custom antique, books and reindeer antler

LINDER, CARL NACHF.
Erholungstr. 10
D-42699 Solingen
GERMANY
212 33 0 856; Fax: 212 33 71 04
info@linder.de; www.linder.de

MARTTIINI KNIVES
PO Box 44 (Marttiinintie 3)
96101 Rovaniemi
FINLAND

MATTHEWS CUTLERY
4401 Sentry Dr, Suite K
Tucker, GA 30084-6561
770-939-6915

MESSER KLÖTZLI
PO Box 104
Hohengasse 3, Ch-3402 Burgdorf
SWITZERLAND
034 422 2378; 034 422 7693
info@klotzli.com; www.klotzli.com

MURAKAMI, ICHIRO
Knife Collectors Assn. Japan
Tokuda Nishi 4 Chome, 76 Banchi,
Ginancho
Hashimagun, Gifu
JAPAN
81 58 274 1960; 81 58 273 7369
www.gix.orjp/~n-resin/

MUSEUM REPLICAS LIMITED
2147 Gees Mill Rd
Conyers, GA 30012
800-883-8838
www.museumreplicas.com

NICHOLS CO.
Pomfret Rd
South Pomfret, VT 05067
Import & distribute knives from EKA (Sweden), Helle (Norway), Brusletto (Norway), Roselli (Finland). Also market Zippo products, Snow, Nealley axes and hatchets and snow & Neally axes

NORMARK CORP.
Craig Weber
10395 Yellow Circle Dr
Minnetonka, MN 55343

PRODUCTORS AITOR, S.A.
Izelaieta 17
48260 Ermua
SPAIN
943-170850; 943-170001
info@aitor.com
Sporting knives

PROFESSIONAL CUTLERY SERVICES
9712 Washburn Rd
Downey, CA 90241
562-803-8778; 562-803-4261
Wholesale only. Full service distributor of domestic & imported brand name cutlery. Exclusive U.S. importer for both Marto Swords and Battle Ready Valiant Armory edged weapons

SCANDIA INTERNATIONAL INC.
5475 W Inscription Canyon Dr
Prescott, AZ 86305
928-442-0140; Fax: 928-442-0342
mora@cableone.net; www.frosts-scandia.com
Frosts knives of Sweden

STAR SALES CO., INC.
1803 N. Central St
Knoxville, TN 37917
800-745-6433; Fax: 865-524-4889
www.starknives.com

SVORD KNIVES
Smith Rd., RD 2
Waiuku, South Auckland
NEW ZEALAND
64 9 2358846; Fax: 64 9 2356483
www.svord.com

SWISS ARMY BRANDS LTD.
The Forschner Group, Inc.
One Research Drive
Shelton, CT 06484
203-929-6391; 203-929-3786
www.swissarmy.com

TAYLOR CUTLERY
PO Box 1638
1736 N. Eastman Rd
Kingsport, TN 37662
Colman Knives along with Smith & Wesson, Cuttin Horse, John Deere, Zoland knives

UNITED CUTLERY CORP.
1425 United Blvd
Sevierville, TN 37876
865-428-2532; 865-428-2267
order@unitedcutlery.com;
www.unitedcutlery.com
Harley-Davidson ® Colt ® , Stanley ®, U21 ®, Rigid Knives ®, Outdoor Life ®, Ford ®, hunting, camping, fishing, collectible & fantasy knives

UNIVERSAL AGENCIES INC
4690 S Old Peachtree Rd, Suite C
Norcross, GA 30071-1517
678-969-9147; Fax: 678-969-9169
info@knifecupplies.com;
www.knifesupplies.com;
www.thunderforged.com; www.uai.org
*Serving the cutlery industry with the finest
selection of India Stag, Buffalo Horn,
Thurnderforged ™ Damascus. Mother of Pearl,
Knife Kits and more*

VALOR CORP.
1001 Sawgrass Corp Pkwy
Sunrise, FL 33323
800-899-8256; Fax: 954-377-4941
www.valorcorp.com
Wide variety of imported & domestic knives

WENGER N. A.
15 Corporate Dr
Orangeburg, NY 10962
800-431-2996
www.wengerna.com
Swiss Army ™ Knives

WILD BOAR BLADES
1701 Broadway, Suite 282
Vancouver, WA 98663
888-476-4400; 360-735-0390
usakopro@aol.com;
www.wildboarblades.com
*Carries a full line of Kopromed knives and
kitchenware imported from Poland*

WORLD CLASS EXHIBITION KNIVES
Cary Desmon
941-504-2279
www.withoutequal.com
Carries an extensive line of Pius Lang knives

ZWILLING J.A. HENCKELS USA
171 Saw Mill River Rd
Hawthorne, NY 10532
800-777-4308; Fax: 914-747-1850
info@jahenckels.com;
www.jahenckels.com
*Kitchen cutlery, scissors, gadgets, flatware and
cookware*

knife making supplies

AFRICAN IMPORT CO.
Alan Zanotti
22 Goodwin Rd
Plymouth, MA 02360
508-746-8552; 508-746-0404
africanimport@aol.com
Ivory

AMERICAN SIEPMANN CORP.
65 Pixley Industrial Parkway
Rochester, NY 14624
800-724-0919; Fax: 585-247-1883
www.siepmann.com
*CNC blade grinding equipment, grinding
wheels, production blade grinding services.
Sharpening stones and sharpening equipment*

ANKROM EXOTICS
Pat Ankrom
22900 HWY 5
Centerville, IA 52544
641-436-0235
ankromexotics@hotmail.com
www.ankromexotics.com
*Stabilized handle material; Exotic burls
and hardwoods from around the world;
Stabilizing services available*

ATLANTA CUTLERY CORP.
P.O.Box 839
Conyers, Ga 30012
800-883-0300; Fax: 770-388-0246
custserve@atlantacutlery.com;
www.atlantacutlery.com

BATAVIA ENGINEERING
PO Box 53
Magaliesburg, 1791
SOUTH AFRICA
27-14-5771294
bertie@batavia.co.za; www.batavia.co.za
*Contact wheels for belt grinders and surface
grinders; damascus and mokume*

BLADEMAKER, THE
Gary Kelley
17485 SW Phesant Ln
Beaverton, OR 97006
503-649-7867
garykelly@theblademaker.com;
www.theblademaker.com
*Period knife and hawk blades for hobbyists
& re-enactors and in dendritic D2 steel.
"Ferroulithic" steel-stone spear point, blades
and arrowheads*

BOONE TRADING CO., INC.
PO Box 669
562 Coyote Rd
Brinnon, WA 98320
800-423-1945; Fax: 360-796-4511
www.boonetrading.com
Ivory of all types, bone, horns

BORGER, WOLF
Benzstrasse 8
76676 Graben-Neudorf
GERMANY
wolf@messerschmied.de;
www.messerschmied.de

BOYE KNIVES
PO Box 1238
Dolan Springs, AZ 86441-1238
800-853-1617; 928-767-4273
info@boyeknives.com;
www.boyeknives.com
Dendritic steel and Dendritic cobalt

BRONK'S KNIFEWORKS
Lyle Brunckhorst
Country Village
23706 7th Ave SE, Suite B
Bothell, WA 98021
425-402-3484
bronks@bronksknifeworks.com;
www.bronksknifeworks.com
Damascus steel

CRAZY CROW TRADING POST
PO Box 847
Pottsboro, TX 75076
800-786-6210; Fax: 903-786-9059
info@crazycrow.com; www.crazycrow.com
Solingen blades, knife making parts & supplies

CULPEPPER & CO.
Joe Culpepper
P.O. Box 690
8285 Georgia Rd.
Otto, NC 28763
828-524-6842; Fax: 828-369-7809
culpepperandco@verizon.net
www.knifehandles.com http://www.
knifehandles.com
www.stingrayproducts.com <http://www.
stingrayproducts.com>
*Mother of pearl, bone, abalone, stingray,
dyed stag, blacklip, ram's horn, mammoth
ivory, coral, scrimshaw*

CUSTOM FURNACES
PO Box 353
Randvaal, 1873
SOUTH AFRICA
27 16 365-5723; 27 16 365-5738
johnlee@custom.co.za
Furnaces for hardening & tempering of knives

DAMASCUS-USA CHARLTON LTD.
149 Deans Farm Rd
Tyner, NC 27980-9607
252-221-2010
rcharlton@damascususa.com;
www.damascususa.com

DAN'S WHETSTONE CO., INC.
418 Hilltop Rd
Pearcy, AR 71964
501-767-1616; 501-767-9598
questions@danswhetstone.com;
www.danswhetstone.com
Natural abrasive Arkansas stone products

**DIAMOND MACHINING TECHNOLOGY,
INC. DMT**
85 Hayes Memorial Dr
Marlborough, MA 01752
800-666-4DMT
dmtsharp@dmtsharp.com;
www.dmtsharp.com
*Knife and tool sharpeners-diamond, ceramic
and easy edge guided sharpening kits*

DIGEM DIAMOND SUPPLIERS
7303 East Earll Drive
Scottsdale, Arizona 85251
602-620-3999
eglasser@cox.net
*#1 international diamond tool provider. Every
diamond tool you will ever need 1/16th of an
inch to 11'x9'. BURRS, CORE DRILLS, SAW
BLADES, MILLING SHAPES, AND WHEELS*

DIXIE GUN WORKS, INC.
PO Box 130
Union City, TN 38281
800-238-6785; Fax: 731-885-0440
www.dixiegunworks.com
Knife and knifemaking supplies

EZE-LAP DIAMOND PRODUCTS
3572 Arrowhead Dr
Carson City, NV 89706
800-843-4815; Fax: 775-888-9555
sales@eze-lap.com; www.eze-lap.com
Diamond coated sharpening tools

FLITZ INTERNATIONAL, LTD.
821 Mohr Ave
Waterford, WI 53185
800-558-8611; Fax: 262-534-2991
info@flitz.com; www.flitz.com
Metal polish, buffing pads, wax

FORTUNE PRODUCTS, INC.
205 Hickory Creek Rd
Marble Falls, TX 78654-3357
830-693-6111; Fax: 830-693-6394
www.accusharp.com
AccuSharp knife sharpeners

GALLERY HARDWOODS
Larry Davis
Acworth, GA
www.galleryhardwoods.com
Stabilized exotic burls and woods

GILMER WOOD CO.
2211 NW St Helens Rd
Portland, OR 97210
503-274-1271; Fax: 503-274-9839
www.gilmerwood.com

GREEN RIVER LEATHER, INC.
1100 Legion Park Rd.
Greensburg, KY 42743
270-932-2212; Fax: 270-299-2471
sherrylott@alltel.net;
www.greenriverleather.com
Complete line of veg tan and exotic leathers, shethmaking hardware, thread, dyes, finishes, etc.

GRS CORP.
D.J. Glaser
PO Box 1153
Emporia, KS 66801
800-835-3519; Fax: 620-343-9640
glendo@glendo.com; www.glendo.com
Engraving, equipment, tool sharpener, books/videos

HALPERN TITANIUM INC.
Les and Marianne Halpern
PO Box 214
4 Springfield St
Three Rivers, MA 01080
888-283-8627; Fax: 413-289-2372
info@halperntitanium.com;
www.halperntitanium.com
Titanium, carbon fiber, G-10, fasteners; CNC milling

HAWKINS KNIVE MAKING SUPPLIES
110 Buckeye Rd
Fayetteville, GA 30214
770-964-1177; Fax: 770-306-2877
Sales@hawkinsknifemakingsupplies.com
www.HawkinsKnifeMakingSupllies.com
All styles

HILTARY-USGRC
6060 East Thomas Road
Scottsdale, AZ 85251
Office: 480-945-0700
Fax: 480-945-3333
usgrc@cox.net
Gibeon Meteorite, Recon Gems, Diamond cutting tools, Exotic natural minerals, garaffe bone. Atomic absorbtion/ spectographic analyst, preciscious metal

HOUSE OF TOOLS LTD.
#54-5329 72 Ave. S.E.
Calgary, Alberta
CANADA T2C 4X
403-640-4594; Fax: 403-451-7006

INDIAN JEWELERS SUPPLY CO.
Mail Order: 601 E Coal Ave
Gallup, NM 87301-6005
2105 San Mateo Blvd NE
Albuquerque, NM 87110-5148
505-722-4451; 505-265-3701
orders@ijsinc.com; www.ijsinc.com
Handle materials, tools, metals

INTERAMCO INC.
5210 Exchange Dr
Flint, MI 48507
810-732-8181; 810-732-6116
solutions@interamco.com
Knife grinding and polishing

JANTZ SUPPLY / KOVAL KNIVES
PO Box 584
309 West Main
Davis, OK 73030
800-351-8900; 580-369-2316
jantz@brightok.net; www.knifemaking.com
Pre shaped blades, kit knives, complete knifemaking supply line

JOHNSON, R.B.
I.B.S. Int'l. Folder Supplies
Box 11
Clearwater, MN 55320
320-558-6128; 320-558-6128
Threaded pivot pins, screws, taps, etc.

JOHNSON WOOD PRODUCTS
34897 Crystal Rd
Strawberry Point, IA 52076
563-933-6504

K&G FINISHING SUPPLIES
1972 Forest Ave
Lakeside, AZ 85929
800-972-1192; 928-537-8877
csinfo@knifeandgun.com;
www.knifeandgun.com
Full service supplies

KOWAK IVORY
Roland and Kathy Quimby
(April-Sept): PO Box 350
Ester, AK 99725
907-479-9335
(Oct-March)
PO Box 693
Bristow, OK 74010
918-367-2684
sales@kowakivory.com;
www.kowakivory.com
Fossil ivories

LITTLE GIANT POWER HAMMER
Harlan "Sid" Suedmeier
420 4th Corso
Nebraska City, NE 68410
402-873-6603
www.littlegianthammer.com
Rebuilds hammers and supplies parts

LIVESAY, NEWT
3306 S Dogwood St
Siloam Springs, AR 72761
479-549-3356; 479-549-3357
Combat utility knives, titanium knives, sportsmen knives, custom made orders taken on knives and after market Kydex© sheaths for commercial or custom cutlery

LOHMAN CO., FRED
3405 NE Broadway
Portland, OR 97232
503-282-4567; Fax: 503-287-2678
lohman@katana4u.com;
www.japanese-swords.com

M MILLER ORIGINALS
Michael Miller
2960 E Carver Ave
Kingman AZ 86401
928-757-1359
mike@milleroriginals.com;
www.mmilleroriginals.com
Supplies stabilized juniper burl blocks and scales

MARKING METHODS, INC.
Sales
301 S. Raymond Ave
Alhambra, CA 91803-1531
626-282-8823; Fax: 626-576-7564
experts@markingmethods.com;
www.markingmethods.com
Knife etching equipment & service

MASECRAFT SUPPLY CO.
254 Amity St
Meriden, CT 06450
800-682-5489; Fax: 203-238-2373
info@masecraftsupply.com;
www.masecraftsupply.com
Natural & specialty synthetic handle materials & more

MEIER STEEL
Daryl Meier
75 Forge Rd
Carbondale, IL 62903
618-549-3234; Fax: 618-549-6239
www.meiersteel.com

NICO, BERNARD
PO Box 5151
Nelspruit 1200
SOUTH AFRICA
011-2713-7440099; 011-2713-7440099
bernardn@iafrica.com

NORRIS, MIKE
Rt 2 Box 242A
Tollesboro, KY 41189
606-798-1217
Damascus steel

NORTHCOAST KNIVES
17407 Puritas Ave
Cleveland, Ohio 44135
www.NorthCoastKnives.com
Tutorials and step-by-step projects. Entry level knifemaking supplies.

OSO FAMOSO
PO Box 654
Ben Lomond, CA 95005
831-336-2343
oso@osofamoso.com;
www.osofamoso.com
Mammoth ivory bark

OZARK KNIFE & GUN
3165 S Campbell Ave
Springfield, MO 65807
417-886-CUTT; 417-887-2635
danhoneycutt@sbcglobal.net
28 years in the cutlery business, Missouri's oldest cutlery firm

PARAGON INDUSTRIES, INC. L. P.
2011 South Town East Blvd
Mesquite, TX 75149-1122
800-876-4328; Fax: 972-222-0646
info@paragonweb.com;
www.paragonweb.com
Heat treating furnaces for knifemakers

POPLIN, JAMES / POP'S KNIVES &
SUPPLIES
103 Oak St
Washington, GA 30673
706-678-5408; Fax: 706-678-5409
www.popsknifesupplies.com

PUGH, JIM
PO Box 711
917 Carpenter
Azle, TX 76020
817-444-2679; Fax: 817-444-5455
Rosewood and ebony Micarta blocks,rivets for
Kydex sheaths, 0-80 screws for folders

RADOS, JERRY
7523E 5000 N. Rd
Grant Park, IL 60940
815-405-5061
jerry@radosknives.com;
www.radosknives.com
Damascus steel

REACTIVE METALS STUDIO, INC.
PO Box 890
Clarksdale, AZ 86324
800-876-3434; 928-634-3434; Fax: 928-634-6734
info@reactivemetals.com; www.
reactivemetals.com

R. FIELDS ANCIENT IVORY
Donald Fields
790 Tamerlane St
Deltona, FL 32725
386-532-9070
donaldfields@aol.com
Selling ancient ivories; Mammoth, fossil &
walrus

RICK FRIGAULT CUSTOM KNIVES
3584 Rapidsview Dr
Niagara Falls, Ontario
CANADA L2G 6C4
905-295-6695
zipcases@zipcases.com;
www.zipcases.com
Selling padded zippered knife pouches
with an option to personalize the outside
with the marker, purveyor, stores-address,
phone number, email web-site or any other
information needed. Available in black cordura,
mossy oak camo in sizes 4"x2" to 20"x4.5"

RIVERSIDE MACHINE
201 W Stillwell
DeQueen, AR 71832
870-642-7643; Fax: 870-642-4023
uncleal@riversidemachine.net
www.riversidemachine.net

ROCKY MOUNTAIN KNIVES
George L. Conklin
PO Box 902, 615 Franklin
Ft. Benton, MT 59442
406-622-3268; Fax: 406-622-3410
bbgrus@ttc-cmc.net
Working knives

RUMMELL, HANK
10 Paradise Lane
Warwick, NY 10990
845-469-9172
hank@newyorkcustomknives.com;
www.newyorkcustomknives.com

SAKMAR, MIKE
1451 Clovelly Ave
Rochester, MI 48307
248-852-6775; Fax: 248-852-8544
mikesakmar@yahoo.com
Mokume bar stock. Retail & wholesale

SANDPAPER, INC. OF ILLINOIS
P.O. Box 2579
Glen Ellyn, IL 60138
630-629-3320; Fax: 630-629-3324
sandinc@aol.com; www.sandpaperinc.com
Abrasive belts, rolls, sheets & discs

SCHEP'S FORGE
PO Box 395
Shelton, NE 68876-0395

SENTRY SOLUTIONS LTD.
PO Box 214
Wilton, NH 03086
800-546-8049; Fax: 603-654-3003
info@sentrysolutions.com;
www.sentrysolutions.com
Knife care products

SHEFFIELD KNIFEMAKERS
SUPPLY, INC.
PO Box 741107
Orange City, FL 32774
386-775-6453
email@sheffieldsupply.com;
www.sheffieldsupply.com

SHINING WAVE METALS
PO Box 563
Snohomish, WA 98291
425-334-5569
info@shiningwave.com;
www.shiningwave.com
A full line of mokume-gane in precious and
non-precious metals for knifemakers, jewelers
and other artists

SMITH ABRASIVES, INC.
/ SMITH WHETSTONE, INC.
1700 Sleepy Valley Rd
Hot Springs, AR 71901
www.smithabrasives.com

SMOLEN FORGE, INC.
Nick Smolen
S1735 Vang Rd
Westby, WI 54667
608-634-3569; Fax: 608-634-3869
smoforge@mwt.net;
www.smolenforge.com
Damascus billets & blanks, Mokume gane
billets

SOSTER SVENSTRUP BYVEJ 16
Søster Svenstrup Byvej 16
4130 Viby Sjælland
Denmark
45 46 19 43 05; Fax: 45 46 19 53 19
www.poulstrande.com

STAMASCUS KNIFEWORKS INC.
Ed VanHoy
24255 N Fork River Rd
Abingdon, VA 24210
276-944-4885; Fax: 276-944-3187
stamascus@hughes.net;
www.stamascus-knive-works.com
Blade steels

STOVER, JEFF
PO Box 43
Torrance, CA 90507
310-532-2166
edgedealer1@yahoo.com;
www.edgedealer.com
Fine custom knives, top makers

TEXAS KNIFEMAKERS SUPPLY
10649 Haddington Suite 180
Houston TX 77043
713-461-8632; Fax: 713-461-8221
sales@texasknife.com;
www.texasknife.com
Working straight knives. Hunters including
upswept skinners and custom walking sticks

TRU-GRIT, INC.
760 E Francis Unit N
Ontario, CA 91761
909-923-4116; Fax: 909-923-9932
www.trugrit.com
The latest in Norton and 3/M ceramic grinding
belts. Also Super Flex, Trizact, Norax and
Micron belts to 3000 grit. All of the popular belt
grinders. Buffers and variable speed motors.
ATS-34, 440C, BG-42, CPM S-30V, 416 and
Damascus steel

UNIVERSAL AGENCIES INC
4690 S Old Peachtree Rd, Suite C
Norcross, GA 30071-1517
678-969-9147; Fax: 678-969-9169
info@knifecupplies.com;
www.knifesupplies.com;
www.thunderforged.com; www.uai.org
Serving the cutlery industry with the finest
selection of India Stag, Buffalo Horn,
Thurnderforged ™ Damascus. Mother of Pearl,
Knife Kits and more

WASHITA MOUNTAIN WHETSTONE CO.
PO Box 20378
Hot Springs, AR 71903-0378
501-525-3914; Fax: 501-525-0816
wmw@hsnp

WEILAND, J. REESE
PO Box 2337
Riverview, FL 33568
813-671-0661; 727-595-0378
rwphil413@earthlink.net
Folders, straight knives, etc.

WILD WOODS
Jim Fray
9608 Monclova Rd
Monclova, OH 43542
419-866-0435

WILSON, R.W.
PO Box 2012
113 Kent Way
Weirton, WV 26062
304-723-2771

WOOD CARVERS SUPPLY, INC.
PO Box 7500-K
Englewood, FL 34223
800-284-6229; 941-460-0123
info@woodcarverssupply.com;
www.woodcarverssupply.com
Over 2,000 unique wood carving tools

WOOD LAB
Michael Balaskovitz
P.O. Box 222
Hudsonville, MI 49426
616-322-5846
michael@woodlab.biz;
www.woodlab.biz
Acrylic stabilizing services and materials

WOOD STABILIZING SPECIALISTS
INT'L, LLC
2940 Fayette Ave
Ionia, IA 50645
800-301-9774; 641-435-4746
mike@stabilizedwood.com;
www.stabilizedwood.com
Processor of acrylic impregnated materials

ZOWADA CUSTOM KNIVES
Tim Zowada
4509 E. Bear River Rd
Boyne Falls, MI 49713
231-348-5416
tim@tzknives.com; www.tzknives.com
Damascus, pocket knives, swords, Lower case
gothic tz logo

mail order sales

A.G. RUSSELL KNIVES INC
2900 S. 26th St
Rogers, AR 72758-8571
800-255-9034 or 479-631-0055;
fax 479-631-8734
lynnd@agrussell.com; www.agrussell.com
The oldest knife mail-order company, highest quality. Free catalog available. In these catalogs you will find the newest and the best. If you like knives, this catalog is a must

ARIZONA CUSTOM KNIVES
Julie Hyman
35 Miruela Ave
St. Augustine, FL 32080
904-826-4178
sharptalk@arizonacustomknifes.com;
www.arizonacustomknives.com
Color catalog $5 U.S. / $7 Foreign

ARTISAN KNIVES
Ty Young
575 Targhee Twn Rd
Alta, WY 83414
304-353-8111
ty@artisanknives.com;
www.artisanknives.com
Feature master artisan knives and makers in a unique "coffee table book" style format

ATLANTA CUTLERY CORP.
P.O.Box 839
Conyers, Ga 30012
800-883-0300; Fax: 770-388-0246
custserve@atlantacutlery.com;
www.atlantacutlery.com

ATLANTIC BLADESMITHS/PETER STEBBINS
50 Mill Rd
Littleton, MA 01460
978-952-6448
Sell, trade, buy; carefully selected handcrafted, benchmade and factory knives

BALLARD CUTLERY
1495 Brummel Ave.
Elk Grove Village, IL 60007
847-228-0070

BECK'S CUTLERY SPECIALTIES
107 S Edinburgh Dr
Cary, NC 27511
919-460-0203; Fax: 919-460-7772
beckscutlery@mindspring.com;
www.beckscutlery.com
Knives

BLADEGALLERY, INC. / EPICUREAN EDGE, THE
107 Central Way
Kirkland, WA 98033
425-889-5980; Fax: 425-889-5981
info@bladegallery.com;
www.bladegallery.com
Bladegallery.com specializes in hand-made one-of-a-kind knives from around the world. We have an emphasis on forged knives and high-end gentlemen's folders

BLUE RIDGE KNIVES
166 Adwolfe Rd
Marion, VA 24354
276-783-6143; 276-783-9298
onestop@blueridgeknives.com;
www.blueridgeknives.com
Wholesale distributor of knives

BOB NEAL CUSTOM KNIVES
PO Box 20923
Atlanta, GA 30320
770-914-7794
bob@bobnealcustomknives.com;
www.bobnealcustomknives.com
Exclusive limited edition custom knives-sets & single

BOB'S TRADING POST
308 N Main St
Hutchinson, KS 67501
620-669-9441
bobstradingpost@cox.net;
www.gunshopfinder.com
Tad custom knives with reichert custom sheaths one at a time, one of a kind

BOONE TRADING CO., INC.
PO Box 669
562 Coyote Rd
Brinnon, WA 98320
800-423-1945; Fax: 360-796-4511
www.boonetrading.com
Ivory of all types, bone, horns

CARMEL CUTLERY
Dolores & 6th
PO Box 1346
Carmel, CA 93921
831-624-6699; 831-624-6780
ccutlery@ix.netcom.com;
www.carmelcutlery.com
Quality custom and a variety of production pocket knives, swords; kitchen cutlery; personal grooming items

CUSTOM KNIFE CONSIGNMENT
PO Box 20923
Atlanta, GA 30320
770-914-7794; 770-914-7796
bob@customknifeconsignment.com; www.customknifeconsignment.com
We sell your knives

CUTLERY SHOPPE
3956 E Vantage Pointe Ln
Meridian, ID 83642-7268
800-231-1272; Fax: 208-884-4433
order@cutleryshoppe.com;
www.cutleryshoppe.com
Discount pricing on top quality brands

CUTTING EDGE, THE
2900 South 26th St
Rogers, AR 72758-8571
800-255-9034; Fax: 479-631-8493
ce_info@cuttingedge.com;
www.cuttingedge.com
After-market knives since 1968. They offer about 1,000 individual knives for sale each month. Subscription by first class mail, in U.S. $20 per year, Canada or Mexico by air mail, $25 per year. All overseas by air mail, $40 per year. The oldest and the most experienced in the business of buying and selling knives. They buy collections of any size, take knives on consignment. Every month there are 4-8 pages in color featuring the work of top makers

DENTON, J.W.
102 N. Main St
Hiawassee, GA 30546
706-896-2292
jwdenton@alltel.net
Loveless knives

DUNN KNIVES INC.
PO Box 204
5830 NW Carlson Rd
Rossville, KS 66533
800-245-6483
steve.greene@dunnknives.com;
www.dunnknives.com

FAZALARE, ROY
PO Box 1335
Agoura Hills, CA 91376
818-879-6161 after 7pm
ourfaz@aol.com
Handmade multiblades; older case; Fight'n Rooster; Bulldog brand & Cripple Creek

FROST CUTLERY CO.
PO Box 22636
Chattanooga, TN 37422
800-251-7768; Fax: 423-894-9576
www.frostcutlery.com

GENUINE ISSUE INC.
949 Middle Country Rd
Selden, NY 11784
631-696-3802; 631-696-3803
gicutlery@aol.com
Antique knives, swords

GEORGE TICHBOURNE CUSTOM KNIVES
7035 Maxwell Rd #5
Mississauga, Ontario L5S 1R5
CANADA
905-670-0200
sales@tichbourneknives.com;
www.tichbourneknives.com
Canadian custom knifemaker has full retail knife store

GODWIN, INC. G. GEDNEY
PO Box 100
Valley Forge, PA 19481
610-783-0670; Fax: 610-783-6083
sales@gggodwin.com;
www.gggodwin.com
18th century reproductions

GOLCZEWS KNIVES
Larry Golczewski, dba New Jersey Knifer
30 Quigley Rd.
Hewitt, NJ 07421
973-728-2386
Medium- to high-priced custom and handmade knives, some production if made in USA, Japan, Germany, or Italy. Practical to tactical. Consignments welcome. Also buy, design, and appraise.

GRAZYNA SHAW/QUINTESSENTIAL CUTLERY
715 Bluff St.
Clearwater, MN 55320
201-655-4411; Fax: 320-558-6128; www.quintcut.com
Specializing in investment-grade custom knives and early makers

GUILD KNIVES
Donald Guild
320 Paani Place 1A
Paia, HI 96779
808-877-3109
don@guildknives.com;
www.guildknives.com
Purveyor of custom art knives

HOUSE OF TOOLS LTD.
#136, 8228 Macleod Tr. SE
Calgary, Alberta, Canada
T2H 2B8

JENCO SALES, INC. / KNIFE IMPORTERS, INC. / WHITE LIGHTNING
PO Box 1000
11307 Conroy Ln
Manchaca, TX 78652
303-444-2882
kris@finishlineusa.com
www.whitelightningco.com
Wholesale only

KELLAM KNIVES CO.
902 S Dixie Hwy
Lantana, FL 33462
800-390-6918; 561-588-3186
info@kellamknives.com;
www.kellamknives.com
Largest selection of Finnish knives; own line of folders and fixed blades

KNIFEART.COM
13301 Pompano Dr
Little Rock AR 72211
501-221-1319; Fax: 501-221-2695
www.knifeart.com
Large internet seller of custom knives & upscale production knives

KNIFEMASTERS CUSTOM KNIVES/J&S FEDER
PO Box 208
Westport, CT 06880
(203) 226-5211
Investment grade custom knives

KNIVES PLUS
2467 I 40 West
Amarillo, TX 79109
800-687-6202
salessupport@knivesplus.com; www.knivesplus.com
Retail cutlery and cutlery accessories since 1987

KRIS CUTLERY
2314 Monte Verde Dr
Pinole, CA 94564
510-758-9912 Fax: 510-223-8968
kriscutlery@aol.com; www.kriscutlery.com
Japanese, medieval, Chinese & Philippine

LONE STAR WHOLESALE
2407 W Interstate 40
Amarillo, TX 79109
806-356-9540
Wholesale only; major brands and accessories

MATTHEWS CUTLERY
4401 Sentry Dr
Tucker, GA 30084-6561
770-939-6915

MOORE CUTLERY
PO Box 633
Lockport, IL 60441
708-301-4201
www.knives.cx
Owned & operated by Gary Moore since 1991 (a full-time dealer). Purveyor of high quality custom & production knives

MORTY THE KNIFE MAN, INC.
4 Manorhaven Blvd
Pt Washington, NY 11050
516-767-2357; 516-767-7058

MUSEUM REPLICAS LIMITED
2147 Gees Mill Rd
Conyers, GA 30012
800-883-8838
www.museumreplicas.com
Historically accurate and battle ready swords & daggers

NORDIC KNIVES
1634-C Copenhagen Drive
Solvang, CA 93463
805-688-3612; Fax: 805-688-1635
info@nordicknives.com;
www.nordicknives.com
Custom and Randall knives

PARKERS' KNIFE COLLECTOR SERVICE
6715 Heritage Business Court
Chattanooga, TN 37422
615-892-0448; Fax: 615-892-9165

PLAZA CUTLERY, INC.
3333 S. Bristol St., Suite 2060
South Coast Plaza
Costa Mesa, CA 92626
866-827-5292; 714-549-3932
dan@plazacutlery.com;
www.plazacutlery.com
Largest selection of knives on the west coast. Custom makers from beginners to the best. All customs, William Henry, Strider, Reeves, Randalls & others available online by phone

RANDALL KNIFE SOCIETY
PO Box 158
Meadows of Dan, VA 24120
276-952-2500
payrks@gate.net;
www.randallknifesociety.com
Randall, Loveless, Scagel, moran, antique pocket knives

ROBERTSON'S CUSTOM CUTLERY
4960 Sussex Dr
Evans, GA 30809
706-650-0252; 706-860-1623
rccedge@csranet.com; www.robertsoncustomcutlery.com
World class custom knives, Vanguard knives-Limited exclusive design

SHADOW, JAY & KAREN
9719 N Hayden Rd
Scottsdale, AZ 85258
866-455-1344; 480-947-2136
service@mustlovepens.com;
www.jaykar.com
Diamonds imported direct from Belgium

SMOKY MOUNTAIN KNIFE WORKS, INC.
2320 Winfield Dunn Pkwy
PO Box 4430
Sevierville, TN 37864
800-251-9306; 865-453-5871
info@smkw.com; www.eknifeworks.com
The world's largest knife showplace, catalog and website

STODDARD'S, INC.
50 Temple Pl
Boston, MA 02116
617-426-4187
Cutlery (kitchen, pocket knives, Randall-made knives, custom knives, scissors & manicure tools) binoculars, lwo vision aids, personal care items (hair brushes, manicure sets mirrors)

VOYLES, BRUCE
PO Box 22007
Chattanooga, TN 37422
423-238-6753; Fax: 423-238-3960
bruce@jbrucevoyles.com;
www.jbrucevoyles.com
Knives, knife auctions

knife services

appraisers

Levine, Bernard, P.O. Box 2404, Eugene, OR, 97402, 541-484-0294, brlevine@ix.netcom.com

Russell, A.G., Knives Inc, 2900 S. 26th St., Rogers, AR 72758-8571, phone 800-255-9034 or 479-631-0055, fax 479-631-8734, lynnd@agrussell.com, www.agrussell.com

Vallini, Massimo, Via G. Bruno 7, 20154 Milano, ITALY, 02-33614751, massimo_vallini@yahoo.it, Knife expert

custom grinders

McGowan Manufacturing Company, 4854 N Shamrock Pl #100, Tucson, AZ, 85705, 800-342-4810, 520-219-0884, info@mcgowanmfg.com, www.mcgowanmfg.com, Knife sharpeners, hunting axes

Peele, Bryan, The Elk Rack, 215 Ferry St. P.O. Box 1363, Thompson Falls, MT, 59873

Schlott, Harald, Zingster Str. 26, 13051 Berlin, GERMANY, 049 030 9293346, harald.schlott@T-online.de, Custom grinder, custom handle artisan, display case/box maker, etcher, scrimshander

Wilson, R.W., P.O. Box 2012, Weirton, WV, 26062

custom handles

Cooper, Jim, 1221 Cook St, Ramona, CA, 92065-3214, 760-789-1097, (760) 788-7992, jamcooper@aol.com

Burrows, Chuck, dba Wild Rose Trading Co, 289 Laposta Canyon Rd, Durango, CO, 81303, 970-259-8396, chuck@wrtcleather.com, www.wrtcleather.com

Fields, Donald, 790 Tamerlane St, Deltona, FL, 32725, 386-532-9070, donaldfields@aol.com, Selling ancient ivories; mammoth & fossil walrus

Grussenmeyer, Paul G., 310 Kresson Rd, Cherry Hill, NJ, 08034, 856-428-1088, 856-428-8997, pgrussentne@comcast.net, www.pgcarvings.com

Holland, Dennis K., 4908-17th Pl., Lubbock, TX, 79416

Imboden II, Howard L., hi II Originals, 620 Deauville Dr., Dayton, OH, 45429

Kelso, Jim, 577 Collar Hill Rd, Worcester, VT, 05682, 802-229-4254, (802) 223-0595

Knack, Gary, 309 Wightman, Ashland, OR, 97520

Marlatt, David, 67622 Oldham Rd., Cambridge, OH, 43725, 740-432-7549

Mead, Dennis, 2250 E. Mercury St., Inverness, FL, 34453-0514

Myers, Ron, 6202 Marglenn Ave., Baltimore, MD, 21206, 410-866-6914

Saggio, Joe, 1450 Broadview Ave. #12, Columbus, OH, 43212, jvsag@webtv.net, www.j.v.saggio@worldnet.att.net, Handle Carver

Schlott, Harald, Zingster Str. 26, 13051 Berlin, GERMANY, 049 030 9293346, harald.schlott@T-online.de, Custom grinder, custom handle artisan, display case/box maker, etcher, scrimshander

Snell, Barry A., 4801 96th St. N., St. Petersburg, FL, 33708-3740

Vallotton, A., 621 Fawn Ridge Dr., Oakland, OR, 97462

Watson, Silvia, 350 Jennifer Lane, Driftwood, TX, 78619

Wilderness Forge, 315 North 100 East, Kanab, UT, 84741, 435-644-3674, bhatting@xpressweb.com

Williams, Gary, (GARBO), PO Box 210, Glendale, KY, 42740-2010

display cases and boxes

Bill's Custom Cases, P O Box 603, Montague, CA, 96064, 530-459-5968, billscustomcases@earthlink.net

Brooker, Dennis, Rt. 1, Box 12A, Derby, IA, 50068

Chas Clements' Custom Leathercraft, Chas, 1741 Dallas St., Aurora, CO, 80010-2018, 303-364-0403, GRYPHONS@HOME.NET, Display case/box maker, Leatherworker, Knife appraiser

Freund, Steve, Tomway LLC, 1646 Tichenor Court, Atlanta, GA, 30338, 770-393-8349, steve@tomway.com, www.tomway.com

Gimbert, Nelson, P.O. Box 787, Clemmons, NC, 27012

McLean, Lawrence, 12344 Meritage Ct, Rancho Cucamonga, CA, 91739, 714-848-5779, lmclean@charter.net

Miller, Michael K., M&M Kustom Krafts, 28510 Santiam Highway, Sweet Home, OR, 97386

Miller, Robert, P.O. Box 2722, Ormond Beach, FL, 32176

Retichek, Joseph L., W9377 Co. TK. D, Beaver Dam, WI, 53916

Robbins, Wayne, 11520 Inverway, Belvidere, IL, 61008

S&D Enterprises, 20 East Seventh St, Manchester, OH, 45144, 937-549-2602, 937-549-2602, sales@s-denterprises.com, www.s-denterprises.com, Display case/ box maker. Manufacturer of aluminum display, chipboard type displays, wood displays. Silk screening or acid etching for logos on product

Schlott, Harald, Zingster Str. 26, 13051 Berlin, GERMANY, 049 030 9293346, harald.schlott@T-online.de, Custom grinder, custom handle artisan, display case/box maker, etcher, scrimshander

engravers

Adlam, Tim, 1705 Witzel Ave., Oshkosh, WI, 54902, 920-235-4589, www.adlamngraving.com

Alfano, Sam, 36180 Henry Gaines Rd., Pearl River, LA, 70452

Allard, Gary, 2395 Battlefield Rd., Fishers Hill, VA, 22626

Alpen, Ralph, 7 Bentley Rd., West Grove, PA, 19390, 610-869-7141

Baron, David, Baron Technology Inc., 62 Spring Hill Rd., Trumbull, CT, 06611, 203-452-0515, bti@baronengraving.com, www.baronengraving.com, Polishing, plating, inlays, artwork

Bates, Billy, 2302 Winthrop Dr. SW, Decatur, AL, 35603, bbrn@aol.com, www.angelfire.com/al/billybates

Bettenhausen, Merle L., 17358 Ottawa, Tinley Park, IL, 60477

Blair, Jim, PO Box 64, 59 Mesa Verde, Glenrock, WY, 82637, 307-436-8115, jblairengrav@msn.com

Bonshire, Benita, 1121 Burlington, Muncie, IN, 47302

Boster, A.D., 3000 Clarks Bridge Rd Lot 42, Gainesville, GA, 30501, 770-532-0958

Brooker, Dennis B., Rt. 1 Box 12A, Derby, IA, 50068

Churchill, Winston G., RFD Box 29B, Proctorsville, VT, 05153

Collins, Michael, Rt. 3075, Batesville Rd., Woodstock, GA, 30188

Cupp, Alana, PO Box 207, Annabella, UT, 84711

Dashwood, Jim, 255 Barkham Rd., Wokingham, Berkshire RG11 4BY, ENGLAND

Dean, Bruce, 13 Tressider Ave., Haberfield, N.S.W. 2045, Sydney, AUSTRALIA, 02 97977608

DeLorge, Ed, 6734 W Main St, Houma, LA, 70360, 504-223-0206

Dickson, John W., PO Box 49914, Sarasota, FL, 34230

Dolbare, Elizabeth, PO Box 502, Dubois, WY, 82513-0502

Downing, Jim, PO Box 4224, Springfield, MO, 65808, 417-865-5953, www.thegunengraver.com, Scrimshander

Duarte, Carlos, 108 Church St., Rossville, CA, 95678

Dubben, Michael, 414 S. Fares Ave., Evansville, IN, 47714

Dubber, Michael W., 8205 Heather Pl, Evansville, IN, 47710-4919

Eklund, Maihkel, Föne 1111, S-82041 Färila, SWEDEN, www.art-knives.com

Eldridge, Allan, 1424 Kansas Lane, Gallatin, TN, 37066

Ellis, Willy B, Willy B's Customs by William B Ellis, 4941 Cardinal Trail, Palm Harbor, FL, 34683, 727-942-6420, www.willyb.com

Engel, Terry (Flowers), PO Box 96, Midland, OR, 97634

Flannery Engraving Co., Jeff, 11034 Riddles Run Rd., Union, KY, 41091, engraving@fuse.net, http://home.fuse.net/ engraving/

Foster, Norvell, Foster Enterprises, PO Box 200343, San Antonio, TX, 78220

Fountain Products, 492 Prospect Ave., West Springfield, MA, 01089

Gipe, Sandi, Rt. 2, Box 1090A, Kendrick, ID, 83537

Glimm, Jerome C., 19 S. Maryland, Conrad, MT, 59425

Gournet, Geoffroy, 820 Paxinosa Ave., Easton, PA, 18042, 610-559-0710, www.geoffroygournet.com

Halloran, Tim 316 Fence line Dr. Blue Grass, IA 52726 563-381-5202

Harrington, Fred A., Winter: 3725 Citrus, Summer: 2107 W Frances Rd Mt Morris MI 48458-8215, St. James City, FL, 33956, Winter: 239-283-0721 Summer: 810-686-3008

Henderson, Fred D., 569 Santa Barbara Dr., Forest Park, GA, 30297, 770-968-4866

Hendricks, Frank, 396 Bluff Trail, Dripping Springs, TX, 78620, 512-858-7828

Holder, Pat, 7148 W. Country Gables Dr., Peoria, AZ, 85381

Ingle, Ralph W., 151 Callan Dr., Rossville, GA, 30741, 706-858-0641, riengraver@aol.com, Photographer

Johns, Bill, 1716 8th St, Cody, WY, 82414, 307-587-5090

Kelly, Lance, 1723 Willow Oak Dr., Edgewater, FL, 32132

Kelso, Jim, 577 Coller Hill Rd, Worcester, VT, 05682

Koevenig, Eugene and Eve, Koevenig's Engraving Service, Rabbit Gulch, Box 55, Hill City, SD, 57745-0055

Kostelnik, Joe and Patty, RD #4, Box 323, Greensburg, PA, 15601

Kudlas, John M., 55280 Silverwolf Dr, Barnes, WI, 54873, 715-795-2031, jkudlas@cheqnet.net, Engraver, scrimshander

Limings Jr., Harry, 959 County Rd. 170, Marengo, OH, 43334-9625

Lindsay, Steve, 3714 West Cedar Hills Drive, Kearney, NE, 68847

Lyttle, Brian, Box 5697, High River AB CANADA, T1V 1M7

Lytton, Simon M., 19 Pinewood Gardens, Hemel Hempstead, Herts. HP1 1TN, ENGLAND

Mason, Joe, 146 Value Rd, Brandon, MS, 39042, 601-824-9867, www.joemasonengraving.com

McCombs, Leo, 1862 White Cemetery Rd., Patriot, OH, 45658

McDonald, Dennis, 8359 Brady St., Peosta, IA, 52068

McKenzie, Lynton, 6940 N Alvernon Way, Tucson, AZ, 85718

McLean, Lawrence, 12344 Meritage Ct, Rancho Cucamonga, CA, 91739, 714-848-5779, lmclean@charter.net

Meyer, Chris, 39 Bergen Ave., Wantage, NJ, 07461, 973-875-6299

Minnick, Joyce, 144 N. 7th St., Middletown, IN, 47356

Morgan, Tandie, P.O. Box 693, 30700 Hwy. 97, Nucla, CO, 81424

Morton, David A., 1110 W. 21st St., Lorain, OH, 44052

Moulton, Dusty, 135 Hillview Ln, Loudon, TN, 37774, 865-408-9779

Muller, Jody & Pat, PO Box 35, Pittsburg, MO, 65724, 417-852-4306/417-752-3260, mullerforge@hotmail.com, www.mullerforge.com

Nelida, Toniutti, via G. Pasconi 29/c, Maniago 33085 (PN), ITALY

Nilsson, Jonny Walker, Tingsstigen 11, SE-933 33 Arvidsjaur, SWEDEN, +(46) 960-13048, 0960.13048@telia.com, www.jwnknives.com

Nott, Ron, Box 281, Summerdale, PA, 17093

Parsons, Michael R., McKee Knives, 7042 McFarland Rd, Indianapolis, IN, 46227, 317-784-7943

Patterson, W.H., P.O. Drawer DK, College Station, TX, 77841

Peri, Valerio, Via Meucci 12, Gardone V.T. 25063, ITALY

Pilkington Jr., Scott, P.O. Box 97, Monteagle, TN, 37356, 931-924-3400, scott@pilkguns.com, www.pilkguns.com

Poag, James, RR1, Box 212A, Grayville, IL, 62844

Potts, Wayne, 1580 Meade St Apt A, Denver, CO, 80204

Rabeno, Martin, Spook Hollow Trading Co, 530 Eagle Pass, Durango, CO, 81301

Raftis, Andrew, 2743 N. Sheffield, Chicago, IL, 60614

Roberts, J.J., 7808 Lake Dr., Manassas, VA, 20111, 703-330-0448, jjrengraver@aol.com, www.angelfire.com/va2/ engraver

Robidoux, Roland J., DMR Fine Engraving, 25 N. Federal Hwy.

Studio 5, Dania, FL, 33004

Rosser, Bob, Hand Engraving, 2809 Crescent Ave Ste 20, Homewood, AL, 35209-2526, www.hand-engravers.com

Rudolph, Gil, 20922 Oak Pass Ave, Tehachapi, CA, 93561, 661-822-4949, www.gtraks@csurfers.net

Rundell, Joe, 6198 W. Frances Rd., Clio, MI, 48420

Schickl, L., Ottingweg 497, A-5580 Tamsweg, AUSTRIA, 0043 6474 8583, Scrimshander

Schlott, Harald, Zingster Str. 26, 13051 Berlin, GERMANY, 049 030 9293346, 049 030 9293346, harald.schlott@T-online.de, www.gravur-kunst-atelier.de.vu, Custom grinder, custom handle artisan, display case/box maker, etcher, scrimshander

Schönert, Elke, 18 Lansdowne Pl., Central, Port Elizabeth, SOUTH AFRICA

Shaw, Bruce, P.O. Box 545, Pacific Grove, CA, 93950, 831-646-1937, 831-644-0941

Shostle, Ben, 1121 Burlington, Muncie, IN, 47302

Slobodian, Barbara, 4101 River Ridge Dr., PO Box 1498, San Andreas, CA 95249, 209-286-1980, fax 209-286-1982, barbara@dancethetide.com. Specializes in Japanese-style engraving.

Smith, Ron, 5869 Straley, Ft. Worth, TX, 76114

Smitty's Engraving, 21320 Pioneer Circle, Hurrah, OK, 73045, 405-454-6968, smittys.engraving@prodigy.net, www.smittys-engraving.us

Spode, Peter, Tresaith Newland, Malvern, Worcestershire WR13 5AY, ENGLAND

Swartley, Robert D., 2800 Pine St., Napa, CA, 94558

Takeuchi, Shigetoshi, 21-14-1-Chome kamimuneoka Shiki shi, 353 Saitama, JAPAN

Theis, Terry, 21452 FM 2093, Harper, TX, 78631, 830-864-4438

Valade, Robert B., 931 3rd Ave., Seaside, OR, 97138, 503-738-7672, (503) 738-7672

Waldrop, Mark, 14562 SE 1st Ave. Rd., Summerfield, FL, 34491

Warenski, Julie, 590 East 500 N., Richfield, UT, 84701, 435-896-5319, julie@warenskiknives.com, www.warenskiknives.com

Warren, Kenneth W., P.O. Box 2842, Wenatchee, WA, 98807-2842, 509-663-6123, (509) 663-6123

Whitehead, James 2175 South Willow Ave. Space 22 Fresno, CA 93725 559-412-4374 jdwmks@yahoo.com

Whitmore, Jerry, 1740 Churchill Dr., Oakland, OR, 97462

Winn, Travis A., 558 E. 3065 S., Salt Lake City, UT, 84106

Wood, Mel, P.O. Box 1255, Sierra Vista, AZ, 85636

Zietz, Dennis, 5906 40th Ave., Kenosha, WI, 53144

Zima, Russ, 7291 Ruth Way, Denver, CO, 80221, 303-657-9378, www.rzengraving.com

etchers

Baron Technology Inc., David Baron, 62 Spring Hill Rd., Trumbull, CT, 06611

Fountain Products, 492 Prospect Ave., West Springfield, MA, 01089

Hayes, Dolores, P.O. Box 41405, Los Angeles, CA, 90041

Holland, Dennis, 4908 17th Pl., Lubbock, TX, 79416

Kelso, Jim, 577 Collar Hill Rd, Worcester, VT, 05682

Larstein, Francine, FRANCINE ETCHINGS & ETCHED KNIVES, 368 White Rd, Watsonville, CA, 95076, 800-557-1525/831-426-6046, 831-684-1949, francine@francinetchings.com, www.boyeknivesgallery.com

Lefaucheux, Jean-Victor, Saint-Denis-Le-Ferment, 27140 Gisors, FRANCE

Mead, Faustina L., 2550 E. Mercury St., Inverness, FL, 34453-0514, 352-344-4751, scrimsha@infionline.net, www.scrimshaw-by-faustina.com

Myers, Ron, 6202 Marglenn Ave., Baltimore, MD, 21206, (acid) etcher

Nilsson, Jonny Walker, Tingsstigen 11, SE-933 33 Arvidsjaur, SWEDEN, +(46) 960-13048, 0960.13048@telia.com, www.jwnknives.com

Schlott, Harald, Zingster Str. 26, 13051 Berlin, GERMANY, 049

030 9293346, harald.schlott@T-online.de, Custom grinder, custom handle artisan, display case/box maker, etcher, scrimshander

Vallotton, A., Northwest Knife Supply, 621 Fawn Ridge Dr., Oakland, OR, 97462

Watson, Silvia, 350 Jennifer Lane, Driftwood, TX, 78619

heat treaters

Bay State Metal Treating Co., 6 Jefferson Ave., Woburn, MA, 01801

Bos Heat Treating, Paul, Shop: 1900 Weld Blvd., El Cajon, CA, 92020, 619-562-2370 / 619-445-4740 Home, PaulBos@ BuckKnives.com

Holt, B.R., 1238 Birchwood Drive, Sunnyvale, CA, 94089

Kazou, Okaysu, 12-2 1 Chome Higashi, Ueno, Taito-Ku, Tokyo, JAPAN, 81-33834-2323, 81-33831-3012

Metal Treating Bodycote Inc., 710 Burns St., Cincinnati, OH, 45204

O&W Heat Treat Inc., One Bidwell Rd., South Windsor, CT, 06074, 860-528-9239, (860) 291-9939, owht1@aol.com

Progressive Heat Treating Co., 2802 Charles City Rd, Richmond, VA, 23231, 804-545-0010, 804-545-0012

Texas Heat Treating Inc., 303 Texas Ave., Round Rock, TX, 78664

Texas Knifemakers Supply, 10649 Haddington, Suite 180, Houston, TX, 77043

Tinker Shop, The, 1120 Helen, Deer Park, TX, 77536

Valley Metal Treating Inc., 355 S. East End Ave., Pomona, CA, 91766

Wilderness Forge, 315 North 100 East, Kanab, UT, 84741, 435-644-3674, bhatting@xpressweb.com

Wilson, R.W., P.O. Box 2012, Weirton, WV, 26062

leather workers

Abramson, David, 116 Baker Ave, Wharton, NJ, 07885, lifter4him1@aol.com, www.liftersleather.com

Bruner, Rick, 7756 Aster Lane, Jenison, MI, 49428, 616-457-0403

Burrows, Chuck, dba Wild Rose Trading Co, 289 Laposta Canyon Rd, Durango, CO, 81303, 970-259-8396, chuck@wrtcleather.com

Clements' Custom Leathercraft, Chas, 1741 Dallas St., Aurora, CO, 80010-2018

Cole, Dave, 620 Poinsetta Dr., Satellite Beach, FL 32937, 321-773-1687, www.dcknivesandleather.blademakers.com. Custom sheath services.

Cooper, Harold, 136 Winding Way, Frankfort, KY, 40601

Cooper, Jim, 1221 Cook St, Ramona, CA, 92065-3214, 760-789-1097, 760-788-7992, jamcooper@aol.com

Cow Catcher Leatherworks, 3006 Industrial Dr, Raleigh, NC, 27609

Cubic, George, GC Custom Leather Co., 10561 E. Deerfield Pl., Tucson, AZ, 85749, 520-760-0695, gcubic@aol.com

Dawkins, Dudley, 221 N. Broadmoor Ave, Topeka, KS, 66606-1254, 785-235-3871, dawkind@sbcglobal.net, ABS member/ knifemaker forges straight knives

Evans, Scott V, Edge Works Mfg, 1171 Halltown Rd, Jacksonville, NC, 28546, 910-455-9834, (910) 346-5660, edgeworks@ coastalnet.com, www.tacticalholsters.com

Genske, Jay, 283 Doty St, Fond du Lac, WI, 54935, 920-921-8019/Cell Phone 920-579-0144, jaygenske@hotmail.com, Custom Grinder, Custom Handle Artisan

Hawk, Ken, Rt. 1, Box 770, Ceres, VA, 24318-9630

Homyk, David N., 8047 Carriage Ln., Wichita Falls, TX, 76306

John's Custom Leather, John R. Stumpf, 523 S. Liberty St, Blairsville, PA, 15717, 724-459-6802, 724-459-5996

Kelley, Jo Ann, 52 Mourning Dove Dr., Watertown, WI 53094, 920-206-0807, ladybug@ticon.net, www.hembrookcustomknives.com. Custom leather knife sheaths $40 to $100; making sheaths since 2002.

Kravitt, Chris, HC 31 Box 6484, Rt 200, Ellsworth, ME, 04605-9805, 207-584-3000, 207-584-3000, sheathmkr@aol.com, www.treestumpleather.com, Reference: Tree Stump Leather

Larson, Richard, 549 E. Hawkeye, Turlock, CA, 95380

Layton, Jim, 2710 Gilbert Avenue, Portsmouth, OH, 45662

Lee, Randy, P.O. Box 1873, 270 N 9th West, St. Johns, AZ, 85936, 928-337-2594, 928-337-5002, randylee@randyleeknives.com, info@randyleeknives.com, Custom knifemaker; www.randyleeknives.com

Long, Paul, 108 Briarwood Ln W, Kerrville, TX, 78028, 830-367-5536, kgebauer@classicnet.net

Lott, Sherry, 1100 Legion Park Rd., Greenburg, KY 42743, phone 270-932-2212, fax 270-299-2471, sherrylott@alltel.net

Mason, Arne, 258 Wimer St., Ashland, OR, 97520, 541-482-2260, (541) 482-7785, www.arnemason.com

McGowan, Liz, 12629 Howard Lodge Dr., Winter Add-2023 Robin Ct Sebring FL 33870, Sykesville, MD, 21784, 410-489-4323

Metheny, H.A. "Whitey", 7750 Waterford Dr., Spotsylvania, VA, 22553, 540-582-3228 Cell 540-542-1440, 540-582-3095, nametheny@aol.com, www.methenyknives.com

Miller, Michael K., 28510 Santiam Highway, Sweet Home, OR, 97386

Mobley, Martha, 240 Alapaha River Road, Chula, GA, 31733

Morrissey, Martin, 4578 Stephens Rd., Blairsville, GA, 30512

Niedenthal, John Andre, Beadwork & Buckskin, Studio 3955 NW 103 Dr., Coral Springs, FL, 33065-1551, 954-345-0447, a_niedenthal@hotmail.com

Neilson, Tess, RR2 Box 16, Wyalusing, PA, 18853, 570-746-4944, www.mountainhollow.net, Doing business as Neilson's Mountain Hollow

Parsons, Larry, 1038 W. Kyle, Mustang, OK 73064 405-376-9408 s.m.parsons@sbcglobal.net

Parsons, Michael R., McKee Knives, 7042 McFarland Rd, Indianapolis, IN, 46227, 317-784-7943

Poag, James H., RR #1 Box 212A, Grayville, IL, 62844

Red's Custom Leather, Ed Todd, 9 Woodlawn Rd., Putnam Valley, NY, 10579, 845-528-3783

Rowe, Kenny, 3219 Hwy 29 South, Hope, AR, 71801, 870-777-8216, 870-777-0935, rowesleather@yahoo.com, www.knifeart.com or www.theedgeequipment.com

Schrap, Robert G., 7024 W. Wells St., Wauwatosa, WI, 53213-3717, 414-771-6472, (414) 479-9765, knifesheaths@aol.com, www.customsheaths.com

Strahin, Robert, 401 Center St., Elkins, WV, 26241, *Custom Knife Sheaths

Tierney, Mike, 447 Rivercrest Dr., Woodstock ON CANADA, N4S 5W5

Turner, Kevin, 17 Hunt Ave., Montrose, NY, 10548

Velasquez, Gil, 7120 Madera Dr., Goleta, CA, 93117

Walker, John, 17 Laber Circle, Little Rock, AR, 72210, 501-455-0239, john.walker@afbic.com

Watson, Bill, #1 Presidio, Wimberly, TX, 78676

Whinnery, Walt, 1947 Meadow Creek Dr., Louisville, KY, 40218

Williams, Sherman A., 1709 Wallace St., Simi Valley, CA, 93065

miscellaneous

Hendryx Design, Scott, 5997 Smokey Way, Boise, ID, 83714, 208-377-8044, www.shdsheaths@msn.com

Kydex Sheath Maker

Robertson, Kathy, Impress by Design, PO Box 1367, Evans, GA, 30809-1367, 706-650-0982, (706) 860-1623, impressbydesign@comcast.net, Advertising/graphic designer

Strahin, Robert, 401 Center St., Elkins, WV, 26241, 304-636-0128, rstrahin@copper.net, *Custom Knife Sheaths

photographers

Alfano, Sam, 36180 Henery Gaines Rd., Pearl River, LA, 70452

Allen, John, Studio One, 3823 Pleasant Valley Blvd., Rockford, IL, 61114

Balance Digital, Rob Szajkowski, 261 Riverview Way, Oceanside, CA 92057, 760-815-6131, rob@balancedigital.com, www.balancedigital.com

Bilal, Mustafa, Turk's Head Productions, 908 NW 50th St., Seattle, WA, 98107-3634, 206-782-4164, (206) 783-5677, mustafa@turkshead.com, www.turkshead.com, Graphic design, marketing & advertising

Bogaerts, Jan, Regenweg 14, 5757 Pl., Liessel, HOLLAND

Box Photography, Doug, 1804 W Main St, Brenham, TX, 77833-3420

Brown, Tom, 6048 Grants Ferry Rd., Brandon, MS, 39042-8136

Butman, Steve, P.O. Box 5106, Abilene, TX, 79608

Calidonna, Greg, 205 Helmwood Dr., Elizabethtown, KY, 42701

Campbell, Jim, 7935 Ranch Rd., Port Richey, FL, 34668

Cooper, Jim, Sharpbycoop.com photography, 9 Mathew Court, Norwalk, CT, 06851, jcooper@sharpbycoop.com, www.sharpbycoop.com

Courtice, Bill, P.O. Box 1776, Duarte, CA, 91010-4776

Crosby, Doug, RFD 1, Box 1111, Stockton Springs, ME, 04981

Danko, Michael, 3030 Jane Street, Pittsburgh, PA, 15203

Davis, Marshall B., P.O. Box 3048, Austin, TX, 78764

Earley, Don, 1241 Ft. Bragg Rd., Fayetteville, NC, 28305

Ehrlich, Linn M., 1850 N Clark St #1008, Chicago, IL, 60614, 312-209-2107

Etzler, John, 11200 N. Island Rd., Grafton, OH, 44044

Fahrner, Dave, 1623 Arnold St., Pittsburgh, PA, 15205

Faul, Jan W., 903 Girard St. NE, Rr. Washington, DC, 20017

Fedorak, Allan, 28 W. Nicola St., Amloops BC CANADA, V2C 1J6

Fox, Daniel, Lumina Studios, 6773 Industrial Parkway, Cleveland, OH, 44070, 440-734-2118, (440) 734-3542, lumina@en.com

Freiberg, Charley, PO Box 42, Elkins, NH, 03233, 603-526-2767, charleyfreiberg@tos.net

Gardner, Chuck, 116 Quincy Ave., Oak Ridge, TN, 37830

Gawryla, Don, 1105 Greenlawn Dr., Pittsburgh, PA, 15220

Goffe Photographic Associates, 3108 Monte Vista Blvd., NE, Albuquerque, NM, 87106

Graham, James, 7434 E Northwest Hwy, Dallas, TX, 75231, 214-341-5138, jamie@jamiephoto.com, www.jamiephoto.com, Product photographer

Graley, Gary W., RR2 Box 556, Gillett, PA, 16925

Griggs, Dennis, 118 Pleasant Pt Rd, Topsham, ME, 04086, 207-725-5689

Hanusin, John, Reames-Hanusin Studio, PO Box 931, Northbrook, IL, 60065 0931

Hardy, Scott, 639 Myrtle Ave., Placerville, CA, 95667

Hodge, Tom, 7175 S US Hwy 1 Lot 36, Titusville, FL, 32780-8172, 321-267-7989, egdoht@hotmail.com

Holter, Wayne V., 125 Lakin Ave., Boonsboro, MD, 21713, 301-416-2855, mackwayne@hotmail.com

Hopkins, David W, Hopkins Photography inc, 201 S Jefferson, Iola, KS, 66749, 620-365-7443, nhoppy@netks.net

Kerns, Bob, 18723 Birdseye Dr., Germantown, MD, 20874

LaFleur, Gordon, 111 Hirst, Box 1209, Parksville BC CANADA, V0R 270

Lear, Dale, 6544 Cora Mill Rd, Gallipolis, OH, 45631, 740-245-5482, dalelear@yahoo.com, Ebay Sales

LeBlanc, Paul, No. 3 Meadowbrook Cir., Melissa, TX, 75454

Lester, Dean, 2801 Junipero Ave Suite 212, Long Beach, CA, 90806-2140

Leviton, David A., A Studio on the Move, P.O. Box 2871, Silverdale, WA, 98383, 360-697-3452

Long, Gary W., 3556 Miller's Crossroad Rd., Hillsboro, TN, 37342

Long, Jerry, 402 E. Gladden Dr., Farmington, NM, 87401

Lum, Billy, 16307 Evening Star Ct., Crosby, TX, 77532

Lum, Mitch 4616 25th Ave. NE #563 Seattle, WA 98105 www.mitchlum.com mitch@mitchlum.com 206-356-6813

McCollum, Tom, P.O. Box 933, Lilburn, GA, 30226

Mitch Lum Website and Photography, mitch@mitchlum.com, www.mitchlum.com

Moake, Jim, 18 Council Ave., Aurora, IL, 60504

Moya Inc., 4212 S. Dixie Hwy., West Palm Beach, FL, 33405

Norman's Studio, 322 S. 2nd St., Vivian, LA, 71082

Owens, William T., Box 99, Williamsburg, WV, 24991

Palmer Studio, 2008 Airport Blvd., Mobile, AL, 36606

Payne, Robert G., P.O. Box 141471, Austin, TX, 78714

Pigott, John, 9095 Woodprint LN, Mason, OH, 45040

Point Seven, 810 Seneca St., Toledo, OH, 43608, 419-243-8880, www.pointsevenstudios.com

Professional Medica Concepts, Patricia Mitchell, P.O. Box 0002, Warren, TX, 77664, 409-547-2213, pm0909@wt.net

Rasmussen, Eric L., 1121 Eliason, Brigham City, UT, 84302

Rhoades, Cynthia J., Box 195, Clearmont, WY, 82835

Rice, Tim, PO Box 663, Whitefish, MT, 59937

Richardson, Kerry, 2520 Mimosa St., Santa Rosa, CA, 95405, 707-575-1875, kerry@sonic.net, www.sonic.net/~kerry

Ross, Bill, 28364 S. Western Ave. Suite 464, Rancho Palos Verdes, CA, 90275

Rubicam, Stephen, 14 Atlantic Ave., Boothbay Harbor, ME, 04538-1202

Rush, John D., 2313 Maysel, Bloomington, IL, 61701

Schreiber, Roger, 429 Boren Ave. N., Seattle, WA, 98109

Semmer, Charles, 7885 Cyd Dr., Denver, CO, 80221

Silver Images Photography, 2412 N Keystone, Flagstaff, AZ, 86004

Slobodian, Scott, 4101 River Ridge Dr., P.O. Box 1498, San Andreas, CA, 95249, 209-286-1980, (209) 286-1982, www.slobodianswords.com

Smith, Earl W., 5121 Southminster Rd., Columbus, OH, 43221

Smith, Randall, 1720 Oneco Ave., Winter Park, FL, 32789

Storm Photo, 334 Wall St., Kingston, NY, 12401

Surles, Mark, P.O. Box 147, Falcon, NC, 28342

Third Eye Photos, 140 E. Sixth Ave., Helena, MT, 59601

Thurber, David, P.O. Box 1006, Visalia, CA, 93279

Tighe, Brian, RR 1, Ridgeville ON CANADA, L0S 1M0, 905-892-2734, www.tigheknives.com

Towell, Steven L., 3720 N.W. 32nd Ave., Camas, WA, 98607, 360-834-9049, sltowell@netscape.net

Valley Photo, 2100 Arizona Ave., Yuma, AZ, 85364

Verno Studio, Jay, 3030 Jane Street, Pittsburgh, PA, 15203

Ward, Chuck, 1010 E North St, PO Box 2272, Benton, AR, 72018, 501-778-4329, chuckbop@aol.com

Weyer International, 2740 Nebraska Ave., Toledo, OH, 43607, 800-448-8424, (419) 534-2697, law-weyerinternational@msn.com, Books

Wise, Harriet, 242 Dill Ave., Frederick, MD, 21701

Worley, Holly, Worley Photography, 6360 W David Dr, Littleton, CO, 80128-5708, 303-257-8091, 720-981-2800, hsworley@aol.com, Products, Digital & Film

scrimshanders

Adlam, Tim, 1705 Witzel Ave., Oshkosh, WI, 54902, 920-235-4589, www.adlamngraving.com

Alpen, Ralph, 7 Bentley Rd., West Grove, PA, 19390, 610-869-7141

Anderson, Terry Jack, 10076 Birnamwoods Way, Riverton, UT, 84065-9073

Bailey, Mary W., 3213 Jonesboro Dr., Nashville, TN, 37214, mbscrim@aol.com, www.members.aol.com/mbscrim/ scrim.html

Baker, Duane, 2145 Alum Creek Dr., Cambridge Park Apt. #10, Columbus, OH, 43207

Barrows, Miles, 524 Parsons Ave., Chillicothe, OH, 45601

Brady, Sandra, P.O. Box 104, Monclova, OH, 43542, 419-866-0435, (419) 867-0656, sandyscrim@hotmail.com, www.knifeshows.com

Beauchamp, Gaetan, 125 de la Riviere, Stoneham, PQ, G0A 4P0, CANADA, 418-848-1914, (418) 848-6859, knives@gbeauchamp.ca, www.beauchamp.cjb.net

Bellet, Connie, PO Box 151, Palermo, ME, 04354 0151, 207-993-2327, phwhitehawk@gwl.net

Benade, Lynn, 2610 Buckhurst Dr, Beachwood, OH, 44122, 216-464-0777, llbnc17@aol.com

Bonshire, Benita, 1121 Burlington Dr., Muncie, IN, 47302

Boone Trading Co. Inc., P.O. Box 669, Brinnon, WA, 98320, 800-423-1945, ww.boonetrading.com

Bryan, Bob, 1120 Oak Hill Rd., Carthage, MO, 64836

Byrne, Mary Gregg, 1018 15th St., Bellingham, WA, 98225-6604

Cable, Jerry, 332 Main St., Mt. Pleasant, PA, 15666

Caudill, Lyle, 7626 Lyons Rd., Georgetown, OH, 45121

Cole, Gary, PO Box 668, Naalehu, HI, 96772, 808-929-9775, 808-929-7371, www.community.webshots.com/album/11836830uqyeejirsz

Collins, Michael, Rt. 3075, Batesville Rd., Woodstock, GA, 30188

Conover, Juanita Rae, P.O. Box 70442, Eugene, OR, 97401, 541-747-1726 or 543-4851, juanitaraeconover@yahoo.com

Courtnage, Elaine, Box 473, Big Sandy, MT, 59520

Cover Jr., Raymond A., Rt. 1, Box 194, Mineral Point, MO, 63660

Cox, J. Andy, 116 Robin Hood Lane, Gaffney, SC, 29340

Dietrich, Roni, Wild Horse Studio, 1257 Cottage Dr, Harrisburg, PA, 17112, 717-469-0587, ronimd@aol

DiMarzo, Richard, 2357 Center Place, Birmingham, AL, 35205

Dolbare, Elizabeth, PO Box 502, Dubois, WY, 82513-0502

Eklund, Maihkel, Föne 1111, S-82041 Färila, SWEDEN, +46 6512 4192, maihkel.eklund@swipnet.se, www.art-knives.com

Eldridge, Allan, 1424 Kansas Lane, Gallatin, TN, 37066

Ellis, Willy b, Willy B's Customs by William B Ellis, 4941 Cardinal Trail, Palm Harbor, FL, 34683, 727-942-6420, www.willyb.com

Fisk, Dale, Box 252, Council, ID, 83612, dafisk@ctcweb.net

Foster Enterprises, Norvell Foster, P.O. Box 200343, San Antonio, TX, 78220

Fountain Products, 492 Prospect Ave., West Springfield, MA, 01089

Gill, Scott, 925 N. Armstrong St., Kokomo, IN, 46901

Halligan, Ed, 14 Meadow Way, Sharpsburg, GA, 30277, ehkiss@bellsouth.net

Hands, Barry Lee, 26192 East Shore Route, Bigfork, MT, 59911

Hargraves Sr., Charles, RR 3 Bancroft, Ontario CANADA, K0L 1C0

Harless, Star, c/o Arrow Forge, P.O. Box 845, Stoneville, NC, 27048-0845

Harrington, Fred A., Summer: 2107 W Frances Rd, Mt Morris MI 48458 8215, Winter: 3725 Citrus, St. James City, FL, 33956, Winter 239-283-0721, Summer 810-686-3008

Hergert, Bob, 12 Geer Circle, Port Orford, OR, 97465, 541-332-3010, hergert@harborside.com, www.scrimshander.com

Hielscher, Vickie, 6550 Otoe Rd, P.O. Box 992, Alliance, NE, 69301, 308-762-4318, hielscher@premaonline.com

High, Tom, 5474 S. 112.8 Rd., Alamosa, CO, 81101, 719-589-2108, scrimshaw@vanion.com, www.rockymountainscrimshaw.com, Wildlife Artist

Himmelheber, David R., 11289 40th St. N., Royal Palm Beach, FL, 33411

Holland, Dennis K., 4908-17th Place, Lubbock, TX, 79416

Hutchings, Rick "Hutch", 3007 Coffe Tree Ct, Crestwood, KY, 40014, 502-241-2871, baron1@bellsouth.net

Imboden II, Howard L., 620 Deauville Dr., Dayton, OH, 45429, 937-439-1536, Guards by the "Last Wax Technic"

Johnson, Corinne, W3565 Lockington, Mindora, WI, 54644

Johnston, Kathy, W. 1134 Providence, Spokane, WA, 99205

Karst Stone, Linda, 903 Tanglewood Ln, Kerrville, TX, 78028-2945, 830-896-4678, 830-257-6117, karstone@ktc.com

Kelso, Jim, 577 Coller Hill Rd, Worcester, VT, 05682

Kirk, Susan B., 1340 Freeland Rd., Merrill, MI, 48637

Koevenig, Eugene and Eve, Koevenig's Engraving Service, Rabbit Gulch, Box 55, Hill City, SD, 57745-0055

Kostelnik, Joe and Patty, RD #4, Box 323, Greensburg, PA, 15601

Lemen, Pam, 3434 N. Iroquois Ave., Tucson, AZ, 85705

Martin, Diane, 28220 N. Lake Dr., Waterford, WI, 53185

McDonald, René Cosimini-, 14730 61 Court N., Loxahatchee, FL, 33470

McFadden, Berni, 2547 E Dalton Ave, Dalton Gardens, ID, 83815-9631

McGowan, Frank, 12629 Howard Lodge Dr., Winter Add-2023 Robin Ct Sebring FL 33870, Sykesville, MD, 21784, 863-385-1296

McGrath, Gayle, PMB 232 15201 N Cleveland Ave, N Ft Myers, FL, 33903

McLaran, Lou, 603 Powers St., Waco, TX, 76705

McWilliams, Carole, P.O. Box 693, Bayfield, CO, 81122

Mead, Faustina L., 2550 E. Mercury St., Inverness, FL, 34453-0514, 352-344-4751, scrimsha@infionline.net, www.scrimshaw-by-faustina.com

Mitchell, James, 1026 7th Ave., Columbus, GA, 31901

Moore, James B., 1707 N. Gillis, Stockton, TX, 79735

Ochonicky, Michelle "Mike", Stone Hollow Studio, 31 High Trail, Eureka, MO, 63025, 636-938-9570, www.bestofmissourihands.com

Ochs, Belle, 124 Emerald Lane, Largo, FL, 33771, 727-530-3826, chuckandbelle@juno.com, www.oxforge.com

Pachi, Mirella, Via Pometta 1, 17046 Sassello (SV), ITALY, 019 720086, WWW.PACHI-KNIVES.COM

Parish, Vaughn, 103 Cross St., Monaca, PA, 15061

Peterson, Lou, 514 S. Jackson St., Gardner, IL, 60424

Poag, James H., RR #1 Box 212A, Grayville, IL, 62844

Polk, Trena, 4625 Webber Creek Rd., Van Buren, AR, 72956

Purvis, Hilton, P.O. Box 371, Noordhoek, 7979, SOUTH AFFRIC, 27 21 789 1114, hiltonp@telkomsa.net, www.kgsa.co.za/member/hiltonpurvis

Ramsey, Richard, 8525 Trout Farm Rd, Neosho, MO, 64850

Ristinen, Lori, 14256 County Hwy 45, Menahga, MN, 56464, 218-538-6608, lori@loriristinen.com, www.loriristinen.com

Roberts, J.J., 7808 Lake Dr., Manassas, VA, 22111, 703-330-0448, jjrengraver@aol.com, www.angelfire.com/va2/ engraver

Rudolph, Gil, 20922 Oak Pass Ave, Tehachapi, CA, 93561, 661-822-4949, www.gtraks@csurfers.net

Rundell, Joe, 6198 W. Frances Rd., Clio, MI, 48420

Saggio, Joe, 1450 Broadview Ave. #12, Columbus, OH, 43212, 614-481-1967, jvsaggio@earthlink.net, www.j.v.saggio@worldnet.att.net

Sahlin, Viveca, Konstvaktarevagem 9, S-772 40 Grangesberg, SWEDEN, 46 240 23204, www.scrimart.use

Satre, Robert, 518 3rd Ave. NW, Weyburn SK CANADA, S4H 1R1

Schlott, Harald, Zingster Str. 26, 13051 Berlin, 929 33 46, GERMANY, 049 030 9293346, 049 030 9293346, harald.schlott@t-online.de, www.gravur-kunst-atelier.de.vu

Schulenburg, E.W., 25 North Hill St., Carrollton, GA, 30117

Schwallie, Patricia, 4614 Old Spartanburg Rd. Apt. 47, Taylors, SC, 29687

Selent, Chuck, P.O. Box 1207, Bonners Ferry, ID, 83805

Semich, Alice, 10037 Roanoke Dr., Murfreesboro, TN, 37129

Shostle, Ben, 1121 Burlington, Muncie, IN, 47302

Smith, Peggy, 676 Glades Rd., #3, Gatlinburg, TN, 37738

Smith, Ron, 5869 Straley, Ft. Worth, TX, 76114

Stahl, John, Images In Ivory, 2049 Windsor Rd., Baldwin, NY, 11510, 516-223-5007, imivory@msn.com, www.imagesinivory.org

Steigerwalt, Jim, RD#3, Sunbury, PA, 17801

Stuart, Stephen, 15815 Acorn Circle, Tavares, FL, 32778, 352-343-8423, (352) 343-8916, inkscratch@aol.com

Talley, Mary Austin, 2499 Countrywood Parkway, Memphis, TN, 38016, matalley@midsouth.rr.com

Thompson, Larry D., 23040 Ave. 197, Strathmore, CA, 93267

Toniutti, Nelida, Via G. Pascoli, 33085 Maniago-PN, ITALY

Trout, Lauria Lovestrand, 1555 Delaney Dr, No. 1723, Talahassee, FL, 32309, 850-893-8836, mayalaurie@aol.com

Tucker, Steve, 3518 W. Linwood, Turlock, CA, 95380

Tyser, Ross, 1015 Hardee Court, Spartanburg, SC, 29303

Velasquez, Gil, Art of Scrimshaw, 7120 Madera Dr., Goleta, CA, 93117

Wilderness Forge, 475 NE Smith Rock Way, Terrebonne, OR, 97760, bhatting@xpressweb.com

Williams, Gary, PO Box 210, Glendale, KY, 42740, 270-369-6752, garywilliam@alltel.net

Winn, Travis A., 558 E. 3065 S., Salt Lake City, UT, 84106

Young, Mary, 4826 Storeyland Dr., Alton, IL, 62002

organizations

AMERICAN BLADESMITH SOCIETY
c/o Jan DuBois; PO Box 1481; Cypress, TX 77410-1481; 281-225-9159; Web: www.americanbladesmith.com

AMERICAN KNIFE & TOOL INSTITUTE***
David Kowalski, Comm. Coordinator, AKTI; DEPT BL2, PO Box 432, Iola, WI 54945-0432;715-445-3781; Web: communications@akti.org; www. akti.org

AMERICAN KNIFE THROWERS ALLIANCE
c/o Bobby Branton; 4976 Seewee Rd; Awendaw, SC 29429; www.AKTA-USA.com

ARIZONA KNIFE COLLECTOR'S ASSOCIATION
c/o D'Alton Holder, President, 7148 W. Country Gables Dr., Peoria, AZ 85381; Web: www.akca.net

ART KNIFE COLLECTOR'S ASSOCIATION
c/o Mitch Weiss, Pres.; 2211 Lee Road, Suite 104; Winter Park, FL 32789

BAY AREA KNIFE COLLECTOR'S ASSOCIATION
Doug Isaacson, B.A.K.C.A. Membership, 36774 Magnolia, Newark, CA 94560; Web: www.bakca.org

ARKANSAS KNIFEMAKERS ASSOCIATION
David Etchieson, 60 Wendy Cove, Conway, AR 72032; Web: www.arkansasknifemakers.com

AUSTRALASIAN KNIFE COLLECTORS
PO BOX 149 CHIDLOW 6556 WESTERN AUSTRALIA TEL: (08) 9572 7255; FAX: (08) 9572 7266. International Inquiries: TEL: + 61 8 9572 7255; FAX: + 61 8 9572 7266, akc@knivesaustralia.com.au

CALIFORNIA KNIFEMAKERS ASSOCIATION
c/o Clint Breshears, Membership Chairman; 1261 Keats St; Manhattan Beach CA 90266; 310-372-0739; breshears@mindspring.com
Dedicated to teaching and improving knifemaking

CANADIAN KNIFEMAKERS GUILD
c/o Peter Wile; RR # 3; Bridgewater N.S. CANADA B4V 2W2; 902-543-1373; www.ckg.org

CUSTOM KNIFE COLLECTORS ASSOCIATION
c/o Jim Treacy, PO Box 5893, Glen Allen, VA 23058-5893; E-mail: customknifecollectorsassociation@yahoo.com; Web: www.customknifecollectorsassociation.com
The purpose of the CKCA is to recognize and promote the ar significance of handmade knives, to advnace their collectio conservation, and to support the creative expression of th who make them. Open to collectors, makers purveyors, a other collectors. Has members from eight countries. Pr calednar which features custom knives either owned o CKCA members.

CUTTING EDGE, THE
1920 N 26th St, Lowell, AR 72745; 479-631-0 36-4618; ce-info@cuttingedge.com
After-market knives since 1968. We offer about al knives each month. The oldest and the most experie siness of buying and selling knives. We buy collections ke knives on consignment or we will trade. Web: www com

FLORIDA KNIFEMAKERS ASSOCIATION
c/o President, Dan Mink, PO Box 861, Crystal beach, Florida, 34681 (727) 786 5408; Web: www.floridaknifemakers.org

JAPANESE SWORD SOCIETY OF THE U.S.
PO Box 712; Breckenridge, TX 76424

KNIFE COLLECTORS CLUB INC, THE
1920 N 26th St; Lowell AR 72745; 479-631-0055; 479-631-8734; lynnd@agrussell.com; Web:www.club@k-c-c.com
The oldest and largest association of knife collectors. Issues limited edition knives, both handmade and highest quality production, in very limited numbers. The very earliest was the CM-1, Kentucky Rifle

KNIFE WORLD
PO Box 3395; Knoxville, TN 37927; 800-828-7751; 865-397-1955; 865-397-1969; knifepub@knifeworld.com
Publisher of monthly magazine for knife enthusiasts and world's largest knife/cutlery bookseller. Web: www.knifeworld.com

KNIFEMAKERS GUILD
c/o Beverly Imel, Knifemakers Guild, Box 922, New Castle, IN 47362; (765) 529-1651; Web: www.knifemakersguild.com

KNIFEMAKERS GUILD OF SOUTHERN AFRICA, THE
c/o Carel Smith; PO Box 1744; Delmars 2210; SOUTH AFRICA; carelsmith@therugby.co.za; Web:www.kgsa.co.za

KNIVES ILLUSTRATED
265 S. Anita Dr., Ste. 120; Orange, CA 92868; 714-939-9991; 714-939-9909; knivesillustrated@yahoo.com; Web:www. knivesillustrated.com
All encompassing publication focusing on factory knives, new handmades, shows and industry news, plus knifemaker features, new products, and travel pieces

MONTANA KNIFEMAKERS' ASSOCIATION, THE
14440 Harpers Bridge Rd; Missoula, MT 59808; 406-543-0845
Annual book of custom knife makers' works and directory of knife making supplies; $19.99

NATIONAL KNIFE COLLECTORS ASSOCIATION
PO Box 21070; Chattanooga, TN 37424; 423-892-5007; 423-899-9456; info@nationalknife.org; Web: www.nationalknife. org

NEO-TRIBAL METALSMITHS
PO Box 44095; Tucson, AZ 85773-4095; Web: www.neo-tribalmetalsmiths.com

NEW ENGLAND CUSTOM KNIFE ASSOCIATION
George R. Rebello, President; 686 Main Rd; Brownville, ME 04414; Web: www.knivesby.com/necka.html

NORTH CAROLINA CUSTOM KNIFEMAKERS GUILD
c/o 2112 Windy Woods Drive, Raleigh, NC 27607 (919) 834-4693; Web: www.nckniveguild.org

NORTH STAR BLADE COLLECTORS
PO Box 20523, Bloomington, MN 55420

OHIO KNIFEMAKERS ASSOCIATION
c/o Jerry Smith, Anvils and Ink Studios, P.O. Box 7887, Columbus, Ohio 43229-7887; Web: www.geocities.com/ohioknives/

directory

OREGON KNIFE COLLECTORS ASSOCIATION
Web: www.oregonknifeclub.org

RANDALL KNIFE SOCIETY
PO Box 158, Meadows of Dan, VA 24120 email: payrks@gate.net; Web: www.randallknifesociety.com

ROCKY MOUNTAIN BLADE COLLECTORS ASSOCIATION
Mike Moss. Pres., P.O. Box 324, Westminster, CO 80036

RESOURCE GUIDE AND NEWSLETTER / AUTOMATIC KNIVES
2269 Chestnut St., Suite 212; San Francisco, CA 94123; 415-731-0210; Web: www.thenewsletter.com

SOUTH CAROLINA ASSOCIATION OF KNIFEMAKERS
c/o Victor Odom, Jr., Post Office Box 572, North, SC 29112 (803) 247-5614; Web: www.scak.org

SOUTHERN CALIFORNIA BLADES
SC Blades, PO Box 1140, Lomita, CA 90717; Web: www.scblades.com

TEXAS KNIFEMAKERS & COLLECTORS ASSOCIATION
2254 Fritz Allen Street, Fort Worth, Texas 76114; Web: www.tkca.org

TACTICAL KNIVES
Harris Publications; 1115 Broadway; New York, NY 10010; Web: www.tacticalknives.com

TRIBAL NOW!
Neo-Tribal Metalsmiths; PO Box 44095; Tucson, AZ 85733-4095; Web: www.neo-tribalmetalsmiths.com

WEYER INTERNATIONAL BOOK DIVISION
2740 Nebraska Ave; Toledo, OH 43607-3245; Web: www.weyerinternational.com

publications

BLADE
700 E. State St., Iola, WI 54990-0001; 715-445-2214; Web: www.blademag.com
The world's No. 1 knife magazine

CUTLERY NEWS JOURNAL (BLOG)
www.cutlerynewsjournal.blog
Covers significant happenings from the world of knife collecting, in addition to editorials, trends, events, auctions, shows, cutlery history, and reviews

KNIFE WORLD
PO Box 3395, Knoxville, TN 37927; www.knifeworld.com

KNIVES ILLUSTRATED
265 S. Anita Dr., Ste. 120, Orange, CA 92868; 714-939-9991; knivesillustrated@yahoo.com; Web: www.knivesillustrated.com
All encompassing publication focusing on factory knives, new handmades, shows and industry news

RESOURCE GUIDE AND NEWSLETTER / AUTOMATIC KNIVES
2269 Chestnut St., Suite 212, San Francisco, CA 94123; 415-731-0210; Web: www.thenewsletter.com

TACTICAL KNIVES
Harris Publications, 1115 Broadway, New York, NY 10010; Web: www.tacticalknives.com

WEYER INTERNATIONAL BOOK DIVISION
2740 Nebraska Ave., Toledo, OH 43607-3245